HOLY SPIRIT
revivals

HOLY✦SPIRIT
revivals

*How you can experience the
joy of living in God's power*

Charles Finney

Whitaker House

HOLY SPIRIT REVIVALS

ISBN: 0-88368-565-5
Printed in the United States of America
Copyright © 1999 by Whitaker House

Whitaker House
30 Hunt Valley Circle
New Kensington, PA 15068

Library of Congress Cataloging-in-Publication Data

Finney, Charles Grandison, 1792–1875.
    Holy Spirit revivals / by Charles G. Finney.
       p. cm.
   ISBN 0-88368-565-5
   1. Finney, Charles Grandison, 1792–1875. 2. Revivals—United States. 3. Revivals—Great Britain. I. Title.
BV3785.F485A3   1999
269'.24'0973—dc21   99-10743

3 4 5 6 7 8 9 10 11 12 13 / 07 06 05 04 03 02 01

Contents

Introduction

C harles Grandison Finney was a man with a message that burned through the religious deadwood and secular darkness of his time. He had the ability to shock both saint and sinner alike. Because he was radical in both his methods and his message, Finney was criticized for almost everything except being boring. Even so, Finney's sermons and writings continue to reappear to each new generation of young Christians as a fresh challenge to holiness and spiritual awakening.

Finney was nearly thirty years of age before he turned from his skepticism regarding Christianity and wholeheartedly embraced the Bible as the true Word of God. He gave up his law profession in order to spread the Gospel, and he soon became the most noteworthy revivalist of the nineteenth century. Finney's travels as an evangelist were largely concentrated in upstate New York, which he refers to here as "the West," but his ministry extended into other northeastern states and even as far as England. It is estimated that over 250,000 souls were converted as a result of his preaching.

The following pages contain Finney's personal record of the many revivals that he witnessed during his lifetime. His complete memoirs were published by the trustees of Oberlin College in 1876. The theological ideas that Finney originally presented here have been abridged, and an elaboration of these ideas can be found in the book *God in You,* also published by Whitaker House.

The substance of Finney's dealings with sinners was "to make them understand that God required of them then to yield themselves entirely to His will, to ground their weapons of rebellion, to submit to Him as their rightful Sovereign, and to accept Jesus as their only Redeemer." Accordingly, it is right to say that Finney's focus was always upon the hearts of his fellowmen, and his ever present wish was that all might be saved and *"come to the knowledge of the truth"* (1 Tim. 2:4).

One

Birth and Early Education

It has pleased God to connect my name and labors with an extensive movement of the church of Christ, especially in relation to revivals of religion. To a considerable degree, this movement involved some views of Christian doctrine that had not been common, along with changes in the means of carrying forward the work of evangelism. Thus, it was very natural that some misunderstanding prevailed so that, to some extent, even good men called into question the wisdom of these measures and the soundness of these theological statements. It was also natural that ungodly men were irritated and, for a time, strenuously opposed to these great movements.

I was connected with these movements, but only as one of the many ministers and servants of Christ who shared prominently in promoting them. Some parts of the church have considered me as an innovator in both doctrine and measures, and many have looked upon me as rather prominent, especially in attacking some of the old forms of theological thought and expression and in stating the doctrines of the Gospel in new language.

For a number of years, I have been asked, by the friends of the revivals with which my name and labors have been connected, to write a history of them. Because so much misunderstanding has prevailed regarding them, it is thought that the truth of history demands a statement from me of the doctrines that were preached, of the measures used, and of the results of preaching those doctrines and using those measures.

My mind seems to recoil instinctively from saying much about myself, but I am obliged to do so in order to speak honestly of the revivals and my relation to them. For this reason I have declined, up to this time, to undertake such a work. However, the trustees of Oberlin College, together with other friends in this country and in England, have laid the matter before me and urged me to undertake it for the cause of Christ. They have insisted that a better understanding needs to exist in the church regarding the revivals that occurred in upstate New York and elsewhere, beginning in 1821, because those revivals have been most misrepresented and opposed.

I approach the subject with reluctance for many reasons. I have kept no diary and consequently must depend on my memory. However, my memory is naturally very tenacious, and the events that I have witnessed in revivals of religion have made a very deep impression on my mind. I remember, with great distinctness, many more events than I will have time to communicate. Anyone who has witnessed powerful revivals of religion is aware that many cases of conviction and conversion are daily occurring. Such cases are frequently so numerous that, if all the highly interesting facts of even one revival were narrated, they would fill a large volume.

I propose only to relate a few of the instances of conversion that occurred in different places, along with an account of the doctrines that were preached and the measures that were used. In this way, the church will be enabled, at least in part, to estimate the power and purity of those great works of God. To give any intelligible account of the part that I was called to play in those scenes, it is necessary that I give a little history of the manner in which I came to adopt the doctrinal views that I have long held and preached and that have been regarded by many people as objectionable.

I must commence by giving a brief account of my birth, my early circumstances and education, my conversion to Christ, my study of theology, and my entering into the work of the ministry. I am not about to write an autobiography, so I will relate the events of my private life only as far as is necessary to give an intelligible account of the manner in which I became related to those great movements of the church.

I was born in Warren, Connecticut, on August 29, 1792. When I was about two years old, my family moved to Oneida County, New York, which was mostly wilderness at that time. No religious privileges were enjoyed by the people, and very few religious books could be found. The new settlers, being mostly from New England, almost immediately established public schools; but they had among them very little intelligent preaching of the Gospel. I attended a public school until I was about fifteen or sixteen years old, and I advanced so far as to be thought capable of teaching in the public school myself.

Neither of my parents were Christians, and among our neighbors there were very few religious people. I seldom heard a sermon, unless it was an occasional one from some traveling minister. I recollect very well that the preachers I heard were so ignorant that the people would return from the meetings and spend a considerable time in irrepressible laughter at the mistakes and absurdities of the preaching.

A church had just been built in my neighborhood, and a minister chosen, when my father was induced to move into the wilderness skirting the southern shore of Lake Ontario, a little south of Sackett's Harbor. Here I lived for several years, again enjoying no better religious privileges than I had in Oneida County.

When I was about twenty years old, I returned to Connecticut, and from there I went to New Jersey in order to teach. I taught and studied as best I could, and twice I returned to New England to attend an academy, for a season. While attending the academy, I considered going to Yale College. My teacher was a graduate of Yale, but he advised me not to go. He said it would be a waste of time, because I could easily study Yale's curriculum myself in two years, whereas it would cost me four years to graduate from there. Because of what he said, I did not pursue my education any further at that time. I later acquired some knowledge of Latin, Greek, and Hebrew, but I was never a classical scholar and never possessed so much knowledge of the ancient languages as to think myself capable of criticizing our English translation of the Bible.

The teacher to whom I have referred asked me to join him in conducting an academy in one of the Southern states. I was inclined to accept his proposal, with the intention of pursuing and completing my studies under his instruction. But when I informed my parents, whom I had not seen for four years, of my contemplated move south, they both came immediately after me and persuaded me to go home with them to Jefferson County, New York. After this, I decided to enter the law office of Squire Wright as a student. His office was located in the town of Adams, in Jefferson County. This was in 1818.

Up to this time I had never enjoyed what might be called religious privileges. I had never lived in a praying community, except during the periods when I was attending the academy in New England; and the religion in that place was not at all calculated to arrest my attention. The preaching there was by an aged clergyman who read his sermons in a manner that left no impression on my mind. He had a monotonous, humdrum way of reading what he had probably written many years before. Although the people paid close and reverent attention to his reading, I must confess that to me it was not much like preaching.

To give a better idea of his preaching, let me say that his sermons were written on a piece of paper just small enough to put into a small Bible. I sat in the balcony and observed that he placed his manuscript in the middle of his Bible and used his fingers as bookmarks for the passages of Scripture to be quoted in his sermon. This made it necessary to hold his Bible in both hands and rendered all hand gestures impossible. As he proceeded, he would read the passages of Scripture where his fingers were inserted, and thus he would liberate one finger after another, until the fingers of both hands were read out of their places. When his fingers were all read out, he was near the close of the sermon. Anyone can judge whether such preaching was calculated to instruct or interest a young man who neither knew nor cared anything about religion.

When I was teaching school in New Jersey, the preaching in the neighborhood was chiefly in German. I do not think I heard half a dozen sermons in English during my whole stay in New Jersey, which was about three years.

Thus, when I went to Adams to study law, I was almost as ignorant of religion as a heathen. I had been brought up mostly in the dark. I had very little regard for the Sabbath and had no definite knowledge of religious truth.

At Adams, for the first time, I regularly heard the preaching of an educated minister. Rev. George W. Gale, from Princeton, New Jersey, became pastor of the local Presbyterian church soon after I arrived there. His preaching was of the old-school and was therefore thoroughly Calvinistic, sometimes resembling what has been called hyper-Calvinism. I was not able to gain very much instruction from his preaching because, as I sometimes told him, he seemed to assume many things that to my mind needed to be proved. He seemed to take it for granted that his hearers were theologians and that he might therefore assume all the great and fundamental doctrines of the Gospel. But I was more perplexed than edified by his preaching.

Until this time I had never lived where I could attend a regular prayer meeting. So I began to attend one that was held near our office every week, as often as I could be excused from business at that hour.

In studying elementary law, I found the old authors frequently quoting the Scriptures and referring especially to the Pentateuch as authority for many of the great principles of common law. This excited my curiosity so much that I went and purchased a Bible, the first I had ever owned. Whenever I found a reference by the law authors to the Bible, I turned to the passage of Scripture. This soon led to my taking a new interest in the Bible, and I read and meditated on it much more than I had ever done before in my life. However, much of it I did not understand.

Mr. Gale frequently dropped by our office and seemed anxious to know what impression his sermons had made on my mind. I used to converse with him freely, and I now think that I sometimes criticized his sermons unmercifully. I raised whatever objections I had against his positions.

In conversing with him, I confirmed my suspicion that he himself was confused and that he did not accurately define to himself what he meant by many of the important terms that he used. Indeed, I found it impossible to attach any meaning to many of the terms he used with great formality and frequency. What did he mean by repentance? Was it a mere feeling of sorrow for sin? Was it altogether a passive state of mind, or did it involve a voluntary element? If it was a change of mind, in what respect was it a change of mind? What did he mean by the term *regeneration?* What did such language mean when applied to a spiritual change? What did he mean by faith? Was it merely an intellectual state? Was it merely a conviction, or persuasion, that the things stated in the Gospel were true? What did he mean by sanctification? Did it involve any physical change in the person, or any physical influence on the part of God? I could not tell, nor did he himself seem to know, in what sense he used these and similar terms.

We had many interesting conversations, but they seemed to raise more questions in my mind rather than to satisfy me in respect to the truth. But as I read my Bible, attended the prayer meetings, heard Mr. Gale preach, and conversed with him and the elders of the church and others from time to time, I became very restless. A little consideration convinced me that I was by no means in a state of mind to go to heaven if I were to die. It seemed to me that religion contained something infinitely important, and so I decided that if the soul was immortal, I needed a great change in my inward state to be prepared for happiness in heaven. But still I was not sure of the truth of the Gospel and the Christian religion, and the question was of too much importance to allow me to rest in any uncertainty on the subject.

I was particularly struck with the fact that the prayers that I had listened to from week to week were not answered. Indeed, from continued prayers and from other remarks, I understood that those who offered them did not regard them as answered. I heard the people pray continually for the outpouring of the Holy Spirit, and just as often I heard them confess that they did not receive what they had asked for. When I read my Bible, I learned what Christ had said in regard to prayer and answers to prayer:

> *Ask, and it will be given to you; seek, and you will find; knock, and it will be opened to you. For everyone who asks receives, and he who seeks finds, and to him who knocks it will be opened.*   *(Matt. 7:7–8)*

I also read that God is more willing to give His Holy Spirit to those who ask Him than earthly parents are to give good gifts to their children (v. 11).

This inconsistency—the fact that they prayed so much and were not answered—was a sad stumbling block to me. I did not know what to make of it. Was I to believe that these people were not truly Christians and therefore did not prevail with God? Did I misunderstand the promises and teachings of the Bible on this subject? Or was I to conclude that the Bible was not true? Here was something inexplicable to me, and at one point it seemed that it would almost drive me into skepticism. It seemed to me that the teachings of the Bible did not at all agree with the facts that were before my eyes.

On one occasion, when I was in one of the prayer meetings, some of the attendees asked if I wanted them to pray for me. I told them no, because I did not see that God answered their prayers. I said, "I suppose I need to be prayed for, for I am conscious that I am a sinner. But I do not see that it will do any good for you to pray for me, for you are continually asking, but you do not receive. You have been praying for a revival of religion ever since I have been in Adams, and yet you have not seen it happen. You

15

have been praying for the Holy Spirit to descend upon you, and yet you complain of your spiritual leanness. You have prayed enough since I have attended these meetings to have prayed the Devil out of Adams, if there is any virtue in your prayers. But here you are, still praying and still complaining." I was quite earnest and probably very irritable as a result of being brought face to face with religious truth, which was a new state of things to me.

On further reading of my Bible, it struck me that their prayers were not answered because they did not comply with the conditions upon which God had promised to answer prayer. They did not pray in faith, in the sense of expecting God to give them the thing for which they asked. For some time this thought only led me to more questions, rather than to anything definite. However, this relieved me. After struggling in that way for two or three years, I firmly concluded that whatever confusion there might be either in my own mind, in my pastor's, or in the mind of the church, the Bible was, nevertheless, the true Word of God.

This being settled, I was brought face to face with the question of accepting Christ and His Gospel or pursuing a worldly life. The Holy Spirit was so much at work in me, though I did not know it then, that I could not leave this question unsettled for much longer.

Two

Conversion to Christ

One Sunday night in the autumn of 1821, I made up my mind that I would settle the question of my soul's salvation, and if it were possible, I would make my peace with God. However, as I was very busy in the affairs of the office, I knew that I would never attend to the subject with any real results unless I was determined. Therefore, I resolved then and there, as far as possible, to avoid all business and everything that would divert my attention, in order to give myself wholly to the work of securing the salvation of my soul. I carried this resolution into execution as sternly and thoroughly as I could. I was, however, obliged to be in the office a good deal. But as the providence of God would have it, I did not have much to do either on Monday or Tuesday of that particular week, and so I had the opportunity to read my Bible and engage in prayer most of the time.

But I was very proud without knowing it. I had supposed that I did not care much about others' opinions of me, and I had in fact been quite obvious in attending prayer meetings and paying attention to religion while in Adams. In this respect I had led the church at times to think that I must be an anxious inquirer. But when I had to face the question, I found that I was very unwilling to have anyone know that I was seeking the salvation of my soul. When I prayed, I would only whisper my prayer, after having plugged the keyhole in the door, lest someone should discover that I was engaged in prayer.

Before that time my Bible lay on the table with the rest of my law books, and it had never occurred to me to be ashamed of being found reading it, any more than I should be ashamed of being found reading any of my other books.

17

But after I had addressed myself in earnest to the subject of my own salvation, I kept my Bible out of sight as much as I could. If I was reading it when anybody came in, I would throw my law books on top of it to create the impression that I had not had it in my hands. Instead of being outspoken and willing to talk with anybody and everybody on the subject as before, I found myself unwilling to converse with anybody. I did not want to see my minister because I did not want to let him know how I felt, and I had no confidence that he would understand my case and give me the direction that I needed. For the same reasons, I avoided conversation with the elders of the church or with any of the Christian people. I was ashamed to let them know how I felt, on the one hand; on the other, I was afraid they would misdirect me. I felt myself left only to the Bible.

During Monday and Tuesday my convictions increased, but still it seemed as if my heart grew harder. I could not shed a tear; I could not pray. I had no opportunity to pray above a whisper, and frequently I felt that I would find relief in prayer if I could be alone where I could use my voice and express myself. I was shy and avoided speaking to anybody on any subject, as much as I could, and I made sure not to arouse any suspicion that I was seeking the salvation of my soul.

Tuesday night I became very nervous, and in the night a strange feeling came over me as if I was about to die. I knew that if I did die, I would sink down to hell, but I quieted myself as best I could until morning.

At an early hour on Wednesday, I started for the office. But just before I arrived at the office, something seemed to confront me, as if an inward voice said to me, "What are you waiting for? Did you not promise to give your heart to God? And what are you trying to do? Are you endeavoring to work out a righteousness of your own?"

At this point, the whole question of Gospel salvation was opened to me in a marvelous manner. I think I then saw, as clearly as I ever have in my life, the reality and fullness of the atonement of Christ. I saw that His work is a finished work and that, instead of needing any righteousness of my own to recommend me to God, I had to submit myself to the righteousness of God through Christ. Gospel salvation seemed to be an offer to be accepted, something that was full and complete, and all that was necessary on my part was to agree to give up my sins and accept Christ. Instead of being a thing to be brought about by my own works, salvation was a thing to be found entirely in the Lord Jesus Christ, who presented Himself before me as my God and my Savior.

Without being distinctly aware of it, I had stopped in the street right where the inward voice had first come upon me. How long I remained in that position I cannot say. But after I contemplated this distinct revelation for a while, the inner voice seemed to ask, "Will you accept it now, today?" I replied, "Yes, I will accept it today, or I will die in the attempt."

North of the village and over a hill lay a stretch of woods in which I walked almost daily when the weather was pleasant. It was now the tenth of October, and the time was past for my frequent walks there. Nevertheless, instead of going to the office, I turned and bent my course toward the woods, feeling that I must be alone and away from all human eyes and ears, so that I could pour out my prayer to God.

But still my pride showed itself. As I went over the hill, it occurred to me that someone might see me and suppose that I was going away to pray. Yet there was probably not a person on earth who would have suspected such a thing, had he seen me going. But so great was my pride, and so much was I possessed with the fear of man, that I skulked along the fence, until I got so far out of sight that no one from the village could see me. I then made my way into the woods nearly a quarter of a mile, went over on the other side of the hill, and found a place where some large trees had fallen across each other, leaving an open place between. There I saw I could make a kind of closet. I crept into this place and knelt down for prayer.

As I turned to go up into the woods, I recollect having said, "I will give my heart to God, or I never will come down from there." I recall repeating this as I went up—"I will give my heart to God before I ever come down again." But when I attempted to pray, I found that my heart would not pray. I had supposed that if I could only be where I could speak aloud without being overheard, I would pray freely. But when I tried it, I was mute; I had nothing to say to God, or at least I could say only a few words, and those without heart. In attempting to pray, I would hear a rustling in the leaves and would stop and look up to see if somebody were coming. I did this several times.

Finally I found myself sinking fast to despair. I said to myself, "I cannot pray. My heart is dead to God, and it will not pray." I then reproached myself for having promised to give my heart to God before I left the woods. When I tried, I found I could not give my heart to God. My soul hung back, and my heart was in no way going out to God. I began to feel deeply that it was too late, that I was past hope, and that God must have given up on me.

I then began to think my promise rash, that I would give my heart to God that day or die in the attempt. It seemed to me as if that were binding upon my soul, and yet I was going to break my vow. A great discouragement came over me, and I felt almost too weak to get up on my knees.

Just at this moment, I again thought I heard someone approach me, and I opened my eyes to see whether it were so. But just then it was distinctly shown to me that my pride was the great difficulty that stood in the way. An overwhelming sense of my wickedness in being ashamed to have a human being see me on my knees before God took such powerful possession of me that I cried at the top of my voice and exclaimed that I would not leave that place if all the men on earth and all the devils in hell surrounded me. "What!" I said. "Such a degraded sinner as I am, on my knees confessing my sins to the great and holy God—how can I be ashamed to have any human being, a sinner like myself, find me on my knees endeavoring to make my peace with my offended God?" The sin appeared awful, infinite. It broke me down before the Lord.

Just at that point, this passage of Scripture seemed to drop into my mind with a flood of light: *"Then you will... pray to Me, and I will listen to you. And you will seek Me and find Me, when you search for Me with all your heart"* (Jer. 29:12–13). Somehow I knew that this was a passage of Scripture, though I do not think I had ever read it. I knew that it was God's Word, and God's voice that spoke to me. I instantly seized hold of this with my heart. I had intellectually believed the Bible before, but never had I known that faith was a voluntary trust instead of an intellectual state. I was conscious of trusting at that moment in God's veracity. I cried to Him, "Lord, I take You at Your Word. You know that I am searching for You with all my heart and that I have come here to pray to You, and You have promised to hear me."

This seemed to confirm that I could, indeed, fulfill my vow that very day. The Spirit seemed to emphasize this idea in the words, *"When you search for Me with all your heart"* (v. 13). I told the Lord that I would take Him at His Word, that I knew He could not lie, and that I was therefore sure that He heard my prayer and that I would find Him.

He then gave me many other promises, from both the Old and New Testaments, especially some regarding our Lord Jesus Christ. I never can, in words, make any human being understand how precious and true those promises appeared to me. I took them one after the other as infallible truth, the assertions of God, who cannot lie (Titus 1:2). They did not seem to fall into my intellect so much as into my heart, to be put within the grasp of the voluntary powers of my mind. I took hold of them and fastened upon them with the grasp of a drowning man.

I continued to pray in this way and to receive and take hold of promises for a long time—I do not know how long. I prayed until my mind became so full that, before I was aware of it, I was on my feet and tripping up the hill toward the road. I did not really think about whether I had been converted, but as I went up, brushing through the leaves and bushes, I recollect saying with great emphasis, "If I am ever converted, I will preach the Gospel."

I soon reached the road that led to the village, and I began to reflect on what had passed. I found that my mind had become wonderfully quiet and peaceful. I said to myself, "What is this? I must have grieved the Holy Spirit entirely away. I have lost all my conviction. I do not have a particle of concern about my soul, and it must be that the Spirit has left me. Indeed, I never was so far from being concerned about my salvation in my life!"

Then I remembered what I had said to God while I was on my knees—that I would take Him at His Word. And so I recalled many things I had said, and I concluded that it was no wonder the Spirit had left me. I imagined that for such a sinner as I was to take hold of God's Word in that way was presumption, if not blasphemy. I concluded that, in my excitement, I had grieved the Holy Spirit and perhaps committed the unpardonable sin.

I walked quietly toward the village, and so perfectly quiet was my mind that it seemed as if all nature listened. I had gone into the woods immediately after an early breakfast, and when I returned to the village I found it was lunchtime. Yet I had been wholly unaware of the time that had passed; it appeared to me that I had been gone from the village only a short time.

But how was I to account for the quiet of my mind? I tried to recall my convictions, to get back again the load of sin under which I had been laboring. But all sense of sin, all consciousness of present sin or guilt, had departed from me. I said to myself, "What is this, that I cannot arouse any sense of guilt in my soul, as great a sinner as I am?" I tried in vain to make myself anxious about my present state. I was so quiet and peaceful that I tried to feel concerned about it, lest it should be a result of my having grieved the Spirit away. But no matter what view I took of it, I could not be anxious at all about my soul and my spiritual state.

The repose of my mind was unspeakably great. I never can describe it in words. The thought of God was sweet to my mind, and the most profound spiritual tranquility had taken full possession of me. This was a great mystery.

I went to lunch and found I had no appetite to eat. I then went to the office and found that Squire Wright had gone to lunch. I took down my bass viol and, as I was accustomed to do, began to play and sing some pieces of sacred music. But as soon as I began to sing those sacred words, I began to weep. It seemed as if my heart were all liquid, and my feelings were in such a state that I could not hear my own voice in singing without causing my tears to overflow. I wondered at this and tried to hold back my tears but could not. After trying in vain to suppress my tears, I put away my instrument and stopped singing.

After lunch, Squire Wright and I were engaged in moving our books and furniture to another office. We were very busy in this and had little conversation all afternoon. My mind, however, remained in that profoundly tranquil state. There was a great sweetness and tenderness in my thoughts and feelings. Everything appeared to be going right, and nothing seemed to ruffle or disturb me in the least.

Just before evening I decided that, as soon as I was left alone in the new office, I would try to pray again—that I was not going to abandon the subject of religion and give it up, at any rate. Therefore, although I no longer had any concern about my soul, I would still continue to pray.

By evening we got the books and furniture adjusted, and I made a good fire in the fireplace, hoping to spend the evening alone. Just at dark, Squire Wright, seeing that everything was adjusted, bade me good night and went home. I accompanied him to the door, and as I closed the door and turned around, my heart seemed to be liquid within me. All my feelings seemed to rise and flow out, and the utterance of my heart was, "I want to pour my whole soul out to God." The rising of my soul was so great that I rushed into the room behind the front office to pray.

There was no fire and no light in that room; nevertheless, it appeared perfectly lit to me. As I went in and shut the door after me, it seemed as if I met the Lord Jesus Christ face to face. It did not occur to me then, nor did it for some time afterward, that it was wholly a mental state. On the contrary, it seemed to me that I saw Him as I would see any other man. He said nothing, but looked at me in such a manner as to break me down right at His feet. I have ever since regarded this as a most remarkable state of mind, for it seemed real to me that He stood before me, that I fell down at His feet and poured out my soul to Him. I wept aloud like a child and made such confessions as I could with my choked utterance. It seemed to me that I bathed His feet with my tears, but cannot recall that I had any distinct impression that I touched Him.

I must have continued in this state for a good while, but my mind was too much absorbed with the interview to recall anything that I said. Yet I know, as soon as my mind became calm enough to break off from the interview, I returned to the front office and found that the fire I had made was nearly burned out. But as I turned and was about to take a seat by the fire, I received a mighty baptism of the Holy Spirit. Without any expectation of it, without ever having thought that there was any such thing for me, without any recollection that I had ever heard the thing mentioned by any person in the world, the Holy Spirit descended upon me in a manner that seemed to go through me, body and soul. I could feel the impression, like a wave of electricity, going through me. Indeed, it seemed to come in waves of liquid love—I cannot express it in any other way. It seemed like the very breath of God. I can recall distinctly that it seemed to fan me like immense wings.

No words can express the wonderful love that was *"poured out"* (Rom. 5:5) in my heart. I wept aloud with joy and love, and I literally bellowed out the unutterable gushings of my heart. These waves came over me and over me, one after the other, until I cried out, "I will die if these waves continue to pass over me!" I said, "Lord, I cannot bear any more!" Yet I had no fear of death.

How long I continued in this state, with this baptism continuing to roll over me and go through me, I do not know. But I know it was late in the evening when a member of my choir—for I was the leader of the choir—came into the office to see me. He found me in this state of loud weeping and said to me, "Mr. Finney, what ails you?" I could not answer him for some time. He then said, "Are you in pain?" I gathered myself up as best I could and replied, "No, but so happy that I cannot live."

He turned, left the office, and in a few minutes returned with one of the elders of the church, Elder B——, whose shop was just across the way from our office. This elder was a very serious man, and I had scarcely ever seen him laugh. In my presence he had been very watchful. When he came in, I was still in a state of loud weeping. Elder B—— asked me how I felt, and I began to tell him. Instead of saying anything, he fell into spasmodic laughter. It seemed as if it were impossible for him to keep from laughing from the very bottom of his heart.

There was a young man in the neighborhood who had been a close friend of mine. Our minister, as I afterward learned, had repeatedly talked with him on the subject of religion and had warned him against being misled by me. Mr. Gale informed him that I was very careless about religion, and he thought that if my friend associated much more with me, his mind would be diverted and he would not be converted. After I was converted, my friend told me that he had said to Mr. Gale several times, when he had admonished him about associating so much with me, that my conversations had often affected him more, religiously, than his preaching. I had indeed shared my feelings a good deal with this young man.

Just at the time when I was giving an account of my feelings to Elder B——, this young man came into the office. I was sitting with my back toward the door and barely noticed that he came in. He listened with astonishment to what I was saying, and the first I knew, he partly fell upon the floor and cried out in the greatest agony of mind, "Do pray for me!" The elder of the church and the other member knelt down and began to pray for him, and when they had prayed, I prayed for him myself. Soon after this they all left me alone.

I then wondered, "Why did Elder B—— laugh so? Did he think that I was deluded or crazy?" This thought brought a kind of darkness over my mind, and I began to ask myself whether it was proper for me—such a sinner as I had been—to pray for that young man. A cloud seemed to come over me; I felt I could not rest in anything. After a little while I retired to bed, not distressed in mind, but still at a loss as to what to make of my present state. Notwithstanding the baptism I had received, my view was so obscured that I went to bed without feeling sure that my peace was made with God.

I soon fell asleep, but almost as soon awoke again on account of the great flow of the love of God that was in my heart. I was so filled with love that I could not sleep. I fell asleep again and awoke in the same manner. When I awoke, this temptation toward unbelief returned upon me, and the love that seemed to be in my heart abated; but as soon as I was asleep, it was so warm within me that I would immediately awake. Thus I continued until, late at night, I obtained some sound repose.

When I awoke in the morning, the sun had risen and was pouring a clear light into my room. Words cannot express the impression that this sunlight made upon me. Instantly, the baptism that I had received the night before returned upon me in the same manner. I rose to my knees in the bed and wept aloud with joy, remaining for some time too much overwhelmed with the baptism of the Spirit to do anything but pour out my soul to God. It seemed as if this morning's baptism was accompanied by a gentle reproof, and the Spirit seemed to say to me, "Will you doubt? Will you doubt?" I cried. "No, I will not doubt; I cannot doubt!" He then cleared the subject up so much that it was in fact impossible for me to doubt that the Spirit of God had taken possession of my soul.

In this state, I was taught that justification by faith is a present experience. I had never distinctly viewed this as a fundamental doctrine of the Gospel. Indeed, I did not know at all what it meant in the proper sense. But I could now see and understand what was meant by the passage, *"Having been justified by faith, we have peace with God through our Lord Jesus Christ"* (Rom. 5:1). I could see that, from the moment I believed while up in the woods, all sense of condemnation had entirely dropped out of my mind, and I could not feel a sense of guilt or condemnation by any effort that I could make. My sins were gone, and my sense of guilt was gone, as if I had never sinned.

This was just the revelation that I needed. As far as I could see, I was in a state in which I did not sin. Instead of feeling that I was sinning all the time, my heart was so full of love that it overflowed. My cup ran over with blessing and with love, and I could not feel that I was sinning against God. Nor could I recover the least sense of guilt for my past sins.

Three

Beginning of My Work

On that same morning, I went to the office, and there I was experiencing the renewal of those mighty waves of love and salvation flowing over me, when Squire Wright came into the office. I said a few words to him on the subject of his salvation. He looked at me with astonishment but made no reply whatsoever. He dropped his head and, after standing a few minutes, left the office. I thought no more of it then, but afterward I found that the remark I made had pierced him like a sword, and he did not recover from it until he was converted.

Soon after Squire Wright had left the office, Deacon B—— came into the office and said to me, "Mr. Finney, do you recall that my case is to be tried at ten o'clock this morning? I suppose you are ready?" I had been retained to act as his attorney. I replied to him, "Deacon B——, I have a retainer from the Lord Jesus Christ to plead His cause, and I cannot plead yours." He looked at me with astonishment and said, "What do you mean?" I told him, in a few words, that I had enlisted in the cause of Christ and that he must go and get somebody else to attend his lawsuit; I could not do it. He dropped his head and went out without making any reply. A few moments later, in passing the window, I observed that Deacon B—— was standing in the road, seemingly lost in deep meditation. He went away, as I afterward learned, and immediately settled his suit. He then committed himself to prayer and soon got into a much higher religious state than he had ever been in before.

I soon set out from the office to converse with all the people I could find about their souls. I had the impression, which has never left my mind, that God wanted me to preach the Gospel and that I must begin immediately. I somehow seemed to know it with a certainty that was past all possibility of doubt, just as I knew that I had received the love of God and the baptism of the Holy Spirit.

When I was first convicted, the thought had occurred to me that if I was ever converted, I would have to leave my profession, of which I was very fond, and begin preaching the Gospel. This at first was an obstacle to me. I thought I had spent too much time and study in my profession to think now of becoming a Christian, if by doing so I would be obliged to preach the Gospel. However, I at last came to the conclusion that I must submit to God, that I had never commenced the study of law out of any regard to God, and that I had no right to place any conditions on Him. I had laid aside the thought of becoming a minister until the thought came to me, as I have related, on my way from my place of prayer in the woods.

But now, after receiving the baptism of the Spirit, I was quite willing to preach the Gospel. Indeed, I found that I was unwilling to do anything else. I no longer had any desire to practice law. Everything in that direction no longer had any attraction for me at all. I had no desire to make money. I had no hungering and thirsting after worldly pleasures and amusements at all. My whole mind was taken up with Jesus and His salvation, and worldly concerns seemed of very little consequence to me. Nothing, it seemed to me, could be put in competition with the worth of souls; and I thought no labor could be so sweet, and no employment so exalted, as that of holding up Christ to a dying world.

With this impression, I went forth to converse with anyone I might meet. I first dropped in at the shop of a shoemaker, who was a pious man and, in my estimation, one of the most praying Christians in the church. I found him in conversation with a son of one of the elders of the church. This young man was defending Universalism. Mr. W——, the shoemaker, turned to me and said, "Mr. Finney, what do you think of the argument of this young man?" The young man then stated what he had been saying in defense of Universalism. I was so ready with an answer that in a moment I was enabled to blow his argument to the wind. The young man saw at once that his argument was gone, and he rose up without making any reply and went out suddenly. But soon I observed, as I stood in the middle of the room, that the young man, instead of going along the street, had passed around the shop, had climbed over the fence, and was heading straight across the fields toward the woods. I thought no more of it until evening, when the young man came out and appeared to be a bright convert, telling of his experience. He had gone into the woods, and there, so he said, had given his heart to God.

I spoke with many people that day, and I believe the Spirit of God made lasting impressions on every one of them. I cannot remember one whom I spoke with who was not soon after converted. In the afternoon, I called at the house of a friend, where a young man lived who was employed in distilling whiskey. The family had heard that I had become a Christian, and as they were about to sit down to tea, they urged me to sit down and have tea with them. The man of the house and his wife were both people of faith, but the wife's sister, who was present, was unconverted. The young man who distilled whiskey, a distant relative of the family, was a rather outspoken and talkative Universalist, a young man with a good deal of energy.

I sat down with them to tea, and they requested me to ask a blessing. Though I had never before asked a blessing, I did not hesitate a moment but commenced to ask the blessing of God as we sat around the table. I had hardly begun before the state of these young people rose before my mind and excited so much compassion that I burst into weeping and was unable to proceed. Everyone around the table sat speechless for a short time while I continued to weep. Suddenly, the young man moved back from the table and rushed out of the room. He fled to his room, locked himself in, and was not seen again until the next morning, when he came out expressing a blessed hope in Christ. He has been for many years an able minister of the Gospel.

In the course of the day, my conversion had created a good deal of astonishment in the village. In the evening, without any appointed time having been set that I could learn, I observed that the people were going to the place where they usually held their prayer meetings. I afterward learned that some time before this, some members of the church had proposed to make me a subject of prayer. I also learned that Mr. Gale had discouraged them, saying that he did not believe I would ever be converted because I was very much enlightened upon the subject of religion but very much hardened. Furthermore, he said he was almost discouraged that, although I led the choir and taught the young people sacred music, they were so much under my influence that they would probably not be converted while I remained in Adams.

After I was converted, I found that some of the wicked people in the town had hidden behind me. One man in particular, a Mr. C——, who had a pious wife, had repeatedly said to her, "If religion is true, why don't you convert Finney? If you Christians can convert Finney, I will believe in religion."

When an old lawyer by the name of M——, living in Adams, heard that I had been converted, he said that it was all a hoax, that I was simply trying to see what I could make Christian people believe.

However, with one consent the people seemed to rush to the place of worship. I went there myself. The minister was there, along with nearly all the principal people in the village. No one seemed ready to open the meeting, but the house was packed to its utmost capacity. I did not wait for anybody but arose and began by saying that I then knew that religion was from God. I went on and told such parts of my experience as it seemed important for me to tell. This Mr. C——, who had promised his wife that if I was converted he would believe in religion, was present. Mr. M——, the old lawyer, was also present. What the Lord enabled me to say seemed to take a wonderful hold upon the people. Mr. C—— got up, pressed through the crowd, and went home, leaving his hat. Mr. M—— also left and went home, saying I was crazy. "He is in earnest," said he, "there is no mistake; but he is deranged, that is clear."

As soon as I had finished speaking, Mr. Gale rose and made a confession. He confessed that he had discouraged the church when they had proposed to pray for me. He said also that when he had heard that day that I was converted, he had promptly said that he did not believe it. He said he had no faith. He spoke in a very humble manner.

I had never before prayed in public. But soon after Mr. Gale was through speaking, he called on me to pray. We had a wonderful meeting that evening; and, from that day, we had a meeting every evening for a long time. The work spread on every side.

As I had been a leader among the young people, I immediately set up a meeting for them, which they all attended. I gave up my time to labor for their conversion, and in a very wonderful manner the Lord blessed every effort that was made. They were converted one after another, with great rapidity; and the work continued among them so that only one of them was left unconverted.

The work spread among all classes of people and extended itself not only through the village, but also out of the village in every direction. My heart was so full that, for more than a week, I did not feel at all inclined to sleep or eat. I literally seemed to have meat to eat that the world knew nothing of (John 4:32). My mind was overflowing with the love of God. I went on in this way for a good many days, until I found that I must eat and sleep or I would become insane. From that point, I was more cautious in my labors, ate regularly, and slept as much as I could.

The Word of God had wonderful power. Every day I was surprised to find that a few words spoken to an individual would stick in his heart like an arrow.

After a short time, I went to Henderson to visit my father. He was an unconverted man, and only one of the family, my youngest brother, had ever made a profession of faith. My father met me at the gate and said, "How do you

do, Charles?" I replied, "I am well, Father, body and soul.
But Father, you are an old man. All your children are
grown up and have left your house, and I never heard a
prayer in my father's house." Father dropped his head,
burst into tears, and replied, "I know it, Charles; come in
and pray." We went in and engaged in prayer. My father
and mother were greatly moved, and in a very short time
they were both converted.

I remained in that neighborhood for two or three days
and conversed with as many people as I could. I think it was
on the following Monday night that a monthly prayer
meeting was held in Henderson. Despite having two small
churches, the town was very much a moral waste, and at
this time religion was at a very low ebb.

My youngest brother attended this monthly prayer
meeting and afterward gave me an account of it. Because
few people typically attended the meeting, it was held at a
private house. A few of the members of the Baptist church
and a few Congregationalists were present.

The deacon of the Congregational church was a feeble
old man by the name of M——. He was quiet in his ways
and had a good reputation for piety but seldom said much
to anyone upon the subject. He was present, and they called
on him to lead the meeting. He read a passage of Scripture
according to their custom. They then sang a hymn, and
Deacon M—— stood up behind his chair and led in prayer.
The other people present, all of them professors of religion,
knelt down around the room.

My brother said that Deacon M—— began to pray, as
usual, in a low, feeble voice but soon began to raise his
voice, which became tremulous with emotion. He proceeded
to pray with more and more earnestness, until soon he began to rise up on his toes and come down on his heels again
and again, so that everyone could feel the jar in the room.
He continued to raise his voice, rise up on his toes, and
come down on his heels more emphatically each time. As
the spirit of prayer led him onward, he began to raise his
chair together with his heels and bring that down upon the

floor, and soon he raised it a little higher and brought it down with still more emphasis. He continued to do this more and more, until he would bring the chair down as if he would break it to pieces.

In the meantime, the believers who were on their knees began to groan, sigh, weep, and agonize in prayer. The deacon continued to struggle, until he was nearly exhausted. When he ceased, no one in the room could get up from his knees. The people could only weep and confess and melt down before the Lord. From this meeting, the work of the Lord spread forth in every direction all over the town. And thus it spread at that time from Adams as a center, throughout nearly all the towns in the county.

I have said that I was converted in a grove where I went to pray and that Squire Wright, in whose office I studied law, was convicted that same day. Very soon after my conversion, several other cases of conversion occurred that were reported to have taken place under similar circumstances; that is, people went up into the grove to pray, and there they made their peace with God. When Squire Wright heard them tell their experiences, one after the other, in our meetings, he insisted that he could pray anywhere and that he was not going up into the woods to have the same story to tell that had been so often told. Although this was a thing entirely immaterial in itself, it was a point on which his pride had become committed; therefore, he could not get into the kingdom of God in this state.

I have since found a great many cases of this kind, where a sinner's pride of heart commits him to some question, perhaps something immaterial in itself. In all such cases, the dispute must be yielded, or the sinner will never get into the kingdom of God. I have known some people to remain for weeks in great tribulation of mind, pressed by the Spirit, but they could make no progress until the point upon which they were committed was yielded.

After Squire Wright was converted, he said that he had been made to see that it was pride that had made him take that stand and had kept him out of the kingdom of God.

Still he had not been willing to admit this, even to himself. He had tried in every way to make himself believe, and to make God believe, that he was not proud. One night he prayed all night in his parlor that God would have mercy on him, but in the morning he felt more distressed than ever. He finally became enraged that God did not hear his prayer and was tempted to kill himself. He was so tempted to use his penknife for that purpose that he actually threw it as far as he could, so that it might be lost and this temptation would not prevail. On another night, after returning from a meeting, he was pressed with a sense of his pride and with the fact that it prevented his going up into the woods to pray. He therefore looked around for a mud puddle in which to kneel down, so that he might demonstrate that it was not pride that kept him from going into the woods. Thus he continued to struggle for several weeks.

But one afternoon I was sitting in our office, in the company of two of the elders of the church, when the young man whom I had met at the shoemaker's shop came hastily into the office and exclaimed as he came, "Squire Wright is converted! I went up into the woods to pray, and I heard someone shouting very loud. I went up to the brow of the hill, where I could look down, and I saw Squire Wright pacing to and fro, singing as loud as he could sing. Every few moments he would stop, clap his hands with his full strength, and shout, 'I will rejoice in the God of my salvation!' Then he would march and sing again, and then stop, shout, and clap his hands." While the young man was telling us this, Squire Wright could be seen coming over the hill. As he came down to the foot of the hill, we observed that he met Father T——, as we all called him, an aged Methodist brother. He rushed up to him and took him right up in his arms. After setting him down and conversing a moment, he came rapidly toward the office. When he came in, he was sweating profusely—he was a heavy man—and he cried out, "I've got it! I've got it!" clapped his hands with all his might, fell to his knees, and began to give thanks to God. He then gave us an account of what had been passing in his mind and why he had not obtained a hope before. He said as soon as he gave up that point and went into the woods, his mind was relieved; and when he knelt down to pray, the Spirit of God came upon him and filled him with unspeakable joy. From that time, Squire Wright took a decided stand for God.

I had been in the habit of rising early in the morning and spending a season of prayer alone in the church, and I finally succeeded in interesting a number of other believers to meet there in the morning for prayer. This was at a very early hour, and we were generally together long before it was light enough to see to read. I persuaded Mr. Gale to attend these morning meetings.

But soon they began to be remiss, and so I would get up in time to go around to their houses and wake them up. Many times I gathered up those whom I thought would be most likely to attend, and we would have a precious season of prayer. But still they attended with more and more reluctance, a fact that greatly distressed me.

One morning I had been to many of the houses to gather the men, and when I returned to the church, only a few of them had arrived. Mr. Gale was standing at the door of the church, and the day was just beginning to dawn. All at once a light perfectly indescribable shone in my soul and almost prostrated me to the ground. In this light, it seemed as if I could see that all nature praised and worshipped God except man. This light seemed to be like the brightness of the sun in every direction. It was too intense for the eyes. I recall casting my eyes down and breaking into a flood of tears, in view of the fact that mankind did not praise God. I think I then knew, at least in part, of the light that prostrated Paul on his way to Damascus. It was surely a light I could not have endured long.

When I burst out into loud weeping, Mr. Gale said, "What is the matter, Brother Finney?" I could not tell him. I found that he had seen no light and that he saw no reason why I should be in such a state of mind. I therefore said very little. I believe I merely replied that I saw the glory of

God and that I could not endure to think of the manner in which He was treated by men. Indeed, it did not seem to me at the time that this vision of His glory was to be described in words. I continued to weep, and the vision, if it may be so called, passed away and left my mind calm.

When I was a young Christian, I would have many seasons of communing with God that cannot be described in words. Very often those seasons would end in an impression on my mind like this: *"See that you tell no one; but go your way"* (Matt. 8:4). I did not understand this at the time, and several times I paid no attention to this injunction but tried to tell my fellow Christians what the Lord had said to me, or rather what seasons of communion I had had with Him. But I soon found that it was not any good to tell my fellow-men what was passing between the Lord and my soul. They could not understand it. They would look surprised and sometimes, I thought, incredulous. I soon learned to keep quiet in regard to those divine manifestations and to say very little about them.

I used to spend a great deal of time in prayer, sometimes literally praying *"without ceasing"* (1 Thess. 5:17). I also found it very profitable, and felt very much inclined, to hold frequent days of private fasting. On those days I would seek to be entirely alone with God. Sometimes I would pursue a wrong course in fasting, attempting to examine myself according to the ideas then entertained by my minister and the church. I would try to look into my own heart and would turn my attention particularly to my motives and the state of my mind. When I pursued this course, I invariably found that the day would end without any perceptible advance being made. Afterward I saw clearly why this was so: I was turning my attention from the Lord Jesus Christ and looking into myself. But whenever I let the Spirit take His own course with me and let Him lead and instruct me, I always found it useful in the highest degree. I found I could not live without enjoying the presence of God; I could not rest, study, or attend to anything with the least satisfaction or benefit unless the way was clear between my soul and God.

The Lord taught me, in those early days of my Christian experience, many very important truths in regard to the spirit of prayer. Not long after I was converted, a woman with whom I had once boarded became very sick. She was not a Christian, but her husband, a brother of Squire Wright, was a Christian. He came into our office one evening and said to me, "My wife cannot live through the night." A sense of burden came upon me, the nature of which I could not at all understand; with it came an intense desire to pray for that woman. The burden was so great that I left the office almost immediately and went to the church to pray for her. There I struggled but could not say much. I could only groan with groanings loud and deep.

I stayed in the church a considerable time, in this state of mind, but got no relief. I returned to the office, but I could not sit still. I could only pace the room and agonize. I returned to the church again and went through the same process of struggling. For a long time I tried to get my prayer before the Lord, but somehow words could not express it. I could only groan and weep, without being able to express what I wanted in words. I returned to the office again and still found I was unable to rest, and I returned a third time to the church. At this time the Lord gave me power to prevail. I was enabled to roll the burden upon Him, and I obtained the assurance in my own mind that the woman would not die and that she would never die in her sins.

Early the next morning, the husband of this woman came into the office. I inquired how his wife was. Smiling, he said, "She's alive, and to all appearance she is better this morning." I replied, "Brother W——, she will not die with this sickness; you may count on it. And she will never die in her sins." I do not know how I was made sure of this, but it was in some way made plain to me, so that I had no doubt that she would recover. She did recover, and soon afterward she obtained a hope in Christ.

At first I did not understand what this all was. But shortly afterward I related it to a Christian brother. He said to me, "Why, that was the travail of your soul." A few minutes of conversation and pointing me to certain Scriptures led me to understand what it was.

Soon after this, I had another experience that illustrates the same truth. You will remember that there was one young person who remained unconverted among those with whom I was acquainted. She was naturally a charming girl, very much enlightened on the subject of religion, but she remained in her sins. One of the elders of the church and I agreed to make her a daily subject of prayer, to continue to present her case at the throne of grace, morning, noon, and night, until she was converted, until she died, or until we became unable to keep our covenant. Though I remained greatly concerned for her soul, I soon found that my prayer partner was losing his spirit of prayer for her. But this did not discourage me. I continued to hold on with increasing importunity. I also availed myself of every opportunity to converse plainly and searchingly with her on the subject of her salvation.

After I had continued in this way for some time, one evening I went to see her just as the sun was setting. As I came up to the door, I heard a shriek from a female voice and a scuffling and confusion inside the door, so I stood and waited for the confusion to be over. The lady of the house soon came and opened the door, holding in her hand a portion of a book that had evidently been torn in two. She was pale and very much agitated. She held out the portion of the book and said, "Mr. Finney, do you think my sister has become a Universalist?" The book was a defense of Universalism. The young girl's sister had detected her reading it in secret and had tried to get it away from her; what I had heard was the struggle to obtain the book.

I then declined to go in. The information struck me very much in the same way as had the announcement that the sick woman was about to die. It loaded me down with great agony. As I returned to my residence, I felt almost as if I would stagger under the burden that was on my mind. I struggled, groaned, and agonized but could not find words to present the case before God.

The discovery that that young woman, instead of being converted, was becoming a Universalist so astounded me that I could not break through with faith and get hold of God in reference to her case. It seemed as if a cloud of darkness had risen up between me and God in regard to prevailing for her salvation. But still the Spirit struggled within me with groanings that could not be uttered (Rom. 8:26).

However, I was obliged to retire that night without having prevailed. But as soon as it was light I awoke, and the first thought that I had was to ask the God of grace again for that young woman. I immediately got out of bed and fell to my knees. No sooner was I upon my knees than the darkness gave way; as soon as I pleaded for her, God said to me, "Yes! Yes!" If He had spoken with an audible voice, it would not have been more distinctly understood. I was instantly relieved, my mind became filled with the greatest peace and joy, and I felt a complete certainty that her salvation was secure.

I expected her to be converted immediately, but she was not. She remained in her sins for several months. I felt disappointed, at the time, that she was not converted at once, and I wondered whether I had really prevailed with God in her behalf. However, several months later, after attending some lectures that I gave on Universalism, this young woman indeed gave her heart to the Lord.

Soon after I was converted, the man with whom I had been boarding for some time, who was a magistrate and one of the principal men in the town, was deeply convicted of sin. He had been elected a member of the legislature of the state. I was praying daily for him, urging him to give his heart to God. His conviction became very deep; but still, from day to day, he deferred submission and did not obtain a hope. My prayers for him increased.

One afternoon, several of his political friends had a long talk with him. That evening, I again attempted to bring his case to God, as the urgency in my mind for his conversion had become very great. In my prayer, I had drawn very near to God in intimate communion. Indeed, His presence was so real that I was bathed in tears of joy, gratitude, and love. In this state of mind I attempted to pray for this friend. But the moment I did so, my mouth was shut; I found it impossible to pray a word for him. The Lord seemed to say to me, "No, I will not hear." An anguish seized me, which I thought at first was a temptation. But the door was shut in my face, and I had no spirit of prayer for him at all. This pained me beyond expression.

The next morning I saw him. As soon as I brought up the question of submission to God, he said to me, "Mr. Finney, I will have nothing more to do with it until I return from the legislature. I stand committed to my political friends to carry out certain measures in the legislature that are incompatible with my first becoming a Christian, and I have promised that I will not attend to the subject until after I have returned from Albany."

As soon as he told me what he had done, I understood why I could no longer pray for him. I could see that his convictions were all gone, and that the Spirit of God had left him. From that time, he grew more careless and hardened than ever. When he returned in the spring, he was an almost insane Universalist. He remained in his sins, finally fell into decay, and died a dilapidated man, in the full faith of Universalism.

Four

My Doctrinal Education and Other Experiences in Adams

S oon after I was converted, I called on my pastor and had a long conversation with him on the Atonement. Since he was a Princeton student, he of course held the limited view of the Atonement—that it was only for the elect. Our conversation lasted nearly half a day. He believed that Jesus suffered for the elect the literal penalty of the divine law, that He suffered just what was due to each of the elect on the score of retributive justice. I objected that this was absurd, for in that case He suffered the equivalent of endless misery multiplied by the whole number of the elect. But Mr. Gale insisted that this was true.

I was a mere child in theology, a novice in religion and biblical learning. But I thought Mr. Gale did not have biblical views, and I told him so. The only book I had read on the subject was my Bible, and all that I had found there on the subject I had interpreted as I would have the same passages in a law book. I thought Mr. Gale had evidently interpreted Scripture to conform to an established theory of the Atonement.

He was alarmed at my obstinacy. I thought that the Bible clearly taught that the Atonement was made for all men, while he limited it to a part. I could not accept his view, for I could not see that he fairly proved it from the Bible. His rules of interpretation did not meet my own; they were much less definite and intelligible than those to which I had been accustomed in my law studies. To my objections, he could make no satisfactory reply. I asked him if the Bible did not require all who hear the Gospel to repent, believe the Gospel, and be saved. He admitted that it did require all to believe and be saved. But how could they believe and accept a salvation that was not provided for them?

This discussion was often renewed, and it continued throughout my whole course of theological studies under Mr. Gale. I believe he had the strongest conviction that I was truly converted, but he felt the greatest desire to keep me within the strict lines of Princeton theology. After this we had frequent conversations, not only on the question of the Atonement, but also on various theological questions.

I had never heard him preach on the subject of the Atonement. I think he feared to present his views to the people. His church, I am sure, did not embrace his view of a limited atonement.

In the spring of that year, the older members of the church began to decline in their zeal for God. This greatly oppressed me and most of the young converts. About this time I read a newspaper article bearing the title, "A Revival Revived." The gist of it was that a revival had taken place during the winter in a certain town, but in the spring it had declined. When earnest prayer was offered for the continued outpouring of the Spirit, the revival was powerfully revived. This article set me into a flood of weeping.

I was at that time boarding with Mr. Gale, and I took the article to him. The article made no such impression on him as it did on me. I was so overcome with a sense of God's divine goodness in hearing and answering prayer, and with an assurance that God would hear and answer prayer for the revival of His work in Adams, that I went through the house weeping aloud like a child. Mr. Gale seemed surprised at my feelings and my expressed confidence that God would revive His work.

At the next meeting of the young people, I proposed that we should all pray individually for the revival of God's work—that we should pray in our prayer closets at sunrise, at noon, and at sunset for one week, until we would come together again and see what more was to be done. No other means were used for the revival of God's work, but the spirit of prayer was immediately poured out wonderfully upon the young converts. Before the week was out, I learned that some of them, when they would attempt to observe this season of prayer, would lose their strength and be unable to rise to their feet or even rise up on their knees in their prayer closets. I also learned that some would lie prostrate on the floor and pray with unutterable groanings for the outpouring of the Spirit of God. Indeed, the Spirit was poured out; and before the week ended, all the meetings were thronged.

In the spring of this year, 1822, I put myself under the care of the presbytery as a candidate for the Gospel ministry. Some of the ministers urged me to go to Princeton to study theology, but I declined, saying that my financial circumstances forbade it. This was true, but they said they would see that my expenses were paid. Still I refused to go; and when I was urged to give them my reasons, I plainly told them that I would not put myself under such an influence as they had been under. I was confident they had been wrongly educated and that they were not ministers who met my ideal of what a minister of Christ should be. I told them this reluctantly, but I could not honestly withhold it. They appointed Mr. Gale to superintend my studies. He offered me the use of his library and said he would give what attention I needed to my theological studies.

But my studies, so far as he was concerned as my teacher, were little else than controversy. He clung to the old-school doctrine of original sin, or that the human constitution was morally depraved. He also believed that men were utterly unable to do anything that God required them to do and that God had condemned men for their sinful nature, for which they deserved eternal death. In addition, he believed that the influences of the Spirit of God on the minds of men were physical, acting directly upon the substance of the soul. I could not receive these doctrines. But he was quite stubborn and sometimes seemed very impatient with me because I did not receive them without question.

He used to insist that if I tried to reason on the subject, I would probably end up in infidelity. He would remind me that some of the students who had been at Princeton had gone away infidels because they would try to reason on the subject and would not accept the Confession of Faith and the teaching of the professors at that school. He furthermore warned me that I would never be useful as a minister unless I embraced the truth—meaning the truth as he believed and taught it. I was quite willing to believe what I found taught in the Bible, and I told him so.

We used to have many lengthy discussions that greatly discouraged me, and several times I was on the point of giving up the study for the ministry altogether. However, there was one member of the church to whom I opened my mind freely on this subject, and that was Elder H——, a very godly, praying man. He had been educated in Princeton views and held pretty strongly the doctrines of Calvinism. Nevertheless, as we had frequent and long conversations, he became satisfied that I was right. He would call on me frequently to have long seasons of prayer with me that lasted well into the night, to strengthen me in my studies and my discussions with Mr. Gale. He also helped me to decide more and more firmly that, come what would, I would preach the Gospel.

One afternoon Mr. Gale and I had been conversing for a long time on the subject of the Atonement, and the hour arrived for us to attend a Bible study. We continued our conversation on that subject while other people continued to arrive. People would sit down and listen with the greatest attention to what we were saying. When we proposed to stop and begin our meeting, they earnestly begged us to proceed with our discussion and let that be our meeting. We did so and spent the whole evening in that way, very much to the satisfaction and edification of those present.

After many such discussions with Mr. Gale in pursuing my theological studies, the presbytery was finally called together at Adams to examine me and, if they could agree to do so, license me to preach the Gospel. This was in March

Holy Spirit Revivals

1824. I expected a severe struggle with them in my examination, but I think they were cautious of getting into any controversy with me because of the blessing that had evidently attended my conversations and my teaching in prayer meetings, Bible studies, and lectures. In the course of my examination, they avoided asking any questions that would naturally bring my views into collision with theirs.

Unexpectedly, they asked me if I received the Confession of Faith of the Presbyterian Church. This large work containing the catechism and confession had not been part of my studies. I replied that I received it for substance of doctrine, so far as I understood it. But I spoke in a way that plainly implied that I did not know much about it. However, I answered honestly, as I understood it at the time. They heard the trial sermons that I had written, and they went through with all the ordinary details of such an examination. When they had examined me, they voted unanimously to license me to preach.

A large congregation was assembled to hear my examination. At this meeting of the presbytery, I first saw Rev. Daniel Nash, a member of the presbytery who was generally known as Father Nash. I got in a little late and saw a man standing in the pulpit speaking to the people. I noticed that he looked at me as I came in and was looking at others as they walked up the aisles.

As soon as I reached my seat and listened, I observed that he was praying. I was surprised to see him looking all over the church, as if he were talking to the people, while in fact he was praying to God. Of course, it did not sound to me much like prayer, and he was at that time indeed in a very cold and backslidden state.

The Sunday after I was licensed, I preached for Mr. Gale. When I came down from the platform he said to me, "Mr. Finney, I will be very much ashamed to have it known, wherever you go, that you studied theology with me." This was so much like him that I made little or no reply to it. I held down my head, felt discouraged, and went my way.

Afterward he viewed this subject very differently and told me that he blessed the Lord that, in all our discussions, he had not influenced me to change my views in the least. He very frankly confessed his error in the manner in which he had dealt with me and said that I would have been ruined as a minister if I had listened to him.

The fact is, Mr. Gale's education for the ministry had been entirely defective. He had imbibed a set of opinions, both theological and practical, that were a straitjacket to him. He could accomplish very little or nothing if he carried out his own principles. I had the use of his library and searched it thoroughly on all the questions of theology that came up for examination. But the more I examined his books, the more I was dissatisfied.

I had been used to the close and logical reasonings of judges in my law books, but when I went to Mr. Gale's old-school library, I found almost nothing proved to my satisfaction. I am sure it was not because I was opposed to the truth, but I was dissatisfied because the positions of these theological authors were unsound and not satisfactorily sustained. They often seemed to state one thing and prove another, and frequently fell short of logically proving anything.

I finally said to Mr. Gale, "If there is nothing better than I find in your library to sustain the great doctrines taught by our church, I must be an infidel." And I have always believed that if the Lord had not led me to see the fallacy of those arguments and to see the real truth as presented in the Scriptures, I would have been forced to be an infidel.

At first, being no theologian, my attitude in respect to Mr. Gale's views was one of negation or denial, rather than one of direct opposition. I often said, "Your positions are not proved." So I thought then, and so I think now. But Mr. Gale would insist that I ought to defer to the opinions of the great and good men who, after much consultation and deliberation, had come to those conclusions. He said it was unbecoming for me, a young man bred to the profession of law and having no theological education, to stand my views against those of the great men and profound theologians whose opinions I found in his library. He told me that if I persisted in requiring full proof of those points, I would indeed become an infidel.

Now, I could not deny that there was a good deal of force in this, but still I found myself utterly unable to accept doctrine on the ground of authority. If I tried to accept those doctrines as mere dogmas, I could not do it; I could not respect myself in doing it. Often when I left Mr. Gale, I would go to my room and spend a long time on my knees over my Bible. Indeed, I read my Bible on my knees a great deal during those days of conflict, asking the Lord to teach me His mind on those points. I had nowhere to go but directly to the Bible and to the workings of my own mind. In opposition to Mr. Gale, I gradually formed views of my own that appeared to be unequivocally taught in the Bible.

Not only were Mr. Gale's theological views an obstacle to his usefulness, but his practical views were equally erroneous. He assured me that, if I addressed the people as I intended to do, the Spirit of God would not approve and cooperate with my labors, the people would not hear me, they would become offended, and my congregation would all fall off. Unless I wrote out my sermons, he predicted, I would immediately become stale and uninteresting and would divide and scatter instead of build up the congregation wherever I preached.

I do not wonder that he was shocked at my views in relation to preaching the Gospel. With his education, I knew it could not be otherwise. He carried out his views with very little practical result. I pursued mine, and by the blessing of God the results were the opposite of those he had predicted. When this fact came out clearly, it completely upset his theological and practical ideas as a minister. This result at first annihilated his hope as a Christian but finally made him quite another man as a minister.

But there was another defect in Brother Gale's education, which I regarded as fundamental. If he had ever been converted to Christ, he had fallen short of receiving the baptism of the Holy Spirit, which is indispensable to ministerial success and the conversion of souls. When Christ commissioned His apostles to go and preach, He told them to wait in Jerusalem until they were *"endued with power from on high"* (Luke 24:49). This power, as everyone knows, was the baptism of the Holy Spirit poured out upon them on the Day of Pentecost. This was indispensable for success in their ministry. I did not suppose then, nor do I now, that this baptism was simply the power to work miracles. The power to work miracles and the gift of tongues were given as signs to attest the reality of their divine commission. But the baptism itself was a divine purifying, an anointing bestowing on them a divine illumination and filling them with faith, love, peace, and power so that their words were made sharp in the hearts of God's enemies, living and powerful, like a two-edged sword (Heb. 4:12). As far as I could learn of Mr. Gale's spiritual state, he did not have the peace of the Gospel when I sat under his ministry.

I have often been surprised and pained that, to this day, so little stress is laid upon the baptism of the Holy Spirit as a qualification for preaching Christ to a sinful world. Without the direct teaching of the Holy Spirit, a man will never make much progress in preaching the Gospel. The fact is, unless he can preach the Gospel as a real experience, his speculations and theories will come far short of preaching the Gospel.

I hope my reader will not suppose, from anything I have said, that I did not love and highly respect Mr. Gale. I did both. He and I remained the firmest friends to the day of his death. I have said what I have in relation to his views because I think it applicable to many of the ministers of the present day. I think that their practical views of preaching the Gospel, whatever their theological views may be, are very defective, and that their lack of the anointing and power of the Holy Spirit is a fundamental defect in their preparation for the ministry. As I have become more and more acquainted with the ministry, I am persuaded that there is a something missing in their views of the best way of presenting the Gospel to men, despite all their training, discipline, and education. Namely, they lack of the power of the Holy Spirit.

Five

Preaching as a Missionary

Having had no regular training for the ministry, I did not expect or desire to labor in large towns or cities or to minister to longstanding congregations. I intended to go into the new settlements and preach in schoolhouses, barns, and groves as best I could. Accordingly, soon after being licensed to preach, for the sake of being introduced to the region where I proposed to labor, I took a commission for six months from a female missionary society located in Oneida County. I went into the northern part of Jefferson County and began my labors at Evans' Mills.

At this place I found two churches, a small Congregational church without a minister, and a Baptist church with a minister. I presented my credentials to the deacons of the Congregational church. They were very glad to see me, and I soon began my labors with them. They had no meeting place, but the two churches worshipped on alternate Sundays in a large stone schoolhouse, so that I was able to have the building only every other Sunday. But I could use it in the evenings as often as I pleased. I therefore divided my Sundays between Evans' Mills and Antwerp, a village some sixteen or eighteen miles still farther north.

I began, as I said, to preach in the stone schoolhouse at Evans' Mills. The people were very much interested, and they thronged the place to hear me preach. They extolled my preaching, and the little Congregational church became hopeful that they would be built up and that there would be a revival. Convictions occurred under nearly every sermon that I preached, but still no general conviction appeared upon the public mind.

I was very much dissatisfied with this state of things. At one of my evening services, therefore, after having preached there two or three Sundays and several evenings in the week, I told the people at the close of my sermon that I had come there to secure the salvation of their souls. After all, I did not come there to please them but to bring them to repentance. It did not matter to me how well they were pleased with my preaching if they rejected my Master. Something was wrong, either in me or in them, and I could not spend my time with them unless they were going to receive the Gospel. I said all of this to them. Then, quoting the words of Abraham's servant, I said, *"And now if ye will deal kindly and truly with my master, tell me: and if not, tell me; that I may turn to the right hand, or to the left"* (Gen. 24:49 KJV). I asked them this question and insisted that I must know what course they proposed to pursue. If they did not plan to become Christians and enlist in the service of the Savior, I wanted to know it, so that I might not labor with them in vain. I said to them, "You admit that what I preach is the Gospel. You profess to believe it. Now, do you intend to receive it or reject it? You must have some idea about it. I now have a right to take it for granted, inasmuch as you admit that I have preached truth, that you acknowledge your obligation at once to become Christians. This obligation you do not deny, but will you meet the obligation? Will you discharge it? Will you do what you admit you ought to do? If you will not, tell me; and if you will, tell me, so that I may turn to the right or to the left."

After I saw that they understood this but still looked greatly surprised at the way I put it, I said to them, "Now I must know your decision. You who are now willing to pledge to me and to Christ that you will immediately make your peace with God, please rise up. On the contrary, you who want me to understand that you are committed to remain in your present attitude, not to accept Christ—those of you who are of this mind may remain seated." They looked at one another and at me, and all sat still, just as I expected.

After looking around at them for a few moments, I said, "Then you are committed. You have rejected Christ and His Gospel. You are witnesses one against the other, and God is witness against you all. You may remember as long as you live that you have thus publicly committed yourselves against the Savior and said, *'We will not have this man* [Jesus Christ] *to reign over us'* (Luke 19:14)." This is the gist of what I urged upon them.

When I thus pressed them, they began to look angry, arose *en masse,* and started for the door. When they began to move, I paused. As soon as I stopped speaking, they turned to see why I did not go on. I said, "I am sorry for you; and I will preach to you again, the Lord willing, tomorrow night."

They all left the house except Deacon McC——, who was a deacon of the Baptist church in that place. I saw that the Congregationalists were confounded. They were few in number and very weak in faith. I presume that every member of both churches who was present, except Deacon McC——, was taken aback and concluded that, by my imprudence, I had ruined all hopeful appearances. Deacon McC—— came up and took me by the hand and, smiling, said, "Brother Finney, you have got them. They cannot rest under this; rely upon it. The brethren are all discouraged, but I am not. I believe you have done the very thing that needed to be done, and that we shall see the results." I thought so myself, of course. I intended to place them in a position that, upon reflection, would make them tremble in view of what they had done. But for that evening and the next day, they were full of wrath. Deacon McC—— and I agreed to spend the next day in fasting and prayer—separately in the morning, and together in the afternoon. I learned in the course of the day that the people were threatening to tar and feather me and to give me walking papers, as they said. Some of them cursed me, said that I had put them under oath, and said that I had drawn them into a solemn and public pledge to reject Christ and His Gospel.

This was no more than I expected. In the afternoon, Deacon McC—— and I went into a grove together and spent the whole afternoon in prayer. In the evening, the Lord gave us great promise of victory. Both of us felt assured that we had prevailed with God and that the power of God would be revealed among the people that night.

As the time came for meeting, we left the woods and went to the village. The people were already thronging to the place of worship. Those who had not already gone, seeing us go through the village, left their stores and places of business or stopped their games that they were playing in the grass and packed the house to its utmost capacity.

I had not thought even once about what I would preach, which was common for me at that time. The Holy Spirit was upon me, and I felt confident that I would know what to preach when the time came for action. As soon as the building was packed so that no more people could get in, I arose and, without any formal introduction, opened with these words:

> *Say to the righteous that it shall be well with them, for they shall eat the fruit of their doings. Woe to the wicked! It shall be ill with him, for the reward of his hands shall be given him.*   *(Isa. 3:10–11)*

The Spirit of God came upon me with such power that it was like opening a firing squad upon them. For more than an hour, the Word of God came through me to them like a sword that was *"piercing even to the division of soul and spirit"* (Heb. 4:12). I saw that a general conviction was spreading over the whole congregation. Many of them could not hold up their heads. That night I did not ask for any reversal of the action they had taken the night before, or for any commitment of themselves in any way, but I took it for granted during the entire sermon that they were committed against the Lord. Then I set a time for another meeting and dismissed the congregation.

As the people withdrew, I observed in one part of the schoolhouse a woman in the arms of some of her friends, who were supporting her. I went to see what was the matter, supposing that she was in a fainting fit. But I soon found that she was not fainting, but that she could not speak. There was a look of the greatest anguish in her face. I advised the women to take her home, pray with her, and see what the Lord would do. They informed me that she was Miss G——, sister of a well-known missionary, and that she was a member of the church in good standing and had been for several years.

That evening, instead of going to my usual lodgings, I accepted an invitation and went home with a family with which I had not before stayed overnight. Early in the morning, I found out that several people throughout the town had tried to find me at my usual residence during the night, so that I might visit certain family members who were under awful distress of mind. This led me to go out among the people, and everywhere I found a state of wonderful conviction of sin and alarm for their souls.

After lying in a speechless state about sixteen hours, Miss G——'s mouth was opened, and a new song was given to her. She was taken from the horrible pit of miry clay, and her feet were set upon a rock. Many saw it and feared. (See Psalm 40:2–3.) She declared that she had been entirely deceived—that for eight years she had been a member of the church and thought she was a Christian, but during the sermon the night before, she saw that she had never known the true God. When His character arose before her mind as it was then presented, her hope "perished," as she expressed it, "like a moth." She said that such a view of the holiness of God was presented that, like a great wave, it annihilated her hope in a moment.

I found at this place a number of Deists, some of them men of high standing in the community. One of them was the manager of a hotel in the village, and others were respectable men of more than average intelligence. These Deists seemed banded together to resist the revival. When I ascertained exactly the ground they took, I preached a sermon that directly addressed them, for on Sundays they would listen to my preaching. I used this passage as my text:

Bear with me a little, and I will show you that there are yet words to speak on God's behalf. I will fetch my knowledge from afar; I will ascribe righteousness to my Maker. (Job 36:2–3)

I went over their whole position, as far as I understood it, and God enabled me to sweep it clean. As soon as I had finished and dismissed the meeting, the hotel keeper, who was the leader among them, came up to me and, taking me by the hand, said, "Mr. Finney, I am convinced. You have met and answered all my difficulties. I would like to converse with you further." I heard no more of their infidelity, and if I remember correctly, almost that entire group of Deists was converted.

There was one old man in Evans' Mills who was not only an infidel, but also a great railer against religion. He was very angry at the revival movement. Every day I heard about his railing and blaspheming but took no public notice of it. He altogether refused to attend any meetings. But in the midst of his opposition, while sitting one morning at the table, he suddenly fell out of his chair and had a stroke. A physician was immediately called. After a brief examination, the physician told him that he could live a very short time and that if he had anything to say, he must say it at once. The man had just enough strength and time, as I was informed, to stammer out, "Don't let Finney pray over my corpse." This was the last of his opposition in that place.

During that revival, my attention was called to a sick woman in the community. She had been a member of a Baptist church and was well-known in the place, but people had no confidence in her piety. She was quickly dying of tuberculosis, and they begged me to call and see her. I went and had a long conversation with her. She told me a dream, which she had had when she was a girl, that made her believe her sins were forgiven. I tried to persuade her that there was no evidence of her conversion in that dream. Her acquaintances affirmed that she had never lived a Christian life and had never evinced a Christian character, and I had

come to try to persuade her to give up her false hope and
see if she would not now accept Jesus Christ so that she
might be saved. I dealt with her as kindly as I could, but she
took great offense and afterward complained that I had
tried to take away her hope and distress her mind. She
called me cruel for trying to distress a woman as sick as she
was, to disturb the repose of her mind. She died not long
afterward. But when this woman came to be actually dying,
her eyes were opened, and she caught such a glimpse of the
character of God, of what heaven was, and of the holiness
required to dwell there, that she shrieked with agony and
exclaimed that she was going to hell. In this state, she died.

One afternoon, a Christian brother called on me and
wished me to visit his sister, who was dying of tuberculosis
and was a Universalist. Her husband, he said, was a Universalist and had led her into Universalism. I was told to go
and see her when her husband was not at home, because he
was determined that his wife's mind should not be disturbed with the question of universal salvation. I went and
found her very uneasy in her views of Universalism. During
my conversation with her, she gave up these views entirely
and embraced the Gospel of Christ. I believe she held fast to
this hope in Christ until she died.

Her husband returned in the evening and learned from
her what had taken place. He was greatly enraged and
swore he would "kill Finney." He armed himself with a
loaded pistol and that night went to the place where I was
to preach. I knew nothing of this at the time. The meeting
that evening was in a schoolhouse outside of the village. As
I was preaching, I saw a powerful looking man, near the
middle of the room, fall from his seat. As he sunk down he
groaned, and then he shrieked out that he was sinking
down to hell. He repeated this several times. The people
knew who he was, but he was a stranger to me.

Of course, this created a great excitement among the
packed house. It broke up my preaching, and so great was
his anguish that we spent the rest of our time praying for
him. When the meeting was dismissed, his friends helped

him home. The next morning I found that he had spent a sleepless night, and that at the early dawn he had gone forth, they knew not where.

He was not heard from until about ten o'clock in the morning. I was walking up the street and saw him coming, apparently from a grove at some distance from the village. He was on the opposite side of the street, coming toward me, when I first saw him. When he recognized me, he came across the street to meet me, and I saw that his countenance was all aglow. I said to him, "Good morning, Mr. C——." "Good morning," he replied. "And," said I, "how do you feel in your mind this morning?" "Oh," he said, "I do not know. I have had an awfully distressed night. In the morning I went into the woods, but when I got there I found I could not pray. I thought I could give myself to God, but I could not. I tried and tried, until I was discouraged. Finally I saw that it was of no use, and I told the Lord that I found myself condemned and lost; that I had no heart to pray to Him and no heart to repent; that I found I had hardened myself so much that I could not give my heart to Him, and therefore I must leave the whole question to Him." "Well, what followed?" I inquired. "Why," said he, "I got up, and my mind was so still and quiet that I found the Spirit of God was grieved away, and I had lost my conviction. But when I saw you, my heart began to burn within me; and instead of feeling as if I wanted to avoid you, I felt so drawn that I came across the street to see you."

But I should have said that not only was his face glowing when he came near me, but he also leaped, took me right up in his arms, turned around once or twice, and then set me down. After further conversation, I left him in a hopeful state of mind. He never opposed my ministry again.

At this place I again saw Father Nash, the man who prayed with his eyes open at the meeting of the presbytery when I was licensed. After he was at that meeting of the presbytery, he was taken with inflamed eyes and was shut up in a dark room for several weeks, during which he gave himself almost entirely to prayer. His whole Christian experience was overhauled; and as soon as he was able to see, with a double black veil before his face, he sallied forth to labor for souls.

When he came to Evans' Mills, he was full of the power of prayer. He was another man altogether from what he had been at any former period of his Christian life. I found that he had a prayer list of the names of people whom he made subjects of prayer every day and sometimes many times a day. Praying with him and hearing him pray in meetings, I found that his gift of prayer was wonderful, and his faith almost miraculous.

There was a man by the name of Mr. D—— who kept a tavern in a corner of the village and whose house was the resort of all the opposers of the revival. The barroom was a place of blasphemy, and he was himself a most profane, ungodly, abusive man. He went about the streets, railing about the revival, and would take particular pains to swear and blaspheme whenever he saw a Christian. One of the young converts lived almost across the way from him. He told me that he meant to sell his house and move out of that neighborhood because every time he was out of doors and Mr. D—— saw him, he would come out and swear, curse, and say everything he could to hurt his feelings. Mr. D—— had not been to any of our meetings, and of course he was ignorant of the great truths of religion and despised the whole Christian enterprise. Father Nash heard us speak of this Mr. D—— as "a hard case" and immediately put his name on his prayer list.

Not many days afterward, as we were holding an evening meeting in a very crowded house, who should come in but this notorious Mr. D——? His entrance created a considerable stir in the congregation. People feared that he had come to make a disturbance. The fear and abhorrence of him had become very general among Christians, so that when he came in, some of the people got up and left. I recognized his face and kept my eyes on him. Very soon I was convinced that he had come not to oppose, but because he was in great anguish of mind. He sat down and seemed very uneasy. He soon arose and tremblingly asked me if he might say a few words. He then proceeded to make one of the most heartbroken confessions that I have ever heard. His confession seemed to cover the whole ground of his treatment of God, of Christians, of the revival, and of everything good.

This thoroughly broke up the fallow ground in many hearts and was the most powerful means that could have been used, just then, to give an impetus to the work. From that time, a prayer meeting was held in Mr. D——'s barroom nearly every night.

Six

Evans' Mills: The Spirit of Prayer Prevails

A little way from the village of Evans' Mills was a settlement of Germans, where there was a German church with several elders and a considerable membership but no minister and no regular religious meetings. Once each year, they were in the habit of having a minister come up from the Mohawk Valley to administer the ordinances of baptism and the Lord's Supper. He would catechize their children and receive into the church those individuals who had made the required attainments in knowledge. This was the way in which they were made Christians. They were required to commit to memory the catechism and to be able to answer certain doctrinal questions in order to be admitted to full Communion in the church. After receiving Communion, they took it for granted that they were Christians and that all was safe.

But when they heard about the revival in Evans' Mills, they asked me to go out there and preach. I consented, and the first time I preached I used this text: *"Without* [holiness]...*no one will see the Lord"* (Heb. 12:14).

The settlement turned out *en masse,* and the schoolhouse where they worshipped was filled to its utmost capacity. They could understand English well. I began by showing what holiness is not. I took everything that they considered to be religion, and I showed that it was not holiness at all. Second, I showed what holiness is. I then showed what is meant by "seeing the Lord," and I explained why those who had no holiness could never see the Lord—why they could never be admitted to His presence and be accepted by Him. I concluded with pointed remarks that were intended to bring the subject home. And it did reach their hearts by the power of the Holy Spirit.

In a few days, the whole settlement was under conviction. Elders and laypeople were all in the greatest consternation, feeling that they had no holiness. At their request, I set up a meeting to give instruction to inquirers. This was during their harvest time. I held the meeting at one o'clock in the afternoon and found the building literally packed. People had thrown down the implements with which they were gathering their harvest and had come to the meeting.

I stood in the center of the house and asked them questions, encouraging them to ask me questions. They became very much interested and were very free in asking questions and in answering the questions that I asked them. I seldom ever attended a more interesting or profitable meeting than that.

One woman came in late and sat near the door. When I spoke with her after the meeting, I said, "You look unwell." "Yes," she replied, "I am very sick. I have been in bed until I came to this meeting. But I cannot read, and I wanted to hear God's Word so much that I got up and came to the meeting." "How did you come?" I inquired. She replied, "I came on foot." "How far is it?" was the next question. "About three miles," she said. I found that she was under conviction of sin and had a remarkably clear understanding of her position before God. She was soon after converted, and what a remarkable convert she was! She was one of the most exceptional women in prayer, and she repeated more Scripture in her prayers than nearly any person I had ever heard.

I addressed another woman, who was tall and dignified, and I asked her about the state of her mind. She replied immediately that she had given her heart to God and went on to say that the Lord had taught her to read since she had learned how to pray. I asked her what she meant. She said she had never learned how to read, and when she gave her heart to God, she was greatly distressed that she could not read God's Word. "But I thought," she said, "that Jesus could teach me to read, and I asked Him if He would teach me to read His Word. When I had prayed, I believed I could read. So I went and got my children's New Testament and tried to read what I had heard them read. I then went to the schoolteacher and asked her if I read correctly, and she said I did. Since then, I can read the Word of God for myself." When I later asked her neighbors about her, they all confirmed that she could not read a syllable until after she was converted.

The revival among the Germans resulted in the conversion of the whole church and of nearly the whole community. It was one of the most interesting revivals that I ever witnessed.

I have only narrated some of the principal facts connected with this revival in Evans' Mills. But I should also say regarding it that a wonderful spirit of prayer and great unity of feeling prevailed among Christians. The little Congregational church had been discouraged and confused after I had pressed them to receive or reject Christ. But as soon as they saw the results of the next evening's preaching, they recovered themselves. They rallied and took hold of the work as best they could; and though they were a feeble and inefficient band, with one or two exceptions, still they grew *"in the grace and knowledge of our Lord and Savior Jesus Christ"* (2 Pet. 3:18) during that revival.

The Baptist minister and I seldom met each other, though sometimes we were enabled to attend meetings together. He preached in the schoolhouse half of the time, and I the other half. Consequently, I was generally away when he was there, and he was generally absent when I was there. He was a good man and worked as best he could to promote the revival. Both churches were so strengthened, and their numbers so greatly increased, that they soon went forward and built each of them a stone meetinghouse, and I believe they have had a healthy state of religion since that time.

The doctrines preached during the revival were those I have always preached as the Gospel of Christ. I insisted on the voluntary, total moral depravity of the unregenerate, and on the unalterable necessity of a fundamental change of heart by the Holy Spirit and by means of the truth.

I laid great stress upon prayer as an indispensable condition of promoting the revival. The atonement of Jesus Christ, His divinity, His divine mission, His perfect life, His vicarious death, His resurrection, repentance, faith, justification by faith, and all the kindred doctrines were discussed as thoroughly as I was able, were pressed home, and were evidently made effective by the power of the Holy Spirit.

The means used were simply preaching, prayer and conference meetings, much private prayer, much personal conversation, and meetings for the instruction of earnest inquirers. These, and no other means, were used for the promotion of that work and the work of many revivals to come. There was no appearance of fanaticism, no bad spirit, no divisions, no heresies, no schisms. At that time, and certainly as long as I was at that place, there was no regrettable or questionable result of that revival.

But there were cases of intensified opposition to this revival. In one nearby region a few years before, there had been a wild excitement passing through that region. They had called it a revival of religion, but it had turned out to be false. It resulted in the impression on many minds that religion was mere delusion. Taking what they had seen as a specimen of a revival of religion, they felt justified in opposing anything that resembled the promoting of a revival.

I found that it had left among Christian people some practices that were offensive—practices meant to arouse ridicule rather than any serious conviction of the truth of religion. For example, in all their prayer meetings I found a custom prevailing like this: everyone who professed religion felt it his duty to testify for Christ, "take up the cross," and say something in the meeting. One would rise and say, essentially, "I have a duty to perform that no one can perform for me. I arise to testify that religion is good, though I must confess that I do not enjoy it at present. I have nothing in particular to say, only to bear my testimony. I hope you will all pray for me." That person would sit down, and another would rise and say, almost to the same effect, "Religion is good, though I do not enjoy it. I have nothing else to say, but I must do my duty. I hope you will all pray for me." Thus the time would be occupied, and the meeting would pass with very little that was more interesting than these remarks. Of course, the ungodly would make sport of this.

It was, in fact, ridiculous and repulsive. But the impression was so rooted in the public mind that this was the way to hold a prayer and conference meeting that it became the duty of every Christian person, whenever an opportunity was afforded, to give such testimony for God. In order to get rid of this custom, I was obliged to hold no such meetings. Consequently, I appointed every meeting for preaching. When we were assembled, I would begin by singing, and then I would pray myself. I would then call on one or two others to pray, naming them. I would name a Scripture and talk for a while. Then, when I saw that an impression was made, I would stop and ask one or two to pray that the Lord might fasten that on their minds. I would proceed with my talk and, after a little while, stop again and ask one or two to pray. Thus I would proceed, not throwing the meeting open at all for remarks on the part of the people. Then they could go away without feeling that they had neglected their duty in not bearing testimony for God. In this way I was enabled to overcome that silly method of holding meetings that created so much ridicule on the part of the ungodly.

After the revival took a thorough hold in this place, opposition entirely ceased so far as I could learn. I spent more than six months in Evans' Mills and in Antwerp, laboring between the two places, and for the latter part of the time I heard nothing of open opposition.

During the whole six months that I labored in that region, I rode on horseback from town to town and preached the Gospel as I had opportunity. When I left Adams, my health had deteriorated a good deal. I had coughed blood, and at the time I was licensed, my friends thought that I could live only a short time. Mr. Gale charged me, when I

left Adams, not to attempt to preach more than once a
week, and then to be sure not to speak more than half an
hour at a time. But instead of this, I visited from house to
house, attended prayer meetings, and preached and labored
every day, and almost every night, through the whole season. Before the six months were completed, my health was
entirely restored, my lungs were sound, and I could preach
two hours or longer without feeling the least fatigue. I
preached out of doors; I preached in barns; I preached in
schoolhouses, and a glorious revival spread all over that
new region.

Seven

Secrets to Successful Ministry

A ll through the earlier part of my ministry, I used to hear from ministers a great many rebuffs and reproofs, particularly in respect to my manner of preaching. You will remember that, when I preached for Mr. Gale immediately after I was licensed, he told me he would be ashamed to have anyone know that I was a pupil of his. The fact is, their education had been so entirely different from mine that they disapproved of my manner of preaching very much. They would reprove me for illustrating my ideas by referring to the common affairs of men of different pursuits around me, as I was in the habit of doing. I borrowed my illustrations from the occupations of farmers, mechanics, and other classes of men. I also tried to use words that they would understand by addressing them in the language of the common people, and I sought to express all my ideas in few words.

People have often said to me, "You do not preach. You just talk to the people. Anybody could preach as you do." A man in London, who had been a skeptic, went home from one of our meetings greatly convicted. His wife, seeing him greatly excited, said to him, "Husband, have you been to hear Mr. Finney preach?" He replied, "I have been to Mr. Finney's meeting. He doesn't preach; he only explains what other people preach." Others have said about my preaching, "It doesn't seem like preaching. Rather, it seems as if Mr. Finney took me alone and was conversing with me face to face."

Before I was converted, I had a different tendency. In writing and speaking, I had sometimes allowed myself to use ornate language. But when I began to preach the Gospel, I was so eager to be thoroughly understood that I earnestly studied to express my thoughts with the greatest simplicity of language. This was extremely contrary to the ideas that prevailed among ministers at that time and still prevail to a very great extent.

In reference to my illustrations they would say, "Why don't you illustrate from events of ancient history and take a more dignified way of illustrating your ideas?" I defended myself by saying that my objective was not to cultivate a style of oratory that would soar above the heads of the people, but to make myself understood. Therefore, without being coarse or vulgar, I would use any language adapted to this end.

But many of my fellow ministers were completely in the dark regarding the results of that method of addressing people. They used to complain that I let down the dignity of the pulpit; that I was a disgrace to the ministerial profession; that I talked like a lawyer at the bar; that I talked to the people in a colloquial manner; that I said "you" instead of saying "they" and instead of preaching about sin and sinners in general; that I said "hell" with such an emphasis that I often shocked the people; furthermore, that I urged the people with such vehemence, as if they might not have a moment to live. And sometimes they complained that I blamed the people too much.

Ministers generally avoid preaching what the people before them will understand. They will preach to them about other people, and the sins of other people, instead of addressing them and saying, "You are guilty of these sins" and "The Lord requires this of you." They often preach about the Gospel instead of preaching the Gospel. They often preach about sinners instead of preaching to them. They studiously avoid being personal, in the sense of making anyone present feel he is the man. I have always pursued a different course. I have often said, "Do not think I am talking about anybody else; for I mean you, you, and you."

Ministers told me at first that people would never endure this but would get up, walk out, and never come to hear me again. But this is all a mistake. Very much depends on the spirit in which something is said. If the people see that it is said in the spirit of love, with a yearning desire to do them good; if they cannot deny that it is telling the truth in love and that it is coming right home to them to save them individually, there are very few who will continue to resent it. At the time they may feel pointed at and rebuked; nevertheless, the conviction is upon them that they needed it, and it will surely ultimately do them great good.

I have often said to people, when I saw that they looked offended, "Now you resent this, and you will go away and say that you will not come again. But you will come again. Your own convictions are on my side. You know that what I tell you is true, that I tell it for your own good, and that you cannot continue to resent it." I have always found this to be true.

After I had preached some time and the Lord had added His blessing everywhere, I used to say to ministers, whenever they contended with me about my manner of preaching and desired me to adopt their ideas and preach as they did, that I dared not make the change they desired. I said, "Show me a more excellent way. Show me the fruits of your ministry, and if they far exceed mine, I will adopt your views. But you yourselves cannot deny that, whatever errors I may have fallen into, or whatever imperfections there may be in my preaching style, the results justify my methods. I intend to improve all I can, but I can never adopt your manner of preaching the Gospel until I have higher evidence that you are right and I am wrong."

Oftentimes, they used to complain that I was guilty of repetition in my preaching. I would take the same thought and turn it over and over, illustrating it in various ways. I assured them that I thought this was necessary in order to make myself understood, and I could not be persuaded to relinquish this practice by any of their arguments. Then they would say, "You will not interest the educated part of your congregation." But facts soon silenced them on this point, too. They found that judges, lawyers, and educated men were converted by scores under my preaching, whereas such a thing seldom occurred under their methods.

I was, from the very first, aware that I would encounter this opposition and that there was this wide gulf between me and other ministers. I seldom felt that I was one of them or that they regarded me as really belonging to their fraternity. I was bred a lawyer. I came right from a law office to the pulpit, and I talked to the people as I would have talked to a jury.

I have always taken their criticisms kindly and given them credit for benevolent intentions. In reply to their objections, I have sometimes told them what a judge of the supreme court said to me on this subject. "Ministers," said he, "do not exercise good sense in addressing the people. They are afraid of repetition. They use language not well understood by the common people. Their illustrations are not taken from the common pursuits of life. They write in too elevated a style and are not understood by the people.

"Now, if lawyers were to take such a course, they would ruin themselves and their cause. When I was at the bar, I used to take it for granted that I would have to repeat my main points about as many times as there were persons in the jury box. I learned that unless I did so, I would lose my cause. Our objective in addressing a jury is to get their minds settled before they leave the jury box. We are not to make a speech in language they can understand only in part; we are not to use illustrations entirely above their comprehension; we are not to display our oratory and then let them go. We are set on getting a verdict.

"Hence, we are determined to be understood. We mean to convince them; and if they have doubts as to the law, we make them understand it, and we rivet it in their minds. In short, we expect to get a verdict and to get it on the spot, so that when they go to their room, they will have understood us and will have been convinced by the facts and arguments. If we do not thus take pains to urge home every thought, every word, and every point, so as to lodge it in their convictions, we are sure to lose our cause.

"Now, if ministers would do this, the effects of their preaching would be unspeakably different from what they are. They go into their study and write a sermon, they go to their pulpit and read it, and those who listen to it poorly understand it, until they go home and consult their dictionaries. Ministers do not address the people, expecting to convince them and to get their verdict in favor of Christ on the spot. They rather seem to aim at making fine literary productions and displaying great eloquence and ornate language."

I could mention many facts illustrative of the views of ministers and of the manner in which they sometimes treated me. But I hope nothing I say on this subject will leave the impression that I thought either my views or my methods perfect, for I had no such thought. I was aware that I was only a child. I had not enjoyed the advantages of the higher schools of learning, and so I had been conscious all along that I lacked those qualifications that would make me acceptable, especially to ministers, but also to the people. Thus, I had never had any higher ambition than to go into the new settlements and places where they did not enjoy the Gospel.

I was often surprised myself, in the first years of my preaching, to find it so edifying and acceptable to the most educated classes. This was more than I had expected and greatly more than my fellow ministers had expected. I always endeavored to improve in everything in which I discovered myself to be in error. But the longer I preached, the less reason had I to think that my error lay in the direction in which my fellow ministers supposed it to lie.

The more experience I had, the more I saw the results of my method of preaching, and the more I conversed with all classes, high and low, educated and uneducated, the more was I convinced that God had led me, had taught me, and had given me right ideas in regard to the best manner of winning souls. I know that God taught me, for surely I never had obtained these ideas from man. I have often thought that I could say with perfect truth, as Paul said, that I was not taught the Gospel by man, but by the Spirit of Christ Himself. (See Galatians 1:11–12.) And I was taught it by the Spirit of the Lord in a manner so clear and forcible that no argument of my ministerial brethren had the least weight with me.

I mention this as a matter of duty, for I am still convinced that the seminaries are spoiling the ministers to a great extent. Ministers in these days have great facilities for obtaining information on all theological questions. They are vastly more knowledgeable in theological, historical, and biblical learning than they perhaps ever have been in any age of the world. Yet with all their learning, they do not know how to use it. They are, after all, much like David in Saul's armor. A man can never learn to preach except by preaching.

As I later learned, it was very common in my earlier years of preaching for ministers to agree among themselves that, if I were to succeed in the ministry, it would bring the seminaries into disrepute. They were afraid that men would come to think it hardly worthwhile to support the schools with their funds if a man could be accepted as a successful preacher without them. I never had a thought of devaluing the education furnished by colleges or theological seminaries, though I did think, and think now, that in certain respects they are greatly mistaken in their modes of training their students. The students should be encouraged to exercise and improve their gifts and calling of God by going out into any places open to them and by holding Christ up to the people in earnest talks. Men cannot learn to preach without practice.

Instead of this, the students are required to write what they call sermons and to present them for criticism. That is, the sermons are read to the class and the professor. Thus, they play preaching. No man can preach in this manner. These so-called sermons will, of course, degenerate into literary essays under the criticism they receive. This reading of elegant literary essays is not preaching; it may be gratifying to literary taste, but it is not spiritually edifying and is not calculated to win souls to Christ. People who want to hear the Word of God have no respect for such sermons. As for real eloquence—that gushing, impressive, and persuasive oratory that naturally flows from an educated man whose soul is on fire with his subject and who is free to pour out his heart to a waiting and earnest people—they have none of it. Our theological schools would be of much greater value if they were much more practical.

My experience has been, even in respect to personal popularity, that "honesty is the best policy" in a minister. If he intends to maintain his hold upon the confidence, respect, and affection of any congregation, he must be faithful to their souls. He must let them see that he is not courting them for any purpose of popularity, but that he is trying to save their souls. Men are not fools. They have no solid respect for a man who will go to the pulpit and preach smooth things. They deeply despise it in their inmost souls. No man will gain permanent respect or will be permanently honored by his people unless he deals faithfully with their souls as an ambassador of Christ.

The great argument in opposition to my views of preaching the Gospel was that I could not give nearly so much instruction to the people as I would if I wrote my sermons. They said it would never do for a pastor to preach extemporaneously. Now, I have the best of reasons for believing that preachers of written sermons do not give their people as much instruction as they think they do. The people do not remember their sermons. In multitudes of instances, I have heard people complain, "I cannot carry home anything that I hear from the pulpit." They have said to me, "We always remember what we have heard you preach. We remember your text and the manner in which you handled it, but written sermons we cannot remember."

I have been a pastor now for many years—ever since 1832—and I have never heard any complaint that I did not instruct the people. My habit has always been to study the Gospel, so that my mind is always pondering the truths of the Gospel and the best ways of using them. I go among the people and learn their needs. Then, in the light of the Holy Spirit, I take a subject that I think will meet their present needs. I think intensely on it, I pray much over the subject, I get my mind full of it on Sunday morning, and then I go and pour it out to the people. One great difficulty with a written sermon is that, after one has written it, he needs to think very little of the subject, and he needs to pray very little. He perhaps reads over his manuscript Saturday evening or Sunday morning, but he does not feel the need for being powerfully anointed, so that his mouth may be opened and that he may be enabled to preach out of a full heart. He is quite at ease. He has only to use his eyes and his voice, and he can preach. It may be a sermon that has been written for years; it may be a sermon that he has written himself within the week. But on Sunday, there is no freshness in it. It does not come as a new, fresh, and anointed message from God to his heart, and through his heart to the people.

I think I have studied all the more for not having written my sermons. I have been obliged to become familiar with the subjects upon which I preached, and to fill my mind with them so that I could then go and talk them off to the people. I simply sketch an outline of the remarks I plan to make and the inferences with which I will conclude. When I first began to preach, and for the first twelve years of my ministry, I wrote not a word. Thus, I commonly preached without any preparation, except what I got in prayer. Oftentimes I went to the pulpit without knowing upon what Scripture I would speak or a word that I would say. I depended on the occasion and the Holy Spirit to suggest the Scripture and to open up the whole subject to my mind, and certainly I preached with great success and power. It seemed that I could see with intuitive clearness just what I ought to say, and whole platoons of thoughts, words, and illustrations came to me as fast as I could deliver them.

I began to make very bare outlines—what I called "skeletons"—to preserve what had been given me, after I had already preached it. When the Spirit of God had given me a very clear view of a subject, I found I could not retain it in order to use it on any other occasion, unless I jotted down an outline of the thoughts. But after all, I have never found myself able to use old skeletons in preaching without remodeling them and having a fresh and new view of the subject given me by the Holy Spirit. I almost always get my subjects on my knees in prayer. It has been a common experience with me, upon receiving a subject from the Holy Spirit, to have it make so strong an impression on my mind as to make me tremble. When subjects are thus given me that seem to go through me, body and soul, I can in a few moments make out a skeleton that will enable me to retain the view presented by the Spirit. I find that such sermons always have great power upon the people.

The power of these sermons was not the result of any productions of my own brain or of my own heart, unassisted by the Holy Spirit. They were not from me, but from the Holy Spirit in me. This higher inspiration is promised to all who have been called by Christ to preach the Gospel. What else did Christ mean when He said, *"Go therefore and make disciples of all the nations...and lo, I am with you always, even to the end of the age"* (Matt. 28:19–20)? All ministers may be, and ought to be, so filled with the Holy Spirit that all who hear them will be impressed with the conviction that "God is surely in them."

Eight

Antwerp: Two Women
Restored to Sanity

I must now give some account of my labors and their result in Antwerp, a village north of Evans' Mills. I arrived there for the first time in April and found that no
religious services of any kind were held in the town. The
land in the township belonged to Mr. P——, a rich land-
holder who resided in Ogdensburgh. To encourage the settlement of the township, he had built a brick church. But
the people had no desire to keep up public worship. Therefore, the church was locked up, and the key was in the possession of Mr. C——, who kept the village hotel.

I very soon learned that there was a Presbyterian
church in that place, consisting of a few members. Some
years before, they had tried to keep up a meeting at the
village on Sundays. But Deacon R——, who conducted their
Sunday meetings, lived about five miles out of the village;
and in approaching the village, he was obliged to pass
through a Universalist settlement. The Universalists had
broken up the village meeting by making it impossible for
Deacon R—— to get through their settlement to the meeting. They would even take the wheels off his carriage, and
finally they carried their opposition so far that he gave up
attending meetings at the village. After that, all religious
services in the township were relinquished.

There were three pious women in the village: the hotel
keeper's wife, Mrs. C——; a Mrs. H——, the wife of a merchant; and a Mrs. R——, the wife of a physician. I arrived
there on a Friday and called on those pious women, asking
them if they would like to have a meeting. They said that
they would, but they did not know that it would be possible.
Mrs. H—— agreed to open her parlor that evening for a

meeting, if I could get anybody to attend. I went around and invited the people, securing the attendance of about thirteen people. After I preached to them in her parlor, I said I would preach on Sunday if I could get the use of the village schoolhouse. I got the consent of the trustees, and the next day the news of a Sunday morning meeting at the schoolhouse was spread among the people.

In going around the village, I heard a vast amount of profanity, more than in any place I had ever visited. It seemed as if the men, no matter what they were doing, were all cursing and swearing and damning each other. I felt as if I had arrived upon the borders of hell. I had an awful feeling as I went around the village on Saturday. The very atmosphere seemed to me to be poison, and a kind of terror took possession of me.

I gave myself to prayer on Saturday, and finally this answer came: *"Do not be afraid, but speak, and do not keep silent; for I am with you, and no one will attack you to hurt you; for I have many people in this city"* (Acts 18:9–10). This completely relieved me of all fear. I found, however, that the Christian people there were really afraid that something serious might happen if religious meetings were again established in that place. But I could see that the news of my preaching at the schoolhouse had passed around the village enough to arouse quite an excitement.

Sunday morning I arose and left my lodgings in the hotel. In order to get alone, where I could let out my voice as well as my heart, I went up into the woods at some distance from the village and remained for a considerable time in prayer. However, I did not find relief, so I went up a second time; but the load upon my mind increased, and I did not find relief. I went up a third time, and then the answer came. I found that it was time for the meeting and went immediately to the schoolhouse. It was packed to its utmost capacity. I had my pocket Bible in my hand and read to them this Scripture: *"God so loved the world that He gave His only begotten Son, that whoever believes in Him should not perish but have everlasting life"* (John 3:16). I cannot

77

remember much that I said, but I know that the point I was trying to bring home was the treatment that God received in return for His love. The subject affected my own mind very much, and I preached and poured out my soul and my tears together.

Attending the meeting were several of the men who had been so profane the day before. I pointed them out and told what they had said—how they called on God to damn each other. Indeed, I let loose my whole heart upon them. I told them they seemed to howl blasphemy in the streets like hellhounds, and it seemed to me that I had arrived on the very verge of hell. Everybody knew that what I said was true, and the people wept about as much as I did myself. I think there were scarcely any dry eyes in the house.

Mr. C——, the keeper of the hotel, had refused to open the church in the morning. But as soon as these first services came to an end, he arose and said to the people that he would open the church in the afternoon.

The people scattered and carried the information in every direction, and in the afternoon the church was nearly as crowded as the schoolhouse had been in the morning. Everybody was at the meeting, and the Lord let me loose upon them in a wonderful manner. My preaching seemed to be something new to them. Indeed, it seemed to me as if I could rain hail and love upon them at the same time—in other words, that I could rain hail upon them in love. It seemed as if my love for God, in view of the abuse that they heaped upon Him, sharpened my mind to the most intense agony. I felt like rebuking them with all my heart and yet with a compassion that they could not mistake. I don't think they ever accused me of severity, although I think I never spoke with more severity, perhaps, in my life.

The labors of this day were effective in convicting most of the population. From that day, no matter when or where I would appoint a meeting, the people would throng to hear. The work immediately commenced and went forward with great power. I preached twice in the village church on Sundays, attended a prayer meeting at intermission, and generally preached somewhere, usually in a schoolhouse in the neighborhood, at five o'clock in the afternoon.

On the third Sunday that I preached there, an aged man came to me as I was approaching the pulpit. He asked me if I would go and preach in a schoolhouse in his neighborhood, about three miles away, saying that they had never had any services there. He wished me to come as soon as I could. I told him I would come the next day, Monday, at five o'clock in the afternoon.

Monday was a warm day. I left my horse at the village and thought I would walk the three miles, so that I would have no trouble in calling on all the people in the neighborhood of the schoolhouse. However, before I reached the place, having worked so hard the day before, I found myself very much exhausted, and I sat down by the road and felt as if I could scarcely proceed. I blamed myself for not having taken my horse. I was therefore not able to call on anyone before five o'clock.

But at the appointed hour, I found the schoolhouse full, and I could only find room to stand near the open door. I read a hymn, and I cannot call it singing, for they seemed never to have had any church music in that place. The people ventured to sing, but it amounted to each one bellowing out in his own way. My ears had been cultivated by teaching church music, and their horrible discord distressed me so much that, at first, I thought I must go out. I finally put both hands over my ears and held them with my full strength. But this did not shut out the discord. I withstood it, however, until they were through. Then I cast myself down on my knees, almost in a state of desperation, and began to pray. The Lord opened the windows of heaven, and the spirit of prayer was poured out, and I let my whole heart out in prayer.

I had not thought about a text upon which to preach but had waited to see the congregation. As soon as I had finished praying, I rose from my knees and said, *"Get up, get out of this place; for the LORD will destroy this city!"* (Gen. 19:14). I then went on to explain this Scripture, telling them about Abraham and his nephew, Lot. I explained their relationship to each other, their separating from each other on account of differences between their herdsmen, and that Abraham took the hill country while Lot settled in the valley of Sodom. I then told them how exceedingly wicked Sodom became, and what abominable practices they fell into. I told them that the Lord decided to destroy Sodom, and so He visited Abraham to inform him of what He was about to do. I said that Abraham prayed to the Lord to spare Sodom, if He found so many righteous people there, and the Lord promised to do so for their sakes. Abraham then asked God to save it for a fewer number of righteous people, and the Lord said He would spare it for their sakes. Abraham kept on reducing the number, until he reduced the number of righteous people to ten. God promised him that, if He found ten righteous people in the city, He would spare it. But no further request was made, and God could find only one righteous person there, and that was Lot, Abraham's nephew.

> *Then the men said to Lot, "Have you anyone else here? Son-in-law, your sons, your daughters, and whomever you have in the city; take them out of this place! For we will destroy this place, because the outcry against them has grown great before the face of the LORD, and the LORD has sent us to destroy it."*
> (Gen. 19:12–13)

While I was relating these facts, I observed the people looking as if they were angry. Many of the men looked at each other and at me as if they were ready to fall upon me and chastise me on the spot. I saw their strange and unaccountable looks and could not understand what I was saying that had offended them. However, it seemed to me that their anger rose higher and higher as I continued the narrative. As soon as I had finished the narrative, I turned upon them and said that I understood that they had never had a religious meeting in that place, and that I therefore had a right to take it for granted that they were an ungodly people. I pressed that home upon them with more and more energy, with my heart full almost to bursting.

I had not spoken to them in this direct manner for more than a quarter of an hour, when all at once an awful solemnity seemed to settle down upon them. The congregation began to fall from their seats in every direction and to cry for mercy. If I had had a sword in each hand, I could not have cut them off their seats as fast as they fell. Indeed, nearly the whole congregation were either on their knees or on the floor in less than two minutes. Everyone prayed for himself who was able to speak at all.

Of course, I was obliged to stop preaching, for they no longer paid any attention. I said to them, "You are not in hell yet. Now let me direct you to Christ." For a few moments I tried to hold forth the Gospel to them, but scarcely any of them paid any attention. My heart was so overflowing with joy at this scene that I could hardly contain myself. It was with much difficulty that I refrained from shouting and giving glory to God.

As soon as I could sufficiently control my feelings, I turned to a young man who was close to me and who was engaged in praying for himself, laid my hand on his shoulder to get his attention, and preached Jesus in his ear. As soon as I got his attention to the cross of Christ, he believed, was calm and quiet for a minute or two, and then broke out in praying for the others. I then turned to another and took the same course with him, with the same result; and then another, and another.

In this way I continued, until the time arrived when I had to leave them and go to fulfill an appointment in the village. I told them this, and I asked the old man who had invited me there to remain and take charge of the meeting while I went to my appointment. He did so. But there was too much interest, and there were too many wounded souls, to dismiss the meeting; and so it was held all night. In the morning, there were still some there who could not get away, and they were carried to a private house in the neighborhood, in order to make room for the school. In the afternoon, they sent for me to come down there, as they could not yet break up the meeting.

When I went down the second time, I received an explanation of the anger shown by the congregation during the introduction of my sermon the day before. I learned that their town was called Sodom, that there was only one pious man in the place, and that they him called Lot. This was the old man who had invited me there. The people supposed that I had chosen my subject, and had preached to them in that manner, because they were so wicked as to be called Sodom. This was a striking coincidence, but as far as I was concerned, it was altogether accidental.

Although this revival came upon them so suddenly and was of such a powerful type, the converts were sound, and the work permanent and genuine. I never heard of any disastrous reaction having taken place.

I have spoken of the Universalists having prevented Deacon R—— from attending religious meetings on Sunday in the village of Antwerp by taking the wheels off his carriage. When the revival got its full strength, Deacon R—— wanted me to go and preach in that neighborhood of Universalists. Accordingly, I made an appointment to preach on a certain afternoon in their schoolhouse. When I arrived, I found the schoolhouse filled, and Deacon R—— sitting near a window by a stand with a Bible and hymnbook on it. I sat down beside him, then arose and read a hymn, and they sang along. After praying, I read this Scripture to them: *"Serpents, brood of vipers! How can you escape the condemnation of hell?"* (Matt. 23:33).

I saw that Deacon R—— was very uneasy, and he soon got up and went and stood in the open doorway. As there were some boys near the door, I supposed, at the time, that he had gone to keep the boys still. But I afterward learned that it was through fear. From my text he concluded that I was going to deal very plainly with them, and he had been made quite nervous about the opposition that he had encountered from them and wanted to keep out of their reach.

I proceeded to pour myself out upon them with all my might, and before I was through, there was a complete upturning of the very foundations of Universalism in that place. It was a scene that almost equaled that of Sodom. Thus, the revival penetrated to every part of the town, and some of the neighboring towns shared in the blessing. The work was very precious in this place.

Among the converts was a considerable number whose friends were Methodists. On a Saturday I learned that some Methodist people were saying to the converts, "Mr. Finney is a Presbyterian. He believes in the doctrine of election and predestination, but he has not preached it here. He dares not preach it, because if he did, the converts would not join his church." This led me to preach on the doctrine of election the Sunday morning before they joined the church. Using Scripture, I explained all that I knew to be true about the doctrine of election: that it is a doctrine of the Bible, that to deny it is to deny the very attributes of God, that it poses no obstacle to the way of the salvation of the non-elect, that all men may be saved if they desire to be, and that it is the only hope that anybody will be saved. The Lord made the doctrine so clear to me and to the people that I believe it convinced the Methodists themselves.

There were many interesting cases of conversion in this place, and there were two very striking cases of instantaneous recovery from insanity during this revival. As I went into a meeting one Sunday afternoon, I saw several ladies sitting in a pew with a woman who was dressed in black and seemed to be in great distress of mind. They were partly holding her, to prevent her from going out. As I came in, one of the ladies came to me and told me that this woman was insane, that she had been a Methodist but had, as she supposed, fallen from grace into despair and finally to insanity. Her husband was an intemperate man. He had brought her to the meeting and had gone to the tavern. I said a few words to her, but she replied that she could not listen to any praying, preaching, or singing; that hell was her portion; and that she could not endure anything that made her think of heaven.

I cautioned the ladies, privately, to keep her in her seat, if they could do so without her disturbing the meeting. I then went to the pulpit and read a hymn. As soon as the singing began, this woman struggled hard to get out. But the ladies held her and kindly but persistently prevented her escape. After a few moments she became quiet but seemed to avoid hearing or listening at all to the singing. I then prayed. For a short time, I heard her struggling to get out. But before I had finished, she became quiet, and the congregation was still. The Lord gave me a great spirit of prayer, along with this Scripture: *"Let us therefore come boldly to the throne of grace, that we may obtain mercy and find grace to help in time of need"* (Heb. 4:16).

My purpose was to encourage faith, not only in ourselves, but also in her and in ourselves for her. As I proceeded with my prayer, she began to raise her head gradually and to look at me from within her long black bonnet. She looked up more and more, until she sat upright and looked me in the face with intense earnestness. As I proceeded to urge the people to be bold in their faith, to launch out and commit themselves with the utmost confidence to God through the atoning sacrifice of our Great High Priest, all at once she startled the congregation by uttering a loud shriek. She then nearly cast herself from her seat, held her head very low, and trembled. The ladies in the pew with her partly supported her and watched her with obvious prayerful interest and sympathy. As I continued, she began to look up again and soon sat upright, with a face wonderfully changed, indicating triumphant joy and peace.

I have seldom seen in any human face the glow that was on her face just then. Her joy was so great that she could hardly contain herself until the meeting was over, and then she soon made everybody around her understand that she had been set free. She glorified God and rejoiced with amazing triumph. When I saw her again two years later, she was still full of joy and peace.

The other case of recovery was that of another woman who had fallen into despair and insanity. I was not present when she was restored, but I was told that it was almost instantaneous, by means of a baptism of the Holy Spirit. Revivals of religion are sometimes accused of making people mad. But the fact is, men are naturally mad on the subject of religion, and revivals restore them rather than make them mad.

Having received the converts and having labored in both Antwerp and Evans' Mills until the fall of the year, I procured for them a young man by the name of Denning, whom they settled as pastor. I then suspended my labors at Antwerp.

Nine

Rutland: Vain Woman Is Converted

At this time I was earnestly pressed to remain at Evans' Mills and finally told them that I would stay for the year. Being engaged to marry Miss Lydia Andrews, I went from there to Whitestown, in Oneida County, and was married in October 1824. My wife was making additional preparations for housekeeping, and a day or two after our marriage I returned to Evans' Mills in order to obtain means to transport our household goods. I told her that she might expect me back in about a week.

The previous fall, I had preached a few times at a place called Perch River, about a dozen miles northwest of Evans' Mills. I spent one Sunday at Evans' Mills, intending to return for my wife about the middle of that week. But a messenger from Perch River came up that Sunday and said there had been a revival working its way slowly among the people ever since I preached there. He begged me to go and preach there at least once more. I finally promised to be there Tuesday night, but I found the interest so deep that I stayed and preached Wednesday night, then Thursday night, until finally I gave up returning that week for my wife and continued to preach in that neighborhood.

The revival soon spread to Brownville, a considerable village several miles southwest from that place. Finally, under the pressing invitation of the minister and church at Brownville, I went there and spent the winter. I had written to my wife and obtained her consent, for the circumstances required me to defer coming for her until God seemed to open the way.

At Brownville there was a very interesting work, but the church was in such a state that it was very difficult to get them into the work. I could not find much soundhearted

piety, and the policy of the minister was to forbid anything
like a revival. I labored there that winter with great pain
and had many serious obstacles to overcome. Sometimes
the minister and his wife were away from our meetings,
and I would learn afterward that they had stayed away to
attend a party.

I was the guest of a Mr. B——, one of the elders of the
church and the most intimate and influential friend of the
minister. One day, as I came down from my room and was
going out to call on some inquirers, I met Mr. B—— in the
hall. He said to me, "Mr. Finney, what would you think of a
man who was praying week after week for the Holy Spirit
and could get no answer?" I replied, "I would think he was
praying with false motives." "But with what motives," said
he, "should a man pray? If he wants to be happy, is that a
false motive?" I replied, "Even Satan might pray with as
good a motive as that." Then I quoted the words of the
psalmist: *"Uphold me by Your generous Spirit. Then I will
teach transgressors Your ways, and sinners shall be converted to You"* (Ps. 51:12–13). "See," said I, "the psalmist
did not pray for the Holy Spirit so that he might be happy,
but so that he might be useful and that sinners might be
converted to Christ." Then we parted.

I remained out until dinner time. When I returned, Mr.
B—— met me and immediately began to confess. "Mr. Finney," said he, "I owe you a confession. I was angry when
you said that to me, and I must confess that I hoped I would
never see you again. What you said caused me to see that I
had never been converted, that I had never had any higher
motive than a mere selfish desire for my own happiness.
After you left the house, I went and asked God to take my
life. I could not endure to have it known that I had always
been deceived. I have been a close friend of our minister. I
have journeyed with him and conversed with him more
than any other member of the church, and yet I saw that I
had always been a deceived hypocrite. The mortification
was intolerable, and I wanted to die, so I asked the Lord to
take my life." He was all broken down, and from that time

he was a new man. His conversion did a great deal of good in that town.

While I was in Brownville, God revealed to me the fact that He was going to pour out His Spirit in Gouverneur and that I must go there and preach. I knew absolutely nothing about the town except that it was a place of much opposition toward the revival in Antwerp the year before. I can never tell how or why the Spirit of God made that revelation to me. But I knew then, and I have no doubt now, that it was a direct revelation from God to me.

Very soon after this, I saw one of the members of the church from Gouverneur, who was passing through Brownville. I told him what God had revealed to me. He stared at me as if he supposed that I was insane. But I told him to go home and tell his fellow church members to prepare themselves for my coming and for the outpouring of the Lord's Spirit. From him I learned that religion was in a very low state in Gouverneur and that he himself was as cold as an iceberg.

Early in the spring of 1825, I left Brownville, with my horse and sleigh, to go after my wife. I had been absent six months since our marriage. I drove about fifteen miles, and the roads were very slippery. My horse was smooth shod, and I found I must have his shoes reset. I stopped at Le Rayville, a small village about three miles south of Evans' Mills. While my horse was being shod, my presence there became known, and I was soon asked to preach at one o'clock in the schoolhouse.

At one o'clock the place was packed. While I preached, the Spirit of God came down with great power upon the people. The outpouring of the Spirit was so great that, in compliance with their earnest entreaty, I decided to spend the night there and preach again in the evening. But the work increased more and more; in the evening I scheduled another meeting in the morning, and in the morning I set up another in the evening. Soon I saw that I would not be able to go any farther after my wife. I asked one of the men to take my horse and sleigh and go after my wife so that I could remain. He did so, and I went on preaching, from day to day and from night to night, and there was a powerful revival. My wife arrived a few days after I had sent for her, and we accepted the invitation of Judge C—— and his wife to become their guests.

After I had labored in Le Rayville a few weeks, the majority of the inhabitants were converted. The people then urged me to go and preach in a Baptist church in the town of Rutland, where Rutland joins Le Rayville. I made an appointment to preach there one afternoon. The weather had become warm, and I walked over, through a pine grove, about three miles to their place of worship. I arrived early and found the church open, but nobody there. I was warm from having walked so far, and I went in and took my seat near the center of the church. Very soon people began to come in and take their seats here and there, scattered all over the church. Soon the number increased so that they were coming continually. I sat still, being an entire stranger there.

One young woman who came in had two or three tall plumes in her bonnet and was rather showily dressed. She was slender, tall, dignified, and quite pretty. I observed, as soon as she came in, that she tossed her head and gave a very graceful motion to her plumes. She looked around just enough to see the impression she was making. The whole thing was so peculiar that it struck me very much. She sat down in the pew directly behind me. I turned partly around and looked at her from head to foot. She saw that I was observing her critically, and she looked a little abashed. In a low voice I said to her, very earnestly, "Did you come in here to get people's attention away from God and His worship, and to make people worship you?" This made her squirm, but I made her hear me out. She began to tremble, and when I had said enough to fasten the thought of her insufferable vanity on her mind, I arose and went to the pulpit. As soon as she saw that I was the minister who was about to preach, her agitation began to increase—so much so as to attract the attention of those around her. The house was soon full, and I read a passage of Scripture and went on to preach.

The Spirit of the Lord was evidently poured out on the congregation. At the close of the sermon, I called upon any who wished to give their hearts to God to come forward and take a seat in the front pews, which were empty. The moment I made the call, this young woman was the first to arise. She burst out into the aisle and came forward like a person in a state of desperation. She seemed to have lost all sense of the presence of anybody but God. She came rushing forward to the front seats, until she finally fell in the aisle and shrieked with agony. A large number arose in different parts of the church and came forward, and many of them appeared to give their hearts to God upon the spot, including this young woman. I found out later that she was an agreeable girl but was regarded by everybody as very vain and showy. Many years afterward, a man informed me that she still resided there, was married, was a very useful woman, and had always been a very earnest Christian since that meeting.

I preached a few times at this place, and then the question of Gouverneur came up again. God seemed to say to me, "Go to Gouverneur; the time has come." Brother Nash had come a few days before this and was spending some time with me. So, because I had two or three appointments in that part of Rutland, I said to Brother Nash, "You must go to Gouverneur, see what is there, and come back and make your report."

He started the next morning. After he had been gone two or three days, he returned, saying that he had found many Christians uneasy in their minds. He was confident that there was a good deal of the Spirit of the Lord among the people but that they were not aware what the state of things really was. I asked Brother Nash to return immediately to Gouverneur, to inform the people there that they might expect me on a certain day that week.

Ten

Gouverneur: Universalists
Are Converted

Brother Nash accordingly returned the next day and made the appointment as I desired. I had to ride nearly thirty miles to reach the place. Because of heavy rains, it seemed that I would not be able to reach my appointment. The people in Gouverneur had given up expecting me that day, but the rains abated enough that I arrived in the evening.

I rode rapidly on, arrived at the church door, and hurried in. Brother Nash stood in front of the pulpit, having just risen up to dismiss the meeting. On seeing me enter, he held up his hands and waited until I came near the pulpit, and then he took me right in his arms. After thus embracing me, he introduced me to the congregation. I informed them that I had come to fulfill my appointment, and, the Lord willing, I would preach at a certain hour.

The people had heard enough, for and against me, to have their curiosity excited. Therefore, when the hour arrived, the room was filled. The Lord gave me a text, and I went to the pulpit and poured my heart out to the people. The Word took powerful effect. I dismissed the meeting and went to get some rest.

The village hotel was at that time kept by a Dr. S——, an avowed Universalist. The next morning I went out, as usual, to call on the people and converse with them about their souls. After making a few calls, I dropped into a tailor's shop, where I found a number of people discussing the subject of the sermon the night before. I had never yet heard of Dr. S——, but I found him at this tailor's shop, defending his Universalist sentiments. The remarks that were made immediately opened the conversation, and Dr.

S—— stepped forward to dispute the positions that I had advanced and to maintain the doctrine of universal salvation. Somebody introduced him to me, and I said to him, "Doctor, I would be very happy to converse with you about your views; but if we are going to have a conversation, we must first agree upon the method of our discussion."

I had had enough discussions with Universalists to know that no good would come from it unless certain terms were agreed upon and adhered to in the discussion. I therefore proposed, first, that we should take up one point at a time and discuss it until we had settled it or had no more to say upon it, and then another, and another, confining ourselves to the point immediately in debate. Second, we should not interrupt each other, but each one should be free to give his views upon the point without interruption. Third, there would be no frivolous objections, but we would observe fairness and courtesy and give due consideration to every argument.

Having settled the preliminaries, we commenced the argument. It did not take long to demolish every position that Dr. S—— assumed. He knew very little of the Bible. As Universalists always do, he dwelt mainly on the utter injustice of endless punishment. He took the position that, whatever the Bible said about it, endless punishment was unjust; therefore, if the Bible threatened men with endless punishment, the Book could not be true. I soon showed him and those around him that he had little ground to stand on, as far as the Bible was concerned. As I proved to them the justice of endless punishment, I saw that his friends became agitated and felt as if the foundations were giving way under them. Pretty soon one of them went out. As I proceeded, another went out. Finally they all forsook him, seeing, one after the other, that their leader was utterly wrong. When he had nothing more to say, I urged upon him the question of immediate attention to salvation. Then I very kindly bid him good morning and went away, feeling sure that I would soon hear from him again.

The doctor's wife was a Christian woman and a member of the church. She told me, a day or two afterward, that the doctor came home from that conversation apparently greatly agitated. She suspected that he had spoken with me, and she said to him, "Doctor, have you seen Mr. Finney this morning?" He was so restless and agitated that this brought him to tears, and he exclaimed, "Yes, and he has turned my own weapons against me!" His agony became intense, and he soon surrendered himself to his convictions and expressed hope in Christ. In a few days his companions were brought in, one after the other, until the revival made a clean sweep of them.

Gouverneur had a Baptist church and a Presbyterian church. As soon as the revival broke out and attracted general attention, the Baptists began to oppose it. They spoke against it and used very objectionable means to arrest its progress. This encouraged a group of young men to join together in opposing the work. The Baptist church was quite influential, and the stand that they took greatly emboldened the opposition and seemed to give it a peculiar bitterness and strength, as might be expected. Those young men seemed to stand like a bulwark in the way of the progress of the revival.

In this state of things, Brother Nash and I made up our minds that this opposition must be overcome and could only be overcome by prayer. We therefore gave ourselves up to prayer until we prevailed and felt confident that no power that earth or hell could present would be allowed to permanently stop the revival.

The next Sunday, after I had preached morning and afternoon and Brother Nash had given himself up almost continually to prayer, the people gathered at five o'clock in the church for a prayer meeting. The meetinghouse was filled. Near the close of the meeting, Brother Nash arose and addressed the group of young men who had joined together to resist the revival. I believe they were all there, and they sat braced up against the Spirit of God. It was too solemn for them to openly ridicule what they heard and saw, and yet their stubbornness was apparent to everybody.

Brother Nash addressed them very earnestly, pointing out the guilt and danger of the course they were taking. Toward the close of his address, he became exceedingly ardent and said to them, "Now, mark my words, young men. God will break your ranks in less than one week, either by converting some of you, or by sending some of you to hell. He will do this as certainly as the Lord is my God." He brought his hand down on the top of the pew before him so as to jar it thoroughly. He immediately sat down, dropped his head, and groaned with pain.

The house was as still as death, and most of the people held down their heads. I could see that the young men were agitated. Personally, I regretted that Brother Nash had gone so far. He had committed himself, that God would either take the life of some of them and send them to hell or would convert some of them within a week. However, on Tuesday morning of the same week, the leader of these young men came to me in the greatest distress of mind. He was all prepared to submit, and as soon as I pressed him he broke down like a child, confessed, and gave himself to Christ. Then he said, "What shall I do, Mr. Finney?" I replied, "Go immediately to all your young companions, pray with them, and exhort them at once to turn to the Lord." He did so, and before the week was out, nearly all of that group of young men were hoping in Christ.

After the conversion of this group of young men and of several others, I thought it was time to put a stop to the opposition of the Baptist church and minister. I therefore said to a deacon of the Baptist church, who had been very bitter in his opposition, "You have carried your opposition far enough. You must be satisfied that this is the work of God. I have made no allusion in public to your opposition, and I do not wish to do so or to appear to know that there is any such thing, but you have gone far enough. If you do not stop immediately, I will feel it is my duty to expose your opposition from the pulpit."

He confessed, said that he was sorry, and promised that he would not oppose the work any more. He said that he had made a great mistake and had been deceived, but that he also had been very wicked about it. Then his minister arrived, and I had a long conversation with them together. The minister confessed that he had been wicked and that his sectarian feeling had carried him too far. He hoped that I would forgive him, and he asked God to forgive him. I told him that I would take no notice whatever of the opposition of his church, provided they stopped it, which they promised to do.

But I then said to him, "A considerable number of the young people, whose parents belong to your church, have been converted. If you start trying to make them Baptists, you will create a sectarian feeling in both churches, and that will be worse than any opposition you have offered thus far. In spite of your opposition, the work has gone on, because the Presbyterian brethren have kept clear of a sectarian spirit and have had the spirit of prayer. But if you start proselytizing, it will destroy the spirit of prayer and will stop the revival immediately." He knew it, he said. Therefore, he would say nothing about receiving the converts into the church until the revival was over, and then the converts would be allowed to join whichever church they pleased.

This was on Friday. The next day was the day for their monthly covenant meeting. When they had gathered, instead of keeping his word, the minister threw the doors of the church open and invited the converts to come forward, give their testimony, and join the church. Those who could be persuaded to do so gave their testimony, and the next day there was a great parade in baptizing them. The minister immediately secured the help of one of the most proselytizing Baptist ministers I ever knew. He came in and began to preach and lecture on baptism.

They traversed the town for converts in every direction, and whenever they could find anyone to join, they would begin to march, sing, and make a great parade in going to the water and baptizing them. This soon grieved the Presbyterian church so as to destroy their spirit of prayer and faith, and the work came to a standstill. For six weeks there was not a single conversion. Everyone, both saints and sinners, was discussing the question of baptism.

A considerable number of men in the village, some of them prominent men, had been under strong conviction and appeared to be near conversion, but they were entirely diverted by this discussion of baptism. Indeed, this seemed to be the universal effect. Everybody could see that the revival had stopped and that the Baptists, although they had opposed the revival from the beginning, were bent upon having all the converts join their church.

On Sunday I finally said to the people, "You see how it is. No conversion has occurred now for six weeks, and you know the reason." I did not tell them that the pastor of the Baptist church had violated his word, nor did I allude to it, for I knew that it would do only harm to inform the people that he had been guilty of taking such a course. But I said to them, "Now, I do not want to take up a Sunday to preach on this subject. But if you will come on Wednesday afternoon at one o'clock, bringing your Bibles and your pencils to mark the passages, I will read to you all the passages in the Bible that relate to the mode of baptism. I will show you the views of the Baptists on all those passages, together with my own, and you will judge for yourselves where the truth lies."

When Wednesday came, the house was crowded. I saw quite a number of the Baptist brethren present. I began to read, first in the Old Testament and then in the New, all the passages that had any reference to the mode of baptism, so far as I knew. I gave the views that the Baptists had of those texts and the reasons for their views. I then gave my own views and my reasons for them. I saw that the people appeared satisfied in regard to the mode of baptism. The Baptists, as far as I knew, were quite satisfied that I had stated their views fairly. Before I dismissed the meeting I said, "If you will come tomorrow, at the same hour, I will read to you all the passages in the Bible that relate to the subject of baptism, and pursue the same course as I have done today."

The next day the house was crowded, if possible more than the day before. Many of the principal Baptists were present, and I observed the old elder, the great proselyter, sitting in the congregation. After the introductory services, I arose and began my reading. At this point the elder arose and said, "Mr. Finney, I have an appointment and cannot stay to hear your readings. But I will wish to answer you. How will I know what course you take?" I replied, "Elder, I have before me a little skeleton, in which I quote all the passages that I will read. You can have these notes, if you wish, and reply to them." He then left and went to his appointment.

I then took up the covenant made with Abraham, and I read everything in the Old Testament that directly dealt with the relation of families and of children to that covenant. I gave the Baptist view of the passages that I read, together with my own, with the reasons on both sides, as I had done the day before. I then went through all the New Testament passages referring to the subject. The people became very mellow, and the tears flowed very freely when I held up that covenant as the covenant that God still makes with parents and their households. The congregation was much moved and melted.

Just before I was through, the deacon of the Presbyterian church had to go out with a child who had sat with him during the long meeting. He told me afterward that, as he went into the vestibule of the church, he found the old elder sitting there with the door ajar, listening to what I was saying, and absolutely weeping.

When I was done, the people thronged around me on every side, and with tears they thanked me for so full and satisfactory a discussion of that subject. The question was intelligently settled, and soon the people ceased to talk about it. I never had to rebuke the opposition of the Baptists publicly. In the course of a few days, the spirit of prayer returned, and the revival went on again with great power.

I have not been in Gouverneur for many years. But I have often heard from there and have always understood that there has been a very healthy state of religion in that place and that they have never had anything like a discussion on the subject of baptism since.

Eleven

De Kalb: Answers to Prayer

From Gouverneur I went to De Kalb, a village about sixteen miles farther north. The town had a Presbyterian church and minister, but the church was small, and the minister seemed not to have a very strong hold upon the people. However, I think he was a good man. I began to hold meetings in different parts of the town. The village was small, and the people were very much scattered. Since the region was new, the roads were new and bad. But a revival commenced immediately and went forward with a good deal of power for a place where the inhabitants were so much scattered.

A few years before, there had been a revival in De Kalb under the labors of the Methodists. It had been accompanied by a good deal of excitement and many cases of what the Methodists call "falling under the power of God." The Presbyterians had resisted this; consequently, a bad feeling had arisen between the Methodists and the Presbyterians— the Methodists accusing the Presbyterians of opposing the revival on the basis of these cases of falling. There seemed to be a good deal of truth in this, and I thought the Presbyterians had been in error.

One evening, at the close of my sermon, I observed a man fall from his seat near the door, and the people gathered around him to take care of him. From what I saw, it was a case of "falling under the power of God," as the Methodists would express it, and so I supposed it was a Methodist. But I later discovered that one of the principal members of the Presbyterian church had fallen. Remarkably, during this revival, there were several cases of this kind among the Presbyterians and none among the Methodists. This led to a state of great cordiality and good feeling among them.

While laboring in De Kalb, I first became acquainted with Mr. F—— of Ogdensburgh. He heard of the revival in De Kalb and came from Ogdensburgh, about sixteen miles, to see it. He was wealthy and very benevolent. He proposed to employ me as his missionary to work in the towns throughout that county, and he would pay me a salary. However, I declined to pledge myself to preach in any particular place or to confine my labors within any given lines.

Mr. F—— spent several days with me, visiting from house to house and attending our meetings. He had been educated in Philadelphia as an old-school Presbyterian and was himself an elder in the Presbyterian church in Ogdensburgh. On going away, he left a letter for me, containing three ten-dollar bills. A few days later, he again visited De Kalb for two or three days. He attended our meetings and became very much interested in the work. When he went away, he left another letter containing, as before, three ten-dollar bills. Thus I now had $60, with which I immediately purchased a buggy. Though I had a horse, I had no carriage, and my young wife and I used to go to meetings a good deal on foot.

One Saturday, just before evening, a German tailor from Ogdensburgh called on me and informed me that Mr. F—— had sent him from Ogdensburgh to take my measurements for a suit. I had begun to need clothes, and not long before I had said to the Lord that my clothes were getting shabby, but it had not occurred to me again. Mr. F——, however, had observed it and sent this man, who was a Roman Catholic, to take my measurements. I asked him if he would stay over the Sunday and take my measurements Monday morning. I said, "It is too late for you to return tonight. If I allow you to take my measurements tonight, you will go home tomorrow." He admitted that he expected to do so. I said, "Then you will not take them. If you will not stay until Monday morning, I will not be measured for a suit." He remained.

The same afternoon, there were other arrivals from Ogdensburgh. Among them was Mr. S——, who was an elder in the same church with Mr. F——. Mr. S——'s son, an unconverted young man, came with him.

Elder S—— attended the meeting in the morning, and at the intermission was invited by Elder B—— to go home with him for some refreshments. Elder B—— was full of the Holy Spirit; on the way home he preached to Elder S——, who was at the time very cold and backward in religion. Elder S—— was very much moved by his words.

Soon after they entered the house, they were invited to sit down and have some refreshments. As they drew around the table, Elder S—— said to Elder B——, "How did you get this blessing?" Elder B—— replied, "I stopped lying to God. All my Christian life I have been making pretenses and asking God for things that I was not truly willing to have. Often I was insincere and really lied to God. As soon as I made up my mind that I never would say anything that I did not really mean to God in prayer, God answered me; the Spirit came down, and I was filled with the Holy Spirit."

At this moment Mr. S——, who had not yet sat down, shoved his chair back from the table, fell on his knees, and began to confess how he had lied to God and how he had played the hypocrite in his prayers as well as in his life. The Holy Spirit fell upon him immediately and filled him with as much as he could hold.

In the afternoon the people had assembled for worship, and I was standing behind the pulpit reading a hymn. I heard somebody talking very loudly and approaching the building, the door and windows being open. Two men then came in: Elder B—— and another man I did not know, who was Elder S——. As soon as Elder S—— came in at the door, he lifted his eyes to me, came straight up to the pulpit, and took me up in his arms. "God bless you! God bless you!" said he. He then told me and the rest of the congregation what the Lord had just done for his soul.

His countenance was all aglow. He was so changed in his appearance that those who knew him were perfectly astonished at the change. His son, who had not known of this change in his father, rose up and was hurrying out of the church as soon as he saw and heard him. His father cried out, "Do not leave the church, my son, for I never loved you before!" He went on to speak, and the power with which he spoke was perfectly astonishing. The people melted down on every side, and his son broke down almost immediately.

Very soon the Roman Catholic tailor rose up and said, "I must tell you what the Lord has done for my soul. I was brought up a Roman Catholic, and I never dared to read my Bible. I was told that if I did, the Devil would carry off my body. Sometimes when I dared to look into it, it seemed as if the Devil was peering over my shoulder and had come to carry me off. But I see now that it was all a delusion." The tailor went on to tell what the Lord had done for him just there on the spot—what views the Lord had given him of the way of salvation by Jesus Christ. It was evident to everybody that he was converted.

This made a great impression on the congregation. I could not preach. The whole course of the meeting had taken on a color that the Lord had given it. I sat still and saw the salvation of God. All that afternoon, conversions were multiplied in every part of the congregation. As they arose, one after another, and told what the Lord had done and was doing for their souls, the impression increased. I had scarcely ever seen so spontaneous a movement by the Holy Spirit in convicting and converting sinners.

The next day Elder S—— returned to Ogdensburgh. But, as I understand, he made many calls on the way, conversing and praying with many families. In this way, the revival was extended to Ogdensburgh.

I have said that the spirit of prayer prevailed in these revivals. It was common for young converts to be greatly troubled in prayer; in some instances, they were constrained to pray whole nights for the conversion of souls around them, until their bodily strength was quite exhausted. There was a great pressure of the Holy Spirit on the minds of Christians, and they seemed to carry around with them the burden of immortal souls. They manifested the greatest solemnity and watchfulness in all their words and actions. It was very common to find Christians, whenever they met in any place, falling on their knees in prayer instead of engaging in conversation.

Not only were prayer meetings greatly multiplied and fully attended, and not only was there great solemnity in those meetings, but there was also a mighty spirit of secret prayer. Christians prayed a great deal, many of them spending several hours in private prayer. It was also the case that two or more would take the promise—*"If two of you agree on earth concerning anything that they ask, it will be done for them by My Father in heaven"* (Matt. 18:19)—and make some particular person a subject of prayer. It was wonderful to see how they prevailed. Answers to prayer were multiplied on every side, so that no one could escape the conviction that God was daily and hourly answering prayer.

If anything occurred that threatened to mar the work, if there was any appearance of any root of bitterness springing up or any tendency toward fanaticism, Christians would heed the alarm and give themselves to praying that God would direct and control all things. It was surprising to see to what extent, and by what means, God would remove obstacles out of the way in answer to prayer.

In regard to my own experience, I will say that I could do nothing unless I had the spirit of prayer. If even for a day or an hour I lost the spirit of grace and supplication, I found myself unable to preach with power and effectiveness or to win souls by personal conversation. My experience has always been such.

For several weeks before I left De Kalb, I was very strongly burdened in prayer and had an experience that was somewhat new to me. I found myself so borne down with the weight of immortal souls that I was constrained to pray without ceasing. Some of my experiences, indeed, alarmed me. A spirit of importunity sometimes came upon me so that I would say to God that He had made a promise to answer prayer, and I could not and would not be denied. I felt so certain that He would hear me and that His faithfulness to His promises and to Himself made it impossible for Him not to hear and answer, that frequently I found myself saying to Him, "I hope You do not think that I can be denied. I come with Your faithful promises in my hand, and I cannot be denied." Unbelief looked incredibly absurd to me, and I was certain that God would answer prayer—those prayers that, from day to day and from hour to hour, I found myself offering in such agony and faith. I had no idea of the shape the answer would take, the locality in which the prayers would be answered, or the exact time of the answer. Even so, my impression was that the answer was near, and I felt myself strengthened in the divine life. I put on the armor for a mighty conflict with the powers of darkness (Eph. 6:11–17), and I expected soon to see a far more powerful outpouring of the Spirit of God.

Twelve

Western: A Family's Children Are Converted

In the early part of October, my wife and I went to Utica to attend the meeting of the synod to which I belonged, and to visit her father's family living near Utica. We spent a few days at the synod and then set out to return to my former field of labor in Saint Lawrence County. We had not gone more than a dozen miles when we met Mr. Gale in his carriage, on his way to Utica. Mr. Gale, my former teacher, had left Adams not long after I left it. He had moved to a farm in the town of Western, in Oneida County, where he was endeavoring to regain his health and was employed in teaching some young men who were preparing themselves to preach the Gospel.

When Mr. Gale saw me, he leaped from his carriage and said, "God bless you, Brother Finney. I was going down to the synod to see you. You must go home with me. I do not believe that I ever was converted. I wrote the other day to Adams, to find out where a letter would reach you, because I wanted to open my mind to you on the subject." He was so importunate that I consented, and we drove immediately to Western.

In Western a series of revivals soon began. As far as I know, these revivals first attracted the notice and excited the opposition of certain prominent ministers in the East.

The churches in that region were mostly Presbyterian. However, there were three Congregational ministers in that county who called themselves the Oneida Association, who, at the time, published a pamphlet against those revivals. But since the pamphlet made no public impression that we could learn, no public notice was ever taken of it. We thought it likely that that association had much to do with the opposition that was raised in the East. It was well known that their leader, Rev. William R. Weeks, insisted very much upon a doctrine he called "the divine efficiency scheme." His views on this subject naturally led him to be suspicious of anything in the revivals that was not connected with those views. But we never supposed that the whole opposition could have originated in the actions of any of the members of that association.

No public replies were made to the letters or to anything that was published in opposition to the revivals. Those of us who were engaged in them had our hands and hearts too full to turn aside to reply to letters, reports, or publications that so obviously misrepresented the character of the work. Of course, this lack of response allowed many people outside the range of the revivals, where the facts were not known, to misunderstand the character of the revivals. So much misunderstanding came to exist that it became common for people, in referring to those revivals, to assume that they contained much disorder and that there was much to deplore in their results.

Now, all this was entirely a mistake. I will relate, as fairly as I can, the characteristics of these revivals, the measures that were used in promoting them, and their real results.

I have said that Mr. Gale had settled on a farm in Western and was engaged in teaching some young men while endeavoring to regain his health. I went directly to his house and was his guest for several weeks. We arrived there Thursday, and that afternoon there was a weekly prayer meeting in the schoolhouse near the church. Mr. Gale invited me to go to the prayer meeting, and I went. The church had no minister, and Mr. Gale was unable to preach. I believe they usually had a minister only part of the time, and for some time prior to my going there, they had had no regular preaching at all in the Presbyterian church. There were three elders in the church, along with a few members; but the church was very small, and religion was at low watermark. There seemed to be no life, courage, or eagerness on the part of Christians, and nothing was happening to secure the conversion of sinners or the sanctification of the church.

They asked me to take charge of the meeting, but I declined, expecting to be there only for that afternoon and preferring to hear them pray and talk, rather than to take part in the meeting myself. The meeting was opened by one of the elders, who read a chapter in the Bible, then a hymn, which they sang. After this he made a long prayer, or perhaps I should say an exhortation, or gave a narrative—I hardly know what to call it. He told the Lord how many years they had been holding that prayer meeting weekly, and that no answer had been given to their prayers. He made some statements and confessions that greatly shocked me. After he finished, another elder took up the same theme. He read a hymn and, after singing, engaged in a long prayer, in which he went over nearly the same ground as the first one. Then followed the third elder in the same strain.

By this time I could say with Paul that my spirit was stirred within me. They were about to dismiss the meeting when one of the elders asked me if I would make a remark before they dismissed. I arose and took their statements and confessions for a text; and it seemed to me, at the time, that God inspired me to give them a terrible searching.

When I arose, I had no idea what I would say, but the Spirit of God came upon me. I took up their prayers, statements, and confessions and dissected them. I asked if it had been understood that that prayer meeting was a mock prayer meeting. Had they come together to mock God by implying that all the blame of what had been going on all this time was to be ascribed to His sovereignty?

At first I observed that they all looked angry. Some of them afterward said that they were on the point of getting up and going out. But I continued on the track of their prayers and confessions, until the elder who had opened the meeting burst into tears and exclaimed, "Brother Finney, it is all true!" He fell on his knees and wept aloud. This was the signal for a general breaking down. Every man and woman went down on his or her knees. There were probably not more than a dozen present, but they were the leading members in the church. They all wept, confessed, and broke their hearts before God. This scene continued for nearly an hour, and a more thorough breaking down and confession I have seldom witnessed.

As soon as they recovered themselves somewhat, they asked me to remain and preach to them on Sunday. I regarded it as the voice of the Lord and consented to do so. This was Thursday night. On Friday, I was greatly troubled. That day I went frequently to the church to engage in secret prayer, and I had a mighty hold upon God. On Sunday the church was full of hearers. I preached all day, and God came down with great power upon the people. It was evident to everybody that the work of grace had begun. I set dates to preach in different parts of the town during the week, and the work increased from day to day.

In the meantime, I was always in prayer, and I found that the spirit of prayer was prevailing in the church. The work went on, spread, and prevailed, until it began to exhibit unmistakable indications of the direction in which the Spirit of God was leading from that place.

The town of Rome was about nine miles away. About halfway there was a small village called Elmer's Hill. There was a large schoolhouse, where I held a weekly lecture, and it soon became evident that the work was spreading in the direction of Rome and Utica. There was a settlement northeast of Rome, about three miles, called Wright's settlement. Many people came down from Rome and from Wright's settlement to attend the meetings at Elmer's Hill, and the work soon began to take effect among them.

But I must relate a few of the incidents that occurred during the revival in Western. Many answers to prayer and many scenes of great interest were presented in this revival.

Mrs. B——, a wife of one of the elders of the church, had a large family. One of the sons was a Christian who

107

lived in Utica, but the rest of the family were at home and were unconverted. The eldest daughter, S——, had been especially regarded by the family as almost perfect. I talked with her several times, but I found that I could not strip away her self-righteousness. She had evidently been made to believe that she was almost a Christian. Her life had been so irreproachable that it was very difficult to convict her of sin. The second daughter was also a very amiable girl, but she did not regard herself as worthy to be compared with the eldest in respect to amiability and excellence of character.

One day when I was talking with S—— and trying to make her see herself as a great sinner, C——, the second daughter, said to me, "Mr. Finney, I think that you are too hard on S——. If you were to talk so to me, I would feel that I deserved it, but I don't think that she does." After being defeated several times in my attempts to secure the conviction and conversion of S——, I made up my mind to bide my time and wait for an opportunity when she was away from home or alone. It was not long before the opportunity came. I entered into conversation with her, and by God's help I stripped the covering from her heart. She was brought under powerful conviction of sin. The Spirit pursued her with mighty power. The family was surprised and greatly distressed for S——, but God pushed the question home until, after a struggle of a few days, she broke down and became as beautiful a convert as I have ever seen. Her convictions were so thorough that when she accepted Christ, she was strong in faith, was clear in her understanding of duty and of truth, and immediately became a power for good among her friends and acquaintances.

In the meantime, C——, the second daughter, became very much alarmed about herself and very anxious for the salvation of her own soul. The mother seemed to be in real travail of soul day and night. I called to see the family almost daily, sometimes two or three times a day. One child after another was converted, and we were expecting every day to see C—— converted. But for some reason she lingered. One day I called to see her and found her in the sitting room alone. I asked her how she was getting on, and she replied, "Mr. Finney, I am losing my conviction. I do not feel nearly as concerned about myself as I have."

Just at this moment, a door was opened, and Mrs. B—— came into the room. I told her what C—— had said. It shocked her so that she groaned aloud and fell on the floor. She was unable to rise, and she struggled and groaned out her prayers in a manner that immediately indicated to me that C—— would certainly be converted. She was unable to say much in words, but her groans and tears showed the extreme agony of her mind. As soon as this scene occurred, the Spirit of God manifestly came upon C—— afresh. She fell on her knees, and before she arose she broke down and became as thorough a convert as S—— was. All the B—— children were converted at that time, I believe, except the youngest, then a little child.

There is one of my own experiences that, for the honor of God, I must not fail to relate here. I had preached and prayed almost continually during the time that I had been at Mr. Gale's. As I was accustomed to using my voice in private prayer, I had spread a buffalo robe, so that I might not be heard, on the hayloft where I used to spend much of my time in secret prayer to God. I would pray whenever I was not visiting or engaged in preaching. Mr. Gale had admonished me several times that, if I did not take care, I would go beyond my strength and become ill. But the Spirit of prayer was upon me, and I would not resist Him. Rather, I gave Him scope and let out my strength freely in pouring my soul out to God.

It was November, and the weather was becoming cold. Mr. Gale and I had been out visiting inquirers with his horse and buggy. We came home, went into the barn, and put out the horse. Instead of going into the house, I crept up into the hayloft to pour out my burdened soul to God in prayer. I prayed until my burden left me. I was so exhausted that I fell down and lost myself in sleep. I must have fallen asleep almost instantly, I judge, from the fact that I had no recollection of any time elapsing after the struggle in my soul was over. The first I knew, Mr. Gale came climbing up into the hayloft and said, "Brother Finney, are you dead?" I awoke, and at first I could give no account why I was there asleep and could form no idea how long I had been there. But I knew that my mind was calm and my faith unwavering. The work would go on—of that I felt assured.

I have said that at Western I was the guest of Mr. Gale, and that he had come to the conclusion that he was never converted. He told me the progress of his mind. He had firmly believed that God would not bless my labors because I would not preach what he regarded as the truths of the Gospel. But when he found that the Spirit of God did accompany my labors, it led him to the conclusion that he was wrong. Ultimately, this led him to such an overhauling of his whole state of mind and of his views as a preacher that he came to the conclusion that he had never been converted and did not understand the Gospel. During the revival in Western, he attended nearly all the meetings. Before many weeks had passed, he told me that he had come into an entirely different state of mind in regard to his own soul. He had changed his views of the Gospel and thought I was right. He said he thanked God that he had had no influence on me to lead me to adopt his views, and that I would have been ruined as a minister if he had prevailed. From this time he became a very effective worker, so far as his health would permit, in the revival in that region.

The doctrine upon which I insisted—that the command to obey God implied the power to do so—at first created considerable opposition in some places. Because I denied that moral depravity is physical depravity and because I believed that the Spirit's influences are those of teaching, persuading, convicting, and, of course, a moral influence, I was regarded by many as teaching new and strange doctrines. Indeed, as late as 1832, when I was laboring in Boston for the first time, Dr. Beecher said that he had never before heard the doctrine preached that the Spirit's influences are moral as opposed to physical. Therefore, to a considerable extent, ministers and Christians regarded this doctrine as virtually a denial of the Spirit's influence. Hence, although I insisted upon the divine agency in conviction, regeneration, and every other Christian exercise, it was a long time before the cry ceased to be heard that I denied the agency of the Holy Spirit in regeneration and conversion. It was said that I taught self-conversion and self-regeneration. I was frequently rebuked for addressing the sinner as if the blame of his impenitence belonged entirely to himself and for urging him to immediate submission. However, I persisted in this course, and it was seen by ministers and Christians that God acknowledged it as His truth and blessed it to the salvation of thousands of souls.

I have spoken of the meetings at Elmer's Hill and have said that people from Rome and Wright's settlement began to come in large numbers. The effect of the Word of God upon those who came plainly indicated that the work was rapidly extending in that direction.

Thirteen

Rome, New York: The Presence of God Is Felt

At this time Rev. Moses Gillett, pastor of the Congregational church in Rome, heard what the Lord was doing in Western and came to see the work that was going on. He arrived with a Miss H——, one of the prominent members of his church. Miss H—— was a very devout and earnest Christian girl. They were both greatly impressed with the work of God. I could see that the Spirit of God was stirring them up in the deepest foundations of their minds. After a few days, Mr. Gillett and Miss H—— came again. On their second visit, Mr. Gillett said to me, "Brother Finney, it seems to me that I have a new Bible. I never before understood the promises as I do now. I never got hold of them before. I cannot rest; my mind is full of the subject, and the promises are new to me." This conversation, which was actually much longer than what I have related, led me to understand that the Lord was preparing him for a great work in his own congregation.

Soon after this, when the revival was in its full strength in Western, Mr. Gillett persuaded me to exchange pulpits with him for a day. I consented reluctantly.

On the Saturday before the day of our exchange, on my way to Rome, I greatly regretted that I had agreed to the exchange. I felt that it would greatly mar the work in Western, because Mr. Gillett would preach some of his old sermons, which I knew very well could not be adapted to the state of things. However, the people were praying, and it would not stop the work, although it might retard it. I went to Rome and preached three times on Sunday. To me it was perfectly evident that the Word took great effect. Many heads were down, and a great number of them were bowed down with deep conviction for sin. I preached in the morning on the verse, *"The carnal mind is enmity against God"* (Rom. 8:7), and followed it up in the afternoon and evening.

When Mr. Gillett returned from Western on Monday morning, I told him what my impressions were in respect to the state of the people. He did not seem to realize that the work was beginning with such power as I supposed. But he wanted to call for inquirers, if there were any in the congregation, and wished me to be present at the meeting. I told him I would be, and that he might circulate information throughout the village that there would be an inquiry meeting on Monday evening. I would go to Western and return just at evening, it being understood that he was not to let the people know that he expected me to be present.

The meeting was called at the house of one of his deacons. When we arrived, we found the large sitting room crowded to its utmost capacity. Mr. Gillett looked around with surprise and obvious agitation, for he found that the meeting was composed of many of the most intelligent and influential members of his congregation, especially the prominent young men in the town. We spent a little while in attempting to converse with them, and I soon saw that the feeling was so deep that there was danger of an outburst of feeling that would be almost uncontrollable. I therefore said to Mr. Gillett, "It will not do to continue the meeting in this shape. I will make some remarks and then dismiss them."

Nothing had been said or done to create any excitement in the meeting. But the work was going on with such power that even a few words of conversation would make the stoutest men writhe in their seats, as if a sword had been thrust into their hearts. It would probably not be possible for one who had never witnessed such a scene to realize what the force of the truth sometimes is under the power of the Holy Spirit. It is indeed a sword, and a two-edged sword. The pain that it produced when searchingly presented in a few words of conversation would create a distress that seemed unendurable.

Mr. Gillett became very irritated. He turned pale, and with a good deal of excitement he said, "What will we do?" I put my hand on his shoulder and in a whisper said, "Keep quiet, keep quiet, Brother Gillett." I then addressed them in as gentle but as plain a manner as I could, calling their attention at once to their only remedy and assuring them that it was a present and all-sufficient remedy. I pointed them to Christ as the Savior of the world, and I continued in this manner as long as they could endure it, which was only a few moments.

Mr. Gillett became so agitated that I stepped up to him and, taking him by the arm, said, "Let us pray." We knelt down in the middle of the room where we had been standing. I led in prayer in a low, unimpassioned voice. I interceded with the Savior to, then and there, lead all these sinners to accept the salvation that He offered and to believe to the saving of their souls. The agitation deepened every moment. As I could hear their sobs and sighs, I closed my prayer and rose suddenly from my knees. They all arose, and I said, "Now please go home without speaking a word to each other. Try to keep silent, and do not break out into a boisterous manifestation of feeling, but go without saying a word."

At this moment a young man by the name of W——, a clerk in Mr. H——'s store, being one of the first young men in the place, so nearly fainted that he fell upon some young men who stood near him. Then all of them partially fainted and fell together. This had nearly produced a loud shrieking, but I hushed them down and said to the young men, "Please prop that door wide open, and let everyone leave in silence." They did as I requested. They did not shriek, but they went out sobbing and sighing, and their sobs and sighs could be heard until they got out into the street.

This Mr. W—— remained silent until he entered the door where he lived, but he could contain himself no longer. He shut the door, fell on the floor, and burst out into a loud wailing, in view of his awful condition. This brought his family around him and scattered conviction among all of them. Similar scenes occurred in other families. Several were converted at the meeting and went home so full of joy that they could hardly contain themselves.

The next morning, as soon as it was dawn, people began to call at Mr. Gillett's to have us go and visit members of their families who, they said, were under the greatest conviction. We had a hasty breakfast and started out. As soon as we were in the streets, the people ran out from many houses and begged us to go into their houses. As we could only visit one place at a time, when we went into a house, the neighbors would rush in and fill the largest room. We would stay and give them instruction for a short time and then go to another house, and the people would follow us.

We found a most extraordinary state of things. Convictions were so deep and universal that we would sometimes go into a house and find some people in a kneeling posture and some prostrate on the floor. We visited, conversed, and prayed in this manner, from house to house, until noon. I then said to Mr. Gillett, "This will never do; we must have a meeting of inquiry. We cannot go from house to house, and we are not meeting the needs of the people at all." He agreed with me. But the question arose: "Where will we have the meeting?"

A Mr. F——, a religious man, at that time kept a hotel at the center of the town. He had a large dining room. Mr. Gillett said, "I will stop in and see if we may have the meeting of inquiry in his dining room." Without difficulty he obtained consent. He then went immediately to the public schools and announced that at one o'clock there would be a meeting of inquiry at Mr. F——'s dining room. We went home, ate lunch, and started for the meeting. We saw people hurrying, some of them actually running, to the meeting. They were coming from every direction. By the time we were there, the room, though a large one, was crammed to its utmost capacity with men, women, and children.

This meeting was very much like the one we had had the night before. The feeling was overwhelming. Some men of the strongest nerves were so cut down by the remarks that were made that they had to be taken home by their friends. This meeting lasted until nearly nightfall. It resulted in a great number of conversions and was the means of greatly extending the work on every side.

I preached that evening, and Mr. Gillett appointed a meeting for inquiry the next morning in the courthouse. This was a much larger room than the dining hall, though it was not so central. However, the courthouse was crowded when it was time for the meeting. We spent a good part of the day in giving instruction, and the work went on with wonderful power. I preached again in the evening, and Mr. Gillett appointed an inquiry meeting the next morning at the church, as no other room in the village was then large enough to hold the inquirers.

In the evening we attempted to hold a prayer and conference meeting in a large schoolhouse. But the meeting was hardly begun before the feeling deepened so much that, to prevent an undesirable outburst of overwhelming feeling, I told Mr. Gillett that we should dismiss the meeting and request the people to go in silence. Christians could then spend the evening in secret or family prayer, whichever seemed most desirable. Sinners were exhorted not to sleep until they gave their hearts to God. After this, the work became so widespread that I preached every night for twenty nights in succession, and twice on Sundays. Our prayer meetings during this time were held in the church in the daytime. The prayer meeting was held one part of the day, and an inquiry meeting the other part. After the work had thus commenced, we held a prayer meeting and an inquiry meeting every day, with preaching in the evening. There was a solemnity throughout the whole place and an awe that made everybody feel that God was there.

Ministers came in from neighboring towns and expressed great astonishment at what they saw and heard. Conversions multiplied so rapidly that we had no way of learning who had been converted. Therefore, every evening, at the close of my sermon, I requested all who had been converted that day to come forward and report themselves in front of the pulpit, so that we might have a little conversation. We were every night surprised by the number and the class of people who came forward.

At one of our morning prayer meetings, the lower part of the church was full. I arose and was making some remarks to the people, when an unconverted man, a merchant, came into the meeting. He found a seat in front of me, near where I stood speaking. He had sat only a few moments, when he fell from his seat as if he had been shot. He writhed and groaned in a terrible manner. I stepped to his pew and saw that he was altogether in agony of mind.

A skeptical physician sat near him. He stepped out of his pew, came over, and examined this man who was thus distressed. He felt his pulse and examined the case. He said nothing but turned away, leaned his head against a post that supported the balcony, and manifested great agitation. He said afterward that he saw at once that it was distress of mind, and it took his skepticism entirely away. He was soon after converted. We engaged in prayer for the man who fell in the pew. Before he left the house, his anguish passed away, and he rejoiced in Christ.

Another physician, a very amiable man but a skeptic, had a little daughter and a praying wife. Little H——, a girl perhaps eight or nine years old, was strongly convicted of sin, and her mother was greatly interested in her state of mind. But her father was quite indignant. He said to his wife, "The subject of religion is too high for me. I never could understand it. Yet you tell me that this little child understands it so as to be intelligently convicted of sin? I do not believe it. I know better. It is fanaticism; it is madness." Nevertheless, the mother of the child held fast in prayer. The doctor had made these remarks with a good deal of spirit. Immediately he took his horse and went several miles to see a patient. On his way, this subject took possession of his mind in such a manner that it was all opened to his understanding, and the whole plan of salvation by Christ was so clear to him that he saw that a child could indeed understand it. He wondered that it had ever seemed so mysterious to him. He regretted what he had said to his wife about little H——, and he hurried home so that he might take it back. He soon came home a changed man, told his wife what had occurred, encouraged his daughter to come to Christ, and both father and daughter have since been earnest Christians and have done much good.

In this revival, as in others that I have known, God did some awe-inspiring things in righteousness. On one Sunday, as we came from behind the pulpit and were about to leave the church, a man came in haste to Mr. Gillett and myself and asked us to go to a certain place, saying that a man had fallen down dead there. I was engaged in conversing with somebody, so Mr. Gillett went alone. When I was through with the conversation, I went to Mr. Gillett's house, and he soon returned and related the event. Three men who had been opposing the work had met that Sunday and spent the day in drinking and ridiculing the work. They went on in this way until one of them suddenly fell dead. When Mr. Gillett arrived at the house and the circumstances were related to him, he said, "There is no doubt that that man has been stricken down by God and has been sent to hell." His companions were speechless. They could say nothing, for it was evident to them that their conduct had brought upon him this awful stroke of divine indignation.

As the work proceeded, it gathered in nearly the whole population, especially those who belonged to Mr. Gillett's congregation. He said to me before I left, "As far as my congregation is concerned, the Millennium has come already. My people are all converted." Mr. Gillett afterward reported that, during the twenty days that I spent at Rome, there were five hundred conversions in that town.

During the progress of this work, a good deal of excitement sprang up in Utica, and some there were inclined to ridicule the work at Rome. Mr. H——, who lived in

Rome, was a very prominent citizen and was regarded as
the head of society there in the areas of wealth and intelligence. He was a skeptic—or, I should say, he held Unitarian
views—but he was a very respectable man and held his
views unobtrusively, saying very little to anybody about
them. The first Sunday I preached there, Mr. H—— was
present. As he afterward told me, he was so astonished at
my preaching that he made up his mind that he would not
go again. He went home and said to his family, "That man
is mad, and I would not be surprised if he set the town on
fire." He stayed away from the meeting for two weeks. In
the meantime, the work became so great that it confused
his skepticism, and he was in a state of great perplexity.

He was president of a bank in Utica and used to attend
the weekly meeting of the directors there. On one of these
occasions, one of the directors began to tease him about the
state of things in Rome, as if they were all running mad
there. Mr. H—— remarked, "Gentlemen, say what you will,
there is something very remarkable in the state of things in
Rome. Certainly no human power or eloquence has produced what we see there. I cannot understand it. You say it
will soon subside. No doubt the intensity of feeling that is
now in Rome must soon subside, or the people will become
insane. But, gentlemen, there is no accounting for that
state of feeling by any philosophy, unless there is something
divine in it."

After Mr. H—— had stayed away from the meeting
about two weeks, a few of us assembled one afternoon to
make him a special subject of prayer. The Lord gave us
strong faith in praying for him, and we felt that the Lord
was working in his soul. That evening he came to the
meeting. When he came into the house, Mr. Gillett whispered to me as we sat in the pulpit and said, "Brother Finney, Mr. H—— has come. I hope you will not say anything
that will offend him." "No," said I, "but I will not spare
him, either." In those days I was obliged to preach without
premeditation, for I had not an hour in a week that I could
take to arrange my thoughts beforehand.

I chose my subject and preached. The Word took a powerful hold, and, as I had hoped and intended, it took a powerful hold of Mr. H——. That night, when at the close of the meeting I requested all those who had been converted that day and evening to come forward and report themselves, Mr. H—— was one who came deliberately, solemnly forward and reported himself as having given his heart to God. He appeared humble and penitent, and I have always supposed he was truly converted to Christ.

The state of things in Rome was such that no one could come into the village without feeling awestruck with the impression that God was there in a strange and wonderful manner. As an illustration of this, I will relate an incident. The sheriff of the county resided in Utica. There were two courthouses in the county: one in Rome, and the other in Utica. Consequently, the sheriff, named B——, had much business in Rome. He afterward told me that he had heard of the state of things in Rome, and he, together with others, had a good deal of laughter over what they had heard.

One day it was necessary for him to go to Rome. He said that he was glad to have business there, for he wanted to see for himself what it was that people talked so much about and what the state of things really was in Rome. He drove on without any particular impression upon his mind at all, until he crossed the old canal, about a mile from the town. As soon as he crossed the canal, a strange impression came over him, an awe so deep that he could not shake it off.

He felt as if God pervaded the whole atmosphere. He said that this increased the whole way, until he came to the village. He stopped at Mr. F——'s hotel, and the hostler came out and took his horse. He observed that the hostler looked just as he himself felt, as if he were afraid to speak. He went into the hotel and found the gentlemen there with whom he had business. He said they were all so much impressed that they could hardly attend to business. Several times during the short time he was there, he had to rise from the table abruptly, go to the window and look out, and try to divert his attention in order to keep from weeping. Everybody else appeared to feel just as he did. Such an awe, such a solemnity, such a state of things he had never had any idea of before. He hurried through his business and returned to Utica, never again to speak lightly of the work in Rome. A few weeks later in Utica, he was converted.

The Spirit's work was so spontaneous, so powerful, and so overwhelming in Rome that it became necessary to exercise the greatest caution and wisdom in conducting all the meetings. An undesirable outburst of feeling would have brought about a reaction. But no reaction followed. The moral state of the people was so greatly changed that Mr. Gillett often remarked that it did not seem like the same place. Whatever was left of sin was obliged to hide its head. No open immorality could be tolerated there for a moment.

A spirit of prayer prevailed in Rome at this time. On the Saturday that I came from Western to exchange with Mr. Gillett, I attempted to make the people understand that God would immediately answer prayer, provided they fulfilled the conditions upon which He had promised to answer prayer, and especially if they expected Him to answer their requests. I observed that they were greatly interested in my remarks, and their faces manifested an intense desire to see an answer to their prayers. Near the close of the meeting, I said, "I really believe, if you will unite this afternoon in the prayer of faith to God for the immediate outpouring of His Spirit, that you will receive an answer from heaven sooner than you would get a message from Albany by the quickest messenger that could be sent."

I said this with great emphasis, and I observed that the people were startled by my expression of earnestness and faith in respect to an immediate answer to prayer. The fact is, I had so often seen this result in answer to prayer, that I made the remark without any misgiving. Nothing was said by any of the members of the church at the time, but I later learned that three or four members of the church determined to take God at His Word and see whether He would answer while they were yet speaking. One of them told me afterward that wonderful faith was given them by the Spirit of God to pray for an immediate answer. He added, "The answer did come quicker than we could have gotten an answer from Albany."

Indeed, the town was full of prayer. No matter where you would go, you heard the voice of prayer. Wherever Christians met, they prayed. Wherever there was an unconverted sinner, especially if he showed any opposition, you would find two or three people agreeing to make him a special subject of prayer.

I should also mention the conversion of Mrs. Gillett during this revival. She was a beautiful woman, considerably younger than her husband, and his second wife. She had been, before Mr. Gillett married her, under conviction for several weeks and had become almost deranged. She had the impression that she was not one of the elect and that there was no salvation for her. Soon after the revival began in Rome, she was powerfully convicted again by the Spirit of the Lord.

She was a woman of refinement, fond of dress, and she wore some trifling ornaments—nothing, however, that I would have thought of as being any stumbling block in her way. Being her guest, I conversed repeatedly with her as her convictions increased. But it never occurred to me that her fondness for dress could stand in the way of her being converted to God. But as the work became more powerful, her distress became alarming. Mr. Gillett, knowing what had formerly occurred in her case, feared that she might fall into the state of despondency in which she had been years before. She asked me frequently what she should do. Almost every time I came into the house, she would come to me, beg me to pray for her, and tell me that her distress was more than she could bear. I could see that she was depending too much on me; therefore, I tried to avoid her.

This went on until, one day, I came into the house and went into the study. As usual, in a few moments she was before me, begging me to pray for her and complaining that there was no salvation for her. I got up abruptly and left her, without praying with her, saying to her that it was of no use for me to pray for her because she was depending on my prayers. When I did so, she sunk down as if she would faint. Nevertheless, I left her alone and went abruptly from the study to the parlor.

After a few moments, she came rushing across the hall into the parlor, with her face all aglow, exclaiming, "Mr. Finney! I have found the Savior! I have found the Savior! Don't you think it was the ornaments in my hair that stood in the way of my conversion? When I prayed, they would come up in my mind, and I would be tempted to give them up. But I thought they were trifles and that God did not care about such trifles. But the ornaments that I wore continually kept coming up in my mind whenever I attempted to give my heart to God. When you abruptly left me, I was driven to desperation. I cast myself down, and these ornaments came up again. I said, 'I will not have these things come up again; I will put them away from me forever.' So I renounced them. As soon as I promised to give them up, the Lord revealed Himself to my soul."

Fourteen

Rome and Utica: Three Thousand People Converted

There were two Presbyterian congregations in Utica, one under Mr. Aiken, the other under Mr. Brace. When I had been in Rome about twenty days, one of the elders of Mr. Aiken's church, a very prominent and useful man, died; and I went to Utica to attend his funeral. Mr. Aiken conducted the funeral, and I learned from him that the spirit of prayer was already evident in his congregation and in that town. He told me that one of the women had been so deeply troubled in her soul about the state of the church and of the ungodly in Utica, that she had prayed for two days and nights, almost incessantly, until her strength was exhausted. She could not endure the burden of her mind unless somebody was engaged in prayer with her— someone upon whose prayer she could lean and who could express her desires to God.

I understood this and told Mr. Aiken that the work had already begun in her heart. He recognized it, of course, and wished me to commence labor with him and his people immediately. I soon did so, and the work began at once. The Word took immediate effect, and the place became filled with the manifested influence of the Holy Spirit. Our meetings were crowded every night, and the work spread and went on powerfully, especially in the two Presbyterian congregations.

Soon after I began work in Utica, I observed to Mr. Aiken that Mr. B——, the sheriff, did not attend the meetings. But a few evenings afterward, just as I was about to begin to preach, Mr. Aiken whispered to me that Mr. B—— had come in. He pointed him out to me, as he made his way up the aisle to his seat. I took a Scripture verse and proceeded to address the congregation. I had spoken a few moments when I observed Mr. B—— rise up in the pew, turn deliberately around, wrap his coat around him, and kneel down. This caught the attention of those who sat near him and knew him, and it produced a considerable sensation in that part of the church. The sheriff remained on his knees during the whole service. He then retired to his room at the hotel in which he was staying.

He afterward told me that, when he went home, his mind was greatly burdened with the subject I had talked about. I had pressed the congregation to accept Christ just as He was presented in the Gospel. After considering all the points I had made, he had said to himself, "My soul, will you consent to this? Will you accept Christ, give up sin, and give up yourself? And will you do it now?" He said he had thrown himself on his bed in the agony of his mind. He said he had brought his soul to accept Christ "here and now," and his distress left him so suddenly that he fell asleep and did not wake for several hours. When he did awake, he found his mind full of peace and rest in Christ. From that moment he became an earnest worker for Christ.

The hotel at which he boarded in Utica was at that time kept by Mr. S——. The Spirit took powerful hold of that house; Mr. S—— himself was soon made a subject of prayer and became converted, along with a large number of his family and his boarders. Indeed, this hotel, the largest in the town, became a center of spiritual influence, and many were converted there. So powerful was the impression in the community that I heard of several cases of people who stopped for a meal or to spend a night and were powerfully convicted and converted before they left the town. Both in Utica and in Rome, it was a common remark that nobody could be in the town or pass through it without being aware of the presence of God. A divine influence seemed to pervade the place, and the whole atmosphere seemed to be empowered by a divine life.

It was in the midst of the revival in Utica that we first heard of the opposition that was springing up in the East.

Mr. Asahel Nettleton had written some letters to Mr. Aiken, in which it was evident that he was very much mistaken as to the character of the revivals. Mr. Aiken showed me the letters. Among them was one in which Mr. Nettleton stated what he regarded as objectionable in the conduct of the revivals, but the things he complained of had not been done, so we took no more notice of the letters. One of the complaints was that women would sometimes pray in the social meetings. It was true that women—and some very prominent women—would sometimes lead in prayer in the daily meetings. However, no opposition was manifested to this either in Utica or in Rome. Indeed, it was not a subject of much conversation or thought in the neighborhood where it occurred.

The work went on with great power, converting all classes, until Mr. Aiken reported the conversion of five hundred in the course of a few weeks—most of them belonging to his own congregation. Revivals were a comparatively new thing in that region, and the majority of the people had not become convinced that they were the work of God. They were not awed by them, as they afterward became. The impression seemed to be that those revivals would soon pass away and would prove to have been a mere excitement of human emotions. Of course, those who were interested in the work had no such idea.

One circumstance occurred, in the midst of that revival, that made a powerful impression. The Oneida presbytery met there while the revival was going on in its full strength. One aged clergyman, a stranger to me, was very much annoyed by the strength and fervor of the revival. He found the public mind all absorbed with the subject of religion, so that there was prayer and religious conversation everywhere, even in the stores and other public places. He had never seen a revival and had never heard what he heard there.

On Friday afternoon, before the presbytery adjourned, he arose and made a vehement speech against the revival. What he said greatly shocked and grieved the Christian people who were present. They felt like falling on their faces before God and crying to Him to prevent what he had said from doing any harm.

The presbytery adjourned just at evening. Some of the members went home, and others remained in Utica overnight. The Christians gave themselves to prayer. There was a great crying to God that night, that He would counteract any evil influence that might result from that speech. The next morning, the clergyman was found dead in his bed.

In the course of these revivals, people came from afar from almost every direction to see for themselves what they had heard the Lord was doing. Many of them were converted to Christ. Among these visitors, Dr. Garnet Judd, who soon afterward went to the Hawaiian Islands as a missionary and became quite well-known, was one.

About the same time a young woman, Miss T——, from some part of New England, came to Utica. She was teaching high school in Newburgh, New York. After having read much in the newspapers about the revival in Utica, Miss T——, along with many others, became filled with wonder and astonishment, wishing to go and see for herself what it meant. She dismissed her school for ten days and took the stagecoach for Utica. As she passed through Genesee Street toward the hotel, she saw the name of B—— T—— on one of the signs. She was an entire stranger in Utica and did not think that she had an acquaintance or relative there. But after inquiring who B—— T—— was, she dropped him a note, saying that the daughter of a Mr. T——, naming her father, was at the hotel and would be pleased to see him. Mr. T—— met her, found that she was a distant relative of his, and invited her immediately to his house. She accepted his invitation. Being an earnest Christian man, he immediately took her to all the meetings and tried to interest her in religion. She was greatly surprised at all that she saw, and a good deal annoyed.

She was an energetic, highly cultivated, and proud young lady. The manner in which people conversed with her and pressed upon her the necessity of immediately giving her heart to God very much disturbed her. The preaching that she heard from night to night took a deep hold upon her. The guilt of sinners was largely insisted upon, and their danger of eternal damnation was made prominent in what she heard. This aroused her opposition, but still the work of conviction went on powerfully in her heart.

After writhing under the truth for a few days, she came to see me. She sat down on the sofa in the parlor. I drew up my chair in front of her and began to press her with the claims of God. She told me that she could not accept my preaching that sinners deserved to be sent to an eternal hell; she did not believe that God was such a being. I replied, "Nor do you yet understand what sin is; if you did, you would not complain that God sends the sinner to an eternal hell." I then explained the subject to her as plainly as I could. As much as she hated to believe it, the conviction of its truth was becoming irresistible. I talked in this strain for some time, until I saw that she was ready to sink under conviction. Then I said a few words about the place that Jesus holds and what is the real situation of things in regard to the salvation of those who thus deserved to be damned.

Her face became pale, she threw up her hands and shrieked, and then she fell forward upon the arm of the sofa and let her heart break. It seemed as though she had never cried before. But now the floodgates were opened, and she let her whole heart gush out before God. I had no reason to say any more to her. She soon arose and went to her own lodgings. She almost immediately gave up teaching, offered herself as a foreign missionary, was married to a Mr. Gulick, and went out to the Hawaiian Islands at the same time that Dr. Judd went there. She has been a very effective missionary and has raised several sons who also are missionaries.

While living in Utica, I preached frequently in New Hartford, a village four miles south of Utica. A precious and powerful work of grace was occurring there under a Mr. Coe, pastor of the Presbyterian church at that time. I also preached at Whitesboro, another beautiful village, four miles west of Utica, where a powerful revival was also taking place. The pastor, Mr. John Frost, was a most effective laborer in the work.

I must point out a circumstance that occurred in this neighborhood. There was a cotton factory on the Oriskany Creek, a little above Whitesboro, a place now called New York Mills. It was owned by Mr. W——, an unconverted man but a gentleman of high standing and good morals. My brother-in-law, Mr. G—— A——, was at that time superintendent of the factory. I was invited to go and preach at that place. I went one evening and preached in the village schoolhouse, which was large and was crowded with hearers. The Word took a powerful effect among the people, especially among the young people who worked in the factory.

The next morning after breakfast, I went to the factory to walk through it. As I went through, I observed a good deal of agitation among those who were busy at their work. On passing through an area where a large number of young women were weaving, I observed one woman eyeing me, then making a comment to her neighbor. They both laughed. I could see that they were quite agitated by my presence. I went slowly toward them, with sorrow filling my eyes. As the one woman saw me coming, her hands trembled so that she could not do her work. I approached slowly, looking at the machinery on each side as I passed. This girl grew more and more agitated and could not proceed with her work. Trying to calm herself, she looked out the window. When I came within eight or ten feet of her, I looked solemnly at her. She sank down and burst into tears. The impression caught almost like gunpowder, and in a few moments nearly everyone in the room was in tears.

This feeling spread throughout the factory. Mr. W——, the owner of the establishment, was present. Seeing the state of things, he said to the superintendent, "Stop the mill, and let the people attend to religion, for it is more important that our souls be saved than that this factory run." The factory was immediately stopped, but no one knew where to assemble. The superintendent suggested that we could assemble in the mule room once the mules were taken out. (A mule is a machine used to draw and twist fiber, in this case cotton, into yarn or thread and to wind it onto spindles.) We did so, and I scarcely ever attended a more powerful meeting. The revival went through the mill with astonishing power, and in the course of a few days nearly everyone in the mill was converted.

Because much has been said about the conversion of Theodore D. Weld in Utica, it may be well for me to give a correct report of the facts. His aunt, Mrs. C———, was a very godly woman who lived in Utica. He was the son of an eminent clergyman in New England, and his aunt thought he was a Christian because he used to lead her family in worship. Before the commencement of the revival, he had become a member of Hamilton College in Clinton. The work in Utica had attracted so much attention that many people from Clinton, and some of the professors of the college, had been to Utica and had reported what was occurring there. A good deal of excitement had resulted. Weld held a very prominent place among the students of Hamilton College, and when he heard what was going on in Utica, his opposition was greatly aroused. He became quite outrageous in his expressions of opposition to the work.

This fact became known in Utica, and his aunt, with whom he had boarded, became very anxious about him. To me he was an entire stranger. His aunt wrote him and asked him to come home and spend a Sunday in order to hear the preaching. He at first declined but finally got some of the students together and told them that he had decided to go to Utica. He said he knew it must be fanaticism, that it would not move him. He came full of opposition, and his aunt soon learned that he did not intend to hear me preach. Mr. Aiken had usually occupied the pulpit in the morning, and I in the afternoon and evening. His aunt learned that he intended to go to Mr. Aiken's church in the morning, when he expected Mr. Aiken to preach, but that he would not go in the afternoon or evening, because he was determined not to hear me.

In view of this, Mr. Aiken suggested that I preach in the morning, and I consented. Mrs. C—— came to the meeting with her family, among them Mr. Weld. She took pains to have him so seated in the pew that he could not easily get out, for she feared that he would leave when he saw that I was going to preach. I knew that his influence among the young men of Utica was very great and that his coming there would have a powerful influence to make them band together in opposition to the work. Mr. Aiken pointed him out to me as he came in and took his seat.

After the introductory exercises, I arose and read this verse: *"One sinner destroys much good"* (Eccl. 9:18). I had never preached from it or heard it preached from, but I began to preach and to show how, in many instances, how the influence of one man might destroy a great many souls. I suppose that I drew a rather vivid picture of Weld, of what his influence was, and of what harm he might do. Once or twice he made an effort to get out, but his aunt made sure that he could not get out without annoying her; therefore, he remained in his seat until the meeting was finished.

The next day I went to a store on Genesee Street to converse with some people there, as it was my custom to do. I found Weld there. For nearly an hour he talked to me in a most abusive manner. I had never heard anything like it. I got an opportunity to say very little to him, for his tongue ran incessantly. He was very gifted in language. It soon attracted the attention of all who were in the store. The news ran along the streets, and the clerks gathered in from the neighboring stores and stood to hear what he had to say. All business ceased in the store, and everyone gave himself up to listening to his vituperation. But finally I appealed to him and said, "Mr. Weld, are you not the son of a minister of Christ? Is this the way for you to behave?" I saw that these words stung him, and after making some very severe comment, he immediately left the store.

I went out also and returned to Mr. Aiken's, where for the time I was lodging. I had been there only a few moments when somebody came to the door. And who should come in but Mr. Weld? He looked as if he wanted to bury his head in a hole. He began immediately to make the most humble confession and apology for the manner in which he had treated me, and he expressed himself in the strongest terms of self-condemnation. I took him kindly by the hand and had a little conversation with him, assured him that I had nothing against him, and exhorted him earnestly to give his heart to God. I prayed with him before he went. He left, and I heard no more of him that day.

The next morning I heard that he had gone to his aunt's, greatly subdued. But when she asked him to pray, his enmity arose so much that he went into one of the most blasphemous strains of verbal abuse that could be uttered. He continued in a most astonishing way, until they all became convulsed with astonishment. His aunt attempted to converse with him and to pray with him, but the opposition of his heart was terrible. She became frightened at the state of mind that he manifested. After praying with him and entreating him to give his heart to God, she went to bed.

He went to his room and alternately paced or lay upon the floor. He spent the whole night in that terrible state of mind—angry, rebellious, and yet so convicted that he could scarcely live. Just at daylight, while walking back and forth in his room, a pressure came upon him that crushed him down to the floor; with it came a voice that seemed to command him to repent, to repent now. He said it broke him down to the floor, and there he lay until, late in the morning, his aunt found him lying on the floor calling himself a thousand fools. To all human appearance, his heart was all broken to pieces. The next night he rose in the meeting and made a very humble, earnest, brokenhearted confession. From that time he became a very effective helper in the work. Being a powerful speaker, he was instrumental for many years in the conversion of a great many souls.

I have said that no public replies were made to the things that found their way into print in opposition to these revivals. Mr. Nettleton, along with Dr. Lyman Beecher, had written several letters of opposition. I have also said that a pamphlet was published, by the ministers who composed the Oneida Association, in opposition to the work. To this I believe no public answer was given. A Unitarian minister residing in Trenton published an abusive pamphlet, in which he greatly misrepresented the work and made a personal attack on me. To this the Reverend Mr. Wetmore, one of the members of the Oneida presbytery, published a reply.

This revival occurred in the winter and spring of 1826, spreading from Rome and Utica in every direction. Ministers came from a considerable distance, attending the meetings and in various ways helping to forward the work. I spread my own labors over as large a field as I could. I cannot now remember all the places where I spent my time. The pastors of all those churches sympathized deeply with the work and, like good and true men, laid themselves upon the altar and did all they could to forward the great and glorious movement; and God gave them a rich reward. About three thousand people were converted.

The doctrines preached in these revivals were the same ones that I had always used. Instead of telling sinners to pray for a new heart, we called on them to make themselves a new heart and a new spirit (Ezek. 18:31), and we pressed the duty of instant surrender to God. We told them the Spirit was striving with them to induce them to give Him their hearts, to believe, and to enter at once into a life of devotion to Christ—a life of faith, love, and Christian obedience. We taught them that if they would yield at once to their own convictions of duty, they would be Christians. We tried to show them that everything they did or said before they had submitted, believed, and given their hearts to God was all sin; it was not what God required them to do but was simply deferring repentance and resisting the Holy Spirit. This teaching was, of course, opposed by many; nevertheless, it was greatly blessed by the Spirit of God.

Fifteen

Auburn in 1826: A Backslidden Church Turns

D r. Lansing, pastor of the First Presbyterian Church in Auburn, came to Utica to witness the revival there, and he urged me to go out and labor for a time with him. In the summer of 1826, I complied with his request and went there and labored with him for a season. I had known that a considerable number of ministers east of Utica were taking an attitude of hostility to the revivals. However, until I arrived in Auburn, I was not fully aware of the amount of opposition I was destined to meet from the ministry. These ministers knew nothing of me personally, but they had been influenced by the false reports that they had heard. But soon after I arrived in Auburn, I learned from various sources that a system of espionage was being carried on that was intended to result in an extensive union of ministers and churches to hedge me in and prevent the spread of the revivals connected with my labors.

My mind soon became very troubled by the extensive working of this system of espionage. Mr. Frost of Whitesboro had come to a considerable knowledge of the facts and communicated them to me. I said nothing publicly or privately to anybody on the subject but gave myself to prayer. I looked to God for His direction with great earnestness day after day, asking Him to show me the path of duty and to give me grace to ride out the storm.

I will never forget what a scene I passed through one day in my room at Dr. Lansing's. The Lord showed me as in a vision what was before me. He drew so near to me while I was engaged in prayer that my flesh literally trembled on my bones. I shook from head to foot under a full sense of the presence of God. At first, and for some time, it seemed more like being on the top of Sinai, amid its full thunderings, than in the presence of the cross of Christ.

Never in my life was I so awed and humbled before God as then. Nevertheless, instead of feeling like fleeing, I seemed drawn nearer and nearer to God—seemed to draw nearer and nearer to that presence that filled me with such unutterable awe and trembling. After a season of great humiliation before Him, there came a great lifting up. God assured me that He would be with me and would uphold me; that no opposition would prevail against me; and that I had nothing to do, in regard to this matter, but to focus on my work and wait for the salvation of God.

I can never fully describe the sense of God's presence and all that passed between God and my soul at that time. It led me to be perfectly trustful, perfectly calm, and to have nothing but the most perfectly kind feelings toward all who were arraying themselves against me. I felt assured that everything would come out right, that my true course was to leave everything to God; and as the storm gathered and the opposition increased, I never for one moment doubted how it would end up. I was never disturbed by it; I never spent a waking hour in thinking of it, though to all outward appearances it seemed as if all the churches of the land, except where I had labored, would unite to shut me out of their pulpits. This was indeed the avowed determination of the men who led the opposition. They were so deceived that they thought there was nothing to do but to unite and, as they expressed it, "put him down." But God assured me that they could not put me down.

A passage in the twentieth chapter of Jeremiah was repeatedly brought to my mind with great power:

O LORD, You induced [enticed] *me, and I was persuaded* [enticed]; *You are stronger than I, and have prevailed. I am in derision daily; everyone mocks me. For when I spoke, I cried out; I shouted, "Violence and plunder!" because the word of the LORD was made to me a reproach and a derision daily. Then I said, "I*

*will not make mention of Him, nor speak anymore in
His name." But His word was in my heart like a
burning fire shut up in my bones; I was weary of holding it back, and I could not. For I heard many mock-
ing: "Fear on every side!" "Report," they say, "and we
will report it!" All my acquaintances watched for my
stumbling, saying, "Perhaps he can be induced
[enticed]; then we will prevail against him, and we
will take our revenge on him." But the LORD is with
me as a mighty, awesome One. Therefore my persecu-
tors will stumble, and will not prevail. They will be
greatly ashamed, for they will not prosper. Their everlasting confusion will never be forgotten. But, O LORD
of hosts, You who test the righteous, and see the mind
and heart, let me see Your vengeance on them; for I
have pleaded my cause before You.   (Jer. 20:7–12)*

I do not mean that this passage literally described my
case or expressed all my feelings, but there was so much
similarity in the case that this passage was often a support
to my soul. The Lord did not allow me to take the opposition to heart, and I can truly say that I never had an un-
kind feeling toward any leading opposer of the work.

I recall having had a strange feeling of horror in regard
to a pamphlet published by Mr. Weeks, to whom I referred
in chapter twelve. Soon after he published it, he began to
write a book that he called *The Pilgrim's Progress in the
Nineteenth Century*. He was a man of considerable talent
but was much deluded and exceedingly off-base in his theology. I do not mention him because I wish to say any evil
of him or of his book, but merely to say that he never
ceased to oppose, directly or indirectly, the revivals that did
not favor his views. But God has disposed of all his influence. I have heard nothing of him now for many years.

Despite the attitude that some of the Christians in
Auburn were taking, along with so many ministers
abroad, the Lord soon revived His work in Auburn. Mr.
Lansing had a large and very intelligent congregation. The

revival soon took effect among the people and became powerful.

It was at that time that Dr. S—— of Auburn was so greatly blessed in his soul as to become quite another man. Dr. S—— was an elder in the Presbyterian church when I arrived there. He was a very timid and doubting kind of Christian who had little effectiveness because he had little faith. He soon, however, became deeply convicted of sin and descended into the depths of humiliation and distress, almost to despair. He remained in this state for weeks, until one night, in a prayer meeting, he was quite overcome with his feelings and sank down helpless on the floor. Then God opened his eyes to the reality of his salvation in Christ. This occurred just after I had left Auburn and gone to Troy, New York, to labor. Dr. S—— soon followed me to Troy. The first time I saw him there, he exclaimed, "Brother Finney, they have buried the Savior, but Christ is risen." He received such a wonderful baptism of the Holy Spirit that he has been the rejoicing and the wonder of God's people ever since.

Partly because of the known disapproval of my labors on the part of many ministers, a good deal of opposition sprang up in Auburn. A number of the leading men in that large village took a strong stand against the work. But the Spirit of the Lord was among the people with great power.

There was a hatter by the name of H—— residing in Auburn at this time. His wife was a Christian woman, but he was a Universalist and an opposer of the revival. He carried his opposition so far as to forbid his wife's attending our meetings, and for several successive evenings she remained at home. One night, as the bell rang for the meeting, half an hour before the assembly met, Mrs. H—— was so troubled about her husband that she withdrew into private prayer and spent the half hour in pouring out her soul to God. She told Him how her husband behaved and that he would not let her attend the meeting, and she drew very near to God.

As the bell was tolling for the people to assemble, she came out of her prayer closet and found that her husband had come in from the shop. As she entered the sitting room, he said that if she wanted to go to the meeting, he would accompany her. He afterward informed me that he had made up his mind to attend the meeting that night to see if he could find something to justify his opposition to his wife, or at least something to laugh about and sustain him in ridiculing the whole work. When he proposed to accompany his wife, she was very much surprised but prepared herself, and they came to the meeting.

I had been visiting and laboring with inquirers the whole day and had had no time to arrange my thoughts or even to decide upon a text. During the introductory services, a text occurred to my mind. It was the words of the man with the unclean spirit, who cried out, *"Let us alone!"* (Mark 1:24). With these words I endeavored to show the conduct of those sinners who wanted to be let alone, who did not want to have anything to do with Christ.

The Lord gave me power to give a very vivid description of the course that this class of men was pursuing. In the midst of my sermon, I observed a person fall from his seat near the aisle and cry out in a most terrific manner. The congregation was very much shocked, and the outcry of the man was so great that I stopped preaching and stood still. After a few moments, I requested the congregation to sit still while I went down to speak with the man. I found him to be this Mr. H——. The Spirit of the Lord had so powerfully convicted him that he was unable to sit on his seat. When I reached him, he had so far recovered his strength as to be on his knees, with his head on his wife's lap. He was weeping aloud like a child, confessing his sins and accusing himself in a terrible manner. I said a few words to him, but the Spirit of God had his attention so thoroughly that I soon desisted from all efforts to make him listen to what I said. When I told the congregation who it was, they all knew him and his character, and it produced tears and sobs in every part of the house. I waited to see if he would be quiet enough for me to go on with my sermon, but his loud weeping rendered it impossible. I can never forget the appearance of his wife as she sat and held his face in her hands upon her lap. There appeared in her face a holy joy and triumph that words cannot express.

We had several prayers, I dismissed the meeting, and some people helped Mr. H—— to his house. He immediately wished them to send for some of his companions, with whom he had been in the habit of ridiculing the work of the Lord in that place. He could not rest until he had sent for a great number of them and had made confession to them, which he did with a very broken heart. He was so overcome that he could not get around for several days, and during this time he continued to warn his friends to flee from the wrath to come. As soon as he was able to get around, he took hold of the work with the utmost humility and simplicity of character, but with great earnestness. Soon afterward, he was made an elder in the church, and ever since, he has been a very exemplary and useful Christian. His conversion was so powerful, and the results were so evident, that it did very much to silence the opposition.

There were several wealthy men in the town who took offense at Dr. Lansing, myself, and the laborers in that revival. After I left, they got together and formed a new congregation. Most of these were, at the time, unconverted men. Let the reader bear this in mind, for I will have occasion to point out the results of this opposition and the formation of a new congregation, and the subsequent conversion of nearly every one of those opposers.

Soon after my arrival in Auburn, a striking thing occurred. My wife and I were guests of Dr. Lansing, the pastor of the church. The church members were much conformed to the world and were accused by the unconverted of being leaders in fashion and worldliness. As usual, I directed my preaching to secure the reformation of the church and to get them into a revival state. One Sunday I had preached, as searchingly as I was able, in regard to their attitude before the world. The Word took deep hold of the people.

At the close of my address, I called, as usual, upon the pastor to pray. He was much impressed with the sermon. Instead of immediately engaging in prayer, he made a short but very earnest address to the church, confirming what I had said to them. At this moment a man arose in the balcony and said in a very deliberate and distinct manner, "Mr. Lansing, I do not believe that such remarks from you can do any good while you wear a ruffled shirt and a gold ring and while your wife and the ladies of your family sit before the congregation, dressed as leaders in the fashions of the day." It seemed as if this would kill Dr. Lansing outright. He made no reply but cast himself across the side of the pulpit and wept like a child. The congregation was almost as shocked and affected as he was. They almost universally dropped their heads upon the seats in front of them, and many of them wept. With the exception of the sobs and sighs, the house was profoundly silent. I waited a few moments, and since Dr. Lansing did not move, I arose and offered a short prayer and dismissed the congregation.

I went home with the dear, wounded pastor, and when all the family had returned from church, he took the ring from his finger—it was a slender gold ring that could hardly attract notice—and said that his first wife, when upon her deathbed, had taken it from her finger and placed it upon his with a request that he wear it for her sake. He had done so, without a thought of its being a stumbling block. Of his ruffles he said he had worn them from his childhood and did not think of them as anything improper. Indeed, he could not remember when he began to wear them, and of course he thought nothing about them. "But," said he, "if these things are an occasion of offense to any, I will not wear them." He was a precious Christian man and an excellent pastor.

Almost immediately after this, the church felt the need to make a public confession of their backsliding and lack of a Christian spirit. Accordingly, a confession was drawn up, covering the whole ground. It was then read before the congregation. The people stood, many of them weeping while the confession was read. From this point, the work went forward with greatly increased power.

The confession was evidently a heart work and no sham; God most graciously and manifestly accepted it, and the mouths of opposers were shut. The fact is that, to a great extent, the churches and ministers were in a low state of grace, and those powerful revivals took them by surprise. I did not much wonder then, nor have I since, that those wonderful works of God were not well understood and received by those who were not in a revival state.

There were a great many interesting conversions in Auburn and its vicinity, and also in all the neighboring towns throughout that part of the state, as the work spread in every direction. In the spring of 1831, I was again in Auburn and saw another powerful revival there.

Sixteen

Troy: A Self-Righteous Judge Is Converted

Early in the autumn of 1826, I accepted an invitation from the Reverend Dr. Beman to labor with him in Troy, New York. I spent the fall and winter there, and the revival was powerful in that city.

Soon after my arrival in Troy, I went to Albany to see Mr. Nettleton. He was the guest of a family with which I was acquainted. I spent part of an afternoon with him and conversed with him in regard to his doctrinal views, especially the views held by the Dutch and Presbyterian Churches regarding the nature of moral depravity. I found that he entirely agreed with me on all the points of theology upon which we conversed. However, when I told him that I intended to remain in Albany and hear him preach in the evening, he manifested uneasiness and remarked that I must not be seen with him. Hence Judge C——, who had accompanied me from Troy and who had been in college with Mr. Nettleton, went with me to the meeting, and we sat in the balcony together. I saw enough to convince me that I could expect no advice or instruction from Mr. Nettleton, and that he was there to take a stand against me. I soon found I was not mistaken.

Mr. Nettleton never attempted to change my views and practices in promoting revivals of religion. His views were so similar to mine at that time that he could have molded me at his discretion, but he said not a word to me about my manner of conducting revivals, nor did he ever write a word to me upon the subject. He kept me at arm's length, and although we conversed on some points of theology then much discussed, it was plain that he was unwilling to say anything regarding revivals. This was the only time I saw him, until I met him again at the convention in New Lebanon, which I will relate later in this chapter.

In Troy we soon began to feel the influence of Dr. Beecher's letters over some of the leading members of Dr. Beman's church. This opposition increased and was undoubtedly stirred up by an outside influence, until finally a complaint was filed against Dr. Beman and his case was brought before the presbytery. For several weeks the presbytery sat and examined the charges against him.

In the meantime, I continued my labors in the revival. Christian people continued praying mightily to God. I continued preaching and praying incessantly, and the revival went on with increasing power. Meanwhile, Dr. Beman had to give almost his entire attention to his case before the presbytery. When the presbytery had examined the charges, they were nearly unanimous in dismissing the whole subject and justifying the course that he had taken. The charge was not for heresy, but for things conjured up by the enemies of the revival and by those who were misled by an outside influence. The failure of this effort to break Dr. Beman down considerably thwarted the opposition to the revival.

In the midst of the revival, it became necessary for me to leave Troy for a week or two in order to visit my family in Whitesboro. While I was gone, Rev. Horatio Foote was invited by Dr. Beman to preach. I do not know how often he preached, but he greatly offended the already estranged members of the church. He bore down upon them with the most searching discourses. A few of them finally made up their minds to withdraw from the congregation. They did so and established another congregation after I had left Troy.

In this revival, as in those that had preceded, there was a very earnest spirit of prayer. We had a daily prayer meeting at eleven o'clock. At one of those meetings, a Mr. S——, cashier of a bank in Troy, was so pressed by the spirit of prayer that, when the meeting was dismissed, he was unable to rise from his knees, as we had all just been kneeling in prayer. He remained on his knees and writhed

143

and groaned in agony. He said, "Pray for Mr. ——," who was president of the bank of which he was cashier. This president was a wealthy, unconverted man. When it was seen that his soul was in travail for that man, the praying people knelt down and wrestled in prayer for his conversion. As soon as the mind of Mr. S—— was relieved so that he could go home, we all retired. Soon afterward, the president of the bank, for whom we had prayed, expressed hope in Christ. He had not attended any of the meetings, and it was not known that he was concerned about his salvation. But prayer prevailed, and God soon took his case in hand.

At that time I was a guest of Judge C——, who had been in Albany with me, and his father was living with him. The old gentleman had been a judge in Vermont. He was remarkably correct in his outward life, a venerable man whose house in Vermont had been the home of ministers who visited the place. To all appearance he was quite satisfied with his amiable and self-righteous life. His wife had told me of her anxiety for his conversion, and his son had repeatedly expressed fear that his father's self-righteousness would never be overcome, and that his natural amiability would ruin his soul.

One Sunday morning, the Holy Spirit opened the case to my understanding and showed me how to reach it. In a few moments, I had the whole subject in my mind. I went downstairs and told the old lady and her son what I was about to do, and I exhorted them to pray earnestly for him. I followed out the divine vision, and the Word took such powerful hold of him that he spent a sleepless night. His wife informed me that he had spent a night of anguish, that his self-righteousness was thoroughly annihilated, and that he was almost in despair. His son had told me that he had long prided himself as being better than members of the church. He soon became clearly converted and lived a Christian life to the end.

Before I left Troy, a young lady, a Miss S—— from New Lebanon, who was an only daughter of one of the deacons of the church there, came to Troy to purchase a dress for a ball that she wished to attend. She had a cousin in Troy who was numbered among the young converts and was a zealous Christian. She invited Miss S—— to attend all the meetings with her. This aroused the enmity of her heart. She was very restless, but her cousin pleaded with her to stay from day to day and to attend the meetings. Before she left, she was thoroughly converted to Christ.

As soon as her eyes were opened and her peace was made with God, she went immediately home to New Lebanon and began labors for a revival in that place. Religion in New Lebanon was, at that time, in a very low state. The young people were nearly all unconverted, and the old members of the church were in a very cold and ineffective state. Miss S——'s father, the deacon, had become very formal, and for a long time religious matters had been largely neglected in the whole town. They had an aged minister—a good man but a man who did not seem to know how to perform revival work.

Miss S—— first began at home, asking her father to give up his "old prayer," as she expressed it, and to wake up and be engaged in religion. As she was a great favorite in the family, especially with her father, her conversion and conversation greatly affected him. He very soon became quite another man and felt deeply that they must have a revival of religion. The daughter also went to the house of her pastor and conversed with a daughter of his who was in sin. She was soon converted. The two girls then united in prayer for a revival of religion and went from house to house, stirring up the people.

In the course of a week or two, there was so much interest excited that Miss S——, at the request of her pastor and the church, came to Troy to beg me to go to New Lebanon to preach. I did so. The Spirit of the Lord was poured out, and the revival soon went forward with great power. Striking conversions were multiplied, and a great and blessed change came over the religious aspect of the whole place.

Because I was outside the region poisoned by the influence of the opposition raised by Dr. Beecher and Mr.

Nettleton, I heard little opposition in this place during the revival, especially from religious people. Everything seemed to go on harmoniously. The people in New Lebanon were soon led to feel that they greatly needed a revival, and they seemed to be very thankful that God had visited them. Most of the prominent men in the community were converted.

Among these was a Dr. W——, who was said to be an infidel. He at first manifested a good deal of hostility to the revival and declared that the people were mad. But he was made a particular subject of prayer by Miss S—— and some others who had great faith that, notwithstanding his fiery opposition, he would soon be converted. One Sunday morning he came to the meeting, and I could see that those who felt for him were burdened. Their heads were down, and they were in a prayerful state during nearly the whole sermon. Before night, however, it was plain that the doctor's opposition began to give way. He listened throughout the day, and he spent that night in a deeply troubled state of mind. The next morning he called on me, subdued like a little child, and confessed that he had been all wrong. He was very frank in opening his heart and declaring the change that had come over him. It was clear that he was another man, and from that day he took hold of the work and went forward with all his might.

I must mention a little incident somewhat connected with the opposition that had been manifested in Troy. The presbytery of Columbia had a meeting while I was in New Lebanon. Upon being informed that I was laboring in one of their churches, they appointed a committee to visit the place and inquire into the state of things. From Troy and other places, and from the opposition of Mr. Nettleton and the letters of Dr. Beecher, they had been led to believe that my method of conducting revivals was so very objectionable that it was the duty of the presbytery to inquire into it. They appointed two presbyters to visit the place.

The news of their upcoming visit reached New Lebanon, and it was feared that it might create some division and disturbance if this committee came. Therefore, some of the Christians made this a particular subject of prayer. For a day or two before the time when the two presbyters were expected, they prayed much that the Lord would overrule this thing and would not allow it to divide the church or introduce any element of discord. The two men were expected to be there on Sunday, but the day before, a violent snowstorm set in. The snow was so deep that they found it impossible to get through, were detained on Sunday, and on Monday found their way back to their own congregations.

Soon after this, I received a letter from Mr. B——, informing me that the presbytery had appointed him one of a committee to visit me and to make some inquiry in regard to my mode of conducting revivals. He invited me to come and spend a Sunday with him and preach for him. I did so. As I understood afterward, his report to the presbytery was that it was unnecessary and useless for them to take further action in the case, that the Lord was in the work, and that they should take heed lest they be found fighting against God. (See Acts 5:39.) I heard of no more opposition from that source. As far as I know, they thereafter sympathized with the work that was going on.

About this time, a proposition was made by somebody to hold a convention on the subject of conducting revivals. It was finally agreed to hold the convention in July 1827, in New Lebanon, where I had been laboring. I had left New Lebanon and had been spending a short time at the village of Little Falls, on the Mohawk River, near Utica. But I was obliged to leave after a very short stay in that place and return to New Lebanon to attend the convention.

Many people misunderstood the intention of this meeting and imagined that it was for a trial before a council regarding some charge against me. But this was by no means the case. The intent was simply to compare views, to get the facts of the revivals that had been so much opposed, and to see if we could come to a better understanding between the Eastern opposers of the revivals and those who had been instrumental in promoting them.

On the appointed day, the invited members arrived. None of us was representing any churches or ecclesiastical bodies whatsoever. We came together with no authority to act for the church or any branch of it, but simply to consult, to compare views, to see if anything was wrong, and if so, to agree to correct what was wrong on either side. There were Dr. Lyman Beecher and Mr. Asahel Nettleton from the East; Dr. Joel Hawes from Hartford; Dr. Dutton from New Haven; Dr. Heman Humphrey, president of Amherst College; Rev. Justin Edwards of Andover; and a considerable number of other men whose names I do not recollect. From the West, that is, from central New York where those revivals had been in progress, there were Dr. Beman of Troy, Dr. Lansing of Auburn, Mr. Aiken of Utica, Mr. Frost of Whitesboro, Mr. Gillett of Rome, Mr. Coe of New Hartford, Mr. Gale of Western, Mr. Weeks of Paris Hill, some others whose names I do not now recall, and myself.

As soon as the convention was organized and the business before us was stated and understood, the inquiry was raised by those from the West in regard to the source from which Dr. Beecher and Mr. Nettleton had received their information. We had been particularly eager to find out who was misleading those men and giving them such a view of the revivals as to make them feel justified in the course they were taking. We wanted to know from where all this mysterious opposition had proceeded. We therefore raised the inquiry at once and wished to know from what source they had received their information about those revivals. It was discovered at once that this was an embarrassing question.

I should mention that no opposition had been manifested by any of the ministers from the East who attended the convention, except Dr. Beecher and Mr. Nettleton. It was not difficult to see from the outset that Dr. Beecher felt himself committed and that his reputation was at stake. As some of his letters had found their way into print, he knew he would be held responsible for them. It was very plain that he and Mr. Nettleton were both very sensitive. It was also very apparent that Dr. Beecher had secured the attendance of the most influential New England ministers in order to sustain himself before the public and to justify himself in the course he had taken. As for Mr. Nettleton, Dr. Beecher had assured him that all the New England church judiciaries would speak out in his favor and sustain him.

When the question was raised as to the sources of the information, Dr. Beecher replied, "We have not come here to be catechized, and our spiritual dignity forbids us to answer any such questions." I thought this was strange, that we were not allowed to know the source from which their information had been obtained. But we found ourselves utterly unable to learn anything about it.

The convention went on several days; but as the facts came out in regard to the revivals, Mr. Nettleton became so very nervous that he did not attend several of our sessions. He plainly saw that he was losing ground and that nothing could be ascertained that could justify the course that he was taking. This must have been very visible also to Dr. Beecher.

I should have said before that, when he was asked how the facts were to be learned about those revivals, Dr. Beecher insisted that the testimony of the believers from the West, who had been engaged in promoting them, should not be received. Because we had been the objects of his censure, he said that we were not admissible as witnesses, and the facts should not be received from us. But to this, the other ministers from the East would not listen for a moment. Dr. Humphrey very firmly remarked that we were the best witnesses that could be produced; that we knew what we had done in those revivals of religion; that we were therefore the most competent and the most credible witnesses; and that our statements were to be received without hesitation by the convention. To this there was a universal agreement, with the exception of Dr. Beecher and Mr. Nettleton. This decision greatly affected both Dr. Beecher and Mr. Nettleton. They saw that if the facts came out from those who had witnessed the revivals, they might entirely overrule all the misunderstandings and all the misstatements that had been made upon the subject.

Our meeting was very fraternal throughout; there was no disputing or bitterness manifested by anyone, with the exception of Dr. Beecher and Mr. Nettleton. The ministers from the East appeared candid, desired to know the truth, and were glad to learn the particulars of the Western revivals.

Near the close of the convention, Mr. Nettleton made it known that he wished to give the reasons he had for the course he had taken. He had what he called "a historical letter," in which he claimed to give the reasons and state the facts upon which he had founded his opposition. A copy of it had been sent to Mr. Aiken when I was laboring with him in Utica, and Mr. Aiken had given it to me. I had it in my possession at the convention, and I would have mentioned it in due time if Mr. Nettleton had not done so.

He read the letter. It was a statement of the things of which he complained, the things that he had been informed were practiced in those revivals, especially by myself. It was evident that the letter was aimed at me, though I was seldom mentioned in it by name. The convention listened attentively to the whole letter, which was as long as a sermon. Thus the convention had before them the facts upon which he had acted—facts that he supposed had justified his course of action.

When he sat down, I arose and expressed my satisfaction that that letter had been read. I then affirmed that not one of the complaints mentioned about me was true. And I added, "All those with whom I have performed all these labors are here, and they know whether I am chargeable with any of these things in any of their congregations. If they know or believe that any of these things are true of me, let them say so now and here."

No one there ventured to justify a single sentence that related to me in Mr. Nettleton's historical letter. Even Mr. Weeks, whom I expected to say something in reply to my explicit denial of Mr. Nettleton's charges, said nothing. This, of course, was astounding to Mr. Nettleton and Dr. Beecher. No doubt they expected him to speak out and justify what he had written. But he said nothing indicating that he had any knowledge of any of the facts that Mr. Nettleton had presented in his letter. The reading of this letter prepared the way for closing the convention.

After this convention, the reaction of public feeling was overwhelming. Late in the fall of the same year, I met Mr. Nettleton in the city of New York. He told me he was there to publish his letters against the Western revivals. I asked him if he would publish his historical letter that he had read before the convention. He again said he would publish his letters in order to justify what he had done. I told him if he published that letter, it would react against himself, because all who were acquainted with those revivals would see that he was acting without a valid reason. He again replied that he would publish his letters and would risk the reaction. He published several other letters, but that one he did not publish, as far as I could learn.

In the biographies of Dr. Beecher and Mr. Nettleton, I find much complaint of the bad spirit that prevailed in those revivals. But I never heard the name of Dr. Beecher or Mr. Nettleton mentioned in public during those revivals, and certainly not censoriously. They were never, even in private conversation, spoken of with the least bitterness. The friends and promoters of those revivals were in a sweet, Christian spirit and as far as possible from being denunciatory. If they had been in a denunciatory spirit, those blessed revivals could never have been promoted by them, and the revivals could never have turned out as gloriously as they did. No, the denunciation was on the side of the opposition, which was grossly deceived at every step.

A quotation from Dr. Beecher's biography will illustrate the governing spirit of the opposition: "Finney, I know your plan, and you know I do. You intend to come to Connecticut and carry a streak of fire to Boston. But if you attempt it, as the Lord lives, I'll meet you at the state line, call out all the artillery men, and fight every inch of the way to Boston, and then I'll fight you there." This, and many other things that I find in his biography, shows how completely deceived he was and how utterly ignorant he was of the character, motives, and doings of those who had labored in the glorious revivals. I had no intention or desire to go to Connecticut or to Boston.

After the convention, I heard no more of the opposition of Dr. Beecher and Mr. Nettleton. Opposition in that form had spent itself. The results of the revivals were to shut the mouths of opposers and to convince everybody that they were indeed pure and glorious revivals of religion, as far from anything objectionable as any revivals that ever were witnessed in this world.

Revivals should increase in purity and power as intelligence increases. Anyone who reads the Acts of the Apostles and the record of the revivals of that day will see the reaction, backsliding, and apostasies that followed. The converts in apostolic times were either Jews, with their prejudice and ignorance, or degraded heathens. The art of printing had not yet been discovered. Copies of the written Word of God were not to be had, except by the rich, who were able to purchase manuscript copies. Christianity had no literature that was accessible to the masses. With so much darkness and ignorance, with so many false ideas of religion, with so much to mislead and debase, and with so few facilities for sustaining religious reformation, it was not to be expected that revivals of religion be pure and free from errors.

We have and preach the same Gospel that the apostles preached. We have every resource for guarding against error in doctrine and practice and for securing a sound Gospel religion. The people among whom these great nineteenth-century revivals prevailed were an intelligent, cultivated people. Abounding in their midst was not only secular education, but also religious education. Nearly every church had an educated, able, and faithful pastor. They were well able to judge the propriety of the measures employed. In a most striking and remarkable manner, God set His seal upon the doctrines that were preached and upon the means that were used to carry forward that great work. The results are now found in all parts of the land. The converts of those revivals are still living and laboring for Christ and for souls, in almost every state in this Union.

Since the opposition made by Mr. Nettleton and Dr. Beecher, it has been assumed that I have been reformed and have given up the measures they complained of. This is completely a mistake. Were I to live my life over again, I think that, with the experience of more than forty years in revival labors, I would, under the same circumstances, use substantially the same measures that I did then.

But this is no credit to myself; no, indeed. It was no wisdom of my own that directed me. I was made to feel my ignorance and dependence and was led to look to God continually for His guidance. I had no doubt then, nor have I ever had, that God led me by His Spirit to take the course I did. I do not doubt that those who opposed the revivals were good men. They were, however, misled and deceived. The fact is, during the spring that followed the convention, it was agreed by Dr. Beecher, Dr. Beman, and others to drop the subject and publish nothing more in regard to those revivals, and I saw nothing further in print about the subject. A truce had been declared between the friends of the revivals and the followers of Dr. Beecher and Mr. Nettleton. In fact, Dr. Beecher's attitude toward the revivals changed so much that, several years later, he invited me to preach in Boston.

To me it does not matter who may have given to Dr. Beecher the supposed facts upon which he acted. Certainly none of the pastors where those revivals prevailed ever gave him any information that justified his course, and no other men understood the matter as well as they did. The truthful record of my labors up to the time of the convention, and from that time onward, will show how little I knew or cared what Dr. Beecher and Mr. Nettleton were saying or doing about me. I bless the Lord that I was kept from being diverted from my work by their opposition, and that I never gave myself any uneasiness about it. When I was in Auburn, as I have related, God had given me the assurance that He would overrule all opposition without my turning aside to answer my opposers. This I never forgot. Under this divine assurance, I went forward with a trustful spirit and a focused mind. Now, when I read about all the misunderstandings that went on, I stand amazed at my opposers' delusion and consequent anxiety concerning myself and my labors.

Seventeen

Stephentown: The Spirit of God Is Poured Out

After the convention, I remained a short time in New Lebanon. I do not think the convention injured the religious state of the people in that place. I believe the people were edified and strengthened by what they knew of the convention. Indeed, everything had been conducted in a spirit tending to edify rather than confuse the people.

Soon after the close of the convention, as I came from behind the pulpit on a Sunday, a young lady by the name of Miss Maria S——, from Stephentown, was introduced to me. She asked me if I could go to her town and preach. I replied that my hands were full and that I did not see how I could go. I saw that she was choked with deep feeling, so that she could not speak; but I did not have time to converse with her then, so I went to my lodgings.

Afterward I inquired about Stephentown, a place north of and adjoining New Lebanon. Many years before, a wealthy individual had bequeathed to the Presbyterian church in that place a fund, the interest of which was sufficient to support a pastor. Soon after this, a Mr. B——, who had been a chaplain in the Revolutionary Army, was settled there as pastor of the church. He remained until the church ran down, and he finally became an open infidel. This had produced a disastrous effect in that town. He remained among them, openly hostile to the Christian religion.

After he had ceased to be pastor of the church, they had had one or two ministers. Nevertheless, the church declined, and the state of religion grew worse and worse until, finally, they held their Sunday services in a small schoolhouse that stood near the church.

Their last minister affirmed that he stayed until not more than half a dozen people in the town would attend on Sundays. And although there was a fund for his support and his salary was regularly paid, he could not think it his duty to spend his time laboring in such a field. He had therefore been dismissed. No other denomination had taken possession of the field, and the whole town was a complete moral waste. Three elders of the Presbyterian church and about twenty members remained. The only unmarried person in the church was this Miss S——. Nearly the whole town was in a state of impenitence.

On the following Sunday, Miss S—— met me again as I came from behind the pulpit, and she begged me to go there and preach. She asked me if I knew anything of the state of things there. I informed her that I did, but I told her I did not know how I could go. Again her feelings were so strong that she was speechless. These facts, coupled with what I had heard, began to take hold of me, and my mind began to be profoundly stirred in respect to the state of things in Stephentown. I finally told her that if the elders of the church desired me to come, she might announce that I would come and preach in their church the next Sunday at five o'clock in the afternoon. This would allow me to preach twice in New Lebanon, after which I could ride to Stephentown. This seemed to light up her countenance and lift the load from her heart. She went home and gave out the notice that I would come.

The next Sunday, after I had preached the second time, one of the young converts in New Lebanon offered to take me to Stephentown in his carriage. When he came in his buggy to take me, I asked him, "Do you have a steady horse?" "Oh, yes!" he replied. "What made you ask that question?" "Because," I said, "if the Lord wants me to go to Stephentown, the Devil will prevent it if he can. If you do not have a steady horse, he will try to make the horse kill me." The young man smiled, and we rode on. Before we got to Stephentown, that horse ran away twice and came close to killing us. The young man expressed the greatest astonishment and said he had never seen such a thing before.

However, in due time we arrived safely at Mr. S——'s, the father of Miss S——. He lived about half a mile from the church, in the direction of New Lebanon. As we went in, we met Maria, who tearfully yet joyfully received us and showed me to a room where I could be alone, as it was not quite time for the meeting. Soon afterward, I heard her praying in a room overhead. When it was time for the meeting, we all went and found a very large gathering. The congregation was solemn and attentive, but nothing very particular occurred that evening. I spent the night at Mr. S——'s, and Maria seemed to be praying over my room nearly all night. I could hear her low, trembling voice, interrupted often by sobs and weeping. I had made no appointment to come to Stephentown again, but before I left in the morning, she pleaded so hard that I consented to have an appointment made for me for five o'clock the next Sunday.

Nearly the same things occurred on the following Sunday, but the congregation was more crowded. I could see an obvious increase of solemnity and interest the second time I preached there. I left after making an appointment to preach again. At the third service, the Spirit of God was poured out on the congregation.

Judge P——, who lived in a small village in one part of the town, had a large family of unconverted children. At the close of the service, as I came from behind the pulpit, Miss S—— stepped up to me and pointed me to a pew in which sat a young woman greatly overcome with feeling. I went to speak to her and found her to be one of the daughters of this Judge P——. Her convictions were very deep. I sat down by her and gave her instructions, and before she left the house she was converted. She was a very intelligent, earnest young woman and became a very useful Christian. She and Miss S—— seemed immediately to unite their prayers. But there was not yet much movement among the older members of the church. Their relationships with each

157

other were such that a good deal of repentance and confession had to pass among them before they could get into the work.

The state of things in Stephentown now demanded that I leave New Lebanon and take up residence there. I did so. The spirit of prayer, in the meantime, had powerfully come upon me, as had been the case for some time with Miss S——. As the praying power spread and increased, the work soon took on a very powerful character, so much so that the Word of the Lord would cut the strongest men down and render them entirely helpless.

I have mentioned the family of Judge P—— as being large. There were sixteen members of that family, children and grandchildren, all of whom were converted and united with the church before I left. There was another family in the town by the name of M——, which was also a large and very influential family. Most of the people in the town lived scattered along a road that, if I recall correctly, was about five miles long. On inquiry I found there was not a religious family on that whole road and not a single house in which family prayer was maintained.

I made an appointment to preach in a schoolhouse on that road, and when I arrived the school was very crowded. I took for my text this Scripture: *"The curse of the LORD is on the house of the wicked"* (Prov. 3:33). The Lord gave me a very clear view of the subject, and I was enabled to bring out the truth effectively. I told them that I understood that there was not a praying family in that whole district. The fact is, the town was in an awful state. The influence of Mr. B——, their former minister who was now an infidel, had borne its legitimate fruit; there was very little conviction of the truth and reality of religion left among the impenitent in that town. This meeting resulted in the conviction of nearly all who were present. The revival spread in that neighborhood, and I recollect that in this M—— family there were seventeen conversions.

But there were several influential and prominent families in the town who did not attend the meetings. It seemed that they were so much under the influence of Mr. B—— that they were determined not to attend. However, in the midst of the revival, this Mr. B—— died a horrible death, and this later put an end to his opposition.

In the meantime, Miss S—— of New Lebanon, who was converted at Troy, heard that these families did not attend, and she came to Stephentown. As her father was a man very well-known and very much respected, she was received with respect and deference by any family that she wished to visit. She called on one of these families, and she persuaded them to accompany her to a meeting. I believe she was acquainted with their daughters. They soon became so interested that they needed no influence to persuade them to attend. She then went to another family, and to another, with the same result. Finally, she secured the attendance of all the families that had stayed away. These families were nearly all converted before I left the town. Indeed, almost all the principal inhabitants of the town were gathered into the church, and the town was morally renovated.

Eighteen

Philadelphia: Lumbermen Miraculously Saved

The preceding summer, Rev. Mr. Gilbert of Wilmington, Delaware, came to New Lebanon while I was laboring there, to visit his father. Mr. Gilbert was very old-school in his theological views but was a good and earnest man. His love for souls overruled all difficulty on theological differences between him and me. He heard me preach in New Lebanon, saw the results, and was very eager that I come and aid him in Wilmington.

As soon as I could see my way clear to leave Stephentown, I went to Wilmington and engaged in labors with Mr. Gilbert. I soon found that his teaching had rendered it nearly impossible to promote a revival among his congregation, until their views could be corrected. They seemed to be afraid to make any effort, lest they should take the work out of the hands of God. They had the oldest of the old-school views of doctrine; consequently, their theory was that God would convert sinners in His own time. Therefore, to urge them to immediate repentance and to attempt to promote a revival was to attempt to make men Christians by human strength, and thus to dishonor God by taking the work out of His hands. I also observed that their prayers contained no urgency for an immediate outpouring of the Spirit, and that this was all in accordance with the views in which they had been educated.

It was plain that nothing could be done unless Mr. Gilbert's views could be changed upon this subject. I therefore spent hours each day in conversing with him on his views. We talked the subject over in a brotherly manner; and after laboring with him in this way for two or three weeks, I saw that his mind was prepared to have my own views brought before his people. The next Sunday, I used this Scripture as my text: *"Get yourselves a new heart and a new spirit. For why should you die?"* (Ezek. 18:31). I went thoroughly into the subject of the sinner's responsibility and showed what a new heart is.

The congregation became intensely interested, and great numbers stood to their feet in every part of the church. The place was completely filled, and there were strange looks in the assembly. Some looked distressed and offended, others intensely interested. Not infrequently, when I brought out strongly the contrast between my own views and the views in which they had been instructed, some laughed, some wept, some were angry; but I do not recall that anyone left the church. It was a strange excitement.

In the meantime, I could hear Mr. Gilbert breathe and sigh behind me, and could not help observing that he was in the greatest anxiety. I knew I had caught him in his convictions, but I did not know whether he would resolve to withstand what would be said by his people. But I was preaching to please the Lord and not man. I thought that it might be the last time I would ever preach there; but I intended to tell them the truth, and the whole truth, on that subject, whatever the result might be.

When I was through, I did not call upon Mr. Gilbert to pray, for I dared not. Instead, I prayed myself that the Lord would bring home the Word, make it understood, and give the people open minds to weigh what had been said, to receive the truth, and to reject what might be erroneous. I then dismissed the assembly and went down the pulpit stairs, Mr. Gilbert following me. The congregation withdrew very slowly, and many seemed to be standing and waiting for something, as if they supposed they ought to hear what Mr. Gilbert had to say. Mr. Gilbert, however, went out immediately.

As I came down the pulpit stairs, I observed two ladies sitting on the left hand of the aisle through which we had to pass. I had been introduced to them, and I knew they were friends and supporters of Mr. Gilbert. They now looked partly grieved, partly offended, and greatly astonished. One of the ladies took hold of Mr. Gilbert as he was following behind me and said to him, "Mr. Gilbert, what do you think of that?" He replied, "It is worth five hundred dollars." That greatly gratified me and affected me very much. She replied, "Then you have never preached the Gospel." "I am sorry to say I never have," he admitted. The other lady said to him almost the same things and received a similar reply. That was enough for me; I made my way to the door and went out. Many of those who had gone out were standing in front of the church, discussing vehemently the things that had been said. As I passed along the streets going to Mr. Gilbert's where I lodged, I found the streets full of excitement and discussion. From what I could tell, the impression was decidedly in favor of what had been said.

From this point the work went forward. The truth was worked out admirably by the Holy Spirit. Mr. Gilbert's views became greatly changed, as well as his style of preaching and his manner of presenting the Gospel.

Meanwhile, I had been persuaded to go to Philadelphia and preach for Rev. James Patterson twice each week. I went on the steamboat and preached in the evening, returning the next day to preach in Wilmington, thus alternating my evening services between Wilmington and Philadelphia. The distance was about forty miles. The Word took so much effect in Philadelphia that it became my duty to go there, leaving Mr. Gilbert to carry on the work in Wilmington.

Mr. Patterson, with whom I first labored in Philadelphia, held the views of theology then held at Princeton, since known as the theology of the old-school Presbyterians. But he was a godly man and cared a great deal more for the salvation of souls than for questions about ability and inability, or any of those points of doctrine upon which the old- and new-school Presbyterians differ. His wife held the New England views of theology; that is, she believed in a general, as opposed to a restricted, atonement.

At this time I belonged to the Presbyterian Church myself. I had been licensed and ordained by a presbytery, composed mostly of men educated at Princeton. When I was licensed to preach the Gospel, I had not yet examined the

Confession of Faith with any attention. But when I came to read and ponder it, I saw there were several points I could not fully accept. I suppose that Mr. Patterson understood this before I went to labor with him, for when I explained my views in his pulpit, he expressed no surprise. Indeed, he did not object at all to my views.

The revival took such hold in his congregation that he became greatly interested. As he saw that God was blessing the Word as I presented it, he stood firmly by me and never, in any case, objected to anything that I advanced. Sometimes when we returned from a meeting, Mrs. Patterson would remark, "Now you see, Mr. Patterson, that Mr. Finney does not agree with you on these points." He would always reply, in the greatness of Christian faith and love, "Well, the Lord blesses it."

The interest became so great that our congregations were packed at every meeting. One day Mr. Patterson said to me, "Brother Finney, if the Presbyterian ministers in this city find out your views and what you are preaching to the people, they will hunt you out of the city as they would a wolf." I replied, "I cannot help it. I can preach no other doctrine; and if they must drive me out of the city, let them do it and take the responsibility. But I do not believe that they can get me out."

However, the ministers did not take the course that he predicted. Instead, nearly all of them received me to their pulpits. When they learned what was going on at Mr. Patterson's church and that many of their own church members were greatly interested, they invited me to preach for them. I think I preached in nearly all of the Presbyterian churches in that city.

At that time, Philadelphia was almost united in regard to the views of theology held at Princeton. It was a most remarkable thing to me that my doctrinal views were not openly called into question by any of the ministers or churches. I did not hesitate anywhere or on any occasion to present my views, and they did not become a stumbling block to anyone in Philadelphia.

Mr. Patterson was himself greatly surprised that I met no open opposition from the ministers or churches on account of my theological views. Yet I did not present them at all in a controversial way. Rather, I simply employed them, in my instructions to saints and sinners, in a way so natural that only discriminating theologians would notice. Many things that I said were new to the people. For example, one night I preached on this Scripture: *"There is one God and one Mediator between God and men, the Man Christ Jesus, who gave Himself a ransom for all, to be testified in due time"* (1 Tim. 2:5–6). This was a sermon on the Atonement in which I presented the view that I have always held of its nature and of its universality. I stated, as strongly as I could, those points of difference between my own views and those that were held by limited atonement theologians. This sermon attracted so much attention and excited so much interest that I was urged to preach on the same subject in other churches. The more I preached on it, the more desirous people were to hear; and the excitement became so general that I preached on that subject seven different evenings in succession, in seven different churches.

The revival spread and took a powerful hold. All our meetings for preaching, prayer, and inquiry were crowded. There were a great many more inquirers than we could well attend to. It was late in the fall when I took my lodgings in Philadelphia, and I continued to labor there without any intermission until the following August, in 1828.

As in other places, there were some cases of very bitter opposition on the part of a few individuals. But still I was not annoyed or hindered by any public opposition. The ministers received me kindly, and in no instance did they speak publicly, if indeed they spoke at all, against the work that was going on.

I found Mr. Patterson to be one of the truest and holiest men with whom I have ever labored. His preaching was quite remarkable. He was a tall man with a striking appearance and a powerful voice. He preached with great earnestness, often with tears rolling down his cheeks; but there was often no cohesiveness in what he said and very little relation to his text. He often said to me, "When I preach, I preach from Genesis to Revelation." He would take a Scripture, and after making a few remarks upon it, or perhaps none at all, some other verse would be suggested to him, upon which he would make some very pertinent and striking remarks, and then another text. Thus, his sermons were made up of compelling and striking remarks on a great number of Scriptures as they arose in his mind.

It was impossible to hear him preach without being impressed with a sense of his intense earnestness and his great honesty. I only heard him preach occasionally; when I first did so, I was pained, thinking that his preaching was of such rambling nature that it could not take effect. However, I found myself mistaken. Notwithstanding the rambling nature of his preaching, his great earnestness and anointing fastened the truth on the hearts of his hearers. I think I never heard him preach without finding that some of his hearers were deeply convicted by what he said.

He used to have a revival of religion every winter. At the time when I labored with him, he told me he had had a revival for fourteen winters in succession. He had a praying congregation. When I was laboring with him, for two or three days the work seemed to be at a standstill, and I began to feel alarmed, lest something had grieved the Holy Spirit. One evening at a prayer meeting, while this state of things was becoming evident, one of the elders arose and made a confession. He said, "Brothers and sisters, the Spirit of God has been grieved, and I have grieved Him. I have been in the habit of praying on Saturday nights until midnight for Brother Patterson and for the preaching. This has been my habit for many years. Last Saturday night, I was tired and omitted it. I thought the work was going on so pleasantly and so powerfully that I might indulge myself and go to bed without looking to God for a blessing on the labors of the Sabbath. On Sunday, I felt that I had grieved the Spirit, and I saw that there was not the usual manifestation of the influence of the Spirit upon the congregation. I have felt convicted ever since and have felt that it was my duty to make this public confession."

When I first began to labor with Mr. Patterson, I felt considerably tried, in some instances, by what he would say to convicted sinners. For example, the number in attendance was very large at the first meeting for inquirers that we had. We spent some time in conversing with different people, moving around from place to place, and giving instruction. Before I knew it, Mr. Patterson arose and in a very excited manner said, "My friends, you have turned your faces Zionward, and now I exhort you to press forward." He went on in an exhortation for a few moments, in which he distinctly made the impression that they were now in the right way, and that they had only to press forward as they were doing then in order to be saved. His remarks pained me exceedingly, for they seemed to me to tend to self-righteousness, to make the impression that they were doing very well, and that if they continued to do their duty as they were then doing it, they would be saved.

This was not my view of their condition at all, and I felt perplexed as to how I should counteract it. At the close of the meeting, when I summed up the results of our conversation and made an address to them, I alluded to what Mr. Patterson had said. I remarked that they must not misunderstand what he had said, that what he had said was true of those who had really turned to God and set their faces Zionward by giving their hearts to God. But they must not think of applying this to themselves if they were convicted but had not yet repented, believed, and given their hearts to God. For if their faces were not turned Zionward, then they were really turning their backs on Christ. If they were still resisting the Holy Spirit, still on the way to hell, and still without submission, repentance, and faith, then they were only increasing their condemnation. Mr. Patterson listened with the greatest attention. I will never forget with what earnestness he looked at me and with what interest he saw the distinctions that I made.

I continued until I could see and feel that I had corrected the impression that had been made by Mr. Patterson.

I then called upon them to kneel down and commit themselves forever to the Lord, renouncing all their sins and giving themselves up to the bestowal of sovereign goodness, with faith in the Lord Jesus Christ. I explained to them, as plainly as I could, the nature of the Atonement and the salvation presented in the Gospel. I then prayed with them and have reason to believe that a great number of them were converted on the spot.

After this I never heard anything from Mr. Patterson that was at all objectionable in giving instruction to inquiring sinners. Indeed, I found him remarkably teachable and open-minded to such distinctions. He seemed particularly quick to get hold of those truths that needed to be presented to inquiring sinners. He was a lovely Christian man and a faithful minister of Jesus Christ.

After preaching in Mr. Patterson's church for several months and in nearly all the Presbyterian churches in the city, it was thought best that I take up a central position and preach steadily in one place. On Race Street there was a large German church, the pastor of which was a Mr. Helfenstein. The elders of the congregation, together with their pastor, requested me to occupy their pulpit. Their church was then the largest house of worship in the city. It was always crowded, and it seated three thousand people when the place was packed and the aisles were filled. There I preached regularly for many months.

About midsummer of 1829, I left for a short time and visited my wife's parents in Oneida County. Then I returned to Philadelphia and labored there until about midwinter. I do not recall exact dates, but think that, in all, I labored in Philadelphia about a year and a half. In all this time, there was no abatement of the revival. The converts became numerous in every part of the city. I never had labored anywhere where I was received more cordially, and nowhere else did Christians, especially converts, appear better than they did there. There was no schism among them, and I never heard of any disastrous influence resulting from that revival.

In the spring of 1829, when the Delaware River was high, the lumbermen came down with their rafts from the region where they had been getting lumber during the winter. At that time, there was a large area in northern Pennsylvania, called by many "the lumber region," that extended up toward the headwaters of the Delaware River in southern New York. Many men were engaged in getting lumber there, summer and winter. Much of this lumber was floated down in the spring of the year, when the water was high, to Philadelphia. They would get their lumber when the river was low, and when the snow melted off and the spring rains came, they would throw it into the river and float it down to where they could build rafts or otherwise embark it for the Philadelphia market.

Many of the lumbermen were raising families in that region, and much of the land there was unsettled and unoccupied except by these lumbermen. They had no schools and, at that time, no churches or religious privileges at all. One minister told me that he was born in that lumber region and that, when he was twenty years old, he had never attended a religious meeting and did not know his alphabet.

These men who came down with the lumber attended our meetings, and quite a number of them were converted. They went back into the wilderness and began to pray for the outpouring of the Holy Spirit. They told the people around them what they had seen in Philadelphia, and they exhorted them to attend to their salvation. Their efforts were immediately blessed, and the revival began to take hold and to spread among those lumbermen. It went on in a most powerful and remarkable manner. It spread to such an extent that, in many cases, people who were almost as ignorant as heathen would be convicted and converted without attending any meetings. Men who were getting lumber and were living in little shanties alone, or where two or more were together, would be seized with such conviction that it would lead them to wander off and inquire what they should do. Then they would be converted, and thus the revival spread. The greatest simplicity was manifested by the converts.

As an example of this, an aged minister who had been somewhat acquainted with the state of things related the following fact to me. He said one man had a little shanty by himself. He began to feel that he was a sinner, and his convictions increased upon him until he broke down, confessed his sins, and repented. The Spirit of God revealed to him so much of the way of salvation that he evidently knew the Savior. But he had never attended a prayer meting or heard a prayer in his life. His feelings became such that he finally felt constrained to go and tell some of his acquaintances, who were getting lumber in another place, how he felt. But when he arrived, he found that many of them felt just as he did and that they were holding prayer meetings. He attended their prayer meetings and heard them pray, and finally he prayed himself. This was the form of his prayer: "Lord, You have got me down, and I hope You will keep me down. And since You have had such good luck with me, I hope You will try other sinners."

I have said that this work began in the spring of 1829. In the spring of 1831, I was in Auburn again. Two or three men from this lumber region came there to see me and to inquire how they could get some ministers to go with them. They said that no fewer than five thousand people had been converted in that lumber region, that the revival had extended itself along for eighty miles, and that there was not a single minister of the Gospel there.

I have never been in that region, but from all I have ever heard about it, I have regarded that as one of the most remarkable revivals that has occurred in this country. It was carried on almost independently of the ministry, among a class of people very ignorant in regard to religious instruction, yet the revival was remarkably free from fanaticism or anything that was objectionable. *"See how great a forest a little fire kindles!"* (James 3:5). The spark that was struck into the hearts of those few lumbermen who came to Philadelphia spread over that forest and resulted in the salvation of a multitude of souls.

Nineteen

Reading: A Lawyer Is Converted

A s I found myself in Philadelphia, in the heart of the Presbyterian Church and where Princeton views were almost universally embraced, the greatest difficulty I met with in promoting revivals of religion was the false instruction given to the people, especially to inquiring sinners. Indeed, in all my life as a minister, in every place and country where I have labored, I have found this difficulty to some extent; and I am certain that multitudes are living in sin who would immediately be converted if they were truly instructed. The foundation of this error is the dogma that human nature is sinful in itself and that sinners are therefore entirely unable to become Christians.

It had been the practice of many ministers, when preaching repentance and urging a sinner to repent, to tell him that he could not repent any more than he could create a world. They would sometimes tell the sinner to do his duty, to press forward, to read his Bible, to use the means of grace—in short, they would tell him to do anything and everything but the very thing that God commands him to do. God commands him to repent now, to believe now, to make himself a new heart now. But the ministers were afraid to urge God's claims in this form, because they were continually telling the sinner that he had no ability to do these things.

Such instructions always pained me exceedingly, and much of my labor in the ministry has consisted in correcting these views and in pressing the sinner to do just what God commands him to do. To a very great extent, the church has instructed sinners to begin with an outward performance of duty in order to secure an inward change of their wills and affections. But I have always treated this as totally wrong, unorthodox, and highly dangerous. I think I have found thousands of sinners, of all ages, who are living under this delusion and would never think themselves called upon to do anything more than merely to pray for a new heart, live a moral life, read their Bibles, attend meetings, use the means of grace, and leave all the responsibility of their conversion and salvation with God.

From Philadelphia, in the winter of 1829–1830, I went to Reading, a city about forty miles west of Philadelphia. In Reading there were several German churches and one Presbyterian church. The pastor of the latter was the Reverend Dr. Greer. At his request and that of the elders of the church, I went there to labor for a time.

I soon found, however, that neither Dr. Greer nor any of his people had any idea of what they needed or what a revival really was. None of them had ever seen a revival. Besides, all revival efforts for that winter had been postponed by an arrangement to have a dance every other week, which was attended by many of the church members and was managed in part by one of the leading elders in Dr. Greer's church. Dr. Greer had never said anything against this. They also had no preaching or religious meetings of any kind during the week.

When I found what the state of things was, I thought it my duty to tell Dr. Greer that those dances would have to be given up very soon or I would not occupy his pulpit, for they would interfere with my preaching. But he said, "You may take your own course." I did so, and I preached three times on Sunday and four times during the week, for about three weeks, before I said anything about any other meetings. We had no prayer meetings, for the reason that the lay members had never been in the habit of taking part in such meetings.

However, on the third Sunday, I announced that a meeting for inquiry would be held in the lecture room, in the basement of the church, on Monday evening. I stated as clearly as possible the purpose of the meeting, and I mentioned the type of person that I desired to attend. I invited those, and only those, who were seriously concerned about the state of their souls, had made up their minds to attend to the subject immediately, and desired to receive instruction on what they should do to be saved. Dr. Greer made no objection to this, as he had left everything to my judgment. But I do not think he had an idea that many, if any, would attend such a meeting and thereby openly acknowledge their concern for their souls.

Monday was a rather snowy, cold day. I observed that conviction was taking hold of the congregation, yet I felt doubtful how many would attend a meeting for inquirers. When evening came, I went to the meeting. Dr. Greer came in and saw that the lecture room—a rather large room, nearly as large as the sanctuary of the church above—was full. On looking around, Dr. Greer observed that most of the impenitent people in his congregation were present, and among them were those who were regarded as the most respectable and influential.

He said nothing publicly. But he said to me, "I know nothing about this kind of meeting; take it into your own hands, and manage it in your own way." I opened the meeting with a short address, in which I explained to them what I wished, which was to have a few moments' conversation with each of them and to have them state to me frankly how they felt on the subject, what their convictions were, and what their difficulties were.

I walked around among them and gave each of them an opportunity to say, in the fewest words, what their state of mind was. Dr. Greer did not say a word but followed me around and heard all that I had to say. He remained near me, for I spoke to each one in a low voice, so as not to be heard by others outside the immediate vicinity. I found a great deal of conviction and feeling in the meeting. Conviction had taken hold of all classes, the high and the low, the rich and the poor.

Dr. Greer was greatly moved. Though he said nothing, it was evident to me that his interest was intense. To see his congregation in such a state as this was what he had never had any conception of. I saw that he controlled his emotions with difficulty at times.

When I had spent as much time as was allowed me in personal conversation, I then went back to the pulpit and summed up the results of what I had found that was interesting in their communications to me. Without naming anyone, I took the representative cases and dissected, corrected, and taught them. I tried to strip away their misunderstandings and mistakes, to correct the impression that they had that they must simply wait for God to convert them. In an address of perhaps half or three-quarters of an hour, I set before them the whole situation as clearly as I could.

After praying with them, I called on those who felt prepared to submit, who were willing then and there to pledge themselves to live wholly for God, who were willing to commit themselves to the sovereign mercy of God in Christ Jesus, and who were willing to give up sin and renounce it forever. I called on them to kneel down and, while I prayed, to commit themselves to Christ and inwardly do what I exhorted them to do. Dr. Greer looked very much surprised at the manner in which I pressed them to instant submission.

As soon as I saw that they thoroughly understood me, I called on them to kneel and knelt myself. Dr. Greer knelt by my side but said nothing. I presented the case in prayer to God, staying close to the point of now submitting, believing, and consecrating themselves to God. There was a solemnity pervading the congregation, with the exception of my own voice in prayer and the sobs, sighs, and weeping that were heard throughout the congregation.

After putting the case before God, we rose from our knees, and without saying anything more I pronounced the blessing and dismissed them. Dr. Greer took me by the hand and said, "I will see you in the morning." He went his way, and I went to my lodgings. At about eleven o'clock, a messenger came to my lodgings and said that Dr. Greer was dead. He had just gone to bed, when he suffered from a stroke and died immediately. He was greatly respected and loved by his people, and I am persuaded he deserved to be. His sudden death was a great shock and became the subject of constant conversation throughout the town.

Although many in the congregation had submitted to Christ at the meeting on Monday evening, the death of Dr. Greer, under such extraordinary circumstances, was a great diversion of the public mind for a week or more. But after his funeral was over and the usual evening services got into their proper routine, the work became very powerful and went forward in a most encouraging manner.

Of course, from day to day, I had my hands, my head, and my heart entirely full. There was no pastor to help me, and the work spread on every side. The elder who had been one of the managers of the regular dances soon humbled his heart before the Lord and entered into the work of the revival. As a result, the members of his family were soon converted. The revival made a thorough sweep in the families of those members of the church who entered into the work.

In this place the influence of the old-school teaching of which I have complained was very evident. Early one morning, a lawyer who belonged to one of the most respectable families in the town called on me at my room, in the greatest agitation of mind. He was a man of first-rate intelligence and a gentleman. He came in, introduced himself, and said he was a lost sinner—that he had made up his mind that there was no hope for him. He then informed me that when he was in Princeton College, he and two of his classmates became very anxious about their souls. They went together to Dr. Ashbel Green, who was then president of the college, and asked him what they should do to be saved. The doctor told them to keep out of all bad company, to read their Bible regularly, and to ask God to give them new hearts. "Continue this," he said, "and the Spirit of God will convert you, or He will leave you and you will return to your sins." "Well," I inquired, "how did it end up?" "Oh," said he, "we did just as he told us to do. We kept out of bad

174

company and prayed that God would put new hearts in us. But after a little while, our convictions wore away, and I did not care to pray any longer. We lost all interest in the subject." Then, bursting into tears, he said, "My two companions are in drunkards' graves, and if I cannot repent I will soon be in one myself."

I tried to instruct him and to show him the error that he had fallen into under such instruction. He had resisted and grieved the Spirit by waiting for God to do what He had commanded him to do. I tried to show him that God could not do for him what He required him to do: God required him to repent, and God could not repent for him; God required him to believe, but God could not believe for him; God required him to submit but could not submit for him. I then tried to make him understand the place that the Spirit of God has in giving the sinner repentance and a new heart—that the Spirit leads him to see his sins and urges him to give them up and to flee from the wrath to come. He presents to him the Savior, the Atonement, and the plan of salvation and urges him to accept these things.

"But hasn't God already given up on me? Isn't my day of grace past?" he asked. I said to him, "No, it is clear that the Spirit of God is still calling you, still urging you to repentance." I then asked him if he would respond to the call, if he would come to Jesus, if he would take hold of eternal life then and there. When I saw that the way was fully prepared, I called on him to kneel down and submit; he did so and became a thorough convert right on the spot. "Oh," he afterward said, "if Dr. Green had only told us this, we would all have been converted immediately. But my friends are lost, and what a wonder of mercy it is that I am saved!"

A great majority of Dr. Greer's congregation were converted in this revival. At first I had considerable difficulty in getting rid of the influence of the daily press. I think there were two or more daily newspapers published there at the time. The people, particularly the German population, were a good deal under the influence of these newspapers. I learned that the editors were drinking men and were often carried home in a state of intoxication on public occasions. These editors began to give the people religious advice and to speak against the revival and the preaching. This threw the people into a state of perplexity. It went on from day to day and from week to week, until finally the state of things became such that I thought it my duty to point it out. I therefore used this Scripture as my text one Sunday: *"You are of your father the devil, and the desires of your father you want to do"* (John 8:44). I then went on to show in what way sinners fulfill the desires of the Devil, pointing out a great many ways in which they perform his dirty work and do for him what he cannot do for himself.

After I had presented the subject to the people, I applied it to the course pursued by the editors of those daily papers. I asked the people if they thought that those editors were fulfilling the desires of the Devil, if they believed the Devil desired them to do just what they did. I then asked them if it was suitable and decent for men of their character to attempt to give religious instruction to the people. I told the people what I understood their character to be, and I expressed my disgust that such men should attempt to instruct the people in regard to their duties to God and their neighbors. I said, "If I had a family here, I would not have such a newspaper in my house. I would fear to have it under my roof and would consider it too filthy to be touched with my fingers; I would use tongs and throw it into the street." The next morning, the newspapers were pretty plentifully scattered in the street, and I neither saw nor heard any more of their opposition.

I remained in Reading until late in the spring. From there I went to Lancaster, Pennsylvania, at that time the home of the late President Buchanan. The Presbyterian church in Lancaster had no pastor, and I found religion in a very low state. They had never had a revival of religion, and they had no idea what it was or what were the appropriate means of securing it. I remained in Lancaster a very short time. However, the work of God was immediately revived, the Spirit of God being poured out almost at once upon the people.

I was the guest of an aged gentleman by the name of K——, who was one of the elders of the church and the leading man in the church. While I was lodging with him, an incident occurred that revealed the real state of religion in that church. A former pastor of the church had invited Mr. K—— to join the church and hold the office of elder. One Sunday evening, after hearing a couple of very searching sermons, the old gentleman could not sleep. He was so greatly troubled in his mind that he could not endure it until morning. He called on me in the middle of the night, stated what his convictions were, and then said that he knew he had never been converted. He said that when he was requested to join the church and become an elder, he knew that he was not a converted man. But he had been so urged until he finally consulted Rev. Dr. C——, an aged minister of a Presbyterian church not far from Lancaster. He stated to him the fact that he had never been converted and that he had been asked to join the church so that he might become an elder. Dr. C——, in view of all the circumstances, advised him to join and accept the office, which he did.

His convictions when he called on me were very deep. I gave him such instructions as I thought he needed, pressed him to accept the Savior, and dealt with him just as I would with any other inquiring sinner. It was a very solemn time. He submitted to and accepted the Savior at that time.

One evening in Lancaster, I preached on a subject that led me to insist on the immediate acceptance of Christ. The meetinghouse was literally packed. At the close of my sermon, I made a strong appeal to the people to decide at once. I called on those whose minds were made up and who would then accept the Savior, to rise up so that we might know who they were and so that we might make them subjects of prayer. There were two men sitting near one of the doors of the church, one of whom was very much affected by the appeal that was made and could not avoid showing very strong emotion, which was observed by his neighbor. However, the man did not rise up, nor did he give his heart to God. I had reminded the people that that might be the last opportunity some of them would ever have to decide this question; that in so large a congregation it was not unlikely that there were those who would then decide their everlasting destiny, one way or the other. It was not unlikely that God would hold some of them to the decision that they then made.

After the meeting was dismissed, these two men went out together, and one said to other, "I saw you were very moved by the appeals Mr. Finney made." "I was," he replied. "I never felt this way before in my life, especially when he reminded us that that might be the last time we would ever have an opportunity to accept the offer of mercy." They continued conversing in this way for some distance and then separated, each one going to his own home. It was a dark night, and the one who had felt so moved and was so pressed with the conviction that he might then be rejecting his last offer, tripped over the curb and broke his neck. This was reported to me the next day.

I established prayer meetings in Lancaster and insisted upon the elders of the church taking part in them. This they did at my earnest request, although they had never been accustomed to do it before. The interest seemed to increase from day to day, and conversions multiplied. I do not recall now why I did not stay longer than I did, but I left at so early a period as not to be able to give a detailed account of the work there.

Twenty

Columbia: A Pastor's Conversion

From Lancaster, about midsummer in 1830, I returned to Oneida County, New York, and spent a short time at my father-in-law's in Whitestown. During my stay, a messenger came from the town of Columbia, in Herkimer County, requesting me to go there and assist in a work of grace that had already commenced. I was induced to go; however, I did not expect to remain there, as I had other, more pressing calls for labor. I went for a short time to lend such aid as I was able.

In Columbia was a large German church, the membership of which had been received, according to their custom, upon examination of their doctrinal knowledge, instead of their Christian experience. Consequently, the congregation had been composed mostly of unconverted people. Both the church and congregation were large.

Their pastor was a young man by the name of H——. He was of German descent and from Pennsylvania. He gave me the following account of himself and of the state of things in Columbia. He said he had studied theology with a German doctor of divinity who did not encourage experiential religion at all. One of his fellow students was religiously inclined and used to pray privately. Their teacher suspected this and in some way came to a knowledge of the fact. He warned the young man against it as a very dangerous practice, said he would become insane if he persisted in it, and said that as his teacher he should be blamed himself for allowing a student to take such a course.

Mr. H—— said that he himself had no religion. He had joined the church in the common way and had not thought that anything else was required, so far as piety was concerned, to become a minister. His mother was a pious

179

woman. She knew better and was greatly distressed that a son of hers, who had never been converted, had entered the sacred ministry. When he had received a call to the church in Columbia and was about to leave home, his mother had a very serious talk with him, impressed upon him the fact of his responsibility, and said some things that powerfully affected his conscience. He said that he could not get this conversation with his mother out of his thoughts, and his convictions of sin deepened until he was nearly in despair.

This continued for many months. He had no one to consult and did not open his mind to anybody. But after a severe and extended struggle, he was converted, came into the light, saw where he was and where he had been, and saw the condition of his church and all churches that admitted members in a similar way.

His wife was unconverted. He immediately gave himself to labor for her conversion and, under God, he soon secured it. His soul was full of the subject; he read his Bible, prayed, and preached with all his might. But he was a young convert and did not have the kind of instruction he needed, and he felt at a loss as to what to do. He went around the town and found that only one or two of his leading elders, as well as several of his female members, knew what it was to be converted.

After much prayer and consideration, he made up his mind what to do. On Sunday he announced that there would be a meeting of the church on a certain day during the week and that he wished all the church members to be present. His own conversion, preaching, visiting, and conversing around the town had already created a good deal of excitement, so that religion came to be the common topic of conversation.

On the day appointed, nearly all the members were present. He then addressed them in regard to the real state of the church and the error they had fallen into in regard to the conditions on which members had been received. He made a speech to them, partly in German and partly in English, so that anyone there could understand him. After talking until they were a good deal moved, he proposed to disband the church and form a new one, insisting that this was essential to the prosperity of religion. He had already come to an understanding with those whom he knew to be truly converted, that they would lead in voting for the disbanding of the church. The motion was put forth, and the converted members arose as requested. They were very influential members, and the people finally kept rising until the vote was nearly unanimous. The pastor then said, "There is now no church in Columbia, and we propose to form one of Christians, of people who have been converted."

He then related his own experience before the congregation, and he called on his wife, who did the same. Then the converted elders and members followed, one after another, as long as any could come forward and relate a Christian experience. In this way, they proceeded to form a church. He then said to the others, "Your church relations are dissolved. You are out in the world, and until you are converted and in the church, you cannot have your children baptized, and you cannot partake of the ordinances of the church." This created a panic, for to them it was an awful thing not to partake of the sacrament and not to have their children baptized, for this was the way in which they themselves had been made Christians.

Mr. H—— then labored among them with all his might. He visited, preached, prayed, and held meetings, and the interest increased. This work had been going on for some time when he heard that I was in Oneida County, and he sent the messenger for me. I found him a warmhearted young convert. He listened to my preaching with almost irrepressible joy. I found the congregation large and interested, and the work was in a very prosperous, healthful state. That revival continued to spread until it reached and converted nearly all the inhabitants of the town.

I found Mr. H——'s views evangelical. He was surrounded by a congregation as thoroughly interested in religion as could well be desired. As I preached to them the Gospel of Christ, they would hang on my every word with great interest, attention, and patience. Mr. H—— himself was like a little child—teachable, humble, and earnest. That work continued for over a year, spreading throughout that large population of farmers.

After I returned to Whitestown, I was invited to visit New York City. Anson G. Phelps, hearing that I had not been invited to the pulpits of that city, rented a vacant church on Vandewater Street and sent me an urgent request to come there and preach. I did so, and there we had a powerful revival. I found Mr. Phelps very much engaged in the work and not hesitating at any expense that was necessary to promote it. He has since become well-known as a great benefactor to the leading charitable institutions of our country.

The church that he rented could be had only for three months. Accordingly, before the three months were out, Mr. Phelps purchased a church on Prince Street, near Broadway. This church had been built by the Universalists. From Vandewater Street, therefore, we went to Prince Street and formed a church, mostly of people who had been converted during our meetings on Vandewater Street. I continued my labors on Prince Street for several months, until the latter part of summer.

During my labors there, I was very much struck with the piety of Mr. Phelps. While we remained at the church on Vandewater Street, my wife and I, with our only child, were guests at his home. While Mr. Phelps was a man literally loaded with business, somehow he preserved a highly spiritual frame of mind. He would come directly from his business to our prayer meetings and would enter into them with a spirit that clearly showed that his mind was not absorbed in business to the exclusion of spiritual things. As I watched him from day to day, I became more and more interested in his interior life, as it was manifested in his outward life.

One night I went downstairs around twelve or one o'clock at night to get something for our little child. I supposed the family was all asleep, but to my surprise I found

Mr. Phelps sitting by his fire, in his pajamas, and saw that I had broken in upon his private devotions. I apologized by saying that I had supposed he was in bed. He replied, "Brother Finney, I have a great deal of business pressing me during the day, and have little time for private devotion. My custom is, after having a nap at night, to arise and have a season of communion with God." After his death, it was found that he had kept a journal during these hours in the night, comprising several volumes. This journal revealed the secret workings of his mind and the real progress of his interior life.

I never knew the number converted while I was on Prince and Vandewater Streets, but it must have been large. There was one case of conversion that I must mention. A young woman visited me one day, under great conviction of sin. While conversing with her, I found that she had many things weighing upon her conscience. She told me she had been in the habit of pilfering since childhood. She had taken from her schoolmates and others whatever she had an opportunity to steal. She confessed some of these things to me and asked me what she should do. I told her she must go and return all that she had stolen and confess to those from whom she had stolen.

This of course greatly tried her, yet her convictions were so deep that she dared not keep what she had taken, and she began the work of confessing and making restitution. But as she went forward with it, she continued to recall more and more instances of the kind. She kept visiting me and confessing to me her thefts of almost every kind of articles that a young woman could use. I asked her if her mother knew that she had these things. She said yes, but she had always told her mother that they were given to her. She said to me on one occasion, "Mr. Finney, I suppose I have stolen a million times. I have many things that I know I stole, but I cannot recollect from whom."

I refused to compromise with her and insisted on her making restitution in every case in which she could recall the facts. From time to time she would come to me and report what she had done. I asked her what the people said when she returned the articles. She replied, "Some of them say that I am crazy, some of them say that I am a fool, and some of them are very much affected." "Do they all forgive you?" I asked. "Oh," she said, "they all forgive me, but some of them think that I had better not do as I am doing." This process continued for weeks, perhaps for months. This girl was going from place to place in all parts of the city, restoring things that she had stolen, and making confession. Sometimes her convictions would be so awful that it seemed as if she would be deranged.

One morning she sent for me to come to her mother's residence. I did so, and when I arrived I was taken to her room and found her pacing the room in an agony of despair and with a look that was frightful, because it indicated that she was nearly deranged. I said, "My dear child, what is the matter?" As she was walking, she held in her hand a little Testament. She turned to me and said, "Mr. Finney, I stole this Testament; I have stolen God's Word. Will God ever forgive me? I stole it from one of my schoolmates, and it was so long ago that I had really forgotten that I had stolen it. It occurred to me this morning, and it seems to me that God can never forgive me for stealing His Word." I assured her that there was no reason for her despair. "But," said she, "what shall I do? I cannot remember where I got it." I told her, "Keep it as a constant remembrance of your former sins, and use it for the good you may now get from it."

This process was exceedingly affecting to me; but as it proceeded, the state of mind that resulted from those transactions was truly wonderful. She gained a depth of humility; a deep knowledge of herself and her own depravity; a brokenness of heart; contrition of spirit; and finally, a faith, joy, love, and *"peace...like a river"* (Isa. 66:12). She became one of the most delightful young Christians that I have known.

When the time drew near that I expected to leave New York, I thought that someone in the church who could watch over her ought to be acquainted with her. Up to this time, whatever had passed between us had been a secret, sacredly kept to myself. But as I was about to leave, I related the facts to Mr. Phelps, and they affected him greatly. He said, "Brother Finney, introduce me to her. I will be her friend; I will watch over her for her good." He did so, and I later discovered that she was considered a very earnest Christian woman and always maintained a consistent Christian character and prayerfulness. I also heard that the woman never again had the temptation to steal, from the time of her conversion, and that she could not remember what it was like to have the desire to do so.

This revival prepared the way for the organization of the Free Presbyterian churches in New York City. Those churches were largely composed of the converts of that revival. Many of them had belonged to the church on Prince Street.

At this point I must give a little account of the circumstances connected with the conversion of Mr. Lewis Tappan and his later association with my own labors. His conversion occurred before I was personally acquainted with him. He was a Unitarian and lived in Boston. His brother Arthur, then a very extensive dry-goods merchant in New York, was an earnest Christian man. The revivals through central New York had created a good deal of excitement among the Unitarians, and their newspapers had much to say against them. There were many strange stories in circulation about myself, representing me as a half-crazed fanatic. These stories had been related to Lewis Tappan by Mr. W——, a leading Unitarian minister of Boston, and he believed them.

While these stories were in circulation, Lewis Tappan visited his brother Arthur in New York, and they fell into conversation about those revivals. Lewis called Arthur's attention to the strange fanaticism connected with these revivals, especially to what was said of myself. He asserted that I was "the brigadier general of Jesus Christ." This and similar reports were in circulation, and Lewis insisted upon their truth. Arthur utterly discredited them and told Lewis that they were all nonsense and false, and that he ought not to believe any of them. Lewis, relying upon the statements of Mr. W——, proposed to bet $500 that he could prove these reports to be true, especially the one already referred to. Arthur replied, "Lewis, you know that I do not bet, but I will tell you what I will do. If you can prove by credible testimony that the reports about Mr. Finney are true, I will give you $500. I make this offer to lead you to investigate. I want you to know that these stories are false and that the source from which they come is utterly unreliable."

Lewis, not doubting that he could find proof—for these things had been so confidently asserted by the Unitarians—wrote to Rev. Mr. P——, a Unitarian minister in Trenton Falls, New York, to whom Mr. W—— had referred him. Lewis authorized him to spend $500, if necessary, to procure sufficient evidence that the story was true. Mr. P——, accordingly, undertook to procure the testimony but after great effort was unable to furnish any, except what was contained in a small Universalist newspaper, printed in Buffalo, in which it had been asserted that Mr. Finney claimed that he was a brigadier general of Jesus Christ. Nowhere could he get the least proof that the report was true. Many people had heard and believed that I had said these things somewhere, but as he followed up the reports from town to town, by his correspondence, he could not learn that these things had been said anywhere in particular.

This, in connection with other matters, led Lewis to reflect seriously upon the nature of the opposition and upon the source from which it had come. Knowing the stress that had been laid upon these stories by the Unitarians, and the use they had made of them to oppose the revivals in New York and other places, his confidence in them was greatly shaken. Thus his prejudices against the revivals and orthodox people became softened, and the result was that he embraced orthodox views.

As soon as Lewis Tappan was converted, he became as firm and zealous in his support of orthodox views and revivals of religion as he had been in his opposition to them. About the time that I left New York, after my first labors there on Vandewater and Prince Streets, Mr. Tappan and some other men became dissatisfied with the state of things in New York. After much prayer and consideration, they decided to organize a new congregation and introduce new measures for the conversion of men. They obtained a place to hold worship and called the Reverend Joel Parker, who was then pastor of the Third Presbyterian Church in Rochester, to come to their aid.

Mr. Parker arrived in New York and began his labors around the time that I finished my labors on Prince Street. The First Free Presbyterian Church was formed in New York, and Mr. Parker became its pastor. They labored especially among the class of the population that had not been in the habit of attending church anywhere, and they were very successful.

Twenty-one

Rochester in 1830: One Hundred Thousand Are Converted

After leaving New York, I spent a few weeks in Whitestown at my father-in-law's. As was common, I was being pressed to go in many directions and was at a loss as to what was my duty. But among others, an urgent invitation was received from the Third Presbyterian Church in Rochester, of which Mr. Parker had been pastor, to go there and supply them for a season.

I inquired into the circumstances and found that, on several accounts, it was a very unpromising field of labor. There were only three Presbyterian churches in Rochester. The Third Church, which had extended the invitation, had no minister, and religion was in a low state. The Second Church, or "the Brick Church," as it was called, had a pastor, an excellent man. But there was considerable division in the church in regard to his preaching, and he was restless and about to leave. There was also a controversy existing between an elder of the Third Church and the pastor of the First Church, which was about to be tried before the presbytery. This and other matters had aroused unchristian feelings, to some extent, in both churches, so it seemed a forbidding field of labor at that time.

Even so, the members of the Third Church in Rochester were exceedingly anxious to have me go there. Being left without a pastor, they felt as if there was great danger that they would be scattered, and perhaps annihilated as a church, unless something could be done to revive religion among them.

With these pressing invitations before me, I felt, as I have often done, greatly perplexed. I remained at my father-in-law's and considered the subject, until I felt that I must work somewhere. Accordingly, I packed my things and went to Utica, about seven miles away, where I had many praying friends.

My family and I arrived there in the afternoon, and in the evening quite a number of the leading church members, in whose prayers and wisdom I had a great deal of confidence, met for consultation and prayer in regard to my next field of labor. I laid all the facts before them in regard to Rochester and the other fields to which I was invited at that time. Rochester seemed to be the least inviting of them all.

After talking the matter over and having several seasons of prayer, interspersed with conversation, the men gave their opinions as to what they thought I should do. They were unanimous in the opinion that Rochester was too uninviting a field of labor to be put in competition with New York, Philadelphia, and some other fields to which I was then invited. They were firm in the conviction that I should go east from Utica, and not west. At the time, this was my own impression and conviction, and I left this meeting with the intention not to go to Rochester, but to New York or Philadelphia.

But after I retired to my lodgings, something seemed to question me, "What are the reasons that deter you from going to Rochester?" I could readily enumerate them, but the question returned: "Ah, but are these good reasons? Certainly you are needed in Rochester all the more because of these difficulties. Do you shun the field because there are so many things that need to be corrected, because there is so much that is wrong? But if all was right, you would not be needed." I soon came to the conclusion that we were all wrong, and that the reasons that had determined us against my going to Rochester were the most cogent reasons for my going. I felt ashamed to shrink from undertaking the work because of its difficulties, and it was strongly impressed upon me that the Lord would be with me and that that was my field. I informed my wife of my decision, and early the next morning we embarked and went westward instead of eastward. The Christian men in Utica were greatly surprised when they learned of this change in our destination, and they awaited the result with a good deal of eagerness.

We arrived in Rochester early in the morning and were invited to take up our lodgings for the time with Mr. Josiah Bissell, who was the leading elder in the Third Church.

There were soon some very noteworthy conversions. Mrs. M——, the wife of a prominent lawyer in that city, was one of the first converts. She was a woman of high standing, a lady of culture and extensive influence. The first time I saw her, a friend of hers came with her to my lodgings and introduced her. The lady who introduced her was a Christian woman who had found that she was very troubled in her mind and who persuaded her to come and see me.

Mrs. M—— had been a worldly woman, very fond of society. I saw that she was a very proud woman. She afterward told me that when I first came to Rochester, she greatly regretted it and feared there would be a revival, which would greatly interfere with the pleasures and amusements that she had promised herself that winter. While conversing with her, I found that the Spirit of the Lord was indeed dealing with her in an unsparing manner. She was bowed down with great conviction of sin. After considerable conversation with her, I pressed her earnestly to renounce sin, the world, and everything for Christ. At the conclusion of our conversation, we knelt down to pray. Knowing the pride of her heart, I very soon introduced the Scripture, *"Unless you are converted and become as little children, you will by no means enter the kingdom of heaven"* (Matt. 18:3). Almost immediately I heard Mrs. M——, as she was kneeling by my side, repeating that verse: "Unless you are converted and become as little children—as little children—Unless you are converted and become as little children." The Spirit of God was pressing upon her heart. I therefore continued to pray, holding that subject before her mind and holding her up before God as someone in need of becoming as a little child in order to be converted.

I felt that the Lord was answering prayer. I felt sure that He was doing the very work that I asked Him to do. Her heart broke down, and before we rose from our knees, she was indeed like a little child. When I stopped praying and opened my eyes and looked at her, her face was turned up toward heaven, tears streaming down. From that moment she was outspoken in her religious convictions and zealous for the conversion of her friends. Her conversion, of course, produced much excitement among her class of people. My meetings soon became thronged with that class. The lawyers, physicians, merchants, and all the most intelligent people became more and more interested, and more and more easily influenced.

Very soon the work took effect extensively among the lawyers in that city. They became very anxious about their souls and came freely to our meetings of inquiry. Numbers of them came forward at the close of my sermons and publicly gave their hearts to God. One evening after I had finished preaching, three of them followed me to my lodgings, all of them deeply convicted. All of them had come forward to give their hearts to God but were not clear in their minds and felt that they could not go home until they were convinced that their peace had been made with God. I conversed with them and prayed with them, and before they left they all found peace in believing in the Lord Jesus Christ.

On one occasion I had an appointment to preach in the First Church. There had been a military parade in the city that day. The militia had been called out, and I had feared that the excitement of the parade might divert the attention of the people and mar the work of the Lord. The church was filled in every part. Dr. Penny, who was pastor there, had introduced the services and was engaged in the first prayer, when I heard something like the report of a gun and the jingling of glass, as if a window had been broken. My thought was that some careless person from the military parade on the outside had fired so near the window as to break a pane of glass. But before I had time to think again, Dr. Penny leaped from the pulpit almost over me, for I was kneeling by the sofa behind him. The pulpit was in the front of the church, between the two doors. The congregation fell into a perfect panic and rushed for the doors and the windows, as if they were all crazy. One elderly woman held up a window in the rear of the church, where several, as I was informed, leaped out into the canal. The rear wall of the church stood upon the brink of the canal. The rush was terrific. Some jumped over the balconies into the aisles below; they ran over each other in the aisles.

Not knowing what had happened, I stood behind the pulpit, put up my hands, and cried at the top of my voice, "Be quiet! Be quiet!" But everyone was getting out in every direction, as fast as possible. Because I did not know that there was any danger, the scene looked so ludicrous to me that I could scarcely refrain from laughing. Bonnets, shawls, gloves, handkerchiefs, and parts of dresses were scattered in every direction. Several people were considerably hurt in the mad rush, but no one was killed.

I afterward learned that the walls of the church had been settling for some time, the ground being very damp from its proximity to the canal. Some people in the congregation were afraid that either the tower, the roof, or the walls of the building would come down. The original alarm had been created some time before by a board falling from the roof and breaking through the ceiling above the lamp in front of the organ. Of this I had heard nothing.

On examining the building, it was found that the walls had spread in such a manner that there was indeed danger of the roof falling in. The pressure that night in the balcony was so great as to spread the walls on each side, until there was real danger. At the time this occurred, I greatly feared that the public attention would be diverted and the work would be greatly hindered. But the Spirit of the Lord had taken hold of the work in earnest, and nothing seemed to hold it back.

The Brick Church was thrown open to us, and from that time our meetings alternated between the Second and

Third Churches. People from the First Church attended as far as they could fit into the church. The three churches, and generally Christians of every denomination, seemed to take up a common cause and went to work with a will to pull sinners out of the fire. We were obliged to hold meetings almost continually. I preached nearly every night and three times on Sundays. After the work became so powerful, we held our meetings of inquiry very frequently in the morning.

There was at that time a high school in Rochester, presided over by a Mr. B——, son of the pastor of the church in Brighton, near Rochester. Mr. B—— was a skeptic but was at the head of a very large and flourishing school. Since the school was made up of both sexes, a Miss A—— was his assistant and associate in the school at that time. Miss A—— was a Christian woman. The students of this school had attended the religious services at which I was preaching, and many of them soon became deeply anxious about their souls. One morning Mr. B—— found that his students could not answer questions about the lesson. When he saw that they were in such a state, it very much perplexed him. He called his associate, Miss A——, and told her that the young people were so troubled about their souls that they could not speak. He asked if they should send for Mr. Finney to find out what to do. She advised him to send for me. He did, and the revival took tremendous hold of that school. Mr. B—— himself was soon converted, along with nearly every person in the school.

A few years afterward, Miss A—— informed me that more than forty people who had then been converted in that school had become ministers. A large number of them had become foreign missionaries.

After remaining a few weeks at Josiah Bissell's, I took lodgings in a more central position, at the house of a lawyer of the city, named Mr. B——, who was a Christian man. His wife's sister was with them and was an impenitent girl. She was a young woman of fine appearance, an exquisite singer, and a cultivated lady. I soon learned that she was engaged to be married to a man who was then judge of the supreme court of the state. He was a very proud man who resisted and opposed coming forward to "the anxious seat," as we called the purposely vacant seats at the front of the church, for prayer after my sermons. He was absent a good deal from the city and was not converted that winter. However, a large number of the lawyers were converted, as well as the young lady to whom he was engaged. I mention this because the judge afterward married her, which no doubt led to his own conversion in a revival that occurred about ten years later.

This revival of 1830 made a great change in the moral state and subsequent history of Rochester. The great majority of the leading men and women in the city were converted. A spirit of prayer prevailed in this revival, which I must not fail to mention. When I was on my way to Rochester, as we passed through a village about thirty miles east of Rochester, I saw a minister whom I knew. He had intended to have only a short conversation with me; however, upon discovering where I was going and what I was doing, he made up his mind to go with me to Rochester. We had been there only a few days when this minister became so convicted that he could not help weeping aloud, one time as he walked along the street. The Lord gave him a powerful spirit of prayer, and his heart was broken. As he and I prayed much together, I was struck with his faith in regard to what the Lord was going to do there. He would often say, "Lord, I do not know how it is, but I seem to know that You are going to do a great work in this city." The spirit of prayer was poured out powerfully, so much so that some people stayed away from the public services in order to pray, being unable to restrain their feelings under preaching.

And here I must introduce the name of Mr. Abel Clary. He was an elder of the church where I had been converted, and he had been converted in the same revival in which I was. He had been licensed to preach, but he was so burdened with the souls of men, and his spirit of prayer was so powerful, that he was not able to preach much. His whole time and strength were being given to prayer. The burden of his soul would frequently be so great that he was unable to stand, and he would writhe and groan in agony. I was well acquainted with him and knew something of the wonderful spirit of prayer that was upon him. He was a very silent man, as almost all are who have this powerful spirit of prayer.

I first learned of his being in Rochester when a gentleman who lived about a mile west of the city called on me one day and asked me if I knew a Mr. Abel Clary, a minister. I told him that I knew him well. "Well," said he, "he is at my house and has been there for some time, and I don't know what to think of him." I said, "I have not seen him at any of our meetings." "No," he replied, "he says he cannot go to the meetings. He prays nearly all the time, day and night, and in such an agony of mind that I do not know what to make of it. Sometimes he cannot even get up on his knees but will lie prostrate on the floor and groan and pray in a manner that quite astonishes me." I said to the brother, "I understand it; please keep still. It will all come out right; he will surely prevail."

I knew at the time a considerable number of men who had the same spirit of prevailing prayer, including Father Nash, who in several of my fields of labor came to aid me. This Mr. Clary stayed in Rochester as long as I did, and he did not leave until after I had left. He never appeared in public but gave himself wholly to prayer.

I have said that the moral aspect of things in Rochester was greatly changed by this revival. It was a young city, full of growth and ambition, and full of sin. The inhabitants were intelligent and enterprising in the highest degree. But as the revival swept through the town and converted the majority of the most influential people, both men and women, the change in the city's order, sobriety, and morality was wonderful. The public affairs of the city were soon largely in the hands of Christian men, and the controlling influences in the community were on the side of Christ.

Among other conversions I must not forget to mention that of Mr. P——, a bookseller and a prominent citizen of that place. Mr. P—— was an infidel—not an atheist, but a disbeliever in the divine authority of the Bible. He was a reader and a thinker, a man of keen, shrewd mind, strong will, and most unwavering character. He was, I believe, highly respected. He came to my room early one morning and said, "Mr. Finney, there is a great movement here on the subject of religion, but I am a skeptic, and I want you to prove to me that the Bible is true." The Lord enabled me at once to discern his state of mind, so far as to decide the course I should take with him.

I said to him, "Do you believe in the existence of God?" "Oh, yes!" he said. "I am not an atheist." "Well, do you believe that you have treated God as you should? Have you respected His authority? Have you loved Him? Have you done what you thought would please Him? Don't you admit that you ought to love Him, worship Him, and obey Him according to the best light you have?" "Oh, yes," he said, "I admit all this." "But have you done so?" I asked. "Why, no," he answered, "I cannot say that I have." "Well then," I replied, "why should I give you further information and further light if you will not do your duty and obey the light you already have? When you make up your mind to live up to your convictions, to obey God according to the best light you have, to repent of your neglect thus far, and to please God just as well as you know how for the rest of your life, I will try to show you that the Bible is from God. Until then, it is of no use for me to do any such thing." He replied, "I do not think that is fair," and left.

I heard no more of him until the next morning. Soon after I arose, he came to my lodgings again. As soon as he entered, he clapped his hands and said, "Mr. Finney, God has worked a miracle! I went down to the store after I left your room, thinking of what you had said; and I made up my mind that I would repent of what I knew was wrong in my relationship to God, and that hereafter I would live according to the best light I had. When I did this, my feelings so overcame me that I fell down. I would have died if it had not been for Mr. ———— who was with me in the store." From that time he was a praying, earnest Christian man.

During this great revival, people wrote letters from Rochester to their friends abroad, giving an account of the work. These letters were read in different churches throughout several states and were instrumental in producing great revivals of religion. Many people came from great distances to witness the mighty work of God and were converted. I recall that a physician was so attracted by what he heard of the work that he came from Newark, New Jersey, to Rochester to see what the Lord was doing, and he was converted there.

The work spread like waves in every direction. Wherever I went, the Word of God took immediate effect. It seemed necessary only to present the law of God and the claims of Christ, and people would be converted by scores.

The greatness of the work at Rochester at that time attracted so much attention of ministers and Christians throughout the state of New York, throughout New England, and in many other parts of the United States, that its fame was an effective instrument in the hands of the Spirit of God in promoting the revival. Years after this, in conversing with Dr. Beecher about this powerful revival and its results, he remarked that this was the greatest work of God, and the greatest revival of religion, that the world has ever seen in so short a time. "One hundred thousand," he remarked, "were reported as having connected themselves with churches as the result of that great revival. This is unparalleled in the history of the church and of the progress of religion."

From the time of the New Lebanon convention in 1827, open and public opposition to revivals of religion was less and less manifested. In Rochester I felt no opposition whatsoever. Indeed, the waters of salvation had risen so high, revivals had become so powerful and extensive, and people had had so much time to become acquainted with them and their results, that men were afraid to oppose them as they had done. Ministers had come to understand them better, and the most ungodly sinners had been convinced that they were indeed the work of God. So thoroughly were individuals and whole communities reformed, and so permanent and unquestionable were the results, that the conviction became nearly universal that these revivals were the work of God.

Twenty-two

Auburn, Buffalo, Providence, and Boston: The Work of God Prevails

D uring the latter part of the time that I was in Rochester, my health was poor. I was worn out, and some of the leading physicians had made up their minds that I would never be able to preach again. My labors in Rochester at that time had lasted six months; near their close, Rev. Dr. Wisner of Ithaca came and spent some time witnessing and helping to forward the work. In the meantime, I was invited to many fields; among others, I was urged by Dr. Nott, president of Union College in Schenectady, to go and labor with him and, if possible, secure the conversion of his numerous students. I made up my mind to comply with his request.

In company with Dr. Wisner and Josiah Bissell, I set out for Schenectady in the spring of 1831. I had left my wife and children in Rochester, as the traveling was too dangerous and the journey too fatiguing for them. When we arrived at Geneva, Dr. Wisner insisted on my going home with him to rest awhile. He pressed me very hard to go and finally told me that the physicians in Rochester had told him that I was going to die and that I would never labor in revivals again. I replied that I had been told this before, but that it was a mistake; that the doctors did not understand my case; that I was only fatigued, and a little rest would be enough for me. Dr. Wisner finally gave up his importunity.

Our travel was so very bad that sometimes we could not go more than two miles in an hour, and we had only reached Auburn, though we had left Rochester two or three days before. As I had many dear friends in Auburn and was very tired, I made up my mind to stop there and rest. I had paid my fare through to Schenectady, but I could stop for one or more days if I chose to. I stopped at the house of Mr. T—— S——, son of Chief Justice S——. He was an earnest Christian man and a very dear friend of mine; consequently, I went to his house instead of stopping at the hotel, and I intended to rest there until the next stagecoach came.

In the morning, after sleeping quietly at Mr. S——'s, I had risen and was preparing to take the stagecoach that was scheduled to arrive in the early part of the day. A gentleman came in with the request for me to remain—a request in writing, signed by many of the influential men who had resisted the revival in that place in 1826. These men had carried their opposition so far in the earlier revival that they had broken from Dr. Lansing's congregation and had formed a new one. In the meantime, Dr. Lansing had been called to another field of labor, and Rev. Josiah Hopkins of Vermont was the pastor of the First Church. The petition, which contained an earnest appeal to me to stop and labor for their salvation, was signed by a long list of unconverted men, most of them among the most prominent citizens in the city. This was very striking to me. In this paper they alluded to the opposition they had formerly made to my labors, and they begged me to overlook it and stop and preach the Gospel to them.

This request did not come from the pastor or from his church, but from those who had formerly led in the opposition to the work. They appeared as much surprised as I was at the change in the attitudes of those men. Of course, the pastor and the members of his church also pressed me to comply with the request of these men. I went to my room, laid the subject before God, and soon made up my mind what to do. I told the pastor and his elders that I was exhausted and nearly worn out but that I would remain upon certain conditions. I would preach twice on Sundays, and on two evenings during the week, but all the rest of the labor I left to them. They were not to expect me to attend any other meetings than those at which I preached, and they would have to take upon themselves the task of instructing inquirers and conducting the prayer meetings and other meetings. I knew that they understood how to labor with sinners, and I could trust them to perform that part of the work. I furthermore stipulated that no one should visit me, except in extreme cases, at my lodgings.

The Word took immediate effect. On the first or second Sunday evening that I preached, I saw that the Word was taking powerful hold. At the close, I called for those whose minds were made up to come forward, publicly renounce their sins, and give themselves to Christ. Much to my own surprise, and very much to the surprise of the pastor and many members of the church, the first man who came forward and led the way was the man who had led the opposition to the former revival. He came forward promptly, followed by a large number of the people who had signed that paper. That evening's demonstration produced a general interest throughout the town.

Mr. Clary, the praying man who lived in Rochester, had a brother, a physician, living in Auburn. The second Sunday that I was in Auburn at this time, I saw the solemn face of my friend Mr. Clary in the congregation. He looked as if he was borne down with an agony of prayer. Being well acquainted with him and knowing the great gift of the spirit of prayer that was on him, I was very glad to see him there. He sat in the pew with his brother, the doctor, who claimed to be religious but knew nothing of his brother Abel's great power with God.

At intermission, as soon as I came from behind the pulpit, Mr. Clary, with his brother, met me at the pulpit stairs. The doctor invited me to go home with him and spend the intermission and get some refreshments. I did so.

After arriving at his house, we were soon summoned to the dinner table. We gathered around the table, and Dr. Clary turned to his brother and said, "Abel, will you ask a blessing?" Brother Abel bowed his head and began, audibly, to ask a blessing. He had uttered only a sentence or two when he broke down, moved suddenly back from the table, and fled to his bedroom. The doctor supposed he had been taken suddenly ill, and rose up and followed him. In a few moments he came down and said, "Mr. Finney, my brother wants to see you." "What ails him?" said I. "I do not know, but he says that you know. He appears to be in great distress, but I think it is the state of his mind." I understood it in a moment and went to his room. He lay groaning upon the bed, the Spirit making intercession for him and in him *"with groanings which cannot be uttered"* (Rom. 8:26). I had barely entered the room, when he said, "Pray, Brother Finney." I knelt down and helped him in prayer. I continued to pray until his distress passed away, and then I returned to the dinner table.

I understood that this was the voice of God. The Spirit was upon him, and I felt His influence and took it for granted that the work would move on powerfully. It did so. I believe that every one of those men who signed that paper was converted during that revival.

I stayed in Auburn for six Sundays, preaching twice on Sundays and twice during the week, and leaving all the rest of the labor to the pastor and members of the church. As in Rochester, there was little or no open opposition. Ministers and laypeople took hold of the work, and everybody who had a desire to work found enough to do, and found good success in labor. The pastor told me afterward that in the six weeks that I was there, five hundred souls had been converted. This revival seemed to be only a wave of divine power, reaching Auburn from the center at Rochester, from which such a mighty influence had gone out over the land.

Near the close of my labors in Auburn, a messenger arrived from Buffalo with an earnest request that I should visit that city. The revival in Rochester had prepared the way in Buffalo, just as it had in Auburn. The work had begun in Buffalo, and a few souls had been converted, but they felt that other means needed to be used. They urged me so much that from Auburn I turned back through Rochester to Buffalo, and I never did make it to Schenectady. I spent about one month in Buffalo, during which time a large number of people were converted. The work in Buffalo, as in

Auburn and Rochester, spread very generally among the
more influential classes.

From Buffalo I went, in June, to my father-in-law's in
Whitestown. I spent a part of the summer in journeying for
recreation and for the restoration of my health and
strength.

Early in the autumn of 1831, I accepted an invitation
to hold a series of meetings in Providence, Rhode Island. I
labored mostly in the church of which Rev. Dr. Wilson was
at that time pastor. I think I remained there about three
weeks, holding meetings every evening and preaching three
times on Sundays. The Lord poured out His Spirit immediately upon the people, and the work of grace commenced
and went forward in a most interesting manner. However,
my stay was too short to secure as general a work of grace
in that place as occurred afterward in 1842, when I spent
two months there.

Several of the men and women who have had a leading
Christian influence in Providence since their conversion
were converted in 1831. I had observed in the congregation
on Sundays a young woman of great beauty sitting in a pew
with a young man who, I afterward learned, was her
brother. She had a very intellectual, earnest look and
seemed to listen with the utmost attention and seriousness
to every word I said. I was the guest of Mr. Josiah Chapin,
and in going with him from the church to his house, I saw
this young brother and sister going up the same street. I
pointed them out to Mr. Chapin and asked him who they
were. He informed me that they were a Mr. and Miss A——,
brother and sister, and remarked that she was considered
the most beautiful girl in Providence. I asked him if she was
a Christian, and he said she was not. I told him I thought
her very seriously impressed by my sermons and asked him
if it would be well for me to call and see her. He thought it
would be a waste of time and that possibly I might not be
cordially received. He thought that she was a girl so spoiled
and flattered that she probably entertained little serious
thought in regard to the salvation of her soul.

I did not call upon her, but a few days after this she called to see me. I immediately asked her about the state of her soul. She was very thoroughly awakened, but her real convictions of sin were not yet ripened into the state that I thought was necessary before she could be really brought to accept the righteousness of Christ. I therefore spent an hour or two in trying to show her the depravity of her heart. She at first recoiled from my searching questions. But her convictions seemed to ripen as I conversed with her, and she became more and more serious.

When I told her what I thought was necessary to secure a ripened and thorough conviction under the influence of the Spirit of God, she got up and left. I was confident the Spirit of God had so thoroughly taken hold of her that what I had said to her would not be shaken off, but on the contrary that it would work the conviction that I sought to produce.

Two or three days afterward, she called on me again. I could see that she was greatly bowed down in her spirit. As soon as she came in, she sat down and threw her heart open to me. With the utmost candor she said to me, "Mr. Finney, when I was here before, I thought that your questions and treatment of me were pretty severe. But I see now that I am all that you told me I was. Indeed, had it not been for my pride and my regard for my reputation, I would have been as wicked a girl as there is in Providence. I can see clearly that my life has been restrained by pride and not by any regard for God or His law or Gospel. I can see that God has made use of my pride and ambition to restrain me from disgraceful iniquities. I have been spoiled and flattered, and I have maintained my reputation from purely selfish motives." Her convictions were thorough and permanent. She was calm and rational in everything that she said. It was evident, however, that she had a fervent nature, a strong will, and an uncommonly well-balanced and cultivated intellect. After conversing for some time, we bowed before the Lord in prayer, and she gave herself unreservedly to Christ.

I mention this case because I have always regarded it as a wonderful triumph of the grace of God over the fascinations of the world. The grace of God was too strong for the world, even in a case like this, in which every worldly fascination was surrounding her.

While I was in Providence, Dr. Wisner, then pastor of the Old South Church in Boston, came to Providence and attended our meetings. I afterward learned that he was sent over by the ministers *"to spy out the land"* (Num. 13:16) and bring back a report. I had several conversations with him, and he manifested an almost fanatical interest in what he saw and heard in Providence.

The work in Providence was of a particularly searching character in regard to those who claimed to be Christians. Old hopes were terribly shaken, and there was a great shaking among the dry bones in the different churches. (See Ezekiel 37:4–7.) A deacon of one of the churches was so terribly searched on one occasion that he said to me as I came from behind the pulpit, "Mr. Finney, I do not believe there are ten real Christians in Providence. We are all wrong; we have been deceived." Dr. Wisner was thoroughly convinced that the work was genuine and, for the time, extensive. He believed that there was no indication of influences or results that were to be deplored.

After Dr. Wisner returned to Boston, I soon received a request from the Congregational ministers and churches to go to that city and labor. I began my labors there by preaching in the different churches on Sundays, and on weeknights I preached in the Park Street Church. I soon saw that the Word of God was taking effect and that the interest was increasing from day to day. But I also perceived that there needed to be a great searching among the Christians. There was no spirit of prayer among them such as had prevailed in the revivals in the West and in New York City. There seemed to be a strange type of religion in Boston, not exhibiting the freedom and strength of faith that I had been in the habit of seeing in New York.

I therefore began to preach some searching sermons to the Christians. On Sunday I announced that I would preach a series of sermons to Christians, in the Park Street Church, on certain evenings of the week. But I soon found that these sermons were not at all palatable to the Christians of Boston. It was something they never had been used to, and the attendance at Park Street became less and less, especially on those evenings when I preached to professing Christians. This was new to me. I had never before seen professing Christians shrink back, as they did at that time in Boston, from searching sermons. Again and again I heard people saying, "What will the Unitarians say if such things are true of us who are orthodox? If Mr. Finney preaches to us in this way, the Unitarians will triumph over us and say that at least the orthodox are no better Christians than the Unitarians." It was evident that they somewhat resented my plain dealing and that my searching sermons astonished, and even offended, very many of them. However, as the work went forward, this state of things changed greatly; and after a few weeks they would listen to searching preaching and came to appreciate it.

In Boston, as everywhere else, there was a method of dealing with inquiring sinners that was very trying to me. I would sometimes hold meetings of inquiry in the basement of the Bowdoin Street Church, of which Dr. Lyman Beecher was pastor. One evening, when there was a large attendance and a feeling of great searching and solemnity among the inquirers, I made a closing address in which I tried to point out to them exactly what the Lord required of them. My intention was to bring them to renounce themselves and give themselves and all they possessed to Christ. I tried to show them that they were not their own but were bought with a price (1 Cor. 6:19–20), and I pointed out to them the sense in which they were expected to forsake all that they had and deliver everything to Christ as belonging to Him.

I made this point as clear as I possibly could, and I saw that the impression upon the inquirers seemed to be very deep. I was about to call on them to kneel down while we presented them to God in prayer, when Dr. Beecher arose and said to them, "You need not be afraid to give up all to Christ, for He will give it right back to you." He made no further distinctions, and I feared that he had made a false impression. After he had finished his remarks, therefore, I led them as wisely and carefully as I could to see that they must not entertain the thought that God would give back their possessions in the sense in which He required them to be given up. I told them that the Lord did not require them to relinquish all their possessions or to leave their businesses, houses, and possessions and never to have possession of them again; but He did require them to renounce the ownership of them, to understand and realize that these things were not theirs but the Lord's. Dr. Beecher made no objection to what I said, and it is probable that he never intended anything inconsistent with this in what he said.

The members of the orthodox churches of Boston, at this time, generally received my views of doctrine without question. I know that Dr. Beecher did, for he told me that he had never met a man with whose theological views he so entirely agreed as he did with mine.

After I had spent several weeks in preaching to the different congregations, I consented to preach regularly at Mr. Green's church on Essex Street for a time. I therefore concentrated my labors upon that field. We had a blessed work of grace, and a large number of people were converted in different parts of the city.

I had become fatigued, since I had labored about ten years as an evangelist without anything more than a few days or weeks of rest during the whole period. My fellow ministers were true men, had taken hold of the work as well as they knew how, and labored faithfully and effectively in securing good results.

By this time, a second Free Presbyterian church had been formed in New York City. Mr. Joel Parker's church, the First Free Church, had grown so large that a group had gone off and formed a second church, to which Rev. Mr.

Barrows had been preaching. Some earnest Christians wrote to me from New York, proposing to lease a theater and make it suitable as a church, on the condition that I would come there and preach. They proposed to get what was called the Chatham Street Theatre, in the heart of the most irreligious population of New York. It was owned by men who were very willing to have it transformed into a church. At this time my wife and I had three children, and I could not easily take my family with me while laboring as an evangelist. My strength, too, had become a good deal exhausted. But after praying and looking the matter over, I concluded that I would accept the call from the Second Free Church and would labor, for a time at least, in New York City.

Twenty-three

New York City in 1832: Five Hundred Are Converted

Mr. Lewis Tappan, with other Christians, leased the Chatham Street Theatre and made it into a church and a suitable place to accommodate the anniversary celebrations of the various charitable societies in the area. I left Boston in April 1832, and commenced labors in that theater, the Second Free Presbyterian Church, at that time. The Spirit of the Lord was immediately poured out upon us, and we had an extensive revival that spring and summer.

About midsummer, the cholera appeared in New York for the first time. The panic became great, and many Christian people fled into the country. The cholera was very severe in the city that summer, more so than it ever has been since, and it was especially fatal in the part of the city where I resided. I recall counting, from the door of our house, five hearses drawn up at the same time at different doors within sight. I remained in New York until the latter part of summer, not being willing to leave the city while the mortality was so great. But I found that the influence of the disease was undermining my own health, and in the latter part of summer I went into the country for two or three weeks. On my return, I was installed as pastor of the church.

During the installation services, I became ill; and soon after I got home, it was plain that I had contracted the cholera. The gentleman next door contracted it about the same time, and before morning he was dead. The means used for my recovery gave my system a terrible shock, from which it took me long to recover. However, toward spring I was able to preach again. I invited two fellow ministers to help me in holding a series of meetings. We preached in turn for two or three weeks, but very little was accomplished. I saw that it was not the way to promote a revival there, and I drew the meeting to a close.

On the next Sunday, I made appointments to preach every evening during the week, and a revival immediately commenced and became very powerful. I continued to preach for twenty evenings in succession, besides preaching on Sunday. My health was not yet vigorous, and after preaching twenty evenings, I suspended that form of my labors. The converts known to us numbered five hundred, and our church became so large that very soon a colony was sent off to form another church. A suitable building was erected for that purpose, on the corner of Madison and Catharine Streets.

The work continued to go forward in a very interesting manner. We held meetings of inquiry once or twice a week, sometimes more often, and found that every week a good number of conversions was reported. The church members were a praying, working people. They were thoroughly united, were well trained in regard to labors for the conversion of sinners, and were a most devoted and effective church of Christ. Both men and women would *"go out into the highways and hedges"* (Luke 14:23) and bring people to hear preaching whenever they were called upon to do so. When we wished to announce any extra meetings, little slips of paper, on which was printed an invitation to attend the services, would be carried from house to house in every direction by the members of the church—especially in the part of the city in which Chatham Street Chapel, as we called it, was located. By the distribution of these slips and by oral invitations, the house could be filled any evening in the week. Even our ladies were not afraid to go and gather people from all classes in the neighborhood.

There were three rooms connected with the front part of the theater—long, large rooms that were set up for prayer meetings and for a lecture room. These rooms had been used for very different purposes while the main building was used as a theater. But when set up for our purpose, they were exceedingly convenient. There were three tiers of balconies, and the three rooms were connected with the balconies respectively, one above the other.

I instructed my church members to scatter themselves over the whole church and to keep their eyes open for any who were seriously affected by the preaching. If possible, my congregation were to detain them after preaching for conversation and prayer. They were true to their teaching and were on the lookout at every meeting to see with whom the Word of God was taking effect. They had faith enough to dismiss their fears and to speak to any whom they saw to be affected by the Word. In this way, the conversion of many souls was secured. They would invite them into those rooms, and there we could converse and pray with them, and thus gather up the results of every sermon.

The firm of Naylor and Company, which was at that time the great cutlery manufacturer in Sheffield, England, had a store in New York and a partner by the name of H——. Mr. H—— was a worldly man, had traveled a great deal, and had resided in several of the main cities of Europe. One of the clerks of that establishment had come to our meetings, had been converted, and felt very anxious for the conversion of Mr. H——. For some time the young man hesitated about asking him to attend our meetings, but he finally ventured to do so; thus Mr. H—— came one evening to the meeting.

It happened that Mr. H—— sat near to where Mr. Tappan sat. Mr. Tappan saw that, during the sermon, he manifested a good deal of emotion and seemed uneasy at times, as if he were on the point of going out. But he remained until the blessing was pronounced. Mr. Tappan kept his eye on him and, as soon as the blessing was pronounced, introduced himself as Mr. Tappan, a partner of Arthur Tappan and Company, a firm well-known to everybody in New York at that time.

Mr. Tappan spoke very kindly to him and asked him if he would remain for prayer and conversation. Mr. H——

tried to excuse himself and get away, but Mr. Tappan was so gentlemanly and so kind that he could not easily get away from him. He was importunate and, as Mr. H—— later expressed it, "held fast to a button on my coat, so that my button was the means of saving my soul." The people went home, and Mr. H——, among others, was persuaded to remain. According to our custom, we had a thorough conversation, and Mr. H—— was either then, or very soon after, converted.

When I first went to Chatham Street Chapel, I informed the people there that I did not wish to fill up the church with Christians from other churches, as my purpose was to gather from the world. I wanted to secure the conversion of the ungodly to the utmost possible extent. We therefore gave ourselves to labor for that class of individuals and, by the blessing of God, were quite successful. Conversions were multiplied, so much that our church soon became so large that we had to send off colony after colony. When I left New York, we had seven Free churches whose members were laboring with all their might to secure the salvation of souls.

These churches were supported mostly by collections that were taken up from Sunday to Sunday. If at any time there was a deficiency in the treasury, there was a number of wealthy men in the congregation who would at once supply the deficiency from their own pockets, so that we never had the least difficulty in meeting the financial demands. I never knew a more harmonious, prayerful, and effective people than the members of those Free churches. They were not among the rich, although there were several wealthy men belonging to them. In general, they were gathered from the middle and lower classes. This was what we aimed to accomplish: to preach the Gospel, especially to the poor.

When I first went to New York, I had made up my mind on the question of slavery and was exceedingly anxious to arouse public attention to the subject. I did not, however, divert the attention of the people from the work of converting souls. Nevertheless, in my prayers and preaching, I so often alluded to slavery and denounced it that a considerable excitement came to exist among the people.

I should have said that in January 1834, I took a sea voyage for my health. I went up the Mediterranean in a small sailing vessel in the middle of winter. We had a very stormy passage. My stateroom was small, I was on the whole very uncomfortable, and the voyage did not much improve my health. I spent a few weeks in Malta, and also in Sicily. I was gone about six months. At the time of my departure, excitement had been increasing on the subject of slavery. Mr. Leavitt took up the cause of the slave and advocated it in the New York *Evangelist,* a small newspaper that we had established as a medium for religious communications. When I was about to leave on the sea voyage, I admonished Mr. Leavitt to be careful not to go too fast in the discussion of the antislavery question, lest he should lose his newspaper.

On my way home, I feared that the revivals would begin to decline throughout the country. I feared that the opposition that had been made to them had grieved the Holy Spirit. My own health had nearly broken down, and I knew of no other evangelist who would aid pastors in revival work. I was so distressed over this thought that one day I found myself unable to rest. My soul was in an utter agony. I spent almost the entire day in prayer in my stateroom or walking the deck in intense agony. In fact, I felt crushed with the burden that was on my soul. There was no one on board to whom I could open my mind or say a word.

The spirit of prayer was upon me. I had often experienced it before, but perhaps never to such a degree and for so long a time. I sought the Lord to go on with His work and to provide Himself with the necessary instruments. It was a long summer day in the early part of July. After a day of unspeakable wrestling and agony in my soul, the subject became clear to me in the evening. The Spirit led me to believe that everything would come out right, that God still had work for me to do, that I might rest, and that the Lord would go forward with His work and give me strength to take any part in it that He desired. But I had not the least idea what the course of His providence would be.

On my return, I found that there was a great excitement in New York. The members of my church, together with other abolitionists in New York, had held a meeting on the Fourth of July and had had an address on the subject of slaveholding. A mob was stirred up, and this was the beginning of a series of mobs that spread in many directions whenever and wherever there was an antislavery gathering or a voice lifted up against the abominable institution of slavery.

However, I went forward with my labors in Chatham Street. The work of God immediately revived and went forward with great interest, many people being converted at almost every meeting. The church continued to flourish and to extend its influence and its labors in every direction.

While I was laboring at Chatham Street Chapel, some events occurred, connected with the presbytery, that led to the formation of a Congregational church and to my becoming its pastor. A member came to us from one of the old churches, and we were soon informed that he had previously committed an offense for which he needed to be disciplined. Since his offense had been committed before he left that church, I supposed that it belonged to them to discipline him. I brought the case before the Third Presbytery of New York, to which I then belonged, and they decided that he was under our jurisdiction and that it was our duty to discipline him. We did so.

But soon another case occurred. Before she came to us, a woman who had come from one of the churches was found guilty of an offense that called for discipline. In accordance with the ruling of the presbytery in the other case, we went forward and excommunicated her. She appealed the case to the presbytery, and they ruled in a manner directly opposite to their former ruling. I told them that I did not know how to act, since the two cases were similar but their rulings on them were entirely opposed to each other. But Dr.

Cox of the presbytery replied that they would not be governed by their own precedent, or by any other precedent, and the presbytery went along with him.

Soon after this, the question came up of building the Tabernacle on Broadway. The men who built it, along with the leading members who formed the church there, built it with the understanding that I would be its pastor, and they formed a Congregational church. I then took my dismissal from the presbytery and became pastor of that Congregational church.

When the Tabernacle was in the process of completion—its walls were up and the roof was on—a story was set in circulation that it was going to be an "amalgamation church," in which colored and white people would be forced to sit together. This report created a great excitement all over New York, and somebody set the building on fire. The firemen refused to put it out and left the interior and roof to be consumed. However, the gentlemen who had undertaken to build the Tabernacle went forward and completed it.

On my return to New York in the fall, Mr. Leavitt came to me and said, "Brother Finney, I have ruined the *Evangelist.* I have not been as prudent as you cautioned me to be, and I have gone so far ahead of public intelligence and feeling on the subject, that my subscription list is rapidly failing. We will not be able to continue its publication beyond the first of January, unless you can do something to bring the paper back to public favor again."

I told him my health was such that I did not know what I could do, but I would make it a subject of prayer. He said if I could write a series of articles on revivals, he had no doubt it would restore the paper immediately to public favor. After considering it a day or two, I proposed to preach a course of lectures to my people, on revivals of religion, which he might report for his paper. He took to the idea right away, and in the next issue of his paper he advertised the course of lectures. This had the effect he desired, and he soon after told me that the subscription list was very rapidly increasing.

I began the lectures immediately and continued them through the winter, preaching one each week. Mr. Leavitt could not write shorthand but would sit and take notes; and then the next day he would sit down, fill out his notes, and send them to the press. I did not see what he had reported until I saw it published in his paper. Of course, my lectures were wholly extemporaneous. Often I did not know what the next lecture would be about until I saw his report of my last. Brother Leavitt's reports were meager, since the lectures averaged at least an hour and three quarters in delivery but could be read in the report in about thirty minutes.

These lectures were afterward published in a book called *Finney's Lectures on Revivals.* Twelve thousand copies of them were sold, as fast as they could be printed. They have been reprinted in England and France; they were translated into Welsh and, I believe, into German; and they were very extensively circulated throughout Europe and the colonies of Great Britain. I presume they could be found wherever the English language is spoken. In Wales, a great revival resulted from the translation of those lectures into the Welsh language. One publisher in London informed me that his father had published eighty thousand volumes of these revival lectures, which have been instrumental in promoting revivals in England, Scotland, Wales, Canada, and on some of the islands of the sea.

In England and Scotland, I have met many ministers and laypeople who had been converted, directly or indirectly, through the instrumentality of those lectures. Some people also became ministers because of them. I found people in England, in all the different denominations, who had not only read those revival lectures, but had also been greatly blessed in reading them. When they were first published in the New York *Evangelist,* the reading of them resulted in revivals of religion in multitudes of places throughout this country.

I believe that all of this was the result of that long day of agony and prayer at sea, that God would do something to forward the work of revivals and would enable me, if He desired to do it, to help forward the work. Through the infinite riches of grace in Christ Jesus, I have witnessed for many years the wonderful results of that day of wrestling with God. In answer to that day's agony, He has continued to give me the spirit of prayer.

Soon after I returned to New York, I commenced my labors in the Tabernacle. The Spirit of the Lord was poured out upon us, and we had a precious revival as long as I continued to be pastor of that church. While in New York, I had many applications from young men to take them as students in theology. However, I had too much on my hands to undertake such a work. But the men who had built the Tabernacle had planned ahead and prepared a room that we expected to use for prayer meetings, but more especially for a theological lecture room. The number of applications had been so large that I had made up my mind to deliver a course of theological lectures in that room each year, which students could attend if they so desired.

But about this time, and before I had begun my lectures in New York, the breaking up at Lane Seminary took place when the trustees prohibited any discussion of the question of slavery among the students. When this occurred, Mr. Arthur Tappan told me that he knew of a place in Ohio, called Oberlin, where I could gather those young men and prepare them for the work of preaching throughout the West. If I would go, he said, he would pay all my expenses. He was very earnest in this proposal, but I did not know how to leave New York. Although I strongly sympathized with Mr. Tappan in regard to helping those young men, I did not see how I could accomplish his wishes.

While this subject was under consideration, in January 1835, Rev. John Jay Shipherd of Oberlin and Rev. Asa Mahan of Cincinnati arrived in New York to persuade me to go to Oberlin as a professor of theology. Mr. Mahan had been one of the trustees of Lane Seminary—the only one who had resisted the prohibition of free discussion. Mr. Shipherd had organized a school in Oberlin about a year before this time and had obtained a charter broad enough for a university.

Mr. Mahan had never been in Oberlin. The trees had been removed from the college square, some dorms and one college building had been erected, and about a hundred pupils had been gathered in the academic department of the institution.

The proposal they laid before me was to take those students who had left Lane Seminary and teach them theology. These students themselves had proposed to go to Oberlin if I would accept the call. I had several consultations with Arthur and Lewis Tappan on the subject. I had understood that the trustees of Lane Seminary had acted over the heads of the faculty and, in the absence of some of the professors, had passed the obnoxious resolution that had caused the students to leave. Therefore, I told Mr. Shipherd that I would not go unless two points were conceded by the trustees. One was that they would never interfere with the internal regulation of the school, but would leave that entirely to the discretion of the faculty. The other was that we should be allowed to receive colored people on the same conditions that we did white people, that there should be no discrimination made on account of color.

When these conditions were forwarded to Oberlin, the trustees were called together. After a great struggle to overcome their own prejudices and the prejudices of the community, they passed resolutions complying with the conditions I had proposed. Once this difficulty was removed, the friends in New York were called together to see what they could do about endowing the institution. In the course of an hour or two, they had a subscription filled for the endowment of eight professorships.

It was difficult for me to give up the admirable place of preaching the Gospel before the large crowds that gathered within the sound of my voice. I also felt that our endeavor would be greatly opposed from many sources. I therefore told Arthur Tappan that I was not sure about leaving New York, that we would encounter great opposition because of our antislavery principles, and that we could hardly expect to get enough funds to put up our buildings and to procure all the necessities of a college. I felt I could not commit my-self unless there could be some guarantee that we would get the funds that were indispensable.

Mr. Tappan had heard that strong efforts were being made to induce me to go to Western Reserve College in Hudson rather than to Oberlin. The college at Hudson, at that time, was already an established college. Oberlin had nothing. It had no permanent buildings; it was composed of a little colony of people settled in the woods, just beginning to put up their houses and clear away the immense forest to make a place for a college. It had its charter, to be sure, and perhaps a hundred students, but everything was still to be done.

Oberlin College was established by Mr. Shipherd, very much against the wishes of the men most concerned in building up Western Reserve. Mr. Shipherd once informed me that the principal financial agent of that college told him that he would do all he could to put our college down. As soon as they heard in Hudson that I had been called to Oberlin as professor of theology, the trustees at Western Reserve College elected me as professor of "pastoral theology and sacred eloquence," so that I had the two invitations at the same time. I did not commit myself in writing to either until I had surveyed each school. Brother Tappan wrote to me to warn me against supposing that I could be instrumental in accomplishing at Hudson what we desired to accomplish at Oberlin.

Arthur Tappan's heart was as large as all New York, even as large as the world. When I told him I was unsure about going to Oberlin, he said, "Brother Finney, my own income averages about $100,000 a year. If you will go to Oberlin, take hold of that work, and see that the buildings are put up and a library and that everything else is provided, I will pledge you my entire income, except what I need to provide for my family, until you are beyond financial need." Having perfect confidence in Brother Tappan, I said, "Then my difficulties are out of the way."

219

But still there was a great difficulty in leaving my church in New York. I had never thought of having my labors at Oberlin interfere with my revival labors and preaching. It was therefore agreed between the church and me that I would spend my winters in New York and my summers in Oberlin and that the church would be at the expense of my going and coming. When this was arranged, I took my family and arrived in Oberlin at the beginning of the summer in 1835.

I went to Oberlin and saw that there was nothing to prevent the building up of a college on the principles that had been proposed for it. Those who were at Oberlin were heartily in favor of building up a school on radical principles of reform. I therefore wrote to the trustees of Hudson, declining to accept their invitation, and took up my abode in Oberlin.

Twenty-four

Oberlin College Is Sustained
through Hard Times

W hen the students from Lane Seminary came to
Oberlin, the trustees put up "barracks" in which
they were lodged, and other students thronged
to us from every direction. After I had agreed to come, the
men at Oberlin wrote, asking me to bring a large tent in
which to hold meetings, as there was no room in the place
large enough to accommodate the people. I made this request known to some of my brethren, who told me to go and
get a tent made, and they would supply the money. It was
a circular tent, a hundred feet in diameter, furnished with
all the equipment for putting it up. At the top of the center pole that supported the tent was a banner, upon which
was written in very large characters, "Holiness to the
Lord."

This tent was very useful. When the weather would
permit, we spread it upon the square every Sunday and
held public services in it. It was also used, to some extent,
for holding regular meetings in the surrounding area where
there were no churches large enough to hold the people.

Arthur Tappan had promised to supply us with funds
until we were beyond financial need. With this understanding between us, I entered into the work. But it was
further understood between us that his pledge would not be
known to the trustees, lest they should fail to make efforts
not merely to collect funds, but also to make the needs and
purposes of the institution known throughout the land. In
accordance with this understanding, the work was pushed
as fast as it could well be, considering that we were in the
heart of a great forest and in a location that was rather undesirable.

We had just begun the work of putting up our buildings and had arranged to borrow a large amount of money, when the economy crashed and left Mr. Tappan, and nearly all the men who had pledged to support the faculty at Oberlin, without adequate funds. The majority of wealthy men in the entire country were affected by this crash. It left us not only without funds for the support of the faculty, but also $30,000 in debt, without any prospect of obtaining funds from those who were friends of the college. Mr. Tappan wrote me at this time, acknowledging the promise he had made me and expressing the deepest regret that he was wholly unable to fulfill his pledge. From a human standpoint, it seemed that the college would be a failure.

Most of the people of Ohio were utterly opposed to our enterprise because of its antislavery stance. The towns around us were hostile to our movement, and in some places threats were made to come and tear down our buildings. A democratic legislature was, in the meantime, endeavoring to find some cause for nullifying our charter. In this state of things there was, of course, a great crying to God among the people at Oberlin.

In the meantime, my revival lectures had been very extensively circulated in England, and we were aware that the British public would strongly sympathize with us if they knew our purpose and our condition. We therefore sent a committee to England, composed of Rev. John Keep and Mr. William Dawes, having obtained for them letters of recommendation and expressions of confidence in our enterprise from some of the leading antislavery men of the country. They went to England and laid our purposes and our needs before the British public. They generously responded and gave us £6,000. This very nearly cancelled our indebtedness.

Our friends who were abolitionists and supporters of revivals were scattered throughout the Northern states; they generously aided us to the extent of their ability. But we had to struggle with poverty and many trials for several years. Sometimes we did not know, from day to day, how we were to be provided for. But with the blessing of God we did as best we could.

At one time, I saw no means of providing for my family through the winter. Thanksgiving Day found us so poor that I had been obliged to sell my traveling trunk, which I had used in my evangelistic labors. I rose on the morning of Thanksgiving and put our needs before the Lord. I finally concluded by saying that, if help did not come, I would assume it was for the best and would be entirely satisfied with any course that the Lord would see it wise to take. I went and preached, and I enjoyed my preaching more than I ever had before. I could see that the people enjoyed it exceedingly, as well.

After the meeting, I was detained a little while in conversation with some people, and my wife returned home. When I reached the gate, she was standing in the open door with a letter in her hand. As I approached she said, "The answer has come, my dear," and handed me the letter containing a check for $200 from Mr. Josiah Chapin of Providence. He had been in Oberlin the previous summer with his wife. I had said nothing about my needs at all, as I never was in the habit of mentioning them to anybody. But in the letter containing the check, he said he had learned that the endowment fund had failed and that I was in need of help. He hinted that I might expect more, from time to time. He continued to send me $600 a year for several years, and on this I managed to live.

I spent my summers in Oberlin and my winters in New York for two or three years. We had blessed revivals in New York whenever I returned to preach there; we also had a revival in Oberlin continually. Very few students came to Oberlin at that time without being converted. My health soon became such that I could not continue in both fields of labor. I therefore took a dismissal from my church in New York, and I spent the winter months in laboring to promote revivals of religion in various places.

I have long been convinced that the higher forms of Christian experience are attained only as a result of a terribly searching application of God's law to the human conscience and heart. The results of my labors up to that time had shown me more clearly than ever the great weakness of Christians. I saw that the older members of the church, in general, were making very little progress in grace. They would fall back from a revival state even sooner than young converts. I saw clearly that this was owing to their early teaching, that is, to the views that they had been led to believe when they were young converts.

I was led into a state of great dissatisfaction with my own lack of stability in faith and love, and I often felt myself weak in the presence of temptation. I frequently needed to hold days of fasting and prayer, and to spend much time in overhauling my own religious life, in order to retain the communion with God and the divine strength that would enable me to labor effectively for the promotion of revivals of religion.

In looking at the state of the Christian church, I was led to earnestly inquire whether there was not something higher and more enduring than the Christian church was aware of. Were there promises and means provided in the Gospel for the establishment of a higher Christian life? I devoted myself earnestly to search the Scriptures and to read whatever I could on the subject, until I was satisfied that an altogether higher and more stable form of Christian life was attainable and was the privilege of all Christians. I was convinced that the doctrine of entire sanctification in this life was a doctrine taught in the Bible, and that abundant means were provided for the securing of this privilege of Christians to live without known sin.

The last winter that I spent in New York, the Lord greatly refreshed my soul. After a season of great searching of heart, He gave me, as He has often done, much of the same divine sweetness in my soul that Jonathan Edwards said he attained in his own experience. That winter, I had a thorough breaking up—so much so that sometimes, for a considerable period, I could not refrain from loud weeping in view of my own sins and of the love of God in Christ.

Such seasons were frequent that winter, and they resulted in the great renewal of my spiritual strength and the enlargement of my views in regard to the privileges of Christians and the abundance of the grace of God.

It is well-known that my views on the question of sanctification have been the subject of a good deal of criticism. There seemed to be a general union of ministerial influence against us. Great effort was extended to represent our views at Oberlin as entirely heretical. Such representations were made to ecclesiastical bodies throughout the land, in order to lead many of them to pass resolutions that would warn the churches against the influence of Oberlin theology. We understood very well what had begun this opposition and by what means all this excitement was raised. But we said nothing. The weapons that were formed against us ended up having a disastrous effect upon those who used them. (See Isaiah 54:17.)

I rarely heard anything said at Oberlin against Hudson, at that time or at any other time. We kept about our own business and felt our strength was to sit still and ignore the opposition. In this we were not mistaken. We felt confident that it was not God's plan to allow such opposition to prevail. We always had as many students as we knew what to do with. Our hands were always full of labor, and we were always greatly encouraged in our efforts.

A few years later, one of the leading ministers who had opposed the work at Oberlin came and spent a day or two at my house. Among other things he said to me, "Brother Finney, Oberlin is a great wonder to us. I have for many years been connected with a college as one of its professors. College life and principles, and the conditions upon which colleges are built up, are very familiar to me. We have always thought that colleges could not exist unless they were patronized by the ministry. We knew that young men who were about to go to college would generally consult their pastors in regard to what colleges they should select, and they would be guided by their judgment. Now, the ministers almost universally arrayed themselves against Oberlin.

They warned their churches against you, they discouraged young men from coming to Oberlin, and still the Lord has built you up. You have been supported with funds better than almost any college in the region; you have had far more students; and the blessing of God has been upon you, so that your success has been wonderful. Now, this is a perfect anomaly in the history of colleges. God has stood by you and sustained you through all this opposition, so that you have hardly felt it."

It is difficult now for people to realize the opposition that we met with when we first established the college. I met one woman who, when she found out I was from Oberlin, said, "From Oberlin! Why, our minister said he would just as soon send a son to state prison as to Oberlin!" This spirit prevailed very extensively when the college was first established. Misrepresentations and misunderstandings abounded on every side, and those misunderstandings extended into almost every corner of the United States.

However, a great number of laypeople and ministers in different parts of the country had no confidence in this opposition. They sympathized with our aims, our views, and our efforts. They stood firmly by us through thick and thin. And knowing the limitations that we experienced because of this opposition, they gave their money and their influence freely to help us go forward.

You will recall that Mr. Chapin of Providence sent me $600 a year on which to support my family for several years. When he had done it as long as he thought it his duty—which he did until financial difficulties rendered it inconvenient for him to do so any longer—Mr. Willard Sears of Boston took his place, and for several years he obliged me to take the same amount annually that Mr. Chapin had given. In the meantime, efforts were constantly made to sustain the other members of the faculty, and by the grace of God we rode out the gale. After a few years the panic subsided to a great extent.

President Mahan, Professor Cowles, Professor Morgan, and I wrote on the subject of sanctification. We established a periodical called *The Oberlin Evangelist,* and afterward *The Oberlin Quarterly,* in which we made sure the public was clear on what our real views were. In 1846, I published two volumes on systematic theology. In this work I discussed the subject of entire sanctification. My writings were reviewed several times; to these different reviews I published replies, and no other system of beliefs has been able to resist our orthodoxy.

Being the professor of theology, the theological opposition was directed, of course, principally toward me. But none of the opposition that we met with ruffled our spirits or disturbed us in such a sense as to provoke us into a spirit of controversy or ill feeling.

During these years of smoke and dust, of misunderstanding and opposition from without, the Lord was blessing us richly within. We not only prospered in our own souls as a church, but we also had a continuous revival. We were in what might properly be regarded as a revival state. Our students were converted by scores, and the Lord overshadowed us continually with the cloud of His mercy. Gales of divine influence swept over us from year to year, producing abundantly the fruits of the Spirit: *"love, joy, peace, longsuffering, kindness, goodness, faithfulness, gentleness, self-control"* (Gal. 5:22–23).

I have always attributed our success in this good work entirely to the grace of God. It was no wisdom or goodness of our own that achieved this success. Nothing but continued divine influence, pervading the community, sustained us under our trials and kept us in an attitude in which we could be effective in the work we had undertaken. We always felt that if the Lord withheld His Spirit, no outward circumstances could make us truly prosperous.

We also had trials among ourselves. Subjects frequently came up for discussion, and we sometimes spent days, or even weeks, in discussing great questions of duty and expediency on which we did not think alike. But none of these questions permanently divided us. Our principle was always to allow each other the right to personal opinions. We generally came to a substantial agreement on subjects on which we had differed, and when we found ourselves unable to see alike, the minority submitted themselves to the judgment of the majority. The idea of breaking the church apart for such disagreements was never entertained by us. To a very great extent, we preserved *"the unity of the Spirit in the bond of peace"* (Eph. 4:3); perhaps no other community has existed for so long and passed through so many trials and changes, that has on the whole maintained a greater spirit of harmony, Christian forbearance, and brotherly love.

When the question of entire sanctification first came up at Oberlin for public discussion, and when the subject first attracted the general attention of the church, we were in the midst of a powerful revival. When the revival was going on, one day President Mahan had been preaching a searching discourse. I observed in the course of his preaching that he had left one point untouched that appeared to me of great relevance and importance. As was his custom, he asked me, at the close of his sermon, if I had any remarks to make. I arose and pressed the point that he had omitted. It was the distinction between desire and will. I saw that pressing this distinction upon the people would throw much light on the question of whether they were really Christians or not, whether they were really consecrated persons, or whether they merely had desires without being in fact willing to obey God.

When this distinction was made clear, the Holy Spirit fell upon the congregation in a most remarkable manner. Many people lowered their heads, and some groaned so that they could be heard throughout the place. It demolished the false hopes of professing Christians who had been deceived on every side. Several arose on the spot and said that they had been deceived and how. This was carried to such an extent that it greatly astonished me and produced a general feeling of astonishment in the congregation.

The work went on with power. Professing Christians obtained new hopes or were reconverted in such numbers that a very great and important change came over the whole community. President Mahan had been greatly blessed, along with some of our professors. He came into a entirely new form of Christian experience at that time.

In a meeting a few days after this, one of our theological students arose and asked if the Gospel provided for Christians all the conditions of an established faith, hope, and love. He asked, "Is there not something better and higher than Christians have generally experienced? Is not sanctification attainable in this life, in such a sense that Christians can have unbroken peace and not come into condemnation or have the feeling of condemnation or a consciousness of sin?" Brother Mahan immediately answered, "Yes." What occurred at this meeting brought the question of sanctification prominently before us as a practical question. We had no theories on the subject, no philosophy to maintain, but simply took it up as a Bible question.

In this form it existed among us, as an experiential truth, which we did not attempt to reduce to a theological formula. Nor did we attempt to explain its philosophy until years afterward. But the discussion of this question was a great blessing to us and to a great number of our students who are now scattered in various parts of the country or have gone abroad as missionaries to different parts of the world.

Twenty-five

Providence: A
Skeptic Is Convinced

Before I return to my revival record, I must dwell a
little more upon the progress of the antislavery or
abolition movement, as it was connected with my
labors not only at Oberlin, but also elsewhere. I have spoken of the state of public feeling all around us on this subject and have mentioned that even the legislature of the
state, at that time democratic, endeavored to find some pre-
text for repealing Oberlin's charter because of our antislavery sentiments.

Some of the early reports were that we intended to encourage marriage between colored and white students, even
to compel them to intermarry, and that our purpose was to
introduce a universal system of racial mixture. Early on, we
had reason to worry that a mob from a neighboring town
would come and destroy our buildings, but we had not been
here long before circumstances occurred that created a
more positive reaction in the public mind.

Oberlin College became one of the points on the Underground Railroad, as it has since been called, where escaped slaves on their way to Canada would take refuge for a
day or two, until the way was open for them to proceed.
Several cases occurred in which these fugitives were pursued by slaveholders; and loud protest was raised, not only
in this neighborhood, but also in the neighboring towns,
when they attempted to carry the slaves back into slavery.

Slavecatchers found no practical sympathy among the
people, and scenes like these soon aroused public feeling in
the surrounding towns and began to produce a reaction. This
caused the farmers and people around us to look more carefully into our aims and views, and our school soon became

known and appreciated. This has resulted in a state of confidence and good feeling between Oberlin and the surrounding region.

In the meantime, the excitement on the subject of slavery was greatly agitating the Eastern cities, as well as the West and the South. Our friend Mr. Willard Sears was braving a tempest of opposition in Boston. In order to open the way for a free discussion on that subject there, and in order to establish a pulpit that was open to the free discussion of all great questions of reform, he had purchased the Marlborough Hotel on Washington Street. He connected with it a large chapel for public worship and for reform meetings that could not be held anywhere else. This he did at great expense. In 1842, I was strongly urged to go and preach for a few months at the Marlborough Chapel. I went and preached with all my might for two months. The Spirit of the Lord was immediately poured out, and there was a general agitation among the dry bones. (See Ezekiel 37:4–7.) Inquirers from all parts of the city visited me at my lodgings almost constantly, during every day of the week, and many were obtaining hope from day to day.

At this time Elder Knapp, a well-known Baptist revivalist, was laboring in Providence under much opposition. He was invited by the Baptists in Boston to come and labor there. He therefore left Providence and came to Boston. At the same time, Mr. Josiah Chapin and many others were insisting very strongly upon my coming and holding meetings in Providence. I felt very much indebted to Mr. Chapin for what he had done for Oberlin and for me personally. It was a great trial for me to leave Boston at this time. However, after seeing Brother Knapp and informing him of the state of things, I left and went to Providence. This was a time of the great revival in Boston. It prevailed wonderfully, especially among the Baptists, and more or less throughout the city. The Baptist ministers took hold with Brother Knapp, many Congregational believers were greatly blessed, and the work was very extensive.

In the meantime, I commenced my labors in Providence. The work began almost immediately, and the interest visibly increased from day to day. There were many striking cases of conversion. After the work had gone on for some time, I observed a very venerable looking gentleman who paid very strict attention to the preaching in our meetings. My friend Mr. Chapin immediately noticed him and informed me who he was and what his religious views were. This old gentleman lived not far from the church where I was holding my meetings, on High Street. His father had been a judge of the supreme court in Massachusetts many years before. Mr. Chapin said the man had never been in the habit of attending religious meetings, and he expressed a very great interest in the man and in the fact that he had been drawn out to the meeting. I observed that this gentleman continued to come, night after night, and I could easily perceive that his mind was very much agitated and deeply interested on the question of religion.

One evening as I came to the close of my sermon, this venerable looking man rose up and asked if he might say a few words to the people. When I said yes, he spoke the following words: "My friends and neighbors, you are probably surprised to see me attend these meetings. You have known my skeptical views and that I have not been in the habit of attending religious meetings for a long time. But hearing of the state of things in this congregation, I came in here, and I wish to have my friends and neighbors know that I believe that the preaching we are hearing now is the Gospel. I have changed my mind; I now believe this is the truth and the true way of salvation. I say this so that you may understand my real motive for coming here. It is not to criticize and find fault, but to attend to the great question of salvation and to encourage others to attend to it." He said this with much emotion and then sat down.

There was a very large Sunday school room in the basement of the church. The number of inquirers had become too large, and the congregation too crowded, to call the inquirers forward as I had done in some places. I therefore requested them to go down, after the blessing was pronounced, to the lecture room below. The room was nearly as large as the whole sanctuary of the church and would seat nearly as many, aside from the balcony. The work increased and spread in every part of the city, until the number of inquirers became so great that that large room was nearly filled. From night to night, after the sermon, that room would be filled with rejoicing young converts and trembling, inquiring sinners. This state of things continued for two months. I was then completely worn out, having labored incessantly for four months—two in Boston and two in Providence. Besides, the time of year had come, or had nearly come, for the opening of our spring term in Oberlin. I therefore took my leave of Providence and started for home.

Twenty-six

Rochester in 1842:
Lawyers Are Converted

After resting a day or two in Boston, I left for home. Being very weary with labor and travel, I called on a friend in Rochester in order to take a day's rest before proceeding farther. As soon as it was known that I was in Rochester, Judge G—— called on me, and with much earnestness he requested me to stop and preach. Some of the ministers also insisted upon my stopping and preaching for them. I informed them that I was worn out and that the time had come for me to be at home. However, they were very insistent. I finally consented to stop and preach a sermon or two, and did so. But this brought upon me a more importunate invitation to remain and hold a series of meetings. I decided to remain and, though wearied, went on with the work.

I began my labors with Mr. George S. Boardman, who was pastor of what was then called the Bethel Church, or Washington Street Church. Mr. Shaw was pastor of the Second Church, also called the Brick Church. Mr. Shaw was very anxious to unite with Mr. Boardman and have the meetings at their churches alternately. But Mr. Boardman was not inclined to take this course, saying that his congregation was weak and needed the concentration of my labors at that point. I regretted this, but I could not overrule it and went on with my labors at the Washington Street Church. Soon afterward, Dr. Shaw secured the labors of Rev. Jedediah Burchard in his church and undertook an extensive effort there.

In the meantime, Judge G—— had united with other members of the bar in a written request to me to preach a course of sermons to lawyers, adapted to their ways of

234

thinking. Judge G—— was then one of the judges of the court of appeals in the state, and he was held in very high regard among the whole profession. I consented to deliver the course of lectures. The members of the bar were in a half skeptical state of mind, many of them still unconverted, although there was still a number of pious lawyers left in the city who had been converted in the revival of 1830–1831.

I began my course of lectures to lawyers by asking this question: Do we know anything? I followed up the inquiry by lecturing, evening after evening. My congregation became very select. Brother Burchard's meetings were interesting to one class of the community, and this made more room in the church where I was preaching for the lawyers who were attracted by my course of lectures. It was completely filled every night. As I proceeded in my lectures, from night to night, I observed the interest constantly deepening.

Since Judge G——'s wife was a friend of mine, I had occasion to see him frequently and was very sure that the Word was getting a strong hold of him. He remarked to me after I had delivered several lectures, "Mr. Finney, you have cleared the ground to my satisfaction thus far, but when you come to the question of the endless punishment of the wicked, you will surely fail to convince me on that question." I replied, "Wait and see, Judge." This hint made me all the more careful, when I came to that point, to discuss it with all thoroughness. The next day I met him, and he immediately remarked, "Mr. Finney, I am convinced. Your dealing with that subject was a success; nothing can be said against it." The manner in which he said this indicated that the subject had not merely convinced his intellect, but had also deeply affected his heart.

I lectured from night to night but had not yet thought that my somewhat new and select audience was prepared for me to call for any decision on the part of inquirers. But now I had arrived at a point where I thought it was time to draw the net ashore. I had been carefully laying the net around the whole mass of lawyers, hedging them in with a line of reasoning that they could not resist. I was aware that lawyers are accustomed to listening to arguments, to feeling the weight of logically presented truths, and I had no doubt that the great majority of them were thoroughly convinced as far as I had gone. Consequently, I had prepared a discourse that would bring them to the point, and if it appeared to take effect, I intended to call on them to commit themselves.

When I was in Rochester before, when his wife was converted, Judge G—— had opposed the anxious seat. I expected he would do so again. But when I came to preach this sermon in which I planned to call forward the inquirers, I observed that Judge G—— was not in the seat he had usually occupied. On looking around, I could not see him anywhere among the members of the bar or the judges. I felt concerned about this, for I had prepared myself with reference to his case. I knew his influence was great and that if he would take a decided stand, it would have a very great influence on all the legal profession in the city. However, I soon observed that he had gone into the balcony and had found a seat just at the head of the balcony stairs, where he sat wrapped in his coat. I went on with my discourse, but near the close of what I planned to say, I saw that Judge G—— had left the stairs. I felt distressed, for I concluded that he had gone home because it was cold where he sat. Hence, I thought that the sermon I had prepared in view of his case had failed to have its effect.

From the basement of the church, there was a narrow stairway into the sanctuary above, coming up just by the side of, and partly behind, the pulpit. Just as I was drawing my sermon to a close, with my heart almost sinking with the fear that I was about to fail in what I had hoped to accomplish that night, I felt someone pulling at the hem of my coat. I looked around, and there was Judge G——. He had gone down through the basement and up those narrow stairs, and had crept up the pulpit steps far enough to reach me and pull me by the coat. When I turned around to him and looked at him with great surprise, he said to me, "Mr. Finney, will you pray for me by name? I will take the anxious seat."

I had said nothing about an anxious seat at all. The congregation had seen Judge G—— as he came up the pulpit stairs, and when I announced to them what he said it produced a wonderful shock. There was a great gush of feeling in every part of the house. Many held down their heads and wept; others seemed to be engaged in earnest prayer. He moved to the front of the pulpit and knelt down immediately. The lawyers arose almost *en masse,* crowded into the aisles, and filled the open space in front, wherever they could get a place to kneel. The movement had begun without my requesting it; but I then publicly invited any who were prepared to renounce their sins, give their hearts to God, and accept Christ and His salvation to come forward, into the aisles or wherever they could, and kneel down. There was a mighty movement. We prayed, and then I dismissed the meeting.

Since I had been preaching every night and could not give up an evening to hold a meeting of inquiry, I scheduled a meeting for inquirers the next day at two o'clock in the basement of the church. When I went, I was surprised to find that the room was nearly full and that the audience was composed almost exclusively of the more prominent citizens. This meeting continued from day to day. I had an opportunity to converse freely with many of the people, and they were as teachable as children. A large number of the lawyers were converted; Judge G—— took the lead in coming out on the side of Christ.

I remained in Rochester for two months. The revival became wonderfully interesting and powerful, and it resulted in the conversion of great numbers.

All the meetings of inquiry were held for the purpose of adapting instruction to those who were in different stages of conviction. After I conversed with the people as long as I had time and strength, I often summed up what had been said and took time to answer all their questions, correct all their errors, strip them of every excuse, and bring them face to face with the great question of present, unqualified, universal acceptance of the will of God in Christ Jesus. Faith in God, and God in Christ, was ever made prominent. Inquirers were informed that this faith is not a mere intellectual assent, but is the consent or trust of the heart—a voluntary, intelligent trust in God as He is revealed in the Lord Jesus Christ.

I taught the certainty that sinners will be endlessly punished if they die in their sins. I presented the Gospel in such a way that they could have no doubt. This was, at least, my constant aim and the aim of all who gave instruction. Sinners were taught that, without the divine teaching and influence of the Holy Spirit, they never would be reconciled to God. They were informed that God required them to pray, but to pray in faith and in the spirit of repentance, and that when they asked God to forgive them they were to commit themselves unalterably to His will. They were taught that mere impenitent and unbelieving prayer is an abomination to God. But if they were truly inclined to offer acceptable prayer to God, they could do it, for nothing but their own obstinacy was in the way of their offering acceptable prayer at once.

They were never left to think that they could do their duty unless they gave their hearts to God. To repent, to believe, and to submit were the first duties to be performed; until these were performed, no outward act was doing their duty. For them to pray for a new heart while they did not give themselves up to God was to tempt God. For them to pray for forgiveness before they truly repented was to insult God. And for them to pray in unbelief was to charge God with lying, instead of doing their duty. In short, I endeavored to get sinners to renounce all sin, all excuse-making, all unbelief, all hardness of heart, and every wicked thing in their hearts and lives, here, now, and forever.

Because I was educated as a lawyer, I have always been particularly interested in the salvation of lawyers and those in the legal profession. I understood pretty well their habits of reading and thinking, and I knew that they were more certainly controlled by argument, by evidence, and by logical statements than any other class of men. Wherever I have labored, I have always found that when the Gospel was properly presented, they were the most accessible class of men. I believe that, in proportion, more lawyers have been converted than any other class. I have found that a clear presentation of the law and of the Gospel of God will convince the minds of judges, of men who are in the habit of weighing arguments on both sides. I have never seen a case in which judges attended meetings in a revival and were not convinced of the truth of the Gospel.

One of the judges of the court of appeals, living in Rochester, seemed to have chronic skepticism. He was a reader and a thinker, a man of great refinement and great intellectual honesty. His wife, having experienced religion under my ministry, was a friend of mine. I have conversed extensively with this man, and he always confessed to me that the arguments were conclusive and that his intellect was affected by the preaching and the conversation. He said to me, "Mr. Finney, your preaching always carries me right along. But while I assent to the truth of all that you say, I do not feel right; somehow my heart does not respond." It was both a grief and a pleasure to converse with him. His candor and intelligence made conversation with him on religious subjects a great pleasure; his chronic unbelief rendered it exceedingly painful. More than once I talked to him when his whole mind seemed to be agitated to its lowest depths. And yet he has never been converted.

After his wife died and his son, his only child, drowned, I wrote him a letter. I referred to a conversation I had had with him, trying to win him to a Source from which he could get consolation. He replied in all kindness, but he said that no consolation could meet a case like his. He was truly blind to all the consolation he could find in Christ. He could not imagine how he could ever accept this dispensation and be happy. He has lived in Rochester through one great revival after another; still, he has mysteriously remained in unbelief. His case illustrates the manner in which the intelligence of the legal profession can be carried by the force of truth.

Several of the lawyers who were at this time converted in Rochester gave up their profession and went into the ministry. Among them was Mr. W——, a young lawyer in Rochester who appeared at the time to be soundly converted. For some reason, with which I am not acquainted, he went to Europe and to Rome and finally became a Roman Catholic priest. For years he has labored zealously to promote revivals of religion among Roman Catholics, holding regular meetings. Mr. W—— seems to be an earnest minister of Christ, given up, heart and soul, to the salvation of Roman Catholics. How far he agrees with all their views, I cannot say. When I was in England, he came to see me, and we had just as pleasant a conversation as we would have had if we had both been Protestants. He told me he was trying to accomplish in the Roman Catholic church what I was endeavoring to accomplish in the Protestant church. Concerning his views, he said only that he was laboring among the Roman Catholics to promote revivals of religion. Many other ministers besides Mr. W—— have been the fruits of the great revivals in Rochester.

When I was laboring in that city, lawyers would come to my room, when they were on the point of submission, for conversation and for light on some point that they did not clearly understand. This fact greatly interested me. Again and again I observed that, when those points were cleared up, they were ready at once to submit. Indeed, as a general thing, lawyers take a more intelligent view of the whole plan of salvation than any other class of men to whom I have ever preached or with whom I have ever conversed.

Very many physicians have also been converted in the great revivals that I have witnessed. I think their studies incline them to skepticism or to a form of materialism. Yet they are intelligent; and if the Gospel is thoroughly set before them, stripped of the features that are embodied in hyper-Calvinism, they are easily convinced and are as readily converted as any other class of people. Their studies, in general, have not prepared them so readily to understand the moral government of God as those of the legal profession. But still I have found them open to conviction and not a difficult class of people to deal with on the great question of salvation.

I have found everywhere that the doctrines of hyper-Calvinism have been a great stumbling block, both to the church and to the world. These doctrines teach that human nature is sinful in itself, that man is totally unable to accept Christ and to obey God, and that men are condemned to eternal death for the sin of Adam and for a sinful nature. All the related dogmas of this school of thought have been the stumbling block of many believers and the ruin of sinners. Universalism and Unitarianism have also been stumbling blocks. But I have learned, again and again, that a man needs only to be thoroughly convicted of sin by the Holy Spirit to give up at once and forever, and gladly give up, all such schools of thought. If a right course is taken with skeptics, they will rejoice to find a door of mercy opened through the revelations that are made in the Scriptures.

Twenty-seven

Another Winter in Boston: A Fresh Baptism of the Holy Spirit

I n the fall of 1843, I was called again to Boston. My previous visit had been during a time of the greatest excitement on the subject of the second coming of Christ. When I arrived there in the fall of 1843, I found that that particular form of excitement had blown over, but many forms of error prevailed among the people. The first winter I labored in Boston, Dr. Beecher had said to me, "Mr. Finney, you cannot labor here as you do anywhere else. You have to pursue a different course of instruction and begin at the foundation. The Unitarians and the Universalists have destroyed the foundations, and the people are all afloat. The majority have no settled opinions; every *'Lo here! or, lo there!'* (Luke 17:21 KJV) finds an audience, and almost any conceivable form of error may get a footing."

I have since found this to be true. The majority of the people in Boston are more unsettled in their religious convictions than in any other place that I have ever labored in, notwithstanding their intelligence, for they are surely a very intelligent group on all subjects but that of religion. It is extremely difficult to make religious truths stick in their minds because the influence of Unitarian teaching has led them to call into question all the principal doctrines of the Bible. Their system is one of denials; they deny almost everything and affirm almost nothing. In such a field, error finds the ears of the people open, and the most irrational views on religious subjects come to be held by many people.

I began my labors there in the Marlborough Chapel, and I found there a very unusual state of things. A church had been formed, composed mostly of radicals, and almost all of the members held extreme views on various subjects.

They had come from orthodox churches and had united in a church of their own at Marlborough Chapel. They were good people, but I cannot say that they were a united people. Their extreme views seemed to be an element of mutual repellence among them. On the whole, however, they were a praying, earnest, Christian people. I found no particular difficulty in getting along with them, but they were not at all in a prosperous state as a church.

A young man by the name of S——, who professed to be a prophet, had risen up among them. I had many conversations with him and tried to convince him that he was wrong. I also labored with his followers, to try to make them see that he was wrong. However, I found it impossible to do anything with him or with them, until he finally committed himself on several points and predicted that certain things would happen at certain dates. One was that his father would die on a certain day. I then said to him, "Now the truthfulness of your predictions will be tested. If these things that you predict come to pass, then we will have reason to believe that you are a prophet. But if they do not come to pass, it will prove that you are deceived." This he could not deny. He had staked his reputation as a prophet on the truth of these predictions, and he awaited their fulfillment. Of course, every one of them failed, and he failed with them. And those who were his followers never regained their former influence as Christians.

During that winter in Boston, the Lord gave my own soul a very thorough overhauling and a fresh baptism of His Spirit. Each time I have labored in Boston, I have been favored with a great deal of the spirit of prayer, and this time was no exception. But that winter, in particular, my mind was exceedingly troubled on the questions of personal holiness in regard to the state of the church and its lack of power with God. The orthodox churches in Boston seemed weak, not only in their faith, but also in their power in the community. The fact that they were making little or no progress in overcoming the errors of that city greatly affected my mind.

I gave myself to a great deal of prayer. After my evening services, I would retire as early as I could. But I rose at four o'clock in the morning because I could no longer sleep, and I immediately went to my study and engaged in prayer. My mind was so deeply troubled and so absorbed in prayer that I frequently continued praying from four o'clock until the bell sounded for breakfast at eight o'clock. My days were spent, as much as I could get time, in searching the Scriptures. I read nothing else all that winter besides my Bible, and a great deal of it seemed new to me. The Lord took me from Genesis to Revelation. He led me to see the connection between things, the promises and the threatenings, the prophecies and their fulfillment. Indeed, the whole Bible seemed to be all ablaze with light—and not only light, but it seemed as if God's Word was infused with the very life of God.

While praying in this way for weeks and months, I had a great struggle to consecrate myself to God in a higher sense than I had ever before conceived as possible or had thought to be my duty. I had often before laid my whole family upon the altar of God and had left them to be dealt with according to His discretion. But this time I had a great struggle about giving up my wife to the will of God. She was in very feeble health, and it was very evident that she could not live long. I had never before seen so clearly what was implied in placing her and all that I possessed upon the altar of God. For hours I struggled on my knees to give her up unqualifiedly to the will of God, but I found myself unable to do it. I was so surprised at this that I perspired profusely with agony. I struggled and prayed until I was exhausted, and I found myself entirely unable to give her up to God's will without any objection to His doing with her just as He pleased.

This troubled me much. I wrote to my wife, telling her what a struggle I had had and the concern that I had felt at not being willing to commit her, without reserve, to the perfect will of God. Very soon after this, the thought occurred to me that, after all my laboring and preaching, my will and my heart were still not really submitted to God. The bitterness of death seemed, for a few moments, to possess me at the thought that my religion might be mere feelings. But after struggling for a few moments with this discouragement and bitterness, which I have since attributed to a fiery dart of Satan, I was enabled to fall back on the infinitely blessed and perfect will of God in a deeper sense than I had ever done before. I then told the Lord that I had such confidence in Him that I felt perfectly willing to let myself, my wife, and my family be dealt with according to His wisdom.

I then had a deeper sense than ever before of what was implied in consecration to God. I spent a long time on my knees, considering the matter and giving up everything to the will of God: the interests of the church, the progress of religion, the conversion of the world, and the salvation or damnation of my own soul, as the will of God might decide. Indeed, I went so far as to say to the Lord, with all my heart, that He might do anything He wanted to do with me or mine. I had such perfect confidence in His goodness and love as to believe that He could agree to do nothing to which I could object. I felt a kind of holy boldness in telling Him to do with me whatever seemed good to Him. I knew that He could not do anything that was not perfectly wise and good; therefore, I had the best of grounds for accepting whatever He could agree to do in respect to me and mine. I had never before known so deep and perfect a rest in the will of God.

What appeared strange to me at this time was that I could not get hold of my former hope. Nor could I recall, with any freshness, any of the former seasons of communion and divine assurance that I had experienced. I seemed to have given up my hope and rested everything on a new foundation. I gave up my hope from any past experience, to the extent that I did not know whether God intended to save me or not. Nor did I feel concerned to know. I was willing to wait and see. I told God that if I found that He kept me, worked in me by His Spirit, was preparing me for heaven, and was working holiness and eternal life in my soul, I would take it for granted that He intended to save me. On the other hand, if I found myself empty of divine strength, light, and love, I would conclude that He saw it wise and expedient to send me to hell. In either case, I would accept His will. My mind settled into a perfect stillness.

The thought that I might be lost did not distress me. Indeed, no matter what I thought throughout the rest of the day, I could not find in my mind the least fear, the least disturbing emotion. Nothing troubled me. I was neither elated nor depressed. I was neither joyful nor sorrowful. My confidence in God was perfect, my acceptance of His will was perfect, and my mind was as calm as heaven.

When evening came, the question arose in my mind, "What if God should send me to hell? What then?" I knew I would not object to it. "But can He send a person to hell who accepts His will in the sense in which you do?" This inquiry was no sooner raised in my mind than settled. I said, "No, it is impossible. Hell could be no hell to me if I accepted God's perfect will." This filled my mind with a joy that kept developing more and more for weeks and months. Indeed, for years my mind was too full of joy to feel troubled on any subject. My prayer that had been so fervent and regular for so long a period seemed to end up as, *"Your will be done"* (Matt. 6:10). It seemed as if my desires were all met. What I had been praying for, for myself, I had received in a way that I least expected. Holiness to the Lord seemed to be inscribed on all the thoughts of my mind.

I had such a strong faith that God would accomplish all His perfect will that I could not be anxious about anything. The great anxieties about which my mind had been troubled during my seasons of agonizing prayer seemed to be set aside. Thus, for a long time when I went to God to commune with Him—as I did very, very frequently—I would fall on my knees and find it impossible to ask for anything with any earnestness, except that His will might be done in earth as it is done in heaven. My prayers were swallowed up in this. I often found myself saying that I did not want anything. I was very sure that He would accomplish all His wise and good pleasure (see Philippians 2:13), and with this my soul was entirely satisfied.

I began to preach to the congregation at Marlborough Chapel in accordance with this new and enlarged experience. A considerable number of people in the church saw that my manner of preaching had changed. I presume the people were more aware than I was of the great change. Of course, my mind was too full of the subject to preach anything except a full and present salvation in the Lord Jesus Christ.

At this time, it seemed as if my soul was wedded to Christ in a sense in which I had never thought possible before. The language of the Song of Solomon became as natural to me as my breath. I thought I could understand well the state of mind Solomon was in when he wrote that book. I concluded then that he wrote it after he had been reclaimed from his great backsliding. The Lord lifted me so much above anything that I had experienced before and taught me so much of the meaning of the Bible and of Christ's power that I often found myself saying to Him, "I had not known or imagined that any such thing was true." I then realized what is meant by the saying that He *"is able to do exceedingly abundantly above all that we ask or think"* (Eph. 3:20). What He taught me about His grace was indefinitely above all that I had ever asked or thought.

The passage, *"My grace is sufficient for you"* (2 Cor. 12:9), meant so much to me then. I was amazed that I had never understood it before. I found myself exclaiming, "Wonderful! Wonderful! Wonderful!" as these revelations were made to me. I could understand what the prophet meant when he said, *"His name will be called Wonderful, Counselor, Mighty God, Everlasting Father, Prince of Peace"* (Isa. 9:6). I spent nearly the rest of the winter, until I was obliged to return home, in instructing the people in regard to the fullness that is in Christ. But I found that I preached over the heads of the majority of the people. They did not understand me. Yet there were many who did, and they were wonderfully blessed in their souls and made more progress in the divine life than they ever had before.

I labored that winter mostly for a revival of religion among Christians. The Lord prepared me to do so by the great work He had brought about in my own soul. Although I had had much of the divine life working within me, at times I could not see that I had ever before been in true communion with God. In light of what I had now been shown, all my former experiences still seemed to be sealed up and almost lost sight of.

As the great excitement of that season subsided and my mind became more calm, I saw more clearly the different steps of my Christian experience. I came to recognize that all of those steps were brought about by God, from beginning to end. Since then, I have never had those great struggles and long seasons of agonizing prayer that I had often experienced. I can now come to God with more calmness because I come with more perfect confidence. He enables me now to rest in Him and let everything sink into His perfect will with much more readiness than before the experience of that winter.

Since then I have felt a religious freedom, a religious buoyancy and delight in God and in His Word, a steadiness of faith, a Christian liberty and overflowing love, that I had only experienced occasionally before. I do not mean that such things had been rare to me before, but they were never as constant as they have been since. My bondage seemed to be entirely broken at that time, and since then I have had the freedom of a child with a loving parent. God is within me in such a sense that I can rest on Him and be quiet, lay my heart in His hand, nestle down in His perfect will, and have no worry or anxiety.

The only time that this experience was broken was in 1860, during a period of sickness. I had a season of great depression and was humbled before God. But the Lord brought me out of it and into an established peace and rest.

A few years after this season of refreshing, my wife died. This was a great affliction to me. However, I did not feel the least resistance to the will of God. I gave her up to God without any resistance whatsoever, but it was still a great sorrow. The night after she died, I was lying in my room alone, and some Christian friends were sitting up the whole night in the parlor. I had been asleep for a little while, and as I awoke, the thought of my bereavement flashed over my mind with fantastic power. My wife was gone! I would never hear her speak or see her face again! Her children were motherless! What would I do? My brain seemed to reel. I rose instantly from my bed, exclaiming, "I will go mad if I cannot rest in God!" The Lord soon calmed my mind for that night, but seasons of sorrow that were almost overwhelming would come over me at times.

One day I was on my knees, communing with God on the subject of my wife. All at once He seemed to say to me, "You loved your wife, didn't you?" "Yes," I said. "Well, did you love her for her own sake or for your sake? Did you love her or yourself? If you loved her for her own sake, why are you sad that she is with Me? Should not her happiness with Me make you rejoice instead of mourn, if you loved her for her own sake? Did you love her for My sake? If you loved her for My sake, surely you would not grieve that she is with Me. Why do you think of your loss instead of thinking of her gain? Can you be sorrowful when she is so joyful and happy?"

I can never describe the feelings that came over me after this. It produced an instantaneous change in the whole state of my mind. From that moment, sorrow on account of my loss was gone forever. I no longer thought of my wife as dead, but as alive and in the midst of the glories of heaven. My faith was, at this time, so strong and my mind so enlightened that it seemed as if I could enter into my wife's state of mind in heaven. If there is any such thing as communing with an absent spirit or with one who is in heaven, I seemed to commune with her—not that I ever supposed she was present in such a sense that I communed personally with her. It seemed as if I knew the profound, unbroken rest that she had in the perfect will of God. I could see that this was heaven, and I experienced it in my own soul. To this day, I have never lost this blessing. I can see why those in heaven are in such a state of blessedness.

My wife had died in a heavenly frame of mind. Her rest in God was so perfect that, in leaving this world, she only entered into a fuller understanding of the love and faithfulness of God. This confirmed and perfected forever her trust in God and her union with His will.

Although these are experiences in which my own soul delights to live, I have found that I cannot preach these truths. At least, I cannot preach them and be understood, except by a very small number. Of course, when preaching to sinners, I am obliged to go back to first principles. But even among mature Christians, I have never found that more than a few people appreciate and receive the views of God and Christ, and the fullness of His free salvation, in which my own soul delights. I am always obliged to come down to the level of the people in order to make them understand me, and for many years the churches have been in such a low state that they are utterly incapable of understanding and appreciating what I regard as the most precious truths of the whole Gospel.

This winter in Boston was spent mostly in preaching to professing Christians, and many of them were greatly blessed in their souls. I felt very confident that, unless the foundations could be re-laid in some sense, and unless the Christians in Boston took on a higher type of Christian living, they would never prevail against Unitarianism. What Unitarians needed was to see Christians living out the pure Gospel of Christ. They needed to hear them say, and prove what they said by their lives, that Jesus Christ was a divine Savior and was able to save them from all sin.

The churches in Boston have always seemed to be in bondage in their prayers. Indeed, I have seldom witnessed in Boston what I call the spirit of prayer. The ministers and deacons of the churches, though good men, are afraid of what the Unitarians will say if, in their efforts to promote religion, they launch out in such a way as to wake the people up.

I have labored in Boston in five powerful revivals of religion, and I am sincerely convinced that the timidity of Christians and of the churches is the greatest difficulty in overcoming Unitarianism and all the forms of error there. Knowing that they are constantly exposed to the criticisms of the Unitarians, they have become overcautious. Their faith has been depressed. And the prevalence of Unitarianism and Universalism there has kept them back from preaching and holding forth the danger of the impenitent as Jonathan Edwards presented it in *Sinners in the Hands of an Angry God.* The doctrines that are calculated to arouse men—the doctrine of endless punishment, the necessity of giving up all sin as a condition of salvation—are not held forth with the frequency and power that are indispensable to the salvation of that city.

The members of the little church at Marlborough Chapel were very desirous that I should become their pastor. I left Boston and came home with this question on my mind. Brother Sears came to visit me, to persuade me to go and take up my abode there. But when he arrived at Oberlin and consulted the brethren about the propriety of my going, they so much discouraged him that he did not present the question to me at all.

Twenty-eight

England: A Unitarian Minister Returns to the True Gospel

Having had repeated and urgent invitations to visit England and labor for the promotion of revivals in that country, I embarked with my second wife[*] in the autumn of 1849. After a stormy passage, we arrived in Southampton early in November. There we met Mr. James Harcourt, the pastor of the church in Houghton, a village situated midway between the market towns of Huntington and Saint Ives. Mr. Potto Brown, a very benevolent man, had sent Mr. Harcourt to meet us at Southampton.

Mr. Brown was a Quaker by birth and by education. He and a partner had been engaged in the milling business and belonged to a congregation of Independents in Saint Ives. They became greatly disturbed by the state of things in their neighborhood. The Established Church, as it is called in England, seemed to them to be doing very little for the salvation of souls. Other than the church schools, there were no schools for the education of the poor, and the majority of the people were greatly neglected. After much prayer and consultation with each other, they agreed to adopt measures for the education of the children in the village where they lived and in the villages around them, and to extend this influence as far as they could. They also agreed to use their means to establish worship and build up churches independent of the Establishment.

Not long after this enterprise was begun, Mr. Brown's partner died. This partner, at his death, begged Mr. Brown not to neglect the work that they had commenced, but to

---

[*]Finney's second wife was Elizabeth Ford Atkinson, from Rochester, New York. She died in 1863.

pursue it with vigor and intense focus. Mr. Brown's heart was in the work. He was a man of simple habits, and he spent little money on himself or his family. He built a chapel for public worship in the village where he resided. He then hired a man who held hyper-Calvinistic views to work there as a minister, but he labored year after year with no results that met the expectations of Mr. Brown.

Mr. Brown had frequent conversations with this minister about the lack of good results. He was paying the minister's salary and giving his money in various ways to promote religion—Sunday schools, teachers, and laborers—but few or none were converted. He laid this matter before his minister so frequently that he finally replied, "Mr. Brown, am I God, that I can convert souls? I preach the Gospel to them, and God does not convert them. Am I to blame?" Mr. Brown replied, "Whether you are God or not, the people must be converted." So this minister was dismissed, and Rev. James Harcourt was employed. Mr. Harcourt was an open-Communion Baptist, a talented man, a rousing preacher, and an earnest laborer for souls. Under his preaching, conversions began to appear, and the work went on with hope. Their little church increased in numbers and in faith. They soon extended their operations to neighboring villages, with good results. But still they did not know how to promote revivals of religion.

The children of Mr. Brown's partner, who had been left under his charge after their father had died, had grown up to be young men and women. There were three daughters and three sons, a fine family with an abundance of property, but they were all unconverted. Mr. Brown was very anxious about the salvation of these children. For the education of his own two sons, he had employed a teacher in his family. A considerable number of young men of respectable families from neighboring towns also studied with his sons. This little family school had created a strong bond of interest between Mr. Brown and these families. Mr. Harcourt's labors, for some reason, did not reach these families. He was successful among the poorer and lower classes, was zealous and devoted, and preached the Gospel. As Mr. Brown said, "He was a powerful minister of Jesus Christ." But still he wanted to reach the class of people that Mr. Brown had more particularly on his own heart. These two men frequently talked the matter over and inquired how they could reach that class and draw them to Christ. Mr. Harcourt said that he had done all that he could and that something else must be done or else this class of people would not be reached at all.

He had read my revival lectures, and he finally suggested to Mr. Brown the propriety of writing to me to see if I would come and labor with them. This led to my receiving a very earnest request from Mr. Brown to visit them. He also conversed with many other people and with some ministers, which led to my receiving various invitations to visit England.

At first these letters made little impression on me, for I did not see how I could go to England. Eventually the way seemed to open for me to leave home, at least for a season, and my wife and I went to England in 1849. I had hardly arrived in England before I began to receive multitudes of invitations to preach, for the purpose of taking up collections for different purposes: to pay the pastor's salary, to help pay for a chapel, or to raise money for the Sunday school. Had I complied with their requests, I could have done nothing else. But I declined and told them I had not come to England to get money for myself or for them. My objective was to win souls to Christ.

When we arrived in Houghton and had rested a few days, I began my labors in the village chapel. I soon found that Mr. Brown was altogether a remarkable man. Although brought up a Quaker, he was laboring, in an independent way, for the salvation of the people around him. He had wealth, and his property was constantly and rapidly increasing. The story of his life has reminded me many times of the proverb, *"There is one who scatters, yet increases more; and there is one who withholds more than is right, but it leads to poverty"* (Prov. 11:24). For religious purposes he would spend his money like a prince; and the more he spent, the more he had to spend.

While we were in Houghton, Mr. Brown threw his house open morning, noon, and evening and invited his friends, far and near, to come and pay him a visit. They came in great numbers, so that his table was surrounded at nearly every meal with various people who had been invited in so that I might have conversation with them and so that they might attend our meetings.

A revival immediately commenced and spread among the people. The children of Mr. Brown's partner were soon interested in religion and converted to Christ. The work spread among those who came from the neighboring villages. They heard and gladly received the Word. So extensive and thorough was the work among Mr. Brown's friends, whose conversion he had long been praying for, that before I left, he said that every one of them was converted.

The conversion of this large number of people, scattered over the region, made a very favorable impression. The house of worship at Houghton was small, but it was packed at every meeting, and the devotedness and zeal of Mr. Brown and his wife were most interesting and touching. There seemed to be no bounds to their hospitality. Gentlemen would come in from neighboring towns, from a distance of many miles, early enough to be there at breakfast. The young men who had been educated with his sons were invited and came; I believe every one of them was converted. Thus his greatest desires in regard to them were fulfilled, and much more was done among the masses than he had expected. The savor of this work at Houghton continued for years. Mr. Harcourt informed me that he preached in a praying atmosphere, and with a melting state of feeling around him, as long as he remained in Houghton.

I remained in Houghton only several weeks. Among those who had written, urging me to come to England, was a Mr. Roe, a Baptist minister in Birmingham. As soon as he was informed that I was in England, he came to Houghton and spent several days attending the meetings and witnessing the results.

About the middle of December, we left Houghton and went to Birmingham to labor in the congregation of Mr. Roe. Soon after our arrival, we were introduced to Rev. John Angell James, who was the principal Nonconformist minister in Birmingham. He was a good man who wielded a very extensive influence in that city, and indeed throughout England.

For the first several weeks in Birmingham, I confined my labors to Mr. Roe's congregation, and there was a powerful revival, such a movement as they had never seen. The revival swept through the congregation with great power, and a very large proportion of the impenitent were turned to Christ. Mr. Roe entered heart and soul into the work. I found him a good and true man. He was not at all prejudiced in his views, but he opened his heart to divine influence and poured out himself in labors for souls.

I soon accepted the invitations of the ministers in Birmingham to labor in their various pulpits. The congregations everywhere were crowded; a great interest was excited; and the number of people who would gather into the vestries after preaching, under an invitation for inquirers, was large. Their largest vestries would be packed with inquirers whenever a call was made to go there for instruction.

Soon I discovered that Mr. James had acquaintances in America, and some of them had written him letters, warning him against my influence. In addition, the same pressure was placed upon him from various parts of his own country. He was very frank with me and told me how the matter stood, and I was as frank with him. I said to him, "Brother James, your responsibility is great. I am aware that your influence is great. These letters show both your influence and your responsibility in regard to these labors. You are being pressured to think that I am heretical in my views. But you listen whenever I preach, and you know whether I preach the Gospel or not."

I had taken with me my two published volumes of *Systematic Theology*. I said to Mr. James, "Have you heard me preach anything that is not the Gospel?" He said, "No, nothing at all." "Well, I have my *Systematic Theology,* which I preach everywhere, and I want you to read it." He was very eager to do so. I soon began to see him at the meetings, always with a very venerable looking gentleman. They would attend the meetings together, and when I called for inquirers, they would go in and stand where they could hear all that was said. For several nights in a row, they came in this way, but Mr. James did not introduce me to the person who was with him, nor did he come near me to speak with me.

After things had gone on in this way for a week or two, Mr. James and his venerable friend called at my lodgings. He introduced me to Dr. Redford, who was one of their most prominent theologians. Mr. James said that he had more confidence in Dr. Redford's theological discernment than he had in his own, and that he had requested him to visit Birmingham, attend the meetings, and especially to unite with him in reading my *Systematic Theology.* He said they had been reading it, from day to day, and Dr. Redford would like to have some conversation with me on certain points of theology. We conversed very freely on all the questions to which Dr. Redford wished to call my attention. Afterward, Dr. Redford said very frankly, "Brother James, I see no reason for regarding Mr. Finney as unsound. He has his own way of stating theological propositions, but I cannot see that he differs from us on any essential point."

Dr. Redford remained in Birmingham for a while longer. When he went home, he took my *Systematic Theology,* with my permission. He promised he would read it carefully and then write to me his views respecting it. He was indeed a thoroughly educated theologian. I was therefore more than willing to have him criticize my theology, so that if there was anything that needed to be retracted or amended, he might point it out. I requested him to do so, thoroughly and frankly. He took it home, gave himself up to a thorough examination of it, and read the volumes patiently and critically through. I then received a letter from him, expressing his strong praise of my theological views, but saying there were a few points upon which he would like to make some inquiries. He wished me, as soon as I could get away from Birmingham, to come and preach for him.

I stayed in Birmingham about three months. There were many interesting conversions in that city, and yet the ministers were not then prepared to commit themselves heartily to the use of the necessary means to spread the revival universally over the city.

There was one case of such an interesting character that I must call attention to it. Unitarianism in England was first developed and promulgated in Birmingham. This was the home of old Dr. Priestley, who was one of the principal, if not one of the first, Unitarian ministers in England. His congregation was still in existence when I was in Birmingham. One evening before I left Birmingham, I preached on this text: *"You stiffnecked and uncircumcised in heart and ears! You always resist the Holy Spirit"* (Acts 7:51). First I dwelt on the divinity and personality of the Holy Spirit. Then I endeavored to show in how many ways, and on how many points, men resist the divine teaching. The Lord gave me liberty that night to preach a very searching discourse. My purpose was to show that, while men are pleading their dependence on the Holy Spirit, they are constantly resisting Him.

In Birmingham, as I did everywhere in England, I found that great stress was placed on the influence of the Holy Spirit. But nowhere did I find any clear distinction between a physical influence of the Spirit, exerted directly upon the soul itself, and the moral, persuasive influence that He exerts over the minds of men. Consequently, I frequently found it necessary to call people's attention to the work in which the Holy Spirit is really engaged; to explain to them the express teachings of Christ upon this subject; and thus to lead them to see that they were not to wait for a physical influence, but to give themselves up to His persuasive influence and obey His teachings. This was the objective of my discourse that particular evening.

After the sermon, a woman who had been in the meeting told me that a Unitarian minister had been present in the congregation. I remarked that my words must have sounded strange in the ears of a Unitarian. She replied that she hoped it would do him good. Not long after this, when I was laboring in London, I received a letter from this minister, giving an account of the great change that occurred in his religious experience as a result of that sermon. This letter follows:

August 16, 1850

Reverend and Dear Sir:

Upon learning that you are about to take your departure from England, I feel it would be somewhat ungrateful of me if I allow you to go without expressing the obligation I have to you for the benefit I received from a sermon of yours, preached in Steelhouse Lane, Birmingham. I think it was the last sermon you preached, and it was on resisting the Holy Spirit, but I have never been able to find the text. In order that you may understand the benefit I received from the sermon, it is necessary that I recount, briefly, my position at the time.

I was educated at one of our Nonconformist colleges for the ministry among the Independents. I entered into the ministry and continued to practice it about seven years. During that time, I gradually underwent a great change in theological views. The change was produced partly by philosophical speculations and partly by the deterioration that had taken place in my spiritual condition. I would say with deepest sorrow that my piety never recovered the tone it lost in my passage through college. I attribute all my sorrows principally to this. My speculations led me, without ever having read Dr. Williams' book on divine sovereignty and equity, to fundamentally adopt his views. The reading of his book fully perfected my system: sin is a defect arising out of the necessary defectiveness of a creature that is without the grace of God. The fall of man, therefore, expresses nothing but the inevitable original imperfection of the human race. The great end of God's moral government is to correct this imperfection by education and revelation, and to ultimately perfect man's condition. I had already, and long previously, adopted Dr. Jenkyn's views of spiritual influence.

Under the influence of such principles, sin became to me a mere misfortune that was temporarily permitted, or rather a necessary evil that was to be remedied by infinite wisdom and goodness. Eternal punishment became a cruelty, not to be thought of for one moment, in the dispensation of a good Being. And the Atonement became a perfect absurdity, founded on nonphilosophical views of sin. I became thoroughly Unitarian, and in the beginning of the year 1848, I professed my Unitarianism and became minister of a church.

The tendencies of my mind, however, were fortunately too logical for me to be able to rest in Unitarianism for very long. I pushed my conclusions to simple deism, and then found they must go still farther. For this I was not prepared. My whole soul started back in horror. I reviewed my principles. A revolution took place in my whole system of philosophy. The doctrine of responsibility was restored to me, in its strictest and most literal sense, and with it a deep consciousness of sin.

About two weeks before I heard you preach, I saw clearly that I must someday readopt the evangelical system. I had never doubted it was the system of the Bible. I became Unitarian upon purely rationalistic grounds. But now I found I must accept the Bible, or else perish in darkness. You may imagine the agonies of spirit I had to endure. On the one hand, my convictions were becoming stronger every day. The sense of sin and the need for Christ were obtaining a firmer hold over my heart, and I was in the miserable condition of withholding the truth I knew from the people who were looking up to me for instruction. On the other hand, if I declared my thoughts, my apparent fickleness would instantly have ruined my character, and I would have thrown myself, my wife, and my children upon the world's mercy. I could not make up my mind to this alternative. I had resolved to wait, to gradually prepare the people's minds for the change, and to prepare for the needs of my family during the period of transition.

In this state of mind, I heard your sermon. I felt the truth of your arguments. Your appeals came home irresistibly to my heart, and that night, on my way home, I vowed before God, come what would, I would at once consecrate myself afresh to the Savior whose blood I had so recently learned to value and whose value I had done so much to dishonor.

The result is, through the kind influence of Mr. ———, I have lately become the minister of the church in this town. The peace of mind I now enjoy does indeed surpass all understanding. I never before found such an absorbing pleasure in the work of the ministry. I enter fully into the significance of what Paul said: "If anyone is in Christ, he is a new creation." I bless God for the kind providence that brought me to hear you. Had I not heard you, my newly awakened religious life would probably have been destroyed by continued resistance to my deep convictions. My conscience would again have become hardened, and I would have died in my sins. May God in His infinite mercy and grace grant you a long life of even greater usefulness than He has already blessed you with.

Yours very truly,

——— ———

When I received this letter, I was laboring with Rev. John Campbell in London. I handed it to him to read. He read it over with obviously deep emotion and then exclaimed, "That is worth coming to England for!"

From Birmingham I went to Worcester, around the middle of March, to labor with Dr. Redford. He had read my *Systematic Theology* and had written to me about it. I had brought with me my replies to the various criticisms that had been published earlier, and these I handed to Dr. Redford. He read them through and then called on me. He said, "These replies have cleared up all the questions on which I wished to converse; therefore, I am fully satisfied that you are right." After that, he never criticized any part of my *Systematic Theology,* and he wrote the preface to the English edition, in which he commended the book to the Christian public.

Some wealthy gentlemen came to me at this time and proposed to build a movable tabernacle or house of worship—one that could be taken down and transported from place to place by train and, at slight expense, set up again with all its seats and all the furniture of a house of worship. They proposed to build it, one hundred and fifty feet square, with seats for five or six thousand people. They said if I would agree to use it and preach in it from place to place for six months, they would pay for the expense of building it. But the ministers in Worcester advised me not to do it. They thought it would be more useful for me to occupy the pulpits in the already established congregations in different parts of England than to go through England preaching in such an independent way.

As I had reason to believe the ministers generally would disapprove of a course then so novel, I declined to pledge myself to occupy it. I have since thought that I probably made a mistake, for when I became acquainted with the congregations and places of public worship of the Independent churches, I found them generally so small, so badly ventilated, so hedged in and circumscribed by the Established Church, that it has since appeared to me doubtful whether I was right. I have since believed that I could have accomplished much greater good in England by carrying, as it were, my own place of worship with me, going where God led me and providing for the gathering of the masses, irrespective of denominations. If my strength were now as it was then, I would be strongly inclined to visit England again and try an experiment of that kind.

There were many very striking conversions in Worcester, and the work was indeed interesting. Dr. Redford was greatly affected by the work there. At the annual meetings in London in May, he addressed the Congregational union of England and Wales and gave a very interesting account of this work. I attended those May meetings, being about to commence labor with Dr. John Campbell in London.

Dr. Campbell was a successor of George Whitefield, the great Methodist open-air preacher, and was pastor of the church at the Tabernacle in Finsbury, London, and also of the Tottenham Court Road Chapel. These chapels are both in London, about three miles apart. They were built for Mr. Whitefield, who occupied them for years. Dr. Campbell was also at that time editor of the British *Banner,* the *Christian Witness,* and one or two other periodicals. His voice was such that he did not preach but gave his time to the editing of those papers. He lived in the parsonage in which Whitefield had resided, and he used the same library that Whitefield had used. Whitefield's portrait hung in his study in the Tabernacle. The savor of his name was still there, yet the Spirit that had been upon him was not very apparent in the church at the time I went there. Although Dr. Campbell did not preach, he still held the pastorate, resided in the parsonage, and drew the salary. He supplied his pulpit by employing, for a few weeks at a time, the most popular ministers that could be employed, to preach to his people. I began my labors there early in May.

Twenty-nine

London: Hundreds of Inquirers Are Led to Salvation

I had accepted Dr. Campbell's invitation to supply his pulpit for a time. After the May meetings, I did all I could to promote a revival, though I said no such thing to Dr. Campbell or anyone else for several weeks. I preached a course of sermons designed to convict the people of sin as deeply and as universally as possible. From Sunday to Sunday, and from evening to evening, I saw that the Word was taking great effect.

On Sundays I preached morning and evening; I also preached on Tuesday, Wednesday, Thursday, and Friday evenings. On Monday evening, we had a general prayer meeting in the Tabernacle. At each of these meetings, I addressed the people on the subject of prayer. Our congregations were very large, and the house was always crowded on Sunday mornings and Sunday evenings.

Religion had so declined throughout London at that time that very few weekly sermons were preached. Dr. Campbell said to me once that he believed I preached to more people during the weeknights than all the rest of the ministers in London together. Dr. Campbell did not use most of his salary for himself; rather, he used it to supply his pulpit while he performed some parochial duties when he was not doing editorial work. I found Dr. Campbell to be an earnest but very belligerent man. He was always given to controversy. In this way he did a great deal of good and, occasionally, some harm.

After preaching for several weeks, I knew that it was time to call for inquirers. But Dr. Campbell, I perceived, had no such idea in his mind. Indeed, he had not sat where he could see what was going on in the congregation, as I

could from the pulpit; even if he had done so, he probably
would not have understood it. The practice in that church
was to hold a Communion service every other Sunday evening. On these occasions, they would have a short sermon,
then dismiss the congregation. Everyone would then go
home, except those who had tickets for the Communion
service, who would remain while that ordinance was celebrated.

On one particular Sunday, I said to Dr. Campbell, "You
have a Communion service tonight, and I must have a
meeting of inquiry at the same time. Have you any room,
anywhere on the premises, to which I can invite inquirers
after preaching?" He hesitated and expressed doubts
whether there were any who would attend such a meeting.
However, as I pressed the matter upon him, he replied,
"Yes, there is the nursery school room, to which you might
invite them." I inquired how many people it could accommodate. He replied, "From twenty to thirty, or perhaps
forty." "Oh," I said, "that is not half large enough. Do you
not have a larger room?" At this he expressed astonishment
and inquired if I thought that there was enough interest in
the congregation to warrant the invitation I had intended to
give. I told him there were hundreds of inquirers in the congregation. But at this he laughed and said it was impossible.

I asked him again if he had a larger room. "Why, yes,"
he said, "there is the British schoolroom. But that will hold
fifteen or sixteen hundred; of course you don't want that."
"Yes," said I, "that is the very room. Where is it?" "Oh,"
said he, "surely you will not venture to appoint a meeting
there. Not half as many would attend, I presume, as could
get into the nursery school room. Mr. Finney, remember
you are in England, and in London; you are not acquainted
with our people. You might get people to attend such a
meeting in America, but you will not get people to attend
here. Remember that our evening service is out before the
sun is down at this time of year. Do you suppose that in the
midst of London, under an invitation to those who are anxiously seeking the salvation of their souls, they will single

themselves out, right in the daytime, to attend such a meeting?" I replied to him, "Dr. Campbell, I know what the state of the people is better than you do. The Gospel is as well adapted to the English people as to the American people, and I have no fears at all that the pride of the people will prevent their responding to such a call, any more than it would the people in America."

After a good deal of discussion, Dr. Campbell reluctantly told me where the room was, but he said that I must take the responsibility on myself, that he would not share it. I replied that I expected to take the responsibility and was prepared to do so. He then gave me directions to the place, which was a little distance from the Tabernacle. The people had to pass up Cowper Street toward City Road and then turn through a narrow passage to the British school-room building.

I preached in the morning and again at six o'clock. I preached a short sermon and then called upon all who were anxious for their souls and who were then wishing to make their peace with God, to attend a meeting for instruction adapted to their state of mind. I was very specific in regard to the class of persons invited. I said, "Christians are not invited to attend this meeting. They should remain here for the Communion service. Careless sinners are not invited to this meeting. Those expected to attend are those who are not Christians but who are anxious for the salvation of their souls and want instruction given to them directly on the question of their present duty to God." This I repeated, so as not to be misunderstood. Dr. Campbell listened with great attention. Since I had restricted my appeal to a particular group of people, I presume he expected that very few, if any, would attend. But I felt entirely confident that there was a great amount of conviction in the congregation, and that hundreds were prepared to respond to such a call at once. I was perfectly confident that I was not premature in making such a call. I then dismissed the meeting, and a great part of the congregation began to leave the church.

Dr. Campbell nervously and anxiously looked out the window to see which way the congregation went. To his great astonishment, Cowper Street was perfectly crowded with people who were pressing to get into the British schoolroom. I went with the crowd and waited at the entrance, until the multitude went in. When I entered, I found the room packed. Dr. Campbell later informed me that there must have been at least fifteen or sixteen hundred present in that large room.

Near the entrance there was a platform on which the speakers stood whenever they had public meetings, which was a frequent occurrence. I soon discovered that the congregation were pressed with conviction in such a manner that great care needed to be taken to prevent an explosion of feeling. It was a very short time before Dr. Campbell came in. Observing such a crowd gathering, he was eager to be present, and consequently he hurried through his Communion services and came into the meeting of inquiry. He looked amazed at the crowd and especially at the amount of feeling manifested. I addressed them for a short time on the question of immediate duty, and I endeavored, as I always do, to make them understand that God required of them then to yield themselves entirely to His will, to ground their weapons of rebellion, to submit to Him as their rightful Sovereign, and to accept Jesus as their only Redeemer.

I had been in England long enough to feel the need to be very particular in giving instructions that would do away their idea of waiting for God's time. London is, and long has been, cursed with hyper-Calvinistic preaching. I therefore aimed my remarks at the subversion of those ideas, in which I supposed many of them had been educated. I supposed that only a few people present were members of Dr. Campbell's congregation. Indeed, he had himself told me that the congregation that he saw from day to day was new to him. Therefore, in my instructions, I tried to guard them on the one hand against hyper-Calvinism, and on the other against the low Arminianism in which I supposed many of them had been educated.

After I had laid the Gospel net thoroughly around them, I prepared to draw it ashore. As I was about to ask them to kneel down and commit themselves entirely and forever to Christ, a man cried out in the midst of the congregation, in the greatest distress of mind, that he had sinned away his day of grace. I saw that there was danger of an uproar, and I hushed it down as best I could. I called on the people to kneel down but to remain so quiet, if possible, that they could hear every word of the prayer that I was about to offer. They did keep still, although there was great sobbing and weeping in every part of the house.

I then dismissed the meeting. After this I held similar meetings, with similar results, on Sunday evenings while I remained with that congregation, which was nine months in all. The interest rose and extended so far that the inquirers could not be accommodated in that large British schoolroom. Thus, I would frequently call on those who were prepared to repent, to stand up in their places in the sanctuary itself, while we offered them to God in prayer. The aisles in the Tabernacle were so narrow and so packed that it was impossible to use the anxious seat or for people to move around in the congregation.

Frequently when I made these calls, many hundreds would arise. On some occasions, if the house seated as many as we thought, no fewer than two thousand people sometimes arose when an appeal was made. It would appear from the pulpit as if nearly the whole congregation arose. And yet I did not call upon church members, but simply upon inquirers, to stand up and commit themselves to God.

In the midst of the work, the extent of the religious interest connected with that congregation at that time became great. The dissenters, or Nonconformists, in England had been for a good while endeavoring to persuade the government to have more regard for the dissenting interests in that country. But they had always been answered in a way that implied that the dissenting interest was small compared with that of the Established Church. So much had been said on this subject that the government decided to take measures to determine the relative strength of the two parties. On a certain Saturday night, without any previous warning or notice, a message was secretly sent to every place of worship in the kingdom. The message requested that individuals be selected to stand at the doors of all the churches, chapels, and places of worship in the whole kingdom on the following Sunday morning, in order to count how many people entered houses of worship of every denomination.

Such a notice was sent to Dr. Campbell, but I did not know it until afterward. In obedience to directions, he placed men at every door of the Tabernacle, with instructions to count every person who went in during the morning service. This was done throughout Great Britain. In this way, they ascertained which party had the most worshippers on Sunday, the dissenters or the Established Church. This census proved that the dissenters were the majority. However, Dr. Campbell told me that the men stationed at the doors of the Tabernacle reported several thousands more than could fit into the church. This arose from the fact that multitudes entered the doors and, finding no place to sit or stand, would leave and give place to others.

Where they all came from, Dr. Campbell did not know, and no one could tell. But there is no reason to doubt that hundreds and thousands of them were converted. Indeed, I saw and conversed with vast numbers, and I labored in this way to the full limit of my strength.

On Saturday evening, inquirers and converts would come to the study for conversation. Great numbers came every week, and conversions multiplied. People came from every part of the city. Many people walked several miles every Sunday to attend the meetings. Soon I began to be accosted in the streets by people who knew me and had been greatly blessed in attending our meetings. Indeed, the Word of God was greatly blessed in London at that time.

One day Dr. Campbell requested me to make a few remarks to the scholars in the British schoolroom. I did so. I began by asking them what they proposed to do with their education, and I dwelt on their responsibility in that respect. I tried to show them how much good they might do, and how great a blessing their education would be to them and to the world, if they used it rightly. I also tried to show them what a great curse it would be to them and to the world if they used it selfishly. The address was short, but this point was strongly urged upon them. Dr. Campbell afterward remarked to me that many of them were at that time awakened, were led to seek the salvation of their souls, and were later admitted into the church.

The fact is, the ministers in England, as well as in America, had lost sight of the necessity of pressing present obligations on the consciences of the people. Dr. Campbell said to me, "I don't understand it. You did not say anything but what anybody else might have said just as well." "Yes," I replied, "they might have said it, but would they have said it? Would they have made as direct and pointed an appeal to the consciences of those young people as I did?" This is the difficulty. Ministers talk about sinners, but they do not make the impression that God commands sinners to repent now. Thus, they throw their ministry away.

I seldom hear a sermon that seems to have the intention of bringing sinners face to face with their present duty to God. Ministers, both in England and America, hardly seem to expect or intend to be instrumental in converting anyone by their preaching.

I was greatly troubled by the moral desolation of the vast city of London. The places of worship in the city were sufficient to accommodate only a small part of the inhabitants. But I was greatly interested in a movement that sprang up among the Episcopalians. Numbers of their ministers came in and attended our meetings. One of the rectors, a Mr. Allen, became very interested and made up his mind that he would try to promote a revival in his own parish. He went around and established twenty prayer meetings in his parish at different points. He began preaching with all his might, directly to the people. The Lord greatly blessed his labors, and before I left, he informed me that no fewer than fifteen hundred people had been converted in his parish.

Several other Episcopal ministers were greatly stirred up in their souls and began holding extended or continuous services. When I left London, there were four or five different Episcopal churches that were holding daily meetings and making efforts to promote a revival. In every instance, they were greatly blessed and refreshed.

It was ten years before I visited London again to labor, and I was told that the work had never ceased. It had been going on, enlarging its borders, and spreading in different directions. Many of the converts, the second time I visited there, were laboring in different parts of London in various ways, and with great success.

I have said that I was greatly troubled about the spiritual state of London. I was never more involved in prayer for any city or place than I was for London. Sometimes when I prayed, especially in public, it seemed as if I could not stop praying. The spirit of prayer would almost draw me out of myself in pleading for the people and for the city in general.

After I had preached for Dr. Campbell about four and a half months, I became very hoarse. My wife's health also became much affected by the climate and by our intense labors. Up to this time, she had attended and taken part only in meetings for women, and those were such a new thing in England that she had done little thus far in that way. But while we were at Dr. Campbell's, a request was made that she attend a tea meeting of poor women without education and without religion. Tea meetings are held in England to bring together people for any special purpose. The meeting was called by some of the benevolent Christian gentlemen and ladies, and my wife was urgently requested to attend it. She consented, having no thought that the gentlemen would remain in the meeting while she made her address.

However, when she got there, she found the place crowded. In addition to the women, there was a considerable number of gentlemen who were greatly interested in the results of the meeting. She waited a little, expecting that they would leave. But as they remained and expected her to take charge of the meeting, she arose and apologized for being called to speak in public, informing them that she had never been in the habit of doing so. She had then been my wife a little more than a year and had never been abroad with me to labor in revivals until we went to England. She made an address at this meeting of about three-quarters of an hour in length, and with very good results.

The poor women present seemed to be greatly moved and interested; and when she had finished speaking, some of the gentlemen present arose and expressed their great satisfaction at what they had heard. They said they had had prejudices against women speaking in public, but they could see no objection to it under such circumstances; they saw that it was obviously meant to do great good. They therefore requested her to attend other similar meetings, which she later did. When she returned from this meeting, she told me what she had done, and she said that she thought her public speaking might excite the prejudices of the people of England and perhaps do more harm than good. I feared this myself and expressed as much to her. Yet I did not advise her to keep still and not attend any more such meetings. In fact, after more consideration I encouraged it. From that time she became more and more accustomed, while we remained in England, to that kind of labor. But after we returned home, she continued to labor exclusively with women wherever we went.

Everyone acquainted with London is aware that from early in November until the following March, the city is very gloomy and has a miserable atmosphere either to breathe or to speak in. We had arrived there early in May. In September my friend Potto Brown of Houghton called on us. Seeing the state of health that we were both in, he said,

"You must go to France, or somewhere on the continent where they cannot understand your language, for there is no rest for you in England as long as you are able to speak at all." After talking the matter over, we concluded to take his advice and go to France for a little while. He handed me £50 to meet our expenses.

We went to Paris and various other places in France. We diligently avoided making any acquaintances and kept ourselves as quiet as possible. My wife recovered her full strength very rapidly. I gradually got over my hoarseness; and after an absence of about six weeks, we returned to our labors in the Tabernacle, where we continued to labor until early in the next April, when we left for home. I left England with great reluctance. But the prosperity of the college at Oberlin seemed to require that I return. We had become greatly interested in the people of England and desired very much to stay there and extend our labors.

On the day that we sailed, a multitude of people who had been interested in our labors gathered upon the wharf. A great majority of them were young converts. While the ship waited for the tide, for several hours there was a vast crowd of people in the open space around the ship, waiting to see us off. As we were pulling away from the dock, I watched the waving of handkerchiefs, until we were swept out of sight. Thus closed our first labors in England.

Thirty

Syracuse: An Example of Faith

W e arrived at Oberlin in May 1851. After the usual labors of the summer, we left in the autumn for New York City, expecting to spend the winter laboring at Rev. Dr. Thompson's church, in the old Broadway Tabernacle, as I had been invited to do. But after preaching there a short time, I found so many hindrances in the way of our work that I feared we would fail in our effort to promote a general revival. One of these hindrances was the practice of renting out the Tabernacle for public lectures. This increased the likelihood of having to cancel our evening services. I therefore left and accepted an invitation to go to Hartford and hold a series of meetings. I was invited by Rev. William W. Patton, who was then pastor of one of the Congregational churches of that city.

Very soon after I began my labors in Hartford, a powerful revival influence was manifested among the people. The work spread into all the congregations and went on very hopefully for a number of weeks. But there was one peculiarity about that work that I have never forgotten. Every Sunday that I was in that city, it stormed furiously. Such a succession of stormy Sundays I almost never witnessed. However, our meetings were fully attended, and for a place like Hartford, the work became powerful and extensive.

Those who are acquainted with Hartford know how fastidious and precise the people are in regard to all that they do. While I was in Hartford, the people were afraid of any measures other than prayer meetings, preaching meetings, and meetings for inquiry. In other words, it was out of the question to call on sinners to come forward, break away from the fear of man, and give themselves publicly to

God. Dr. Hawes, one of the Congregational pastors in Hartford, was especially afraid of any such measures. One night, while attending a meeting of inquiry in his vestry, the number of inquirers present was large. At the close I called on those who were willing to give themselves up to God, to kneel down, but only if they did it cheerfully and of their own accord. This startled Dr. Hawes. They did kneel down, and we prayed with them. Dr. Hawes remarked to me, as the inquirers rose and were dismissed, "I have always felt the necessity of some such measure but have been afraid to use it. I have always known that something was needed to bring people to act on their present convictions, but I have not had the courage to propose anything of the kind." I said to him that I had found such measures indispensable to bring sinners to the point of submission.

In this revival there was a great deal of praying. The young converts, especially, gave themselves to very much prayer. One night after the evening services, one of the young converts invited another to go home with him, and they held a season of prayer together. The Lord was with them, and the next evening they invited others, and the next evening more still, until the meeting became so large that they were obliged to divide it. The second meetings soon became too large, and those were divided. These meetings multiplied, until the young converts were almost universally in the habit of holding meetings for prayer, in different places, after the preaching service. Finally, to these meetings they invited inquirers and those who wished to be prayed for. This led to quite an organized effort among the converts for the salvation of souls.

A very interesting state of things sprang up at this time in the public schools in Hartford. Ministers had agreed that they would not visit the public schools or make any religious efforts there because it excited jealousy among the different denominations. One morning a large number of students, when they came together, were so affected that they could not study, and they asked their teacher to pray for them. He was not a Christian, so he sent for one of the pastors, informing him of the state of things and requesting him to come and hold some religious service with them. But the pastor declined, saying that there was an understanding among the pastors that they would not go to the public schools to hold any religious services.

The teacher sent for another, and another, but they all told him he must pray for the students himself. This brought a severe pressure upon him. But it resulted in his giving his own heart to God and in his taking measures for the conversion of the school. A large number of the students in the various public schools were converted at that time.

The inhabitants of Hartford are a very intelligent people; all classes of people there are educated, and there is perhaps no other city in the world where education of such a high order is so general. When the converts came to be received, about six hundred united with their churches. Dr. Hawes said to me before I left, "What will we do with these young converts? If we form them into a church by themselves, they would make admirable workers for the salvation of souls. If, however, we receive them to our churches, where we have so many elderly men and women who are always expected to take the lead in everything, their modesty will make them fall in behind these staid Christian men and women; they will live as they have lived before and be as ineffective as they have been." However, the young converts formed themselves into a kind of city missionary society and organized themselves for the purpose of making direct efforts to convert souls throughout the city.

One of the young ladies, perhaps as well-known and as much respected as any lady in the city, undertook to reclaim and, if possible, save a group of young men who belonged to prominent and wealthy families but had fallen into bad habits and moral decay and had lost the respect of the general population. The position and character of this young lady rendered it possible and proper for her to make such an effort without creating a suspicion of any impropriety on her part. She sought an opportunity to converse with this group of young men, and she brought them together for religious conversation and prayer. She was very successful in reclaiming a number of them. If I have been rightly informed, the converts of that revival were a great power for good in that city. Many of them remain there still and are very active in promoting religion.

While we were in Hartford, Mrs. Finney established prayer meetings for ladies, which were held in the vestries of the churches. These meetings were largely attended and became very interesting. The ladies were entirely united and very much in earnest, and they became a principal power, under God, in promoting His work there.

We left Hartford around the first of April and went to New York City on our way home. There I preached a few times for Rev. Henry Ward Beecher in Brooklyn. There was a growing and deepening religious influence among the people when I arrived. But I preached only a few times because my health gave way, and I was obliged to desist. We came home and went on with our labors in Oberlin as usual, with the result of a great degree of religious influence among our students and extending generally to the inhabitants of the town.

The next winter we left Oberlin and went east to accept an invitation. While we were in Hartford the previous winter, we had received a very pressing invitation to go to the city of Syracuse to labor. The minister of the Congregational church had come to Hartford to persuade me, if possible, to return with him. I could not see it my duty to go at that time, and I thought no more about it. But on our way east at this time, we met this minister in Rochester. He was not then the pastor of the Congregational church in the city of Syracuse. But he felt so much interest for them that he finally made me promise him that I would stop there and spend at least one Sunday. We did so, and we found the little church very much discouraged. Their number was small. The church was mostly composed of people of very radical views on all the great questions of reform. The Presbyterian churches, and the other churches in general, did not sympathize at all with them, and it seemed as if the Congregational church would become extinct.

I preached one Sunday, and I learned so much about the state of things that I was induced to remain another Sunday. Soon I began to perceive a movement among the dry bones. (See Ezekiel 37:4–7.) Some of the leading members of the Congregational church began to confess to each other, and to the public, of their wanderings from God and of other things that had created prejudice against them in the city. This affected the people in the town, who began to come to church. Soon their house of worship was too small to hold the people. Although I had not expected to stay more than one Sunday, I could not see my way clear to leave, and I continued from Sunday to Sunday. The interest continued to increase and to spread. The Lord removed the obstacles and brought the Christian people closer together.

The Presbyterian churches were thrown open to our meetings, and conversions were multiplied on every side. However, as in some other cases, I directed my preaching very much to the Christian people. There had been very little sympathy existing between them, and a great work was needed among the religious people before the way could be prepared outside of the churches. Thus I continued to labor in the different churches, until the Second Presbyterian Church was left without a pastor. After this we concentrated our meetings there in a great measure and remained throughout the winter.

In Syracuse Mrs. Finney established her ladies' meetings with great success. She generally held them in the lecture room of the First Presbyterian Church, a large and convenient room for such meetings. In her meetings that winter, Christians of different denominations seemed to flow together after a while, and all the difficulties that had existed among them seemed to be done away with. The Presbyterian and the Congregational churches were all without pastors while I was there. Hence, none of them opened their doors to receive the converts. This was agreeable to me, since I knew that there was great danger of jealousies springing up and marring the work if anyone began receiving converts.

As we were about to leave in the spring, I announced from the pulpit that on the next Sunday we would hold a Communion service, to which all Christians who truly loved the Lord Jesus Christ and gave evidence of it in their lives were invited. That was one of the most interesting Communion seasons I ever witnessed. The church was filled with communicants. There was a great melting in the congregation, and I think I never saw anywhere a more loving and joyful Communion of the people of God.

After I left, the churches all secured pastors. I have been informed that that revival resulted in great and permanent good. The Congregational church built a larger house of worship and has been a healthy church and congregation ever since. The Presbyterian churches and the Baptist churches were much strengthened in faith and increased in numbers.

The work was very deep there among many Christians. There is one circumstance that I have often heard Mrs. Finney relate that occurred in her meetings and is worth notice here. Her ladies' meetings were composed of the more intelligent ladies in the different churches. Many of them were quite fastidious. But there was an elderly and uneducated old woman who attended their meetings and who used to speak at every meeting, to the annoyance of the ladies. Sometimes she would get up and complain that the Lord laid it upon her to speak in the meetings, while so many educated ladies were allowed to attend and take no part. She seemed always to speak in a whining and complaining manner. This woman's behavior also annoyed and discouraged my wife. She saw that it did not interest the ladies, and it seemed to be an element of disturbance.

But after things had gone on in this way for some time, one day this same old woman arose in meeting, and a new spirit was upon her. As soon as she opened her mouth it was apparent to everybody that a great change had come over her. She had come to the meeting full of the Holy

Spirit, and she poured out her fresh experience, to the astonishment of all. The ladies were greatly interested in what the old woman said; and she went forward with an earnestness, in relating what the Lord had done for her, that carried conviction to every mind. All turned and leaned toward her to hear every word that she said. The tears began to flow, and a great movement of the Spirit seemed to be visible at once throughout the meeting. Such a remarkable change brought immense good, and the old woman became a favorite.

I found in Syracuse a Christian woman who was called Mother Austin, a woman of most remarkable faith. She was poor and entirely dependent on the charity of the people. She was an uneducated woman, but she had such faith that she secured the confidence of all who knew her. The conviction seemed to be universal among both Christians and unbelievers that Mother Austin was a saint. I do not think I ever witnessed greater faith in its simplicity than the faith this woman manifested. Many facts showed her trust in God and showed in what a remarkable manner God provided for her needs from day to day. She said to me on one occasion, "Brother Finney, it is impossible for me to suffer for any of the necessities of life, because God has said to me, *'Trust in the LORD, and do good; so shalt thou dwell in the land, and verily thou shalt be fed'* (Ps. 37:3 KJV)."

One Saturday evening a friend of hers, an impenitent man, called to see her. After conversing awhile with her, he offered her a five-dollar bill as he was leaving. She felt an inward admonition not to take it because she felt that it would be an act of self-righteousness on the part of that man, and it might do him more harm than it would do her good. She therefore declined to take it, and he went away. She had just enough wood and food in the house to last through Sunday, and that was all; she had no means of obtaining any more. But still she was not at all afraid to trust God in such circumstances, as she had done for so many years.

Syracuse: An Example of Faith

On Sunday there came a violent snowstorm. On Monday morning the snow was several feet deep, and the streets were blocked so that there was no getting out without clearing the way. She had a young son who lived with her, the two composing the whole family. They arose in the morning and found themselves snowed in on every side. They mustered enough fuel for a little fire, and soon the boy began to inquire what they would have for breakfast. She said, "I do not know, my son, but the Lord will provide." She looked out, and nobody could pass through the streets. The lad began to weep bitterly and concluded that they would freeze and starve to death. However, she set her table, believing that breakfast would come in due season. Very soon she heard a loud talking in the street and went to the window to see what it was. Several men were outside, shoveling the snow so that a horse could get through. They came up to her door; and when she opened it, she saw that they had brought her plenty of fuel and food, everything to make her comfortable for several days. It was well-known throughout the city that Mother Austin's faith was like a bank; she never suffered for lack of the necessities of life because she drew on God.

Thirty-one

Western in 1854–1855:
Young Backslider Returns to Christ

The next winter, at Christmastime, we went again to Western, in Oneida County, where I had labored in the autumn of 1825. The people were again without a minister, and we spent several weeks there in very interesting labor, with very remarkable results.

Many striking things occurred in the revival this time. There was a young man who was the son of pious parents and had long been made the subject of prayer. His parents were prominent members of the church. Indeed, his father was one of the elders of the church, and his mother was a godly, praying woman. When I began my labors there, to the great surprise and grief of his parents, and of the Christian people generally, the young man became exceedingly bitter against the preaching, the meetings, and all that was done for the promotion of the revival. He committed himself with all the strength of his will against it, and he affirmed that "neither Finney nor hell could convert him." He said many very hateful and profane things, until his parents were deeply grieved, but I am not aware that he had ever been suspected of any outward immorality.

Yet the Word of God pressed him from day to day, until he could stand it no longer. He came one morning to my room. His appearance was truly startling; I cannot describe it. I seldom ever saw a person whose mind had made such an impression on his countenance. He appeared to be almost insane, and he trembled in such a manner that when he was seated, the furniture of the room was evidently jarred by his trembling. When I took his hand, I observed that it was very cold. His lips were blue, and his whole appearance was quite alarming. The fact is, he had stood against his convictions as long as he could endure it. When he sat down, I said to him, "My dear young man, what is the matter with you?" "Oh," said he, "I have committed the unpardonable sin." I replied, "What makes you say so?" "Oh," said he, "I know that I have; I did it on purpose."

He then related this fact of himself: "Several years ago a book was put into my hands, called *The Pirate's Own Book*. I read it, and it produced a most extraordinary effect on my mind. It inspired me with a kind of terrible and infernal ambition to be the greatest pirate that ever lived. I made up my mind to be at the head of all the highway robbers, bandits, and pirates whose history was ever written. But my religious education was in my way. The teaching and prayers of my parents seemed to rise up before me, so that I could not go forward. But I had heard that it was possible to grieve the Spirit of God away, and to quench His influence so that one would feel it no more. I had also read that it was possible to sear my conscience so that it would not trouble me. After my resolution was taken, my first business was to get rid of my religious convictions, so as to be able to go on and perpetrate all manner of robberies and murders without any compunction of conscience. I therefore set myself deliberately to blaspheme the Holy Spirit." He then told me in what manner he did this and what he said to the Holy Spirit, but it was too blasphemous to repeat.

He continued: "I then felt that the Spirit of God would leave me and that my conscience would trouble me no more. After a little while I made up my mind that I would commit some crime and see how it would affect me. There was a schoolhouse across the way from our house. One evening I went out and set it on fire. I then went to my room and went to bed. Soon the fire was discovered. I arose and mingled with the crowd that gathered to put it out. But all efforts were in vain, and it burnt to the ground." To burn a building in that way was a crime punishable by imprisonment. He was aware of this. I asked him if he had gone further in the commission of crime. He replied, "No; my conscience was not at rest about it, as I had expected." I asked him if he had ever been suspected of having burnt it. He did not know that he had, but other young men had been suspected and talked about. I asked him what he proposed to do about it. He replied that he was going to the trustees to confess it, and he asked me if I would accompany him.

I went with him to one of the trustees, who lived nearby, and the young man asked me if I would tell him the facts. I did so. The trustee was a good man and a great friend of the parents of this young man. The announcement affected him deeply. The young man stood speechless before him. After conversing with the trustee for a little while, I said, "We will go and see the other trustees." The gentleman replied, "No, you need not go; I will see them myself and tell them the whole story." He assured the young man that he himself would freely forgive him; and he presumed that the other trustees and the people in the town would forgive him and not subject him or his parents to any expense about it.

I then returned to my room, and the young man went home. Still he was not at rest. As I was going to the meeting in the evening, he met me at the door and said, "I must make a public confession. Several young men have been suspected of this thing, and I want the people to know that I did it, that I had no accomplice, that nobody but God and myself knew it. Mr. Finney, will you tell the people? I will be present and say anything that may be necessary to say if anybody should ask any questions, but I do not feel as if I can open my mouth. You can tell them all about it."

When the people were assembled, I arose and related to them the facts. The family was so well-known and so much beloved in the community that the statement made a great impression. The people sobbed and wept all over the congregation. After he had made this full confession, he obtained peace. I have recently learned that he regained his hold on Christ and did not seem to backslide. He went into the army during the Rebellion and was slain at the battle of Fort Fisher.[*]

In many of the revivals I witnessed, a great number of people came to me who had committed crimes. They came to me for advice and told me the facts. In many instances, restitution, sometimes to the amount of many thousands of dollars, was made by those whose consciences troubled them.

The first winter that I spent in Boston had resulted in many such revelations. I had preached there one Sunday morning on this text: *"He who covers his sins will not prosper"* (Prov. 28:13). In the afternoon I had preached on the remainder of the verse: *"But whoever confesses and forsakes them will have mercy."* The results of those two sermons were extraordinary. For weeks afterward, men and women of almost all ages came to me for spiritual advice, disclosing to me the fact that they had committed various frauds and sins of almost every description. Some young men had defrauded their employers in business; some women had stolen watches and almost every article of female apparel. Indeed, it seemed as if the Word of the Lord had such power in that city that it uncovered a very den of wickedness. It would certainly take me hours to mention the crimes that came to my personal knowledge through the confessions of those who had perpetrated them. But in every instance, the people seemed to be thoroughly repentant and were willing to make restitution to the utmost of their ability.

But I must continue with the events at Western. The revival was of a very interesting character, and many souls were born to God. I remember the conversion of one young lady with a good deal of interest. She was teaching in the village school. I had heard that this young woman did not attend our meetings much and that she manifested

---

[*]Fort Fisher was the last major Confederate stronghold during the Civil War. The fort protected Wilmington, North Carolina, the South's last open seaport on the Atlantic coast. When it fell in January 1865, the Confederate cause was near its end.

considerable opposition to the work. In passing the school-house one day, I stepped in to speak with her. At first she appeared surprised to see me come in. I had never been introduced to her, and I would not have known her if I had not known to look for her in that place. She knew me, however, and at first appeared as if she recoiled from my presence. I took her very kindly by the hand and told her that I had dropped in to speak with her about her soul. "My child," I said, "how is it with you? Have you given your heart to God?" This I said while I held her hand. Her head fell, and she made no effort to withdraw her hand. I saw in a moment that a subduing influence came over her—such a deep and remarkable influence that I felt almost assured that she would submit to God right on the spot.

The most that I expected when I went in was to have a few words with her that I hoped might set her to thinking. I had also hoped to set a time to converse with her more. But she seemed to break down in her heart so readily that, with a few sentences quietly and softly spoken to her, she seemed to give up her opposition and to be ready to lay hold of the Lord Jesus Christ. I then asked her if I should say a few words to the students, and she said she wished I would. I did so and then asked her if I should present her and her students to God in prayer. She said she wished I would and became very deeply affected in the presence of the students. We engaged in prayer, and it was a very solemn time. From that time, the young lady seemed to be subdued and to have *"passed from death to life"* (1 John 3:14).

These two seasons of my being in Western were about thirty years apart. Another generation had come to live in that place. I found, however, a few of the old members there. But the congregation was mostly new and composed of younger people who had grown up after the first revival. The state of religion in Western has improved considerably since this last revival. The ordinances of the Gospel have been maintained, and I believe considerable progress has been made in the right direction.

In both revivals, the people in Rome heard what was occurring in Western and came in considerable numbers to attend our meetings. After a few weeks, this led to my going and spending some time in Rome.

When I was in Rome the first time, and for many years after, the church was Congregational. But a few years before I was there the last time, they had settled a Presbyterian minister, a young man, and he felt that the church ought to be Presbyterian instead of Congregational. He proposed and recommended this to the church, and he succeeded in bringing it about, to the great dissatisfaction of a large number of influential persons in the church. This created a very undesirable state of things in Rome. When I arrived there from Western, I was made aware of this very serious division of feeling in the church. Their pastor had lost the confidence and affection of a considerable number of very influential members of his church.

When I learned the state of things, I felt confident that little could be done to promote a general revival unless that difficulty could be healed. But it had been talked over so much, and the people first concerned in it had so committed themselves, that I labored in vain to bring about a reconciliation. It was not a thing to preach about, but in private conversation I tried to pluck up that root of bitterness. I found the parties did not view the facts alike. I kept preaching, however; and the Spirit of the Lord was poured out, conversions were occurring very frequently, and I trust great good was done.

But after endeavoring in vain to secure a union of feeling and effort such as God would approve, I made up my mind to leave them. I have heard since that some of the disaffected members left the church. I presume the pastor did what he deemed to be his duty in that controversy, but the consequent divisions were exceedingly painful to me, since I felt a particular interest in that church.

Thirty-two

Rochester in 1855: More Lawyers Are Converted

In the autumn of 1855, we were called again to the city of Rochester to labor for souls. At first I had no wish to go, but a messenger arrived with a pressing request, bearing the signatures of a large number of Christians and non-Christians alike. After much deliberation and prayer I consented. We commenced our labors there, and it was very soon apparent that the Spirit of God was working among the people. Some Christians in that place, and especially the brother who had sent for me, had been praying earnestly all summer for the outpouring of the Spirit there. A few souls had been wrestling with God until they felt that they were on the eve of a great revival.

When I arrived in Rochester, I was soon convinced that my going there was of God. I began preaching in the different churches. The First Presbyterian Church in that city was old-school and did not open its doors to our meeting. But the Congregational church, and the two other Presbyterian churches with their pastors, took hold of the work and entered into it with spirit and success. The Baptist churches also entered into the work at this time, and the Methodist churches labored in their own way to extend the work. We held daily noon prayer meetings, which were largely attended and in which a most excellent spirit prevailed.

Soon after I began my labors there, a request was sent to me, signed by the members of the bar and several judges—two judges of the court of appeals, and one or two judges of the supreme court who resided there—asking me to again preach a series of lectures to lawyers about the moral government of God. I complied with their request. I began the course this time by preaching on the verse, *"Commending ourselves to every man's conscience in the sight of God"* (2 Cor. 4:2). I began by remarking that this Scripture assumed that every man has a conscience. I then gave a definition of *conscience* and proceeded to show what every man's conscience truly affirms: that every man knows himself to be a sinner against God; that therefore he knows that God must condemn him as a sinner; and that every man knows that his own conscience condemns him as a sinner.

I shaped my lectures from evening to evening with the intention to convince the lawyers that, if the Bible was not true, there was no hope for them. I endeavored to show that they could not infer that God would forgive them because He was good, for His goodness itself might prevent His forgiving them. Without the Bible to throw light upon this question, it is impossible for human reason to come to the conclusion that sinners could be saved. I endeavored to show them that the Bible reveals the only rational way in which they could expect salvation.

I was aware that there were some skeptics among the lawyers. Indeed, one of them had, a few months before, declared that he would never again attend a Christian meeting, that he did not believe in the Christian religion, and that his mind was made up to pay no more respect to the institutions of Christianity. At the close of my first lecture, this lawyer told a friend, as he went home, that he had been mistaken, that he was satisfied there was more in Christianity than he had supposed, and that he did not see any way to escape the argument to which he had listened. Furthermore, he thought that he should attend all those lectures and make up his mind in view of the facts and arguments that would be presented.

I continued to show them that the Bible is the only means of salvation, until I felt that they knew their only hope was in Christ and the revelations made in the Gospel. However, I had not yet presented Christ but left them shut up under the law, condemned by their own consciences, and sentenced to eternal death. This, as I expected, effectively prepared the way for an eager reception of the blessed Gospel. When I introduced the Gospel as revealing the only possible way of salvation for sinners, they gave way, as other lawyers had done under a former course of lectures in former years. They began to break down, and a large proportion of them were converted.

A remarkable fact is that all three revivals that I have witnessed in Rochester began among the higher classes of society. This was very favorable to the general spread of the work and to the overcoming of opposition. The work in this particular revival spread and excited so much interest that it became the general topic of conversation throughout the city and the surrounding region. Merchants even arranged to have some of their clerks attend one day, and some of them the next day. The work became so widespread throughout the city that in all places, in stores and saloons, in banks, in the street, on public transportation, and everywhere, the work of salvation that was going on was the absorbing topic.

Many men who had stayed out of the former revivals bowed to Christ in this one. Some men who had been open Sabbath breakers, others who had been openly profane—indeed all classes of people, from the highest to the lowest, from the richest to the poorest—were visited by the power of this revival and were brought to Christ. I remained there throughout the winter, the revival increasing continually until the end. Rev. Dr. Anderson, president of the University, engaged in the work with great eagerness, and a large number of the students in the University were converted at that time. The pastors of the two Baptist churches took hold of the effort, and I preached several times in their churches.

Mrs. Finney was well acquainted with the people in Rochester, having lived there for many years and having witnessed the two great revivals in which I had labored before this. She took an absorbing interest in this revival and labored, as usual, with great zeal and success. Many of the ladies in Rochester exerted their utmost influence to bring all classes of people to the meetings and to Christ. Some of them would visit the stores and places of business and use all their influence to secure the attendance of the people working in these establishments. As on former occasions, I found the people of Rochester ready to receive the Word *"with all readiness, and* [to search] *the Scriptures daily to find out whether these things were so"* (Acts 17:11). Many men connected with the operations of the railroad were converted, and finally, much of the Sunday business of the railroads was suspended because of the great religious movement in the city and among those employed on the railroads.

The blessed work of grace extended and increased until it seemed as if the whole city would be converted. As in the former revivals, the work spread to the surrounding towns and villages. It has been quite remarkable that revivals in Rochester have had so great an influence upon other cities and villages far and near.

There was manifested, as there had previously been, an earnest and candid attention to the Word preached, along with a most intelligent inquiry after the truth as it really is taught in the Bible. I never preached anywhere with more pleasure than in Rochester. The people there are a highly intelligent people and have always exhibited a candor, an earnestness, and an appreciation of the truth excelling anything I have seen in any other place on so large a scale. I have labored in other cities where the people were even more highly educated than in Rochester. But in those cities, the views and habits of the people were more stereotyped; the people were more fastidious, more afraid of new things than in Rochester. In New England I have found a high degree of general education, but a timidity, a stiffness, a formality, and a stereotyped way of doing things that has rendered it impossible for the Holy Spirit to work with freedom and power.

When I was laboring in Hartford, I was visited by a minister from central New York who had witnessed the glorious revivals in that region. He attended our meetings in Hartford and observed the type and progress of the work there. I said nothing to him concerning the formality of our prayer meetings or about the timidity of the New Englanders in the use of new measures for saving souls, but he remarked to me, "Brother Finney, your hands are tied; you are hedged in by their fears and by the stereotyped way of doing everything. They have even put the Holy Spirit into a straitjacket." This was a strong statement, and to some it may appear irreverent and profane, but he intended no such thing. He was a godly, earnest, humble minister of Jesus Christ, and he expressed just what he saw and felt, and just what I saw and felt. The Holy Spirit was indeed restrained greatly in His work by the fears and the self-wisdom of the people in New England.

I do not think the people of that region can at all comprehend the restraints that they impose on the Holy Spirit in working out the salvation of souls. Nor can they appreciate the power and purity of the revivals in places where these fears, prejudices, restraints, and self-wisdom do not exist.

In an intelligent, educated community, great freedom may be given in the use of means of saving sinners, without danger of disorder. But wrong ideas of what constitutes disorder are indeed very prevalent. Most churches call anything "disorder" to which they have not been accustomed. They consider their stereotyped ways to be "God's order," and whatever differs from these is disorder and shocks their ideas of propriety. But nothing is disorder that simply meets the needs of the people. In religion, as in everything else, good sense and sound discretion will, from time to time, judiciously adapt means to ends. The measures needed will be naturally suggested to those who witness the state of things; if these are prayerfully and cautiously used, great freedom will be given to the influence of the Holy Spirit in all hearts.

Thirty-three

Boston in 1856–1858: Worldly Woman Becomes Earnest Christian

I n the fall of 1856, we accepted an invitation to labor again in Boston. We began our labors at Park Street, and the Spirit of God immediately manifested His willingness to save souls. The first sermon that I preached was directed to the searching of the church, for I always began by trying to stir up a thorough and pervading interest among Christians, to secure the reclaiming of those who were backslidden, and to search out those who were self-deceived and, if possible, bring them to Christ.

After the congregation was dismissed and the pastor was standing with me behind the pulpit, he said to me, "Brother Finney, I wish to have you understand that I need to have this preaching as much as any member of this church. I have been very much dissatisfied with my religious state for a long time. I have sent for you on my own account and for the sake of my own soul, as well as for the sake of the souls of the people." We had many lengthy and very interesting conversations. He seemed to give his heart thoroughly to God. One evening at a prayer and conference meeting, he related his experience to the people and told them that he had been converted that day.

This of course produced a very deep impression on the congregation and quite extensively on the city. Some of the pastors thought that it was injudicious for him to make a thing of that kind so public. But I did not regard it in that light. It was the best means he could use for the salvation of his people, and it was highly calculated to produce among Christians in general a very great searching of their hearts.

The work was quite extensive that winter in Boston, and many very striking cases of conversion occurred. We

labored there until spring and then thought it necessary to
return to our labors at home. But it was very obvious that
the work in Boston was by no means done, and we left with
the promise that, the Lord willing, we would return and
labor there the next winter. Accordingly, the next autumn
we returned to Boston.

In the meantime, one of the pastors of the city, who
had been in Europe the previous winter, had been writing
some articles opposing our return that were published in
the *Congregationalist*. He regarded my theology, especially
on the subject of sanctification, as unsound. This opposition
produced an effect, and we felt at once that there was discord among the Christian people. Some of the leading
members of his church, who the winter before had entered
heart and soul into the work, stood aloof and did not come
near our meetings. It was evident that his whole influence,
which was considerable at that time in the city, was against
the work. This made some of his good people very sad.

In Boston we had to struggle against a divisive influence that set interest in religion a good deal back from
where we had left it the spring before. However, the work
continued to increase steadily in the midst of these unfavorable conditions. It was evident that the Lord intended to
make a general sweep in Boston. Finally it was suggested
that a businessmen's prayer meeting should be established,
at twelve o'clock, in the chapel of the Old South Church,
which was very central for businessmen. We were guests of
a Christian friend who secured the use of the room and advertised the meeting. But whether such a meeting would
succeed in Boston at that time was considered doubtful.
However, this brother called the meeting; and to the surprise of almost everybody, the place was not only crowded,
but multitudes could not get in at all. This meeting was
continued, day after day, with wonderful results. The place
was, from the very first, too small for them, and other daily
meetings were established in other parts of the city.

Mrs. Finney held ladies' meetings daily at the large
vestry of Park Street Church. These meetings became so

crowded that the ladies would fill the room and then stand around the door on the outside, as far as they could hear on every side.

One of our daily prayer meetings was held at Park Street Church, which would be full whenever it was open for prayer. This was also the case with many other meetings in different parts of the city. The revival became too general to keep any account at all of the number of conversions or to allow for any estimate that would approximate the truth. All classes of people were inquiring everywhere. Many of the Unitarians became greatly interested and attended our meetings in large numbers.

This winter of 1857–1858 will be remembered as the time when a great revival prevailed throughout all the Northern states. A divine influence seemed to pervade the whole land. It swept over the land with such power that, for a time, it was estimated that no fewer than fifty thousand conversions occurred in a single week. This revival had some very interesting features. It was carried on to a large extent through lay influence, so much so as almost to throw the ministers into the shadows. Daily prayer meetings were established throughout the length and breadth of the Northern states. In one of our prayer meetings in Boston that winter, a gentleman arose and said, "I am from Omaha, Nebraska. On my journey east, I have found a continuous prayer meeting all the way. It is about two thousand miles from Omaha to Boston, and there seemed to be a prayer meeting about two thousand miles long."

Of course, slavery seemed to shut out the divine influence from the South. The people there were in such a state of irritation, of vexation, and of committal to the institution of slavery, which had come to be assailed on every side, that the Spirit of God seemed to be grieved away from them. There seemed to be no place found for Him in the hearts of the Southern people at that time. But it was estimated that, during this revival, no fewer than five hundred thousand souls were converted in this country.

This revival was carried on very much through the instrumentality of prayer meetings, by personal visitation and conversation, by the distribution of tracts, and by the energetic efforts of the men and women of the laity. Ministers everywhere universally sympathized with it. There was such a general confidence in the power of prayer, that the people very extensively seemed to prefer meetings for prayer to meetings for preaching. The general impression seemed to be, "We have had instruction until we are hardened; it is time for us to pray." The answers to prayer were constant and striking enough to arrest the attention of people throughout the land. It was evident that in answer to prayer, the windows of heaven were opened and the Spirit of God poured out like a flood. *The New York Tribune* at that time published several extras, filled with accounts of the progress of the revival in different parts of the United States.

I have said that there were some very striking instances of conversion in this revival in Boston. One day I received an anonymous letter from a lady, asking my advice in regard to the state of her soul. Usually I took no notice of anonymous letters. But the handwriting, together with the unmistakable earnestness and obvious talent of the writer, led me to give it unusual attention. She concluded by requesting me to answer it, direct it to Mrs. M——, and leave it with the sexton of the church where I was to preach that night, and she would get it. I was at this time preaching in different churches from evening to evening. I replied to this anonymous writer that I could not give her the advice that she sought because I was not well enough acquainted with her history or with the real state of her mind. But I would venture to call her attention to one fact, which was very apparent not only in her letter, but also in the fact of her not putting her name to it: she was a very proud woman, and she needed to thoroughly consider this fact.

I left my reply with the sexton, as she had requested, and the next morning a lady called to see me. As soon as she came in, she informed me that she was the lady who had written that anonymous letter. She had called to tell me that I was mistaken in thinking that she was proud. She said that she was far enough from that, but she was a member of the Episcopal church and did not want to disgrace her church by revealing the fact that she was not converted. I replied, "It is church pride, then, that kept you from revealing your name." This affected her so deeply that she arose and left the room. I expected to see her no more, but that evening I found her, after the preaching, among the inquirers in the vestry.

She was obviously a woman of intelligence and education, and I could see that she belonged to cultivated society. But as yet I did not know her name, for our conversation that morning had not lasted more than a minute or two before she left the room. As I observed her, I remarked to her quietly, "And you here?" "Yes," she replied, and dropped her head as if she felt deeply. I had a few words of kind conversation with her, and it passed for that evening.

In the inquiry meetings, I always urged the necessity of immediate submission to Christ and brought the inquirers face to face with that duty. I then called on those who were prepared to commit themselves unalterably to Christ, to kneel down. When I made this call at this particular meeting, this woman was among the first who made a movement to kneel. The next morning she called on me again at an early hour. She opened her mind to me and said, "I see, Mr. Finney, that I have been very proud. I have come to tell you who I am and to tell you of my history, so that you may know what to say to me."

She was the wife of a wealthy gentleman who was himself a skeptic. She had made a profession of faith but was unconverted. She was very frank in this interview and threw her mind open to instruction very earnestly. She soon expressed hope in Christ and became a very earnest Christian. She is a remarkable writer and could more accurately record my sermons, without shorthand, than any person I ever knew. She used to come and write my sermons with a rapidity and an accuracy that were quite astonishing. She sent copies of her notes to many of her friends and exerted herself to the utmost to secure the conversion of her friends in Boston and elsewhere.

With this lady I have had much correspondence. She has always shown the same earnestness in religion that she did at that time. She always has some good work in hand and is an earnest laborer for the poor and for all classes that need her instruction, her sympathy, and her help. She has passed through many mental struggles, surrounded as she is by such temptations to worldliness. But I trust that she has been and will be a useful laborer in the church of Christ.

The revival extended from Boston to Charlestown and Chelsea. In short, it spread on every side. I preached in East Boston and Charlestown, and for a considerable time in Chelsea, where the revival became very general and precious. We continued to labor in Boston that winter, until it was time for us to return to our labors at Oberlin. When we left, the work was in its full strength without any apparent abatement at all.

The church and ministry in this country had become so very extensively engaged in promoting the revival, and such was the blessing of God accompanying the exertions of laypeople as well as of ministers, that I made up my mind to return to England for another season, to see if the same influence would not pervade that country.

Thirty-four

Second Visit to England: Physician's Family Saved

W e sailed for Liverpool in December 1858. Our friend Mr. Brown came to Liverpool to meet us, to persuade us to labor in Houghton for a season before we committed ourselves to any other field. Immediately upon our arrival, I received a great number of letters from different parts of England, expressing great joy at our return and inviting us to come and labor in many different fields. However, I spent several weeks laboring in Houghton and Saint Ives, where we saw precious revivals.

At this time we found in Saint Ives a very unusual state of things. Saint Ives had never had a revival before. There was only one Independent church, the pastor of which had been there a good many years but had not succeeded in doing much as a minister. He was a mysterious sort of man. He was very fond of wine and a great opposer of total abstinence. We held our meetings in a hall that would accommodate more people, by far, than the Congregational church. I sometimes preached in the church, but it was a less desirable place to preach in than the hall, as it was a very small and incommodious church.

The revival took powerful effect there, notwithstanding the position of the minister. He stood firmly against it until the interest became so great that he left the town and was gone for several weeks. Since that time, the converts of the revival, along with my friend Mr. Brown and some of the older members of the church, have put up a fine chapel, and the religious condition of the place has been exceedingly different from what it ever had been before.

Mr. Harcourt, the former pastor at Houghton, had proved himself a very successful minister and had been called to London, to Borough Road Chapel. I found him there on my second visit to England. He had been awaiting, with anticipation, our return to England. As soon as he heard we were there, he used most strenuous efforts to secure our labors with him in London. The church over which he presided in London had been torn apart during disagreements on the subject of temperance. They had had a lovely pastor, whose heart had been almost broken by their feuds upon that subject, and he had finally left the church in utter discouragement. Their deacons had been compelled to resign, and the church was in a sad state of disorganization. Brother Harcourt informed me that unless the church could be converted, he was satisfied he never could succeed in doing much in that field.

As soon as we could leave Saint Ives, we went to London to see what could be done in Mr. Harcourt's congregation. We found them, as he had said, in so demoralized a state that it seemed questionable whether the church could ever be resuscitated and built up. However, we went to work—my wife working among the ladies of the congregation—and I began preaching and searching them to the utmost of my strength. It was very soon perceptible that the Spirit of God was poured out and that the church members were very generally in a state of great conviction. The work deepened and spread until it reached every household belonging to that congregation. All the old members of the church were so searched that they confessed to one another and settled their difficulties. Mr. Harcourt told me, before I left, that his church was entirely a new church, that the blessing of God had been universal among them, so that all their old animosities were healed, and that he had the greatest comfort in them. Indeed, the work in that church was really most wonderful.

Some years after my return to England, Mr. Harcourt came to America and paid me a visit. This was a little while after the death of my second wife. He then told me that the work had continued in his church up to that time. His people felt that if there were not conversions every week, something was entirely wrong. They were frightened if the work was not perceptibly and constantly going forward. He said they stood by him, and he felt every Sunday as if he was in the midst of a praying atmosphere. His report of the results of that revival was deeply interesting. Considering what the church had been and what it was after the revival, it is no wonder that Mr. Harcourt's heart was as full as it could be of thanksgiving to God for such a blessing.

In this place, as had been the case before at Dr. Campbell's, many Christians revealed sins that had been covered up for a long time. These cases were frequently brought to my notice by people coming to me to ask for advice. Not only did Christians come, but also many who had never made a profession of faith and who became terribly convicted of sin.

Soon after I began my labors at this time in London, Dr. Tregelles, a distinguished literary man and theologian, wrote to Dr. Campbell, calling his attention to what he regarded as a great error in my theology. Strange to tell, instead of going to my *Systematic Theology* book and seeing just what I did say, Dr. Campbell agreed with Dr. Tregelles and wrote several articles in opposition to what he supposed to be my views. Both of them strangely misunderstood my position and created a good deal of opposition to my labors in England at this time. However, I paid no attention publicly to Dr. Campbell's criticisms on the subject. He has since written me a letter, in which he claimed to subscribe fully to my views, but said that I wrote over the heads of the common people. The fact is, a great many people understood my writings better than Dr. Campbell did himself.

When I began to preach, Dr. Campbell and his colleagues were surprised that I reasoned with the people. Dr. Campbell did not approve of it and insisted that it would do no good. But the people felt otherwise. It was not uncommon for me to hear that my reasonings had convinced people of what they had always doubted, and that my preaching was logical instead of dogmatic and therefore met the needs of the people.

Before I was converted, I had felt greatly the lack of instruction and logical preaching from the pulpit. This experience always had a great influence upon my own preaching. I knew how thinking men felt when a minister took for granted the very things that needed proof. I therefore used to take great pains to meet the needs of people who were in this state of mind. I knew what my difficulties had been, and therefore I endeavored to meet the intellectual needs of my hearers.

I told Dr. Campbell this, but at first he had no faith that the people would understand me and appreciate my reasonings. But when he came to receive the converts and to converse personally with them, he confessed to me again and again his surprise that they had so well understood my reasonings. He would say, "Why, they are theologians!" He was very frank and confessed to me how erroneous his views had been upon that subject.

After I had finished my labors at Borough Road Chapel, we left London and rested a few weeks at Houghton. Such was the state of my health that I thought I must return home. But Dr. F——, an excellent Christian man living in Huntington, urged us to go to his house, finish our rest, and let him do what he could for me as a physician. We accepted his invitation and went to his house. He had a family of eight children, all unconverted. The oldest son was also a physician. He was a young man of remarkable talents, but a thorough skeptic. He had embraced Comte's philosophy and had settled down in extreme views of atheism, or I should say, of nihilism. He seemed not to believe anything. He was a very affectionate son, but his skepticism had deeply wounded his father, who had come to feel an unutterable longing for his son's conversion.

After staying at the doctor's two or three weeks, without medicine, my health became such that I began to preach again. There never had been a revival in Huntington, and they really had no concept of what a revival would be. I occupied what they called Temperance Hall, the only large hall in the town. It was immediately filled, and the

Spirit of the Lord was soon poured out upon the people. I soon found opportunity to converse with young Dr. F——. I took some long walks with him and entered fully into an investigation of his views. Finally, under God, I succeeded in bringing him to a perfect standstill. He saw that all his philosophy was in vain.

While in Huntingdon, I preached one Sunday evening on the Scripture,

> *The hail will sweep away the refuge of lies, and the waters will overflow the hiding place. Your covenant with death will be annulled, and your agreement with Sheol will not stand.*   *(Isa. 28:17-18)*

I spent my strength in searching out the refuges of lies and exposing them, and I concluded with a picture of the hailstorm and the descending torrent of rain that swept away what the hail had not demolished. The impression on the congregation was at the time very deep, and this young doctor was among them.

That night young Dr. F—— could not sleep. His father went to his room and found him in the greatest consternation and agony of mind. At length he became calm, and he *"passed from death to life"* (1 John 3:14). The prayers of the father and the mother for their children were heard. The revival went through their family and converted every one of them. It was a joyful house, one of the loveliest families that I ever had the privilege of staying with. We remained at their house while we continued our labors in Huntington.

The revival took a very general hold of the church and of Christians in that town, and it spread extensively among the unconverted. The entire religious tone of the town seemed to be altered. At that time there were two or three churches of the Establishment, one Methodist, and one Baptist in Huntington. Since then, the converts of that revival, together with Mr. Brown and his son and those Christians who were blessed in the revival, have united and built a large chapel in Huntington, as they did in Saint Ives.

Mr. Brown had pushed his work of evangelization with so much energy that, when I arrived in England the second time, I found that he had seven churches in as many different villages in his neighborhood and was employing twenty preachers, teachers, and laborers. When I first arrived in England, he was running a flouring mill, with ten pairs of millstones. The second time I was there, in addition to this, he was running a mill that he had built at Saint Ives, at an expense of £20,000, with sixteen pairs of millstones. He afterward built, at Huntington, another mill of the same capacity. God poured into Mr. Brown's treasury as fast as he poured out into the treasury of the Lord.

From Huntington we returned to London and labored for several weeks in the northeastern part of the city in several chapels occupied by a branch of the Methodist Church. One of the places of worship was in Spitalsfield. The church was originally built by the Huguenots and was a large place of worship. We had a glorious work of grace there, which continued until late in the summer.

Thirty-five

Scotland and England: Conversions Abound

While I was in London at this time, I was invited very urgently to visit Edinburgh in Scotland. About the middle of August, we left London for Edinburgh. I had been urged to go there by the Reverend Dr. Kirk of Edinburgh, who belonged to the portion of the church in Scotland called the Evangelical Union Church. Their leading theologian was a Mr. Morrison, who presided over a theological school in Glasgow. I found Dr. Kirk an earnest man and a great lover of revival work. This Evangelical Union, or E. U. Church, as they called it, had grown out of a revival effort made in Scotland at the time of the first publication of my revival lectures in that country. A considerable number of Scottish ministers and a much larger number of laypeople had been greatly stirred up and had made many successful revival efforts. But they had expended their strength very much in a controversy over the hyper-Calvinistic views maintained by the Scotch Presbyterians.

I remained in Edinburgh three months, preaching mostly in Dr. Kirk's church, which was one of the largest places of worship in Edinburgh. We had a very interesting revival in that place, and many souls were converted.

Church members were greatly blessed, and Dr. Kirk's hands were full, day and night, of labors among inquirers. But I soon found that he was surrounded by a wall of prejudice. The Presbyterian churches were strongly opposed to this E. U. branch of the church, and I found myself without many openings for labor in other churches. Dr. Kirk was at that time not only pastor, but also professor in a theological school in Glasgow. In addition, he was editor of *The Christian News,* which was published in Glasgow. Dr. Kirk insisted in this newspaper that he entirely accepted my views as he heard me preach them, and that they were the views of the E. U. Church. Thus, by insisting that my views were identical with theirs, he unintentionally shut the doors of the other pulpits against me. Undoubtedly, this kept multitudes of people from our meetings who otherwise would have come and heard me.

Mrs. Finney's labors in this place were greatly blessed. Mrs. Kirk, the wife of the pastor, was a very earnest Christian lady. The two of them established a ladies' prayer meeting that has continued to this day. The answers to prayer that were granted there were wonderful. Requests were sent from many parts of Scotland to them, to pray for various places and people. The history of that meeting has been one of uncommon encouragement. From it, similar meetings have sprung up in various parts of Scotland.

After remaining in Edinburgh three months and seeing a blessed work of grace there, we accepted an invitation to go to Aberdeen. In November we found ourselves in that city, which is near the northern extremity of Scotland. We were invited there by a Mr. Ferguson, also a minister of the E. U. Church and an intimate friend of Dr. Kirk. When we arrived, Mr. Ferguson had been very much irritated by the opposition from the Presbyterian and Congregational churches. His congregation was even more closely hedged in by prejudice than Mr. Kirk's. He was an earnest Christian man, but he had been chafed exceedingly by the opposition that had enclosed him like a wall. At first I could find no audience except with his own people. I became a good deal discouraged, and so did Brother Ferguson.

At the time of this discouragement, Mr. Davison, a Congregational minister of Bolton, in Lancashire, wrote me a very pressing letter to come and labor with him. The state of things was so discouraging in Aberdeen that I indicated that I would go. But in the meantime, the interest greatly increased in Aberdeen, and other ministers and churches began to feel the influence of what was going on there. The

Congregational minister invited me to preach in his church
for a Sunday, which I did. A Mr. Brown in one of the Presbyterian churches also invited me to preach. But at the
time, my hands were too full to accept his invitation,
though I intended to preach for him at another time. The
work in Mr. Ferguson's congregation had begun and was
getting into a very interesting state. Numbers had been
converted, and a very interesting change was evidently
coming over his congregation and over that city. But in the
meantime, I had so committed myself to go to Bolton that I
found I must go.

While I was with Mr. Ferguson in Aberdeen, I was
urged by his son, who was a pastor over one of the E. U.
churches in Glasgow, to labor with him for a season. This
had been urged upon me before I left Edinburgh. But I was
unwilling to continue my labors longer with that denomination—not because they were not good men and earnest
workers for God, but because their controversies had shut
me out from all sympathy and cooperation with the surrounding churches. I had been accustomed to working
freely with Presbyterians and Congregationalists in America, and I desired greatly to preach among the Presbyterians and Congregationalists of Scotland. But in laboring
with the E. U. churches, I found myself in a bad position.
What had been said in *The Christian News,* and the fact
that I was laboring in that denomination, led to the infer-
ence that I agreed entirely with their views, and only their
views, while in fact I did not.

I thought it was not my duty to continue any longer in
this false position. I declined, therefore, to go to Glasgow.
Although I regarded the brother who invited me as one of
the best of men, and his congregation as a godly, praying
people, there were other godly, praying people in Glasgow,
and many more of them than could be found in the E. U.
Church. I felt that in confining my labors to that denomination, I was greatly restricting my own usefulness. We therefore left Aberdeen and went to Bolton, where we arrived on
Christmas Eve, 1859.

I found Bolton to be a city of about thirty thousand inhabitants, lying a few miles from Manchester. It was in the heart of the great manufacturing district of England. In this place the work of the Lord commenced immediately. We were received as guests by Mr. J—— B——. He belonged to the Methodist denomination and was a man of sterling piety, very nonsectarian in his views and feelings. The evening after we arrived, he invited a few friends for religious conversation and prayer. Among them was a lady who had been for some time in an inquiring state of mind. She was brought up as a Quaker but had married a man who was Methodist. After we had had a little conversation, we decided to have a season of prayer. My wife knelt near this lady, and during prayer she observed that she was much affected. She had been for a long time uneasy about the state of her soul but had never been brought face to face with the question of present, instantaneous submission. As we rose from our knees, Mrs. Finney took her by the hand and beckoned to me across the room to come and speak with her.

I responded to the call of my wife, went across the room, and spoke with her. I saw in a moment that her distress of mind was profound. I therefore asked her if she wanted to talk in private. She readily complied, and we crossed the hall into another room. Then I brought her face to face with the question of instant submission and acceptance of Christ. I asked her if she would then and there renounce herself and everything else and give her heart to Christ. She replied, "I must do it sometime; I may as well do it now." We knelt down, and she submitted to God. After this, we returned to the parlor, and the scene between her and her husband was very touching. As soon as she came into the room, he saw such a change in her countenance that they spontaneously hugged each other and knelt down before the Lord.

We were hardly seated before the son of Mr. B—— came into the parlor, announcing that one of the servants was deeply moved. In a very short time, that one also gave evidence of submission to Christ. Then I learned that another was weeping in the kitchen, and I went immediately to her. After a little conversation and instruction, she, too, appeared to give her heart to God. Thus the work had begun. Mrs. B—— herself had been in a doubting and discouraged state of mind for years, and she appeared to melt down and get into a different state of mind almost immediately. The report of what the Lord was doing was soon spread abroad, and people came in daily, almost hourly, for conversation. The first week of January had been appointed as a week of prayer, as it has been since from year to year, and the different denominations agreed to hold united meetings during the week.

Our first meeting was in the chapel occupied by Mr. Davison, who had sent for me to come to Bolton. He was an Independent, or what Americans call a Congregationalist. His chapel was filled the first night. The meeting was opened by a Methodist minister, who prayed with great fervency and a liberty that plainly indicated to me that the Spirit of God was upon the congregation. I knew we would have a powerful meeting. I was invited to follow him with some remarks. I did so, and I took a little time to speak on the subject of prayer. I tried to impress upon the people that their prayers would be immediately answered if they took the stumbling blocks out of the way and offered the prayer of faith. This seemed to thrill the hearts of Christians. The people were immediately stirred up to lay hold of God for a blessing. This was a powerful meeting.

Throughout that week, the spirit of prayer seemed to be increasing, and our meetings had greater and greater power. About the third or fourth day of our meetings, the meeting was held in the chapel of Mr. Best, also a Congregational minister in Bolton. There, for the first time in that city, I called for inquirers. After addressing the congregation for some time, I called for inquirers, and Mr. Best's vestry was thronged with them. We had an impressive meeting with them, and many of them submitted to God.

In Bolton there was a hall that would accommodate more people than any of the chapels. After this week of prayer, the hall was secured for preaching. I began to preach there twice on Sundays, and four evenings in the week. Soon the interest became very widespread. The hall would be crowded every night, so that not another person could get inside the door. The Spirit of God was poured out copiously.

I then recommended that the Christians begin to canvass the whole city, to go in pairs, to visit every house, and if permitted, to pray in every house in the city. They immediately and courageously rallied to perform this work. They got great numbers of tracts, posters, and all sorts of invitations printed, and began the work of canvassing. The Congregationalists and Methodists took hold of the work with great earnestness.

The Methodists were very strong in Bolton and always have been since the day of Wesley. They have always had an able ministry and strong churches there. I found among them both ministers and laypeople who were excellent and earnest laborers for Christ. The Congregationalists also entered into the work with great spirit and energy; and while I remained there, at least, all sectarianism seemed to be buried. They gave the town a thorough canvassing, and the canvassers met once or twice a week to make their reports and to consider further arrangements for pushing the work. It was very common to see a Methodist and a Congregationalist going together from house to house with tracts, praying in every house, warning men to flee from the wrath to come, and urging them to come to Christ.

Of course, in such a state of things, the work spread rapidly among the unconverted. All classes of people—high and low, rich and poor, male and female—became interested. I was in the habit, every evening I preached, of calling on inquirers to come forward and take seats in front of the pulpit. Great numbers would come forward, pushing through the dense crowds that filled every nook and corner of the house. The hall was not only large on its ground floor, but it also had a balcony, which was always crowded. After the inquirers had come forward, we engaged in a prayer meeting, having several prayers in succession while the inquirers knelt before the Lord.

The Methodists were quite noisy and demonstrative in their prayers when sinners came forward. Their impression was that the greater the excitement, the more rapidly the work would go forward. They therefore would pound the pews and pray loudly, sometimes more than one at a time. This distracted the inquirers and prevented their becoming truly converted; although the number of inquirers was constantly increasing, conversions did not multiply as fast as I had been in the habit of seeing them, even where the number of inquirers was far fewer.

After letting things go on like this for two or three weeks, one evening after calling the inquirers forward, I suggested that we should take a different course. I told them that the inquirers needed more opportunity to think than they had when there was so much noise, and that there should not be any confusion, or anything bordering on it, if we expected them to listen and become intelligently converted. I asked them to try for a short time to follow my advice and see what the result would be. They did so, and at first I could see that they were a little in bondage when they attempted to pray, and a little discouraged because it went against their ideas of what constituted powerful meetings. However, they soon recovered from this because many more were converted from evening to evening.

The fame of this work spread abroad, and soon people began to come in large numbers from Manchester to Bolton to attend our meetings. This created a considerable excitement in Manchester and a desire to have me come there as soon as I could. However, I remained in Bolton about three months. The work became so powerful that it broke in upon all classes.

Brother B—— had an extensive cotton mill in Bolton and employed many men and women. I went with him to his mill once or twice and held meetings with his employees. The first time we went, we had a powerful meeting. No fewer than sixty were converted that evening among his own workers. These meetings were continued until nearly all his employees expressed hope in Christ. There were many striking cases of conviction and conversion at the time.

There was a case in Rochester that I have forgotten to mention but that may just as well be mentioned here. A wealthy man was converted in one of the revivals in Rochester and was greatly affected by the principle of loving your neighbor as yourself and doing to others what you would have them do to you. He had been transacting some business for a widow in a village not far from Rochester, and the business consisted in the transfer of some real estate, for which he had been paid for his services about $1500. As soon as he was converted, he thought of this case and realized that he had not done for the widow and her fatherless children what he would want another to do for his own widow and fatherless children if he were to die. He therefore went to see her and told her his thoughts. She replied that she did not see it in that light at all, that she had considered herself very much obliged to him for transacting her business in such a way as to give her all she could ask or expect. She declined, therefore, to receive the money that he offered to refund.

But still he was dissatisfied. He asked her to call in some of her most trustworthy neighbors so that the situation could be presented to them. She called in some Christian friends, men of business, and the whole matter was laid before them. These judges said that the affair was a business transaction, and it was evident that the man had transacted the business to the acceptance of the family and to their advantage. They therefore saw no reason why he should refund the money. He heard what they had to say. But before he left the town, he called on the lady again and said, "My mind is not at ease. If I were to die and leave my wife a widow and children fatherless, and a friend of mine were to transact such a piece of business for them, I would feel as if he should do it for free, since it was for a widow and fatherless children. I cannot see it any other way than this." And he laid the money on her table and left.

Another case occurs to me that illustrates the manner in which the Spirit of God will work in the minds of men when their hearts are open to His influence. Once when I was preaching, I was dwelling on the dishonesties of business, the over-reaching plans of men, and how they justify themselves in violations of the Golden Rule. Before I was through with my discourse, a gentleman arose in the middle of the sanctuary and asked me if he could propose a question. He then presented a case and asked me if that case would come under the Golden Rule. I said, "Yes, I think that it clearly would." He sat down and said no more. But I afterward learned that he went away and made restitution in the amount of $30,000.

The work went on and spread in Bolton, until one of the ministers who had been engaged in directing the movement of canvassing the town said publicly that the revival had reached every family in the city.

If we had had any place of worship large enough, we would probably have had ten thousand people in the congregation each evening. All we could do was fill the hall as full as it could be crowded, and then do whatever else we could to reach the multitudes in other places of worship.

At this place, Mrs. Finney's meetings were also largely attended. She held them, as she always did, in the daytime. Sometimes the ladies would nearly fill the hall. The Christian ladies of different denominations took hold with her and encouraged her, and great good was done through those ladies' meetings.

Both my wife and I were a good deal exhausted by these labors. But in April we went to Manchester. In Manchester the Congregational interest was greater than that of other denominations. I had not been there long, however, before I saw that there was a great lack of mutual confidence among the Christians. Frequently, to my grief, I heard expressions that indicated a lack of real heart-union in the work.

This grieved the Spirit and crippled the work. And although the Spirit of God accompanied the Word from the beginning, the work never thoroughly overcame the sectarian feeling and disagreements of the brethren so that it could spread over the city in the way it had done in Bolton. When I went to Manchester, I expected that the Methodist and Congregational brethren would work harmoniously together as they had in Bolton, but in this I found myself mistaken. Not only was there a lack of cordiality and sympathy between the Methodists and Congregationalists, but there was also a great lack of confidence and sympathy among the Congregationalists themselves. However, our meetings were very interesting, and great numbers of inquirers were found on every side. Still, what I longed to see was a general overflowing of the Spirit's influences in Manchester, as we had witnessed in Bolton. I am sure that large numbers of people were converted there, for I saw and conversed with many of them myself. But the barriers did not break down so as to give the Word of the Lord, and the Spirit of the Lord, free course among the people.

We remained in Manchester until about the first of August 1860, and then went down to Liverpool. A good number of our friends went with us and remained there overnight. On the morning of the third, we left for New York. We found that large numbers of our friends had assembled from different parts of England to bid us good-bye. We took an affectionate and touching leave of them, and we were on our way home.

Thirty-six

Revival Continues at
Oberlin College

I had had very little rest in England for a year and a half, and those who are used to sea voyages will not wonder that I did not rest much during our voyage home. Indeed, we arrived a good deal exhausted, and I was hardly able to preach at all. However, the state of things and the time of year at Oberlin were such that I could not afford to rest. There were many new students, and strangers had been moving into the town, so that there was a large number of impenitent people residing here at that time. The brethren were of the opinion that an effort must be made immediately to revive religion in the churches and to secure the conversion of the unconverted students.

During my absence in England, the congregation had become so large that the church could not comfortably contain them. After considering the matter, the people had concluded to divide and form the Second Congregational Church. The new church worshipped in the college chapel, and the First Church continued to occupy their usual place of worship. The Second Church invited me to preach part of the time to them in the college chapel. But that would hold barely more than half as many as the church, and I could not think it my duty to divide my labors and preach part of the time to one congregation and part of the time to the other. I therefore took steps immediately to secure a revival of religion, holding our meetings at the large church. The Second Church people came in and labored as best they could, but the responsibility of preaching rested almost entirely on me.

We held daily prayer meetings in the church, which were largely attended. Besides preaching twice on Sundays and holding a meeting of inquiry every Sunday evening, I also preached several evenings during the week. In addition to these labors, I was obliged to use up my strength in conversing with inquirers, who were almost constantly visiting me when I was not in the church. These labors increased in intensity and pressure from week to week. The revival became very prevalent throughout the place and seemed likely to make a clean sweep of the unconverted people in the town. But after continuing these labors for four months, during which I had very little rest day or night, I came home one Sunday afternoon and was taken with a severe chill. From that time I was confined to my bed for two or three months.

The change of preaching soon let down the tone of the revival, and gradually it ceased. The conversions grew less frequent, and from week to week, the weekday meetings gradually fell off in their attendance. By the time I was able to preach again, I found the state of religion interesting but not what one would call a revival of religion.

Before I went to England the last time, I saw that an impression seemed to be growing in Oberlin that, while classes were in session, we could not expect to have a revival. Our revivals were now expected to occur during the long vacations in the winter, whereas I had always traveled in the winter in order to labor for revival elsewhere. This was not deliberately stated by anyone, yet it was plain that that was coming to be the impression. While I was in England and was receiving urgent letters to return to America, I spoke of this impression and said that if this was going to be the prevalent idea, then Oberlin was not the place for me. I had come to Oberlin and resided here for the sake of the students, to secure their conversion and sanctification. I had remained here from year to year only because there was so great a number of them here and I had a good opportunity to work upon so many young minds in the process of education. It was principally for their salvation that I remained, but our students were gone during our long vacation.

I had frequently almost made up my mind to leave and give myself wholly to the work of an evangelist. But my health would not enable me to sustain revival labor all year round; therefore, I could do more good here in the spring, summer, and early autumn than I could anywhere else. This I myself believed to be true, and therefore I had continued to labor here during term time.

I had also been greatly afflicted by finding, when an effort was made to secure the conversion of the students during term time, that some planned excursion, amusement, or entertainment would often counteract all that we could do to secure the conversion of the students. I never supposed that this was the intention, but such was the result. I had become almost discouraged. In my replies to letters received while I was in England, I was very free in saying that, unless there could be a change, Oberlin was not my field of labor any longer.

It became increasingly difficult to secure a powerful revival during the summer term. During the summer months in Oberlin, there is a great pressure upon the people. The students are engaged in preparing for the annual meetings of their various college societies, for their examinations, and for commencement. The excitement over these preparations is unfavorable to the progress of a revival of religion. As college societies increased in number, and the class exhibitions and other interesting occasions multiplied, revivals were more and more difficult to initiate. This ought not to be.

Our fall term is properly our harvest here. It begins about the first of September, when we have a large number of new students, many of them unconverted. I have always felt that that term was the time to secure the conversion of our new students. This was secured to a very great extent the year we returned from England. The idea that while classes were in session we could not expect a revival of religion seemed to be demolished. The people took hold of the work, and we had a powerful revival.

Since then we have been much less hindered in our revival efforts in term time. Our revival efforts have taken effect among the students from year to year, because they were aimed to secure the conversion especially of the students. Our general population is a changing one, and we very frequently need a sweeping revival through the whole town to keep up a healthy tone of piety. A great number of our students learn to work in promoting revivals and are very effective in laboring for the conversion of their fellow students. The efforts of brothers and sisters in the church have been increasingly blessed from year to year. We have had a revival continually, summer and winter.

Since 1860, although continually pressed by churches in the East and the West to come and labor as an evangelist, I have not dared to comply with their requests. I have been able, by the blessing of God, to perform a good deal of labor here at Oberlin, but I have felt inadequate to the labor of attempting to secure revivals abroad.

In the winter of 1866–1867, the revival was more powerful among the inhabitants of Oberlin than it had been since 1860. However, as before, I became weak and was unable to attend any more meetings. The work went forward, however, and it continued with great interest until spring.

Thus I have brought these memoirs to the present time, January 13, 1868. Yesterday, Sunday, we had a very solemn day in the First Church. I preached about resisting the Holy Spirit. At the close of the afternoon service, I called on all Christians who were willing to commit themselves against all resistance offered to the teachings of the Holy Spirit, to rise up and unite with us in prayer. Nearly all the Christians rose up without hesitation. I then called on those who were not converted to rise up and take the same stand. Nearly every person in the church stood up under these calls. We then had a very solemn season of prayer and dismissed the meeting.

Conclusion

C harles Finney remained pastor of the First Church in Oberlin until he resigned in 1872. However, he still retained his connection with the seminary and completed his last course of lectures in July 1875, only a few days before his death. He preached as his strength permitted; and during the last month of his life, he preached one Sunday morning in the First Church, and another in the Second.

Notwithstanding the abundant and exhausting labors of his long public life, the burden of years seemed to rest lightly upon him. He still stood as tall as a young man, retained his faculties to a remarkable degree, and exhibited the quickness of thought, feeling, and imagination that always characterized him. His life and character perhaps never seemed richer than in these closing years and months. His public labors were of course very limited, but the quiet power of his life was felt as a benediction upon the community that he had guided, molded, and blessed during forty years.

His last day on earth was a quiet Sunday, which he enjoyed in the midst of his family, taking a walk with his wife* at sunset to listen to the music at the opening of the evening service in the church nearby. When he went to bed that night, he was seized with pains that seemed to indicate some heart trouble, and after a few hours of suffering he died on August 16, 1875, two weeks before his eighty-third birthday.

---

*Finney's third wife was Rebecca Allen Rayl, who had been an assistant principal of the ladies' department at Oberlin College.

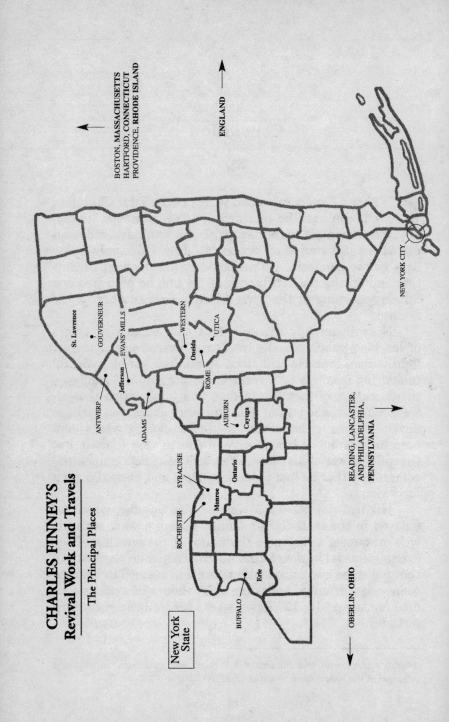

**CHARLES FINNEY'S
Revival Work and Travels**

The Principal Places

New York State

BOSTON, MASSACHUSETTS
HARTFORD, CONNECTICUT
PROVIDENCE, RHODE ISLAND

ENGLAND

St. Lawrence

GOUVERNEUR

EVANS' MILLS

WESTERN

UTICA

Jefferson

Oneida

ROME

ANTWERP

ADAMS

AUBURN

Cayuga

SYRACUSE

Ontario

Monroe

ROCHESTER

Erie

BUFFALO

NEW YORK CITY

READING, LANCASTER,
AND PHILADELPHIA,
PENNSYLVANIA

OBERLIN, OHIO

Albania

the Bradt Travel Guide

Gillian Gloyer

edition
6

www.bradtguides.com

Bradt Travel Guides Ltd, UK
The Globe Pequot Press Inc, USA

SERBIA

REPUBLIC OF MACEDONIA

KOSOVO/A

Komani ferry: one of the world's great boat trips pages 168–9

Kruja: fortress of Albania's national hero, Skanderbeg pages 98–102

Prizreni

Gjakova

Gjakova

Debar

Struga

Shishtaveci

Kukësi

Kruma

Korabi 2753m

Peshkopia

Black Drin

Bulqiza

Shebenik–Jabllanica Nat Pk

Lura

Lura Nat Pk

Tropoja

Gashi Strict Nature Reserve

Fierza

Lake Fierza

Valbona Valley Nat Pk

Bajram Curri

Valbona

Oroshi

Fushë-Arrëzi

Lake Komani

Puka

Rrësheni

Mat

Mt Dajti Nat Pk

Dajti 1613

Tunnel

Vermoshi

Gucia

Jezerca 2693m

Thethi Nat Pk

Thethi

Komani

Rubiku

Fani

Milloti

Qafa-Shtama Nat Pk

Burrelli

Mulleti

Lepusha

Boga

Kiri

Bushati

Ulza

Kruja

Petrela

Lake Shkodra

Razma

Kopliku

Mesi Bridge

Shkodra

Drini

Lezha

Shëngjini

Fushë-Kuqe

Cape Rodoni

Preza

Airport

Vora

TIRANA

Podgorica

Buna

Velipoja

Durrësi

Ulqini, Ulcini

MONTENEGRO

Thethi: a taste of traditional highland life, superb for hiking pages 211–18

Shkodra: the cultural capital of northern Albania pages 187–203

Adriatic Sea

Tirana: Albania's capital city since 1920, an essential stop for museums and nightlife pages 59–86

Durrësi: Roman remains, beaches and seafood pages 87–98

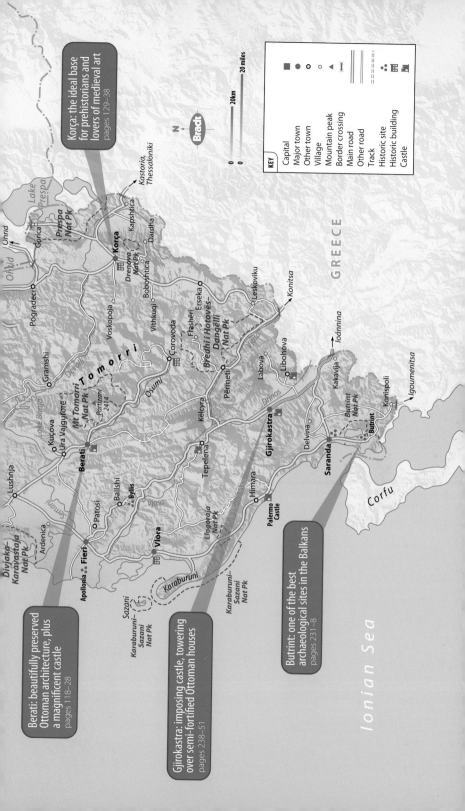

Korça: the ideal base for prehistorians and lovers of medieval art
pages 129–38

Berati: beautifully preserved Ottoman architecture, plus a magnificent castle
pages 118–28

Gjirokastra: imposing castle, towering over semi-fortified Ottoman houses
pages 238–51

Butrint: one of the best archaeological sites in the Balkans
pages 231–8

KEY

■	Capital
●	Major town
○	Other town
○	Village
▲	Mountain peak
⌇	Border crossing
‖‖	Main road
	Other road
┄┄┄	Track
⁘	Historic site
⌂	Historic building
⌘	Castle

20km

20 miles

N

Bradt

GREECE

Ionian Sea

Corfu

Lake Prespa
Ohrid
Lake Ohrid

Prespa Nat Pk

Gorica
Kapshtica
Korça
Dardha
Kastoria, Thessaloniki
Drenova Nat Pk
Boboshtica
Vithkuqi

Pogradeci

Voskopoja

Corovoda
Flasheri
Erseka
Leskoviku
Konitsa

Gramshi

Devoli

T o m o r r i

Mt Tomorri Nat Pk
Partizani 2414

Bredhi i Hotovës-Dangëlli Nat Pk

Permeti

Ura Vajgurore
Kuçova

Lake Banja

Osumi

Kelcyra

Labova
Libohova
Ioannina
Kakavija

Lushnja

Berati

Ballshi
Byllis

Tepelena

Patosi

Vjosa

Drinos

Gjirokastra

Delvina
Saranda
Butrint Nat Pk
Butrint
Konispoli
Igoumenitsa

Ardenica

Divjaka-Karavastaja Nat Pk

Apollonia Fieri

Vlora

Himara

Palermo Castle

Llogoraja Nat Pk

Karaburuni

Sazani

Karaburuni-Sazani Nat Pk

Vjosa

Seman

Albania
Don't
miss...

Communist Heritage
The Unknown Partisan advances
on the enemy, above a plaque
commemorating the Battle for the
Liberation of Tirana (PF/A)
pages 79–83

Gjirokastra
The Skëndulaj family of Gjirokastra
has used this room for betrothal
ceremonies since the 18th century
(DD) page 248

Thethi
The 'lock-in tower'
in Thethi was used
during negotiations
to resolve blood-
feuds (GG)
pages 211–14

Orthodox frescoes
The beautifully restored
frescoes in Shelcani were
painted in 1554 by the
great Albanian icon-
painter Onufri (DD)
pages 116–17

Butrint
The theatre at Butrint,
still used for drama
festivals today, is as it
was in the 2nd century BC
(V/S) pages 233–4

Albania in colour

above   Tirana's central square, pedestrianised in 2017, is the ideal place to start exploring the city (AS/S) pages 72–3

left   The Mosque of Et'hem Bey dates from the 18th century and is one of the best-preserved old buildings in the capital, with frescoes inside and out (DD) page 73

below   Warriors, intellectuals and workers rally around Mother Albania in the 1981 mosaic above the National Historical Museum (JMTP/S) pages 73–4

right   The imposing statue called 'Mother Albania' looks down over Tirana from the Martyrs' Cemetery (O/S) pages 82–3

below left   The Tanners' Bridge is one of the few remnants of Tirana's Ottoman past (JG/S) page 77

below right   Tirana is full of surprises; this Bektashi shrine, the Tyrbe of Kapllan Pasha, nestles below a modern business hotel (GG) page 77

above   Saranda's little harbour, with Lëkurësi castle in the background (SS) pages 230–1

left   The azure Valbona River is renowned for its dramatic gorges and spectacular waterfalls (A/D) pages 171–4

below   The boat-trip along Lake Komani is a highlight of any visit to northern Albania (PW/S) page 168

AUTHOR

Gillian Gloyer studied ancient languages at Wadham College, Oxford. After university, she spent most of her professional career overseas, working in Spain, Chile, Belgium and Bosnia before finding herself, slightly by accident, in Albania. She lived in Tirana for four years, directing a long-term training programme with political parties. Her training schedule took her all over the country and gave her the chance to discover Albania's astonishingly rich history and culture, then almost unknown outside the country. She studied the language and speaks it well.

Gillian is now based in Edinburgh, but she visits Albania at least once a year, for both work and pleasure. She has led tour groups to the country for several UK-based tour operators. She is a keen hillwalker and enjoys hiking in Albania's wildernesses.

CONTRIBUTORS

Malcolm Barrès-Baker is a military historian. He has visited Albania several times.

Catherine Bohne is a naturalist. She lives in Tropoja, in the Albanian highlands.

AUTHOR'S STORY

I first tried to visit Albania in 1982, when it was one of the world's most closed countries. Needless to say, this early attempt was a resounding failure; it was not until 1998 that Albania and I became acquainted. The four years that I went on to spend there were professionally rewarding and politically exciting, but – more to the point – gave me the opportunity to travel to more parts of the country than most Albanians ever do. As I was getting ready to leave, in the spring of 2002, a couple of Albanian friends suggested that my knowledge of their country made me the ideal person to write a travel guide to it.

The seed was sown. Back in Scotland, I contacted Bradt Travel Guides, who, fortuitously, were already thinking of commissioning a guide to Albania. Bradt had published earlier guides, in 1989 and 1995, but since then the country had changed beyond recognition and they realised that a completely new book was called for. I knew nothing about writing travel guides, but I thought I knew a lot about Albania. Unfortunately, much of what I knew tended to be of little practical use to the traveller – the political affiliation of the mayor, for example, or how many women were members of the local election commission – and I swiftly discovered that the project was going to require quite a lot more work than I had anticipated. It was fortunate that Bradt's editorial staff were such skilled hand-holders, coaxing out of me what was needed without plunging me into total despair.

For most visitors, the greatest revelation about Albania is the hospitality and kindness of the Albanian people. They won my heart long ago; having to update this book is nothing more than an excuse for me to go back to the country again and again.

The closest I've been to Albania was gazing at its misty blue mountains across the narrow stretch of sea that separates it from Corfu. It seemed as remote and mysterious as any country in Europe – as indeed it was in the 1960s, gripped by communism's iron fist and inaccessible to tourists. Our first guide to Albania was an illustrated account of a tightly controlled trip under the communist regime in 1989. But, since then, tourism in Albania has evolved dramatically as more and more 'ordinary' people visit what is still nevertheless one of Europe's lesser-known countries. Gillian Gloyer continues to change our perceptions with her thorough and reassuring book.

Sixth edition published March 2018
First published 2004

Bradt Travel Guides Ltd
IDC House, The Vale, Chalfont St Peter, Bucks SL9 9RZ, England
www.bradtguides.com
Print edition published in the USA by The Globe Pequot Press Inc,
PO Box 480, Guilford, Connecticut 06437-0480

Text copyright © 2018 Gillian Gloyer
Maps copyright © 2018 Bradt Travel Guides Ltd. Includes map data © OpenStreetMap contributors
Photographs copyright © 2018 Individual photographers (see below)
Project Manager: Susannah Lord
Cover research: Pepi Bluck, Perfect Picture

ISBN: 978 1 78477 078 5 (print)
e-ISBN: 978 1 78477 547 6 (e-pub)
e-ISBN: 978 1 78477 447 9 (mobi)

British Library Cataloguing in Publication Data
A catalogue record for this book is available from the British Library

Photographs Alamy Stock Photo: Peter Forsberg (PF/A), Olena Kachmar (OK/A); AWL images: Walter Bibikow (WB/AWL); Derek Drescher (DD); Dreamstime.com: Altinosmanaj (A/D), milosk50 (m50/D); Gillian Gloyer (GG); Alma Lahe (AL); Shutterstock.com: Dritan Zaimi Albania (DZA/S), Justinas Galinis (JG/S), Itinerant Lens (IL/S), JM Travel Photography (JMTP/S), Pargovski Jove (PJ/S), YingHui Liu (YHL/S), MehmetO (MO/S), milosk50 (m50/S), ollirg (o/S), Ppictures (Pp/S), Daniel Reiner (DR/S), Elzbieta Sekowska (ES/S), Alla Simacheva (AS/S), VVlasovs (V/S), Przemyslaw Wasilewski (PW/S); SuperStock (SS)
Front cover Berati (OK/A)
Back cover Saranda cove (GG), Thethi valley (SS)
Title page Inside dome of Et'hem Bey mosque, Tirana (YHL/S), Orthodox Cathedral, Korça (IL/S), Sheep herd, Boga (MO/S)

Maps David McCutcheon FBCart.S; Base mapping, modified by Bradt Travel Guides, provided by ITMB Publishing Ltd *(www.itmb.com)* 2018

Typeset by Dataworks, and Ian Spick, Bradt Travel Guides Ltd
Production managed by Jellyfish Print Solutions; printed in India
Digital conversion by www.dataworks.co.in

Acknowledgements

Many people have helped in the preparation of this book from the earliest days of the project. Alban, Elvis and bison-grass vodka are responsible for the original idea. Rather than again listing everyone who contributed to previous editions, I thank them all collectively. I am grateful to everyone at Bradt Travel Guides, past and present, who were far-sighted enough to undertake the first edition; I would probably have given up halfway through, had it not been for the encouragement of Hilary Bradt and Tricia Hayne.

Albania is an exceptionally difficult country for which to obtain accurate maps. The Albanian Military Geographical Institute (IGUS) kindly gave permission to use its town plans and maps. Some of these have been updated for this edition using w openstreetmap.org. Mimoza Hysaj, Egda Rapo and Gjorgj Kasarosi drew the maps which served as the basis for the town plans of Durrësi, Himara and Shkodra, respectively. Ylli Asllani, Arben Hoxha, Daniel Lee and Gjergj Mano provided source maps for Gjirokastra, Korça, Përmeti and Saranda, respectively.

For this sixth edition, I am grateful once again to my friends Kristina Fidhi in Gjirokastra, Ndriçim Mlika and Ols Kabashi in Shkodra, Catherine Bohne in Tropoja, Gjon Pjetri in Mirdita, Destan Spahiu in Kukësi, Alma Lahe and Guri Daco in Tirana and Gjergj Mano in Saranda, who provided not only their local knowledge but also their always excellent company. Ilir Neziri's advice and logistical support in Mati was invaluable; Klodian Pandelejmoni taught me more than I thought possible about Orthodox iconography and church architecture. Finally, Charlie Nuytens has again been invaluable with his advice on campsites and other aspects of caravanning in Albania.

I always appreciate input from readers. My thanks to all those who took the trouble to write.

FOLLOW BRADT

For the latest news, special offers and competitions, subscribe to the Bradt newsletter via the website w bradtguides.com and follow Bradt on:

- ⓕ BradtTravelGuides
- 🐦 @BradtGuides
- 📷 @bradtguides
- 𝓅 bradtguides

Contents

LIST OF MAPS

HOW TO USE THE MAPS IN THIS GUIDE

KEYS AND SYMBOLS Maps include alphabetical keys covering the locations of those places to stay, eat or drink that are featured in the book. Note that regional maps may not show all hotels and restaurants in the area: establishments may be located in towns shown on the map.

GRIDS AND GRID REFERENCES The maps of Tirana use grid lines to allow easy location of sites. Map grid references are listed in square brackets after the name of the place or sight of interest in the text, with page number followed by grid number, eg: [62 C2].

EXTRACTS

The excerpts on pages 81 and 82 are from Bradt's first guide to Albania, Peter and Andrea Dawson's *Albania: A Guide and Illustrated Journal*, which charted their travels in the country towards the end of the communist period. First published by Bradt in 1989, this book is now out of print.

The extracts of Albanian folk tales on pages 196–7 and 207 are translated (by me) from the versions by Mitrush Kuteli, first published in 1965 as *Tregime të Moçme Shqiptare* and republished in Tirana in 1998 by Shtëpia Botuese Mitrush Kuteli.

A NOTE ABOUT PLACE NAMES

Albanian has two forms of every place name. The definite form is that used in the text of this book. The indefinite form is used on road signs and maps. The forms are usually similar enough to be easily recognisable; a glossary on pages 278–9 of this book lists the definite and indefinite forms of those towns or districts that are less obvious.

The name 'Kosova' is used in this book for the country or province that borders Albania to the northeast. Kosova declared its independence on 17 February 2008; at the time of going to press, its status had not been recognised by the United Nations. The country that borders Albania to its east is referred to in this book as 'Macedonia'. Its official name, 'Republic of Macedonia', is used where confusion might otherwise arise with the modern Greek region of Macedonia or with the ancient kingdom of Macedon.

Introduction

Albania has been independent only since 1912. It was the last country in Europe, apart from Macedonia, to gain its independence from the Ottoman Empire and, in its first 30 years as a modern state, it was invaded and occupied, at different times, by all its neighbours. The government that took over in 1944 used a combination of terror, nationalism and isolation to retain power until long after the communist regimes elsewhere in Europe had fallen. Civil unrest bordering on anarchy overwhelmed the country in 1991–92 and 1997.

Given this history, it is not surprising that Albania is so little known. During the communist period, practically the only Westerners who visited the country were in organised groups – ornithologists, art historians or curious adventurers coming in on bus tours from neighbouring Yugoslavia – which were carefully escorted by watchful 'tour guides'. During the 1990s, Albania stayed off the holiday companies' itineraries. It is only in the past few years that travellers in any numbers have started to discover Albania's beauty; its hidden medieval churches and very visible castles; its magnificent archaeological sites, with remains dating back 2½ millennia; and, of course, its delicious fruit, vegetables, lamb and fish.

Albania is easy to get to, by land, sea or air. Road infrastructure continues to improve across the whole country. It becomes easier every year to drive around, and car hire is a more appealing option than it was only a few years ago. It is still true, however, that using public transport is not for those who are easily discouraged or short of time. There are hotels of a reasonable or better standard everywhere.

Since the first edition of this book (although not, I am afraid, solely because of it!), tourism in Albania has changed from being the preserve of the resident expatriates and their visiting family and friends, plus a few ornithologists, art historians and hard-core adventurers. It is now a country which people travel to for their annual holidays. Many of them are drawn to Albania's spectacular, remote wildernesses and, in this new edition, I have continued to pay special attention to hiking and cycling routes. Increasing numbers of visitors are coming to Albania in their own cars or mobile homes and I have tried to enhance the information for those driving themselves. The basic structure of the guide, however, remains the same.

ALBANIA ONLINE

For additional online content, articles, photos and more on Albania, why not visit **w** bradtguides.com/albania?

Part One

GENERAL INFORMATION

1

Background Information

GEOGRAPHY AND CLIMATE

Albania's surface area of 28,748km² (11,100 square miles) makes it slightly smaller than Belgium and slightly larger than the US state of Maryland. Much of its surface is mountainous – the average height above sea level is 708m, and its highest peak, Mount Korabi on the Macedonian border northeast of Peshkopia, is 2,751m high. Most of the population lives in the southern central lowlands and on the coastal plain.

Albania is in the southwest of the Balkan peninsula, bordered by Greece, the former Yugoslav republics of Macedonia and Montenegro, and Kosova. It is separated from Italy by the Adriatic and Ionian seas, which divide at the Bay of Vlora, about 170km up the Albanian coast; at the narrowest point, the Straits of Otranto, the two countries are only 72km apart.

The climate is Mediterranean, with hot dry summers and mild rainy winters in the lowlands. The higher altitudes further inland make temperatures lower, and winter precipitation there often falls as snow. In the highest mountains, snow lies in the northeastern corries all year round. The lowlands have between 270 and 300 days of sunshine a year, and the sea is warm enough to swim in (comfortably) from May to October. The coldest month is January, when the mean lowland temperature is 5–10°C and inland it can fall to below –10°C. The hottest month, July, can be very hot indeed, sometimes topping 40°C inland. Sea breezes keep the coastal towns cooler.

The southern Balkans are located on the boundary between the Eurasian and African tectonic plates, which makes them susceptible to seismic activity. Albania's complex geological development means the country has rich mineral resources – its silver mines were probably one of the attractions for the Greek colonists of the 7th century BC. It has fairly large oil reserves, which in recent years have attracted some Western investment. Under communism, Albania was the world's second-biggest producer of chrome, although production is now a fraction of what it was then.

Albania has 362km of sea coast, with the Adriatic running from the Montenegrin border south to the Bay of Vlora, where the Ionian Sea begins. In all but a few stretches the Adriatic coast is low-lying, with large protected bays (such as those of Vlora and Durrësi) that have been used as harbours since ancient times. The Ionian coast is very rugged, with rocky coves along the narrow coastal strip and steep mountains rising almost straight up along much of its length. The highest point is at the Llogoraja Pass, over 1,000m high. Abrasion and karstic activity have created many caves at the base of the cliffs, some of which were inhabited in prehistoric times.

The country is criss-crossed with rivers, which rise in the high mountains and pass through steep gorges, before reaching the plain and making their way to the sea. The main rivers – and, increasingly, many smaller ones – are managed to generate hydro-electricity; the country's largest hydro-electric system is powered by its longest and most constant stream, the River Drini, which is 285km long and drains nearly 6,000km² within Albania. The longest rivers in southern Albania are the Semani, formed by the confluence of the Devolli and Osumi, and the Vjosa, which rises as the Aoos in northern Greece and runs northwestwards through the beautiful gorges between Përmeti and Tepelena.

NATURAL HISTORY AND CONSERVATION

Over a third of the territory of Albania – more than a million hectares – is forested, and the country is very rich in flora. More than 3,000 different species of plant grow in Albania and about 5% of those are either endemic or sub-endemic (meaning they also grow in neighbouring countries, but the centre of their distribution is in Albania). The box on pages 216–17 has more information about the flora of northern Albania. Many plants are used for medicinal purposes, in cities as well as villages; more information about these can be found in the box on pages 6–7.

The natural vegetation in the coastal strip is *maquis*, the scrubby bushes found all around the Mediterranean; in the north, where the coastal plain is wider, it is almost entirely under cultivation, while in the south many of the hillsides have been terraced and planted with olive trees. As the land rises, the scrub gives way to deciduous forest of beech and oak, with scattered patches of the rare Macedonian pine (*Pinus peuce*). Birch, fir and pine begin to predominate until the treeline is reached at around 2,000m; thereafter only mountain pastures break the harsh landscape. This subalpine and alpine zone occupies about one-eighth of Albania's territory. The forests are home to a great variety of wild animals, including wolves, bears, wild boar and chamois.

The rivers that flow into the low-lying Adriatic coast have created fertile alluvial plains and, at their mouths, exceptionally rich wetlands, which are home to many waterfowl and migratory birds. The coastal marshes were extensively drained in the 20th century to create agricultural land and eradicate malaria. Albania's flora and fauna have also been affected by pollution, as well as unregulated hunting and fishing. The Albanian government introduced a moratorium on hunting in 2014, which has subsequently been extended to 2021. However, illegal hunting continues, especially in the more easily accessible coastal wetlands.

The most outstanding wetlands – the Ramsar sites – are Lake Shkodra, the Karavastaja Lagoons, the Prespa Lakes and part of the Butrint National Park. Even non-ornithologists will find many attractive birds to observe in these wetlands, including pelicans, cormorants, spoonbills, corncrakes and avocets. Among the rare ducks that winter in the Albanian wetlands are the ferruginous duck, or white-eyed pochard (*Aythya nyroca*), and the white-headed duck (*Oxyura leucocephala*), whose fully plumaged male is instantly recognisable from its extraordinary bright blue beak.

Albania's large freshwater lakes also offer good opportunities for birdwatchers. The biggest of these is Lake Shkodra – indeed, at 370km² it is the largest lake in the Balkans – which straddles the border between Albania and Montenegro. Thousands of cormorants (*Phalacrocorax carbo* and *Phalacrocorax pygmeus*) winter on this lake. It is relatively shallow (44m at its deepest point) and is fed by many different rivers, as well as by springs, making it very varied in its fish life.

By contrast, the Ohrid and Prespa lakes, in the southeast of the country, are tectonic lakes. Lake Ohrid, which is shared between Albania and Macedonia, is exceptionally deep and fed mainly by karstic springs around the edges of the lake and on its bed. These springs, in turn, are fed from the Prespa Lakes, high up in the mountains, where Greece, Macedonia and Albania meet. Unique species of fish have evolved in Lake Ohrid, among them the delicious *koran* (*Salmo letnica*) and *belushka* (*Salmothymus ohridanus*).

The Prespa Lakes have very important breeding populations of Dalmatian and white pelicans (*Pelecanus crispus* and *Pelecanus onocrotalus*) and pygmy cormorants (*P. pygmeus*); their breeding sites are on the Greek and Macedonian sides of the lake, but they can be seen foraging all around the shores. Black-necked grebes (*Podiceps nigrocollis*) and coots (*Fulica atra*) winter on the Greater Prespa Lake. Additionally, whiskered terns (*Chlidonias hybridus*) and little bitterns (*Ixobrychus minutus*) are known to breed on the Lesser Prespa Lake. Lake Ohrid is also an important site for wintering waterfowl, with tens of thousands of coots recorded in different bird censuses of the 1990s. Black-necked grebes, pygmy cormorants, goldeneyes (*Bucephala clangula*) and red-crested pochard (*Netta rufina*) also winter at Lake Ohrid. See pages 210–11 for more information about birdwatching in the Albanian coastal wetlands.

Some of the forests and wetlands that present particularly valuable ecosystems are designated as National Parks or Nature Reserves, which is supposed to give them special protection. However, in Albania's case, this legal designation failed to prevent illegal felling of trees, pasturing of livestock, or hunting. A new Law on Protected Areas was passed in May 2017, which should improve the management

BATS IN ALBANIA   *With thanks to Eva de Hullu*

Albania has no fewer than 32 species of bat, including some whose population is declining. Without specialist bat-detecting equipment, it is next to impossible to determine the species of the bats flying around you in the evening. It is easier to go looking for bats in caves or empty sheds – some of the large bunkers might be good places, too.

In caves you are likely to spot different species of horseshoe bat, as well as the bentwing, or Schreiber's long-fingered bat (*Miniopterus schreibersii*), which is recognisable by its long, elegant wings. Colonies of Schreiber's bats can be very large – sometimes comprising as many as 10,000. Horseshoe bats usually fold their wings around their bodies when they sleep, which makes them easy to recognise.

The Albanian NGO Protection and Preservation of Natural Environment in Albania (PPNEA; page 55) has conducted bat-monitoring in caves and bunkers in the Vjosa River area. This project identified six species, including the greater horseshoe bat (*Rhinolophus ferrumequinum*), the lesser horseshoe bat (*Rhinolophus hipposideros*) and – observed for only the second time in Albania and with IUCN (International Union for Conservation of Nature) 'near-threatened' status – Bechstein's bat (*Myotis bechsteinii*). Other species that you might find in Albanian caves are Blasius's horseshoe bat (*Rhinolophus blasii*) and the long-fingered bat (*Myotis capaccinii*). Colonies of Savi's pipistrelle (*Pipistrellis savii*), a southern European species that is widespread in Albania, can be found in cracks in rocks or in buildings.

Sleeping bats are easily disturbed, which can endanger them while they are hibernating (from autumn to spring). You should take care not to pollute their environment, for example by smoking, and leave the bats in peace as soon as you have enjoyed looking at them. Under no circumstances should you ever try to catch a bat. They can give painful bites and some harbour serious diseases such as rabies.

Albanians use many different plants for medicinal purposes; stalls selling them can be found in every town's market and villagers sometimes also sell them from the roadside. In recent years, producers have started to package the more common varieties of medicinal herb in a more controlled and hygienic environment, for sale in shops and supermarkets in Tirana and other towns.

The most popular herbal tea in Albania is *çaj mali*, '**mountain tea**', which is a type of ironwort (*Sideritis raeseri*). Its medicinal effectiveness is a matter of some dispute, but Albanians of all ages drink *çaj mali* to treat virtually any kind of minor ailment, from the common cold to indigestion.

Some of the most widely used herbal remedies are described below, with their Albanian and Latin names. It should be borne in mind, however, that some of them are toxic in the wrong doses or if the wrong part of the plant is used; this list should not be used for self-medication.

Wild **chamomile** (*lule kamomili, Chamomilla recutita*) is one of the most widely used medicinal herbs, and is native to southern and southeastern Europe. The flower heads with their stalks are gathered in the summer and dried – bundles of the herb can be bought all over Albania. Chamomile is used for digestive and nervous disorders, and as an anti-inflammatory; it is usually drunk as an infusion, but it can also be added to bathwater to soothe dermatitis.

St John's wort (*lule basani, Hypericum perforatum*), used in northern Europe as an anti-depressant, is very widely used in Albania to treat a variety of other ailments. Bundles of its long stems can often be seen on market and street stalls. It is used to treat diseases of the digestive and respiratory tracts, as well as kidney problems. It improves the circulation of the blood and helps against sleeplessness. St John's wort also has antiseptic properties, and an extract made from its flowers is used externally to prevent infection of wounds or burns.

The **lime** tree (*bliri i bardhë, Tilia*) has about 20 documented species, two of which are used medicinally. The flowers have anti-inflammatory, diuretic and mild anti-spasmodic properties, and also induce perspiration. The infusion made from them is used to treat colds and flu, and diseases of the kidneys and urinary tract. It helps to lower high temperatures and soothes nervous complaints.

The blue flowers of **borage** (*shaja, Borago officinalis*) have diuretic, antiseptic and anti-inflammatory properties, as well as being a culinary herb. Infusions of borage are used to treat urinary infections and problems of the nervous system; borage solution can also be applied externally to skin injuries and inflammations.

of these vulnerable areas. This Law established a new National Agency for Protected Areas (AKZM), with regional offices in each of the country's 12 prefectures. Information, in English, about all of Albania's national parks and nature reserves can be found on the Agency's website (**w** *akzm.gov.al*). Ornithologists or others wishing to access the most sensitive areas should request permission in the regional office of the respective prefecture.

HISTORY

PREHISTORY The country now known as Albania has been inhabited for more than ten millennia. The first Palaeolithic settlements to be excavated were in caves at Gajtan, near Shkodra, and Konispoli in the far southwest. More recent work has

Marshmallow (*mullanjadhja, Althaea officinalis*) has been cultivated in Europe for its medicinal properties since the Middle Ages, when it was grown in monasteries. Albanians use marshmallow, as an infusion of the roots and leaves, to treat coughs and stomach disorders; the leaves are made into poultices to heal external wounds and soften bruises.

Extracts of **hawthorn** (*murrizi, Crataegus laevigata* and other *Crataegus* species) are used commercially in drops and pills for the treatment of heart and vascular problems. In Albania, the flowers and leaves of hawthorn are made into an infusion that improves heart rhythm and lowers blood pressure.

Fennel (*maraja, Foeniculum vulgare*) is a component of many commercially available herbal tea mixtures. As an infusion, the fruit is used to treat diseases of the digestive system and respiratory tract; a similar infusion can also be used as an eye wash for minor inflammations of the eyelid or conjunctivitis.

White horehound (*kapinoku, Marrubium vulgare*) has anti-inflammatory and antiseptic properties, and its flowering stems are used to treat mild digestive disorders and inflammation of the upper respiratory tract.

Cowslip and **oxlip**, both members of the primrose family (*aguliçore, primulaceae*) contain complex organic substances called saponins, which have an expectorant effect. Their roots or flowers are made into decoctions or infusions that are drunk to ease bronchitis and other diseases of the respiratory tract.

Blackthorn, or **sloe** (*kullumbria, Prunus spinosa*), is a spiny shrub whose white flowers have mildly diuretic and laxative properties. In Albania it is administered as an infusion to those suffering from problems of the digestive system, kidneys and urinary tract; it is also good for preventing chills and treating the symptoms of rheumatism.

Lungwort (*pulmonaria, Pulmonaria officinalis*) is one of the oldest medicinal herbs, used since the Middle Ages to treat respiratory problems. In Albania, its flowering stems are administered in the form of an infusion to treat those suffering from bronchitis.

Heartsease (*manushaqja tringjyrëshe, Viola tricolor*) is used internally and externally for its antiseptic and anti-inflammatory properties. The flowering stems are steeped in water and either administered as an infusion, to treat inflammation of the upper respiratory passages and infections of the urinary tract or kidneys; or used to soak gauze pads, which are applied as compresses to treat external wounds and dermatitis.

identified some open-air sites: Shkreli in the northwest and the area around Apollonia in central Albania, for example. The Neolithic period in this region is c6000–c2100BC and the Bronze Age is c2100–c1200BC; the Korça region is full of sites from these periods, including the tumulus site at Kamenica (page 140). It is in the Iron Age, starting around 1200BC, that it begins to be possible to recognise the culture known as Illyrian. Some archaeologists take the view that, during the Bronze Age, the inhabitants of the Balkan peninsula began to develop tribal differences and that one of the tribes that emerged as a result was the Illyrian people, who are the ancestors of modern Albanians. Others think that the Illyrians came from elsewhere and invaded Albania at some point between the 13th and the 10th centuries BC.

There is also considerable controversy over the question of where the boundary was between Hellenes (Greeks), Epirotes (whom the Hellenes considered to be sort of Greek, in the same way as Macedonians were) and Illyrians (who were definitely barbarians, ie: not Greek). It may be that Illyrian and Epirote settlements were interspersed in what is now southern Albania and northern Greece.

ILLYRIANS What is not in question is that Illyrian culture had many distinctive features and that the ancient Greeks considered the various Illyrian tribes as similar enough to each other to form a distinct group. They built large, well-fortified cities (almost all of which were in stunning locations with magnificent views), they traded with the Greek colonies on the Adriatic coast and beyond and they minted coins. The silver and copper that they mined was also used for personal adornments: *fibulae* (brooches) such as fibulae (brooches) in spiralling figure-of-eight shapes; metal coils, which women twisted into their hair; and the unique *byzylyk*, bracelets that were placed on the arms and legs of a dead person as part of the burial process. In one tumulus a skeleton was found with no fewer than six *byzylykë* on each limb.

In the 3rd century BC, a northern Illyrian tribe called the **Ardiaeans** established its capital in Shkodra. The Ardiaeans were seafarers – their coins (and the modern 20-lek coin) show a small, fast galley called a *liburnis*, which was a particular favourite of pirates – and in 229BC their attacks on Italian ships brought them to war with Rome, then emerging as the most powerful state in Italy. Queen Teuta of the Ardiaeans was forced to make terms, and the Romans gained their first foothold on the other side of the Adriatic. Sixty years later, in 168BC, they defeated the Ardiaeans in battle and besieged their king, Genti (known to the Romans as Gentius), in Rozafa Castle until he surrendered. Genti was the last Illyrian king.

ROMANS From the middle of the 2nd century BC, Roman control brought peace and prosperity to Albania. To connect the Adriatic coast with Thessalonica and Byzantium, the Romans built one of their great arterial roads, the Via Egnatia. The road was named after a Roman proconsul of Macedonia, Gnaeius Egnatius, who laid it and built bridges along it in the 2nd century BC, using an ancient route that linked southern Illyria with Macedonia. The starting points were Dyrrachium (now Durrësi) and Apollonia, and at the place where these two branches joined a town grew up, which later acquired the name of Elbasani. The Romans built other roads too – one down the coast from Shkodra through Durrësi to Butrint and beyond, another from Shkodra east through Prizreni to Niš.

Julius Caesar visited the province of Illyricum in 56BC, while it was under his command, but the first time he is known to have come specifically to what is now Albania was in 48BC, pursuing his opponent in the Civil War, Pompey. Octavian studied in Apollonia before he became the Emperor Augustus, and rewarded the city afterwards with tax-free status. Many Roman citizens bought estates or settled in Albania. Lissus (Lezha) had a community of Roman citizens when Mark Antony landed there with Caesar's reinforcements in 48BC; a friend of Cicero's owned land near Buthrotum (Butrint). Dyrrachium, a free city in the Republic, became a Roman colony under Augustus, who also founded colonies at Byllis and Buthrotum.

On the final division of the Roman Empire in AD395, Albania came under Constantinople's authority, rather than Rome's. This meant that when the Western Empire collapsed in the 5th century, Albania became part of the Byzantine Empire.

BYZANTINES The 4th, 5th and 6th centuries saw destabilising invasions of Albania by Visigoths and then Ostrogoths, who occupied Dyrrachium in AD480 and used it as a base from which to invade Italy and set up a kingdom there. Shkodra was sacked in AD380 and Onchesmus (now Saranda) was completely destroyed in

AD551. However, in between invasions, life went on. Bishops were installed and churches were built. The great builder-emperor, Justinian (AD527–65), ordered the fortification or refortification of several cities, including Dyrrachium and Byllis.

In the 10th century, Bulgaria captured large swathes of the Balkans, including all of Albania. The Byzantines were only able to recover this territory after 1018. However, the respite was short. In 1081, a large Norman army, under Robert Guiscard, landed at Avlona (Vlora) and proceeded up the coast to Dyrrachium. The ensuing battle is described in great detail by Anna Comnena, the daughter of the Byzantine emperor Alexius I Comnenus. (Among his allies were a people called the Albanoi.) Despite initial success, the Battle of Dyrrachium was a crushing defeat for Byzantium. Many of the empire's officers were killed; the European troops who had formed the backbone of its army proved to be undisciplined and useless and were replaced with foreign mercenaries. The decisive moment in the battle was a shock charge by the Norman cavalry, holding their lances ahead of them instead of throwing them. This innovation had been tested at the Battle of Hastings, and would be used to even more devastating effect in the First Crusade 15 years later.

After a siege lasting several months, the Normans went on to take Dyrrachium and other coastal towns, as a prelude to an advance to the east two years later; by the middle of the following year, the whole of Illyria was in their hands. Alexius I fought back, however. Allied with the Venetians, who wanted (and got) control of Dyrrachium and Corfu, Byzantium had retaken most of its Balkan territories by the end of 1083.

Constantinople fell to the Fourth Crusade in 1204, and for the rest of that century competing successor states vied for pre-eminence. One of these became known as the **Despotate of Epirus**, whose capital was at Arta (now in northwestern Greece) and whose boundaries extended north to Dyrrachium and, at times, east to Macedonia and Thessalonica. It was founded soon after the fall of Constantinople by Michael I Comnenus Ducas, an illegitimate grandson of Alexius I Comnenus. His own illegitimate son, Michael II Comnenus Ducas, who ruled from about 1237 to 1271, seems to have been the first to use the title of Despot of Epirus. A despot was a kind of imperial regent and provincial administrator, and the title was usually awarded by the emperor.

In 1256, Michael II embarked on a campaign to capture Thessalonica, a city then held by one of the other mini empires, that of Nicaea, and by early summer he was at the city's gates. Early in 1258, however, Durrësi, Vlora and Butrint fell to Prince Manfred of Sicily; Michael II reacted by offering him his daughter in marriage, with the conquered territory as her dowry, and forming an alliance with the kingdoms of Sicily and Achaia against Nicaea. The newly crowned co-Emperor of Nicaea, Michael Palaeologus, dispatched a large army to the Balkans which took the Epirote army by surprise at Kastoria. Michael II Comnenus Ducas regrouped with his allies at Vlora, but they were conclusively defeated at Pelagonia (now Monastir, in Macedonia) in the summer of 1259. The Nicaeans captured Arta and Michael II took refuge on the island of Cephalonia. He made his way back to Arta the following year, but it was too late for the Despotate of Epirus to reassert itself. On 15 August 1261, Michael VIII Palaeologus entered Constantinople in triumph after the fall of the Latin Empire.

Meanwhile, Albania continued to be tussled over. Manfred Hohenstaufen, by then King of Sicily, died in battle in 1266 against the crusade of Charles of Anjou, the younger brother of King Louis of France. In 1275, the Byzantines retook Butrint and Berati, driving the Angevins back to the Adriatic coast. Five years later, Charles dispatched an army of about 8,000 eastwards across Albania to Berati;

the garrison and people in the fortified citadel there held out until a relief army from Constantinople reached them in March 1281 and inflicted a crushing defeat on the Angevin troops. Albania was now back in Byzantine hands.

However, the Byzantine Empire had been fatally weakened during its years of exile from Constantinople and, in the 14th century, it was able to devote less and less energy to its western periphery. The Angevins recaptured Durrësi in 1307; the Serbian king Stefan Dušan invaded Albania in 1343, and got as far south as Vlora and Berati. The Serbs never exercised full control over the country, however. Instead it became a patchwork of semi-independent states run by powerful Albanian families; on Stefan Dušan's untimely death in 1355, they were left as the only functioning authorities. They included the Balshajs in northern Albania, the Muzakajs in the south, and the Topias in central Albania – in the 1380s, Karl Topia rebuilt the church of St Gjon Vladimir near Elbasani (pages 117–18).

THE OTTOMAN CONQUEST The Ottomans had first settled on European soil in 1354, much to the alarm of John VI Cantacuzenus, the Byzantine historian and – at the time – co-emperor. In 1371, Sultan Murad I's troops routed the Serbian army at the river Maritsa; and in June 1389 a coalition of Serbs, Hungarians, Bosnians, Bulgarians and Albanians, under the leadership of the Serbian prince Lazar, met the Ottoman troops on the Field of Blackbirds (Kosovo Polje, in Serbian). The sultan was killed, but the coalition was routed and Prince Lazar executed. The few Serbian nobles who survived were obliged to swear a personal oath of allegiance to the new sultan, Murad's son Bayezid.

Bayezid marched against Constantinople in 1394, and the city remained under siege for eight years, until the Mongol army under **Tamurlane** swept into Asia Minor and defeated the Ottomans in 1402. Bayezid was taken prisoner and died in captivity. His successor as sultan, Mehmed I, returned to Albania; in 1417, Ottoman forces captured Vlora and then Gjirokastra. But their grip on the country was weak and Albania had not yet given up. The early 1430s saw rebellions, put down in 1433. In 1443, the Ottoman army was defeated at the Serbian town of Niš, by a crusade under a multi-national leadership, which included the Hungarian hero János Hunyadi. At this point Skanderbeg, an Albanian nobleman who had been trained as a soldier in the Ottoman army, raised a rebellion from his family seat at Kruja (see box, pages 206–7). Thanks to Skanderbeg's ability to unify the Albanian clans against the enemy, they resisted the occupiers until 1479 – 26 years after the Ottomans had taken the Byzantine capital.

Under Islamic law, non-Muslims living under Muslim sovereignty are treated as 'protected infidels', a status quite different from that of non-Muslims under non-Muslim sovereignty, who can legitimately be killed or enslaved. The Christians in Albania (and elsewhere) were not obliged to convert to Islam, but they did have to pay a capitation tax. It was by virtue of this tax that their lives and property enjoyed legal protection.

Perhaps even more significant for Christian peasants was the 'Collection', or *devshirme*, whereby non-Turkish families throughout the empire were required to give up one of their sons to the sultan. Between the 14th and late 16th centuries, the Collection was the main source of recruitment into imperial service, and it must have been a huge sacrifice for peasant families who needed their sons to work their land (although if a family had only one son, he was spared). The best-looking youths in each intake were educated in the Palace Schools and sometimes worked their way up to become governors or other senior officials. Most of the 'collected' boys, though, became **Janissaries**, members of the sultan's personal infantry corps.

Originally, the Janissaries consisted of a few hundred men who served as the sultan's bodyguards. Although their numbers grew over the years, they remained a small, elite corps – during the 16th century, they numbered around 10,000 at any one time. They were fiercely loyal to the Ottoman dynasty, although not necessarily to individual sultans; Janissary rebellions forced at least two sultans to abdicate.

As for those selected for the Palace Schools, after their education was complete they could become pages to the sultan, serve in the military palace guard or join one of the cavalry divisions attached to the palace; if they had a particular interest in Islamic law, they could become *imams*; if their aptitude lay in languages, they might become clerks. It was the sultan's personal pages, however, who stood the best chance of achieving the great offices of the empire – *viziers*, imperial treasurers and chancellors. Many Albanians became Grand Viziers, such as Daud Pasha, who was Grand Vizier from 1485 to 1497, and Koja Sinan Pasha a century later.

INDEPENDENCE In many cases, in fact, it was Ottoman civil servants who provided the intellectual framework and the creative impulse for the **Albanian nationalist movement** that began to emerge in the late 19th century. Abdyl Frashëri (see box, pages 152–3), for example, was Director of Finance for the *vilayet* (province) of Ioannina. He was a senior figure in the Prizren League, whose original goal was merely the unification of the four Albanian-speaking *vilayets*, but which by 1881 was campaigning for autonomy within the Ottoman Empire. The League succeeded in expelling the imperial administrators from Kosova, but it was crushed shortly afterwards and its leaders were imprisoned.

The nationalist movement now realised that the Albanian language could be a tool with which to build a sense of national unity, and the focus of its campaigning shifted to cultural and linguistic demands. Albanian books and magazines were published and Albanian-medium schools (ie: schools that taught subjects in the Albanian language) were opened (page 136). A generation of great Albanian poets emerged, who embodied the national cultural renaissance (Rilindja Kombëtare) under way.

One obstacle to national unity was the fact that Albanians of different religious faiths wrote their language in different alphabets – Muslims used the Arabic script, Orthodox southerners the Greek alphabet, and northern Catholics the Roman. Agreement on a common alphabet therefore became a pressing aim of the Rilindja movement, and in 1909 a congress in Elbasani formally adopted the Roman alphabet, which is used today.

The **First Balkan War** started on 8 October 1912 when Montenegro attacked northern Albania, which was still part of the Ottoman Empire. The other Balkan countries immediately joined in, the Ottoman army crumbled and Albania found itself invaded from all sides. Practically abandoned by their Ottoman rulers, the Albanians realised that if they did not obtain independence their territory would be swallowed up by their Balkan neighbours. Meanwhile, Austria-Hungary had become concerned that Greek, Serb and Italian designs on Albania would reduce its own influence in the Balkans – its southern backyard. Ismail Qemali, who had been one of the 26 Albanians elected to the Istanbul parliament after the Young Turk revolution of 1908, travelled to Vienna and Budapest to obtain diplomatic support for Albanian independence.

By the time the war began, much of Albania was already up in arms and Albanian soldiers were deserting the Ottoman army, although others fought bravely with the Ottoman forces against the Montenegrins. Rebels led by the Kosovar Isa Boletini occupied Skopje, took control of Kosova, and captured large tracts of what is now

Albanian territory. When Ismail Qemali returned from his diplomatic tour, he learned that Serbian troops were approaching the Adriatic. Northern Albania was being invaded by the Balkan League and the Greek navy was attacking in the south – it was in difficult circumstances indeed that on 28 November 1912, 83 delegates from all parts of Albania gathered in Vlora and proclaimed Albania's independence.

The Great Powers – Austria-Hungary, Britain, France, Germany, Italy and Russia – formally recognised independent Albania in May 1913. In June, after 500 years, the last Ottoman troops left Albanian soil. The Great Powers appointed an International Commission of Control to draft a constitution, and Frontier Commissions to demarcate its borders. They refused to recognise the provisional government set up in Vlora and appointed a German prince as a puppet monarch. Prince Wilhelm of Wied never governed beyond Durrësi and gave up altogether after only six months (for more about this interlude, see box, page 97). Albania sank into anarchy as its leaders fought among themselves for power and, during World War I, it fragmented into a mess of 'autonomous' statelets under the influence of the various countries that had designs on its territory. It would not begin to recover until the 1920s.

KING ZOG One of the leaders who emerged during this chaotic period was Ahmed Zogu, a clan chief from the Mati district in northern central Albania. He participated in the Congress of Lushnja in January 1920, which appointed a senate and a cabinet to restore political order, and a High Council of State to oversee them. Zogu was made Interior Minister in the new government. Over the next few years he went on to consolidate his power base, and in December 1924 – after a brief period out of power – he marched on Tirana and overthrew the Democratic Party government of Fan Noli. He quickly abolished the High Council of State, became president, and set about rewriting the constitution and eliminating his opponents.

By the mid 1920s, Italian influence over Albania was increasing. Italian companies were building roads and improving harbours, Italian colonists were settling in parts of the south and, in November 1927, a large Italian military mission was installed in the country, with Italian officers attached to Albanian military units. In 1928, Zogu crowned himself Zog I, King of the Albanians, and promulgated a new constitution that gave him practically unrestricted powers.

Meanwhile, Italian 'advisers' were installing themselves in the ministries, Italian architects were redesigning Tirana and Italian businessmen were taking over the country's economy. By 1938, Italy accounted for 68.4% of Albania's exports and 36.3% of its imports. Eventually, on 7 April 1939, Mussolini annexed Albania and Italian troops invaded and occupied it. The king sent his wife, Queen Geraldine, and two-day-old son, Leka, to safety across the Greek border, following them himself later in the day. Zog would never return to Albania; he died in Paris in 1961, from where his remains were repatriated in 2012, as part of the centenary of Albanian independence. His widow and son both died in Tirana: Geraldine, who by then styled herself the Queen Mother (Nëna Mbretëresha), in October 2002; Leka, in 2011.

WORLD WAR II Events in Albania during World War II are a matter of extreme controversy and political polarisation. The various liberation groups can be broadly categorised as 'nationalist', meaning those who wanted the post-war borders of Albania to include Kosova and other Albanian-speaking lands, and 'partisan', meaning those who ultimately came out on top and took power after liberation. The former group included supporters of King Zog, such as Abas Kupi, who came to call themselves the Legality (Legaliteti) Movement, and supporters of the Noli government, such as

M C Barrès-Baker

The Special Operations Executive (SOE) was created in July 1940. Placed under the Minister of Economic Warfare and intended 'to co-ordinate ... subversion and sabotage, against the enemy overseas', it combined Section D of MI6, the propaganda branch of the Foreign Office and a research branch of the War Office.

In November 1940, the exiled King Zog planned a revolt in northern Albania. SOE feared, possibly wrongly, that Zog was so unpopular that supporting him would actually weaken Albanian resistance. In any case the plan was opposed by the Greeks and just about everybody else; nothing came of it.

In April 1941, SOE sent Lieutenant-Colonel Dayrell Oakley-Hill, who had helped organise Zog's gendarmes before the war, into northern Albania, along with 300 resisters. He was to foment a rebellion but, when Germany invaded Yugoslavia, the operation turned into a diversion to support the Yugoslavs. The tiny invasion received little support and the situation rapidly became hopeless. Oakley-Hill eventually surrendered to the Germans in Belgrade.

In early 1942, SOE headquarters in Cairo began to plan subversion in Albania again. Until 1944, the ethnographer Margaret Hasluck (see box, pages 116–17) ran the SOE Albania desk from Cairo. Since the British didn't recognise an Albanian government-in-exile, they were prepared to work with all Albanian resisters. In April 1943, Major Neil 'Billy' McLean and Captain David Smiley entered from northern Greece and contacted the National Liberation Movement (LNÇ, predominantly partisan) and the anti-communist, anti-Zog Balli Kombëtar. Weapons drops began in June. Initially the aircraft flew from Cyrenaica, moving in December to Italy from where sea sorties were also made. Most supplies went to the partisans, despite McLean and partisan leader Enver Hoxha having developed a growing mutual antipathy. A series of meetings between the LNÇ and Balli Kombëtar, possibly brokered by SOE and the Zogist Abas Kupi, led to the short-lived Mukje Agreements in August.

The Italian surrender exacerbated the divisions between the LNÇ and the nationalists, and civil war threatened. In October 1943, SOE sent in an enlarged mission under Brigadier E F 'Trotsky' Davies, withdrawing McLean. Davies and his men continued to work with the resistance and carry out sabotage, despite growing civil conflict and large-scale German anti-partisan offensives over the winter. He was also charged with uniting the Albanians, or with recommending which group Britain should recognise. 'It sounded so simple,' Davies wrote later. 'In Albania I was to find the whole matter very complex and difficult.' Initially Davies recommended supporting all groups that fought the Germans, but in December he recommended limiting support to the partisans – by far the most active resisters. Davies was captured in January 1944.

SOE, now based in Bari, followed his first recommendation. Norman Wheeler, and later Alan Palmer, took over in the south. In April 1944, McLean and Smiley, along with Julian Amery, returned to northern Albania as part of a mission to Kupi. McLean became very close to Kupi, and hoped he could be built up as an alternative to the partisans. The aims of the two SOE missions rapidly diverged.

M C Barrès-Baker

By April 1944, the partisans were organised like a regular army. They had 13,000 soldiers, formed into 12 brigades. Despite their communist leadership, they were a broad-based popular resistance movement. Abas Kupi had only 5,000 men, and they were far less active than the partisans. Hoxha clearly mistrusted his SOE liaison officers, but his troops killed Germans. 'Billy' McLean's attempt to convince SOE in Bari to consider Kupi as a serious alternative to the partisans was therefore doomed. Although Bari officially supported both groups, the partisans continued to receive the bulk of air-dropped supplies.

Between spring 1943 and late 1944, about 50 British officers were sent to Albania. They were a varied group: Smiley was happiest when 'blowing things up'; Peter Kemp had fought as a nationalist volunteer in the Spanish Civil War; Davies ended the war in Colditz; Reginald Hibbert would become British Ambassador in Paris; and Julian Amery, who would later become a Conservative MP, got into trouble for wearing a beard while in uniform at Bari and, while moving in disguise around a Tirana full of occupying German soldiers in light summer uniforms, had a sudden insight into what it must be like to be a colonial subject of the British Empire. A sort of *Boy's Own* adventure atmosphere comes across in some SOE men's memoirs, but this was frustrating, gruelling and dangerous work. Several SOE men (not just officers) have graves in the Tirana Park Memorial Cemetery. The highest-ranking man buried there, Brigadier Arthur Nicholls, developed severe frostbite during the German offensive over the winter of 1943/44. Despite medical assistance from his Albanian colleagues, he died three days after his 33rd birthday. He was awarded a posthumous George Cross.

In July 1944, the partisans launched a major offensive, entering Kupi's heartland. Fearing all-out civil war, SOE stopped supplying them, but further partisan successes against the Germans led to this decision being reversed. Bari now signed military agreements with the LNÇ. Faced with this clear British move towards the partisans, Kupi and the Ballists both engaged the Germans more forcefully, but SOE was not impressed. In September 1944, it gave up on them completely. McLean and Smiley were ordered to return to Bari. Dismayed by the lack of support for Kupi, Smiley and Amery later claimed that SOE was bedazzled

Mit'hat Frashëri, who founded the National Front (Balli Kombëtar) Party in April 1939, immediately after the Italian invasion. The latter group included Enver Hoxha and Mehmet Shehu, and its core was the Albanian Communist Party.

Albania remained part of Italy for more than four years, although the Greek army occupied parts of the south when the Italian invasion of Greece went awry in late 1940. When Italy surrendered in September 1943, the occupying army in Albania disintegrated – some Italian soldiers became servants on Albanian farms in order to get enough food to survive. As in Italy itself, the Wehrmacht stepped into the gap; a Council of Regency was set up, consisting of four Albanian politicians who were prepared to collaborate with the Germans, and the country was formally independent once more.

Many Albanians, however, refused to accept the German occupation. In the vicious war that followed, Albanians fought both against and alongside the Germans, and against each other. Beyond the intellectual elite of Tirana, Albanian politics is still essentially based on who did what to whom during World War II.

by the partisans and infiltrated by communist agents. The books in which they made these claims were widely read, unlike Hibbert's memoir of his work with the partisans, and for many years their views became the accepted version.

Fearing a partisan victory, many nationalists were by now fighting alongside the Germans. Kupi refused to do this, disbanding his forces instead. The British authorities in Italy refused to evacuate him, but he still managed to get out of Albania and across the Adriatic.

In October, British commandos helped liberate Saranda, making Hoxha very suspicious. Long Range Desert Group forward observers directed RAF air support during the battle for Tirana and SOE men accompanied the partisan brigades into the city.

The end of the war was not the end of British involvement in Albania. From 1949 to 1953, the American CIA and British military intelligence attempted to overthrow Hoxha by covert means. It has been claimed that Cambridge spy Kim Philby gave Moscow details of the operation, but the plans overestimated the ability of ordinary Albanians to rise up against the regime. Many infiltrators, code-named 'pixies' by their Anglo-American handlers, lost their lives.

After the war, Hoxha denied, or greatly played down, British aid to the partisans. Indeed, he destroyed all trace of the British War Cemetery, moving the bodies to an unmarked collective grave, with the result that, until 1995, men who had died in Albania had to be commemorated at Phaleron War Cemetery in Greece. Even now, the grave markers at Tirana Park Memorial Cemetery do not correspond precisely to where the men lie. On the other hand, some in the West accused the SOE of having enabled the communists to seize power. Most historians now accept that the aid was very useful to the partisans, but that they would have defeated the other groups anyway. Several SOE agents who served in Albania subsequently wrote memoirs. For details of these, see page 281.

Initially, the post-communist government only recognised the achievements of SOE personnel who had not worked with the partisans, but for the Liberation Day celebrations in November 1994 they invited all the wartime British Liaison Officers they could. Only two managed to attend – Hibbert, who had worked with the partisans, and Smiley, who had not. Both men were awarded the Order of Liberty, First Class.

Both nationalists and partisans were assisted by British officers, infiltrated into Albania from 1943 by the Special Operations Executive, or SOE (see boxes, above and page 13). Gradually, however, Britain gave greater support to the partisans, supplying them with weapons, ammunition and clothing. In May 1944, at a congress in the southern town of Përmeti, a provisional government was elected. The Congress of Përmeti consolidated the exclusion that had begun the previous year of the non-communist forces, annulled various decisions and agreements made by the pre-war monarchist government, and specifically banned King Zog from returning to Albania.

In September, partisan brigades began to advance on Tirana. The Battle for the Liberation of Tirana lasted 19 days, from 29 October to 17 November; intense street fighting raged up and down the city, with the partisans receiving some air support from RAF Beaufighters. By the end of November, the Germans had been driven out of Shkodra, their last foothold in Albania, and the communist government controlled the whole country.

COMMUNISM Albania was impoverished and devastated at the end of World War II. An estimated 28,000 people had been killed and thousands more were homeless. The United Nations implemented a relief programme and the new government – under its prime minister, Enver Hoxha – organised brigades of peasants to repair roads and rebuild houses. Meanwhile, industry, banking and transport were nationalised, the property of those who had fled the country for political reasons was confiscated and, in 1945, an agrarian reform law broke up and redistributed privately owned estates. The following year all surplus agricultural land was taken over by state farms or co-operatives.

At this time, the relationship between Albania and Yugoslavia was still good – Belgrade gave generous economic assistance to its neighbour, despite its own need for reconstruction. As far as Britain and the USA were concerned, however, Albania suspected their embassies of encouraging opponents of the regime (probably with some justification) and started to restrict their diplomats' movements. Britain withdrew its diplomatic mission in April 1946, followed later that year by the USA.

Relations between Britain and Albania became even worse after the **Corfu Channel incident** of October 1946, when two British destroyers hit mines in the narrow strait between Ksamili and Corfu, and more than 40 crew members were killed. The mines had been recently laid, rather than forming part of a wartime minefield, and Britain accused Albania of deliberately laying them. The matter was the first-ever case referred to the International Court of Justice, which ruled against Albania and ordered it to pay compensation. Many historians now think that Yugoslav ships were responsible, although Albania's (and Britain's) role in the episode is still far from clear.

When Yugoslavia was expelled from Cominform (the post-war body that replaced Comintern) in 1948, Albania immediately sided with the Soviet Union and annulled all its economic agreements with its neighbour. This was also the year that the Albanian Communist Party changed its name to the Party of Labour (Partia e Punës së Shqipërisë; PPSH).

The 1950s was a decade of **industrialisation**, with hydro-electric plants built to provide power for the new factories and mines. In 1954, the year after Stalin's death, Mehmet Shehu took over the position of prime minister, although Enver Hoxha stayed on as First Secretary of the party and continued to wield considerable power. Shehu had been one of the partisans' most illustrious generals; before the war he had attended Italian military school, been expelled for left-wing activities and fought in the Spanish Civil War. He was interned in France and returned to Albania on his release in 1942.

By the late 1950s, relations between China and the Soviet Union were deteriorating and Albania took China's side. In 1961, this culminated in a complete severance of diplomatic links between Albania and the USSR and, in 1968, Albania withdrew from the Warsaw Pact. In 1967, in the wake of the Chinese Cultural Revolution, Albania banned the practice of religion and declared itself the **world's first atheist state**. Christian and Muslim clerics were shot or imprisoned, and churches and mosques were demolished or converted into warehouses or sports halls. Only a few very old or exceptionally beautiful religious buildings were spared.

After Mao's death in 1976, China lost interest in Albania and in 1978 it ended its aid programmes there. Albania now had no powerful ally to protect and subsidise it, and had little option but to begin to improve relations with its neighbours – first with Yugoslavia and later, after the restoration of democracy there, with Greece. However, most Albanians – those who did not take part in sporting or cultural delegations or get to attend trade fairs – were almost completely cut off from the rest of the world.

Rapprochement with Yugoslavia caused divisions within the party and the government, which Hoxha usually resolved by eliminating those who disagreed with him. Mehmet Shehu fell out of favour and was found dead in December 1981. It was rumoured that Hoxha had shot him, but Shehu's own sons believe their father committed suicide. They and their mother were imprisoned; Shehu's widow died in prison, while his sons were released in 1991. Hoxha himself died in 1985 and was succeeded as First Secretary by Ramiz Alia (1925–2011), one of the few northerners to have gained prominence in the PPSH.

Alia attempted to improve relations with Albania's neighbours, but internally there was little liberalisation of any sort until after the Berlin Wall had fallen. Then a few minor political reforms were announced and religious worship was again tolerated. In 1990, thousands of Albanians climbed over the walls of the Western embassy buildings in Tirana, in an attempt to flee the country. Students began demonstrations and hunger strikes, demanding, first of all, better living conditions in their halls of residence, then the removal of Enver Hoxha's name from that of Tirana's university, and finally 'freedom [and] democracy'. On 11 December 1990, the government at last agreed to allow independent political parties. When the Democratic Party (DP) was formed the following day, it was the first opposition party in Albania for half a century.

THE 1990S In February 1991, a march in support of the striking students turned into a symbolic and historic event, when the demonstrators poured into Skanderbeg Square and pulled down the 10m-high statue of Enver Hoxha which dominated it. A few weeks later tens of thousands of young men climbed aboard ships docked in the ports of Durrësi and Vlora, and forced their crews to take them across the Adriatic to the Italian port of Brindisi. It was in this tense environment that, on 31 March 1991, Albania's first multi-party elections were held. The DP and other newly formed parties contested the elections, but were unable to make much headway against the PPSH electoral machine. Despite the parliamentary arithmetic, however, the PPSH government was brought down only weeks later by a general strike. A cross-party government took over and new elections were held on 22 March 1992, which the DP won by a landslide.

The PPSH subsequently rebranded itself as the Socialist Party and carried out internal reforms, in particular allowing considerable autonomy to its youth wing, whose members were not tainted by association with the party's communist past.

The DP governed until 1997, when it, too, was brought down. This time the cause of the unrest was the failure of pyramid investment schemes, which had sprung up in 1995 and 1996. The 'pyramids' offered a rate of return that people with any experience of Western capitalism would have known was unsustainable. The Albanians, however, isolated as they had been, were easily convinced to deposit their savings there; some sold their houses or farms to raise cash to invest in the pyramids. Even educated people who knew deep down that it was too good to be true allowed themselves to be carried along. Towards the end of 1996, some of the smaller pyramid 'banks' began to fail, as was inevitable, and savers began to panic, which was also inevitable.

Street demonstrations spread and soon became riots. In the generally anti-DP cities of the south, the riots grew from simple protests against the disappearance of people's savings to a full-scale rebellion against the government, which quickly spread to other parts of the country. Police and army officers fled and looters broke into their weapons stores. Anything connected to the state was ransacked and destroyed, from DP offices and police stations to state-owned hotels and children's swing-parks.

The anarchy lasted for weeks and was only brought under any sort of control by the arrival of an international peacekeeping force, the promise of new elections, and the establishment of a caretaker, cross-party government. The elections of June 1997 were conducted in circumstances in which normal campaigning was impossible and voter intimidation was widespread. Nonetheless, the results were accepted by the DP president, who resigned just before the new, socialist-dominated parliament convened.

The incoming government restored its authority gradually over central Albania, but there was still considerable instability in much of the rest of the country. Over half a million weapons had been looted in the spring of 1997, and attempts to persuade people to hand them back were largely unsuccessful. In September 1998, the political situation took a turn for the worse with the assassination of a DP Member of Parliament, Azem Hajdari. For a few days, violence returned to the streets of Tirana, fortunately without spiralling out of control.

Gradually Albania pieced itself back together. Its central and local authorities won widespread praise for their response to the crisis in Kosova, which brought half a million refugees across its borders. Its Interior Ministry and police chiefs cleared the car-jackers off the highways and locked up the armed gangs who controlled some towns and cities. Ordinary Albanians were horrified by what happened to their country in 1997. This, perhaps more than anything else, has ensured that Albania has subsequently avoided sliding into similar turmoil, even when political tensions have run high.

GOVERNMENT AND POLITICS

Albania is a parliamentary democracy, governed by a constitution passed in 1998. One hundred and forty members, elected through regional party lists, sit in its parliament. Their mandate runs for four years and the last elections were held in June 2017, when the Socialist Party obtained an overall majority. The largest opposition parties are the Democratic Party and the Socialist Movement for Integration (LSI). Every five years, the parliament elects the country's president, who is the head of state; Ilir Meta of LSI was elected president in April 2017.

Local government is conducted by 61 municipal councils and their directly elected mayors. In addition, there are 12 prefectures, each headed by an appointee of central government. The prefects co-ordinate the regional departments of the various ministries and have some oversight over the local councils' work. For macro-planning purposes, each local council elects delegates from its number to a regional authority (*qark*) whose boundaries correspond with those of the prefecture.

ECONOMY

The Democratic Party government elected in 1992 inherited an economy in ruins, where GDP had fallen by more than 50% since 1989. It launched an economic reform programme that included price and exchange system liberalisation, fiscal consolidation, monetary restraint and an incomes policy. These were complemented by a comprehensive package of structural reforms, including privatisation, enterprise and financial sector reform, and creation of the legal framework for a market economy and private sector activity.

These reforms were similar to those applied in other newly democratic countries of central and eastern Europe, and were popularly known as 'shock therapy'. The growth and currency stabilisation that they brought were accompanied by unemployment and a sharp reduction in state benefits. In 1995, GDP growth began to stall and inflation to increase – in 1996, it approached 20% and in 1997, the year of the civil uprising, it reached 50%.

Since 1998, however, the economy has stabilised and GDP has increased every year since, thanks mainly to the expansion of the services sector, which accounts for nearly half of GDP. Agriculture, mostly on small family farms, accounts for about half of employment but about 20% of GDP. The construction industry has fallen back from its peak in 2008 to about 9% of GDP. The economy is further bolstered by remittances from Albanians abroad, mainly in Greece and Italy, which, although they have declined in recent years, still account for 7% of GDP.

The grey economy may be as large as 50% of official GDP. Much of this comes from the cultivation and export of cannabis, which is widely grown throughout the country. Spectacular police raids on the cannabis producers of Lazarati and elsewhere make international headlines from time to time.

ETHNIC GROUPS

Most people who live in Albania are ethnically Albanian. There are several minority groups in the country, but accurate figures for their numbers are not available. The most recent census, conducted in 2011, was the first to include a question about ethnic and cultural affiliation, but this was one of several optional questions and nearly 16% of respondents chose not to answer it. The nationwide figures also give a misleading impression because most ethnic minorities are clustered in specific districts, rather than being evenly spread throughout the country.

The largest minority is the Greek-speaking community, which is concentrated in southern Albania. There are state-funded Greek-medium schools in that part of the country, and ethnic Greeks are active in the political and commercial life of Albania. The nationwide figure for the Greek community in the 2011 census is 0.87%, although it is likely that there is some underreporting. The Roma and the Vlachs make up the second-largest ethnic groups, with 0.3% each at national level. As in most other countries, Roma are almost completely excluded from the political process and many live in extremely precarious conditions of great poverty.

Vlachs (also known as Aroumanians) were originally transhumant shepherds and they are found all over the Balkans. The main centres of Vlach population in Albania are in villages in the Korça district (Voskopoja is one; Mborja is another) and across the central lowlands in towns such as Lushnja and Berati. Their language is very similar to Romanian and many Albanian Vlachs have emigrated to study or work in Romania. It is not known when the two groups divided, but the languages are close enough that a modern Romanian and an Albanian Vlach can converse with each other.

Egyptians and Slavs are the other main minorities in Albania. The Egyptian, or Jevg, community claims to be descended from Egyptian mercenaries who came to Albania with Alexander the Great's army. This community, too, exists in other Balkan countries; in Albanian-speaking lands their mother tongue is Albanian. Egyptians are often lumped in with Roma, but they look different and are more integrated into Albanian society. The main thing the two communities have in common is the extreme discrimination they face.

There are Slav-speaking settlements around Lake Prespa, where they are ethnically Macedonian; in the border area between Peshkopia and Kukësi, where they are Gorani, like their cousins (often literally) across the border in Kosova; and around Lake Shkodra and in Malësia e Madhe, where they are ethnically Montenegrin.

Albanian is an Indo-European language, in the same large family as Greek, Italian and Serbo-Croat (and English), but in a separate linguistic branch from all of them. It shares certain grammatical features with Romanian, and the point at which the two languages diverged is a matter of great controversy among philologists of both countries.

Albania was part of the Ottoman Empire for more than 400 years (pages 10–11), and Turkish words have naturally become assimilated into the Albanian language, including *reçel* (jam), *koltuk* (armchair), *sahat* (clock), *çantë* (handbag) and *kusur* ([small] change). Greek words have also made their way into Albanian, and are used particularly in the south (eg: 'Are you hungry?', *A ke oreks?*).

The grammatical structure of Albanian is instantly recognisable to anyone who has studied other Indo-European languages. People who speak French or another Romance language will notice cognates such as *furrë* (*four*, oven), *qen* (*chien*, dog) and the numbers *dy* and *katër* (two and four). That said, however, it must be admitted that Albanian grammar is difficult and much of its vocabulary does not look familiar on first acquaintance.

Albanians themselves are secretly rather pleased that their language is reputed to be so difficult. They will waste no time in telling you with glee that the Albanian alphabet has 36 letters; they will regale you with stories of elderly peasants from opposite ends of the country who are unable to understand each other's dialect. They will be delighted if you learn some of their language, but somewhat taken aback if you speak it well.

THE ALPHABET The 36 letters of the alphabet include two letters with diacritic marks (*ë* and *ç*) and nine digraphs, meaning letters that are written using two consonants but that are considered to be a single letter (*dh, gj, ll, nj, rr, sh, th, xh* and *zh*). This makes the printed language look scarier than it really is – most of the 36 letters will cause no difficulty at all. Each of the consonants is always pronounced in the same way, wherever it appears in the word; vowels can be short or long, but the language is fairly phonetic, which makes it very easy to learn phrases. A guide to pronunciation and a list of everyday words and phrases can be found on pages 272–8.

DIALECTS A dialect is a language variant that is sufficiently different from another variant of the same language, and sufficiently consistent within itself, to be more than just an accent. Three dialects of Albanian are normally recognised: Arbëresh is spoken in parts of southern Italy, where Albanians settled after the Ottoman conquest of their country; Gheg is spoken in northern Albania, Kosova, Montenegro and northwestern Macedonia; and Tosk is spoken in southern Albania, southern Macedonia and Skopje, and in some mountain villages of northern Greece. Some argue that the language used in central Albania (Durrësi and Tirana) might also qualify as a dialect.

Within Albania a standard form of the language is used, known as 'the literary language' (*gjuha letrare*). The literary language was an official attempt to combine elements of Gheg and Tosk, although northern Albanians would contend that Tosk elements preponderate in it. It has been taught in Albanian schools for more than 50 years and is universally understood. People may use their own dialect when talking among themselves, but with anyone who is not local (ie: not only foreigners) they will switch to this standardised Albanian. Of course, it is true that an elderly shepherd is likely to be less fluent in 'literary language' than a 30-year-old bank clerk, but the chances are the shepherd will also make more of an effort to ensure that, as a guest in his or her land, you are happy and understand what is going on.

RELIGION

E mos shikoni kisha e xhamia/feja e shqyptarit asht shqyptaria!
(Pay no attention to churches and mosques/the Albanian's faith is Albanian-ness!)
O Moj Shqypni!, Pashko Vasa (1825–92)

During the five centuries that they formed part of the Ottoman Empire, Albanians converted to Islam in larger numbers than anywhere else in Ottoman Europe. Catholicism survived in the high mountains of the north and in coastal cities such as Shkodra; Orthodox Christians clung to their faith in the south. However, it is fairly clear that many (if not most) of those who converted did so for entirely pragmatic reasons, such as reducing their tax demands, gaining the right to bear arms or keeping their sons from the *devshirme* (pages 10–11). Often the man of the household would convert, while his wife retained her Christian faith. There were also cases of 'crypto-Christianity', where people would adopt Islamic names and attend prayers in the mosque, but in private would follow their old Christian rituals.

Perhaps this attitude helps to explain how it was possible for religion to be completely banned in 1967. In that year, Albania's communist government prohibited religious worship and the country became the world's only officially atheist state (page 16). Churches and mosques were demolished or turned into warehouses or sports halls, and the practice of religion remained an offence until 1990. Albania remains an extremely secular society today.

The 2011 census was the first to include a question about the respondent's religious affiliation, but it was one of several optional questions and over 16% of people chose not to answer it. Unreliable though the data may be, they reveal an interesting shift from the traditional breakdown of 70% Muslim, 20% Orthodox and 10% Catholic. The 2011 figures show just under 57% Muslim, with a further 2% answering 'Bektashi', 10% Catholic and only 7% Orthodox. A fraction of 1% identified themselves as belonging to another Christian religion – the evangelical Protestant churches that have become popular in the cities in the past decade or so – and 2.5% continue to describe themselves as atheists.

THE AUTOCEPHALOUS CHURCH The Albanian Orthodox Church is autocephalous, meaning that it ordains its own bishops and is its own authority. Autonomy from the Greek Church was a campaign issue for Orthodox Albanians in the Rilindja years of the early 20th century, particularly in Korça and among diaspora Albanians in the USA (many of whom were originally from Korça). The first liturgy in Albanian was celebrated in Boston in 1908, by a priest who had been ordained two weeks before by the Russian Archbishop of New York. The Albanian priest's name was Fan Noli, and in 1924 he also served for six months as Prime Minister of Albania.

After the end of communism and the restoration of religious freedom, a new archbishop was enthroned in 1992, and the Albanian Church has regained its autocephalous status. The website of the Orthodox Autocephalous Church (w *orthodoxalbania.org*) has information about the Church's history and activities, although not all of it is translated into English. There is also a breakaway Orthodox Autocephalous Church, based in Elbasani (page 115).

THE CATHOLIC CHURCH Albania's Catholics are mostly concentrated in the northwest of the country: Shkodra, Mirdita and villages hidden in the mountains, too remote for the Ottomans to have bothered trying to convert them to Islam. Their perceived allegiance to Rome brought them under particular suspicion from the communists who came to power in 1944. Priests were arrested and shot; others were imprisoned and died in labour camps. Lay Catholics were arrested too, including a young woman from Mirdita called Marie Tuci, who had been a postulant with the Stigmatine Sisters in Shkodra until the government closed the convent. Imprisoned in 1949, she died the following year, aged only 21. Some of the Catholics who died for their faith under communism are commemorated in Shkodra Cathedral and (in Albanian) on the website of the Catholic church in Shkodra (w *kishakatolikeshkoder.com*).

JUDAISM Despite the German occupation of Albania, the country's small Jewish community survived World War II; indeed, during the war, Albania provided a haven for Jewish refugees from other countries. Some of the Albanians who sheltered Jews are honoured at the Yad Vashem Holocaust memorial in Jerusalem as 'Righteous among the Nations'. Nor were Jews treated any worse than members of other religions during the atheism campaign. The Jewish community emigrated *en masse* to Israel as soon as the borders opened, not because they had been badly treated in Albania but simply because, unlike most Albanians, they were lucky enough to have a country that would welcome them.

BEKTASHISM Albania's 'fourth religion' is Bektashism, a Sufi order of Islam founded in the 13th century. The Ottoman Empire's 'official' Islam was Sunni, and was followed mainly by the intelligentsia, the civil servants and functionaries. Ordinary people in the Balkan provinces were much more attracted by the Sufi sects, whose rituals and rite system were closer to folk beliefs. The followers of Sufism believe that individuals can achieve communion with God through their own personal qualities and experience, with the help of contemplation.

Bektashism came to Albania gradually, brought by clerics known as dervishes or *babas* (fathers) travelling alone or in very small groups. They actively sought to assimilate local traditions into the religious ideas they taught, including relics of paganism such as mountain worship. Their religious centres – places of preaching, study and initiation called *teqe* (spelt '*tekke*' in Turkish, and sometimes in English too) – were often established near the tomb of some righteous person, who with time became venerated in the same way as Christian saints.

Bektashism took hold in Albania and began to expand dramatically in the early 19th century; Ali Pasha Tepelena (see box, pages 254–5) was a convert. Alarmed by the sect's popularity, the Ottoman authorities attempted to suppress it; in response, the *babas* moved up into the mountains and built *teqes* in high, remote places such as Mount Tomorri in Skrapari and Melani, above Libohova. Many of these *teqes* are still used today, especially for pilgrimages on holy days.

The Bektashi order was expelled from Turkey in 1925 and its leadership of the time decided to move its world headquarters to Albania. The World Bektashi Centre, in the outskirts of Tirana, welcomes visitors (pages 85–6).

EDUCATION

School education in Albania follows a pattern that is unfamiliar to British visitors. Most children attend the same school for nine years, then go on to either a General High School (Shkolla e Mesme e Përgjithshme) or a Professional High School (Shkolla e Mesme Profesional). The latter trains students for specific professions – for example, economics and accounting, mechanics, construction, hotel management or sports. In very rural areas, the elementary schools tend to take only five classes; after their fifth year, the children have to commute to school in a larger village or town, or even board with relatives or in a school dormitory (*konvikt*).

More than half of those who finish high school go on to higher education. Albania's state university was founded in the 1950s. It has branches in each city, offering a range of faculties such as engineering, medicine, science, law and economics; the Agricultural Institute in Kamza (near Tirana) and the Conservatoire (in Tirana) are also part of the state university system. The first private university in the country opened its doors in 2002 and since then there has been a huge increase in the number of such institutions. They are of varying quality; some are very good and have close academic relations with universities in Italy, France or other western European countries. Many Albanian families continue to make huge sacrifices so that their children can go to universities abroad.

CULTURE

LITERATURE The earliest documents written in Albanian were religious works produced by Catholic priests – a 16th-century missal and some doctrinal poetry survive. However, Albanian literature did not emerge until the 19th century, in a cultural phenomenon known as the National Renaissance (Rilindja Kombëtare), which was closely linked to the rise of Albanian nationalism.

The 19th-century writers included essayists and dramatists, but the predominant literary form was lyric poetry, and its exponents came from all parts of the Albanian-speaking world. Pashko Vasa (1825–92) and Gjergj Fishta (1871–1940) were Shkodran; Çajupi (1866–1930) and Naim Frashëri (1843–1900) came from the south; Jeronim de Rada (1814–1903) was Arbëresh; and Fan Noli (1880–1965) was born in an Albanian settlement near Adrianople, now the Turkish city of Edirne. Other notable literary figures of the period were Asdreni (1872–1947), the author of the poem that later became the national anthem, and the essayist Faik Konica (1875–1942), who was Albania's ambassador to the USA from 1926 until his sudden death in 1942.

The lyric tradition continued into the 20th century, represented by the Shkodran poets Migjeni (1911–38) and Martin Çamaj (1925–93), and was complemented with novels, plays and short stories. The extracts from Albanian folk tales throughout this book are translated from the versions by Mitrush Kuteli (the pseudonym of Dhimitër Pasko, 1907–67). Dritëro Agolli (1931–2017) made a delightful translation of some of Robert Burns's poems into Albanian. These writers, like others such as Fatos Arapi (b1930), the Kosovar Rexhep Qosja (b1936) and Vath Koreshi (1936–2006), are almost unknown in the English-speaking world.

The only novelist of that generation who is at all widely read there is Ismail Kadare, born in Gjirokastra in 1936. Kadare's works, in addition to being fine literature, make very good background reading if you are planning to visit Albania. *Chronicle in Stone*, *Broken April* and *The General of the Dead Army* are perhaps the most accessible. These novels are available in English, but the translations are made from the French version rather than coming directly from Albanian. Those who read the language may well prefer the French translations, which were made by the great Albanian–French translator Jusuf Vrioni (1916–2001), and give a more accurate flavour of the original. Affordable paperback editions are published in Fayard's *Le Livre de Poche* series. See pages 246–7 for further information about Kadare and his work.

The next generation of Albanian writers includes Bardhyl Londo (b1948), Besnik Mustafaj (b1958), Preç Zogaj (b1957) and Visar Zhiti (b1952), whose first volume of poetry was deemed so subversive that it earned him ten years in communist labour camps.

FILM In the 1960s and 1970s, Albania developed a thriving film industry. A film studio, Kinostudio, was opened in 1952 and *Skanderbeg*, a Soviet–Albanian co-production, was released the following year. Initially, post-production was done in the Soviet Union or Yugoslavia; the first feature film entirely produced in Albania was *Tana*, in 1958. By the 1970s, Kinostudio was making 14 films a year. There were 26 cinemas, in towns all over the country, and portable cinemas took films to the villages. The Albanian Film Archive (w *aqshf.gov.al*) holds a huge stock of communist-era films, much of it in very precarious condition. Work is under way to conserve, restore and digitise some of the films and, in due course, they may become commercially available on DVD.

In the late 1990s, Albanian scriptwriters and directors began to produce films again and several have had international success. Directors to look out for include Kujtim Çashku (*Colonel Bunker*, 1996), Gjergj Xhuvani (*Slogans*, 2001; *Dear Enemy*, 2004; *East West East*, 2009) and Fatmir Koçi (*Time of the Comet*, 2008). Art-house cinemas in Britain and other western European countries screen Albanian films from time to time, and they can sometimes be sourced from the internet.

MUSIC There are three distinct strands to Albanian folk music – the diatonic music of the north, the pentatonic tradition of the south and the urban music of the north (*ahengu qytetar*) in which chromatic melodies often prevail.

The music of northern Albania (and of Albanians in Montenegro and Kosova) is characterised by solo male singers, accompanied on long-necked stringed instruments called *çiftelia* and *lahuta*. The *lahutë* is a bowed instrument, making it suitable for accompanying diatonic melodies, while the *çifteli* has frets and is used to create a kind of drone effect, which is very atmospheric. A single-drone bagpipe called the *gajde* is also played in the north and sounds remarkably Celtic.

Albanian polyphonic music has a very wide geographic spread. It is found not only in southern Albania, but also across the modern borders in Greek Epirus and southwestern Macedonia, as far north as parts of Kosova, and in the Arbëresh settlements in southern Italy. In its core area of southwestern Albania, its basis is pentatonic and it is usually sung unaccompanied, by two or three – or in rare cases four – voices (in the musical sense of 'voices'; there might well be more than three or four people singing). The most characteristic instrument of the south is the clarinet.

The chromatic intervals of Albanian urban folk music were inherited from Turkish musical traditions during the Ottoman period. This type of music is found mainly in the towns of central Albania, especially Elbasani, and also in Shkodra and Berati. It can be sung with an instrumental accompaniment, or played by a small orchestra. Musical instruments typical of this tradition are the accordion, the mandolin, the tambourine and a fretted instrument called the *sharki*. Urban folk music has heavily influenced the development of 'popular music', *musika popullore*, which is the only type of traditional music that is at all easy to hear live in Albania.

The folklore festivals at Gjirokastra (every four years, more or less) and Peshkopia (annually, in September) are the best places to hear all the different Albanian musical traditions, including performers from other Albanian-speaking lands. Smaller festivals of traditional music take place from time to time in other parts of the country; the Përmeti Folk Festival, held annually in June, brings together traditional musicians from all over the Balkans, with a special focus on a different country each year.

2

Practical Information

WHEN TO VISIT

For most purposes, the best times of year to visit Albania are spring and autumn. The countryside is particularly beautiful in those seasons; in autumn the orchards blaze with the bright orange of the persimmons and the cooler colours of the citrus fruits, while in spring the apple and cherry blossoms form little pastel-toned drifts by the roadside. The long spring evenings are a good time to enjoy the terrace cafés in Tirana and the coastal towns. In September and October it is still warm enough to swim at the Ionian beaches. In addition, spring and autumn are ideal for relatively low-level hiking or cycle-touring.

Albania has a Mediterranean climate and in the lowlands it never gets really cold. The southwest coast in particular is very clement, with average winter temperatures of 8–10°C. The problem in winter tends to be rain, which makes the city streets and minor roads muddy and slippery. Most of Albania's annual rainfall occurs between late autumn and early spring; outside the high mountain areas, it is unusual for it to rain in summer.

In the highlands, winter is a much more serious proposition; snow can fall from November until March. Major roads, such as those linking Shkodra with Kukësi or Përmeti with Korça, are cleared quickly (usually within a day), but the high passes on minor roads are normally closed for two or three months – or even longer in a harsh winter. Mountain towns such as Korça and Peshkopia are very cold at this time of year. In Tirana, however, it is unusual for temperatures to stay below zero for more than a few days at a time, while on the coast, snow is practically unheard of.

In summer, on the other hand, inland towns can become oppressively hot; July is usually the warmest month, and sightseeing in high summer is an exhausting business. In Tirana, for example, temperatures in the high 30°Cs are common, and there are a few days in most summers when the thermometer tops 40°C. Hotels and restaurants of a reasonable standard have air conditioning, but museums do not. On the coast, sea breezes keep the average temperatures down to a more tolerable 25–30°C; but during July and August the coastal resorts are crowded and the beaches covered in litter. The best place to be at the height of summer is in the high mountains. Hikers and cyclists should be sure to have enough water with them; everyone else will never be far from a café.

HIGHLIGHTS

Albania has something for almost everyone. Lovers of the outdoors will be happy just about anywhere in the country. The Albanian Alps in the far north and the mountains between Berati and Përmeti in the south are probably the best organised in terms of accommodation, guides and so forth. The Lura Lakes, between Rrësheni and Peshkopia, and the Lunxhëria and Nemerçka ranges in the southwest, are more remote but offer fantastic hiking and cycling opportunities.

Those who are interested in archaeology and history will find Albania full of delights. In the southwest of the country, the ancient city of Butrint already draws hundreds of thousands of visitors every year. It richly deserves its status as the country's best-known archaeological site, but there are many other interesting Illyrian, Greek and Roman remains. No visit to southern Albania would be complete without the ancient cities of Gjirokastra and Berati, with their hilltop castles and unique architecture. In the north, the castles of Shkodra and Kruja embody centuries of history, one layer upon another.

Lovers of medieval art should visit the icon collections in Berati, Korça and Tirana; the whole of central and southern Albania is full of half-forgotten churches with magnificent frescoes. Ornithologists will want to head for the coastal wetlands at Karavastaja, Kune-Vaini and Velipoja. Finally, connoisseurs of beaches could easily spend a couple of weeks happily working their way up or down the Albanian Riviera.

SUGGESTED ITINERARIES

Where you go in Albania depends not only on what you like doing, but also where you enter the country. The main points of entry are Tirana International Airport and Saranda, on the ferry from Corfu. Those who approach Albania from other directions – perhaps via a budget flight to Montenegro, Kosova or Macedonia, or on a ferry from Italy – will need to tweak these suggested routes to suit their starting points. All the itineraries that follow can be done by public transport, although the occasional taxi or hire-car will speed things up considerably.

LONG WEEKEND
Coming from Corfu
Friday: Arriving in Saranda on the morning hydrofoil will allow you to head straight for Butrint, possibly spending the night at the Livia Hotel there.
Saturday: Gjirokastra: visiting the castle and one or two of the traditional houses; staying overnight there or returning to Saranda in the evening.
Sunday: The Riviera: Ali Pasha's fortress at Porto Palermo; possibly Borshi Castle; a swim at Borshi or Himara; back to Saranda for the Monday-morning hydrofoil to Corfu.

It is possible to rent a car in Saranda and for such a short visit this would be advisable (page 41).

Flying into Tirana
Friday: Day in Tirana: National Historical Museum; National Gallery of Arts; a walk around town.
Saturday: Visit one or all of Tirana's museums of the communist period; hike to Pëllumbasi Cave, returning to Tirana that evening; or visit Durrësi (beach or archaeological sites and museum, depending on weather and preferences), either returning to Tirana or staying overnight in Durrësi.
Sunday: Travel to Kruja; visit the castle and museums; straight to the airport for the evening flight, or stay overnight and travel to the airport from Kruja the next morning.

ONE WEEK
Coming from Corfu
Day 1: As Friday, *Long Weekend*

Day 2: As Saturday, *Long Weekend*, staying overnight in Gjirokastra.
Day 3: Visit Antigonea and/or Libohova area; overnight in Gjirokastra.
Day 4: Day trip to Byllis; return to Gjirokastra or Saranda in the afternoon.
Days 5–6: The Riviera: as Sunday, *Long Weekend*, but staying at Borshi, Himara or Dhërmiu; swim and eat fish, or continue to the Llogoraja Pass and go hiking in the forest (a hire car would be especially useful on these two days).
Day 7: Return to Saranda; afternoon ferry back to Corfu.

Flying into Tirana
Day 1: As Friday, *Long Weekend*.
Day 2: Berati: visit the castle and Ethnographic Museum; walk around town; stay overnight.
Day 3: Day trip to Byllis; overnight in Berati.
Day 4: Return to Tirana via Elbasani.
Day 5: As Saturday, *Long Weekend*.
Day 6: Day in Tirana: combination of cable-car trip to Mount Dajti; Petrela Castle; Archaeological Museum; Tirana Mosaic; a walk around the city.
Day 7: As Sunday, *Long Weekend*.

TWO WEEKS
Coming from Corfu
Day 1: As Friday, *Long Weekend*.
Day 2: Further exploration of Butrint site; boat trips and/or hiking. Overnight in Saranda or Gjirokastra.
Days 3–5: As days 2–4, *One Week*, with final night in Gjirokastra or Përmeti.
Day 6: To Korça via Përmeti and Erseka.
Day 7: Korça and environs (archaeological sites or Prespa Lakes, depending on preferences).
Days 8–10: To Tirana; follow Tirana weekend itinerary (staying a third night in Kruja or Tirana).
Day 11: Vlora.
Days 12–13: As days 5–6, *One Week*, returning slowly to Saranda down the Riviera.
Day 14: Morning or afternoon ferry back to Corfu.

Flying into Tirana
Days 1–4: As above, with night 4 in Elbasani.
Day 5: To Korça (archaeological sites or Prespa Lakes, depending on preferences); overnight in Korça.
Day 6: To Gjirokastra via Erseka and Përmeti.
Day 7: Gjirokastra: visiting the castle and the traditional houses; staying overnight there or continuing to Saranda in the evening.
Day 8: Saranda and Butrint.
Day 9: Return to Tirana via Riviera (Himara and Vlora).
Day 10: As day 6, *One Week*.
Day 11: As day 5, *One Week*.
Days 12–13: Lezha, Shkodra and Drishti or Rubiku. Overnight in Shkodra.
Day 14: As day 7, *One Week*.

THREE WEEKS A three-week itinerary might combine the two one-week itineraries (regardless of the point of entry into Albania; the order of the itineraries can be tweaked so that you finish where you want to leave from, rather than at the other end of the country), and then focus on either (a) cultural and historical heritage or (b) outdoor activities in the mountains (see following sections).

Option (a) Add three nights to 'Corfu' days 1–3, staying in Gjirokastra and Saranda, to visit the Islamic sites at Delvina, Phoinike and Hadrianopolis.

Add two nights to 'Tirana' day 5, to allow a day trip to Voskopoja, a detour to Selca e Poshtme and more time to explore Korça.

Days 19–20: Add two nights to 'Tirana' days 12–13, for an overnight trip to Thethi, Puka or Mirdita.

Day 21: As day 7, *One week*.

Option (b) Add two nights to 'Tirana' days 2–3, continuing from Berati to Çorovoda for rafting or hiking, depending on the time of year.

Day 16: To Shkodra.

Days 17–20: Bus to Thethi; overnight there; hike to Valbona; overnight in Tropoja; return to Shkodra on Komani ferry.

Day 21: Return to airport either directly from Shkodra or with detour to Kruja (as day 7, *One week*), depending on flight departure time.

ONE MONTH If you are lucky enough to have a whole month to spend in Albania, you will probably have torn up any itinerary by the end of your first week. Those who like mountains will want to spend more time in the Albanian Alps or perhaps explore Puka or Mirdita. Those interested in cultural heritage may want to spend an extra day or two in Shkodra and then visit Mati and Mirdita on the way back to Kruja (or Saranda). Or perhaps you will have had enough of travelling and just want to relax on the Riviera or at one of the lakes. It is worth repeating that Albania has something for almost everyone.

TOUR OPERATORS

The number and range of organised tours to Albania from western Europe increases every year. The tours range from general introductions, often including one or more of Albania's neighbouring countries, to specialist archaeological or cultural visits. The doyen of the UK-based tour operators is Regent Holidays, which has been leading trips to Albania since 1971. Regent also offers a four-night city break to Tirana and – like other agencies – can tailor-make individual itineraries.

Although there are many travel agencies within Albania, almost all of them cater for the outbound market. As a rule, those that act as agents for foreign tour operators also offer tours and bespoke itineraries for independent travellers.

IN THE UK
Andante Travels The Old Barn, Old Rd, Alderbury, Salisbury SP5 3AR; 01722 713800; e tours@andantetravels.co.uk; w andantetravels.co.uk

Brightwater Holidays Eden Park Hse, Cupar, Fife KY15 4HS; 01334 657155; e info@brightwaterholidays.com; w brightwaterholidays.com

Regent Holidays 6th Fl, Colston Tower, Colston St, Bristol BS1 4XE; 020 7666 1244; w regent-holidays.co.uk; see ad, 2nd colour section

IN THE USA
Kutrubes Travel 328 Tremont St, Boston, MA 02116; +1 617 426 5668; e adventures@kutrubestravel.com; w kutrubestravel.com; see ad, page 55. Offers tours to Albania of various durations.

IN ALBANIA
Albania Holidays Tirana; 04 223 5688, 04 223 5498; e contact@albania-holidays.com; w albania-holidays.com; see ad, 2nd colour section

Elite Travel Elbasani; ☎ 05 424 4094, 425 9934; e info@elitetravel-albania.com; w elitetravel-albania.com; see ad, page 55

Gjolek Mera Elbasani; m 069 21 22 555; e gjolekmera@yahoo.com

Past & Present Journeys Tirana; ☎ 04 237 3975; e info@pastandpresent.al; w pastandpresent.al

Tours Albania & Balkans Tirana; m 068 40 29 914; e toursalbania@yahoo.com; w tours-albania. com; see ad, page 55

OUTDOOR HOLIDAYS

Caravan Travel Gjirokastra; m 069 53 75 743, 069 22 34 137; e travelcaravan@ymail.com; w caravanhorseriding.com; ☐ Caravan Riding Centre Albania. Runs horseback tours in the mountains of southwest Albania. Experienced riders only; local horses & kit provided. English spoken.

Cycle Albania Tirana; ☎ 04 432 4884; m 069 24 75 728; e info@cyclealbania.com; w cyclealbania. com; see ad, 2nd colour section. Guided or self-guided tours on bicycles or motorcycles; bikes & motorbikes also available to hire.

Drive Albania 16–18 Palace Gates Rd, London N22 7BN, UK; ☎ 020 3393 9989 (UK); m 069 81 17 716 (Albania); e info@drivealbania.com; w drivealbania.com; see ad, page 222. Off-road

driving, mountain-biking & hiking tours in Albania's wildest corners.

Outdoor Albania Rr Gjin Bue Shpata 9/1, Sh 2, Ap 4, Tirana; ☎ 04 222 7121; Ⓢ Outdoor Albania; e info@outdooralbania.com; w outdooralbania. com; see ad, 2nd colour section. Albania's 1st specialist outdoors operator, organises guided hiking holidays of varying durations throughout spring & summer. In winter, offers guided ski tours & snowshoeing trips, led by an experienced climber & skier. 1-day & w/end activities, including day hikes in the countryside around Tirana; bespoke tours for individuals or small groups, to suit participants' abilities & interests. English spoken.

Walks Worldwide Long Barn South, Sutton Manor Farm, Bishop's Sutton, Alresford SO24 0AA, UK; ☎ 0845 301 4737, 01962 737565; e sales@ walksworldwide.com; w walksworldwide.com. Offers several hiking tours in northern & southern Albania & can also arrange tailor-made walking holidays there.

Zbulo! (Discover Albania) m 069 21 21 612, 069 67 31 932; e welcome@zbulo.org; w zbulo. org; ☐ Zbulo - Discover Albania; see ad, page 221. Can arrange visas for cross-border hikes (pages 43–4), & offers some unusual hiking itineraries. English spoken.

RED TAPE

Citizens of most Western countries are not required to obtain Albanian visas in advance. Countries to which this visa-free system applies include all those in the European Union and EFTA, all of Albania's neighbours (including Serbia), Australia, Canada, Japan, New Zealand, the USA and Turkey. Visitors to Albania are no longer required to pay an entry tax.

The Albanian Foreign Ministry's website (w *punetejashtme.gov.al*) carries information in English about visa requirements, and information on Albanian embassies throughout the world.

EMBASSIES

ALBANIAN EMBASSIES OVERSEAS Albanian embassies do not provide guidance to tourists beyond visa requirements and similar queries. Nor does the country have any tourist information offices overseas.

Ⓔ **Canada** 130 Albert St, Suite 302, Ottawa, Ontario, K1P 5G4; ☎ +1 613 236 3053; e embassy. ottawa@mfa.gov.al; w ambasadat.gov.al/canada/en/

Ⓔ **UK** (also covers the Republic of Ireland) 33 St George's Dr, London SW1V 4DG; ☎ 020 7828 8897;

e embassy.london@mfa.gov.al; w ambasadat.gov. al/united-kingdom/en

Ⓔ **USA** 2100 S Street NW, Washington DC 20008; ☎ +1 202 223 4942; e embassy.washington@mfa. gov.al; w ambasadat.gov.al/usa/en

WESTERN EMBASSIES IN TIRANA The Albanian Foreign Ministry's website (w *punetejashtme.gov.al*) has a full list of diplomatic representation in Albania, with contact details and consular opening hours, including for countries (such as Canada and Sweden) which cover Albania from their embassies in other countries.

Ⓔ Austria Rr Frederik Shiroka 3; `04 227 4855/6; e tirana-ob@bmeia.gv.at; w bmeia.gv.at/botschaft/tirana.html (also consulate in Shkodra)

Ⓔ Denmark Rr Nikolla Tupe 1, 4th Fl; `04 228 0600; e tiaamb@um.dk; w albanien.um.dk

Ⓔ France Rr Skënderbeu 14; `04 238 9700; e ambafrance.tr@adanet.com.al, consulat.tirana-amba@diplomatie.gouv.fr; w ambafrance-al.org

Ⓔ Germany Rr Skënderbeu 8; `04 227 4505; e info@tirana.diplo.de; w tirana.diplo.de

Ⓔ Greece Rr Frederik Shiroka 3; `04 227 4670, 04 227 4669, 04 223 4668; e gremb.tir@mfa.gr; w www.mfa.gr/tirana (also consulates in Korça & Gjirokastra)

Ⓔ Italy Rr Gjon Pali II 2; `04 227 5900; e segramb.tirana@esteri.it; w ambtirana.esteri.it (also consulates in Gjirokastra, Shkodra & Vlora)

Ⓔ Netherlands Rr Asim Zeneli 10; `04 224 0828; e tir@minbuza.nl; w nederlandwereldwijd.nl/landen/albanie

Ⓔ Poland Rr e Durrësit 123; `04 451 0020; e tirana.amb.sekretariat@msz.gov.pl; w tirana.msz.gov.pl

Ⓔ Spain Rr Skënderbeu 43; `04 227 4960/1; e emb.tirana@maec.es; w exteriores.gob.es/Embajadas/Tirana

Ⓔ Switzerland Rr Ibrahim Rugova 3/1; `04 223 4888, 04 225 6535; e helpline@eda.admin.ch; w eda.admin.ch/tirana

Ⓔ UK Rr Skënderbeu 12; `04 223 4973/4/5; e british.embassytirana@fco.gov.uk; w gov.uk/government/world/organisations/british-embassy-tirana

Ⓔ USA Rr e Elbasanit 103; `04 224 7285; e TiranaUSConsulate@state.gov; w tirana.usembassy.gov

GETTING THERE AND AWAY

BY AIR At the time of writing, Tirana was Albania's only international airport. A second may open at Kukësi during the lifetime of this guidebook; it is likely that this will be used mainly by budget airlines. Budget airline Wizz Air will start flights from London Luton to Tirana in May 2018. There are also budget flights from the UK to Podgorica and Prishtina. For information about getting to Albania from Montenegro, see pages 168, 190 and 220, and from Kosova, see pages 167 and 174.

Officially called 'Mother Teresa International Airport' and usually referred to as Rinas (the name of the village which once existed there), Tirana airport has been completely modernised and has a bright and airy passenger terminal with all the usual facilities, including free Wi-Fi. Smoking is prohibited throughout, except in an airside smoking lounge in departures. British Airways (w *ba.com*) has direct flights from London Gatwick to Tirana (TIA). A full list of airlines that operate scheduled flights into Tirana, with their websites and the telephone numbers of their offices in Tirana, is available on Tirana International Airport's website (w *tirana-airport.com*). This also has real-time listings for arrivals and departures, details about flight schedules and other useful information.

An ATM in the baggage reclaim area accepts Visa, MasterCard and Maestro cards, and issues Albanian lek. There is also a bureau de change (currency-exchange desk). There are reasonable toilet facilities in baggage reclaim. Beyond customs control are car-hire agencies (page 41), mobile-phone shops, cafés and a bookshop. There are several hotels in the vicinity of the airport (see opposite).

It takes about half an hour by car from the airport to Tirana, 17km away. A slip road in the opposite direction leads to the Fushë–Kruja junction of the main north–south highway, 2.8km from the airport; this is the most convenient route to northern Albania.

Approved airport taxis can be booked online in advance on w atex.al, hired from one of the taxi drivers who wait where passengers exit into the arrivals hall, or arranged at the kiosk just outside the exit from the terminal. You should agree a fare with the driver before accepting his services – the going rate into Tirana is €20. Unofficial taxis wait in the car park across the road from the airport perimeter fence and may charge slightly less.

From 06.00 to 18.00, an hourly bus service runs from the airport into the centre of Tirana, dropping passengers off as required at the two bus stations on Rruga e Durrësit. The one-way fare for this journey is 250 lek. In the city centre, the bus-stop is behind the National Theatre of Opera and Ballet [69 E2]. There are also bus services from the airport to Durrësi (*480 lek;* \ *052 225 539*) and Fieri (*1,000 lek;* m *069 67 40 073*). A taxi to Shkodra from the airport should cost no more than €50.

On the way out of Albania, airport check-in and security procedures are reasonably efficient. Leks can be changed back into euros, US dollars or sterling at the landside bureau de change, but the rates are as poor as one might expect. It is likely to be a better deal to spend any surplus leks in the airside duty-free shops. These sell Albanian souvenirs and foodstuffs such as olive oil and mountain tea (see box, page 6), as well as the usual things one finds in airports.

Where to stay at Tirana International Airport *Map, page 58*

Ark Hotel (56 rooms) \ 450 0515/0616; m 068 80 30 234; e info@arkhotel.al; w arkhotel. al. Part of Best Western's Premier chain, just beyond the airport perimeter fence & 5mins' walk from the terminal building. The quiet, generously sized rooms have good-size beds, AC, TV, & nicely designed en suites with bath & separate shower. Good English spoken at reception; lifts; restaurant; bar; well-equipped gym, spa & sauna; plus a small outdoor pool (summer only). B/fast served from 03.30 to 10.00, bar & restaurant open until 23.00. **$$$$**

Hotel Airport Tirana (50 rooms) \ 450 0190; m 068 20 04 243, 068 20 47 964, 068 20 55 133; e info@hotel-airportirana.com; w hotel-airportirana.com. Located just outside airport perimeter fence; hotel shuttle service provides free pick-up & drop-off on request. Restaurant, garden bar, outdoor swimming pool with wooden loungers, lift, laundry service & free parking. Nicely furnished, soundproofed rooms all en suite with AC, flatscreen TV, balcony, hairdryer & internet access; some have minibar, spa shower. **$$$$**

Jürgen (7 rooms) m 069 22 30 663; e hoteljurgen@yahoo.com. Right at entrance to airport perimeter fence; free parking; friendly, efficient reception staff. Restaurant with terrace; bar; garden. All rooms en suite with AC, TV & free Wi-Fi. **$$**

Verzaçi (30 rooms) m 068 20 25 542; e verzaci_hotel@yahoo.com; w verzaci-airport. com. 100m (5mins' walk) from airport roundabout; free pick-up & drop-off on request. Restaurant (**$$$**), terrace bar; lift; English spoken at reception; free parking; good Wi-Fi. Bedrooms surprisingly quiet, great views of parked planes & Kruja. All rooms with nice en-suite bathroom with excellent shower; flatscreen TV, AC, small balcony. **$$**

BY SEA For many northern Europeans, the cheapest and most convenient way to get to southern Albania is to take a flight to Corfu and from there the hydrofoil to Saranda. The journey takes about 40 minutes. There is at least one hydrofoil crossing a day, all year round (pages 223 and 226).

Albania has good sea connections with Italy. The busiest route is Bari–Durrësi (page 91), with several ferry companies operating throughout the year. The crossing takes about 9 hours. There are also ferries to Durrësi from Ancona and Trieste (18 and 24 hours, respectively), and to Vlora from Brindisi (8 hours overnight;

page 261). The Italian ferry websites (eg: w *traghetti.it*, w *traghettiamo.it*) have details of all the routes between Italy and Albania.

Those fortunate enough to have the use of a **private yacht** will find their mooring options rather limited in Albania. The country's only marina (at least at the time of writing) is on the Bay of Vlora, at Orikumi (pages 270–1). It is also possible to anchor or berth in Durrësi, Shëngjini, Vlora and Himara. Official port fees and other information are available from the National Coastal Agency (Agjencia Kombëtare e Bregdetit). Sail Albania, based in Vlora, are port agents for Vlora and the Orikumi marina; they also charter yachts and motorboats. There are other maritime agents in Albania, though most of them focus on commercial shipping.

National Coastal Agency m 067 60 96 010;
w bregdeti.gov.al
Orikum Yachting Club (Marina e Orikumit)
✪ 40° 20′ 32″ N 19° 28′ 18″ E; ☎ 0391 22248;
☎ +39 05 6525 2040 (Italy); m 069 53 50 233;
e marinaorikum@hotmail.it; w orikum.it

Sail Albania Rr Murat Terbaçi, Uji i Ftohtë, Vlora;
m 069 73 24 138, 069 77 10 739; e sailalbania@
gmail.com; w sail-albania.com

BY LAND Visitors who bring their own **cars** into Albania should ensure that their vehicle insurance is valid there. There is no longer a 'circulation tax'. Petrol and diesel are widely available everywhere except the most remote mountain areas. Liquid Petroleum Gas (LPG) is available in cities and large towns.

Crossing into Albania by **bus** is usually a straightforward process. Finding out about these cross-border buses, however, can be more of a challenge. At Greek bus stations and tourist information offices, staff will often deny the existence of any public transport to Albania. It is unclear whether this is because they are genuinely unaware of the many buses that travel between Greek and Albanian towns and cities, or are trying to prevent tourists from leaving their country.

There is always the alternative of taking a local bus to the border, going through both passport controls on foot, and continuing onward in one of the taxis or minibuses waiting on the Albanian side. At the major land crossings – Kakavija and Kapshtica from Greece, Qafë-Thana from Macedonia and Hani i Hotit from Montenegro – there will always be onward transport during the daytime. At the smaller crossings the drivers tend to have given up waiting for custom by about noon.

If crossing into Albania from Kosova, there are practically no formalities beyond showing your passport. Women aged under 18 travelling without either of their parents should carry a notarised authorisation; this is intended to make life difficult for criminals trafficking women, rather than for the legitimate female traveller. In the other direction, the Kosovar authorities require a minimum of 15 days' (additional) insurance to be purchased for foreign-registered vehicles (€30 for a car, at the time of writing). Vehicles with Kosova or Albania plates are exempt. This means that, unlike at other international crossings, local buses and minibuses travel freely across the border at Qafë e Morinës. See page 174 for further information about public transport on this route.

There are no international passenger **trains** at the time of writing, although the line from Podgorica to Shkodra is open and used for freight.

HEALTH *With thanks to Dr Felicity Nicholson*

BEFORE YOU GO Albania is no more dangerous from a health point of view than any other country in southeastern Europe. It is a good idea in general to keep up to date with **vaccinations** against tetanus, polio and diphtheria. In the UK these are normally given together and should be boosted every ten years. Other vaccinations that are worth considering are those against hepatitis A, hepatitis B and rabies.

For other journey preparation information, consult w travelhealthpro.org.uk (UK) or w wwwnc.cdc.gov/travel/ (USA). All advice found online should be used in conjunction with expert advice received prior to or during travel.

OTHER PRECAUTIONS Albanian **tap water** is treated and is fine for brushing teeth, but the pipes are old and most urban Albanians prefer mineral water. In the mountains, everybody drinks spring water, often piped from their own spring.

You should try to avoid drinking **unpasteurised milk** while you are in Albania; there is TB and brucellosis in the Albanian dairy herd. Dairy products in supermarkets and restaurants are commercially produced and properly pasteurised. Safe UHT milk is always available, even in small shops which stock homemade butter and cheese. The problem only really arises if you are staying with a family in a rural area, when you will almost certainly be offered fresh milk for breakfast and soft cheese or yoghurt at lunch or dinner. If you are concerned, you might want to think in advance about how to refuse it tactfully; the Albanian for 'I don't eat dairy products' is *'nuk ha bulmet'*.

HEALTH CARE IN ALBANIA If you are involved in an accident or a medical emergency, you should get yourself or the injured person into a taxi and say to the driver *'tek urgjenca'*, meaning 'to accident and emergency'. You will be given the best treatment possible. There is also an ambulance service, reached by dialling 127, but a taxi is probably quicker, at least outside the big cities.

In Tirana and other cities, there are now good non-state hospitals, with the latest technological equipment, which offer a full range of medical services up to and including heart bypasses and neurosurgery.

✚ **American Hospital** ☎04 235 7535/7011; w spitaliamerikan.com. 3 hospitals in Tirana (☎*04 235 7535*), medical centre in Durrësi (☎*05 222 2333*) & hospital in Fieri (☎*034 232 123*).

✚ **Hygeia Hospital** Opposite Casa Italia (Kthesa e Kamzës); ☎04 232 3000 (emergency), 04 239 0000 (info); w hygeia.al

In small towns and rural areas, health care can be a problem. State hospitals are often short-staffed and their equipment is old and sometimes does not work at all; many rural clinics have closed altogether. If you intend to travel outside the cities and are reliant on a specific medication, you should ensure you take an adequate supply with you.

For minor ailments, pharmacies can sell you almost anything over the counter. Opticians can make repairs to spectacle frames or replace lenses fairly quickly. Disinfecting solution for contact lenses is stocked by a few opticians in Tirana, but not widely elsewhere. The standard of dental practices is very variable – there are some good ones in Tirana – and you should seek local advice, perhaps at your hotel. The international-style supermarkets in Tirana and other large cities stock tampons.

HEALTH RISKS IN ALBANIA
Hepatitis A This viral infection is transmitted by contaminated food or water. Washing your hands before and after eating, and taking care over what you consume will greatly reduce the risk of contracting hepatitis A. If you plan to camp wild or stay in mountain-village homes, where it may be more difficult to take these precautions, you might consider being vaccinated before you travel.

Hepatitis B Hepatitis B is transmitted by sexual contact with an infected person, or by puncture wounds from contaminated instruments, such as needles. In the UK, the course of vaccinations is usually given only to health workers and other people who are likely to be at high risk. Albania is considered to have an intermediate carriage rate for hepatitis B of 2–8%. For travellers, the risk of hepatitis B can be avoided by not indulging in risky behaviour such as unsafe sex, body piercing, tattooing or acupuncture. There is also an increased risk when working with small children or playing contact sports. There are two types of vaccination, but even the shorter course (Engerix) must be started at least 21 days before travel for those aged 16 or over.

Insect-borne diseases These include tick-borne encephalitis and leishmaniasis; malaria was eradicated from Albania in the 1930s.

Leishmaniasis Leishmaniasis is transmitted by sandflies, very small insects (a third the size of mosquitoes) that bite mainly between dusk and dawn. They breed quickly in unsanitary conditions, so if you are in this kind of environment you should minimise outdoor activities after dusk, use protective clothing and insect repellent, and consider using a fine-meshed bed net (the mesh in mosquito nets is too big to keep sandflies out). The bite is painful, so you will know if you have been bitten. Leishmaniasis has two forms: cutaneous, which causes skin ulcers and lesions; and visceral, which weakens the immune system and can be fatal. There is no vaccine to prevent leishmaniasis, but both forms can be treated.

Tick-borne encephalitis This is spread through the bites of infected ticks. You can protect yourself to a large extent by preventing ticks from attaching themselves to you, and removing any that succeed. If you are hiking in the forests, you should cover your arms and legs; wear long trousers tucked into your boots, and a hat. There is some evidence that insect repellents containing DEET or permethrin can discourage ticks. Tick repellent and tick-removal gadgets can be bought before you travel, but they are not available in Albania.

Always check for ticks at the end of your day out. Ticks should be removed as soon as possible; the longer they are on your body, the greater the chance of infection. Grasp the tick as close as you can to your skin, with tick tweezers or your fingernails, and then pull it steadily and firmly away, at right angles to your skin. The tick will come away complete, as long as you do not jerk or twist. Clean the skin, and your hands, afterwards with soap and water or skin disinfectant, if possible. Don't try to burn the tick off or remove it with Vaseline, alcohol or other irritants, since they can cause the ticks to regurgitate and therefore increase the risk of disease. If you are travelling with a companion, you can check each other for ticks; if you are hiking with small children remember to check their heads, and particularly behind the ears.

Seek medical attention if you feel flu-like symptoms within one to four weeks after being bitten by a tick. In 20–30% of cases, the disease can then progress, with symptoms including a high fever and headache. There is a safe and effective vaccine (TicoVac and TicoVac Junior) available in the UK, although not on the NHS – the full schedule is three doses over 12 months. Two doses given a minimum of two weeks apart will offer some protection, although you should continue to take the precautions outlined above.

Rabies Rabies is not commonly reported – the last recorded case of human rabies in Tirana was in 1978 – but Albania is nonetheless classified as a high-risk country. Rabies can be passed from animals to humans through a bite, scratch or a lick and also through saliva getting into the eyes, nose or mouth. If you are bitten, scratched or licked by any mammal, wash the wound thoroughly with soap and under running water for at least 15 minutes, then pour on a strong iodine (if available) or alcohol solution. Seek medical advice as soon as possible.

Post-exposure prophylaxis should be given as soon as possible, but there is no time limit. Those who have not been immunised (see below) will need five doses of rabies vaccine and rabies immunoglobulin (RIG). The latter is unlikely to be found in Albania as there is a world shortage. Having three pre-exposure doses means you no longer need RIG, but just two further doses of rabies vaccine given three days apart which will be available. Pre-exposure vaccinations for rabies are ideally advised for everyone, but are particularly important if you intend to have contact with animals and/or are likely to be more than 24 hours away from medical help. Remember, if you do contract rabies, mortality is 100%.

SAFETY

Albania is a safe country for visitors. Its traditions of hospitality mean foreigners are treated with great respect; almost all Albanians will go out of their way to help you if you are lost or in trouble. In general, violent crime in Albania happens either within the underworld of organised crime or in the context of a blood feud. A foreign visitor is highly unlikely to come into contact with either of these categories.

Nevertheless, there are poor and desperate people in Albania, as there are in any other country, and thefts and muggings do occur. It is foolish to flash expensive watches or cameras around, especially in the peripheral areas of towns where the poorest people tend to live. Some travellers carry a dummy wallet with a small amount of cash in it, so that in the event of a mugging they can hand this over instead of their 'real' wallet full of dollars or euros.

The greatest risk most people in Albania face is on the roads, where traffic accidents are very frequent and the fatality rate is one of the highest in Europe. Until a decade ago, Albanian roads were so bad that it was difficult to drive fast enough to kill anyone. Now, though, cars zip along newly upgraded highways which are also used by villagers and their livestock. There is no stigma attached to drink-driving and little attempt is made to check it.

WOMEN TRAVELLERS

Foreign women are treated with respect in Albania, although the same respect is not always shown to Albanian women. Domestic violence, in particular, is very prevalent and almost always unreported. Outside the home, however, women are at less risk of sexual assault or rape than in any northern European country. Of course these crimes are not completely unknown, but they are rare enough to make headline news when they happen.

BLACK AND MINORITY ETHNIC TRAVELLERS

Black and minority ethnic (BAME) visitors to Albania sometimes find themselves on the receiving end of treatment that, although not racist in its intent, can make the visitor feel uncomfortable – for example, children or even adults stroking or pinching your skin out of curiosity. Occasionally, however, BAME visitors have been verbally and even physically abused by groups of racists. There have also been sporadic reports of racist treatment by some hotel owners. Saranda seems to be especially problematic.

LGBTI TRAVELLERS

Homosexuality is legal in Albania. A law passed in 2010 specifically protects its citizens against discrimination on grounds of sexual orientation, while a 2013 amendment to the criminal code added sexual orientation and gender identity to the grounds for charges of hate crimes. However, it is still rather taboo and the LGBTI (lesbian, gay, bisexual, transgender and intersex) community generally keeps a low profile. Almost no public figures are openly gay. A contestant on Albania's version of *Big Brother* came out in 2010, after the anti-discrimination law had been passed, but this led to his parents being driven out of their home town. That said, however, LGBTI travellers are unlikely to encounter hostility or discrimination in Albania, assuming they behave with reasonable discretion (as they probably would in an unfamiliar town in their own country). A couple of bars in Tirana advertise 'gay-friendly' evenings.

The National Network for LGBTI Rights, launched in 2017, is a non-formal structure that aims to promote LGBTI rights at local and national level, to increase the involvement of the LGBTI community in decision making, and to lobby for policies and laws that support LGBTI rights. The lead organisation is the Pink Embassy/ LGBT Pro (w *pinkembassy.al*), which has been active since the mid 2000s.

TRAVELLERS WITH A DISABILITY With thanks to Clare Sears

In 2010, Albania signed the UN Convention on the Rights of People with Disabilities. The next step in the journey towards achieving a society based on equality for all will be the ratification of this Convention, which will set targets for improving legislation, access and employment for people with disabilities. While this is all positive, Albania remains a deeply problematic destination for people with physical disabilities, particularly users of wheelchairs. Most pavements in Albania are not accessible, which makes independent movement nearly impossible, and most communist-era public and cultural buildings are entirely inaccessible, often with steep stairs. Outside central Tirana, traffic lights do not have acoustic signals; public transport is completely inaccessible for wheelchair users; and the use of Braille is pretty much non-existent. All that said, however, people with reduced mobility will find Albanians eager (possibly overeager) to assist when necessary.

Some more recent buildings have been designed to take people with disabilities

INFORMATION FOR TRAVELLERS WITH A DISABILITY

The UK's **gov.uk** website (w *gov.uk/guidance/foreign-travel-for-disabled-people*) provides general advice and practical information for travellers with disabilities preparing for overseas travel. **Accessible Journeys** (w *disabilitytravel.com*) is a comprehensive US site written by wheelchair users who have been researching wheelchair-accessible travel full-time since 1985. There are many tips and useful contacts (including lists of travel agents on request) for slow walkers, wheelchair travellers and their families, plus informative articles, including pieces on disabled travelling worldwide. The company also organises group tours. **Global Access News** (w *globalaccessnews.com/index.htm*) provides general travel information, reviews and tips for travelling with a disability. The **Society for Accessible Travel and Hospitality** (w *sath.org*) also provides some general information.

into account. The Sheraton and Rogner Europapark hotels are accessible and have specifically designed guest rooms. Tirana International Airport is accessible throughout, including the toilets, and has dedicated parking spaces at the entrance to the terminal. Some of the new shopping malls in Tirana and other big cities are also accessible. See page 54 for contact information for the Albanian Disability Rights Foundation.

TRAVELLING WITH CHILDREN

Older children are likely to have a wonderful time in Albania, as long as they are reasonably flexible when things do not go exactly as planned. Travelling with young children, however, does present some practical problems. Pavements tend to be rather high, which can make pushchairs awkward to manoeuvre, and restaurants rarely have high chairs available. Outside Tirana, health care is not up to Western standards and it may be hard to find exactly the medication you need, should this be required. Entertainment specifically for children is not usually available, apart from the swing-parks that abound in every town. On the outskirts of Tirana, strung out along the Elbasani road, there are several day resorts that have pools and other activities for children.

Two particularly appealing places for children of almost any age are the Llogora Tourist Village, between Vlora and Saranda, and Farma Sotira, in the mountains between Përmeti and Korça. The Llogora resort (page 260) has sports facilities including tennis courts and a large indoor swimming pool. Activities are organised for youngsters and a babysitting service is offered. The whole resort, over 1ha in extent, is designed to blend in harmoniously with the natural beauty of the park. Several roe deer live in a large enclosure at the edge of the forest and are let out during the day to wander freely around the complex. Farma Sotira (page 148) is a working farm, with sheep, cattle, chickens and horses. There is an outdoor pool with a separate shallow section for children. It is surrounded by meadows and forests; more strenuous hikes are also possible.

WHAT TO TAKE

It is not strictly necessary to take anything at all to Albania; imported toiletries, first-aid items, standard chargers for mobile phones and alkaline batteries can all be bought in any reasonable-sized town. Tampons are available in the Western-style supermarkets in Tirana and other cities, and the street markets have the same cheap imported clothes as those sold in Western supermarkets, at similar prices.

The most useful item to bring is undoubtedly a pocket- or head-torch (flashlight). The electricity supply in towns is much more reliable than it used to be, but there are still power cuts from time to time. In rural areas, these are more frequent and the lights can occasionally be out for several hours. Even if you are not planning to venture out of the cities, you will find a torch useful. The streets of Albanian towns are badly lit, as are some museums – a torch can come in very handy for seeing what is in the display cases.

Electrical sockets are the European two-pin standard; British travellers should remember to pack an adaptor for their phone, camera or other electronic equipment. For trips into the mountains of more than a day or two, a portable solar charger is a good way to keep phones and cameras powered up.

Mosquitoes can be a problem in the summer, especially on the coast. Insect repellent can be purchased in Albania, but you may prefer to come prepared with an extra-powerful brand. Plug-in devices which emit repellent are useful at night but, if you are likely to be staying anywhere with an uncertain power supply, a mosquito coil is more practical.

If you plan to travel around the country, particularly by public transport, a supply of baby wipes or a tube of antibacterial hand gel will come in useful. The roadside restaurants where the buses and minibuses stop for breaks usually have running water, but not always anything with which to dry your hands. Grabbing a couple of paper napkins from the restaurant-table on your way to the toilet is a useful precaution.

In the cities, especially Tirana, the summer dust can irritate eyes and throats; eye drops and cough sweets help, and some contact lens wearers give up and revert to wearing glasses.

MONEY

CURRENCY The Albanian monetary unit is called the lek, which is also one of the words for 'money'. The currency floats freely but is fairly stable; at the time of going to press, there are 152 lek to the pound sterling, 133 to the euro, and 114 to the US dollar. Up-to-date rates can be consulted on many websites, such as w exchangerates. org.uk. On the rate boards in banks and bureaux de change, the initials 'ALL' are sometimes used instead of the word 'lek'.

In the 1970s, the lek was revalued and a zero was dropped. Albanians of all ages still insist on using the old number of zeros, although people who have regular dealings with foreigners sometimes try to remember not to. The systems are differentiated by the adjectives 'old' (*të vjetra*) and 'new' (*të reja*). In modern supermarkets the prices are displayed in 'new' lek; in markets and small shops, particularly outside the cities, if prices are displayed at all they might be in either system. While it is fairly easy to guess that the price of a bottle of mineral water is about 30p rather than £3.00 (50 'new' lek rather than 500), it can in other cases be quite unclear which is meant. Fortunately, most Albanians are very honest about this and will put you right if you try to give them ten times more money than they expect.

Matters are made even more confusing by a tendency to quote large numbers without mentioning the word 'thousand' – so a hotel receptionist might well quote a room rate simply as 'fifty'. The only way to find out if this means 50 euros or 5,000 (new) lek is by asking.

CHANGING MONEY All towns have ATMs (cash machines, known in Albanian as *bankomat*). Some ATMs (eg: those of the ProCredit and Raiffeisen banks) can issue euro notes as well as Albanian lek. A few cash machines are still not linked to the international networks and only accept cards issued by that bank; the security guard will usually put you right if he spots you approaching the wrong sort of ATM.

Credit cards can be used to withdraw cash from ATMs and, increasingly, to pay for goods or services in city shops, hotels and the more upmarket restaurants. Some hotels have card machines that accept payment only in lek, even if the room rate is quoted in euros; the conversion rate is usually worse than the bank rate. The receptionist really ought to check first that you are happy with this, but you may wish to double-check before authorising the payment, especially if you have a Eurozone card.

Outside the cities, you should not rely on being able to use your credit card at all. This is especially important to bear in mind if you are setting off to travel in the Albanian mountains, where you will need sufficient cash to pay for all your accommodation and, if you are driving, fuel. The Albanian Riviera is also a cash-only economy along almost the whole of its length. Locations of ATMs in the Albanian Alps and Riviera are given in the relevant sections of this guidebook.

Foreign currency can be changed in banks, at bureaux de change, and on the street; the euro is by far the most widely accepted. The more upmarket hotels offer currency-exchange services, although often only for euros and usually at a less favourable rate than on the street. Banks and bureaux de change will have rates for major currencies other than the US dollar and the euro. Bureaux de change provide a speedier, less bureaucratic procedure than banks, and offer practically the same rate for the amounts most visitors will be changing. Where a bureau de change exists, the money changers on the street do not offer a significantly better rate. In Tirana and other big cities a minority of unscrupulous on-street changers circulate counterfeit notes.

You will almost certainly be able to pay for your hotel room in euros even if you have been quoted a price in lek, although the hotel will use a rule-of-thumb exchange rate which may not be in your favour. Restaurants also sometimes accept euros, especially in the far north where they are used to visitors from Montenegro and Kosova, where the euro is the official currency.

Visitors from the United States, in particular, should note that travellers' cheques are not accepted as payment anywhere in Albania and can no longer even be cashed.

BUDGETING

How much you spend in Albania depends on what you want to do and where you want to sleep. If you base yourself in Tirana, stay in one of the top-of-the-range hotels, hire a car with a driver to move around in, and eat in the best fish restaurants, you could just about get through €300 a day (hotel: €130–160; car: €100 a day, if long tours are involved; dinner with wine in an expensive restaurant: €40–50 per head). If, at the other budgetary extreme, you stay in backpackers' hostels (€12–15 per person), travel everywhere by bus (an hour-long journey costs about €1), buy lunch from the market (bread, cheese, tomatoes and fruit for under €5), and dine on pasta or pizza (€10 maximum), you could equally easily keep within a budget of a tenth of that amount.

Most people will probably fall somewhere between these two extremes. A 1.5-litre bottle of water in a shop (as opposed to a café) costs between 50 and 70 lek; a half-litre bottle of Albanian beer in a bar usually ranges from 150 to 200 lek; a small loaf of bread from a bakery costs between 40 and 50 lek; small, triangular *byrek* (page 48) are usually 30 lek; a medium-sized Mars bar, or similar imported chocolate, costs 60 lek in a supermarket, a bit more in a kiosk; and a litre of petrol or diesel, at the time of writing, is around 160 lek. Bars and cafés on the coast tend to charge more, especially in summer, than their inland equivalents.

Most museums, castles and archaeological sites have a small admission charge, usually 200 lek. A few of the most recently remodelled museums charge 500 or even 700 lek per visitor. Some sites are still unstaffed and do not have any explanatory information for visitors; when access is possible, it is free. Increasingly, mosques and churches charge a fixed admission fee; where they do not, a contribution of 100 or 200 lek per person is expected.

GETTING AROUND

MAPS After many years when almost all road maps of Albania were based on an out-of-date and inaccurate source from the early 1990s, it is a huge relief that usable maps are at last available. While they are usable, however, none is absolutely reliable – distances and spot heights, in particular, vary wildly from one map to another – and the speed of Albania's road improvement programme means that road classification is likely to go out of date quite quickly (this warning even applies to the maps in this guide).

The only commercially available **hiking maps** are published by the German company Huber Kartographie. At the time of going to press, only the far north of Albania is covered: 1:50,000 maps of Tropoja (pages 166–74), Thethi and Kelmendi (pages 211–21), and a 1:60,000 map of the cross-border hiking trail known as Peaks of the Balkans (pages 43–4). Further maps in this series are planned. The maps have contours at 50m intervals and include descriptions, in English, of selected hiking trails and cycling routes. Better still, they show, in grey dotted lines, the routes of old paths; these were the best routes 40 years ago and many of them are still used by local people.

Once you get to the Albanian Alps, 1:30,000 hiking maps of the mountains in the north can also be purchased, at very reasonable cost, from Journey to Valbona, a multi-faceted organisation based in Tropoja (w *journeytovalbona.com*). The only reliably marked trails in Valbona are being maintained and expanded by a group of local volunteers, and these beautiful maps are being produced in tandem with that work. They differentiate between marked trails, unmarked but clear trails, and invisible but plausible routes for confident navigators. Contours are shown at 10m intervals, 4x4 tracks are also indicated and there are extensive trail notes. The maps are printed to a high quality on waterproof paper. Maps of five different areas are available; the whole map, with hiking routes from Thethi to Gashi, can be consulted at the Rilindja Hotel (at the time of writing; page 172), where the smaller maps can be bought. Some of the purchase price goes to finance the work of maintaining and expanding the trail system.

The Albanian Military Geographical Institute (IGUS) has mapped the whole country in 1:50,000, but at the time of writing the sheets are not on sale. The only option at that scale, outside the Albanian Alps, is to refer to the 1:50,000 Soviet topographic maps, available to download for a small charge at w mapstor.com. These maps are based on very old data but are still useful for planning hikes or cycling tours in most of Albania. In some parts of the country the topography has changed quite substantially since they were produced – for example, the old village of Kukësi is now under Lake Fierza – and they should be used with caution everywhere, since new roads and dams have been built and old tracks have become blocked by landslides or washed away by floods. The names on the maps are in the Cyrillic alphabet. It should also be noted that the projection used is one from which amateur GPS equipment is unlikely to be able to set co-ordinates.

Freytag & Berndt *Albania*, 1:400,000, single-sided, index on reverse, some topographical detail, also covers all of Montenegro & Kosova, most of Macedonia & part of northern Greece.

Freytag & Berndt *Albania*, 1:200,000, double-sided, index booklet, some topographical detail, shows administrative boundaries.

Huber Kartographie GmBH *Peaks of the Balkans*, 1:60,000, contoured, GPS-compatible, relief shading, shows national park boundaries & recommended overnight stops. Detailed route description on reverse, with GPS waypoints.

Huber Kartographie GmBH *Tropoja–B. Curri–Valbona & Vermoshi–Tamare–Razma–Thethi*, 1:50,000, contoured at 50m intervals, spot heights, GPS-compatible, extensive topographic information. Recommended hiking & cycling routes are prominently marked & cross-referenced to descriptions on the reverse of each map. The old, traditional paths are also shown.

ITMB *Albania*, 1:210,000, double-sided, indexed, some topographical details, street plans of 7 cities & towns. Not a hiking map, but shows many of the old, traditional paths. Inexplicably, some well-established roads are missing altogether, including at least 2 border crossings.

Reise Know-How *Albanien*, 1:220,000, double-sided, indexed, waterproof, tear-resistant, good topographical detail with contour colouring & spot heights. Awkward to use on the road.

CAR HIRE Self-drive cars can be hired in Tirana, the airport and a handful of other locations. Car-hire rates have reduced substantially in recent years, making this an attractive option. Only Tirana Car Rentals currently offers the option of dropping the vehicle off in a different town from where it was picked up. For some of the routes described in this book, a small saloon will not be adequate. Some of the car-hire agencies have 4x4 vehicles available, although of course these are considerably more expensive.

The car-hire desks at the airport are not open 24 hours a day; in any case, if you want to be sure of being able to rent a car as soon as you arrive, you should book it in advance. Several small, local companies also offer car hire from offices located just beyond the airport perimeter fence, across the road.

It is reasonably economical to hire a taxi with its driver, either through Albania Holidays (page 28) or any other local travel agency, or independently at the main taxi rank in each town.

🚗 **Avis** Sheraton Hotel; 📞 04 226 6389; or Rogner Hotel; 📞 04 223 5011; w avis.com
🚗 **Europcar** Rr e Durrësit 61; 📞 04 222 7888; w europcar.com
🚗 **Hertz** Tirana International Hotel, Skanderbeg Sq; 📞 04 226 2511; w hertz.com

🚗 **Sixt** Volkswagen dealership, Rr e Kavajës 116; m 068 20 68 500; w sixt.com
🚗 **Tirana Car Rentals** Rr Abdyl Frashëri 11, Sh 4 (offices also in Durrësi, Vlora & Saranda); 📞 04 630 1255; m 068 40 30 505; w tirana-car-rentals.com

CYCLING *Thanks to Bruce Logan, Jaap de Boer and others for their comments on cycling in Albania*

Cyclists will be spoilt for choice with all the ancient tracks across Albania's mountain passes and along remote valleys. Suitable bikes cannot be hired in Albania, except as part of an organised excursion or for day trips from Tirana. Some ideas for routes are suggested in the relevant chapters.

Road surfaces are very variable and 'touring' or off-road tyres are essential. The cobbled surfaces of some of the old Italian-built roads become very slippery in wet weather and may not be rideable then. Gradients are often much steeper than cyclists used to the Alps, for example, might expect. The unreliability of maps of Albania (see opposite) can make these gradients even more of a surprise (or shock). Softies can always fall back on the option of putting the bikes on a bus and doing the toughest stretches the easy way. See below, and throughout for advice on public transport.

Albanian drivers are now becoming more used to sharing their roads with foreign cyclists and, in the main, they are reasonably courteous to them. However, it is safer as well as more enjoyable to travel as much as possible during the day and on roads with light traffic. On busy highways, extreme caution and defensiveness are advisable. On some of the new highways, there are signs indicating that cyclists are not allowed. If there is an alternative route, it will probably make for more enjoyable riding; if there is not, it seems that the prohibition is not enforced, at least not on foreign cyclists.

As for security, if you are camping you should remove all loose items and lock the bike as securely as you possibly can, perhaps by chaining it to a tree. Hotel owners will be happy to find a space for your bike in the courtyard or somewhere else secure, although you should nonetheless lock it and keep loose items with you.

INTERURBAN TRANSPORT Albanians use three main methods of public transport between towns: buses, minibuses and shared taxis. Buses have about 40 seats and run to timetables. Minibuses have 10–15 seats and leave when they are full. Where both types of vehicle operate, the bus is cheaper and tends to take a bit longer, but is often more comfortable. Rural and mountainous routes are often not served by buses at all, only minibuses and taxis. Buses and minibuses operate **daily**, except on some very remote routes where there is no service on a Sunday. The cost of a shared taxi is based on four paying passengers, including children and luggage if necessary. The trains are cheap, but they are so slow and infrequent that nobody uses them for any but the shortest journeys. There are no internal civilian flights at the time of writing.

When travelling, the crucial thing to bear in mind is that Albanians are early risers. Bus services start very early indeed, often before 06.00. Where there are minibuses, the earliest ones fill up quickly with people who are travelling all the way to the final destination. Later in the morning, you could spend half an hour, or more, waiting around for more passengers to turn up. The earlier you set off, the quicker your journey will be. Getting to the terminus early also gives you a choice of vehicles; for example, some models of minibus have more room for luggage than others and newer buses tend to have better suspension.

The time of departure of the **last bus** depends to some extent on how far away the destination is – Tirana–Shkodra, for example, is only a couple of hours, and there are buses until 17.00. The latest departures from provincial towns tend to be earlier than those from Tirana; for example, the last bus from Shkodra to Tirana leaves at 16.00. As a rule, you should not rely on being able to find any public transport much later than midday, unless otherwise specified in this guide. After the last bus has left, there are likely to be taxis hanging around hopefully but, unless you are prepared to pay for all four seats in the taxi, you may still have a long wait.

Getting to and from Tirana is easy – every town in Albania has daily transport to the capital, although from very faraway places the bus might leave unfeasibly early. Links between minor towns and their regional capitals are usually good. The bus or minibus will usually have a sign in the windscreen with the name of their destination. If not, there are always lots of people around to ask.

There is always some kind of public transport between the main **villages** and their district capitals (the 'main village' is referred to in Albanian as *komuna*, the old name for the administrative centre of a group of villages). But the 'early start' logic has an extra twist to it in these cases: rural buses (or minibuses) are normally driven by somebody who lives in the village, not the town, which means that the bus spends the night in the village and is driven down to the town in the early morning, to arrive there at the start of the working day. The passengers then go off and do whatever administrative tasks or shopping they have come to town to do. Then, when everybody has finished, the driver takes them all back to the village. This is usually around lunchtime – 13.00 or thereabouts – but the only way to be certain is to ask the driver. This means if you want to go to a village by bus (and there are a lot in this guide, either as attractive destinations in their own right or as the nearest accessible point to an archaeological site), you will probably spend quite a lot of time hanging around, sitting alone on the bus or drinking coffee with the driver. You will probably also have to spend the night in the village, unless you plan to walk out. In very remote areas, it is sometimes possible to hitch a lift on the school buses that ferry the teachers, first thing in the morning, from the district capital to the elementary schools in the villages.

Bus (and minibus) terminuses are often on the outskirts of towns, but there are almost always taxis hanging around to provide onward transport.

INTRA-URBAN TRANSPORT In most Albanian towns and cities, the urban **bus** system is – frankly – opaque. It is designed for people who live in that town and who know that Ilir's boy drives the bus that goes up past the tractor factory. Visitors who do not know Ilir, or what his son looks like, or that those ruined buildings on the hill used to be the tractor factory, until it was burnt down in 1991, have little chance of identifying the bus which will take them where they want to go. In Tirana things are somewhat easier – at least there the buses display their routes – but the buses get so crowded at peak times of day that using them then is not a comfortable option.

Fortunately, there are plenty of **taxis** in every town of any size. They usually have a meter or a flat fare for short journeys within the town centre; for longer journeys you should agree a fare before getting into the car. Taxis can be hired for half a day, or a day, or even longer – the Albanian expression for this is *'në dispozicion'* – and again the rate should be negotiated in advance. If meal breaks are involved you will be expected to pay for the driver's food, unless this has been specifically excluded from the deal.

Taxi licences are issued by the relevant local council. Licensed taxis have yellow registration plates with the word TA-XI on them, and a shield-shaped sticker on the door with the licence number on it. In Tirana and some other cities, the cars themselves are often yellow too. In very small towns the cars might have only the council's stickers, not the yellow number plates. Pirate taxis are not usually any cheaper for short journeys. Licences are quite expensive and the legitimate taxi drivers are understandably resentful of the pirates.

Taxis do not usually cross international borders (the Kosova–Albania border does not count as international). At the busier, longer-established crossings, there are usually taxis or minibuses waiting on the Albanian side to collect people who have been dropped off on the other side and walked across. This is common practice and the drivers will have a going rate for the trip, although whether they let a foreigner in on this secret is another matter. The smaller, less traditional crossings do not have reliable transport of this sort.

It can sometimes be a challenge to find museums, galleries and other places of interest. Street names are rarely used in Albania and, even when they are, matters are complicated by the fact that everybody still uses the old, communist-era names instead of the new ones that are on street maps. Albanians navigate by landmarks rather than addresses so that, if you ask for directions to, say, the Vila Bekteshi restaurant in Shkodra, you will not be told it is on Rruga Hazan Riza Pasha, but that it is behind the mosque, near the Orthodox cathedral.

HIKING AND SKIING Albania offers magnificent opportunities to explore wild, remote places, on foot, on skis or with snowshoes. However, only a few of the national parks have any kind of infrastructure in place to support outdoor activities; accommodation, where it exists at all, is usually in family homes with conditions that are sometimes rather basic. Indeed, just reaching many of Albania's national parks and nature reserves involves a difficult journey by 4x4 or several hours' walk from the nearest village served by public transport.

The mountain areas of Albania are now very sparsely populated, because many villagers have given up subsistence farming in exchange for a slightly less tough life in a town or city. If you sprain your ankle or run into other problems, the nearest help could well be several hours' walk away. Remote mountain areas do not usually have mobile-phone coverage. You should never set off on a hike alone. Great caution is also needed when approaching sheepdogs in the mountains; they are trained to attack anything which they think might be a threat to the livestock they are protecting. If you are confronted by a sheepdog, stop; if you have the presence of mind, back slowly away from it. Do not go any further into the dog's territory until the shepherd, who will be somewhere around, makes his or her way to you and calls the dog off.

Long-distance hiking Two long-distance, cross-border hiking trails have been developed in recent years: Peaks of the Balkans (**w** *peaksofthebalkans.com*) and

Via Dinarica (w *viadinarica.com*). The main problem with both of these initiatives is that it is practically impossible for an independent hiker to obtain permission to cross the borders between Montenegro, Kosova and Albania. In theory, all three countries have systems in place to enable this; in practice, you need to be physically present at the relevant police station in order either to pay the permit fee (Montenegro) or to process the paperwork (Albania and Kosova). Zbulo (page 29; w *zbulo.org*) can submit your paperwork, chase up your application and inform you when your permit is approved, for a small fee. If you are travelling as part of an organised hiking tour, the agency you have booked with will deal with permits for the whole group.

Hikers are unlikely to be robbed, but it is not impossible either; if you are attacked, your assailant is almost certain to be armed with a gun.

An increasing number of guesthouses in the Albanian mountains provide space and facilities for campers. Often these will be shared with people travelling in campervans or mobile homes, which is usually fine but can sometimes lead to friction, if the two groups have different views of what time days should start and finish. There are also campsites on the Riviera beaches, most of them open only in summer.

Wild camping is tolerated, but you should follow the usual codes of conduct (the Mountaineering Council of Scotland's website – w *mcofs.org.uk/assets/pdfs/ wildcamping.pdf* – has useful guidelines, although obviously its legal advice does not apply in Albania). In particular, it is not always easy to tell if you are pitching your tent on private property. If there is an inhabited house within sight, you should make yourself known to the inhabitants. Apart from anything else, if they discover in the middle of the night that there are strangers roaming around their property, they are almost certain to reach for their guns before leaving the house to find out who is there. Albanian highlanders have ancient traditions of hospitality and may well invite you to sleep in their house. If you prefer to be in your tent, a polite compromise might be for you to camp in their garden. If the head of the family refuses payment, it is a nice gesture to press a few hundred lek, 'for the children' ('*për femijët*'), into the hand of the oldest child.

Sleeping rough in the Albanian mountains might also bring you into closer proximity with the carnivorous fauna of the country than you would like. Wolves do not eat people, although hearing them howl around your tent is probably quite disconcerting; bears, on the other hand, have been known to attack humans and they don't howl first. Albania also has some venomous snakes, among them the dangerous nose-horned viper (*Vipera ammodytes*).

Skiing In the communist era, skiing was quite a popular pastime and several small resorts were developed. They do not have Western-style infrastructure, but for adventurous skiers they can be interesting to visit. The first snow usually falls in November and lasts until March or April, with average snowfall of 40–60cm and low maximum temperatures. At the time of writing, the best place to ski in Albania is **Puka**, in the north of the country, where skis (and ice skates) can be hired and which has a choice of good accommodation (pages 163–6). For those who are prepared to bring their own skis, other resorts are:

Dardha 20km south of Korça; page 166.
A traditional village, 1,344m above sea level, which is a tourist attraction in the summer, too. Hotel & guesthouse accommodation is available.

Shishtaveci 31km from Kukësi; pages 177–8.
The plateau is over 2,000m above sea level. There are several guesthouses & a small hotel in the village. The road from Kukësi is now asphalted all the way to the border with Kosova.

Voskopoja 26km west of Korça; pages 138–40. The Akademia Hotel, 2,286m above sea level, was used in the communist period to accommodate groups of students on skiing trips. Alternative accommodation is available with local families in Voskopoja.

People who actually live in the Albanian mountains do not use skis to get around in winter, but **snowshoes**. These are an enjoyable way for non-skiers to explore the mountains in winter. Outdoor Albania (page 29; w *outdooralbania.com*), the Tirana-based specialist agency, runs snowshoeing excursions throughout the winter in the mountains around Tirana, as well as ski tours in different parts of the country. In spring and summer it offers treks of varying lengths and levels of difficulty.

ACCOMMODATION

Communist-era hotels in Albania were built to provide accommodation either for individuals travelling on official business or for families on holiday at the beach or in the mountains. Very few foreign tourists visited Albania and so – unlike other communist countries in central and eastern Europe – there were no hotels specifically built for them.

Every provincial capital had a centrally located hotel, with its own bar and restaurant, and usually with a large number of rooms. This was invariably referred to as 'Turizmi' ('The Tourism'), and it was where foreign tour groups stayed as well as Albanian sports teams or cultural ensembles. In coastal and mountain resorts, there were similar hotels, usually called 'Kampi' (i Punëtorëve, 'The Workers' Camp'), to accommodate student groups and holidaying families. Because these hotels had been state-owned, they were often targeted by rioters during the civil uprising of spring 1997 and several were completely destroyed. Of those that survived, all have now been privatised.

It has taken a while for all the new owners to make the investment required, but most of these hotels now meet reasonable international standards, with en-suite bathrooms, constant hot (and cold!) running water, air conditioning and a TV with some cable channels as a minimum. In some towns, the former 'Turizmi' is of a very high standard indeed.

In a few cases, the owners have not yet upgraded the whole hotel. Typically this means that some rooms – one or two floors – now have en-suite bathrooms, some form of heating in winter and a television set; these rooms usually cost about €30–40 for two people. Rooms on the remaining floors still share toilets and showers. These are not always offered to foreign visitors, but they are cheaper than the upgraded rooms, usually 1,000 lek per person per night, and you will be allocated one if you ask for it.

More recently built hotels are also very variable in their quality. Some target Albanians travelling for work reasons – bus drivers, sales representatives, etc – and are cheap but basic. Others have opted for the smaller but wealthier market of Albanian professionals and foreign visitors. The conditions in these hotels range from the comfortable to the very comfortable, although their room rates do not always reflect the facilities offered. These mid-range hotels have en-suite bathrooms, air conditioning and cable television as standard. In Tirana, such hotels typically charge €60–70; in the rest of the country it is usually €10–20 less. At the beach resorts in July and August, hotels charge whatever they think they can get away with; demand exceeds supply at the height of the Albanian holiday season and so haggling is unlikely to be successful at that time of year. When the quoted price is for the room, not per person, single travellers can often negotiate a discount.

Room rates are usually given in euros, except at the budget end of the market where they tend to be quoted in lek. It is always possible to pay in either currency, although you may be given your change in lek. Sterling and US dollars are not usually accepted. Breakfast is sometimes included, sometimes not; it will almost always be available, even if you have to pay extra for it. Albanian hotel breakfasts usually consist of toast or bread with a hard-boiled or fried egg, cheese, jam, honey and/or ham. Often you will be invited to choose one or two of these options. Milk or tea is traditionally served with breakfast; coffee is not always included but can be ordered separately.

Increasing numbers of hotels in Albania now have their own websites through which rooms can be booked. Otherwise, hotel accommodation throughout the country can be reserved through the Tirana-based agency **Albania Holidays** (\ 04 223 5688, 04 223 5498; w *albania-hotel.com*) and through international websites such as w hostelworld.com and w booking.com. Information about rural guesthouses – and suggestions for hiking itineraries – can be found on w albanian-mountains.com, a website funded by Italian and German development agencies.

CAMPING Campsites for mobile homes are a relatively new phenomenon in Albania and the standards are variable. Some close in the off-season. Details of some of the longer-standing campsites are given in the relevant chapter. They usually also provide spaces where tents can be pitched.

In summer, many of the beaches on the Riviera (pages 253–9) have tented sites, of varying degrees of comfort, where travellers can either rent a tent or pitch their own. Information about these seasonal campsites is available on the usual travellers' websites. Advice on wild camping is given on page 44.

EATING AND DRINKING

FOOD Albanian cuisine is rich in Mediterranean ingredients such as olive oil, tomatoes and pimentos, although garlic is not widely used. Lamb, as you would expect in a mountainous country, is excellent, as is fish from Albania's rivers, seas and lakes. Those who like offal will welcome the chance to try dishes that BSE and changing consumer tastes have eliminated from northern European menus.

Fruit and vegetables Fruit and vegetables in Albania are delicious. The tomatoes taste of tomato, the watermelons remind you of something other than water, and the citrus fruit is tangy and refreshing. Aubergines, courgettes, green beans and okra figure prominently in summer, with cabbages, carrots and potatoes taking over in winter. It is a frequent boast in restaurants that all the food is organic (*bio*), but there is no system in Albania yet for certifying organic produce.

Meat The classic way to eat lamb is spit-roasted (*mish në hell*), and the classic place to eat it is at one of the out-of-town restaurants that specialise in this. At weekends and on public holidays these places are filled with extended families at huge tables, tucking into lamb, salad, chips and carafes of wine. A variation is *paidhaqe*, lamb ribs grilled over charcoal. Town restaurants are more likely to serve pork or veal (the calves are not kept in crates and are much older when they are slaughtered than the milk-fed veal calves which used to be eaten in Britain). Veal escalopes are ubiquitous; *biftek* is a cross-cut steak from the shoulder or loin, which can be fried or braised; and *rosto* is boned shoulder, oven-roasted and served with gravy.

Sheep's heart, liver, kidneys, brains and other organs are very popular. In the big cities, it is not always easy to find restaurants that serve these things, but they always exist and can be tracked down by asking. Albanian specialities include *paçë koke*, a thick soup made with sheep's head that is a traditional breakfast dish, and *kukurec*, chopped innards in a gut casing.

Fish and seafood The lake fish *koran* (a species of trout unique to Lake Ohrid) and carp are usually available only near the lakes where they are fished, although you can sometimes find them in Tirana, at a price. River trout, too, seldom travel far. Fresh sea fish is readily available all along the coast and in the inland cities. The varieties that appear most frequently on menus are *levrek* (sea bass) and *kocë* (sea bream), both usually farmed, *barbun* (red mullet) and *merluc* (hake). Eels (*ngjalë*) are caught in the lakes and coastal lagoons and are much sought after there; they rarely make it to the cities. Prawns (*karkalec*) are landed by Albanian fishermen, and on the coast they are likely to be fresh; elsewhere you may wish to ask if they are frozen (ie: imported). Fresh lobster is sometimes available, although it is not cheap. Mussels (*midhje*) are farmed in the Butrint Lagoon. Clams seem to be served only with pasta dishes in Italian restaurants. Finally, although it is not a fish, the edible variety of frog (*bretkosë*) is bred and its legs eaten – usually grilled – in central and southern Albania.

Traditional meals Traditional Albanian home cooking uses vegetables, yoghurt and cheese to make meat go further. Potatoes, aubergines, courgettes, peppers and cabbage are all stuffed with minced meat. Pieces of veal are simmered with aubergine, spinach or green beans, or braised in a terracotta pot with pickling onions (*mish çomlek*). For *turli*, different vegetables – carrots, aubergines, potatoes, okra or anything else the cook has to hand – are layered with slices of tomato around a veal joint and simmered. *Fergesë* is made with green peppers and onions, fried together and then mixed with egg and *gjizë*, a dry curd cheese, before being baked. Pieces of meat or liver are sometimes added to *fergesë*. In *tavë Elbasani*, or *tavë kosi*, yoghurt and eggs are beaten together and poured over pieces of lamb or mutton, before the whole thing is baked in the oven.

Shish qebap is cubes of meat – lamb, pork or beef – marinated and then grilled on skewers, alternated with onion slices; *qebap në letër* is the same ingredients plus chunks of feta cheese, wrapped in tinfoil and baked in the oven. *Qofta* are rissoles of minced lamb bound with egg: sometimes they are round and flat, like hamburgers, and sometimes they are cylindrical; sometimes they are served grilled with salad and chips, and sometimes with a tomato-based sauce, when they are usually called *qoftë Korçe*.

Albanian housewives preserve vegetables in vinegar for the winter, when salads consist mainly of different sorts of pickle – not only the familiar gherkin, but also preserved peppers, aubergines and other treats.

Albanian fast food *Qofta* also appear as fast food, sold at street kiosks straight from the grill. Doner kebab, called *sufllaqë* in central Albania and *pita* in the south, is served either in a circular piece of unleavened bread or in a hot-dog roll, topped with salad, chips and tomato ketchup or mustard. The other big player in the Albanian fast-food world is the *byrek*, which comes in many guises but is essentially filo pastry with something inside. The classic *byrek* is round and flat, and alternates layers of pastry with *gjizë*, or minced meat fried with chopped onions, or leeks. As a starter for the family lunch, it can be bought whole at the *byrektore* or made at home; as fast food, it is cut into quarters and eaten on the street. Another variant is the small triangular *byrek*, which can contain meat, or *gjizë*, or spinach, or tomato and onion, and is crispier and lighter than its circular relative. Finally there is the *pita*, for which the filo pastry is rolled up around the filling to make a long sausage shape, then coiled around itself and baked. All of these are tasty options when a full meal is not required.

Desserts Desserts are not usually eaten after meals in Albanian homes. On special occasions *xupa* might be served, a kind of blancmange sprinkled with walnuts. Sweetmeats are more often eaten with coffee during the *xhiro*, the early evening promenade. *Kadaif* and *halva* will be familiar to anyone who has visited Turkey or Greece, or indeed ever been in a Turkish café. *Tullumba* are cylinders of dough, deep-fried and tossed in syrup. *Sheqerpare* is made from little balls of sweet dough, baked in butter. *Shëndetlli* is a kind of fruit cake, steeped in honey.

Vegetarians and vegans Except in upmarket, Westernised establishments, there is almost never a specifically vegetarian option among the meals on offer in restaurants. In restaurants that are used to foreigners, vegetarians will always be offered something they can eat; elsewhere, it will generally be possible to persuade the kitchen to rustle up an omelette or a simple tomato sauce for pasta. Fish-eaters will be fine in the cities and on the coast. The Albanian highlands are resolutely carnivorous; non-meat-eaters will struggle to convince their puzzled hosts that all they want is cheese or eggs. Delicious though the cucumbers and tomatoes are, vegans are likely to have become quite tired of them after a couple of weeks in Albania.

DRINK The draught **wine** in provincial restaurants is normally rather young, but can be very drinkable. Albanian wine in bottles is often excellent. The main wine-producing areas are around Korça and Berati and between Lezha and Shkodra. The Bardha vineyard near Tirana produces outstanding wine in small quantities, difficult to track down but on the wine lists of a few Tirana restaurants. Most Albanian vineyards use well-known grapes such as Sauvignon and Cabernet, which

RESTAURANT PRICE CODES

Prices are based on the average cost of a main course.

$$$$$	Expensive	1,500 lek+
$$$$	Above average	1,000–1,500 lek
$$$	Reasonable	500–1,000 lek
$$	Good deal	under 500 lek
$	Cheap	snacks, less than 200 lek per item

are easy for them to sell in quantity. A few, however, are now moving towards a more high-end product using indigenous grapes such as Shesh (red and white), Pulës (white) and Kallmet (red). Some of these vineyards, listed below, can arrange tours of their production facilities and offer tastings of their own wines. For those who are unable to visit the vineyards, these wines are usually on sale in the duty-free shops at Tirana International Airport.

Çobo Winery Ura Vajgurore, near Berati; ☎0361 22088; e info@cobowineryonline.com; w cobowineryonline.com

Kantina Arbëri Rrësheni; ☎0216 22486; e info@kantina-arberi.com; w kantina-arberi.com

Kantina Nurellari Fushë-Peshtani, near Berati; ☎032 238 551; e fatosnurellari@yahoo.com; w nurellariwinery.com

Beer is brewed commercially in Tirana, Korça (the oldest brewery in Albania) and Vlora; the Tirana and Korça breweries produce dark beer as well as the more widely available lager. Locally produced beer is available in a few other towns, such as Puka.

Of the other Albanian alcoholic drinks, **raki** is the most widely consumed. Despite its Turkish name, Albanian raki is not flavoured with aniseed as it is in Turkey. It is a clear spirit, usually distilled from grape juice, and drunk as a morning pick-me-up, an aperitif, a digestif, or at any other time of day. Albanians also make raki from mulberries (*mani*), brambles (*manaferre*) and practically any other soft fruit they can lay their hands on. In Slav-speaking villages raki is distilled from plums, as it is across the border in former Yugoslavia. The Berati-based vineyard Çobo makes excellent walnut raki. Another unusual raki is that made from the fruit of the strawberry tree (*Arbutus unedo*) called *mare* in Albanian. The best raki is homemade; commercially bottled products are widely available in shops.

Albanian brandy (*konjak*) can be quite good, or it can be appalling; the commercially available Skënderbeu brand is in the former category. *Fernet*, a drink made from herbs that tastes nothing like the Italian Fernet-Branca, is a popular aperitif, though something of an acquired taste.

Coffee is an even more integral part of Albanian life than raki. Over coffee, deals are done, jobs are offered and marriages arranged. Having a coffee with an Albanian takes an absolute minimum of half an hour. Traditionally it was made in the usual Balkan way, with very finely ground coffee, water and sugar all boiled together in an individual pot – in Albanian it is called *kafe turke*. This is usually what you will be offered in Albanians' houses. In cafés and restaurants in all but the very smallest towns, Italian espresso machines are the norm, when there is electricity to operate them. During power cuts, *kafe turke* comes back into its own. You will be asked how you take it, meaning how much sugar you want. Four possible answers are: '*e ëmbël*' (sweet); '*e mesme*' (standard, which is quite sweet); '*me pak sheqer*' (with a little sugar); and '*sade*' (unsweetened).

PRACTICAL INFORMATION Most restaurants in Albania do not have fixed opening hours. They are family-run and open when the owners think people might want to start eating – in the countryside this will be around 09.00 or 10.00, when Albanian farmers have breakfast (*paçë koke*, for example), while in towns it is usually a bit later. They close when there are no more customers – in the countryside this tends to be quite early in the evening, in small towns it will be around 21.00 and in cities an hour or so later. Some restaurants, particularly those that serve very traditional food, are open only in the mornings and at lunchtime; the listings in each section of the guide specify where this is the case.

It is rarely necessary to book a table in advance; indeed, most restaurants do not even have telephone numbers, other than the mobile phone of the owner. Where reservations are advisable, numbers are given in the listings in each section.

Restaurant bills are always in lek, although euros are usually accepted if necessary; however, the exchange rate is unlikely to be in the customer's favour. In restaurants, tips are expected though not obligatory – rounding up to about 10% of the total bill is fine. Tipping practice in cafés is to leave a couple of coins on your table after you have paid your bill.

PUBLIC HOLIDAYS

Albania shuts down on the following national holidays: 1 and 2 January (New Year); 1 May (International Workers' Day); and 28 November (Independence Day).

On other public holidays, including the major feast days of each of Albania's religions, banks and government offices are closed, while shops, bureaux de change and other private firms may or may not open. It varies to some extent from town to town – in Catholic Mirdita, for example, you will not find much commercial activity on 25 December. The holidays are: Orthodox Christmas (6 January); Summer Day (14 March); the Bektashi festival of Nevruz (22 March); Catholic and Orthodox Easters (moveable, usually on different Sundays in April); Beatification of Mother Teresa Day (19 October); Liberation Day (29 November; liberation from the Germans, that is – which, since it led to 45 years of Communist rule, not everybody in Albania agrees is a reason for celebration); Bajram i Vogël (Eid al-Fitr, the end of Ramadan, moveable); Bajram i Madh (Eid ul-Adha, moveable); and Catholic Christmas (25 December).

'National' museums close on Mondays; others are more likely to be closed on Saturdays and Sundays. The difference is not always obvious.

SHOPPING

The best places in Albania to shop for souvenirs are Kruja (page 102) and Gjirokastra (page 241), where all the shops are close together in the bazaar. In Kruja, there are traditional felt-makers, who produce slippers and the felt caps called *qeleshe*; shops selling hand-woven *qilime* (this is the same word as the Turkish *kilim*, a woven rug); and antique dealers. Many of the Kruja shops sell small souvenirs such as Albanian flags, copper plates and ashtrays in the shape of bunkers. Gjirokastra's bazaar has a stonemason, a woodworker, lacemakers and shops selling woven textiles and *qilime*, as well as other souvenirs.

Elsewhere it can be quite difficult to find traditional crafts for sale; there are a few shops in Tirana and souvenir stalls at Butrint. Please refer to the relevant chapters of this guide for further information. If all else fails, small souvenirs and bottles of wine, raki and cognac can be purchased at the airport.

ARTS AND ENTERTAINMENT

Albania, like many formerly communist countries, has a strong tradition of classical music. The country's main venue for this is the National Theatre of Opera and Ballet on Tirana's Skanderbeg Square; forthcoming concerts, operas and ballet performances are advertised outside the theatre. Classical recitals also take place in the Academy of Arts in Tirana and, occasionally, in other venues around the country (eg: the theatre at Butrint). Plays and similar performances are staged, generally in Albanian, in the main theatres in Tirana, Shkodra, Durrësi and Korça. It is far from easy to find out about these events; asking at the nearest tourist information office might yield results. Public institutions, such as theatres and museums, cannot normally deal with telephone enquiries from members of the public. The cinemas in several towns and cities usually screen Hollywood films, in the original version with Albanian subtitles. Screenings of Albanian films are much rarer.

It is almost as difficult to find performances of traditional Albanian music or dance. The best way to stumble across them is to be staying in a hotel where a wedding is being celebrated; Albanian weddings last three days, with the final big celebration always on a Sunday night. There are folk festivals at Gjirokastra (every four years, roughly), Peshkopia (annually, in September) and Përmeti (annually, in June). Please refer to the relevant chapters of this guide for further information.

PHOTOGRAPHY

Albanians are usually delighted to have their photographs taken but, like people in any other country, they prefer to be asked first. Once permission has been requested, you may well end up having to take photos of the entire family.

Again like everywhere else, the security and armed forces tend not to be very happy about people taking photos of military or government buildings. Bunkers are fine, as long as they are not surrounding a military base.

MEDIA AND COMMUNICATIONS

MEDIA Albanian **television** is very diverse. In addition to the state-owned public broadcaster, TVSH, several privately owned stations are licensed to broadcast nationwide, with additional local channels in many cities. The main news broadcasts are generally between 07.00 and 08.00, between 15.00 and 16.00, and at around 19.00. The 24-hour news channels have rolling headlines and occasional news summaries in English. Where cable television is provided in hotels, it rarely includes any English-language channels. There are always dozens of Italian channels, plus a few in German and an apparently random selection of other languages. Monoglot news junkies may want to hunt out a hotel with BBC World or CNN.

Radio plays a less significant role in Albania than in some other countries. There are many radio stations, but most of them are music channels. To the great dismay of many Albanians, the BBC World Service ended its Albanian service in 2011. The Voice of America broadcasts to Albania on medium and short wave; its website (**w** *voa.gov*) has details of frequencies.

Newspapers are often very partisan – indeed, three widely available papers are actually owned by political parties. There are two English-language newspapers, the *Albanian Daily News* and the weekly *Tirana Times*, which carry summaries of the previous day's Albanian press as well as their own articles. Hard copies can be obtained at the upmarket hotels in Tirana and in the Adrion bookshop (page 72) on Skanderbeg Square; for details of the subscription-only websites at which they can be read online, see page 285. In Tirana it is also possible to buy newspapers such as the *International Herald Tribune*, the *Financial Times* and the *Guardian*; they are transmitted digitally and printed locally, so that they are available in the mornings. If you have internet access, of course, you can access your preferred media source online, which will be substantially cheaper.

PEOPLE Communicating with Albanians is much easier than might be expected. They are among the most polyglot people in Europe, perhaps because the country was isolated for so long and so few foreigners speak their language. It is mainly younger people who speak English; it is not at all unusual for a young Albanian to have a good command of three or four languages. Most older people do not know English, but they may well speak good French, Greek or Italian.

Italian is widely spoken in coastal towns, such as Shkodra, Durrësi and Vlora, thanks to their historical links with, and geographical proximity to, Italy. Even during the later years of the communist regime, Albanians on the coast and in Tirana could watch Italian television, and so people now in their 30s and 40s more or less grew up with the language and often speak it extremely well. Younger people, however, are more likely to have English as their first foreign language.

Enver Hoxha (see box, page 83) studied in France, at the University of Montpellier, and during communism the French *lycées* in Korça and Gjirokastra continued to operate. Particularly in these towns, therefore, but also elsewhere, a sizeable number of Albanians speak French. In the south of the country, Greek is very widely spoken, including by people who are ethnically Albanian rather than Greek.

Those who were at school or university in the 1950s and 1960s learned Russian, although many of them have not used the language for 40 or more years and have forgotten most of it. In areas that border the former Yugoslavia, there are Slavic-speaking ethnic minorities (page 19). Some people who are now in their 60s learned Chinese, usually because they studied in China; some academic exchanges have resumed since the advent of democracy in Albania, and one occasionally comes across younger people, too, who have studied in China and learned the language.

POST AND TELEPHONES The **fixed network** in Albania is run by a privatised monopoly, called Albtelecom but known locally as 'Telekomi'. Numbers in Tirana have seven digits; numbers elsewhere in the country have five or six. Every town in the country now has direct dialling, as do many villages, but calls are expensive and most people prefer to use their mobile phones. There are fewer than 240,000 fixed-line subscribers in Albania, whereas there are 2.3 million active mobile-phone numbers.

There are several **mobile phone** companies in Albania. Between them, they have agreements with most other European companies, so if you have roaming enabled on your phone you should be able to use it in Albania. Alternatively, if your phone is network-unlocked, an Albanian prepay SIM card will cost a few hundred lek, most of it as call time. If you need a local phone with a call and data package, they can be rented in Tirana, for example at easy shop (*Rr Grigor Heba 45/1;* m *069 83 22 228;* e *admin@easy-shop.al;* f *easyshopalbania*). Tariffs have come down in recent years and coverage is as good as it is ever likely to get in a mountainous country like Albania.

To make a phone call in Albania, other than from a mobile phone, the cheapest option is Albtelecom, where you can book your call, have it transferred to a booth in the phone centre and pay for it after you have made it. In cities, the other option is to use a public phone in the street. These take cards, not coins; you can buy credit either at an Albtelecom office or from one of the people hanging around the phones. Luxury (**$$$$$**) and many upmarket (**$$$$**) hotels allow guests to make calls, directly or through their switchboard, but – like hotels everywhere – they add a hefty charge for this facility.

The Albanian **postal service** (Albapost) is not 100% reliable, although it is not especially bad either. Important documents should be sent by courier; Western Union, DHL and FedEx all have offices in Tirana and other cities.

ALBANIAN TIME AND BUSINESS

Albania is 1 hour ahead of GMT from October to March, and 2 hours ahead in summer; this is the same time as Italy and the countries of former Yugoslavia, but 1 hour behind Greece.

The traditional Albanian working day begins at 08.00, or in rural areas even earlier, and ends at 15.00, when everybody goes home for lunch, the main meal of the day. Many people then take a siesta, particularly in summer when the tarmac on the streets is melting, and re-emerge in the early evening for the *xhiro*. This is when families go out together and walk up and down the town's boulevard or – if it has a waterfront – its promenade. The *xhiro* may include an ice cream or a coffee, or a chat with casually met friends, but it does not have to involve anything other than walking.

Shops are usually open from 09.00 or 09.30 to 15.00, and then again from about 18.00 to about 20.00. Other private businesses do not usually reopen in the evenings, but if you wish to meet the owner or manager, it is almost always possible to do this over a coffee at any reasonable hour. In cities, especially in national and local government offices, working hours have increasingly moved closer to a northern European norm of 08.30 or 09.00 to 16.30 or 17.00, but if you have business to do in Albania, it is best accomplished early in the day.

Doing business or buying property in Albania is fraught with difficulty owing to the prevalence of corruption, the presence of organised crime, and the weakness of the judicial system. Anyone considering investing in the country should seek the advice of the commercial attaché at their embassy in Tirana.

CULTURAL ETIQUETTE

Albanians shake hands not only on being introduced to somebody but also on greeting or leaving people they already know. With friends, a kiss on both cheeks is exchanged by men as well as women. This is often combined with a hand on the other person's shoulder. After a long separation, or with really close friends, the number of kisses increases.

Normal Albanian etiquette is for people to shake hands the first time they see each other every day, and then again when they part. This is beginning to break down a little in office environments in Tirana, but is still very much expected everywhere else.

The usual way to indicate 'yes' is by moving the head horizontally from side to side. During a conversation, this movement is also used to indicate general agreement with what the other person is saying, or simply to show that you are listening. The usual sign for 'no' is a slight raising of the eyebrows, sometimes accompanied by a gentle click of the tongue. Raising the whole chin is a very emphatic 'no'. Unfortunately, exposure to foreign visitors has confused this simple state of affairs and people (especially in Tirana) sometimes try to be helpful by using non-Albanian head signals. The result is that it can be hard to tell whether the person shaking his or her head at you is saying 'yes' in Albanian, or 'no' in your language. Sometimes you just have to ask.

Albanians usually remove their shoes inside their homes or other people's houses. If you are visiting an Albanian home, you will be offered a pair of slippers or plastic sandals to wear while you are indoors.

Smoking is widespread. A ban on smoking in enclosed public places was introduced in 2007, but it is fully enforced in only a handful of restaurants and hotels. However, there is no smoking allowed on public transport, and people almost always respect this. On long journeys, the bus will stop for a couple of cigarette breaks.

As might be expected in a country that for 50 years was starved of contact with foreigners, Albanians are always very keen to engage visitors in conversation, for example, on bus journeys. Their questions often become very personal very quickly, although usually they do not mean to be intrusive. Unmarried women can expect to be grilled about their entire sexual history, as their puzzled interlocutor attempts to work out the reason for this extraordinary state of affairs.

TRAVELLING POSITIVELY

The charitable sector in Albania is very weak compared with northern Europe or (especially) North America. Most Tirana-based not-for-profit organisations conduct research or lobbying rather than hands-on humanitarian assistance. The main organisations that actually feed hungry people and treat sick babies are the churches and mosques.

Albanian Disability Rights Foundation (ADRF) Rr Mujo Ulqinaku 26, Tirana; 04 226 6892, 04 226 9426; e adrf@albmail.com; f. Set up by Oxfam GB in 1994, ADRF (its Albanian acronym is FSHDPAK) promotes the rights of people with disabilities, mostly through lobbying & training.

Albanian Red Cross 04 225 7532/3; e kksh@ albaniaonline.com; w kksh.org.al. The oldest humanitarian organisation in Albania, founded in 1921. It has been a member of the Federation of the International Red Cross & Red Crescent since 1923.

THE ENVIRONMENT AND SUSTAINABLE TOURISM One area where there are some organisations actively trying to make a difference is that of the environment and sustainable tourism; they tend to call themselves 'Associations' (*Shoqata*) to differentiate them from the lobbying and research NGOs. The longest standing is the **Outdoor Albania Association (OAA)** (*Rr e Bogdanëve 3, Tirana; m 068 31 33 451; e outdooralbaniaassociation@yahoo.com; w outdooralbania-association.com*), founded in 2005 by people who were also involved in setting up the specialist tour operator Outdoor Albania (page 29). OAA works with local communities to improve access to remote attractions, bring visitors to these places, and train local people to create businesses that are sensitive to the environmental impact and the sustainability of their enterprises. For example, it is thanks to OAA that the Pëllumbasi Cave, near Tirana, is so easy to visit (pages 83–4). Every summer, it brings foreign and Albanian volunteers together in a village in southern Albania to work on projects such as rubbish collection, path clearing and signposting. OAA can always use donations of money as well as of time and labour; its website gives details of its bank account.

The **Balkans Peace Park Project (B3P)** (e *enquiries@balkanspeacepark.org; w balkanspeacepark.org*) has activities throughout the area proposed for this cross-border park (see box, page 219); specifically in Albania, it ran a summer programme in the village of Thethi (pages 211–18) from 2008 to 2016 and, more recently, also in Kelmendi and Valbona (pages 220–1 and 171–4). Albanian tutors train the local adults in environmental studies and in agricultural improvement techniques, while foreign volunteers teach English to both children and adults, as well as other skills – music, sports, photography, etc. B3P is registered as a charity in England and has a partner organisation, B3P-Albania, registered in Shkodra. Again, they welcome donations as well as volunteers.

Protection and Preservation of Natural Environment in Albania (PPNEA) (*Rr Vangjush Furxhi p16 sh1 a10, Tirana;* ☏ *04 225 6257;* e *contact@ppnea.org;* w *ppnea. org*) focuses on research and policy advocacy. Two of the major international projects PPNEA is involved in are the Balkan Lynx Recovery Programme (page 217) and Save the Blue Heart of Europe, a campaign to protect the wild rivers of the Balkans from unbridled hydro-electric developments. PPNEA also has a number of smaller-scale but no less important projects, including monitoring pelicans and other waterbirds and campaigning against the keeping of bears in captivity. Donations can be made through its website.

The **Organisation to Conserve the Albanian Alps (TOKA)** (*261/1 Rr e Dibres, Tirana;* m *067 30 14 638;* e *contact@toka-albania.org;* w *toka-albania.org*) is a new non-profit organisation, building on the achievements of an informal group which has run successful projects in the Valbona Valley National Park for several years. TOKA (meaning 'earth') is particularly active in protecting and managing the natural resources of the Alps, especially in legally protected areas; creating and promoting sustainable growth; and representing local stakeholders.

Part Two

THE GUIDE

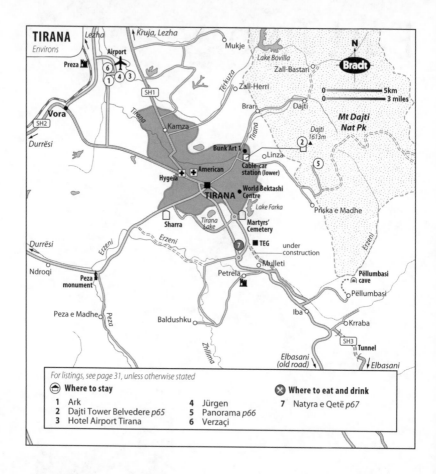

TIRANA
Environs

Lezha
Kruja, Lezha
Mukje
Preza
Airport
SH1
Vora
SH2
Durrësi
Kamza
Tërkuza
Zall-Herri
Zall-Bastari
Lake Bovilla
Brari
Dajti
Dajti
1613m
Mt Dajti
Nat Pk
0 ————— 5km
0 ————— 3 miles

Bunk'Art 1
Linza
Cable-car
station (lower)
American
Hygeia
TIRANA
World Bektashi
Centre
Lake Farka
Priska e Madhe

Durrësi
Erzeni
Erzeni
Sharra
Tirana
Lake
Martyrs'
Cemetery
TEG
under
construction
Erzeni

Ndroqi
Peza
monument
Mulleti
Petrela
Pëllumbasi
cave
Pëllumbasi

Peza e Madhe
Peza
Baldushku
Iba
Krraba
SH3
Tunnel
Zhilima
Elbasani
(old road)
Elbasani

For listings, see page 31, unless otherwise stated

🛏 **Where to stay**

1	Ark
2	Dajti Tower Belvedere *p65*
3	Hotel Airport Tirana
4	Jürgen
5	Panorama *p66*
6	Verzaçi

✖ **Where to eat and drink**

7 Natyra e Qetë *p67*

3

Tirana

Telephone code: 04

Tirana was founded in the early 17th century by Sulejman Pasha of Mulleti, who built a settlement in the area around the modern intersection of Rruga e Barrikadave and Rruga Luigj Gurakuqi. His statue stands today in the little square near that crossroads. Until it was designated as the capital in 1920, Tirana was a small, unimportant town, whose main virtue for Albania's political leaders was its geographical position more or less in the centre of the recently independent country, on the fault line dividing the northern Ghegs from the southern Tosks. It remained a bit of a backwater town for several years afterwards, as Albania struggled to stabilise itself in the face of internal lawlessness and invasions by its hostile neighbours.

It was not until Italian influence became pervasive in the late 1920s that the centre of Tirana took on the appearance of a capital city. Italian planners created the huge new square – which was named after the national hero Skanderbeg – and the wide, typically Fascist Boulevard (now known as Bulevardi Dëshmorët e Kombit); Italian architects designed the ministry buildings, the National Bank and the City Hall around the square, as well as the Dajti Hotel, the royal palace on Rruga e Elbasanit, and some of the embassies. During the communist era, the few older buildings still standing on Skanderbeg Square were demolished and the opera house, the National Historical Museum and the Hotel Tirana (now the Tirana International Hotel) were added, as were the public buildings further down the Boulevard. All these 20th-century accretions, plus the destruction caused by various earthquakes and by the Battle for the Liberation of Tirana in 1944, means that there is not very much left of Ottoman Tirana. A good deal of what survived into the 1990s has subsequently disappeared under glittering high-rise apartment blocks and shopping centres.

Tirana has become well known for its brightly painted apartment blocks. This initiative began in the wake of the 2000 local elections, which saw an artist and former Minister of Culture becoming Mayor of Tirana. The new mayor, Edi Rama (at the time of writing, he is the country's prime minister), began by restoring to the ministries on and around Skanderbeg Square the ochre colour that they had when they were first built in the 1930s; he went on to give a lick of paint to the tatty apartment buildings in the streets nearby, choosing bold colours which – although they did not convince everybody – at least had the merit of brightening up the city. The colours and patterns became livelier and livelier, until even the more progressive of Tirana's citizens began to complain that their city was starting to look like a circus. Happily for them, the harsh summer sun bleaches out the most migraine-inducing colours after a year or two.

As well as its intriguing mix of architectural styles, Tirana has several very good museums and a range of cultural activities. It has hundreds of cafés; dozens of modern bars, popular with younger people; numerous clubs, some with live music, particularly at the weekends; and an array of restaurants, many of them excellent. New bars and restaurants open all the time, and a complete list would certainly become out of date in the lifetime of a guide such as this. The more ephemeral *Tirana in Your Pocket* (w *inyourpocket.com*) lists all the latest fashions in eating, drinking and dancing. Pages 66–7 and 70–1 give details of some of the longer-established places.

Tirana also has some infuriating aspects, mainly the appalling traffic congestion and noise. In general, however, the city centre is an attractive place to stay; and its excellent public transport links make it the best base for exploring the rest of Albania.

GETTING THERE AND AWAY

BY AIR Tirana is Albania's only international airport, 17km and about 30 minutes' drive from the city. Approved airport taxis can be booked online (w *atex.al*) or in the baggage reclaim area. You should agree a fare with the driver before accepting his services – the going rate into Tirana is €20. From 06.00 to 18.00, an hourly bus service runs from outside the perimeter fence into the centre of Tirana; the one-way fare is 250 lek. In the city centre, the bus leaves from the junction of Rruga e Durrësit with Rruga Mine Peza [68 C2], where there is a clearly marked bus stop.

There are several hotels located near the airport, useful for early-morning departures or late-night arrivals (page 31). Tirana International Airport's website (w *tirana-airport.com*) has real-time arrival and departure data, as well as flight schedules and other useful information. See pages 30–1 for further information about flying into Albania.

BY ROAD Buses and/or minibuses run to Tirana from all other parts of Albania. At long last, Tirana now has inter-city bus stations, which are located in different parts of the city according to destination (see map, pages 62–3). Buses and minibuses to Shkodra, Bajram Curri and other destinations in the north leave from the North Station (Stacioni i Veriut), on Rruga e Durrësit, about halfway between the Zogu i Zi and Shqiponja ('Eagle') roundabouts. Buses to Durrësi, Berati and the southwest leave from the 'Shqiponja' bus station, near the Shqiponja roundabout (also known as 'Dogana', or 'Customs'). For Elbasani and the southeast, the bus station is behind the Faculty of Economics building (Fakulteti i Ekonomisë) on Rruga e Elbasanit.

The international bus station [62 B3] is behind the Asllan Rusi Sports Centre (Pallati i Sportit) on Rruga e Durrësit. International buses run to and from the main cities in all the neighbouring countries (Greece, Macedonia, Kosova and Montenegro), and further afield.

The Tirana e Re service (see below) and the urban buses for Vora and Kamza pass the international, North and Shqiponja bus stations. Several urban buses, such as the Qendër–Sauk line, pass the Faculty of Economics on Rruga e Elbasanit.

BY RAIL Tirana's railway station, at the northern end of Boulevard Zogu i Parë, was demolished in 2013 and the railway lines have been asphalted over to build yet another new highway. The city authorities intend to create a woodland park in this area, which will no doubt be nice, although perhaps not as nice for the environment as a functioning rail network would have been.

GETTING AROUND

Urban buses are run by private companies and licensed by the Municipality of Tirana. They can get very crowded in rush hour, but they are incredibly cheap, with a flat fare of 40 lek which is collected by a conductor on the bus. The two routes that are most useful for visitors to the city are the Unaza, which goes around the north of the city in a big loop and then along the Lana River – or vice versa – and the Tirana e Re, which starts on Bulevardi Zogu I and goes straight down the main Boulevard, before turning off along Rruga Abdyl Frashëri, looping right around the ring road and then continuing past the bus stations for the north, southwest and international destinations. Other buses depart from the various bus stops around the edges of the pedestrianised Skanderbeg Square. The buses are different colours, depending on the line they serve, and can be boarded or alighted at any of the bus stops along their route.

Licensed Tirana taxis are metered, although it is worth checking that the driver has turned the meter on when you set off. A short journey in the city centre should cost between 400 and 500 lek. For longer journeys, you may prefer to agree a fare before setting off. Taxis can be hailed on the street. There are also taxi ranks at several places in the city centre: along the sides of The Block (page 71); behind the National Historical Museum on Bulevardi Zogu I, convenient for getting to the airport and the bus stations on that side of the city; and beside the Academy of Arts on Mother Teresa Square. To book a taxi, a reliable firm is City Taxi (**tf** *0800 0000*; **w** *citytaxi.al*).

Cars can be hired in the city centre and at the airport (page 41). Tirana's cycle-hire scheme has bikes in racks at various points around the centre (*60 lek/hr*); the backpacker hostels also have bikes available to rent. There are some segregated cycle-tracks in the city centre, but it should be noted that cycling, or indeed driving, in the centre of Tirana is not for the faint-hearted.

TOURIST INFORMATION

Tirana's tourist information office is located on Rruga Ded Gjo Luli, behind the National Historical Museum [68 D2]. Unfortunately, it is open only from 08.00 to 16.00 on weekdays and is closed altogether at weekends. It stocks a range of free leaflets and brochures about Tirana and other towns in Albania. English is spoken.

Tirana in Your Pocket (**w** *inyourpocket.com*) is updated (a bit) about twice a year and is a good source of information about new restaurants, bars and clubs. The PDF version can be downloaded from its website. The Municipality of Tirana's website (**w** *tirana.gov.al*) has information about the city in Albanian; the unofficial website (**w** *visit-tirana.com*) is more useful.

The local travel agencies listed on pages 28–9 can arrange one-day (or longer) tours of Tirana on request. The backpacker hostels (page 66) organise one-day hikes and cycling tours in the countryside around Tirana. Favourite destinations are Mount Dajti and the Pëllumbasi Cave (Shpella e Pëllumbasit; pages 83–4). These day trips are an excellent option for outdoors enthusiasts who don't have enough time in Albania to embark on a more ambitious trek. Walking tours of Tirana can also be arranged.

WHERE TO STAY

Tirana has a wide range of hotels to suit every pocket. At the very top of the market, charging in excess of €100 a night (**$$$$$**), are the Sheraton, down by the university off Mother Teresa Square, the Rogner, on the Boulevard opposite the Checkpoint memorial, and the Grand Spa, on Rruga Ismail Qemali opposite Hoxha's villa. All are very well appointed, with comfortable rooms, good restaurants and swimming pools (indoor at the Grand Spa, outdoor at the Rogner, both at the Sheraton).

There is a good range of comfortable hotels with rates around the €70–80 mark (**$$$$**). Reception staff almost always speak some English and you can be

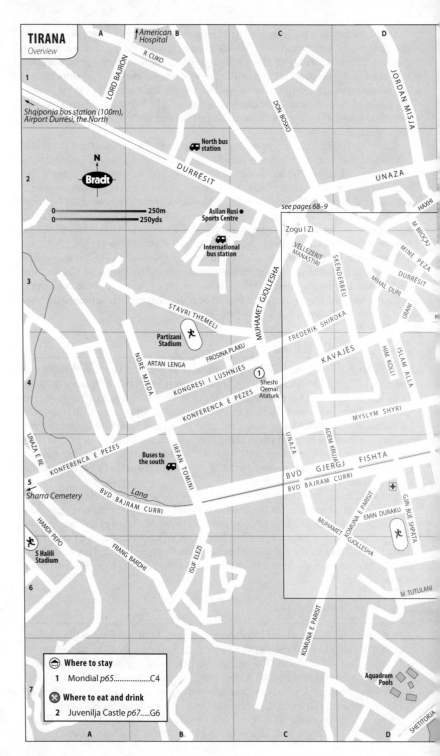

TIRANA
Overview

A   B   C   D

1

↑ American Hospital

LORD BAJRON

R CUKO

DON BOSKO

JORDAN MISJA

← *Shqiponja bus station (100m),*
Airport Durrësi, the North

North bus station

2

DURRËSIT

UNAZA

N

Bradt

HAXHI

see pages 68–9

Asllan Rusi ● Sports Centre

Zogu I Zi

M BROÇAU

MINE PEZA

0   250m
0   250yds

International bus station

VËLLEZËRIT MANASTIRI

SKENDERBEU

MIHAL DURI

DURRËSIT

URANI

3

MUHAMET GJOLLESHA

STAVRI THEMELI

FREDERIK SHIROKA

Partizani Stadium

KAVAJËS

HIM KOLLI

ISLAM ALLA

FROSINA PLAKU

NDRE MJEDA

ARTAN LENGA

4

KONGRESI I LUSHNJES

① Sheshi Qemal Ataturk

MYSLYM SHYRI

KONFERENCA E PEZES

UNAZA E RE

KONFERENCA E PEZES

Buses to the south

IRFAN TOMINI

UNAZA

ADEM KRUJA

FISHTA

BVD GJERGJ FISHTA

5

Lana

BVD BAJRAM CURRI

← *Sharra Cemetery*

BVD BAJRAM CURRI

HAMDI PEPO

GJIN BUE SHPATA

S Halili Stadium

FRANG BARDHI

ISUF ELEZI

MUHAMET GJOLLESHA

KOMUNA E PARISIT

EMIN DURAKU

6

M TUTULANI

KOMUNA E PARISIT

7

Aquadrom Pools

🏃 **Where to stay**
  1 Mondial *p65*.................C4

❌ **Where to eat and drink**
  2 Juvenilja Castle *p67*.....G6

SHETITORJA

A   B   C   D

62

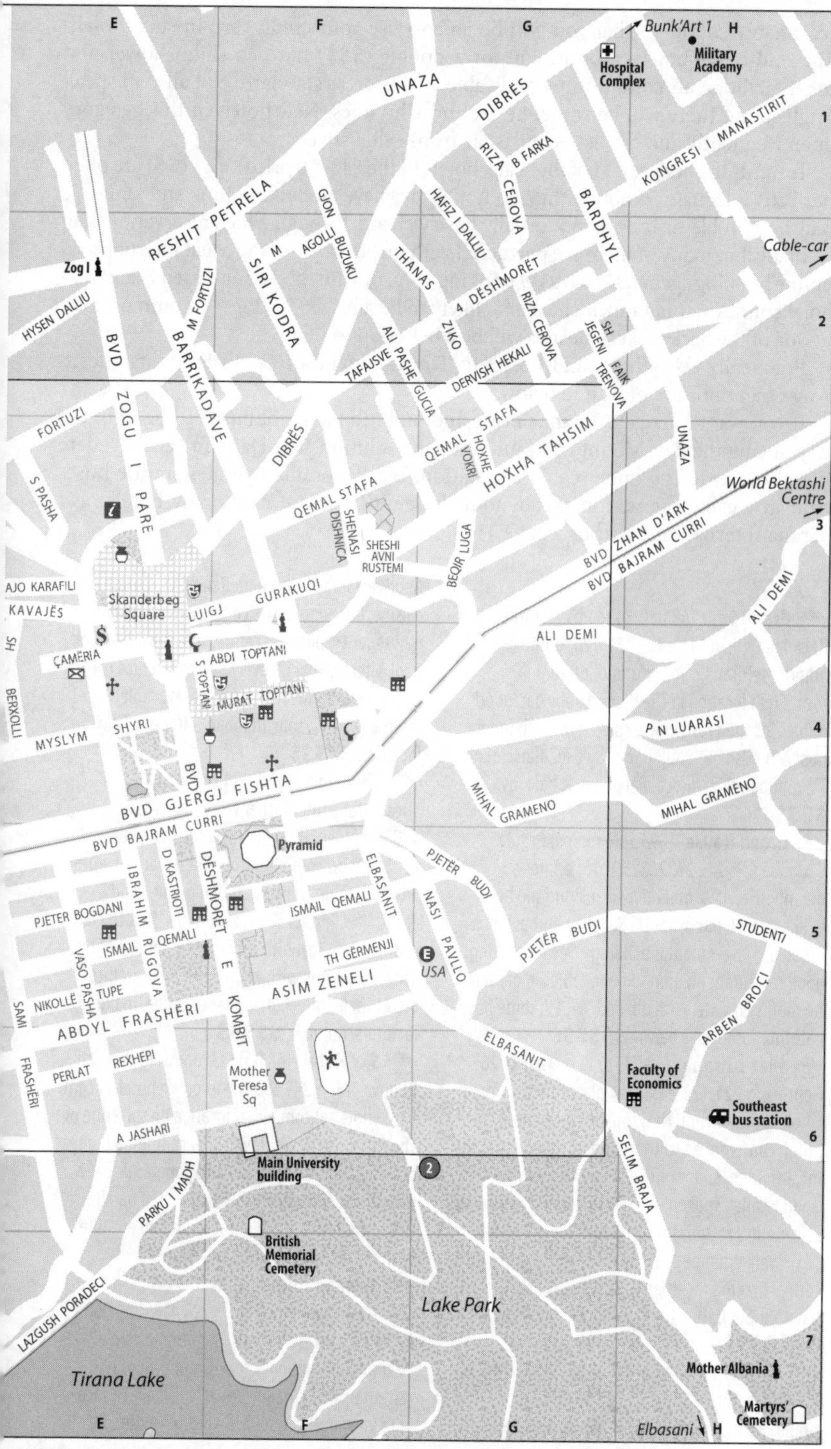

Tirana WHERE TO STAY

3

reasonably confident that you will be able to use your credit card in such hotels. The **mid-range** hotels, around €60 for a double (**$$$**) have en-suite shower and toilet facilities, air conditioning and cable television as standard. Not all staff speak English, but there will be someone around who does. New hotels in this category open frequently and the list below is far from exhaustive.

Towards the **budget** end of the scale, hotels in the €40–50 price range (**$$**) are often perfectly adequate, although they do not always have air conditioning and language may be a problem. They do not usually have websites through which reservations can be made, but many of them are partnered with one or other of the usual international online booking agencies, such as w booking.com, or with the Tirana-based w albania-hotel.com. Anything much cheaper is likely to be a bit seedy; dorm accommodation in one of the backpackers' hostels will be a better option.

Practically every hotel and hostel in Tirana provides free Wi-Fi for its guests. Any exceptions are indicated below.

If you want to escape Tirana's noise and pollution at night but need to be in the city during the day, Mount Dajti might be the solution. The Dajti Tower Belvedere is right next to the upper cable-car station; the Panorama operates shuttle buses from the cable-car station throughout the day. There are now many hotels near Tirana International Airport (page 31).

LUXURY

🏠 **Grand Spa** [68 D6] (31 rooms, 3 suites) Rr Ismail Qemali 11; ☎ 225 3219/20; e info@grandhoteltirana.com; w grandhoteltirana.com. Great location in The Block. Lobby bar, good Italian-inspired restaurant; spa & gym with indoor pool & Turkish bath. All rooms have AC, flatscreen TV, minibar, safe, direct-dial phone & balcony. **$$$$$**

🏠 **Green House** [69 F5] (6 rooms) Rr Jul Variboba 6; ☎ 222 2632, 225 1015; e info@greenhouse.al; w greenhouse.al. Boutique hotel in a quiet street, handy for US & Italian embassies & Albanian governmental buildings. Secure parking; good restaurant on ground floor, tables in garden. All rooms en suite, with dbl bed, AC, TV; some have bathtub, some have balcony. **$$$$$**

🏠 **Plaza Tirana** [69 E3] (190 rooms) Rr 28 Nëntori; ☎ 221 1221; e info@plazatirana.com; w plazatirana.com. New, business-oriented hotel; conference facilities, underground parking inc, lift, gym, spa, same-day laundry service. Good English spoken. All-day informal restaurant, fine-dining restaurant evenings only. All rooms have well-equipped en suite, smart TV, minibar, coffee-making facilities & safe. Deluxe rooms have slipper bath with magnificent views of Mt Dajti. **$$$$$**

🏠 **Rogner Europapark** [69 E6] (137 rooms) Bd Dëshmorët e Kombit; ☎ 223 5035; e info.tirana@rogner.com; w hotel-europapark.com.

Good restaurant with Albanian & international cuisine; bar popular with politicians & expats; lift, newsagent's, business centre, spa, gym. Open-air pool & terrace bar in lovely gardens, tennis courts, fitness centre. All rooms have AC, TV, cabled internet access , safe, minibar, coffee-making facilities. **$$$$$**

🏠 **Sheraton** [69 F7] (151 rooms) Sheshi Italia, off Mother Teresa Sq; ☎ 227 4707; e reservations.tirana@sheraton.com; w starwood.com/sheraton. Piano bar, restaurant with Albanian & international menu, food court, lifts. Indoor & outdoor pools, health club, business lounge with cabled internet & printer. Spacious rooms with king-size beds, satellite TV, AC, safe, direct-dial phone, coffee-making facilities, minibar. **$$$$$**

🏠 **Sky Hotel** [68 D5] (33 rooms) Rr Ibrahim Rugova 5/1; ☎ 241 5995; e info@skyhotel-al.com; w skyhotel-al.com. Great location on the edge of The Block, in the Sky Tower – once Tirana's highest building. Ground-floor bar, lift, panoramic bar & restaurant, fitness centre & spa, secure parking. Large, well-appointed guest rooms, all en suite with rain shower, AC, TV, safe. **$$$$$**

🏠 **Tirana International** [69 E2] (158 rooms, 12 suites) Skanderbeg Sq; ☎ 223 4185; m 068 22 34 185; e reservation@hoteltirana.com.al; w tiranainternational.com. Ground-floor bar; restaurant with mainly Italian cuisine & terrace with view over the square; secure parking; lift.

Indoor pool, spa centre, extensive conference room capacity. All rooms have AC, HD TV, minibar, safe; deluxe rooms have unbeatable views over the city. **$$$$$**

🏠 **Xheko Imperial** [69 E7] (25 rooms) Rr Ibrahim Rugova; ☎ 225 9574/5/6/7; m 068 20 29 777; e contact@xheko-imperial.com; w xheko-imperial.com. Lift to all floors; wine bar; restaurant & bar on roof terrace. Rooms have AC, satellite TV, phone, safe; well-equipped bathrooms with underfloor heating & hairdryers. **$$$$$**

UPMARKET

🏠 **Arbër** [69 E2] (24 rooms, 1 suite) Rr Bardhok Biba 59; ☎ 227 3811; e reservation@hotelarber. com; w hotelarber.com. Lift, laundry service, free car parking for guests, terrace bar, restaurant with Albanian & Italian menu. All rooms en suite, with CH, AC, satellite TV, minibar, direct-dial phone. Rooms are a good size – sgls have 1.2m beds, twins have an armchair & desk; 1 suite with 1 dbl bedroom, 2 bathrooms & a sitting room. **$$$$**

🏠 **Iliria** [69 G7] (20 rooms) Rr e Elbasanit; ☎ 237 1700; m 068 40 27 112; e info@hoteliliriatirana. com; w www.hoteliliriatirana.com. Handy for US embassy and buses to southeast. Restaurant & terrace bar, secure parking, lift. All rooms good sized, with well-appointed en suite, CH, AC, satellite flatscreen TV (with BBC!), minibar, laundry service, safe, balcony; some have balcony overlooking Tirana Park. **$$$$**

🏠 **Mondial** [62 C2] (36 rooms) Rr Muhamet Gjollesha 90; ☎ 223 2372; m 068 20 04 642; e info@hotelmondial.al; w hotelmondial.al. Away from the busy centre, convenient for the airport & highways to the west & north. Helpful reception staff; lift. Good restaurant, rooftop & indoor bars, rooftop pool (in summer), sauna, laundry service, business services, computer in lobby with internet access for guests' use. All rooms have satellite TV, AC, safe, desk, minibar, direct-dial phone; suites have balcony. **$$$$**

🏠 **Theranda** [68 C5] (14 rooms) Rr Andon Z Çajupi 6&7; ☎ 227 3766; e reservations@ therandahotel.com; w therandahotel.com; see ad, page 86. Slightly hard to find but signposted off Rr Çajupi. The only mid-range hotel in Tirana that meets UK health & safety standards (eg: fire exits). 2 quiet villas linked by an attractive courtyard, bar, secure parking, computer for guests' use. No restaurant on site, but b/fast inc. All rooms with

alarmed door locks, good-sized en-suite bathroom, minibar, AC, TV, cabled internet. **$$$$**

🏠 **Vila Alba** [69 F3] (24 rooms & 3 in annexe) Rr Xhorxhi Martini 10; ☎ 225 5937; e office@vila-alba.com; w vila-alba.com. On a quiet side street, b/fast room on top floor with views over city; lift. Nicely furnished, large rooms, all with en-suite bathroom & shower, LCD TV, minibar, AC, dressing table. **$$$$**

MID-RANGE

🏠 **Dajti Tower Belvedere** [map, page 58] (24 rooms) Mt Dajti; m 067 40 11 035; e marketing@dajtiekspres.com; w dajtiekspres. com. Part of the complex around the upper station of the Dajti cable-car; magnificent views over Tirana on one side, forested mountainside on the other. Panoramic restaurant, revolving bar on top floor, free transport on cable-car (*closed Tue*) for hotel guests. All rooms en suite with AC, satellite TV, free Wi-Fi, minibar, phone. **$$$**

🏠 **Gloria** [69 F2] (5 rooms, 1 suite) Rr Qemal Stafa; ☎ 222 0036; m 069 20 53 310; e brpgloria@ hotmail.com; w hotelboutiquegloria.al. Helpful, English-speaking reception staff; secure parking; laundry service. Good, long-established restaurant/pizzeria on top floor (separate entrance, also direct access from hotel). All rooms have AC, flatscreen TV, safe, minibar with free water, well-equipped bathroom with luxurious shower; 4 rooms have balcony. **$$$**

🏠 **Millennium** [69 E3] (7 rooms) Rr Murat Toptani 5; ☎ 225 1935; m 069 95 97 629; e tiranahotelmillennium@gmail. com; w hotelmillennium.eu. Good location on pedestrian street, opposite Millennium cinema. English spoken at reception; nice b/fast room with espresso machine. All rooms have AC, TV, nice en-suite bathroom; 2 have balcony. **$$$**

🏠 **Nobel** [68 D2] (6 rooms, 1 apt) Rr Uran Pano; ☎ 225 6444; m 068 20 20 757; e reservations@hotelnobeltirana.com; w hotelnobeltirana.com. Good location, just off Skanderbeg Sq, behind the Tirana International. Restaurant & 24hr bar. Dbl, sgl & trpl rooms, all en suite with AC, TV, fridge. **$$$**

🏠 **Stela** [69 F1] (9 rooms) Rr e Dibrës; ☎ 222 1547; m 068 20 13 978; e reservations@ hotelstela.al; w hotelstela.al. Bar & restaurant in same building, separate entrance. All rooms en suite with cable TV, AC. **$$$**

🏠 **Villa Tafaj** [68 C2] (25 rooms) Rr Mine Peza 86; ☎222 7581 (reception), 223 4287 (restaurant); m 068 20 21 013, 068 20 78 055; e reservations@ villatafaj.com; w villatafaj.com. Converted 1920s villa; charming, but might be awkward for the less mobile. English spoken; good restaurant, with tables outside in vine-shaded courtyard; reliable Wi-Fi only in public areas. All rooms en suite (some have bathtub), AC, minibar, satellite TV, cabled broadband. **$$$**

THRIFTY

🏠 **Freddy's Hotel** [68 D1] (18 rooms) Rr Bardhok Biba 75; ☎226 6077; m 068 20 35 261, 068 26 01 909; e alfredsalku@yahoo.com; w freddyshostel.com. Centrally located, very good value; good English spoken at reception; friendly, helpful staff & management. Fast reliable Wi-Fi throughout; laundry service; generous buffet b/ fast inc. Airport transfers can be booked through website, excursions can be arranged; small library with guidebooks (including this one) & Albanian literature in translation. Sgl, twin, dbl, trpl & 4-bed rooms, all en suite with good shower-screen & toiletries, TV, fridge; most have AC; ample electrical sockets; bedside light. **$$**

🏠 **Lugano** [68 C2] (8 rooms) Rr Mihal Duri 34; ☎222 2023; m 069 53 08 143; e lugano_hotel@ yahoo.com. Can be booked through AirBNB. Some English spoken at reception. Laundry service. All rooms en suite with AC, TV, fridge. **$$**

🏠 **Panorama** [map, page 58] (5 rooms, 4 chalets) Mt Dajti; ☎236 3124; m 069 20 23 936, 068 20 23 936; e panorama@albaniaonline.net. Friendly staff, some English spoken. A Panorama shuttle bus waits for passengers at the exit from the upper cable-car station. Dbl rooms below the restaurant, chalets to the side, all at ground level.

All rooms & chalets have beautiful views (if it is clear, to the Adriatic), en-suite shower & toilet, TV & heating. **$$**

BUDGET

🏠 **Backpacker Hostel** [68 B2] (48 beds) Rr e Bogdanëve 3; m 068 46 82 353, 068 31 33 451; e tiranabackpacker@hotmail.com; w tiranahostel. com. Albania's 1st backpackers' hostel. Italian-era villa, large garden with bar, hammocks, relaxing area, small pool; camping possible. Well-equipped kitchen with wood stove; lounge with open fire (in winter); computers for guests' use, lockers. Bikes available to hire; car hire can be arranged; day trips organised. 7 dorms (1 with AC) & 2 dbls (**$$**), 3 chalets in garden (**$$**), sharing 3 toilets & 3 showers on each floor; sheets & towels provided; b/fast inc. **$**

🏠 **Hostel Albania** [68 A3] (24 beds) Rr e Kavajës 80/7; m 069 67 48 778; e hostelalbania@ gmail.com; 📘. A new location for this long-established hostel, now above Bar Angolo just off Rr e Kavajës (map on 📘). Kitchen, washing machine; rooftop terrace with pool, barbecue, bar. Free city tours & day trips organised. Summer camping on roof-terrace. 1 dbl en suite (**$$**); 3 dorms, with lockers, sharing 3 toilets & 3 showers; bed linen & b/fast inc. **$**

🏠 **Milingona City Center** [69 G2] (44 beds) Rr Vehbi Agolli; m 069 20 49 836, 069 61 02 875, 069 20 70 076; e milingonahostel@gmail.com; w milingonahostel.com. Located 30m down an alley off Rr Beqir Luga; yellow & green gate, directions on website. Kitchen, washing machine; large garden with fruit-trees, 1st-floor terrace, bar, parking; b/ fast inc. Day trips & airport transfers organised. Bed linen & towel provided; lockers. Camping possible in garden. 5 dorms of varying sizes, 1 dbl & 1 twin (**$$**), each named after an Albanian town. **$**

✖ WHERE TO EAT AND DRINK

Tirana is probably the only capital city in Europe which does not have a McDonald's, although an ersatz McDonald's, called **Kolonat**, has branches across the city centre. Instead, it has a huge number of real restaurants, many of them excellent. In all but the most expensive establishments listed below, a main course with a salad or soup and a beer or a glass of wine should come in at around €15. Fish and seafood are always dearer than meat.

The Albanian fast-food option is a 'grill' – cafés serving shish kebab, grilled *qofta* (meatballs), or *sufllaqë* (doner kebab, the Greek *souvlaki*), usually washed down with beer. There are many such grill restaurants; the Zgara Korça chain is reliable. Vegetarians will have to make do with *byrek* (page 48).

At weekends, Tirana families head out to one of the restaurants on Mount Dajti (page 85), or off the Elbasani road, for spit-roasted or barbecued lamb, accompanied by salad, chips and red wine. A recommended option there is **Natyra e Qetë** [map, page 58] (**m** *068 24 68 334*; **$$**), just beyond the huge shopping mall called Tirana East Gate (TEG).

EXPENSIVE

✕ Otium [68 C5] Rr Brigada VIII; 🔊 222 3570; **m** 069 20 50 778; 🕓 Tue–Sun. Small, intimate restaurant; excellent service; unusual but effective menu blending high-quality Albanian ingredients with Western culinary inventiveness. **$$$$$**

✕ Piazza [68 D2] Rr Ded Gjo Luli, in the corner behind the fountain; 🔊 223 0706. Excellent menu, particularly the fish; outstanding wine list with the best Albanian wines; highly professional service; formal atmosphere. No longer has the monopoly on these virtues that it once had, but still very high quality. The **Piazza Café** (**$$$**) next door serves great sandwiches & burgers until late at night. **$$$$$**

ABOVE AVERAGE

✕ Amor [68 B6] Rr Muhamet Gjollesha; 🔊 224 1573; **m** 069 26 84 952, 068 40 10 403; 🕓 Mon–Sat. High-quality Italian dining in a weirdly out-of-the-way corner of Tirana. No printed menu; the waiter tells you what the chef proposes, based on what they liked the look of in the market that morning. Difficult to find, in an alleyway among residential buildings behind the Dinamo Stadium. **$$$$**

✕ Juvenilja Castle [63 G6] Rr Gjeneral Niko Pushkini; 🔊 226 6666; **w** juvenilja.com. Lovely setting, in a curious castle-style building just on the edge of the Big Park (Parku i Madh). The usual range of salads & Italian dishes, with an unusually interesting selection of Albanian-style antipasti. Tables in garden right next to the park are for drinks only; the restaurant has a roofed gallery overlooking the garden & the park. **$$$$**

✕ Oda [69 F2] Rr Luigj Gurakuqi; 🔊 224 9541; **m** 069 20 94 911. The best traditional Albanian food in Tirana, with specialities from southern & central Albania, inc various offal dishes. In an old house near the central market; 2 small dining rooms, 1 with *sofra* (low wooden tables), the other with Western tables & chairs; English spoken. Excellent selection of raki, inc *mani* & *mare* (page 49). **$$$$**

✕ Sky Club [68 D5] Rr Ibrahim Rugova ; 🔊 222 1666, 222 1143. On the top floor of the Sky Tower on the eastern edge of The Block, is a restaurant with, as one might expect, magnificent views of the city. The Sky Tower is also home to Tirana's only revolving bar. The revolution is quite slow – it takes almost an hour to turn the whole 360°. For those who prefer not to revolve, drinks are also served at tables on the terrace around the outside of the restaurant. **$$$$**

✕ Vila Era [69 F6] Rr Papa Gjon Pali II; **m** 068 90 24 561. Airy, modern interior; garden at rear. Traditional Albanian specialities, plus the usual Italian-influenced dishes; good wine list with several Albanian vineyards represented. **$$$$**

REASONABLE

✕ Amsterdam [69 F6] Rr Asim Zeneli, opposite the Netherlands embassy (hence the name). Pleasant walled garden, pasta & pizzas, grilled meat, instant-heart-attack dishes such as fried cheese. **$$$**

✕ Berlin [68 D6] Rr Pjetër Bogdani, between Sami Frashëri & Vaso Pasha; 🔊 226 0737. Famous for its schnitzels; also has homemade pasta, good pizza, grilled meat & fish; good Albanian wine. **$$$**

✕ Era [68 C6] Rr Ismail Qemali, between Vaso Pasha & Sami Frashëri; 🔊 225 7805, 226 0749. A good selection of traditional Albanian food, plus pizzas & pasta; the terrace is heated in winter; can get crowded, especially inside; one of the few restaurants in Tirana that stays open really late (until midnight at w/ends). **$$$**

✕ Green House [69 F5] Rr Jul Variboba 6; 🔊 223 1015. Reliably good Italian-influenced menu, with a range of interesting meat & fish dishes, plus pizza from wood-fired oven. Sometimes has game dishes such as hare. Friendly, professional service. Tables outside in pleasant courtyard. **$$$**

✕ Juvenilija [68 C5] Rr Sami Frashëri, at the T-junction with Rr Brigada VIII; **m** 068 20 22 802. Juvenilija is a Tirana institution; go with friends & share a couple of pizzas & cold beers. Also offers pasta, risotto, escalopes & some traditional Albanian dishes. **$$$**

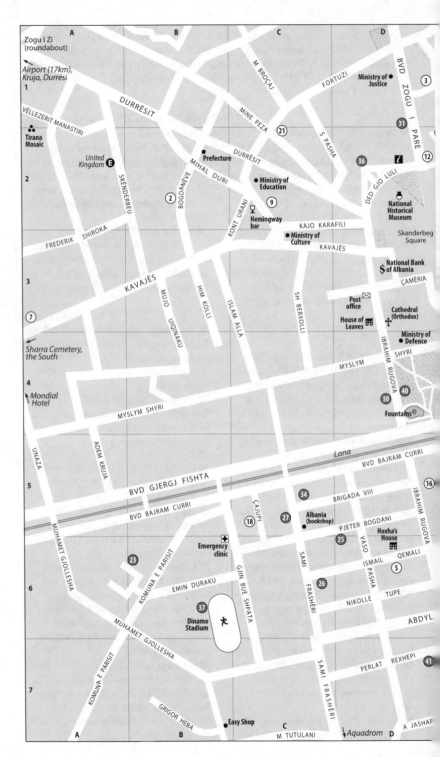

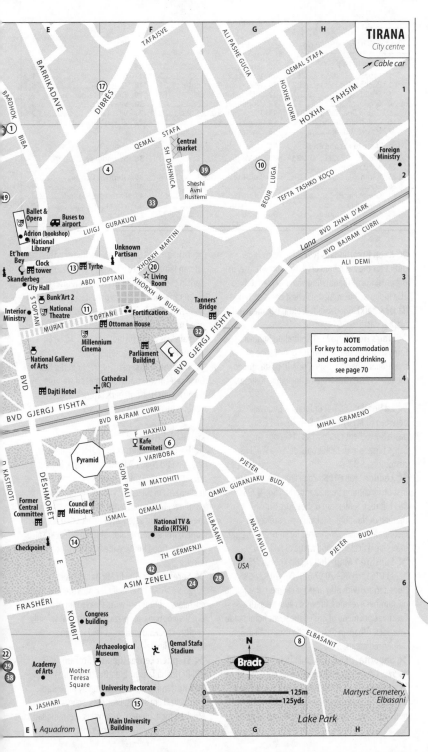

BARDHOK BIBA

E

BARRIKADAVE

DIBRES

TAFAJSVE

F

ALI PASHE GUCIA

G

QEMAL STAFA

HOXHE VOKRI

H

HOXHA TAHSIM

1

⓵

⓾ 17

QEMAL STAFA

SH DISHNICA

STAFA

Central market

BEQIR LUGA

TEFTA TASHKO KOÇO

Foreign Ministry

2

⓵⓽

4

33

39

Sheshi Avni Rustemi

10

Ballet & Opera

Buses to airport

LUIGJ GURAKUQI

XHORXH MARTINI

Lana

BVD ZHAN D'ARK

BVD BAJRAM CURRI

Adrion (bookshop)

National Library

Unknown Partisan

20

ALI DEMI

Et'hem Bey

Clock tower

13 🏛 **Tyrbe**

☆ **Living Room**

3

Skanderbeg

City Hall

ABDI TOPTANI

XHORXH W BUSH

Interior Ministry

S TOPTANI

🎭 **National Theatre**

🚠 **Bunk'Art 2**

11

TOPTANI

Fortifications

Tanners' Bridge

🏛 **Ottoman House**

32

BVD GJERGJ FISHTA

MURAT

Millennium Cinema

National Gallery of Arts

BVD

Parliament Building

🛏 **Dajti Hotel**

✝ **Cathedral (RC)**

NOTE
For key to accommodation and eating and drinking, see page 70

4

MIHAL GRAMENO

BVD GJERGJ FISHTA

BVD BAJRAM CURRI

D KASTRIOTI

DESHMORET

Pyramid

F HAXHIU

♀ **Kafe Komiteti** 6

J VARIBOBA

M MATOHITI

PJETER BUDI

QAMIL GURANJAKU

5

Tirana WHERE TO EAT AND DRINK

NASI PAVLLO

PJETER BUDI

Former Central Committee

Council of Ministers

ISMAIL

QEMALI

National TV & Radio (RTSH)

ELBASANIT

Checkpoint

14

TH GERMENJI

42

24

28

🄴 USA

6

FRASHERI

ASIM ZENELI

KOMBIT

Congress building

ELBASANIT

Archaeological Museum

🚶 **Qemal Stafa Stadium**

N

8

22

29

38

Academy of Arts

Mother Teresa Square

University Rectorate

Bradt

0 ___ 125m

0 ___ 125yds

Martyrs' Cemetery, Elbasani

7

A JASHARI

15

Main University Building

E ↓ *Aquadrom*

E

F

G

Lake Park

H

3

TIRANA *City centre*
For listings, see pages 64–70

Where to stay

1 Arbër E2	8 Iliria G7	16 Sky D5
2 Backpacker Hostel B2	9 Lugano C2	17 Stela F1
3 Freddy's D1	10 Milingona City Center G2	18 Theranda C5
4 Gloria F2	11 Millennium E3	19 Tirana International E2
5 Grand Spa D6	12 Nobel D2	20 Vila Alba F3
6 Green House F5	13 Plaza Tirana E3	21 Villa Tafaj C2
7 Hostel Albania A3	14 Rogner Europapark E6	22 Xheko Imperial E7
	15 Sheraton F7	

Where to eat and drink

23 Amor B6	30 La Voglia D4	38 Serendipity E7
24 Amsterdam F6	31 London D1	Sky Club (see 16)
25 Berlin D6	32 Lulishte 1 Maji F4	39 Stephen Center G2
26 Era C6	33 Oda F2	40 Taiwan D4
Green House (see 6)	34 Otium C5	41 Taverna e Kasapit D7
27 Juvenilija C5	35 Paidhaqe Dajkua E2	42 Vila Era F6
28 Kaon Brewhouse G6	36 Piazza D2	
29 King's House E7	37 Saporita B6	

Kaon Brewhouse [69 G6] Rr Asim Zeneli. Outlet for the Kaon brewery (also a brewhouse, in the outskirts of Tirana), huge beer garden, tables also indoors. One of Albania's best beers on tap (lager & dark). Good salads & antipasti; meat grills; pizza & pasta. $$$

King's House [69 E7] Rr Ibrahim Rugova. Fairly formal restaurant with a good range of traditional Albanian dishes, salads, pasta, grilled meat, etc. Extensive winelist, including Kallmet. $$$

La Voglia [68 D4] Rr Ibrahim Rugova, between Rr Myslym Shyri & the river. Pizzas, pasta & excellent sandwiches of various sorts. Large terrace with tables outside. Free Wi-Fi for customers. $$$

London [68 D1] Bd Zogu I, on the left of the first block coming from Skanderbeg Sq; 223 8851. Italian & Mexican dishes; nice British-themed decoration; smoking ban enforced in restaurant; conservatory area for smokers. The bar offers a particularly good range of raki. $$$

Lulishte 1 Maji [69 F4] Bd Xhorxh W Bush; 223 0151; m 069 20 97 621, 069 20 92 668. Huge terrace with play area for children; live music on summer evenings. Brews its own beer, to a Czech recipe; menu of grilled meat, inc homemade sausages, Albanian dishes & the usual Italian-influenced meals. $$$

Saporita [68 B6] Rr Emin Duraku; m 067 23 48 520. Large new building at main entrance to Dinamo Stadium; at the time of writing, the best pizzas in Tirana (where the bar is high). Tables in non-smoking conservatory area as well as indoors. $$$

Taiwan [68 D4] Rr Ibrahim Rugova. The Taiwan (albanicised as 'Tajvani') complex in the park in the centre of Tirana (Parku i Rinisë) has 3 restaurants within it. Casa di Pasta, on the ground floor, has a range of interesting salads, fresh bread, good pizzas & a selection of pasta dishes. More formal steak & fish restaurants ($$$$$) on upper floors (lift available). $$$

Taverna e Kasapit [68 D7] Rr Perlat Rexhepi. Good selection of traditional meat dishes (its name means 'The Butcher's Tavern'), *fergesë*, etc. Vegetarians will get a salad. $$$

GOOD DEAL

Paidhaqe Dajkua [69 E2] In an alleyway between Bd Zogu I & Rr Bardhok Biba, behind the Arbër Hotel. Dajkua is one of the few restaurants in the city centre to specialise in *paidhaqe*, barbecued lamb or veal ribs, which are traditionally eaten with Greek salad & chips. Superb grilled vegetables; chicken & fish are also available. Good house wine from Përmeti; friendly service. $$

Serendipity [69 E7] Rr Ibrahim Rugova; 225 9377. An essentially Tex-Mex menu – fajitas, enchiladas, burgers – with a leavening of Albanian & Italian options, inc pizza. Live music at w/ends. English-speaking waiters, mixed foreign & Albanian clientele. $$

Stephen Center (Qendër Stefan) [69 G2] Rr Hoxha Tahsim 1, on the corner of Sheshi Avni Rustemi; Mon–Sat. Run by American evangelical Christians. Brunches, soup, salads, Mexican food, burgers. Also offers accommodation, 6 twin rooms (w *stephencenter.com*; **$$$**). $$

ENTERTAINMENT AND NIGHTLIFE

In recent years, Tirana – and specifically the small area in the city centre known as The Block (Blloku) – has become a major nightlife destination. The Block is about 1km², reserved until 25 years ago for the townhouses of the country's leaders, and now absolutely crammed with bars, restaurants and beautiful people. Tirana City Council clamped down several years ago on noise in The Block after midnight, much to the relief of the many people who live in the area; this has meant that the fashionable nightclubs have moved out of town, along the old road to Elbasani. Closer to the city centre, the **Living Room** [69 F3] (*Rr Xhorxh W Bush, roughly opposite Parliament*) is perennially popular. Word of mouth is likely to be the best source of information about the constantly changing trends in the club scene.

Albania, like many formerly communist countries, has a strong tradition of **classical music**. The **National Theatre of Opera and Ballet (TKOBAP)** [69 E2], on Skanderbeg Square, displays the current season's schedule on the outside wall beside the ticket booth. The box office is open 09.00–14.00 and 19.00–20.00 Monday–Friday; tickets can be reserved by phone (m *067 24 17 167*). Tickets are very reasonably priced (the first night is more expensive) and the performances are often excellent, although the level of noise from the audience can be rather irritating. The theatre's website (w *tkob.gov.al*), although unfortunately only in Albanian, has a calendar of forthcoming events and information about past performances. Classical **concerts** usually take place in the Academy of Arts, on the western side of Mother Teresa Square [69 E7], opposite the Archaeological Museum. The box office is just to the right of the main entrance, looking towards the building; prices vary according to the programme and performers.

It is hard to find live folk music in Tirana. The National Ensemble of Folk Song and Dance (Ansambli i Këngëve dhe Valleve Popullore) occasionally performs at the TKOBAP. (See page 24 for information about the regular folk festivals held in other parts of Albania.) Jazz fans should visit the Hemingway bar (m *069 20 22 303*), in the little square at the junction of Rruga Mihal Duri and Rruga Kont Urani, which sometimes has live jazz.

Theatre performances in languages other than Albanian are rare and it is quite difficult to find out even about plays in Albanian. From time to time, the various western European cultural institutes hold festivals of their own countries' films, theatre or music. These festivals tend not to be well publicised and the best way to find out about them is by consulting the *Tirana Times* or *Albanian Daily News*.

The Albanian national **football** team played in the UEFA European Championship for the first time ever in 2016, generating huge excitement throughout the country. A new football stadium [69 F7] is scheduled to open in 2018, when it will become the home of the national side. Until then, the only place to watch football matches in Tirana will be the small stadium on the other side of town [68 B6], whose official name is 'Selman Stërmasi' but which is always called by its Communist-era name of the Dinamo Stadium. Albanian matches are interesting cultural experiences, even for people who are not big football fans.

SHOPPING

The centre of Tirana is full of shops, and the outskirts full of shopping malls, selling imported goods at higher prices than in the UK. There are a few places that stock things likely to be of interest to the visitor – the jewellery and ceramics shops on

Bulevardi Gjergj Fishta between Ibrahim Rugova and Vaso Pasha, the souvenir shops on Rruga Luigj Gurakuqi on the way up to the central market, and a cluster of kiosks on Rruga e Barrikadave near the roundabout. Kruja, less than an hour's drive away (pages 98–102) is a better place than Tirana to shop for souvenirs; the choice is wider and all the shops are together in a compact area.

The **Albania** bookshop [68 C5] on Rruga Sami Frashëri and **Adrion International Bookstore** [68 E3] on Skanderbeg Square stock books in English about Albania and the Balkans, and translations of Albanian literature.

The **central market** [69 F2] (*Pazari i Ri*), between Sheshi Avni Rustemi and Rruga Qemal Stafa, is a brand-new building that has replaced the charming but slightly chaotic warren of stalls that were previously here. As well as meat, fish and dairy products, the market is a cornucopia of fruit and vegetables, different sorts of olives and nuts, honey, eggs and homemade raki. Smaller, neighbourhood markets can still be found elsewhere in the city; there is one along Rruga Mihal Grameno, for example, and another on Rruga Fortuzi.

OTHER PRACTICALITIES

There are ATMs (cashpoints, known in Albanian as *bankomat*) all over the city. See page 38 for some tips on using Albanian ATMs.

Cash euros, sterling, Swiss francs and dollars of the Australian, Canadian and US varieties can all be readily changed in Tirana. There are many bureaux de change throughout the city, with clusters on Bulevardi Zogu I and around the junction of Rruga Myslym Shyri and Rruga Ibrahim Rugova. In general, they stay open until at least 17.00; some close earlier on Saturdays and almost all are shut on Sundays. There are also money changers on the streets, particularly around the National Bank; the rate they offer for small sums is not significantly better than that of the bureaux, and counterfeit notes sometimes circulate on the street. Foreign currency can also be changed in any of the numerous banks in the city, although the process is swifter in the bureaux de change.

The central **post office** [68 D3] is on Rruga Çamëria, across from the National Bank of Albania. It is open from 07.30 to 20.00 Monday to Saturday, and from 07.30 to 14.00 on Sundays.

The city's accident and emergency clinic (*Urgjenca* in Albanian) is on Rruga Gjin Bue Shpata, near the Dinamo Stadium. Tirana has good private **hospitals**; see page 33 for details.

Tirana is a safe city, and the biggest danger is being struck by a bike or motorcycle jumping a red light, or whizzing the wrong way up a one-way street. Outside the city centre, pavements are often rather uneven and, although young Albanian women seem to negotiate them flawlessly in precipitous heels, the less gazelle-like will find it easier to get around in flatter shoes. Along the main shopping streets in the city centre, an unexpected risk is that of falling down the (completely unprotected) steps of one of the many basement shops.

WHAT TO SEE AND DO

SKANDERBEG SQUARE [68 D3] Skanderbeg Square was once the hub of Tirana's commercial and social life. Before World War II, the main market was here; the 18th-century mosque was where men met to chat, as well as to worship; and around the edges of the square were small shops and cafés. In the 1920s and 30s, the square became the city's administrative centre, with imposing new buildings designed by

Italian architects. Now it has been completely closed to traffic and an underground car park has been built beneath its paved expanse.

On Skanderbeg Square's northern side are the National Historical Museum and the Tirana International Hotel; to the west is the National Bank; and the eastern side is entirely taken up with what was once known as the Palace of Culture, which still houses the opera house and the National Library. Bisecting the square is the wide **Boulevard**, designed by Mussolini's emissaries and perfect for Fascist parades. To the south, down to the main university building, it is called Boulevard Dëshmorët e Kombit (the Martyrs of the Nation Boulevard). The northern section is Boulevard Zogu i Parë (Zog the First Boulevard); a statue of King Zog I now stands at its junction with the ring road.

An equestrian statue of **Skanderbeg** (see box, pages 206–7) stands at the head of Dëshmorët e Kombit. The sculptor was Odhisë Paskali (1903–85), a native of Përmeti in the far south of the country. Across the road from the statue are the **Mosque of Et'hem Bey** and, behind it, the clock tower. The 18th-century mosque is one of the few really old buildings left in Tirana, and is perhaps also the most beautiful. Its minaret was shattered in the Battle for the Liberation of Tirana (page 15), but it was subsequently repaired, and the mosque's status as a Cultural Monument kept it from being damaged or destroyed during the atheism campaigns of the late 1960s. There are frescoes on its exterior walls and more paintings inside the mosque. Visitors are admitted except during prayers; shoes must be removed at the entrance, before stepping on the carpet, and women must cover their hair.

Excellent views of the city can be enjoyed from the top of the 35m-high **clock tower**, built in the 1820s (⊕ *09.00–18.00 Mon–Fri, 09.00–14.00 Sat, closed Sun*). There is also a small exhibition of models of clock towers in Albania, which can be seen on request.

MUSEUMS AND GALLERIES
National Historical Museum [68 D2] (*Muzeu Historik Kombëtar;* ⊕ *10.00–17.00 Tue–Sat, 09.00–14.00 Sun, last admission 30mins before closing; 200 lek*) Dominating Skanderbeg Square is the National Historical Museum, with its huge mosaic mural above the entrance. The museum was opened in 1981 and the mural is an excellent example of the triumphalist art of the time. It depicts victorious Albanians from various points in history, from Illyrians to partisans via the fighters and intellectuals who won independence from the Ottoman Empire, all being led into the glorious future by a Mother Albania figure.

You should allow an absolute minimum of 2 hours to look round the whole museum.

There are many interesting things on display, with helpful maps and information on multi-lingual panels. Each display case usually has a summary in English and French. On the ground floor – the prehistory, antiquity and late antiquity sections – some of the individual exhibits are labelled in English and French as well as Albanian. The exhibition is arranged in rough chronological order, and starts with prehistoric finds from the Stone, Copper, Bronze and Iron ages. There are maps of Illyrian tribes and city-states at different points in time, and examples of Illyrian jewellery, coins and votive objects in terracotta and bronze from the 3rd to the 1st centuries BC. Two outstanding works of art date from the 4th century BC: a head of Apollo, discovered in the *orchestra* of the theatre at Butrint (pages 231–6), and known as 'The Goddess of Butrint'; and the first mosaic ever discovered in Albania, which portrays a woman's head and is called 'The Belle of Durrësi'. There is pottery from the Greek colonies in what is now Albania, 3rd-century armour and reconstructions of 2,000-year-old agricultural implements. Maps on the walls show the sites of uprisings and invasions during the turmoil of the 11th and 12th centuries.

The first floor covers the rise of the feudal states in the medieval period, the Ottoman conquest and Albania under Ottoman rule. The highlight of the medieval section is the 'Epitaph' of Gllavenica, a beautiful embroidered altar-cloth from 1373. The complete doorway of the church of St Gjon Vladimir, near Elbasani (pages 117–18), has been re-erected and a relic of the saint is in a display case nearby. There are also interesting exhibits from other medieval churches, including a fragment of fresco from the 13th-century church at Vau i Dejës, near Shkodra, which was demolished (by *art students*) during the atheism campaign of 1967. A whole room is devoted to the role of Skanderbeg as leader of the Albanian resistance to the Ottomans. The section covering the 16th to 18th centuries gives a good overview of Ottoman administration and the development of Albania's cities.

The second floor of the museum covers the National Renaissance (Rilindja Kombëtare), the cultural and political movement of the late 19th and early 20th centuries, which culminated in Albania's declaration of independence on 28 November 1912. The explanatory panels are in English and French, although some prior knowledge of the Rilindja movement would be an advantage in understanding the exhibition. There are nice displays of 19th-century textiles, weapons and ethnographic items. The icon gallery on this floor is home to the magnificent iconostasis from the church of St Gjon Vladimir, by the 17th-century artist Kostandin Ieromonaku. There is a good selection of icons, including works by Onufri; however, the cream of Albania's Byzantine art is in Korça, home of the National Museum of Medieval Art (pages 132–3), and in the Onufri Museum in Berati Castle (pages 123–4).

Although the World War II exhibition still predominantly consists of displays about the communist-led LNÇ (see box, page 13) and the activities of the partisans, the curators have made an effort to include other sides of the story. There are panels explaining the parts played by Balli Kombëtar and the Legalitet movement, for example, and a display of photographs of the Councils of Regency that governed Albania in the period between Italy's capitulation and liberation. The role of SOE (see boxes, pages 13 and 14–15) and the contribution made during the war by the USA are also presented. The World War II section is quite extensive and it could easily take over an hour to study it all in detail. It is possible to access it by the back stairs, without passing through the whole of the rest of the museum, and those with a particular interest in this period might want to consider visiting it separately.

The last hall of the museum is devoted to a fascinating exhibition about Albania during the communist period. Unfortunately, the information panels in the display cases are not translated, which makes it difficult for non-Albanian visitors to follow the historical development of the exhibition. A life-size mock-up of a solitary confinement cell brings home the terrible conditions in which so many Albanians were imprisoned. A rolling video, with some English subtitles, includes film of the student protests in 1991 that ultimately brought about the end of communist rule in Albania.

The museum shop stocks postcards, souvenirs and books. There are civilised toilets on the ground floor.

Archaeological Museum [69 E7] (*Muzeu Arkeologjik; Sh Nënë Tereza;* ⊕ *10.00–14.30 Mon–Fri; 300 lek*) Although the National Historical Museum holds the best-known objects from Albania's archaeological heritage, the collection in the

Archaeological Museum, located within the Centre for Albanology Studies in Mother Teresa Square, is much more extensive. Few of the artefacts are labelled in English, but in most cases the labels merely indicate provenance, so geographical rather than linguistic knowledge is what is required. Some of the curators speak good English and, their time permitting, they are usually pleased to explain the collection to visitors.

The first two rooms are devoted to the Stone, Bronze and Iron ages, with some particularly nice spear- and axe-heads, and a fine iron helmet. Then the artefacts from Illyrian cities begin, which will be of greater interest to visitors who are not prehistory specialists. Lovely little figurines in bronze and terracotta, including a delightful little bronze dog from Antigonea (pages 249–50), are perhaps the most attractive items in these cases, but there is also jewellery and pottery to admire, and a well-preserved helmet complete with nose and cheek guards. The Roman period is represented with statuary, some fine glassware, inscribed tombstones (some with Illyrian names), and inscriptions from Victorinus's Wall, built around the ancient city of Byllis.

On the walls there are enlarged photographs of archaeological sites and of some of the mosaics that have been discovered there. The museum has a selection of

THE MYSTERY OF THE MARTINI RIFLES

With thanks to M C Barrès-Baker

Fans of the 1964 film *Zulu* may wonder why the .45" Martini-Henry rifle, the weapon used to defend Rorke's Drift, appears in so many Albanian paintings and museum display cases. The answer is that they are not Martini-Henrys at all.

The British adopted the Martini-Henry in 1871, naming it after Friedrich von Martini, who designed its breech mechanism, and Scotsman Alexander Henry, who designed the barrel. In 1872, Khedive Ismail of Egypt gave the Ottoman sultan 50,000 Martini-Henrys. The sultan was so impressed that he ordered 600,000 copies from the Providence Tool Company of Rhode Island, USA. These were called Peabody-Martinis, after Henry O Peabody, an American who had patented the earliest version of the Martini breech.

Peabody-Martini rifles played a significant role during the 1877 siege of Plevna, inflicting heavy casualties on the attacking Russian (and Romanian) troops. Turkish payments for the rifles were constantly in arrears, however, and in 1885 this drove Providence Tool bankrupt. Its president was reduced to burning Peabody-Martini rifle butts to keep warm.

A few years later the Turkish army went over to using Mauser magazine rifles; Edith Durham, however, travelling in the early years of the 20th century, describes Albanian gendarmes 'armed with Peabody-Martini rifles of American pattern, which they call "Martinas" and cherish dearly'. By then the rifle had also become the weapon of choice among the Albanian civilian population, both because the cartridge cases were easy to refill and because it was a better man-stopper than more expensive bolt-action rifles.

Martinis could be used as part-payment in a *besa* (see box, pages 192–3) or to buy a wife; but keeping one's Martini in powder and lead could be nearly as expensive as keeping a wife. Men often decorated their Martinis with silver filigree or with silver coins, one for each life taken. In High Albania, Durham describes a man singing a song to his Martini, 'in which he addressed it as his wife and his child, for he wanted no other.'

books for sale, some of them in English translation, about Albanian archaeology and archaeological sites.

National Gallery of Arts [69 E4] (*Galeria Kombëtare e Arteve; Bd Dëshmorët e Kombit;* w *galeriakombetare.gov.al;* ⊕ *10.00–18.00 Wed–Sun; closed Mon & Tue; 200 lek*) The National Gallery of Arts has a fascinating collection of Albanian art, which puts into context the Socialist Realist work that can be seen in so many public spaces around the country. The chronological exhibition begins in the late 19th century with Albania's first non-religious painters, whose portraits and depictions of idealised rural life give an insight into the cultural atmosphere in Albania at that time. Albania's first art school was founded in 1931 and the paintings from the pre-war period show greater realism. The next rooms move Albanian art into the communist period, with the historical tableaux of artists such as Fatmir Haxhiu (1927–2001) and the Socialist Realist portrayals of idealised workers, including some splendid sculptures.

At the beginning of the 1970s, Albanian artists began to experiment with Formalism and produced some outstanding work in this genre. Although they tried to keep within the limits of Socialist Realism, their experimentation was not without risk: one of their number, Edison Gjergjo (1939–89) was arrested in 1974 for painting work 'displaying a pessimistic outlook and formalist traits'. The permanent exhibition ends with a display of post-1990 Albanian painting and sculpture, with work by artists such as Ksenofon Dilo (b1932) and Edi Rama (b1964), who at the time of writing is the Prime Minister of Albania.

The rear hall on the ground floor of the gallery is used for temporary exhibitions, which are often worth a look if you have time. Hidden behind the building is a collection of discarded communist-era statues: Lenin, Stalin, Hoxha, a couple of idealised workers and Shote Galica, a heroine of the struggle for Albanian independence. It is not always possible to gain access to this part of the gallery's grounds; it seems to depend on the mood of the security guard on duty at the time.

The gallery's website (w *galeriakombetare.gov.al*) is an excellent introduction, in English, not only to the collection, but also to the history of Albanian art. The gallery also houses a reference-only art library, with over 4,200 titles in various languages, which is open to the public free of charge.

The Tirana Mosaic [68 A2] (⊕ *08.00–17.00 daily; free admission*) Tirana's only visible Roman remains, the Tirana Mosaic, was discovered during construction work in 1972. The original Roman building seems to have been the villa of a 1st-century AD winemaker. Two of his (or her?) amphorae are on display at the site, along with other items excavated there. The mosaic floor was laid in the 4th or 5th century AD, when the villa was converted into a basilica. It has been conserved and stabilised to make it one of the few mosaics in Albania that can be viewed *in situ* by the general public (another is in Saranda; page 231).

The mosaic site is slightly to the south of Rruga e Durrësit, just inside the ring road (Unaza). It is hidden among residential buildings and is a little tricky to find, although it is signposted from the ring road. It should take about 15 minutes to walk there from Skanderbeg Square, or you could board any of the buses that go from the centre to the Zogu i Zi roundabout.

WALKS AROUND TIRANA A **half-hour walk** around some of Tirana's architectural highlights starts at the clock tower [69 E3] just off Skanderbeg Square. Following the alleyway between the clock tower and the rear entrance to the Italian-designed

City Hall will bring you out on to Rruga Abdi Toptani. The Toptanis were one of the Albanian families that rose to power in the 18th and 19th centuries, during the Ottoman period. These feudal lords were known as *pashas*; there is more information about this phenomenon on pages 254–5. The Toptani family's original power base was Kruja and one of their houses can be visited there (pages 100–1). Another, dating from 1780, can be seen about halfway along Rruga Abdi Toptani, behind a tree-shaded courtyard. The exterior of the building has been sympathetically restored and for many years it functioned as a restaurant, Sarajet ('the Seraglio'). It is well worth a visit, if it reopens to the public in the lifetime of this book.

Directly across Rruga Abdi Toptani from the City Hall is a replica bunker that forms the entrance to Bunk'Art 2. This and its sister-installation, Bunk'Art 1, are dedicated to the interpretation of aspects of the Communist period. (See pages 79–80 for details of the two Bunk'Art sites.) If (for now) you continue past the replica bunker along Rruga Sermedin Toptani, you will see the **National Theatre** and Experimental Theatre on your left, separated by an attractive garden with an outdoor swimming pool beyond it.

This street leads to Rruga Murat Toptani, an attractively pedestrianised street that, in summer, is full of stalls and street performers. The **National Gallery of Arts** is just to the left across the street and the Boulevard is visible on your right. To continue this walking tour, though, turn left on to Rruga Murat Toptani. A short stretch of the Ottoman-era city wall still stands, on the right just beyond the Millennium Cinema. The path to the side of the cinema complex leads to an Austrian-designed villa built for King Zog (page 12) in 1929, now returned to the ownership of his descendants and used as the Albanian Royal Court. The archaeological remains that can be seen towards the end of the pedestrian street are traces of fortifications, which date from the struggle for control of Tirana in the 18th century, between the Toptanis and another feudal family.

To the right of the archaeological site is the **Albanian Parliament** [69 F4], built in 1924 to an Italian design and set in attractive gardens. Information panels at the northern entrance to the gardens show the location of the various buildings. The city's main mosque stood in these gardens until it was destroyed in 1944, during the Battle for the Liberation of Tirana; the large new mosque that replaced it is not on exactly the same site. From here, cross Rruga Xhorxh [George] W Bush to the attractive Italian-period villa that is now the headquarters of the Association of Politically Persecuted People. Down to the left, past the Lulishte 1 Maji restaurant, is a cute little 19th-century bridge called the **Tanners' Bridge** (Ura e Tabakëve) [69 G3].

Now retrace your steps up Rruga Xhorxh W Bush, past the junction with Rruga Murat Toptani and the entrance to the underground car park. In the little park at the junction with Rruga Luigj Gurakuqi, the Socialist Realist monument to the Unknown Partisan (page 82) towers above the modest statue of Tirana's founder, Sulejman Pasha Mulleti. As you turn left here, to return to Skanderbeg Square, you will see, sheltered under a curving roof of the Plaza Hotel (page 64), a curious circular construction, called the **Tyrbe of Kapllan Pasha** [69 E3]. A *tyrbe* is a Bektashi shrine (page 22) commemorating the burial place of a holy person. Kapllan Pasha was the son of Ismail Toptani, who built the beautiful house in Kruja that is now the Ethnographic Museum there (pages 100–1). Kruja was the northernmost stronghold of Bektashism and Kapllan Pasha was the first Toptani to settle in what is now Tirana. It is thanks to the *tyrbe*'s designation as a Cultural Monument that it survived the frenzy of building that overwhelmed Tirana in the first 15 years of this millennium. It is now sympathetically presented in the shadow of the modern architecture that has been built over and around it.

A **longer walk** will let you explore two of Tirana's parks. The relentless pace of construction over the last decade or so has meant the loss of many of Tirana's green spaces, but two of the city's best-loved parks have survived: those known in the Communist era as the Youth Park (Parku i Rinisë) and the Big Park (Parku i Madh).

From Skanderbeg Square, walk down the wide Boulevard Dëshmorët e Kombit (Boulevard of the Martyrs of the Nation) – alternatively, you could jump on a Tirana e Re bus for a couple of stops (*40 lek*). On the left of the Boulevard, just beyond the ministries that line the square, is the National Gallery of Arts (page 76); across the road is the central park, which older Tirana residents still refer to as the Youth Park [68 D4].

In fine weather, the park fills with people of all ages, relaxing with their friends or family. All sorts of traders set out their goods: everything from books and children's toys to pumpkin seeds and candy-floss. A massive monument to Albania's centenary of independence occupies most of the corner between the Boulevard and Rruga Myslym Shyri. The large building on the opposite side of the park – facing on to Rruga Ibrahim Rugova – is a recreation complex known as 'Taiwan' (albanicised as 'Tajvani'), in honour of the country that donated the splendid fountains beside it.

Once you have looked around the Youth Park, continue beyond the Pyramid and the governmental buildings, the Rogner Europapark hotel and the Congress Building (pages 81–2). The square where the Boulevard ends is Mother Teresa Square [69 E7]; the imposing building that occupies most of the southern end is the University of Tirana. In 1990, it was students from this university, then called Enver Hoxha University, who lit the spark that eventually ended single-party rule in Albania (page 17). If you now cross the square and turn right at the university, then slightly uphill to your left, you will find one of the entrances to the Big Park or 'the Lake Park' (Parku i Liqenit) [63 F6]. Now there are two main options: keep going uphill, or bear right.

If you keep going uphill (bearing left), you will get to an attractively painted wooden sign indicating the start of the 'Memorials'. The first memorial you come to is the graveyard of German soldiers who died in Albania during World War II; a little further on are the graves and busts of four highly influential figures in the Albanian cultural renaissance (Rilindja Kombëtare) of the late 19th and early 20th centuries – the three Frashëri brothers, Abdyl, Naim and Sami (see box, pages 152–3); and, a little apart from them, Faik Konica (page 23).

A little beyond the Frashëris, the **British Memorial Cemetery** [63 F6] commemorates 46 British and Commonwealth soldiers and airmen who died in Albania during World War II. (See pages 13–15 for further information about their war work.) They are not buried here, however; their remains were painstakingly collected and reburied by the British Army's Graves Registration Unit in 1946, but were later dug up and moved. Nobody knows where the bodies lie now. The British embassy organises a memorial service here on Remembrance Sunday (around 11 November) every year, which anyone can attend.

If you bear right instead of left at the park entrance, you will come to the **Lake** [63 E7], the reservoir around which the park was created, and the promenade along the top of its dam. On the other side of the dam, the **Aquadrom swimming-pool complex** [62 B7] (⊕ *1 May–1st w/end in Oct; adult admission Jul/Aug: 09.00–14.00 500 lek, 14.00–19.00 300 lek; cheaper in spring/autumn*) has several separate pools, including a dedicated high-diving pool, and a flume. There is a café and a sandwich bar within the complex.

Of course, you might choose simply to wander around the park and see what you come across; it might be a fine Socialist Realist statue, a small Catholic church, a restaurant or a chess-match. Wandering from west to east, you will emerge on Rruga e Elbasanit, with lots of buses back into the centre. The southern shore of the lake has now become a residential suburb, separated from the lake by a stretch of Tirana's outer ring road, inaugurated in September 2017.

COMMUNIST HERITAGE For the first 25 years of Albania's post-communist history, the last thing people wanted to be reminded of was the political repression and economic hardship they had so recently succeeded in getting rid of. Recently, however, national and local authorities have begun to invest in conserving some of the more notable communist sites and curating them so that Albanians and visitors can learn about this difficult and controversial period. There are three such sites in Tirana:

Bunk'Art 1 [map, page 58] (*Rr Fadil Deliu;* m *068 48 34 444;* w *bunkart.al;* ⊕ *09.00–16.00 Wed–Mon; 500 lek*) A fascinating exhibition about how that repressive and isolationist regime developed has been installed within a bunker complex in the northwestern outskirts of Tirana. Built in the 1970s but never used, this vast network of underground tunnels was intended to shelter the entire government apparatus in the event of invasion or nuclear attack (as with similar bunkers built in the UK and elsewhere, one can only wonder whom they expected to be governing after a nuclear attack). There were offices and dormitories for government officials, apartments for the party leaders, communications rooms, an assembly hall and a canteen: 106 rooms in total. A state-of-the-art air purification system was installed and a telephone network linked the party leaders with their officials. You can explore the apartment set aside for Enver Hoxha (page 83): an office, with an anteroom for his secretary (and a wonderful communist-era map of Albania), a sparsely furnished bedroom and an equally sparse en-suite bathroom. The only touch of luxury was the carpeting throughout and the lino cladding over the reinforced concrete walls. The whole complex was top-secret at the time; even the commanders of the military base above ground, which is still operational, were not allowed access to it.

As you go through the tunnels, each room has a display of photographs and other archive material, illustrating the phases of World War II and the subsequent chilling of relations with one set of former allies after another. Some rooms are used for modern art installations inspired by this aspect of Albania's history. You can download an app at the site to access additional information about the exhibits as you go round (free Wi-Fi is provided).

The main public entrance leads through a tunnel, with spooky piped sound effects, to the ticket kiosk. A fair bit of walking is involved, including several flights of steps. It would take over 2 hours to look attentively at the whole exhibition.

Bunk'Art 1 is in the northwestern outskirts of Tirana. From the city centre, the 'Linzë' buses leave from near the clock tower and stop near the main entrance to Bunk'Art 1.

Bunk'Art 2 [68 E3] (*Rr Sermedin Toptani;* m *067 20 72 905;* e *info@bunkart.al;* w *bunkart.al;* ⊕ *09.00–16.00 Wed–Mon; 500 lek*) In the 1980s, the communist authorities constructed a bomb-proof tunnel under the Ministry of the Interior, home to the police force in its various incarnations throughout Albania's 100-year history. Archive photographs and film illustrate the development of policing in the country, from the Dutch-trained gendarmerie (see box, page 97) of the first years after independence, through the Italian occupation (the ministry itself was built by Italian architects in the 1930s), to the terrifying period from 1944 to 1991.

Between 1949 and 1990, nearly a thousand Albanian citizens were killed by the Border Forces; the so-called State Security (Sigurimi i Shtetit) spied on, tortured and imprisoned Albanians on the flimsiest of pretexts.

You can visit the interrogation rooms and the holding cells in the tunnel, as well as the decontamination room that would have been used in the event of a nuclear or chemical attack. There are 24 rooms, including a far-from-luxurious apartment for the Minister of the Interior and a telecommunications centre. The exhibition of photographs and artefacts is very extensive and it would take at least 2 hours to absorb all the information presented. As in Bunk'Art 1, there are also contemporary art installations. Additional information can be accessed in each room by means of Bunk'Art's free phone app, downloadable at the site.

As you leave the tunnel, there is a chance to see the original structure that would have protected it from attack: nearly 2.5m of reinforced concrete. The actual exit and entrance were installed when the exhibition site centre was opened. The decision to erect a replica bunker in the centre of Tirana generated considerable controversy at the time.

The House of Leaves [68 D3] (*Shtëpia e Gjethëve; Rr Ibrahim Rugova;* \ *222 2612, 225 0055;* ◷ *09.00–19.30 daily; 700 lek*) The most recently opened of Tirana's communist-era buildings is the former surveillance centre of the Sigurimi, Albania's secret police. It was built in 1931 as a maternity clinic, founded by Zog I's personal physician, and taken over secretly by the Sigurimi for use mainly by the technicians who tapped people's telephones and installed bugs in their apartments. Also based there was the department responsible for spying on foreign visitors and residents, intercepting communications in hotels and embassies in Tirana and maintaining detailed notes about every foreigner in the country.

The House of Leaves museum displays original items used by the Sigurimi to spy on 'the enemy within' (ie: virtually everyone in Albania) and 'the external enemy' (everybody else). The collection includes original recording devices, photographic equipment and bugs, along with illustrations of how the bugs were concealed. Archive film screened in various rooms document statements given by individuals under interrogation, show trainers explaining how to use the equipment and give a voice to some of the survivors. In a video room, you can watch and listen through headphones to a huge number of further films, documentaries, feature films and interviews. Photographs, reproduced documents, plans and diagrams complement the films and artefacts. A replica living room with made-in-Albania household items from the communist period provides a moment of light relief.

Like the Bunk'Art exhibitions, the House of Leaves presents a vast amount of information, and about 2 hours should be allowed to look around it.

Historic buildings In Skanderbeg Square, the **Tirana International Hotel** [69 E2] and the huge building that houses the opera [69 E3] were both designed by Soviet architects in the 1960s. Only the exterior of these buildings reminds one of those times. The hotel has been completely overhauled; the opera house is being renovated at the time of writing and is likely to lose its faded communist grandeur in the process.

Communist slogans can still occasionally be spotted on the walls of the older-style, four-storey apartment buildings. They were created by setting differently coloured bricks into the structure, which makes them rather difficult to remove, although the passage of time is wearing them out gradually. An easy-to-find example is the party's initials, PPSH, on a building about 90m on the left down Rruga Fortuzi, which goes off Zogu I alongside the Ministry of Justice [68 D1].

Back on the Boulevard, the **Dajti Hotel** [69 E4] played a pivotal role in its first half-century – during the communist period, at least until what is now the Tirana International opened, almost all foreign visitors stayed here. Ordinary Albanians were not allowed through the doors until the advent of democracy. Countless treaties were negotiated and plots hatched in the Dajti Hotel. The doors of this historic hotel closed in December 2005 and the building has become increasingly derelict. Peter and Andrea Dawson described the Dajti in Bradt's first guide to Albania, in 1989; it was still almost the same ten years later, although obviously the statues of Lenin and Stalin had gone by then.

> We decide that the other large hotel in Tiranë, the Dajti, is worth investigation. We walk down the Avenue of the Martyrs of the Nation, past the bronze Lenin statue and the National Art Gallery, and, behind the trees opposite the statue of Stalin, are the party cars: Mercedes and black Volvos. The red 'Dajti' lettering fronts a heavy stone and glass canopy, shielding the steps to the entrance.
>
> Inside, a vast reception area and hall contains a bookshop, a souvenir shop and, in a lounge, a television is showing Albanian programmes, watched by some of the foreign businessmen, who, along with trade and political delegations, form the bulk of the Dajti's clientele.
>
> A corridor to the right leads to the bar, and we have cappuccinos and bottled Albanian beer, sitting in comfortable armchairs at a low walnut table.
>
> Peter and Andrea Dawson, *Albania: A Guide and Illustrated Journal*

The Pyramid, just across the little Lana River from the Dajti, is a remarkable piece of architecture, with its sloping walls at the front leading round to vertical faces at the back. It was commissioned as a memorial museum to Enver Hoxha (see box, page 83); after the end of one-party rule and until the end of the first decade of the 21st century, it was used for conferences and trade fairs, with offices at the rear let to various companies, including a privately owned national TV station. It was designed by Hoxha's daughter, Pranvera, and her husband; they were also the architects of the Congress Building (Pallati i Kongresëve), just beyond the Rogner Hotel further down the Boulevard, and of the Skanderbeg Museum in Kruja (page 100). An ill-advised proposal to demolish the Pyramid appears to have been abandoned and it is to be hoped that the white marble tiles that used to clad its walls will now be restored.

The large bell hanging above the walkway outside the Pyramid is the Bell of Peace, an initiative of schoolchildren from northern Albania who collected spent bullet casings from the 1997 uprising (pages 17–18), and used them to cast this testimonial to the country's near-collapse.

Just across the street that runs behind the Pyramid is a Communist-nostalgia bar called **Kafe Komiteti** [69 F5] (*Rr Fatmir Haxhiu*), furnished and decorated with original items from Albanian households of the 1970s and 80s. It also has an excellent selection of different kinds of raki (page 49).

On the Boulevard next to the Pyramid is the prime minister's office building, known as the **Council of Ministers** [69 E5], which used to house the government in communist days as well – a Socialist Realist bas-relief has been preserved on the wall facing the Boulevard. Across the road is the **Checkpoint** [69 E6] memorial, an installation commemorating Albania's isolation under communism. A piece of the Berlin Wall, a real bunker and – most chilling of all – part of the concrete mineshaft supports from the prison camp at Spaçi (pages 160–1) have been set in a little garden. The memorial has been installed opposite the building where the party's Central Committee met and where its senior members, including Hoxha, had their offices; this now houses various state institutions, such as the Parliament and the Constitutional Court. It is said that there is a tunnel from this building to **Enver Hoxha's house** [68 D6], 270m down Rruga Ismail Qemali. This street and those around it – almost a square mile – were closed to ordinary Albanians until the fall of the Communist regime. The area was called 'The Block' (Blloku) and it was reserved for the families of the party elite, who were later referred to disparagingly as 'Bllok-men'. The bunker in the Checkpoint memorial came from one of the entrances to the Block. Hoxha's house is between Ismail Qemali and Vaso Pasha; the white section surrounded by lawns was his private office (it is still a government building, hence the guards), and he and his family lived in the half of the building closer to Rruga Vaso Pasha. Part of that section has now been taken over by an English-language school, while the other part is occupied by one of the Block's trendy bars – both of which must have the xenophobic Hoxha turning in his grave (read on to find where that is).

Statues and cemeteries Tirana has several good examples of Socialist Realist statues, apart from those in and behind the National Gallery of Arts (page 76). The **monument to the Unknown Partisan** [69 F3] stands in a little square beside the junction of Xhorxh W Bush and Luigj Gurakuqi. The partisan rises above the people and the traffic, waving his comrades on into battle with one hand and gripping his rifle in the other. In the Big Park (pages 78–9), there is a charming statue of a partisan girl offering water to a soldier. Most imposing of all is **Mother Albania**, who overlooks the city at the **Martyrs' Cemetery** (Varreza e Dëshmorëve) [63 H7]. The cemetery is a long walk from the city centre up Rruga e Elbasanit; alternatively, a taxi will take between 15 and 45 minutes, depending on the traffic on Rruga e Elbasanit. The Qendër–Sauk buses can be boarded near the clock tower and pass the entrance gates to the cemetery, on the left-hand side of the road. The cemetery is open on weekdays until early afternoon. A flight of steps on the left of the path leads up to the *parvis* where Mother Albania stands, clutching a laurel wreath with a star and looking out over Tirana spread below her.

In April 1985 Enver Hoxha, former teacher of French, tobacconist and partisan leader, secretary of the Party of Labour, was buried here, and his polished red granite tombstone is on the stepped platform next to Mother Albania. A small red and black double-eagle flag flies at the head of the tombstone, and it is guarded by two soldiers at attention, with high black polished boots and automatic rifles: the smartest soldiers in Albania, according to Andrea.

Nearby are the graves of the party officials, and down the gentle slopes are the graves, many with star and laurel denoting a People's Hero, of 900 men and women killed during the War of National Liberation.

From here you can look down on Tiranë, with the minaret, clock-tower and Hotel Tirana clearly visible. On the left, almost hidden by poplars, is the former palace of King Zog, which was an important seizure for the partisan brigades liberating the capital.

Peter and Andrea Dawson, *Albania: A Guide and Illustrated Journal*

The inscription below Mother Albania reads 'Eternal Glory to the Martyrs of the Fatherland', a reminder that this cemetery is much more than a relic of communism – it commemorates many of those who died in World War II, struggling against Fascist Italy and then Nazi Germany. Resistance fighters who were opposed to the nascent Communist Party were not buried here. The rows of graves run down the hillside beyond the statue, beginning with the best-known partisan fighters, including women such as Margarita Tutulani, who was shot by the Italians in 1943

ENVER HOXHA

Enver Hoxha was born in Gjirokastra in 1908; his reconstructed family home is now that city's Ethnographic Museum (page 248). Hoxha studied in Gjirokastra and Korça and was then given an Albanian state scholarship to attend the University of Montpellier. During his time in France, he met Ali Kelmendi, the most senior of the small number of Albanian communists at the time. When Hoxha returned to Albania in 1936, he got a job teaching at his old school, the French *lycée* in Korça, and became involved in the fledgling Communist Party there.

The party remained very small and fragmented until, in 1941, the Yugoslav communists sent two delegates to help reorganise it and recruit new members. The Albanian Communist Party was officially founded in November 1941, and the following year Enver Hoxha was appointed party secretary. He became Prime Minister of the Provisional Government of Albania in October 1944, and went on to consolidate his power within the party over the next few years. He continued as prime minister until 1954, when he handed over the position to his wartime comrade Mehmet Shehu (pages 16–17); but Hoxha continued to exercise considerable authority over the government, the party and the country until his death in April 1985.

aged only 19. Hundreds of others follow in approximate alphabetical order of their first names, as was standard practice in Albania. Beside Mother Albania is the tomb of the young partisan Qemal Stafa, a founding member of the Albanian Communist Youth; next to that is a rectangular patch where Enver Hoxha's body lay until April 1992, when it was exhumed and reburied in the public cemetery (Sharra Cemetery), on the other side of the city.

To get to Sharra from the Martyrs' Cemetery, transport is required. The nearest taxi rank is just over 1km back down the hill, opposite the Faculty of Economics. Alternatively you could walk, or catch any passing bus, to Skanderbeg Square. On the way back downhill, the gated estate on the left is the 'former palace of King Zog' to which the authors of the first Bradt Guide to Albania refer. As they say, its capture was a key point in the Battle for the Liberation of Tirana in 1944; it was renamed the Palace of the Brigades and became a governmental residence.

Sharra Cemetery (Varreza e Sharrës) is just off Rruga e Kavajës; there are frequent buses to Kombinat, a 10-minute walk away. The turn-off uphill to the cemetery can easily be recognised by the flower stalls just before it. The graves are grouped chronologically, but you need to bear in mind that Hoxha's coffin was exhumed and reburied in 1992, and so that is his chronological position, rather than 1985 when he died. Once you are in roughly the right section, the large brown marble headstone is easy to spot; there are often fresh flowers on the grave. Mehmet Shehu, Albania's prime minister until his fall from grace in 1981, has also been reinterred in the main cemetery. The whereabouts of his remains were unknown until 2001, when one of his sons tracked down his unmarked grave in a village near Tirana.

PËLLUMBASI CAVE (w *pellumbascave.weebly.com;* ⬛ *The Cave of Pellumbas; 100 lek*) The hike up to Pëllumbasi Cave (Shpella e Pëllumbasit) makes for a very pleasant day out if the weather is good. Also known as the Black Cave, it was home to humans at various points between the Stone Age and the early Middle Ages, and to cave bears (*Ursus spelaeus*) a long time before that. (Cave bears became extinct about 27,500 years ago.) The cave is 360m long and has chambers filled with wonderful stalagmites and stalactites. There are also, as one would expect, many bats (see box, page 5).

The path up to the cave starts at the village of Pëllumbasi, 25km from Tirana off the Elbasani road. The caretaker and guide lives near the start of the path and will accompany you if you wish; the loan of a head-torch is included in the price of admission. The path climbs steeply through fields and then emerges at the side of the beautiful Skorana Gorge, with the Erzeni River flowing far below you. There are wooden signs, steps at the steepest parts and handrails at the most slippery parts. It takes about an hour to walk up to the cave entrance.

The turn-off for Pëllumbasi is just before the village of Iba; it is signposted at the junction for 'Ujvara Resort' and, less obviously, 'Pëllumbasi 2km'. A shop at the junction sells drinks and torches; there are a couple of cafés in the village. There are two buses to Pëllumbasi from Tirana in the early morning, returning at 18.00; otherwise, you can take a minibus to Iba and walk from there. Full directions, a map of the hiking route and a diagram of the cave can be downloaded from the Pëllumbasi Cave website. All these developments – the map, the website, the signs, the handrails and everything else besides – are thanks to the efforts of the Outdoor Albania Association, which first reopened the path and began to take hiking groups on this lovely excursion. For further details of how to contact the Outdoor Albania Association, see page 54, or the OAA website (w *outdooralbania-association.com*).

CASTLES South of Tirana, the old road to Elbasani (pages 112–14) starts to climb gradually. As it crosses the Erzeni River, which rises in the mountains to the east of the city, **Petrela Castle** (and the completely incongruous restaurant built on one of its towers) can be seen perched high up on a rock on the other side of the river. Petrela was a strategic link in the defensive system used by Skanderbeg (see box, pages 206–7), and is said to have been where his sister Mamica lived. The restaurant within it opens at 11.00, after which time it is possible to enter the castle precincts and look around the surviving walls and towers. A good, asphalted road just after the bridge runs up to the village of Petrela, to the right, off the main road. Cars can be parked in the village square, from where it is a 5-minute walk up to the castle.

In the other direction, towards the airport, **Preza Castle** occupies a splendid position overlooking the plains westward to the Adriatic and eastward to Mount Dajti. It was probably built in the mid 15th century, as an element in the Ottomans' efforts to capture Kruja (pages 98–102), then reconstructed in the 16th century. It is so close to the airport and has such good views that it makes a nice farewell stop, if you have a little time to spare before checking in.

MOUNT DAJTI The Mount Dajti National Park, 25km to the east of Tirana, is one of the most accessible mountain reserves in the country. It covers 3,000ha centred on Mount Dajti, which overlooks Tirana and can be seen, smog permitting, from Skanderbeg Square. At 1,613m, Mount Dajti is not very high by Albanian standards (although it is 269m higher than Ben Nevis, Britain's highest mountain); this means that there is forest almost all the way to the summit, which makes for very pleasant, shady walking, especially in the heat of summer.

The woodland is mostly beech, with some pines and firs. In the summer, alpine strawberries grow among the trees, and foxes, hares, red squirrels, weasels and beech martens live in the forest.

The Backpacker and Milingona hostels in Tirana (page 66) offer an exciting excursion to Mount Dajti: participants go up in the cable-car while bikes are brought up in a van to meet them. The group spends the day cycling around the network of paths on the mountain and having a picnic lunch, before cycling (or freewheeling) back down to the city. It is perfectly possible to hike around the park independently; a map of the path network is posted at the exit from the upper cable-car station. You should wear sensible footwear and be sure to take sufficient water with you.

Getting there and away By far the best way to get up to Mount Dajti, unless you are very uncomfortable with heights, is on the **cable-car** (*teleferiku; w dajtiekspres. com;* ⊕ *summer 09.00–21.00 Wed–Mon, winter 09.00–19.00 Wed–Mon; 500 lek sgl, 800 lek return; bicycles transported free*). It takes about 15 minutes to travel the 1,000m between the two cable-car stations. The lower station is on the outskirts of Tirana, at the end of Rruga e Dibrës; it is tricky to find if you are driving (or cycling) yourself. Follow the (sporadic) signs through the brand-new apartment buildings, even when you are sure you are lost.

By public transport, the 'Porcelan' **buses** go from the clock tower in the city centre up Rruga Hoxha Tahsim to their terminus, *Teleferiku*, a few minutes' walk from the cable-car station. 'Kinostudio' buses terminate at the stop called I.K.V., from where Dajti Ekspres shuttle buses leave for the lower cable-car station every half hour or so. The upper station is within the national park, but well before the summit.

It is also possible to drive up the mountain, although the road is in rather poor condition now that it is rarely used. It takes about an hour from the western outskirts, through urban sprawl and then into beautiful forests with occasional views out over Tirana. There is a car park at the upper cable-car station.

✖ Where to eat and drink

✖ **Ballkon i Dajtit** m 068 40 11 021; w dajtiekspres.com. Part of the complex around the upper station of the cable-car (see page 65 for details of the hotel in this complex). Standard Albanian restaurant fare – pasta, salads, pizza, grilled meat – with amazing views over Tirana &, on a clear day, out to the Adriatic. $$$

✖ **Gurra e Përrisë** m 068 20 60 720. A trout farm, with the fish in pools in the restaurant's grounds. As well as fish, spit-roasted lamb is a speciality. In summer, tables outside around the trout pools; in winter, traditional-style dining room with log fire. Lovely views of the forested hillsides. $$$

✖ **Panorama** ☎236 3124; m 069 20 23 936, 068 20 23 936. The speciality is spit-roasted lamb, served with chips, salad & red wine; the restaurant is also well known for its game dishes, such as hare & pheasant. It is famous, too, for the spectacular views of Tirana from the dining room & terrace. The Panorama also has rooms & chalets (page 66). $$$

WORLD BEKTASHI CENTRE (*Kryegjyshata; Rr Dhimitër Kamarda;* ☎ *235 5090;* ⊕ *10.00–13.00*) As explained on page 22, the Sufi order known as Bektashism has had its world headquarters in Albania since 1929, when King Zog gave them land for a *teqe* and associated buildings. When Albania was declared an atheist state in 1967 (page 16), the buildings were confiscated and used as an old people's home. Most of the property was returned to the Bektashis in 1991, the old people were relocated to another care home, and the *teqe* was reopened in the presence of Mother Teresa.

In 2015, the crowning glory of the World Bektashi Centre was inaugurated: a great prayer-hall known as the Odeon. Around the entrance stand 16 black pillars, representing the 16 babies killed at the Battle of Karbala, a central event in Shi'a tradition. Visitors may enter the Odeon and admire the exquisite architecture and decoration – the columns of Indian marble (one for each of the 12 martyrs of Islam), the magnificent wall-paintings and, an architectural curiosity, pillars on either side of the *qibla* that spin on their axis. This has nothing to do with Bektashi beliefs but is an ingenious seismic warning system; in the event of an earthquake, the pillars will freeze in place, thus alerting the building's caretakers that there is a problem with the building.

In the basement of the Odeon is an interesting museum with artefacts and panels illustrating the history of Bektashism. At the time of writing, the information is only in Albanian; the Centre hopes that translations into English will be added in time.

The World Bektashi Centre is in the eastern suburbs of Tirana, south of Rruga Ali Demi. It is not at all easy to find and taking a taxi will be the simplest way to get there.

4

Excursions from Tirana

The headland at the north of Durrësi Bay forms a natural harbour in which ships have anchored since the 7th century BC. In antiquity it was known as Epidamnos, and the city that was built around it was called Dyrrhachion. In the 5th century BC, a popular uprising in Dyrrhachion became one of the causes of the Peloponnesian War that engulfed the whole of Greece from 431BC to 404BC.

Under Roman rule, Dyrrachium (as it was by then known) became a vital staging post, one of the two starting points of the Egnatian Way (Via Egnatia), the great road that linked the Adriatic coast with Byzantium. The city thrived during the Roman and Byzantine periods, and the amphitheatre that the Romans built there was the largest in the Balkan peninsula. In the Middle Ages Dyrrachium was coveted by Normans, Angevins and Venetians, and for a few years after independence Durrësi was the capital of Albania. This rich past is reflected in the town's Archaeological Museum, with its collection of Illyrian, Greek and Roman artefacts.

Most Albanians visit Durrësi not for its history but for its beaches, with their golden sand and safe swimming. In the summer, these beaches become very crowded; out of season, in late spring and early autumn, the sea is still warm enough to swim in and the evenings are pleasantly cool. In the city, a lively promenade runs along the seafront, parallel with Taulantia Boulevard, and ends in a small area of beach.

HISTORY   Durrësi has probably been inhabited for about 3,000 years, but it enters history in 627BC, when it was colonised by settlers from the Greek island of Corfu (Corcyra), who may have been attracted by the silver mines further inland in Illyria. The new colony prospered for many years, until internal political unrest led to a war between Corcyra and Corinth. The Athenian historian Thucydides describes the aftermath of this war as one of the causes of the great war fought, between 431BC and 404BC, between Athens and its allies on the one hand, and the Peloponnesians, including Sparta, on the other.

Dyrrhachion flourished during the 4th–2nd centuries BC. The city continued to benefit from Greek cultural influence, and temples were built to Greek deities such as Aphrodite and Artemis. The late 4th-century mosaic known as the 'Belle of Durrësi' is the best example of the Hellenistic art of this period. Politically and economically, too, Dyrrhachion was thriving. The Illyrian kings Glaukias (late 4th century BC) and Monun (around 280–270BC) ruled over a city whose population was growing and which had minted its own coins since the middle of the 4th century BC – some of these can be seen in Durrësi's Archaeological Museum.

After the Roman conquest of 229BC (page 8) the city, its name by now Latinised to Dyrrachium and with a population of around 40,000, became a major transit

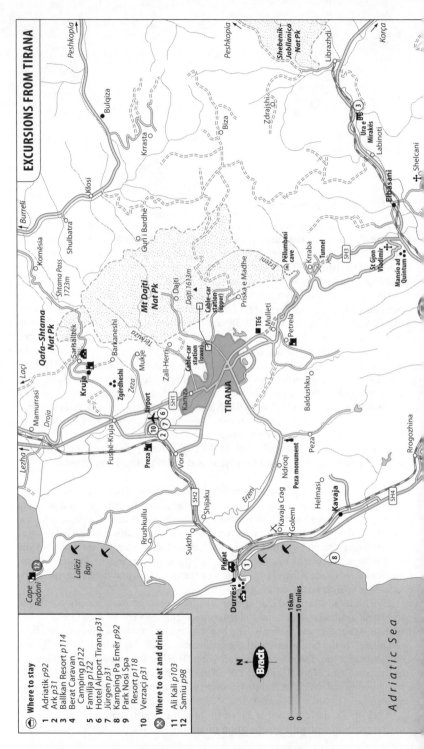

EXCURSIONS FROM TIRANA

Adriatic Sea

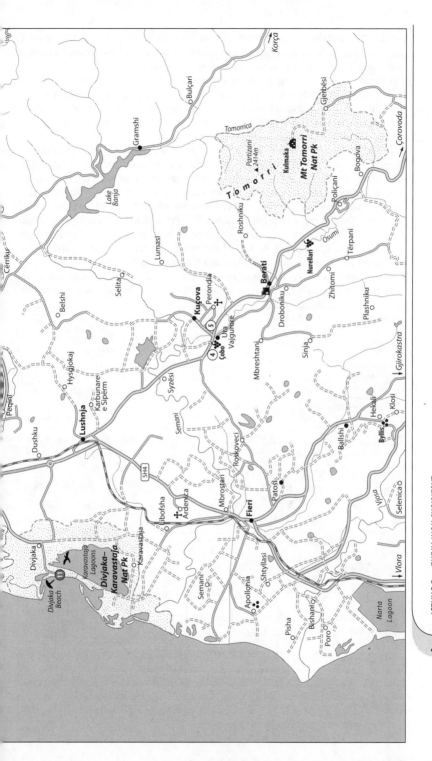

point between Italy and points further east. The Via Egnatia was built by Roman engineers along the route of an already ancient road that had been used by Illyrian and other traders for centuries; its two starting points were Dyrrachium and Apollonia (pages 105–7), and it carried goods and people all the way to Byzantium, later called Constantinople. Excavations in 2016 revealed stonework that, it is thought, may be the starting point of the Via Egnatia. The Roman poet Catullus (84–54BC), mentions the city in one of his poems (C36.15), calling it – as one might expect of a port – 'the road-house of the Adriatic'.

In the second phase of the Roman Civil War, between Julius Caesar and Pompey, Dyrrachium was the Pompeian forces' main arsenal and therefore a key target for Caesar after he landed in Albania in 48BC. Caesar managed to cut Pompey off from his arsenal, but in response Pompey entrenched his army in what must have seemed an impregnable position – the crag to the south of the city which is now called Shkëmbi i Kavajës and which the Romans called Petra. With typical audacity, Caesar decided to blockade Petra and, although his forces were much smaller than Pompey's, not to mention less well fed, he almost succeeded in starving the Pompeian troops into surrender. Pompey then broke through Caesar's lines and, in the ensuing battle, inflicted heavy losses on the opposing side. Caesar managed to free his army and retreated east, where the third and final phase of the civil war would unfold in Thessaly.

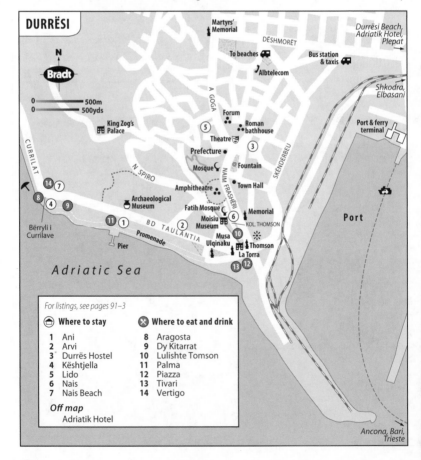

DURRËSI

N

0 — 500m
0 — 500yds

Martyrs' Memorial
DËSHMORËT
Durrësi Beach, Adriatik Hotel, Plepat
To beaches
Bus station & taxis
Albtelecom
Shkodra, Elbasani
King Zog's Palace
A GOGA
Forum
Roman bathhouse
5
Theatre
Port & ferry terminal
Prefecture
3
N SPIRO
Mosque
Fountain
CURRILAT
Amphitheatre
Town Hall
NAIM FRASHËR
SKËNDERBEU
14 7
Archaeological Museum
8
4 9
Fatih Mosque
Memorial
Bërryli i Currilave
11 1
Moisiu Museum
6
KOL. THOMSON
Port
BD TAULANTIA
2
Musa Ulqinaku
10
Promenade
Thomson
Pier
La Torra
13 12

Adriatic Sea

For listings, see pages 91–3

⊜ **Where to stay**

1	Ani	8	Aragosta
2	Arvi	9	Dy Kitarrat
3	Durrës Hostel	10	Lulishte Tomson
4	Kështjella	11	Palma
5	Lido	12	Piazza
6	Nais	13	Tivari
7	Nais Beach	14	Vertigo

✗ **Where to eat and drink**

Off map
Adriatik Hotel

Ancona, Bari, Trieste

GETTING THERE AND AWAY

By land Buses to Durrësi leave Tirana from the Shqiponja bus station, near the Shqiponja ('Eagle') roundabout at the western entrance to the city. There are frequent departures throughout the day until at least 18.00, and the journey takes about 45 minutes.

There are buses to Durrësi from all other cities in Albania. Buses for Tirana are always more frequent and, from the south of the country, any bus going to Tirana will let you alight at the Plepat bus station, a few kilometres south of Durrësi; there are always taxis waiting there to ferry passengers along to the city centre.

Durrësi was the country's main **rail** terminus, although nowadays there are only a couple of trains a day, to Elbasani and Shkodra. Departure times are shown on the timetable outside the station. Sadly, there is no longer a railway service to Tirana. Trains are agonisingly slow and, unless you are a rail devotee, the only journey that makes any kind of sense is the short run down the coast to Golemi. Durrësi station has a certain scruffy charm and the trains themselves are worth a look, even when they are stationary.

By sea Durrësi is served by ferries from three different ports in Italy, the most frequent – and cheapest – being the daily car ferry crossings from Bari, a 9-hour journey. All year round, the ferries travel overnight, leaving Bari at 23.00 and arriving in Durrësi at around 08.00 the following morning. In the summer there are, additionally, daytime sailings. Several operators run ferries on this route; up-to-date schedules can be found on the Italian ferry website w traghetti.it.

In addition to the crossings from Bari, car ferries operate to Durrësi from the Italian ports of Ancona and Trieste. These routes are operated by **Adria Ferries** (+39 (0)71 5021 1621; w www.adriaferries.com), three days a week in each direction. From Ancona, the journey takes 20 hours; from Trieste, slightly longer. The ferries run all year round, with more frequent departures in summer.

The Port of Durrësi has been completely redeveloped, with a new passenger terminal.

By air Durrësi is less than an hour's drive from Albania's only international airport. An airport bus departs from Durrësi from 07.00 to 16.30; in the other direction, the first departure from the airport is at 09.45 and the last at 19.00. The one-way fare is 480 lek. Further information about the airport bus schedule and details of the airlines that fly to Albania can be found on the airport's website (w tirana-airport. com). For further information about the airport, including accommodation there and details of the airlines that fly to Albania, see pages 30–1.

GETTING AROUND The main sights in the city are all fairly central and walking between them is not at all arduous, except in very hot or very wet weather. There is a taxi rank at the bus station in Durrësi, where a driver can be hired for a single journey or for a day's or a half-day's sightseeing.

Red city buses run frequently to the beaches south of Durrësi from the little square on Rruga Dëshmorët, from early morning until about 21.00 in the summer.

WHERE TO STAY *Map, opposite, unless otherwise stated*
There is no shortage of hotels in Durrësi, ranging from the expensive and luxurious to the cheap and cheerful. Several of them can be booked through the Tirana-based agency Albania Holidays (w albania-hotel.com) and through international websites such as w booking.com.

The coast to the south of the town has become heavily built up as far as Kavaja, with dozens of hotels lining the beaches and climbing inexorably higher up the hillside on the other side of the road. In high summer (July and August) the beaches are crowded and dirty, and there are often problems with the water supply in cheaper hotels during this time. Currilat Beach, to the north of the city centre at the curve in the road known as Bërryli i Currilave ('the Currilat Elbow'), is quieter and has better hotels.

Adriatik [map, pages 88–9] (63 rooms, 6 suites) Rr Pavarësia, Plazh; ☎260 850/1; e info@adriatikhotel.com; w adriatikhotel.com. 2 restaurants, bars, large swimming pool in palm-fringed garden, reserved section of sandy beach with sun-loungers & parasols, casino, tennis court, sauna, gym, children's pool & playgrounds. Wi-Fi throughout; free parking, business facilities, souvenir shop. Airport pickups & tours can be arranged for guests. All rooms have en-suite bathroom with tub or jacuzzi; AC, satellite TV, direct-dial phone, minibar, safe; 'standard' rooms have view of gardens, others have sea view, 'executive' rooms have balcony. $$$$$–$$$$

Arvi (35 rooms, 7 suites) Bd Taulantia; ☎230 403; m 068 60 47 177; e arvishpk@msn.com. Modern & well appointed, excellent location on the seafront but close to city centre; English spoken. Restaurant, bars, business facilities, secure parking. Twin & dbl rooms all en suite, AC, satellite TV, Wi-Fi, direct-dial phone & minibar, some with sea view, some also with balcony. $$$$

Ani (14 rooms) Bd Taulantia; ☎224 228; m 069 86 58 612; e anihoteldurres@yahoo.it. Good location on the seafront; English spoken; bar, secure parking. Twin & dbl rooms, some with sea view, all en suite with AC, satellite TV, Wi-Fi & fridge. $$$

Kështjella (13 rooms) Bd Taulantia, Bërryli i Currilave; ☎221 817; m 068 90 38 684; e keshtjella01@hotmail.com; ◻ Hotel Keshtjella Durres. Large beachside restaurant, terrace bar, friendly service. Room rate inc secure parking & use of sun-loungers & parasols on the hotel's section of the beach. Pedalos & boats for hire. All rooms have 1 dbl & 2 sgl beds, en-suite toilet & shower, Wi-Fi, TV, AC, phone, hairdryer, balcony with sea view. $$$

Lido (13 rooms, 1 suite) Rr A Goga; ☎227 941; m 068 20 43 719. Opposite Byzantine forum,

set back from main road. Friendly, helpful staff; English spoken; bar & restaurant. Spacious rooms, twin & dbl, all en suite with Wi-Fi, AC, TV, direct-dial phone, fridge. $$$

Nais (16 rooms) Rr Naim Frashëri 46; ☎230 375, 224 940; e hotelnais@hotmail.com; w hotelnaisdurres.com; ◻ hotelnaisdurres. Lift; friendly, helpful staff, English spoken; bar & conference room. All rooms en suite with Wi-Fi, flatscreen TV, fridge, phone, AC, some have balconies. $$$

Nais Beach (24 rooms) Bd Taulantia, Bërryli i Currilave; ☎223 130; e info@hotelnais.al; w hotel-nais-beach.durres.hotels-al.com. Lift; free parking; English spoken; b/fast room; arrangement with Vertigo restaurant (see opposite). All rooms en suite with Wi-Fi, flatscreen TV, fridge, AC, radio, balcony; upper floors have sea view. $$$

Durrës Hostel (8 rooms) Sheshi Liria; m 069 89 16 810; ◻ durreshostel. Superb location, just off Durrësi's main square, but quiet, in a modernised old townhouse with beautiful tree-shaded gardens. Bar open to public; garden areas reserved for hostel guests; balconies at front & rear of building; roof terrace; fully equipped kitchen; indoor sitting area; laundry; lockers. English spoken; Wi-Fi throughout; bikes available to hire; day trips organised. All rooms high-ceilinged & airy; 2 en-suite dbls $$, 6 dorms sharing ample shower & toilet facilities $

Kamping Pa Emër [map, pages 88–9] Synej-Karpen, near Kavaja; m 066 41 51 502, 066 41 52 854; e reservation@kampingpaemer.com; w kampingpaemer.com. About 10km from the highway, set in lovely grounds 30m from the beach; open year-round; has been poorly maintained & managed in past. Bar & restaurant overlooking the sea; boats for hire; some French spoken. Chalets ($$$$) & rooms ($$$) also available. Beachside pitches for 50 mobile homes & 50 tents. $

✖ WHERE TO EAT AND DRINK *Map, page 90*
The promenade behind Boulevard Taulantia is lined with a string of restaurants, most of them offering the standard Italian dishes such as pasta, risotto and pizza, all of which

Albanian chefs often do very well, plus fish, which is usually fresh and good. All of the promenade restaurants have outside tables available during the summer months.

✗ **Aragosta** Bd Taulantia (Bërryli i Currilave); 226 477, 232 669; w aragosta.al. Lovely setting overlooking the sea on the outskirts of town; hotel rooms also available (**$$$$**). Good fresh fish & seafood, excellent antipasto buffet. Service is disappointing for such an upmarket establishment. **$$$$$**

✗ **Piazza** Bd Taulantia, opposite the Musa Ulqinaku statue. Good-quality seafood & fish; professional service. **$$$$$–$$$**

✗ **Vertigo** Bd Taulantia (Bërryli i Currilave) on top floor of Nais Beach Hotel (under different management). Spectacular sea views, Italian-influenced menu, good service, live music at w/ ends. **$$$$**

✗ **Dy Kitarrat** Bd Taulantia; 235 802. The usual Italian menu, with the added attraction of live music every evening in the summer months. The owner joins other performers in Albanian traditional music as well as Neapolitan & Greek songs. Very popular in the summer; advisable to book. Hotel rooms also available (**$$$$**). **$$$**

✗ **Palma** Bd Taulantia. Reasonably priced fish & meat, pizzas, pasta, etc; tables outside in garden with sea view. **$$$**

✗ **Tivari** Bd Taulantia. Lovely location on the seafront where the promenade begins, tables outside on large terrace. The usual fish, grilled meat, pasta & pizza; also serves Italian-style sandwiches. **$$$**

✗ **Lulishte Tomson** Rr Naim Frashëri. Set in a shady garden (*lulishte*) behind Lodewijk Thomson's statue (page 97). An unpretentious menu of grilled meat & chicken, salads, etc. **$$**

WHAT TO SEE AND DO

The amphitheatre (⊕ 09.00–19.00 daily; 300 lek, inc admission to Archaeological Museum; English-speaking guides sometimes available) The huge Roman amphitheatre, which is one of Durrësi's main attractions, was built in the early 2nd century AD. The largest in the Balkans, it is elliptical in shape, about 130m at its longest point, with the arena itself measuring about 60m by 40m across. On the terraced seats there would have been room for about 15,000 spectators, about a third of the capacity of the Colosseum in Rome.

You can go down into the vaults below the rows of seats – the original steps, supplemented with less slippery modern ones, are just after the ticket booth – and see how the amphitheatre was constructed. The Romans alternated rows of brick with *opus incertum*, a mixture of stones and mortar, a technique designed to resist earthquakes. You can see this *opus incertum* in several places around the amphitheatre, including three full rows, well over 2m high, in one of the galleries. The technique was evidently quite successful, since most of the amphitheatre is still standing, despite Durrësi being hit by several strong earthquakes over the centuries. Behind the gallery, you can see the pens where the wild animals were kept; leading out from it is the tunnel through which the gladiators entered the arena. When the site was first excavated, 40 skeletons were discovered with their necks broken – could they have been unsuccessful gladiators?

When gladiatorial combat was banned in the 5th century, the amphitheatre took on a new life as a Christian funerary space. The arena became a cemetery and small chapels were created in the galleries. One of these has 10th- or 11th-century mosaics of saints and archangels on the walls. They are the only wall mosaics ever found in Albania, and those on the back wall are rather badly damaged. The mosaic on the side wall is thought to depict the sponsor of the whole chapel, a man identified only as Alexandros, and his wife. There is a baptismal well at the entrance.

Back out in the arena, the entrance halfway round the terracing is where Dyrrachium's aristocracy arrived in their carriages. The horses were led off to the left while their owners took their seats above the entranceway. The tunnel through

4

which they rode is said to extend right to where the town centre is now, nearly half a kilometre away. Further round to the left, through the beautifully built tunnel where the horses were led, is another chapel, with faint traces of badly damaged fresco still just about visible.

The amphitheatre was discovered only in 1966 and has not been fully excavated, because people still live in the houses which were unwittingly built on top of it. The Albanian Institute of Archaeology and various Italian universities continue to research the site. Excavations between 2004 and 2007 revealed the southern exit from the amphitheatre, which was destroyed by an earthquake in the 13th century. Several important medieval structures have also been discovered in this area, including shops that were still in use within living memory.

The Archaeological Museum (*Bd Taulantia;* ⊕ *winter 09.00–16.00 Tue–Sat, summer 09.00–14.00 & 16.00–19.00 Tue–Sat, 09.00–14.00 Sun; 300 lek, inc entry to amphitheatre*) Durrësi's Archaeological Museum, closed for several years for structural maintenance and object conservation, reopened in 2014. The exhibition has been reorganised, with helpful information panels in English and Albanian, and good new lighting installed. It covers the prehistoric, Hellenistic and Roman periods; the museum's Byzantine collection will eventually be displayed on the upper floor.

The fact that the city has been more or less continuously inhabited throughout its history means that most of it has never been systematically excavated. Many of the items in the museum were discovered by chance, as local people ploughed their land or as foundations were dug for the new high-rise apartment blocks.

The port that is now Durrësi was colonised by Greek settlers in the 8th century BC. These colonists and the local people interacted and intermarried; evidence of this can be seen in the display of cylindrical grave markers. Their inscriptions, in Greek, have names that mingle Greek and Illyrian. One is to a certain Quintus Dyrracinus Phileros, the middle name showing that people were beginning to identify themselves as being from this city.

Around the middle of the 4th century BC, Dyrrhachion began to mint and circulate its own coins. The silver *stater* bore the old Corcyran emblem of a cow suckling a calf, with the Greek initials DYRR. Lower-denomination bronze coins were also minted. Dyrrhachion's currency has been found as far away as the Danube territories of Dacia (modern Romania) and Thrace.

A highlight of the museum is a whole case of terracotta faces and other body parts. These were votive offerings and were excavated in the 1970s at a sanctuary site northwest of the city. An incredible 1,800kg of fragments were recovered, of which those on display are obviously a selection. Many of the figurines represent Aphrodite, the Greek goddess of love; Catullus, in his *Poem 36* (page 90), indicates that Dyrrachium was a centre of worship of Venus (the Roman name for Aphrodite). Other female deities are represented too, including Artemis, the goddess of the hearth. Some scholars believe that the sanctuary was dedicated to her rather than to Aphrodite.

The development of the Via Egnatia (page 8), one of whose branches began in Dyrrachium, consolidated the city's position as a major trading centre. A fascinating map shows the extent of this trade route and how it connected with other Roman roads. A collection of amphorae (two-handled urns), some of them encrusted with shells from centuries of immersion in the sea, illustrates the city's importance as a maritime trading centre – their lids are marked with the initials of the exporter. Milestones from the Via Egnatia are displayed nearby.

Other interesting exhibits are a large kiln for firing pottery, found intact near Currilat Beach, a limestone door frame with elegantly carved dolphins, and a case of locally produced glassware, mostly the long-necked jars in which, it was popularly supposed, the tears of a deceased's loved ones were collected so that they could be interred with the body (in unromantic fact, they probably just contained ointments and perfumes). Fragments of fresco came from the rescue excavation of a domestic bathhouse, discovered while the foundations were being dug for one of the new high-rise apartment blocks.

At the ticket-desk, there are attractive replicas for sale of some of the artefacts on display, as well as books in Albanian and English about the history of Durrësi and other archaeological sites.

The city walls Durrësi was first fortified in the Hellenistic period and then refortified shortly after the Roman conquest, in the 1st century BC. However, the oldest surviving walls are Byzantine, built during the reign of the emperor Anastasios (AD491–518) to replace earlier fortifications that a catastrophic earthquake in AD348 had destroyed. These walls protected the city for several centuries, until the Byzantine Empire began to collapse and Dyrrachium and its valuable port fell prey to one invader after another. The medieval city within the walls covered an area of around 120ha.

Dyrrachium – or Durazzo, as it was by then known – was part of the Venetian Republic for the whole of the 15th century. One of the towers that the Venetians built, at the southern corner of their walls, can even be seen from within – it has been converted into a bar, called **La Torra**, with tables in the alcoves where cannons would once have stood. Finally, in 1502, the Ottomans rebuilt the old fortifications and garrisoned their troops within them. An information panel at the city gate, which leads to the amphitheatre, shows an outline map of the fortifications as they changed over the centuries. There is a very good view of the line of the Venetian fortifications – and of the amphitheatre – from the rooftop bar in the high-rise building called the Fly Tower.

The forum and baths Turning in from La Torra, up Rruga Naim Frashëri, will bring you to Durrësi's main square, with the town hall and the theatre facing each other across it and the city's main mosque to your left. Behind the theatre is the circular forum, thought to date from the end of the 5th century AD. This may have been a *macellum*, or food market, rather than a traditional multi-purpose forum. A paved area, 40m in diameter, was surrounded by 40 marble Corinthian columns. In its centre was a stepped podium, which may have marked the start of the Via Egnatia. Shops were built around the perimeter of the colonnade. The whole complex had fallen out of use by the 7th century.

While the modern theatre on the main square was being built in 1960, a Roman bathhouse was discovered. It was excavated and preserved below the new building, which forms a protective canopy over it. A helpful illustrated panel at the entrance shows the layout of the *caldarium* and *tepidarium*, with a cheerful-looking slave stoking the fire. The first section of the baths is the *caldarium*, the hot room, with its black-and-white tiled floor. Further in are the remains of the hypocaust, the warm transitional area called the *tepidarium*, the black-and-white tiles of other sections of the baths, a drainage channel and part of the Roman street. In the Byzantine period, a complex drainage system was added and part of the bathhouse was used as a burial site. Excavation work continues. Access to the bathhouse is by a gate which is generally kept locked; the café next door may be able to locate the key-holder.

Ottoman buildings Durrësi was occupied by the Ottomans in August 1501, and a period of economic and cultural decline began. The harbour that had been such an important link across the Adriatic was of little interest to an empire centred far to the east. For the next 200 years, Durrësi became an insignificant little town of no more than 120 houses.

Almost immediately after the occupation, the Ottomans built a mosque on the site of a 10th- or 11th-century basilica, which they called the **Fatih Mosque**; Sultan Mehmed II, who was called the Conqueror (Fatih) after he took Constantinople in 1453, was dead by then, but his memory was not. The mosque is on a corner of a side street off Rruga Naim Frashëri, a restrained, whitewashed building with intricate wrought-iron windows. The minaret is a recent addition.

Just before the corner on which the mosque stands, a left turn will bring you to one of Durrësi's few remaining Ottoman houses, a delightful building with a traditional *çardak* or enclosed balcony. This was the home of Alexander Moisiu, an Albanian actor who was renowned across Europe in the early part of the 20th century. Moisiu was born in 1879, to an Italian mother and Albanian father in Trieste. He applied for Albanian citizenship five years after the country became independent, but was awarded it only in 1934. He died in Switzerland the following year, aged 55. Alexander Moisiu's house is now a **museum** (⊕ *09.00–13.00 Tue–Sat; 100 lek*), which contains an exhibition of photographs and documents relating to the actor's family and professional career, and (perhaps of greater interest to most non-Albanian visitors) a display of folk costumes and other ethnographic material. Those with a particular interest in Alexander Moisiu might like to visit his father's family home in nearby Kavaja, which has also been preserved as a museum.

King Zog's Palace It was not until the Balkan Wars and Albania's independence that the city re-emerged from obscurity; it was the new nation's capital in 1914, under Prince Wilhelm of Wied (see box, opposite), and then again from 1918 until the final decision to site the capital in Tirana. King Zog I (page 12) had a palace built here in 1927, a cream-and-pink villa up on the hill with marvellous views over the city and the bay. The building has now been returned to Zog's descendants and is not open to the public.

Monuments On 7 April 1939, Italian troops disembarked in Durrësi as part of their mission to occupy Albania. British-trained gendarmes, under the command of Abas Kupi (pages 13–15), resisted the invasion but were outnumbered and eventually defeated. Across from La Torra (page 95) stands a Socialist Realist monument to this attempt, which the anti-communist Kupi would probably have hated. Perhaps it is just as well, therefore, that it is not a statue of Kupi, but of one of his fellow resisters, **Musa Ulqinaku**. Nearby, a fierce **partisan** brandishes his rifle at the enemy across the sea. On the other side of La Torra, set in a little garden, is a bust – inaugurated in 2003 – of an earlier gendarmerie commander, Major Lodewijk Thomson, who died in action in Durrësi in June 1914 (see box, opposite).

The beaches If you are staying in the town centre and want a quick dip, the best option is the shore at Currilat, just to the north of the town. The Kështjella Hotel (page 92) and several of the restaurants along this stretch have reserved sections of sandy beach.

The beaches to the **south** of Durrësi have become very built up and cannot be recommended, particularly in the peak tourist season (July and August), when huge numbers of Albanians from landlocked Kosova and Macedonia fill the hotels and

MAJOR LODEWIJK THOMSON AND THE DUTCH PEACEKEEPERS

With thanks to Charlie Nuytens

Albania declared its independence on 28 November 1912, shortly after the outbreak of the First Balkan War (pages 11–12). However, the armed forces of the Balkan League continued to invade and attack their newly independent neighbour. In December, a Conference of Ambassadors was hastily convened in London; its remit was to consider the organisation of the new Albanian state and its international status. It was May 1913 before the London Conference concluded its deliberations and formally recognised Albania. It decided that Albania would be ruled not by the government established in November 1912 under Ismail Qemali, but by a foreign prince chosen by the Great Powers, and that its internal order would be maintained by a gendarmerie under Dutch officers.

The Dutch mission arrived in Albania in October 1913, commanded by Major Lodewijk Thomson, whose military career had included postings in Aceh, South Africa and Greece. (Tintin fans will be happy to learn that Edith Durham, who met him in June 1914, spells his surname 'Thompson'.) The Dutch officers' task was far from easy. Not only did they have to try to create a disciplined Albanian force, changing ingrained habits such as looting after a victory; they were also supposed to oversee the handing in of the weapons that practically every Albanian man held. The only real incentive at their disposal was that anyone who volunteered as a gendarme could keep his weapons.

Prince Wilhelm of Wied, Albania's appointed ruler, landed at Durrësi on 7 March 1914, and made the mistake of appointing Essad Pasha as his Minister of National Defence. Essad had been the military commander of Shkodra who surrendered the city to Montenegro in 1912; since then he had done his best to undermine the Qemali government, with encouragement and probably financial support from Serbia. Almost as soon as Wied arrived in Albania, fighting broke out between supporters of Qemali (by now in exile in Italy) and Essad.

By early June, the political and military situation was deteriorating. Insurgents were advancing on Durrësi; the Dutch-trained gendarmerie tried to contain them by firing on the crowd, killing several people. In the early hours of 15 June, Edith Durham awoke to the sound of rifle fire and rushed to find out what was happening. She soon learned that Thomson had been fatally wounded in the first hours of the battle; he died in a roadside guardhouse, in the arms of *The Times's* correspondent, Arthur Moore.

Thomson's remains were taken back to the Netherlands, where he was buried in the city of Groningen. A few weeks later World War I broke out and the Dutch mission was ordered back home. Prince Wilhelm of Wied left Albania on 3 September, never to return. Thomson, however, is still honoured with statues and street names in the countries of his birth and death. In Durrësi, the bust next to La Torra (page 95) is a replica of the original in Groningen. Behind it is a pleasant café called (another variant of his name!) 'Tomson Garden Grill'. A little further up Rruga Naim Frashëri, a group of columns forms a memorial to Thomson and to the others who died that day; a plaque affixed to one of the columns dates the inauguration of this memorial to Independence Day 1927. The parallel street, where Alexander Moisiu's house stands, is called Rruga Koloneli Thomson.

holiday apartments with which the coast is lined. At this time of year you should expect to find crowded beaches covered in litter, with the sea full of empty plastic bottles and crisp packets. On the positive side, Durrësi Beach has lively nightlife during the tourist season.

Quieter beaches, in or out of season, lie to the **north** of Durrësi, on Lalëzi Bay (Gjiri i Lalëzit) and beyond, at Cape Rodoni (Kepi i Rodonit). The road from Durrësi is asphalted as far as the Franciscan church of Shën Ndout, just before the last beach at Rodoni. A small charge is levied on cars to enter this area. From here, it is possible to **kayak** to remoter beaches and to Rodoni Castle, the medieval sea fortress said to have been built in 1465 by Skanderbeg (see box, pages 206–7). Outdoor Albania organises one-day sea-kayaking excursions to Rodoni from Tirana (page 29). Samiu's restaurant [map, pages 88–9] (really just a hut with tables overlooking the beach; $$) serves fish and prawns pretty much straight from the sea.

KRUJA   *Telephone code: 0511*

Kruja has been fortified since ancient times – ceramics and coins from the 3rd century BC have been excavated there. The name comes from the Albanian word for the spring (*krua*), within the castle, which provided its inhabitants with water. The castle of Kruja was the centre of Albanian resistance to the Ottoman invasion in the 15th century, which was led by the great national hero Gjergj Kastrioti, also known as Skanderbeg (see box, pages 206–7). The buildings and museums within the castle walls, combined with the attractively restored bazaar area just outside them, provide an excellent introduction to Albanian history and traditions. Kruja is the only town in Albania, apart from Saranda in the far south, which is really geared towards tourists and it is the best place in the country to shop for souvenirs.

Kruja was the northernmost stronghold of Bektashism (page 22) – it was the Kruja *baba* (father) who is said to have converted Ali Pasha Tepelena (see box, pages 254–5). Apart from the lovely *teqe* within the castle, there is a link with the Sufi saint Sari Salltëk: the *teqe* dedicated to him in the mountains above the town and, a few kilometres downhill, beside the road that leads up to the town, a rock where his foot is supposed to have left its print in the stone as he strode up from the plain.

GETTING THERE AND AWAY Kruja is about an hour's drive from both Tirana and Durrësi. Minibuses leave Tirana from the North bus station (page 60), with departures between 10.00 and 18.00; the fare is 200 lek. You should take care to board a vehicle that is going all the way up the hill to Kruja; there are more frequent minibuses that go only as far as Fushë-Kruja ('Kruja on the Plain'), the town at the junction on the main Durrësi–Shkodra highway. The drivers will keep you on the right track if you ask; if you do end up having to get off at Fushë-Kruja, it is easy enough to transfer to a local minibus for the Kruja you want. If you do stop in Fushë-Kruja, it is worth having a look at the statue of US President George W Bush, who visited the town in 2007 (and allegedly had his watch stolen during his visit). Once in Kruja, the minibuses go into the centre of town and terminate just beyond the statue of Skanderbeg. The last minibuses usually leave Kruja towards the middle of the afternoon.

Kruja is less than half an hour's drive from Tirana International Airport. This makes it an attractive option to spend your last night, or your last morning, in Kruja and go from there directly to the airport. A taxi from Kruja to the airport should cost €15–20.

For those with their own transport, an alternative route from the north is over the Shtama Pass (Qafa e Shtamës). It is about 50km to Kruja from Burreli (pages 182–5). This road is now asphalted, but the pass is closed when there is snow.

⌂ WHERE TO STAY *Map, below*

There are a couple of hotels in the town centre and another next to the Bektashi *teqe* at Sarisalltëk, about 7km above Kruja. There is an asphalted road to the *teqe* and also a steep footpath; it takes about 1 hour to get there on foot.

⌂ **Panorama** (18 rooms) Rr Kala; 📞 23092;   e hotelpanoramakruje@hotmail.com;
m 069 20 34 533, 069 20 98 528;   w hotelpanoramakruje.com. Unbeatable location

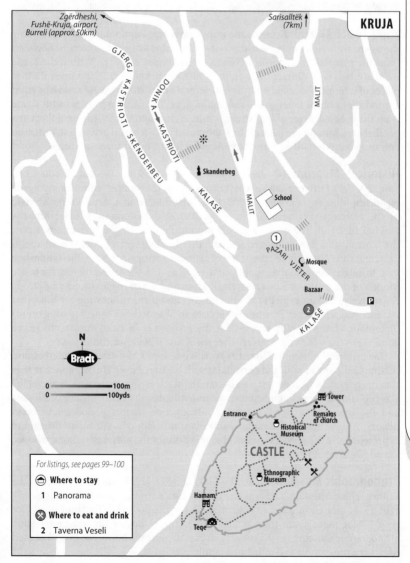

at the lower end of the bazaar, with superb views of the castle from many rooms. Restaurants, terrace bar, lift, secure parking, airport transfers

arranged, free Wi-Fi throughout. All rooms en suite with AC, LCD TV, telephone, hairdryer; some have balconies looking out on to the castle & bazaar. **$$**

✗ WHERE TO EAT AND DRINK *Map, page 99*

There are restaurants within the castle walls, some in family homes and others with seats outside from where you can admire the view. In the bazaar, several traditionally furnished restaurants serve good Albanian food.

✗ Taverna Veseli `24416; m 069 24 24 079.
At the top of the bazaar, the closest restaurant to the castle. Traditional Albanian dishes, plus the usual pasta & pizza. Good service, non-smoking, nicely decorated with traditional agricultural implements & old photographs. **$$$$$–$$$**

WHAT TO SEE AND DO Kruja Castle stands on a crag overlooking the plain below the town, with views on a clear day out to the Adriatic (it can sometimes be seen from the plane as you approach Tirana International Airport). Within the castle walls are two very different museums, a historic Bektashi *teqe* and several other places of interest; you could easily spend several hours visiting these and wandering around the cobbled lanes in the residential area. The usual approach to the castle is up the cobbled street of the bazaar, which is closed to traffic. The road that runs parallel to it, around the back of the Panorama Hotel, lets you drive up to the castle entrance, but it is hard to park there. Allow at least 2 hours for your visit.

Historical Museum (⊕ *09.00–14.00 & 16.00–19.00 Tue–Sat, 09.00–19.00 Sun; 200 lek*) On your left as you emerge from the vaulted entranceway is the Historical Museum, a modern (1982) building designed in a sort of castle-ish style by the architects Pranvera Hoxha – daughter of the communist leader Enver – and her husband. The displays on the ground floor cover the Illyrian city-states, the Roman and Byzantine periods and the development of Albania's medieval principalities. Then comes the story of Albania's struggle against the Ottomans, told through maps, murals, books and replicas. On the upper floors, there are models of the castles at Kruja, Petrela, Rodoni and Berati (pages 84, 98 and 123–5, respectively) and an exhibition of documents and pictures showing the links that Albania had with other European countries in Skanderbeg's time, focusing on his diplomatic efforts to rally support for the resistance. In clear weather, there are good views from the upper terrace over the Kruja Plain towards the sea.

The historical museum is sometimes criticised for its idolatry of Skanderbeg and the implied parallel with the personality cult around Enver Hoxha, and it is true that the relentless 'Skanderfest' can become a little wearing. In fairness, however, he was probably the most significant single individual in the entire history of Albania and the museum is a well-presented introduction to this period of Albanian history. Almost none of the information is translated; non-Albanian visitors are expected to use the services (free of charge) of one of the museum's guides, who are knowledgeable and multi-lingual.

Ethnographic Museum (⊕ *09.00–13.00 & 16.00–19.00 Tue–Sun; 300 lek*) The Ethnographic Museum, opposite the entrance gate (from where the sign is clearly visible), is located in a house built in 1764 for the powerful Toptani family (see page 77 for more about these feudal lords). This is one of the most interesting ethnographic museums in the country, in part because the house itself was designed for such a prosperous and influential family.

The ground floor of the house is where the livestock were kept, the produce from the family's lands was processed and where the tools were made or repaired. There is a raki still (page 49), an olive press and (in replica) the equipment for making felt, one of Kruja's traditional industries. The herdsman slept in the stable, with the sheep and/or goats; the family lived upstairs, in rooms accessed from the covered balcony that was used as the living space in summer. The doorways off the balcony have a stepped threshold, to keep out draughts once the door was closed, and an arch so that those entering had to lower their heads, thus showing respect to those within. Some of the rooms have been maintained with their original 18th-century furniture, frescoes and carved wooden panelling. The reception room, where (male) visitors would be welcomed and entertained by the men of the house, has a beautifully painted ceiling and an enclosed gallery, with a couple of small windows, where the women could sit without being seen by their male relatives' visitors. The room in which the family ate and slept also has a gallery, although it is not walled; this was where the children slept and played, out from under their parents' feet. The large fireplace heated not only the room, but also the water for the house's own steam bath, or *hamam*. The museum also has a rich collection of traditional costumes and jewellery.

A walk around the citadel Ordinary families still live within Kruja Castle, although in less luxurious houses than the Toptani house. A network of cobbled alleyways spreads downhill from the open area where the museums are. Down one of these is the castle's beautiful little Bektashi *teqe*. Bektashism (page 22) is a Sufi order, founded in Persia in the 13th century; it was introduced to Albania in the wake of the Ottoman conquest and became widespread there in the early 19th century. The Kruja *teqe* was built in 1770 (1191 in the Islamic *hijri* calendar) and is one of the oldest in the country. The olive tree in its garden is said to have been planted by Skanderbeg himself, as part of his campaign to encourage the other landowners of Kruja to plant olives.

A *teqe* is not a mosque, but it is a holy place; visitors must remove their shoes before entering. The Kruja *teqe* was used for storage after religion was banned in 1967; it was restored by local Bektashis after freedom of worship was regained in 1990. It is a small, simple building, housing the tombs of past *babas* and is decorated inside with rugs, embroideries and pictures given to the *teqe* by Bektashis around the world. The atheism campaigners (page 16) attempted to destroy the frescoes on the ceiling and walls, but fortunately the local people managed to convince them in time that the *teqe* was a Cultural Monument, and saved these beautiful paintings. The guardian will explain the building's history and the items in it to you, if you are able to establish a common language. A small donation is expected at the end of your visit.

To find the *teqe* from the open area between the museums, look for its dome and head down the winding paths aiming for it. It is reached up a flight of steps through a stone arch. Across from the foot of the steps is a **bathhouse** (*hamam*), five centuries old; the earthenware pipes which can be seen were installed, it is said, by Skanderbeg as a technological innovation that he had learned during his years at court in Constantinople.

At the other end of the citadel, up at the top beyond the museums, the **tower** was originally a lookout and signalling post. Skanderbeg used this castle as part of a chain of communication running the length of Albania – a beacon lit here could be seen by the garrison at Lezha Castle to the north and in Petrela, to the south of Tirana. Beside the tower, on the other side of a retaining wall, are the **remains of a medieval church**, with a couple of surviving fragments of fresco. The lack of maintenance of this church is disgraceful and the frescoes are unlikely to survive much longer.

The bazaar The bazaar was restored in the mid 1960s, but the wood-built shops and cobbled streets have a very authentically Ottoman feel. The extra-long eaves and the gutter in the middle of the road mean that rain, or wet snow, falls off the roofs and drains downhill straight away – an unusual but effective architectural device. Many of the shops sell small souvenirs such as Albanian flags, copper plates and ashtrays in the shape of bunkers. There are also traditional felt-makers, who produce slippers and the felt caps called *qeleshe*; carpet shops, in some of which you can watch the local women weaving the next batch of *qilime* (woven rugs; this is the same word as the Turkish *kilim*) with their ancient patterns; and antique dealers, where wooden butter paddles, cradles and intricately carved dowry chests pause in their journeys from highland villages to modern cities. Kruja's bazaar is a laid-back place and nobody will mind if all you want to do is window-shop.

Zgërdheshi Archaeologists think that the Illyrian ruins at Zgërdheshi may have been the city of Albanopolis, mentioned by Ptolemy (in the 2nd century AD) as the capital of Arbanon, the name from which Albania has taken its modern name. Built, like all Illyrian cities, on a hilltop, Zgërdheshi was fortified in two stages – first the acropolis, in the early Iron Age (c1000BC), and then a larger area, with the construction of defensive walls, in the 4th or 3rd century BC. A third phase, in the 2nd century BC, saw the city expand beyond the western fortifications. The first section you come to is the Illyrian circuit wall, built with the huge stone blocks characteristic of Illyrian fortification, and the remains of watchtowers that were positioned along this wall. The main fortified area covers 10ha and the buildings within it were constructed on terraces. Traces of the terrace walls are still visible, as are postholes and drainage channels in the bedrock. The acropolis is difficult to interpret without a specialist guide, but it is worth the climb for the views westwards to the Adriatic. Wild flowers and herbs grow all around. (I am grateful to Oliver Gilkes for the information on Zgërdheshi in his *Archaeological Guide*; see page 283 for bibliographical details.)

The turn-off for Zgërdheshi is about 5km out of Fushë-Kruja on the road towards Kruja itself. It is signposted at the junction, but not thereafter. You can drive as far as the circuit wall and towers, although the road is unpaved most of the way. Any Kruja minibus will let you off at the junction; it takes 15–20 minutes to walk up to the circuit wall.

DIVJAKA-KARAVASTAJA NATIONAL PARK

The Karavastaja Lagoons to the south of Durrësi are an internationally recognised wetland area – a Ramsar site. It is the winter home of several rare bird species and is the most westerly breeding ground of the Dalmatian pelican. The main wetland area comprises a shallow inner lagoon, and a smaller outer lagoon. The large inner lagoon is an atmospheric, slightly spooky place, full of small, low islands, ideal for pelicans' nests. Between the two lagoons is a large, forested sandbar where there is a small beach resort, with fish restaurants and hotels. The forest consists mainly of maritime pine (*Pinus pinaster*), Aleppo pine (*Pinus halopensis*) and umbrella pine (*Pinus pinea*).

The pinewoods and lagoons are a Category II National Park, Divjaka-Karavastaja, which makes them quite well protected, at least on paper. The local villagers have the right to collect dead wood but not to chop down the trees. In the inner lagoon only artisanal fishery is allowed, although there are more intensive fisheries in the outer one. See pages 5–6 for more information about recent efforts by the Albanian government to protect wildlife and protected areas.

The park's biggest drawback, reasonably enough given it is in the middle of the largest wetland in Albania, is that it is infested with huge, thirsty mosquitoes from late spring to early autumn. If you visit at these times of year, you should take strong insect repellent and, if you plan to stay overnight, mosquito coils to put outside your window – electrically powered devices will be of no use if the electricity goes off while you are asleep. The small resort on the sandbar would make a pleasant overnight stop for birdwatchers or beach lovers.

GETTING THERE AND AWAY The national park is near the village of Divjaka, northwest of the town of Lushnja. It is clearly signposted at the roundabout on the main north–south highway, just beyond the bridge over the Shkumbini River. The village of Divjaka is about 15 minutes' drive down this minor road; to get to the park, 3–4km further on, go through the village and turn right at the crossroads, following the signpost 'Plazh' ('beach'). The road leads through the pine woods and ends at the sandbar. Vehicles entering the national park are charged a small fee. The journey from Tirana takes about 1½ hours.

To get to Divjaka by **public transport** from Tirana (or Durrësi), you can take any bus going south beyond Kavaja – to Lushnja, Fieri or Berati, for example – and ask the driver to let you off at the roundabout. Divjaka taxis wait near the junction until at least midday (probably later in the summer). The usual system is for the driver to wait until his car is full, although obviously he will take you at once if you pay four fares. You should specify at the outset that you are going to Divjaka Beach (Plazhi i Divjakës), to avoid arguments about the fare when you get to the village.

WHERE TO EAT AND DRINK There are several restaurants at Divjaka Beach, serving fresh fish and grilled meat (**$$$**).

Ali Kali [map, pages 88–9] One of the weirdest dining experiences in Albania is at Ali Kali ('Ali the Horse'), which is at the end of a track soon after you enter the Divjaka-Karavastaja national park – sculptures of horses indicate the turn-off; the restaurant tables are set up outside, concealed behind a house. There is no menu; Ali rides up to your table on a white horse (hence the name) with your food and serves it to you from horseback. Then he brings you more, and more, until you can convince him to stop. Fresh fish, meat and bread, all grilled, feature prominently, perhaps thanks to their aerodynamic qualities. Rough red wine and honey from the comb complete the meal. Further surprises await when you come to pay. The toilets are pleasantly civilised, with running water and hand wash. (*Full meal, with wine* **$$$**)

WHAT TO SEE AND DO Apart from the long, sandy beach (and Ali Kali), the main reason to go to Divjaka-Karavastaja is to see the pelicans and other birds. There are no restrictions on walking along the beach; birdwatchers who wish to access the western side of the sandbar, or the islands in the inner lagoon, should request permission in the regional capital, Fieri (page 104). It may be possible to obtain informal access with the park rangers; try asking in the police station in the national park.

The Dalmatian pelican (*Pelecanus crispus*) is listed as 'vulnerable' owing to its small and declining population. The total European breeding population is only about 1,500 pairs. Commercial trade in it is prohibited; it is the only member of the

Pelecanidae on any of the CITES appendices, which regulate trade in endangered species. However, conservation measures are resulting in a population increase in Europe, particularly at the world's largest breeding colony at Lesser Lake Prespa (pages 145–6). Karavastaja is the only place in Albania where the Dalmatian pelican breeds – the colony at Prespa is on the Greek side of the lake – and in the 1990s there were between 40 and 90 resident pairs here, although the numbers seem to have declined. The breeding season runs from April to July, although the pelicans winter at Karavastaja (and elsewhere in Albania) and can thus be seen at other times of year too.

The site is also important for wintering waterbirds – BirdLife International censuses recorded 45,000 individual birds in 1996 and 68,171 in 1997. These include wigeons (*Anas penelope*), northern shovelers (*Anas clypeata*) and teals (*Anas crecca*). Over 1,000 avocets (*Recurvirostra avosetta*) have been recorded at Karavastaja. As well as the pelicans, collared pratincoles (*Glareola pratincola*) and little terns (*Sterna albifrons*) also breed there. The 'vulnerable' spotted eagle (*Aquila clanga*) winters there and has also been observed at other times of year, although it does not breed. Cormorants (*Phalacrocorax carbo*), pygmy cormorants (*Phalacrocorax pygmeus*) and great egrets (*Casmerodius albus*) are all present. The site is also potentially very important for the extremely rare ('critically endangered') slender-billed curlew (*Numenius tenuirostris*). See pages 210–11 for further details of the bird species that can be observed in the Albanian wetlands.

APOLLONIA AND ARDENICA

The ancient city of Apollonia and the 18th-century monastery at Ardenica can easily be combined into a day trip from Tirana, Berati, Durrësi or Vlora. Apollonia was founded in the 6th century BC and became one of Roman Albania's most important cities; there is a medieval monastery beside the ancient site, which houses an excellent museum. The Church of St Mary, part of the Ardenica Monastery, has frescoes painted by the Zografi brothers, who were renowned throughout the southern Balkans during their lifetimes.

GETTING THERE AND AWAY The nearest town to both Apollonia and Ardenica is Fieri, on the main highway south from Durrësi, just north of where it divides for Gjirokastra and Vlora. Apollonia is about 12km west of Fieri, on a reasonably good, asphalted road. It is signposted from the city and at the turn-off to the site. Ardenica is about half an hour's drive north of Fieri and about an hour from Tirana. The turn-off for the monastery is signposted in Albanian and English.

By **public transport**, there are frequent buses and minibuses to Fieri from all major towns in southern and central Albania. However, there is no onward public transport to Apollonia or Ardenica. The main **taxi** rank in Fieri is on the main square, where the Prefecture building is.

WHAT TO SEE AND DO

Ardenica The 18th-century Church of St Mary, part of the monastery at Ardenica, is decorated with frescoes by Kostandin and Athanas Zografi, famous icon-painters in the tradition known as the Korça School (page 133). The monastery is surrounded with high walls, but it is usually possible to gain access; this is the only monastery in Albania that still has monks in residence. A church was first built on this site during the 13th century, possibly on the site of a pagan temple, and the monastery gatehouse dates from 1474.

The 1744 church is a long building of creamy-coloured stone, with a colonnaded narthex. Stones from more ancient sites were used in its building; in the wall nearest the entrance you can see fragments of column capitals and Byzantine Greek inscriptions. The entrance to the church is up a flight of steps beside the bell tower (added in 1924). The beautiful gilded iconostasis is by Kostandin Shpataraku (page 133). The walls are covered in paintings of various saints and of New Testament scenes. A wooden staircase in the narthex leads to more frescoes, a *Last Judgement* and the icon of the church above the entrance.

On the other side of the steps is an elegant cloister of stone arches supporting a wooden terrace, which gives shade to the monks' cells on the first floor. In 1967, the monastery became a military barracks and was later used as a hotel.

Apollonia ($\oplus$ *Oct–Mar 09.00–17.00 daily, Apr–Sep 08.00–20.00 daily; 300 lek*)

History The city of Apollonia was the second Greek settlement on the Illyrian mainland, after Epidamnos (now Durrësi; page 87). Founded, according to tradition, in 588BC and named for the god Apollo, it was settled first by Corinthians, who were followed by others, especially from nearby Corcyra (Corfu). At the time, Apollonia lay only a kilometre from the Aoos River (the Vjosa, in Albanian) and it became a major port. The city grew in importance and, by the time of the Roman conquest in the middle of the 2nd century BC, its coins were in wide circulation, especially in the Danube provinces where Roman coinage was not accepted. With its rival Dyrrachium (the Romans' name for Durrësi), it was one of the starting points of the Via Egnatia, the great arterial road that linked the Adriatic coast with Byzantium (page 8).

In addition to its importance as a trading and military port, the Roman elite considered Apollonia a centre of higher learning. The young Octavian studied there before he was given the title of Augustus – indeed, he had to rush back to Rome to claim power after the Ides of March, 44BC, when his adoptive father, Julius Caesar, was assassinated. Most of the remains that can be seen at Apollonia date from the Roman period. Augustus later awarded Apollonia the status of a 'free and immune city' – immune, that is, from the obligation to pay taxes. Apollonia's status meant that – unlike Dyrrachium and other colonies – it continued to elect its local authorities, its everyday language was Greek, not Latin, and its coins had Apollonia's own symbols on them.

In late antiquity, a series of earthquakes shifted the course of the Aoos – the Vjosa River – far to the south and left Apollonia without the port which had brought its prosperity. The ancient city now stands, isolated and forlorn, on its hill overlooking the fertile Myzeqeja Plain and, a few miles to the west, the Adriatic.

The ancient city Apollonia is a complex, multi-layered site and it is estimated that only about 10% of the city has been excavated to date. Good information panels, in Albanian and English, have now been installed around the site, with computer-generated images of how archaeologists believe the buildings would have looked at the time they were being used. These make it very much easier to get a sense of the layout of the city. A large map at the entrance to the site shows the various buildings, with a key in Albanian and French.

The city was first excavated by the French archaeologist Léon Rey, between 1924 and 1938. It was Rey and his team who uncovered the building that immediately draws the visitor's eye: the **Bouleuterion**, where the city council met. It was built in the late 2nd century AD by the brother of a military commander who had died on

Rome's eastern front. Both brothers held the position of *agonothetes*, the official who presided over and judged the games, and so this building is also sometimes known as the Monument of the Agonothetes. We know all of this from the Greek inscription on the pediment above the columns. These were restored in the 1970s by Albanian archaeologists, who fortunately made it very obvious which bits are restored and which are original.

Behind the Bouleuterion, and built around the same time, is a little theatre known as the **Odeon**. This was not the city's public theatre, but a venue for cultural and musical events for the elite, seating only about 300 people. The line of four marble-clad column bases, between these two buildings, is all that remains of a triumphal arch, through which all traffic into the square would have had to pass.

Leading off this civic area to the northwest is the portico known as **Stoa B**. At 75m long and 12m wide, the stoa predates the Bouleuterion and Odeon by some five centuries. Built to a Corinthian pattern, its ground floor was separated with Doric columns into two parallel walkways. Above these walkways, an upper promenade, probably with Ionic columns, allowed Apollonia's rich citizens to enjoy the marvellous views over their thriving port and the Adriatic Sea. The whole structure backed on to the slope of the hill leading up to the city's acropolis; to reinforce it, 17 niches were built into the hillside on the ground floor. The stone for these was brought, by sea, from the Karaburuni Peninsula, 70km away. During Léon Rey's excavations, several busts of famous philosophers were found around these now-empty niches, placed there to inspire intellectual conversations.

A restored arch at the northwestern end of the stoa marks the site of one of the shops that once stood there. In the area around it are the remains of a cistern, in which rainwater was collected (Apollonia has no aqueduct), and a rectangular building that had a mosaic floor and which archaeologists believe may have been a shrine. The city's public **theatre** can be reached by following the track between the end of the stoa and the arch. It was built in the 3rd century BC, on a magnificent site on the western edge of the city. The curve of the seats can still be seen, cut into the hillside facing the Adriatic, but most of the stonework of the theatre's structure has gone, re-used over the centuries for other buildings. The 18th-century governor of Berati, Kurt Pasha (page 126), notoriously removed huge quantities of stonework from Apollonia for his own building projects.

Like all Greek cities, Apollonia had a reserved area called the *temenos*. This was dedicated to a god, or to several gods, and was not in everyday use. In Apollonia, the *temenos* was on the hill to the east of the Bouleuterion, which Rey called Hill 104. It was surrounded by a wall, part of which can be seen by following the path uphill from the Bouleuterion, on either side of the beautiful archway which was the entrance to the *temenos*. Neatly cut from limestone and sandstone, some of the rectangular blocks are marked with a monogram consisting of the Greek letters D and A: 'belonging to the state of Apollonia' – in other words, the *temenos* wall was a public work.

This path follows the *temenos* wall to the eastern edge of the city. In the valley below was the necropolis, or cemetery, used from the Iron Age onwards. There is an array of Communist-era bunkers on the opposite side of the valley. A little further on are the remains of the city's southeastern **gate**, with its watchtowers. In ancient times, the Vjosa River curved round the head of this valley and the gate provided access to and from the port. Looking south across the valley from this gate, you will see a single column on a little hill. This is the only surviving column of a Greek temple, built (probably in the 5th or 4th century BC) to mark the entrance to the harbour. Known today as the Temple of Shtyllas (*shtylla* means 'column' in Albanian), it may have been dedicated to the city's patron god, Apollo, or to the god of the sea, Poseidon.

The later buildings The site **museum,** located on the first floor of the monastery building, is full of well-presented information about the history of Apollonia and its excavations. There are three rooms of lovely, interesting artefacts: imported and locally made Greek vases, bronzes and busts; armour, including a 4th-century shield, which was excavated in hundreds of pieces and took 27 years to restore; and a case of coins minted in Apollonia and elsewhere. You should try to allow at least 45 minutes to look around the museum. Outside, the 13th-century **church** and the 14th-century refectory are also well worth a look. The well-head in the exonarthex of the church is a repurposed Doric column from the ancient city; you can lift the lid to see the rope-marks worn into the marble by years of lowering and raising buckets. On the church wall behind it is a patch of 13th-century fresco, depicting three Byzantine emperors. There are beautiful frescoes in the refectory, including scenes from the life of Christ and various saints; the eyes of some of the saints were scratched out by believers, who would mix the paint and plaster from them with water and drink this potion as a miracle cure.

There are two cafés at Apollonia: one, named after Léon Rey, is at the summit of 'Hill 104' (the *temenos* hill) and has good views; the other is straight ahead as you enter the fenced-off area of the archaeological site. There are reasonable toilets behind this bar, which visitors to the site may use; the monastery building also has public toilets.

BYLLIS

[Map, page 109] (⊕ *Mar–Oct 08.00–18.00 daily, Nov–Feb 08.00–16.00 daily; 300 lek)* Byllis is a vast archaeological site spread over 30ha of hilltop overlooking the River Vjosa. The ancient walls that surround the site were built in the second quarter of the 4th century BC. Within them are the remains of Illyrian private houses, Roman public buildings, including an impressive theatre, and Byzantine basilicas paved with outstanding mosaics. It is easy to linger for hours in the haunting atmosphere of this remote hilltop, surrounded by the ruins of buildings that are two-and-a-half millennia old. Good interpretative panels around the site, in Albanian and English, mean that it can be readily understood by non-specialists. A well-surfaced and fairly level path leads the visitor around the most important remains.

It was the British traveller Henry Holland who, in the early 19th century, first identified this site as the ancient Byllis, mentioned by Caesar and Cicero. Systematic excavation began in the winter of 1917/18, under the direction of the Austrian archaeologist Camillo Praschniker. Several eminent Albanian archaeologists have excavated at Byllis, among them Neritan Ceka and Skënder Muçaj, who have written a guide to the site, *Byllis: History & Monuments* (page 283). It is worth buying a copy of this book just for the photographs of the Byzantine mosaics, which are usually kept covered to protect them from the elements. Several interesting objects discovered at Byllis can be seen in the National Archaeological Museum in Tirana (pages 74–6).

HISTORY Byllis was the capital of the small republic (*koinon*) of the Byllines and it was the largest city in southern Illyria. The Byllines had a sophisticated system of government, minted bronze coins and controlled an area of about 20km². Their state flourished until 229BC, when the Romans occupied Apollonia and Byllis became a battleground between Rome and Macedonia, thanks to its strategic position overlooking the River Vjosa and the route from Apollonia to Epirus and Macedonia. The advantages of this location would later encourage Rome to make Byllis one of its colonies. The colonial period saw the city flourish again, as Roman veterans built luxurious houses and sponsored public works such as bridges and bathhouses.

Byllis was sacked by the Visigoths towards the end of the 4th century AD, and its enclosing wall was repaired using the original blocks. The sections that were repaired can be identified from the cement used to stick the blocks together. Between AD547 and AD551, Byllis was attacked again. It was rebuilt and it was decided a new wall should be erected, enclosing a much smaller area than the old Illyrian city. The order to construct the new fortification was given by the Emperor Justinian (AD527–65), but it was implemented by a general called Victorinus, and so it is known as Victorinus's Wall. It follows the line of the Hellenistic wall on the western and southern sides of the city, where the hillside is steeper. For the new defences to the north and east, Victorinus re-used some of the old limestone blocks and built a new wall 2.2m thick, interspersed with 12m-high towers. A touching inscription on one of the blocks of his wall, now in the Archaeological Museum in Tirana (page 75), reads: 'I am no longer worried or frightened about barbarians, because I was destined to be built by the hand of great Victorinus.'

GETTING THERE AND AWAY Byllis is about half an hour's drive from the nearest town, Ballshi, which is approximately 2½ hours from Tirana. Local **taxis** can be hired in the centre of Ballshi, beside the war memorial. The 'Ancient City of Bylis' is signposted, in Albanian and English, off to the right on the brow of a hill a couple of kilometres south of Ballshi. It is 5km from the junction to the site; the road is well surfaced and a 4x4 is not required. A **minibus** operates between Ballshi and the village of Hekali, about 1km short of the entrance to the site; the owner of the café at the junction is very helpful and will be able to advise on bus timings. For those on two wheels or with 4x4, an alternative route is the minor road up from the Levan–Tepelena highway, which passes below Byllis; the turn-off is signposted for Hekali, not Byllis.

On the way up to the site, many small oil rigs and other installations can be seen. The oil field under this part of Albania stretches from Ballshi and Fieri to the district of Kuçova, north of Berati; parts of it are now being exploited with modern technology by multi-national companies.

Cars can be parked at the entrance to the site, beside the café where entry tickets are sold and where there are toilets. It carries a small stock of publications about archaeology in Albania. Admission is free on the last Sunday of the month, except in the summer, and on certain dates such as International Museums Day.

WHAT TO SEE AND DO The walls that enclosed the Illyrian city form a rough triangle more than 2km around. On the southern edge there is a gap in the wall where the hillside drops away in a steep cliff for about 200m. The Hellenistic (Illyrian) walls were 8–9m high, built with large rectangular blocks of limestone. These were laid in two lines 3.5m apart, and the gap between the rows was then filled with small stones laid at right angles to the blocks. There were six entrance gates, each guarded by a tower, and additional towers were built at the corners of the walls, to protect and strengthen them.

Between 230BC and 167BC, Byllis's protection was enhanced with the addition of a fortified courtyard at the northern apex of the triangle of its walls. The courtyard was guarded in its turn from a round tower, nearly 9m in diameter and 9m high. The remains of this fortified courtyard are on the right of the modern road as you approach the site.

From the site entrance next to the café, follow the path to the *agora*, the area of the city which the Byllines reserved for public spaces and civic buildings. A wall

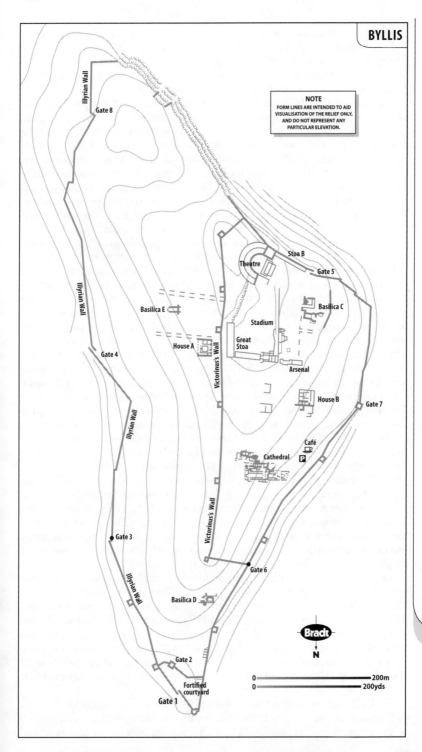

BYLLIS

NOTE
FORM LINES ARE INTENDED TO AID
VISUALISATION OF THE RELIEF ONLY,
AND DO NOT REPRESENT ANY
PARTICULAR ELEVATION.

Illyrian Wall

Gate 8

Illyrian Wall

Gate 4

Illyrian Wall

Gate 3

Illyrian Wall

Gate 2

Fortified
courtyard

Gate 1

Theatre

Stoa B

Gate 5

Basilica E

Basilica C

Stadium

House A

Great
Stoa

Victorinus's Wall

Arsenal

House B

Gate 7

Café

Cathedral

Victorinus's Wall

Gate 6

Basilica D

Bradt

N

0 _____ 200m
0 _____ 200yds

divided this public area from the residential quarter, which was laid out in a grid, with the houses in blocks known as *insulae*. Covering 4ha, the agora was completed during the 3rd century BC, with buildings including the **Great Stoa** (to the east), the Stadium and the vaulted Cistern. On the southern edge of the agora, the Theatre is perhaps the most imposing of Byllis's ancient monuments.

The limestone vaults of the **Cistern** were originally covered with stone tiles to form an underground reservoir, with a capacity of about 1,200m³, which supplied the city with water. Even more remarkably, the roof of the reservoir formed the northern part of the Stadium. Limited suitable space meant that Byllis's **Stadium** had only one track, rather than the more usual oval form. The spectators stood on the steps rising up to the east of the track, which continued as far as the Theatre. The steps were made of rectangular limestone blocks; some can still be seen. Associated with the Cistern is a much later **Bathhouse**, which dates from the reconstruction of the city during Justinian's reign; the baths used water from the Cistern, which was thus still in working order seven centuries after it had been built.

To the west of the Stadium steps is another underground building, the **Arsenal**. Although it was originally built in the middle of the 3rd century BC, it was rebuilt at the beginning of the 1st century AD, when the beautiful wall at the far end was constructed in *opus reticulatum*, the 'netting' pattern that gives it its Latin name.

The **Theatre**, also dating from the middle of the 3rd century BC, would have held about 7,500 spectators. The semicircle of its seating used the slope of the hill as a natural rake; the seats themselves were almost all broken up and re-used over the years for other buildings (including Victorinus's Wall). One section of VIP seating, with carvings on the back, can be seen at the foot of the slope. The best view of the layout of the theatre is obtained by climbing up to the top of the seating rows. The semicircular *orchestra* – the space where the chorus stood during the performance – was drained by a stone-lined channel. In the Hellenistic period, the stage was a 3m-high platform supported on columns. When the theatre was rebuilt during the Roman colony, this stage was replaced with a stone base and a brick backdrop.

The capacity of the theatre shows that it was intended not only for the citizens of Byllis, but also for people from other Bylline towns, who would normally have entered the city by the nearest gate to the theatre, now known as **Gate 5**. This is the best preserved of the Illyrian gates and clearly shows the double entrance created by running a corridor between the two parallel lines of the wall. This structure protected the gate from attacks with catapults or fire and meant that invaders could be picked off from above if they tried to storm the gate. In addition, a tower stood on the arch of the gate. A stoa led from the gate to the entrance to the theatre seats. Gate 5 was rebuilt when the Roman colony was established and the Latin inscription on its southern flank reads: 'Augustus, son of the divine emperor Caesar, gave it' ('it' meaning the reconstruction).

Several basilicae were built at Byllis during the Byzantine period; five have been excavated to date. They are all paved with beautiful mosaics, but (sadly for visitors) these are normally kept covered with protective layers of sand and plastic sheeting. The largest and most impressive Byzantine structure at Byllis is the religious complex known as the **Cathedral**. It is fenced off from the main part of the site, just before the café, and it consists of a church (Basilica B), a baptistery and an episcopal palace. It is of great archaeological importance, because of the complexity of its architecture, the richness of its decorative elements and the large number of objects excavated, which included many coins.

The Cathedral was built in three distinct phases: the original construction, in the late 4th century, was a three-naved church with a narthex (entrance) and portico, and a simple baptistery; in the AD470s, this was expanded with an atrium and galleries; and finally, when the Cathedral was rebuilt during Justinian's reign, the episcopal complex was added. In its completed state, the basilica was a long, narrow building – an astonishing 67m in length – with side-naves, narthex, exonarthex (the room leading into the church, separating it from the outdoors) and porticos, and with galleries on the upper floor. The body of the church (*naos*) is 24.7m long and consists of three differently sized naves, the central one measuring 7.75m across. The naves were separated from each other by columns set on a high base; these columns were not only carved, but also painted, following the Illyrian tradition. At the southern end of the central nave is a platform on which the lectern stood. The atrium is a rectangular hallway surrounded by four porticos, one of which is the exonarthex. A staircase led from the northeastern corner of the exonarthex to the first floor and galleries of the church.

The floors of several sections of the church are paved with magnificent mosaics, which are usually covered to protect them from the elements. One shows a rustic scene; others depict the fishermen of Nazareth and the brothers Simon and Andrew (and an especially cute jellyfish); smaller panels bear different kinds of animals and birds. The basilica's walls were decorated with frescoes, but only a few of these remain, geometric patterns from the first phase of construction.

In AD586, Byllis was sacked and burned once again, this time by invading Slavs. After this destruction, the city was abandoned and the bishopric moved to the nearby town whose name, Ballshi, is a corruption of Byllis.

ELBASANI   *Telephone code: 054*

Elbasani's origins lie in the 2nd century BC, when a trading post called Scampa grew up at the junction of the branches of the Via Egnatia, the great Roman road running between the Albanian coast and Byzantium, whose starting points were Dyrrachium and Apollonia. By the 2nd century AD, this had developed into a sizeable way-station called Mansio ad Quintum. During the upheavals and invasions of the 4th century AD, the Romans fortified the settlement and stationed a legion there to protect the Via Egnatia. The castle that they built is right in the centre of the modern town of Elbasani and covers almost a square kilometre.

The city walls were rebuilt by the Ottomans in 1466, during Mehmed II's expedition against Skanderbeg (see box, pages 206–7). Their plan was to use the fortress as a base for extending their conquest and they gave it the name 'Elbasan', which in Turkish means 'the place for raiding other people's territory'. The town flourished under the Ottomans, and by the 17th century it had become an important commercial centre, exporting its leather, fabrics and silverwork throughout the Ottoman Empire. In the 20th century, Elbasani was for many years the home of Margaret Hasluck, a British archaeologist and ethnographer who went on to direct the SOE's activities in Albania (see boxes, pages 13–15).

The metallurgical complex called the Steel of the Party was built in 1974, with technical and financial support from China, and it employed over 8,000 people in its heyday. Now, most of the plant lies idle; it is almost impossible to bring it up to international environmental standards, and the result has been unemployment and emigration. For many people, it is the only thing they know about Elbasani and so they drive straight past the town without realising that its history goes back much, much further.

GETTING THERE AND AWAY A new highway, with tunnels blasted through the mountains, has cut the journey time between Tirana and Elbasani to under an hour.

Kostandin Kristoforidhi was an illustrious figure in the 19th-century cultural nationalist movement, Rilindja Kombëtare. He was prolific as a translator of religious texts into Albanian, but his life's work was as a lexicographer and grammarian. He was born in Elbasani in 1826 and studied in Ioannina, where he assisted in the preparation of the first Albanian–German dictionary. His first translation was of the New Testament, which he published in both of the main dialects of Albanian, Gheg and Tosk. He would continue throughout his life to translate into both dialects, as a way of demonstrating their similarity to each other.

After living for a time in Istanbul, Malta and Tunis, he returned to Istanbul in 1865 as a translator for the London-based Bible Society. He worked for it until 1874, when the Society dismissed him on the grounds that he did not believe the Bible was divinely inspired.

Unemployed, Kristoforidhi returned to Tirana, where he scraped a living selling wood and charcoal, and opened a bar. Meanwhile, like many other Rilindja figures, he gave clandestine Albanian lessons. In 1884, he returned to Elbasani, where he continued to teach secretly. He was a member of the Commission on the Alphabet that met in the late 1860s to try to agree on a common alphabet in which to write Albanian; it would not be until 1909, 14 years after Kristoforidhi's death, that the congress held in his native town would formally adopt the Roman alphabet for this purpose.

His surviving religious translations are versions of the Four Gospels (1866), the Psalms (1868 in Tosk and 1869 in Gheg), the New Testament (1869 in Gheg and 1879 in Tosk), Genesis and Exodus (1880), Deuteronomy (1882), the Song of Solomon and the Book of Isaiah (both 1884). Kristoforidhi's Tosk translation is the authorised version still used in the Albanian Orthodox Church today. He published a Gheg ABC in 1867, and a Tosk ABC the following year. He also wrote Albanian-language textbooks for his students, and a story called *Gjahu i malësorëve* (*The Highlanders' Hunt*). His scientific work on the Albanian language – his *Dictionary of the Albanian Language* and *Grammar of the Albanian Language* – laid the foundations for the establishment of a unified national language.

Kostandin Kristoforidhi died in Elbasani in 1895 and is buried in the churchyard of St Mary's Church within the castle walls. A statue of him stands on the corner of Rruga Qemal Stafa and Rruga Rinia and a plaque depicting him giving one of his clandestine language classes can be seen on the castle wall near the Bazaar Gate. The words on the plaque read: 'Albania will never learn anything, will never be illuminated, will not be at all civilised with foreign languages, but only with its mother tongue, which is Albanian.'

Buses leave Tirana from the Southeast bus station, behind the Faculty of Economics [63 H6]; the fare is 150 lek. There are buses to Elbasani from every other major town in central and southern Albania.

The main **bus station** in Elbasani is in the square in front of the sports centre. The Tirana buses leave from a little further down and on the opposite side of the street. Local buses and minibuses (eg: for Llixhat and Belshi) leave from a bus stop on Rruga Thoma Kalfi, just beyond the market.

For those with their own transport, the old Tirana–Elbasani road is slow and precipitous, but has spectacular views over the Martanesh Mountains. The highest

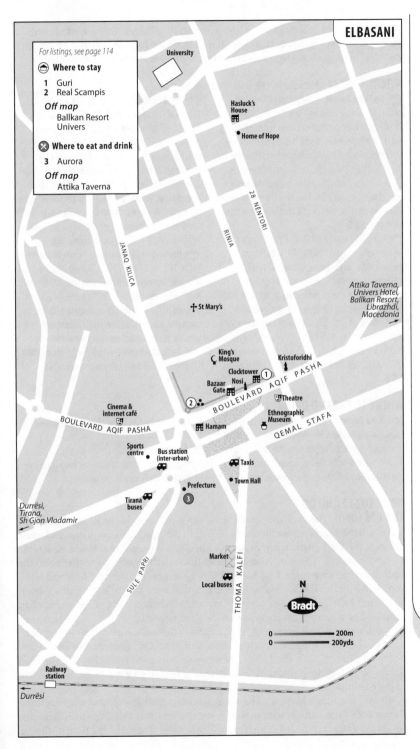

ELBASANI

For listings, see page 114

Where to stay

1 Guri
2 Real Scampis

Off map
   Ballkan Resort
   Univers

Where to eat and drink

3 Aurora

Off map
   Attika Taverna

University

Hasluck's House

Home of Hope

28 NENTORI

RINIA

JANAQ KILICA

Attika Taverna,
Univers Hotel,
Ballkan Resort,
Librazhdi,
Macedonia

St Mary's

King's Mosque

Kristoforidhi

Clocktower

Nosi

Bazaar Gate

Theatre

Cinema & internet café

BOULEVARD AQIF PASHA

Ethnographic Museum

Hamam

QEMAL STAFA

Sports centre

Bus station (inter-urban)

Taxis

Town Hall

Prefecture

Tirana buses

*Durrësi,
Tirana,
Sh Gjon Vladamir*

SULE PAPRI

Market

THOMA KALFI

Local buses

N

Bradt

0 _____ 200m
0 _____ 200yds

Railway station

Durrësi

4

point of the road is almost 931m above sea level; it then hairpins back downhill, passing a series of large Socialist Realist murals on the hillside wall, until Elbasani's vast steel plant comes into view, spreading for miles at the foot of the mountain.

🏠 WHERE TO STAY *Map, page 113, unless otherwise stated*

🏠 **Ballkan Resort** [map, pages 88–9] (18 rooms) Miraka, Rr Elbasan-Librazhd; m 069 44 39 601; e info@resortballkan.com; 🇫 Ballkan Hotel. Country setting in hills between Labinoti & Librazhdi; modern building in lovely gardens on the Shkumbini River; English spoken at reception. Large outdoor swimming pool, restaurant, terrace bar, contemporary cocktail bar; Wi-Fi throughout. All rooms en suite with AC, TV, minibar; some have a balcony. **$$$**

🏠 **Guri** (12 rooms) Bd Qemal Stafa, Lagja Kala (in the castle); m 069 20 83 089; e hotelguri@ hotmail.com. An old house within the castle walls, nicely renovated; has small art gallery & museum within one of the towers of the wall, with outdoor bar area at the tower's foot. Generously sized rooms, all with good en-suite bathrooms inc superb shower; AC, LCD TV, Wi-Fi, phone, fridge. Rooms on 1st floor have Juliet balcony overlooking castle walls; top floor have skylights & attic ceiling. **$$$**

🏠 **Real Scampis** (7 rooms) Bd Qemal Stafa, Lagja Kala (in the castle); ☎ 255 575; f 240 162. Fantastic location within the castle walls, with archaeological remains visible under the café & around the extensive, beautiful gardens. The best restaurant in town, with traditional Elbasani dishes & interesting chef's specials, as well as the usual grilled meat. Vehicle entrance at rear of hotel, with car park. Live music in gardens in summer. Good-sized rooms, all en suite (some have jacuzzi) with AC, satellite TV, Wi-Fi, balcony, phone. **$$**

🏠 **Univers** (14 rooms) Lagja Emin Matraxhiu; ☎ 256 193; m 069 40 71 278, 069 40 71 277; e univers.hotel@yahoo.com, univershoteli@gmail. com; w univershotel.eu. On the eastern outskirts of town (Ura e Bakallit); English spoken. Quiet, modern & comfortable, good restaurant, bar, parking, Wi-Fi throughout; outdoor swimming pool, gardens. All rooms en suite with AC, satellite TV, phone; most have balcony or terrace. **$$**

✕ WHERE TO EAT AND DRINK *Map, page 113*

✕ **Attika Taverna** Rr Kozma Naska (near Ura e Bakallit); ☎ 243 583; m 068 20 71 290. A range of unusual & delicious dishes, neither traditionally Albanian nor, despite the restaurant's name, noticeably Greek. Carnivores will enjoy Sofra e Pashait ('the Pasha's Table'); lots of cheese treats for vegetarians. **$$$**

✕ **Aurora** Around the corner from the Prefecture, has a shady terrace, set back from the road, particularly nice in the summer. **$$$**

WHAT TO SEE AND DO

The old town The surviving castle walls run along one side of Rruga Aqif Pasha and down the streets perpendicular to it. Within them lie Roman remains, including traces of the Via Egnatia (page 8), one of the oldest mosques in Albania, and a fine Orthodox church. There are four entrances through the walls, one of them also the pedestrian entrance to the Real Scampis Hotel. Descending the steps here will bring you right into the archaeological excavations that were carried out while the hotel was being built. Some of the remains are actually beneath the raised terrace bar, protected by a Perspex covering so that they can be seen.

On the other side of Rruga Aqif Pasha, outside the walls, is a *hamam*, an Ottoman bathhouse, whose current structure dates from the 19th century, but which has occupied this site since the 1670s. The exterior is in good condition and the tiled domes on its roof are particularly attractive. The 60m-high clock tower, set into one of the bastions of the wall, was built in 1899.

To find the **King's Mosque** (Xhamia e Mbretit), enter the old town through the **Bazaar Gate** – the archway with the lion fountains on either side. The street forks just inside the entrance; the left-hand fork will bring you straight to the King's Mosque

– one of the oldest in Albania. Construction began in 1492, the year Columbus discovered the New World. The building was neglected under communism, though not deliberately damaged, and the interior has been substantially, though faithfully, renovated.

From the mosque, **St Mary's Church** (Kisha e Shënmërisë) is a couple of hundred metres deeper into the old town, bearing in the same direction. A church was first built on this site in 1486, with renovations and additions made over the centuries. In the garden, as you enter the churchyard, is the tomb of the 19th-century lexicographer and grammarian Kostandin Kristoforidhi (see box, page 112). The church was used by the army for storage after the atheism campaign of 1967, but the fabric of the building was saved from wanton destruction by the cobbled streets of Elbasani's old town, which are too narrow for bulldozers. The interior walls of the church were covered in frescoes until they were whitewashed during the atheism campaign; the only ones that survive are the Pantocrator in the dome and the early 20th-century fresco on the south wall. The iconostasis, however, is the original, intricately carved in boxwood in 1870 by craftsmen from the district of Dibra, famous at the time for the skill of its woodworkers. The icons of St Michael and St Gabriel, the protective saints of all Orthodox churches, were painted in 1659 by the great Albanian artist Onufri (page 123).

Ethnographic Museum (⊕ *09.00–15.00 Mon–Fri; 200 lek*) Elbasani was an important commercial centre in the 17th century, exporting its leather, fabrics and silverwork throughout the Ottoman Empire. Its craftsmen were organised in no fewer than 45 guilds; the Tanners' Guild had a written statute as early as 1658. The city's traditional crafts are given special attention in Elbasani's museum, in addition to the more usual displays of traditional furniture and costumes. The collection is housed in an 18th-century building where, in 1908, the city's first Albanian-medium school was opened. The following year, Elbasani would be the venue for a famous congress, at which the Roman alphabet was formally adopted as the script for the Albanian language. The Congress of Elbasani also chose the town as the site of Albania's first teacher-training college, which opened later the same year.

The ground floor of an Albanian house was traditionally used for workshops, storage, and – in rural areas – the stabling of livestock. The Ethnographic Museum has used this space to display the tools used in the various crafts practised in Elbasani, alongside examples of the items produced. One room is devoted to wool-working, including the making of felt. The different types of *qeleshe*, or fez, are also displayed and explained.

Another room contains blacksmith's and carpenter's tools, and some of the things that these craftsmen produced. An intriguing bladed device is a tobacco-cutter, of a design still used in the countryside today – the whole leaves are bundled into the hopper and pushed through with one hand while the other works the chopper. Another interesting exhibit is a set of bells, in different sizes for different animals, including an extraordinarily heavy cow bell.

Upstairs, in what would have been the living quarters, the central area is open to a covered wooden balcony (*çardak*). In the summer, the family spent much of its time out here, where the breeze could circulate. The rooms leading off the central space each had their own function and they have been furnished accordingly. In the 'women's room', with its intricately carved wooden ceiling, a beautiful cradle and a tiny embroidered jacket show that this was more like a nursery. The wooden cradle has dragons carved on the ends, to keep the baby from harm. Next to the nursery is where the women spun and wove silk for their embroideries and tapestries. Some

4

The combination of archaeology, ethnography and wartime special operations is not a classic career path, yet Margaret Hasluck achieved success in all three fields. She spent 16 years in Albania, researching and publishing on topics as diverse as Roma customs, Albanian grammar and blood feud. In 1935, she settled in Elbasani, where she is remembered to this day as *anglezka*, 'the little Englishwoman'.

The 'Englishwoman' was born in northeast Scotland in 1885, the daughter of a farmer, John Hardie. Despite her humble origins, she went on to study classics at Aberdeen, one of Scotland's four ancient universities, which had opened its faculties to women in 1892. She graduated from Aberdeen in 1907 and went south, to continue her studies at Cambridge University, where (it should be recalled) women were not awarded degree titles until 1921.

This remarkable young woman then turned her attention to archaeology. She studied at the prestigious British School in Athens (known as the BSA) and took part in excavations in Turkey. In 1912, she married Frederick Hasluck, whom she had met at the BSA.

Their married life would be short, however; Frederick Hasluck died of tuberculosis in 1920. He had published research on the followers of Bektashism (page 22), and his widow used a travel grant from Aberdeen University to return to Albania and conduct her own ethnographic fieldwork there. She became an expert on the customs and traditions of the northern clans, including blood feud – her comprehensive study, *The Unwritten Law in Albania*, was published posthumously; she learned the language well enough to publish *Këndime anglisht-shqip*, a collection of stories which illustrate points of Albanian grammar and vocabulary; and she conducted extensive field research in the mountain villages of Shpati, near Elbasani (see below). There, she became friendly with Lefter (Lef) Nosi, an intellectual and politician who was a signatory of Albania's Declaration of Independence and had served in the country's first government. Over the years, they worked together investigating Albanian folklore and ethnography. In 1936, Nosi sold her a plot of land in Elbasani on which she had a house built.

In April 1939, just before Italy invaded and annexed Albania, Margaret Hasluck was expelled from the country. She ended up in Cairo where, in early

---

raw silk is on the spinning wheel, and some part-woven fabric is on the loom, so that you can see the process; some of the embroideries hang on the walls.

The 'men's room' has a fine plaster fireplace (*oxhak*) and is panelled in wood. Like the nursery, there is a brazier in the middle of the floor. Finally, the 'couple's room' has beautifully embroidered bed linen, a 250-year-old mirror and a wooden dowry chest. The traditional wedding clothes on display include the long surcoat typical of Elbasani.

The museum's rich collection has been well laid out and makes a very interesting display, taking an hour or so to look round. There are explanatory panels in Albanian and English. Access for groups can be arranged outside normal opening hours by calling ☎ 259 626.

EXCURSIONS FROM ELBASANI Top of the excursions list, for anyone with even the slightest interest in religious art, is the Church of St Nicholas at **Shelcani**. This 14th-century church somehow escaped the whitewashers of the atheism campaign. Its interior walls are completely covered with magnificent frescoes painted, in

1942, SOE (see boxes, pages 13–15) recruited her to explore possible ways to encourage resistance in occupied Albania. By 1943, she was the head of SOE's Albanian section. She briefed SOE operatives before they were parachuted into Albania, taught them the rudiments of the language, and provided and collated intelligence.

As SOE came to concentrate on supporting the partisans, at the expense of the non-communist resistance, Margaret Hasluck became increasingly disillusioned. She resigned from SOE in 1944, around the same time as she was diagnosed with leukaemia and told she had only a short time left to live. She was awarded the MBE for her services in 1944.

Meanwhile, Lef Nosi had agreed to participate in the Council of Regency, the Albanian quisling government set up by the Germans after Italy's capitulation. After Albania's liberation, not surprisingly, he was tried and shot. Margaret Hasluck wrote a personal letter to Enver Hoxha, pleading for clemency for her friend. Not only was her appeal unsuccessful, but the communist government put it about that she and Nosi had been lovers, in an attempt to destroy both of their reputations.

Margaret Hasluck died of her leukaemia in October 1948, and is buried with her parents, brothers and sisters in the churchyard of the Scottish village of Dallas. The Marischal Museum at her alma mater, Aberdeen University, holds many of the ethnographic artefacts that she sent back there from Albania, including unusual items such as medicinal minerals and herbs, amulets and children's toys. (The Marischal Museum is no longer open to the public; access to the 'virtual museum' may be requested by emailing e kingsmuseum@abdn.ac.uk.) Some of the folk tales that she and Nosi collected and translated together have been collected and published; see page 282 for details of this and *The Unwritten Law in Albania*.

Margaret Hasluck's house in Elbasani, built on the land she bought from Lef Nosi, is now a state kindergarten. Across the street, also on her land, is a children's home, on the wall outside which is a plaque, unveiled by her nephew in 2010, to commemorate the 125th anniversary of her birth. A statue of her friend Lef Nosi now stands in front of the castle walls on the city's main street.

1554, by the great Albanian artist Onufri (page 123). Better still, the frescoes have recently been cleaned by specialists from the Albanian Institute of Monuments. Images of saints and scenes from the New Testament, such as Lazarus rising from the grave and Christ entering Jerusalem on Palm Sunday, glow in radiant colours. Shelcani is in the Shpati Mountains to the southeast of Elbasani, where Margaret Hasluck conducted much of her ethnographic research (see box above). The road is asphalted most of the way, apart from the last 100m or so up to the church, and it takes about 45 minutes to get there from Elbasani. At the start of the track up to the church, there is a small signpost ('Kisha Shën Kollit') and space to park.

The National Historical Museum in Tirana (page 74) has the original doorway and several icons from the church of **St Gjon Vladimir**, part of a medieval monastery about 5km from Elbasani on the old road to Tirana. According to the inscriptions on the lintel, the church was built by Karl Topia, 'lord of Arbër', in 1382, after an earthquake had destroyed the church that previously stood on the site. Karl Topia was one of the powerful feudal princes, who between them ruled Albania from the middle of the 14th century until the Ottoman conquest (page 10). The church itself is set in a peaceful garden, with the monastic buildings to the side. They are attractive buildings, but the church has been completely restored internally, apart from a large fresco which survives in poor condition behind the altar. It is known locally (for example, by taxi drivers) as Kisha e Shijonit, the Church of Shijoni.

The best-preserved piece of Elbasani's Roman heritage is **Mansio ad Quintum**, a few minutes' drive southwest out of town. The original trading post that grew up at the junction of the Apollonia and Dyrrachium branches of the Via Egnatia (page 8) developed over the years into something much more substantial – an official roadhouse, or *mansio*. Every major Roman road had these; they were intended to provide accommodation and entertainment for government officials and others travelling on important business. Mansio ad Quintum had a bathhouse (how could it not?) and shops as well as accommodation; the baths' hypocausts are particularly impressive. The site is up a track just off the main road towards Durrësi, near the village of Bradasheshi. It is unattended and can be accessed at any time.

Llixhat, the Albanian word for 'spa', is an area of thermal springs about 12km from Elbasani. Over the last decade or so, several new hotels have opened there, but the very first was **Park Nosi Spa Resort** [map, pages 88–9] (*Stacioni Termal Park Nosi; 78 rooms;* \ *04 235 687;* m *068 20 66 546;* w *llixhat.com;* **$**), built in 1932, to an Austrian design, by Lef Nosi's brother Grigor. This lovely historic building requires major investment to bring the accommodation up to international standards, but the quality of the waters has been undisputed since they were first analysed scientifically in 1924. (See box, page 154, for more information about this and other thermal baths in Albania.) The spa has immersion pools and mud baths in which clients are treated for a range of ailments, supervised by specialist doctors. The surrounding grounds – over 50,000m^2 – are partly wooded and partly laid out as gardens. There are eight en-suite rooms; others share toilets and showers on each corridor. Park Nosi is about 30 minutes' drive from Elbasani, following the road towards Gramshi. 'LLixha' buses operate from the bus stop just beyond the market in Elbasani.

Just over halfway between Elbasani and Librazhdi, within walking distance of the Ballkan Resort hotel, the **Miraka Bridge** (Ura e Mirakës) crosses the Shkumbini River. The structure is Ottoman, but there has been a bridge here since at least Roman times – this is the route of the Via Egnatia, which connected the Adriatic coast with Constantinople. The Biçaku restaurant (**$$**) in Librazhdi, with its terrace overlooking the river, is a pleasant spot for a drink or for lunch.

Two nice places for **day hikes** around Elbasani are Lake Banja, an artificial lake created in the 1980s for hydro-electric power generation, but never used; and the gently rolling hills around the (natural) lakes of Belshi, both about half an hour's drive away. There is no public transport to Lake Banja. Local minibuses to Belshi leave from near the market. If you have your own transport (with two or four wheels), it is possible to continue on the same road as far as Kuçova, in Berati region. The drive from Elbasani to Kuçova takes about 2 hours, the second half on a rough road for which a 4x4 would probably be needed in wet weather.

BERATI   *Telephone code: 032*

Berati is one of the oldest cities in Albania and one of the most attractive; the view of its white houses climbing up the hillside to the citadel is one of the best-known images of Albania. The citadel walls themselves encircle the whole of the top of the hill. Within them are eight medieval churches, one of which houses an outstanding collection of icons painted by the 16th-century master Onufri. Berati also has an excellent Ethnographic Museum and several other interesting buildings, including two of the oldest mosques in Albania. Thanks to their historical value, the religious buildings in the citadel were protected from the worst ravages of the atheism campaign (page 16), and in 1976 the government designated Berati a 'museum city', which saved the town centre from communist urban planning.

Berati has been inhabited since the Bronze Age, over 4,000 years ago. The great Tomorri Massif, which rises behind it, was a sacred mountain from very early times and it still hosts a huge Bektashi festival every August. The first traces of building on the citadel date from the second half of the 4th century BC, when the Illyrian Parthini controlled the area.

Berati thrived in the Middle Ages, thanks to its strategic location at the point where the trading routes from the south met the lowland plain. This made it an appetising conquest for successive invaders. The Bulgarian Empire took the city in AD860 and held it – barring a 40-year period during which it was reconquered by Byzantium – until 1018. Berati's second return to the Byzantine fold lasted longer, despite a determined attack by the Angevins, who besieged the citadel for seven months in 1280–81. By the mid 14th century, however, as Byzantium's power waned, Berati and much of the rest of Albania became part of Stefan Dušan's 'Empire of the Serbs and the Greeks'. (For more background to this confusing period in Albania's history, see pages 9–10.)

After Stefan Dušan's death in 1355, the whole of what is now southeast Albania, reaching as far as Kastoria (now in northern Greece) came under the control of the Muzakaj family of Berati, one of the powerful Albanian clans that emerged as the only functioning authorities in the period before the Ottoman conquest. The citadel of Berati fell to the Ottomans in 1417 and, despite an attempt to retake it, led by Skanderbeg (see box, pages 206–7) in 1455, it remained in their hands for nearly 500 years. The mountains of the Berati region were a hotbed of partisan activity during World War II, and the city was the first seat of the Interim Government that came to power in October 1944, under the leadership of Enver Hoxha (see box, page 83).

The name of the city may come from the Turkish word *berat*, meaning an order conferring a decoration, a sort of royal warrant; or it might derive from 'Beligrad', the name the Slavs gave the town, although there is debate about whether this is philologically possible. Berati won recognition as a UNESCO World Heritage Site in July 2008.

GETTING THERE AND AWAY Berati is easy to get to from almost everywhere in central and southern Albania, having good **bus** connections with Vlora, Durrësi and Elbasani as well as Tirana. A new road bridge, on the western outskirts of the city, now takes traffic across the Osumi River, effectively replacing the narrow Gorica Bridge.

The buses from **Tirana** leave every 45 minutes, from 04.30 until about 14.30, from the Shqiponja bus station (page 60). The journey takes about 2 hours and the fare is 400 lek. In Berati, the buses terminate a kilometre or so before the city centre, in the Kombinat district; local buses and taxis are on hand to take passengers into town.

There are several interesting routes **by bike or on foot**, to and from Berati. See pages 127–8 for details.

TOUR OPERATORS The Castle Park Hotel just outside Berati (page 122) offers **rafting** weekends (April to June) through the spectacular canyons on the Osumi River, with two nights' accommodation and a full day on the river. The hotel also organises excursions to places of interest in the Berati area, including the castle and the Çobo vineyard (w *cobowineryonline.com*).

4

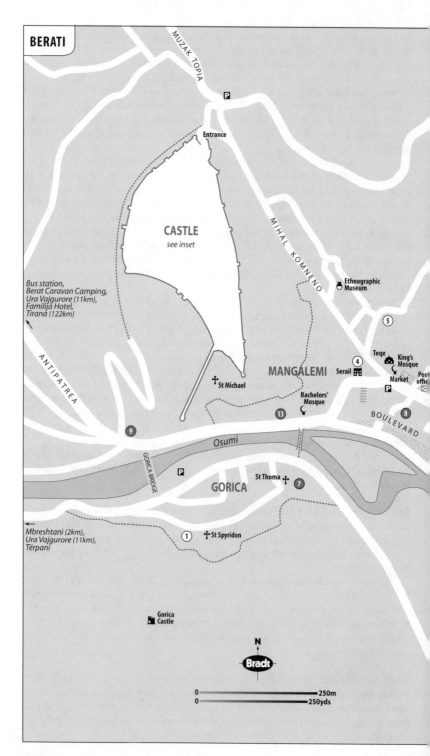

BERATI

MUZAK TOPIA

P

Entrance

CASTLE
see inset

MIHAL KOMNENO

Bus station,
*Berat Caravan Camping,
Ura Vajgurore (11km),
Familija Hotel,
Tirana (122km)*

Ethnographic
Museum

⑤

ANTIPATREA

Teqe
King's
Mosque

Serail ④
Market

Post
offic

MANGÁLEMI

P

† St Michael

Bachelors'
Mosque

⑬

BOULEVARD

⑧

⑨

Osumi

P

GORICA BRIDGE

GORICA

St Thoma †
⑦

Mbreshtani (2km),
*Ura Vajgurore (11km),
Tërpani*

① † St Spyridon

Gorica
Castle

N

Bradt

0 ————— 250m
0 ————— 250yds

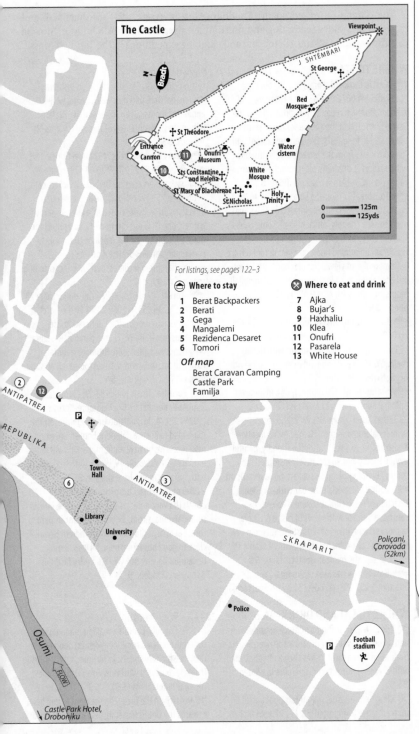

The Castle

J SHTEMBARI

Viewpoint

St George

Red Mosque

St Theodore

Onufri Museum

Water cistern

Entrance
Cannon

11

10

Sts Constantine and Helena

White Mosque

St Mary of Blachernae

St.Nicholas

Holy Trinity

| 0 | 125m |
| 0 | 125yds |

For listings, see pages 122–3

🛏 Where to stay

1 Berat Backpackers
2 Berati
3 Gega
4 Mangalemi
5 Rezidenca Desaret
6 Tomori

Off map
Berat Caravan Camping
Castle Park
Familja

✕ Where to eat and drink

7 Ajka
8 Bujar's
9 Haxhaliu
10 Klea
11 Onufri
12 Pasarela
13 White House

ANTIPATREA

REPUBLIKA

Town Hall

ANTIPATREA

Library

University

SKRAPARIT

Poliçani,
Çorovoda
(52km)

Police

Football stadium

Osumi

FLOW

Castle Park Hotel,
Droboniku

The Tirana-based company Outdoor Albania (page 29) has qualified and experienced guides for **rafting** and, in summer, **river-hiking** trips. Outdoor Albania can also organise hiking, ski touring and climbing expeditions in the Tomorri Massif.

⌂ WHERE TO STAY *Map, pages 120–1, unless otherwise stated*

⌂ **Castle Park** (8 rooms) Rr e Drobonikut; ☎235 385; m 067 20 06 623; e castlepark_2003@ yahoo.it. On the left bank (the Gorica side) of the Osumi River, 1.3km (uphill) out of town; shuttle bus available for guests. Excellent restaurant with splendid views from the terrace; lovely grounds with terraces & children's playground. All rooms en suite with AC, cable TV, balcony, fridge. **$$$**

⌂ **Tomori** (47 rooms, 3 suites) ☎234 462; m 068 20 24 225. Centrally located on the town's main square. Friendly, efficient staff, some English spoken. Lift to all floors; free parking. Good restaurant on ground floor; pizzeria on roof terrace with magnificent views; popular bar, with tables outside in summer, ideal for people-watching. All rooms en suite, with AC, CH, Wi-Fi, TV, minibar, phone. **$$$**

⌂ **Gega** (22 rooms) Rr Antipatrea; ☎234 429; m 069 53 84 435; e hotel.gega@yahoo.com; w hotelgega.com. Bar, restaurant with Italian menu, Wi-Fi, free parking. All rooms en suite with AC, flatscreen TV, fridge. **$$**

⌂ **Mangalemi** (20 rooms, plus 6 in annexe) Rr Mihal Komneno; ☎232 093; m 068 23 23 238; e hotel_mangalemi@yahoo.com; w mangalemihotel.com. Named for its location & also known as Tomi's, after the friendly, helpful owner. Family-run, in sensitively restored 18th-century buildings; English spoken. Good restaurant with traditional specialities; bar with excellent selection of rakis. Çardak (covered balcony), courtyard, terrace with views of castle & city; laundry service; generous b/fast inc. All rooms en suite (some also with bathtub), with AC, cable TV, Wi-Fi, desk, safe, minibar, good curtains. **$$**

⌂ **Rezidenca Desaret** (5 rooms) Lagja 13 Shtatori; ☎237 593; m 069 77 72 732. Spectacular setting high up in Mangalemi; good restaurant; garden; bar; free parking; Wi-Fi. Large, well-appointed rooms, all en suite with AC, TV; large balcony with lovely views of the city towards Mt Tomorri. **$$**

⌂ **Berat Backpackers** (32 beds) Gorica 295; m 069 78 54 219, 069 30 64 429; e info@ beratbackpackers.com; w beratbackpackers.com. Renovated 250-year-old house in Gorica quarter; directions on website; closed in winter. Terraced garden, bar, chill-out room, Wi-Fi, computers for guests, kitchen, washing machine. Day tours to surrounding area. 3 dorms, 4 private rooms, all sharing bathroom facilities; bed linen inc; camping spaces. B/fast inc. **$**

⌂ **Berati** (9 rooms) Rr Veli Zaloshnja, Lagja 28 Nëntori; ☎236 953; m 069 20 74 199; e hotel_berati@yahoo.com. Traditional Berati house, modernised within; Wi-Fi; free parking. Restaurant on ground floor, plus more intimate traditional dining room. Dbl, twin & 4-bed rooms, all en suite with AC, TV, CH, balcony. **$**

⌂ **Familja** [map, pages 88–9] (5 rooms, 1 suite) Rr Kombëtare Ura Vajgurore-Kuçova; ☎0361 22474. Just outside Ura Vajgurore, off the main road to Kuçova. Friendly, English-speaking management; good restaurant, parking. All rooms en suite with AC, cable TV, Wi-Fi; suite has corner bath, smaller rooms have shower. **$**

⚑ **Berat Caravan Camping** [map, pages 88–9] Ura Vajgurore; m 069 42 63 697; e info@ sarandaholidays.com; w beratcaravancamping. com. Set in beautiful garden; 12km from Berati, close to good bus route; open all year. Bar & restaurant on site; free Wi-Fi; laundry facilities; 2 showers, 2 toilets. **$**

✖ WHERE TO EAT AND DRINK *Map, pages 120–1*

✖ **Ajka** Next to St Thoma's Church in Gorica, with a lovely view of Berati across the river. Serves traditional Berati meat dishes such as steak stuffed with cheese or mushrooms. Open fire in winter. **$$$**

✖ **Klea** In the castle, roughly straight ahead from entrance (signposted); ☎234 970; m 069 76 84 861. Friendly, English-speaking management; superbly prepared traditional dishes, good house raki; nice modern toilets. In summer, tables outside in lovely courtyard with views over Osumi Valley. Also has hotel rooms (**$$**). **$$$**

✖ **Onufri** In the castle, on the right as you head towards the Onufri Museum; also known as Koço

Plaku, after the owner. Huge spreads of traditional dishes in cosy, welcoming atmosphere. $$$

✗ **Pasarela** In the modern building opposite the Leaden Mosque. Meat specialities such as stuffed steak & *qofta*. $$$

✗ **White House** On the main road, just beyond the pedestrian bridge on the way out of Berati. Excellent Italian-based menu, best fish in town, wood-fired pizzas, good risotto & pasta. $$$

✗ **Bujar's** In an alleyway off the street opposite the market that connects Rr Kryesore with the Bd; ⏲ lunchtime only. Good-value traditional dishes such as *tavë kosi* & *turli* (page 47). $$

✗ **Haxhaliu** Just beyond the Gorica Bridge on the way out of Berati. The entrance is up the stairs around the corner of the building. Friendly service, good traditional meat dishes such as steak stuffed with cheese. $$

WHAT TO SEE AND DO

The castle The citadel of Berati was first fortified in the 4th century BC by the Illyrian Parthini. At the same time, they also fortified the hill opposite, on the left bank of the Osumi River; the remains of the massive walls there, known as Gorica Castle, can still be seen. The pair of fortresses ensured that the whole river valley could be controlled and defended.

To get to Berati Castle on foot, the easiest way is to walk up Rruga Mihal Komneno (also known as Rruga e Kalasë, 'Castle Street') – the steep cobbled road through Mangalemi, one of the city's protected 'museum zones'. It is also possible to drive this way, although an easier driving route leaves the main road just where it enters Berati from the north and curls around the back of the castle hill; it is signposted in Albanian and English for 'Kala, Castle'. Cars can be parked just outside the outer entrance gate. There are short cuts up the winding stone staircases through Mangalemi, and then through the trees below the citadel, but it is difficult to find the way without a guide.

On the wall by the archway, which forms the outer entrance to the castle, a cross can be seen with the initials MK. This probably dates from a refortification of the citadel undertaken in the 13th century, during the reign of Michael II Comnenus Ducas, Despot of Epirus (page 9). Next to the vaulted inner entrance is a kiosk where a small admission charge is payable, although because the citadel is still inhabited, like Kruja Castle (pages 100–2), by several hundred people, the entrance is never closed. The walls follow the contour of the hilltop in a rough triangle and a network of narrow cobbled streets connects the stone-built houses within them. The huge bust of Constantine the Great (AD306–37) near the entrance was installed in 2003, on the curious grounds that he was one of the Illyrian emperors (even though he was from Niš, hundreds of miles from Berati in what is now Serbia).

Of the 42 churches that the castle walls once contained, only eight remain and, with one exception, they were locked up after the atheism campaign of the late 1960s. The exception was the Church of the Dormition of St Mary (Kisha e Fjetjes së Shënmërisë), a three-naved basilica that was built in 1797 on the foundations of a 10th-century church and which now houses the **Onufri Museum** (⏲ *summer 09.00–13.00 & 16.00–19.00 Tue–Sun, winter 09.00–16.00 Tue–Sat, 09.00–14.00 Sun; 200 lek*), signposted from the inner entrance to the castle.

Onufri was the greatest of a group of Albanian icon-painters – many of them anonymous – of the 16th century. He worked throughout the Balkans, but many of his finest icons were painted for the churches of the Berati citadel. Onufri followed and developed the Byzantine traditions of icon-painting, but his work is special because of his mastery of colour; the red paint he used has the technical name of 'Onufri red'.

The museum was redesigned in 2016 and the exhibition now covers two floors. Over a hundred beautiful icons, from churches in Berati and the surrounding area, are displayed. The earliest are from the 14th century, before icon-painters began to put their names to their work (this is because their purpose was to glorify God, not themselves). Later painters whose names we know, apart from Onufri, include his son Nikolla, David Selenica, Kostandin Shpataraku and the Çetiri (or Katro) family from Korça. Some of the icons combine traditional Byzantine iconography with Ottoman images – a round table, like the *sofra* that can be seen in the Ethnographic Museum, in an icon of the Last Supper (anonymous, 18th century), and the minarets of mosques peeking above the city walls in the icon called 'The Life-Giving Source'. The collection also includes liturgical items, such as crucifixes and Bible covers, examples of the beautiful work of Berati's silver- and goldsmiths.

A preview of some of these lovely icons and objects can be enjoyed on the Berati museums' website (w *muzeumet-berat.al*); the museum shop has a good selection of cards and books about Albanian art. There are toilets behind the shop.

The entrance to the museum is through the church, which is also worth looking around. The ornate iconostasis (altar screen) at the far end was carved in walnut wood and decorated with gold leaf by master craftsmen from the Berati school of the 19th century. The three main icons were the work of Onufri and placed in the church at the time it was built; others were done in the mid 19th century by Johan Katro (pages 132–3). The two manuscripts known as the *Codices of Berat* were discovered in 1968, buried behind the altar – the 6th-century *Purple Codex* is one of the oldest such manuscripts ever found, anywhere – and are now conserved in the State Archive in Tirana.

A walk around the perimeter walls to the **viewpoint** will give you a feel for the size and layout of the castle, as well as offering great views of the city below and the mountains across the river. The 13th-century **Church of St Michael** nestles into the hill below and can be seen to good effect from the Gorica quarter across the river. A path leads up to this church from the main road, but it is not usually possible to gain access. Above the viewpoint, just within the walls, is the **Church of St George** (Shën Gjergji; 14th century), which was converted into a restaurant during the communist period but has now been restored by the parishioners. The Church of St Theodore (Shën Todri) has some surviving frescoes by Onufri. **St Mary of Blachernae** (Shën Mëri Vllaherna) is the oldest church in the castle; local tradition holds that this church was built to celebrate the defeat of the Angevin besiegers in 1281. It was rebuilt in 1578, as the inscription about the narthex door reveals, and its frescoes were painted by Nikolla, Onufri's son.

Almost as old is the beautiful **Holy Trinity** (Shën Triadha), which stands on the slope of the hill just below the inner fortification of the castle (the English text on the information board refers to this, a little confusingly, as the 'citadel'). This part of the castle was built at roughly the same time as the church, in the 13th century. Up in the corner near the entrance is an underground water cistern, dug deep into the rock on which the castle stands, and supported with brick columns and elegant arches. In the 1930s, the Italians adopted a different approach to ensuring the citadel's water supply; they piped spring water across-country from Mount Shpiragu (the 'striped' mountain that faces Mount Tomorri to the west). Sections of the piping can still be seen in the area around the cistern. Information panels have been installed outside each of the churches and at some other points around the castle.

Berati fell to the Ottomans in 1417 and the conquerors wasted no time in refortifying the citadel. They also built two mosques there, the Red and White mosques. Now ruined, both date from the 15th century and are among the oldest in Albania. The **White Mosque**, so called because of the beautiful white stone of which it was built, stands at the corner of the inner fortification opposite the water cistern. The **Red Mosque** lies just outside this area; it was badly damaged by German bombs during World War II and there are plans to restore it, using early 20th-century photographs as reference.

Set into an archway in the outer walls, above the first entrance gate, is a **cannon** that bears the date 1684 and which local tradition claims is English. In fact it may well have been made by the British gun founder Thomas Western (1624–1707). Western carried out contract work for export to the Republic of Venice in 1684; some of his Venetian mortars are in Corfu and one is displayed in the Tower of London. The cannon in Berati is probably a large saker, a widely used gun that fired a cast-iron solid shot of 6–9lb. The emblem engraved on it seems to be the Lion of St Mark, the symbol of the Venetian Republic. The saker may have been captured in battle from Venice (which briefly occupied nearby Vlora in 1690–91), or simply acquired through trade. (I am grateful for this information to Nicholas Hall of the Royal Armouries.)

The town Just off Rruga Mihal Komneno is a beautiful traditional house, built in the late 18th century and inhabited until it was turned into the **Ethnographic Museum** (⏰ *winter 09.00–16.00 Tue–Sat, summer 09.00–13.00 & 16.00–19.00 Tue–Sat, 09.00–14.00 Sun; 200 lek*). A visit to the museum is an excellent opportunity to learn about Berati architecture and find out more about people's way of life until only a few decades ago.

Like traditional houses elsewhere in Albania, the ground floor was not used for living in, but for storage and household activities such as pressing olive oil or distilling raki. Part of the ground floor of this house has been converted to represent a medieval bazaar, with examples of traditional costumes and displays about the crafts traditionally practised in Berati, such as metalwork, felt-making and embroidery. The first floor, where the family lived, is accessed by an external stone staircase that leads to the *çardak* – a vast balcony on which they spent most of their time in the hot summer months, with raised covered sections, called *qoshke*, which functioned like outdoor rooms, with carpets, divans and windows. In the centre of the first floor is the kitchen, lit by a skylight; all the rooms are furnished with items that the inhabitants used in their day-to-day lives, such as looms for wool and silk, cooking utensils and dinner services. Two rooms were used for entertaining guests and have screened galleries (*mafil*) in which the women of the household sat while their menfolk ate and drank in the room below. In one of these visitors' rooms, the door is ingeniously designed so that when the head of the family opened it to his guests, it closed the access to the steep wooden steps to the women's gallery. In the centre of this room is a beautiful dinner service of engraved copper, set out on a *sofer* – a low, circular table around which the diners sat on the carpeted floor. Images of the building and its contents can be viewed on the Berati museums' website (w *muzeumet-berat.al*); the Albanian text about the Ethnographic Museum is very interesting but, unfortunately, almost none of it is translated.

Berati's historic mosques are located fairly close together near the modern town centre. The **Bachelors' Mosque** (Xhamia e Beqarëve), on the main boulevard, was built in 1827 for the use of the city's (unmarried) shop assistants, and its external walls are beautifully decorated with wall paintings. The **Leaden Mosque** (Xhamia e Plumbit), so called from the covering of its dome, dates from 1555. The oldest of the three – and one of the oldest mosques in Albania – is the **King's Mosque** (Xhamia e Mbretit), behind the market at the foot of Rruga Mihal Komneno, the street up to the castle. It has a beautifully carved and painted wooden ceiling, and a large women's gallery. It is possible to see inside the mosque immediately after prayer times; at other times it is usually locked.

The two-storey building with the arched porch across the courtyard from the King's Mosque was a *teqe* of the Sufi order of the Khalwati (or Halveti). It has a beautifully painted ceiling surrounded by frescoes, stained-glass windows and painted wall-cupboards. The inscription above the door reveals that the *teqe's* construction was funded by Ahmed Kurt Pasha, who governed Berati and much of the rest of central Albania in the second half of the 18th century (see box, pages 254–5, for more about the Albanian *pashaliks*). It is thought that he was buried in a now-empty grave behind the *mihrab*. Ahmed Kurt Pasha was also responsible for building the Gorica Bridge and the governor's palace (Seraglio, *Sarayet*) on the other side of Rruga Mihal Komneno, using stonework he plundered from Apollonia (pages 105–6). The buildings of the Mangalemi Hotel (page 122) once formed part of the Pasha's palace. There are informative and helpful panels, in English and Albanian, next to the various historic buildings around the town.

Three neighbourhoods of Berati are designated as 'museum zones', with restrictions on the alterations which may be made to the properties within them. Mangalemi and Kalaja (the castle) are two; the third, Gorica, lies on the other side of the Osumi River. The two sides of the town are connected by the **Gorica Bridge**, a narrow stone bridge built in the 18th century to replace the wooden bridge that had been used until then.

After the Ottoman conquest, Gorica became the Christian quarter; two churches survive there. A modern footbridge leads from opposite the Bachelors' Mosque to just below the little **Church of St Thoma**, tucked into a corner of the cliff at the eastern end of Gorica. A shrine behind the church marks where a local saint is said to have left his footprint in the rock. This is also the best end of Gorica from which to see the citadel and the houses of Mangalemi below it. **St Spyridon's** is the larger of the two churches; it is clearly visible from the castle viewpoint above, but it can be a little tricky to find once you are into the narrow paths in the heart of Gorica. To get to the Illyrian fortifications known as Gorica Castle, turn right over the Gorica Bridge and then head left up the hillside until you reach the top.

Those who are interested in Byzantine religious architecture might also visit the 12th-century church in the nearby village of **Perondia**. It is usually kept locked, but it is sometimes possible to gain entry by asking around in the village for the key-holder. The carved wooden iconostasis dates from 1786; a small amount of badly damaged fresco survives on the walls. The icon of The Birth of St Mary in the Onufri Museum came from this church. Perondia and its church are about 15km from Berati, signposted to the right, off the road to Kuçova from Ura Vajgurore.

The mountains Mount Tomorri is a long, complex massif, most of it over 2,000m high. It runs roughly north–south to Çorovoda from Lake Banja south of Elbasani, with its highest peak, Çuka e Partizanit (2,414m), pretty much halfway along it. An easy way to see some of the spectacular mountain scenery of the Berati area is by taking the good, asphalted road (about 50km) down to Çorovoda, the district capital of Skrapari. Buses leave Berati for Çorovoda at 08.20, 09.00 and 11.00 and take about 1½ hours each way; they are supplemented by minibuses which can be picked up at the eastern end of town, near the stadium.

About half an hour out of Berati, just off the main road in the village of Fushë-Peshtani, is **Kantina Nurellari** (w *nurellariwinery.com; see page 49 for further contact details*), where visits and wine-tastings can be arranged. A few miles further on, about halfway between Berati and Çorovoda, is the little town of Poliçani, one of communist Albania's main arms production centres. The huge factory complex on the valley floor once employed 4,500 people; now the factory lies almost idle, with the only work being the production of ammunition for the Albanian police and other clients. The main source of employment in the area nowadays is the quarrying and preparation for export of the decorative stone tiles that you will see stacked by the roadsides as you drive through the area. After Poliçani, the river valley narrows and the mountains become even more dramatic. Bogova is a pleasant spot to stop, for a drink or something to eat in one of its cafés.

The buses from Berati stop in Çorovoda, an uninspiring communist-era town which serves as the transport hub for trips out to the stunning scenery that surrounds it. Rural buses operate from Çorovoda to the main villages in the district and taxis can be hired in the main square. It has reasonable hotels and restaurants; there is an ATM below the Turizmi Hotel.

A couple of kilometres out of Çorovoda, along the Gjerbësi road, is a lovely little Ottoman bridge over the Çorovoda River. Once this linked trans-continental trade routes; now it's in the middle of nowhere. The village of Gjerbësi is high up on the northeastern flank of Mount Tomorri; the road to it is rough, reaching 1,200m above sea level at one point, but the scenery is spectacular, with beautiful cliffs that give way to strangely coloured mountains of an almost lunar barrenness. There are cafés in Gjerbësi that can arrange meals, given a couple of hours' notice.

This road continues up Mount Tomorri as far as the Kulmaka *teqe*, where the Bektashi saint **Abaz Aliu** is buried. This is said to be the oldest *teqe* in Albania and it is one of the holiest sites of Bektashism (page 22), the focal point of a great pilgrimage every August. The scenery is wonderful, with little villages and farms clinging to the mountains on either side of the Tomorrica River. A 4x4 is needed to reach the *teqe*; from Çorovoda, you should allow at least 4 hours there and back.

The **Osumi Canyons** are several kilometres of stunning multi-coloured cliffs, which drop down to the fast-flowing Osumi River below. Rafting excursions to the canyons can be arranged at the right times of year; see pages 119 and 122. The Osumi Canyons are 20 minutes' drive along the road to Çepani; there is a lovely picnic spot at the top of the cliffs.

Where to stay, eat and drink

Turizmi (17 rooms) Çorovoda; m 068 20 57 424, 068 40 10 042. Also known locally as 'ish-VEFA'. Constant water & electricity, large restaurant with terrace. Good-sized dbl bedrooms, slightly smaller twins, all en suite with small TV. **$$**

Walking, hiking and cycling Mount Tomorri offers magnificent hiking opportunities, but the seriousness of this mountain should not be underestimated. There are no neatly marked footpaths, no hiking maps and no mountain rescue service. Your hotel may be able to arrange a guide for you. Appropriate footwear and clothing are essential, and you should be in reasonable physical shape. Do not assume that you will have a mobile-phone signal; leave a note of your planned route with someone – perhaps the management of your hotel.

A less intimidating option is to head towards Mount Shpiragu on the left bank of the Osumi River. A minor road leads more or less westwards through Gorica, then starts to climb past some destroyed barracks and other military buildings, with tunnels into the hillside visible on the other side of a small river. After an hour or so you reach a pretty reservoir, just before the village of Mbreshtani, which is a nice spot for a picnic. An alternative walk is to the village of Droboniku, a couple of kilometres up past the Castle Park Hotel (page 122); this is especially nice in springtime when the cherry trees are in blossom.

If you have your own 4x4 or two-wheeled transport, you could approach or leave Çorovoda using the ancient trading route along the Tomorrica River, between the

Tomorri and Kosnica ranges. This route connects with the town of Gramshi, at the southern end of Lake Banja (page 118). It is only passable in dry summer weather, since it follows the river, crossing and recrossing it, and there are no bridges between Gjerbësi and Gramshi. It is essential to be well equipped on this route, since there is almost no habitation and there is unlikely to be any other traffic. It takes the villagers about 6 hours to walk from the Gjerbësi Bridge to Gramshi. From Gramshi you could continue north to Elbasani, or you could head for Macedonia or northern Greece along the Devolli River. (See page 141 for information about that route.)

With rugged cycles or motorbikes, or on foot, another route out of Berati takes you via Çorovoda to the district of Përmeti, continuing south on the Çepani road and then on to Frashëri (pages 152–3), or to Këlcyra via Prishta; it is about 40km from Çorovoda to Përmeti as the crow flies. Another possibility, on foot only, is to cross the Ostrovica mountain range from Çorovoda to Vithkuqi or Voskopoja, in the district of Korça. The road is reasonable as far as the village of Potomi, in Skrapari district. A minibus operates between Çorovoda and Backa (check times locally). From Backa a path leads east-northeast to Çemerica; the track to Vithkuqi goes off to the east there. For Voskopoja, continue through Marjani, a beautiful stone village, to Gjergjavica. From there it is an easy walk to Voskopoja (thanks to John Shipton for his route notes). Two days should be allowed for this hike. See the rough map at the start of the next chapter (page 130) for guidance on these routes.

The Italian-built road over the 900m-high Gllava Pass to Këlcyra is, at the time of writing, impassable for any but the most rugged of 4x4 vehicles. It is fine as far as Tërpani on the Berati side and Ballabani on the Këlcyra side; the problem is the pass, where lack of maintenance has caused the road to deteriorate in recent years.

5

The Southeast

KORÇA   *Telephone code: 082*

Southeastern Albania is a fascinating and little-explored corner of the country, with dozens of medieval churches, a wealth of prehistoric sites, the wild Gramoz mountain range and the beautiful Ohrid and Prespa lakes. Korça, the regional capital, is an ideal base from which to visit these attractions. It is also home to the magnificent National Museum of Medieval Art. The city itself is refreshingly civilised, with streets relatively free of the litter that disfigures most of the rest of the country, traffic that recognises the existence of some sort of highway code, and clean mountain air. Its altitude (850m above sea level) and inland position make it very cold in winter and spring, and delightfully cool in summer.

The people of Korça are justifiably proud of their town's cultured and tolerant traditions. It was one of the main centres of the Albanian cultural renaissance (Rilindja Kombëtare), which created the sense of national identity that ultimately led to the country's independence from the Ottoman Empire (page 11). The first Albanian-medium school was opened here in 1887, with the first girls' school following four years later, and the town was one of the focal points of the movement to standardise the Albanian alphabet.

Korça's history became rather chequered in the early 20th century. The Epirote Insurrection of 1913 saw much of southern Albania raided and terrorised by Greek irredentists, who sought its incorporation into Greece. Korça was occupied and its Albanian-medium schools closed, until the Greek government ordered its troops home in June 1914. This respite was short-lived, however, and a year later a Greek army returned to occupy Korça and Berati, laying waste to Muslim villages and farmlands and driving streams of refugees across the country to Vlora. In November 1916, the French occupied Korça and set up the so-called Autonomous Albanian Republic of Korça. As leader, they appointed the Rilindja activist Themistokli Gërmenji, who made French and Albanian the official languages of the autonomous republic and set up Albanian schools. The following year, however, he was accused (probably wrongly) of collaborating with the Axis Powers, sentenced to death by a French military court and executed in November 1917. Not surprisingly, this turbulent period saw a great deal of emigration, mainly to the USA, where Korçans still make up a large proportion of the Albanian-American community.

GETTING THERE AND AWAY   From northern **Greece**, several bus companies run up to Korça from Kastoria (called Kosturi in Albanian), 70km away. There are also buses from Thessalonica (Selaniku) and Athens. If you have your own transport, the small crossing at Tre Urat (called Mertzani by the Greeks), between Konitsa in Greece and Leskoviku in Albania, will take you on to the beautiful mountain road up to Korça via Erseka.

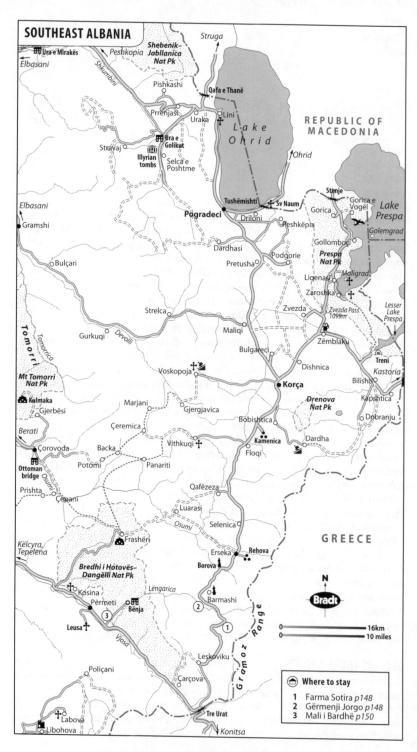

SOUTHEAST ALBANIA

Struga

Elbasani

Ura e Mirakës

Peshkopia

Shebenik–
Jabllanica
Nat Pk

Shkumbini

Pishkashi

Qafa e Thanë

Prrenjasi

Lini

Uraka

Lake
Ohrid

REPUBLIC OF
MACEDONIA

Stravaj

Ura e
Golikut

Illyrian
tombs

Selca e
Poshtme

Ohrid

Elbasani

Tushëmishti

Stenje

Gorica e
Vogël

Lake
Prespa

Gramshi

Pogradeci

Driloni

Sv Naum

Gorica

Golemgrad

Peshkëpia

Dardhasi

Podgorie

Gollomboçi

Prespa
Nat Pk

Bulçari

Pretusha

Liqenasi

Maligrad

Zaroshka

Lesser
Lake
Prespa

Strelca

Zvezda

Zvezda Pass
1099m

Gurkuqi

Devolli

Maliqi

Zëmblaku

Treni

Bulgareci

Kastoria

Voskopoja

Dishnica

Bilishti

Mt Tomorri
Nat Pk

Korça

Drenova
Nat Pk

Kapshtica

Kulmaka

Gjerbësi

Marjani

Gjergjavica

Bobishtica

Dobranju

Berati

Çeremica

Vithkuqi

Kamenica

Dardha

Çorovoda

Backa

Floqi

Ottoman
bridge

Potomi

Panariti

Osumi

Prishta

Çepani

Qafëzeza

Këlcyra,
Tepelena

Luarasi

Selenica

GREECE

Osumi

Frashëri

Rehova

Bredhi i Hotovës-
Dangëlli Nat Pk

Lëngarica

Erseka

Borova

N

Kosina

Barmashi

Përmeti

Bënja

Bradt

Leusa

Vjosa

2

1

0   16km

0   10 miles

Leskoviku

Poliçani

Çarçova

Gramoz Range

Where to stay

1 Farma Sotira p148
2 Gërmenji Jorgo p148
3 Mali i Bardhë p150

Labova

Tre Urat

Libohova

Konitsa

From **Macedonia**, there are two main border crossings into Albania, one at Qafa e Thanë, southwest of Struga, and the other at Tushëmishti, at the southern end of Lake Ohrid. If you are travelling without your own transport via Qafa e Thanë, you will probably have to arrange for a Struga taxi to take you up to the border; during daylight there are always Albanian taxis and minibuses on the other side. See page 141 for information about crossing the border at Tushëmishti.

Within Albania, there are frequent buses to Korça from Tirana, running from early morning until early afternoon. They leave from the Southeast bus station, behind the Faculty of Economics [63 H6]; in Korça, the bus station is across the boulevard (Boulevard Fan Noli) from the Old Bazaar. The journey takes about 3½ hours; the fare is 600 lek. Buses also serve Korça from other cities, including Vlora and Berati. Some minibuses to Erseka leave from near the town hall, others from the main bus station (see page 147 for further details).

See pages 146–8 for the long but scenic route through the Gramoz Mountains and along the beautiful Vjosa River. Buses serving this route leave Gjirokastra at 07.00 every day except Sundays, and Përmeti at 07.00 every day. In the other direction, they leave Korça every day at 06.00 (for Gjirokastra) and 13.00 (for Përmeti).

For suggested routes on foot or by bike into the Korça area, see pages 128 and 141–2.

TOURIST INFORMATION The tourist information office (w *korca.al*; ⊕ *summer 09.00–21.00, winter 09.00–19.00*) is in the stone building on the corner of Theatre Square (the pedestrianised main square). The friendly, English-speaking staff can advise on where to stay and what to do, not only in the town but also in the rest of the Prefecture, which includes Pogradeci, Voskopoja, the Prespa Lakes and the Gramoz Mountains. The office stocks maps, brochures and souvenirs; 19 cycling itineraries, of various length and difficulty, are also available, with a route map which can be downloaded free on to your smartphone. Guided city tours and excursions can be arranged. A good, detailed town plan is posted outside.

In the piazza in front of the cathedral is an information board with maps of the town and the surrounding region. Information plaques around the city explain the main places of interest.

WHERE TO STAY *Map, pages 134–5*

🏠 **Grand Hotel Palace** (84 rooms) Theatre Sq; 243 168, 244 339; e info@grandhotelpalacekorca.com; w grandhotelpalacekorca.com. Great location overlooking the main square. English spoken at reception; lift; good restaurant; Wi-Fi on ground floor; free parking for clients; conference facilities. All rooms en suite (some with bathtub), with CH, TV, bedside light, minibar & direct-dial phone. **$$$**

🏠 **Life Gallery** (15 rooms, 4 suites) Bd Republika 55; 246 800, 243 388; m 066 70 90 222; e info@lifegallery.al; w lifegallery. al. Sophisticated contemporary-styled rooms in a traditional 1924 building. English spoken; professional service; lift. Restaurant, bars, courtyard with water-feature, conference facilities.

All rooms have large, well-equipped bathrooms with superb shower, fluffy dressing-gown & slippers, good toiletries & mirror; excellent lighting, thick curtains, AC, LCD TV, Wi-Fi, well-stocked minibar, phone, desk. **$$$**

🏠 **Regency** (16 rooms, 2 suites) Rr Ismail Qemali 7; 243 868/9, +1 516 520 5227 (US); m 068 20 30 070; e info@hotelregencyalbania. com; w hotelregencyalbania.com. English spoken; professional service. Restaurant, bar, lift, Wi-Fi; conference facilities. All rooms en suite with AC, CH, TV, phone. **$$$**

🏠 **Behar Koçibelli** (530 rooms) Bd Sh Gjergji; 243 532, 230 925; m 069 98 17 654; e hotel. kocibelli@gmail.com. Great location overlooking the main square. Some English spoken at reception; parking for guests. Lift; good restaurant with some Korça specialities (**$$**); bars; Wi-Fi; casino; gym; conference facilities. All rooms en suite, with shower screen & hairdryer (some also bathtub), AC, CH & cable TV. 3 luxury rooms (**$$$$$**) have jacuzzi & excellent shower. **$$**

🏠 **George** (37 rooms) Rr e Mborjës; ☎ 243 794; **m** 069 20 83 112; **e** hotel.george@hotmail.com; **w** hotelgeorge.info. 1.2km from town centre (walking distance, though uphill on the way back to the hotel!), quiet & set in attractive grounds; free parking; terrace bar, formal restaurant & bar; Wi-Fi. All rooms en suite with CH, TV & bedside lights; some have balcony with mountain views. **$$**

🏠 **Kristal** (82 rooms) Rr Konferenca e Labinotit; ☎ 248 992/3; **m** 069 20 98 321, 068 58 88 555; **e** rezeartkote@yahoo.com. On the hillside above the town, the former Workers' Camp (Kampi

i Punëtorëve) has been well modernised & is comfortable. Wonderful views – city to the front & pine forest to the rear. Large restaurant; parking. For those on foot, there are shortcuts which, for the fit & energetic, would make it a 20–30min climb from the town centre. A range of room types, inc apts (**$$$$**), all rooms en suite. **$$**

🏠 **Vila Themistokli** (2 rooms) Bd Sh Gjergji 7; **m** 069 94 45 029; **e** vilathemistokli@gmail.com. A restaurant-with-rooms in the former home of Themistokli Gërmenji (page 129). English spoken; good restaurant with open fire. Excellent cooked b/fast inc freshly squeezed orange juice. Rooms have period furniture, art on walls, thick curtains, CH, flatscreen TV, bedside light, ample electrical sockets, & modern, well-lit bathroom with good shower. **$$**

✗ WHERE (AND WHAT) TO EAT AND DRINK Map, pages 134–5

Korça specialities include *kërnaca*, small cylindrical meatballs, and *lakror*, a large, round *byrek* (filo-pastry pie). There are several restaurants in the city that serve these traditional dishes; two of the best are listed below. Korça families, though, are more likely to go out of town for their family lunches at weekends. One popular destination is the village of Boboshtica, a few kilometres south of Korça – it is signposted at the turn-off from the main road to Erseka; one option is Taverna Antoneta (**m** *068 22 64 963*; **$$$**). Boboshtica is also well known for another Korça speciality, raki distilled from mulberries (*mani*). Another popular destination for family lunches is Dardha, in a lovely alpine setting (1,344m above sea level) and with a good hotel (*Hotel Dardha*; **m** *068 20 60 362*; **$$$**).

✗ **Liceu** Rr Sotir Gura; ☎ 211 208; **m** 069 23 98 529; 069 36 62 303. Opposite the former Lycée Française, in a traditional Korça house; open fire in winter, tables in garden in summer. Grilled meat, *kërnaca, lakror*; friendly, informal atmosphere. **$$$**

✗ **Secret** Bd Republika 31. Grilled meat & fish, pizza, pasta, etc. English menu, English spoken. **$$$**

✗ **Taverna Vasili** Rr Kostandina Gaçe 11; ☎ 246 610; **m** 069 21 48 583. Formal dining; interesting photographs of the town displayed in restaurant. Excellent local specialities, good service. **$$$**

WHAT TO SEE AND DO

National Museum of Medieval Art (*Muzeu Kombëtar i Artit Mesjetar; Bd Fan Noli*; **m** *067 51 38 333*; ⊕ *09.00–14.00 & 17.00–19.00 Tue–Sun; 700 lek*) Located in a new, purpose-built gallery, the National Museum of Medieval Art has the largest collection of icons in Albania, with 7,500 objects spanning seven centuries. It also has a fine collection of other liturgical art, such as hammered silver Bible covers and gold-plated crucifixes. Around 400 works are on permanent display, and the new museum provides space for conservation and restoration laboratories. The exhibition is spread over two floors and there is a lift.

The ground floor displays some of the most famous works by Albania's best-known icon-painters: the 16th-century Berati artist Onufri (page 123), the 18th-century David Selenicasi and the 19th-century Katro (Çetiri) and Zografi families. But there was a long tradition of icon-painting before artists began to sign their work – Byzantine painters believed their work was to glorify God, not themselves – and the earliest works in the museum were painted by these anonymous artists. They include a 13th-century icon of St Nicholas, in lovely warm colours, from one of the churches in Vithkuqi, and 14th-century icons from St Mary's Church in Mborja (page 138): another St Nicholas, this one almost monochromatic, and the stunning Archangel Michael in his armour. Dozens of icons fill the full height of the wall of the gallery, with a viewing platform from which to study them.

In the 16th century, a school of artists began to emerge in Berati, a powerful diocese and an economic centre. The best known of the icon-painters there was called Onufri; almost a whole room on the first floor is devoted to his work. They include a set of Royal Doors (the central double doors in the iconostasis, through which only the priest may pass), with six scenes painted on carved, gilded wood. There are several dramatic, complex icons which tell stories such as the Nativity (with a very Albanian-looking shepherd playing a flute), the Raising of Lazarus, the Transfiguration and the Descent into Hell. Many other works by Onufri and other painters of the Berati School are displayed in the Onufri Museum in Berati Castle (pages 123–4).

The Berati School influenced all other Albanian artists right into the 18th century, but new influences were beginning to creep in too. Kostandin Jeromonaku's *Christ Pantocrator*, dated to 1694, portrays Christ seated on a throne decorated with motifs from Islamic art. Contact with western European artistic schools, inspired by the Enlightenment, brought new developments in the 18th century. An early example of this is the complex and detailed *Akathistos Hymn* by the 18th-century artist Kostandin Shpataraku, with its portrayal of the Western image of the Coronation of St Mary.

Two icon-painting families dominated the later 18th and 19th centuries: the Zografi brothers and their sons, and the Katro family. Kostandin and Athanas Zografi worked all over the Balkans and many of their frescoes have survived in the churches of Voskopoja (pages 138–9). Their work shows clear Venetian influence, with careful brushwork and a more realistic portrayal of the human figure than had been seen before. A particularly interesting painting here is Athanas Zografi's depiction of the Council of Nicaea (*The First Ecumenical Council*), dated to 1765. The Zografis' sons worked with the family of Johan Katro (also known as Johannes Çetiri), whose icons of John the Baptist and St George, surrounded by scenes from his life, are displayed in the room at the end of the first floor. Dominating this room is an entire iconostasis, with most of its original icons, salvaged from the Church of St Nicholas in Rehova (page 147) when the churches were closed during the atheism campaign (page 16).

The early 19th century marked the end of the old style of Albanian icon-painting. Early 20th-century work, such as the icons on display from Dardha, saw a complete break with the post-Byzantine tradition.

Back on the ground floor, there are civilised toilets and a museum shop, which stocks high-quality publications for sale about Albanian religious art, reproductions of some of the icons in the collection, and smaller souvenirs such as mugs. At least 2 hours should be allowed for this fascinating and beautifully laid-out museum.

Archaeological Museum (*Rr Mihal Grameno;* ⊕ *09.00–14.00 & 17.00–19.00 Tue–Fri, 09.00–noon & 17.00–19.00 Sat–Sun; 200 lek*) The items displayed in Korça's Archaeological Museum come from sites all over the southeast region, including the neighbouring districts of Devolli, Kolonja and Pogradeci. The whole region is a prehistorian's paradise, with many very large tumuli (raised barrows)

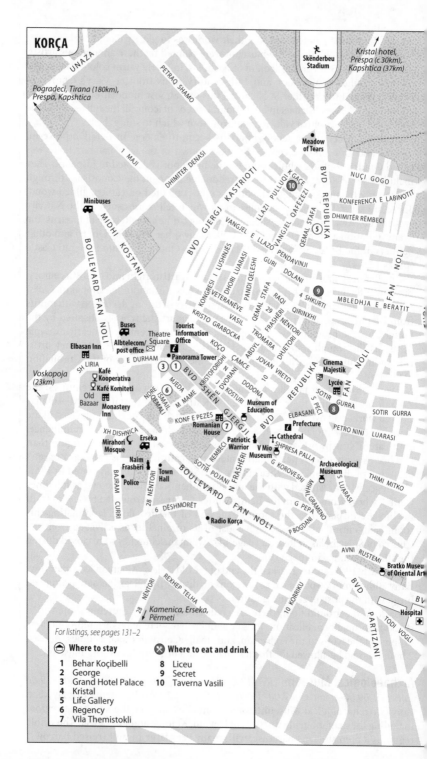

KORÇA

Skënderbeu Stadium

Kristal hotel, Prespa (c 30km), Kapshtica (37km)

Pogradeci, Tirana (180km), Prespa, Kapshtica

UNAZA

PETRAQ SHAMO

Meadow of Tears

NUÇI GOGO

KONFERENCA E LABINOTIT

DHIMITËR RËMBECI

1 MAJI

DHIMITER DENASI

BVD GJERGJ KASTRIOTI

BVD REPUBLIKA

FAN NOLI

Minibuses

MIDHI KOSTANI

LLAZI PULLUQI K GAÇE

10

VANGJEL E LLAZO PENDAVINJI

QEMAL STAFA

5

VANGJEL QAFEZEZI

BOULEVARD FAN NOLI

KONGRESI I LUSHNJES

VANGJEL E LLAZO PENDAVINJI

GURI DOLANI

DHORI LUARASI

PANDI QELESHI

QEMAL STAFA

RAQI QIRINXHI

4 SHKURTI

9

MBLEDHJA E BERATIT

VETERANËVE

VASIL

29 FRASHËRI

NENTORI

KRISTO GRABOCKA

TROMARA

Buses

Theatre Square

Tourist Information Office

Panorama Tower

KOÇO

CAMCE

ABDYL

JOVAN VRETO

DHJETORI

Cinema Majestik

Elbasan Inn

Albtelecom/ post office

E DURHAM

3 1

BVD SHEN GJERGJI

KRISTOFORIDHI

N DYORANI

10

DODONA

REPUBLIKA

Lycée

SOTIR GURRA

SH LIRIA

Kafé Kooperativa

Kafé Komiteti

Old Bazaar

Monastery Inn

NDRE ISMAIL QEMALI

MJEDA

M MAME

N KOSTURI

Museum of Education

ELBASANI

8

SOTIR GURRA

XH DISHNICA

KONF E PEZES

Romanian House

7

Prefecture

PETRO NINI LUARASI

Mirahori Mosque

Erseka

Naim Frashëri

Town Hall

SOTIR POJANI

REMBECI

FRASHËRI

Patriotic Warrior

V Mio Museum

Cathedral

SHPRESA PALLA

Archaeological Museum

THIMI MITKO

Police

BAJRAM CURRI

28 NËNTORI

BOULEVARD FAN NOLI

G KOROVESHI

MIHAL GRAMENO

S LUARASI

6 DËSHMORËT

Radio Korça

G PEPA

P BOGDANI

AVNI RUSTEMI

Bratko Museu of Oriental Art

REXHEP TELHA

NENTORI

10 KORRIKU

BVD PARTIZANI

TODI VOGLI

BV

Hospital

28

Kamenica, Erseka, Përmeti

For listings, see pages 131–2

Where to stay

1 Behar Koçibelli
2 George
3 Grand Hotel Palace
4 Kristal
5 Life Gallery
6 Regency
7 Vila Themistokli

Where to eat and drink

8 Liceu
9 Secret
10 Taverna Vasili

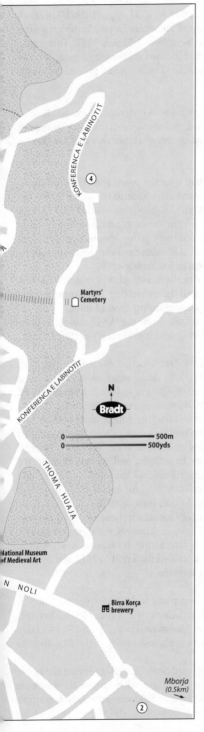

Martyrs'
Cemetery

KONFERENCA E LABINOTIT

KONFERENCA E LABINOTIT

Bradt

0 ————————— 500m
0 ————————— 500yds

THOMA HUAJA

National Museum
of Medieval Art

N NOLI

Birra Korça
brewery

Mborja
(0.5km)

excavated – one of these, Kamenica, is open to the public and has an excellent site museum (page 140). There is a model of a tumulus in the Korça museum, showing how the graves were arranged concentrically.

The exhibition begins with a display of examples of the different types of tools used by Neolithic people (made of bone and horn as well as stone), their ceramics and their cult figurines. From very early on, they built lake-dwellings, using water to protect themselves from wild animals or human enemies. The site at Maliqi, excavated in the 1960s, was the largest in the Balkans (15ha) and was inhabited continuously from the Chalcolithic (3000–2200BC) to the Archaic period (8th–7th century BC). A scale model of the Maliqi settlement illustrates how these wooden houses were constructed on stilts.

Ceramics from the Bronze and Iron ages (from about 2100BC) show the developing influence of Greek city-states such as Corinth, which began to colonise the coast of what is now Albania in the 7th century BC. Other interesting items on display include bronze and silver bracelets and brooches, grave markers (*stelae*) and one of only three Archaic helmets ever found in Albania. In the courtyard the mosaic floor of a Roman bathhouse has been relaid. Here there are also Ottoman-period gravestones, one with a Star of David, and a sarcophagus from the 1st century AD.

The house in which the museum is located dates from the early 19th century, and is in two separate parts. The main building, where the museum's offices and workshops are, was the family residence, with the traditional covered balcony (*çardak*) on the first floor. The archaeological exhibition is in the *han i mysafirëve*, the guest quarters, where visitors to the family were received and accommodated. The Neolithic section is in what used to be a kind of drawing room, where weddings and other parties were held – the band used to play on the little stage behind the stairwell.

Museum of Education (*Bd Shën Gjergji;* m *069 28 34 720;* ⊕ *09.00–14.00 &*
17.00–20.00 daily; 200 lek) The very first school anywhere in which subjects were
taught in the Albanian language opened in Korça on 7 March 1887. This was a
triumph for the Rilindja campaigners who had focused on the language as the key
to building an Albanian national consciousness. The Rilindja's polemicist, Sami
Frashëri, wrote:

> The sign of nationhood is language; every nation supports itself on its language. Those
> who forget their language, and leave it behind, and speak another tongue, in time
> become people of that other nation whose language they speak, and they abandon their
> own nationality.

The Korça school went through ups and downs over the years, getting closed down
intermittently whenever the country's Ottoman rulers noticed its existence, but the
movement it began proved unstoppable. A girls' school was opened in Korça in
1891 – the first girls' school in Albania of any kind, never mind the first to teach in
Albanian – and teachers travelled around the country giving lessons in impromptu
classrooms or even the open air. The first Albanian-medium teacher-training
college (Shkolla Normale) opened in Elbasani in December 1909.

The Korça school is now a Museum of Education, with photographs of the first
pupils and teachers of both 'first schools' and an interesting collection of early
textbooks. There are usually temporary exhibitions on the ground floor.

The Museum of Education is easily identifiable from the 'ABC' sculpture in its
garden. If the building appears to be closed during opening hours, try rattling the gate.

Bratko Museum of Oriental Art (*Muzeu i Artit Oriental Bratko; Bd Fan Noli;*
m *069 21 56 561;* ⊕ *10.00–13.00 &* *17.00–18.00 daily; small charge*) The most
unexpected museum in Korça – perhaps in all of Albania – is the private collection
of Oriental art donated to his home town by Dhimitër Borja, who made his fortune
in the USA from film and photograph laboratories. The collection is housed in a
purpose-built museum, an attractive modern building on Fan Noli Boulevard, just
beyond the new court buildings. It includes one whole room of lovely Oriental
carpets and another of objects from the Far East, India and Africa, all collected
by Mr Borja or given to him during his travels around the world. Chinese and
Japanese prints and paintings hang on the walls. A third room contains a display of
signed photographs of famous Americans and other memorabilia.

The Bratko museum is very much a collector's museum; those who find modern
museums too thematic and interactive will love it. Many of the items on display
are quite beautiful and the whole collection is fascinating. It takes about an hour to
look carefully at everything. The museum was closed for a refit in 2017 and some of
the above details may have changed when it reopens.

A walk around the town centre The best place to begin exploring Korça is
the city's main square, where the tourist information office is (page 131). Dwarfing
everything else in the square is the modern **Panorama Tower**. A lift (*50 lek*) takes
you to a viewing platform from which there are good views of the city and the
mountains that surround it.

From the square, the pedestrianised Boulevard Shën Gjergji leads past the house
of Themistokli Gërmenji (page 129) now a restaurant-with-rooms, the Museum
of Education (see above), the so-called Romanian House – a beautiful example
of Korça architecture – and the former Greek Consulate, still the property of the

Greek state and sadly derelict. Looking down the boulevard is the statue of the kilted **Patriotic Warrior** (cast by Odhisë Paskali, the sculptor of imposing statues in several other Albanian towns and cities), above its water-feature. The road running across the end of Boulevard Shën Gjergji is Boulevard Republika, which bisects the historic centre of Korça. Directly across from the Patriotic Warrior is the Orthodox Cathedral, built in the 1990s near the site of the original cathedral, demolished during the atheism campaign (page 16). On the other side of the piazza is the Prefecture for the Korça region; the information panel on the piazza has maps of the city and the region. A whole neighbourhood of 19th-century houses lies in the warren of streets behind the cathedral, built of local stone, slaked with lime and roofed with small, curved tiles. The Archaeological Museum (pages 133–5) is a beautiful example of a traditional house of this period. Another that is open to the public, in theory (✆ 244 332 *for access*), is the former house and studio of the Albanian Impressionist painter, **Vangjush Mio** (1891–1957). Many of his paintings are exhibited here; others hang in the National Gallery of Arts in Tirana (page 76).

Along Boulevard Republika, and in the cobbled side streets on either side of it, the buildings are a little later and generally in better condition. These houses, with their columns and wrought-iron gates, have a more European feel than the fortress-like houses of Gjirokastra or Berati – a sign of the French influence on Korça in the early 20th century. The Cinema Majestik, on the right a few minutes' walk down the boulevard, was built in 1926 and recently restored by the Imperial cinema chain. It screens subtitled Hollywood movies and, from time to time, Albanian-language films. Down the side street just before the cinema is the French **Lycée** (Liceu Francez), where Enver Hoxha went to school and was later a teacher.

At the end of the boulevard is the **Meadow of Tears** (Lëndina e Lotëve), a small park that marks the spot where, in the 19th and early 20th centuries, families would gather to wave goodbye to their emigrant men or to wait for them to return – at the time, it was where the town ended and the open road began. At the little shrine here, people still light candles for their faraway loved ones. There are good views of the town and the surrounding countryside from the **Martyrs' Cemetery** (Varreza e Dëshmorëve; access by steps is signposted from Boulevard Republika).

Return to the main square along Boulevard Gjergj Kastrioti, or meander back through the side streets to see more traditional architecture. To the west of the square, across Boulevard Fan Noli, is the recently restored **Old Bazaar** (Pazari i Vjetër). Korça's geographical location made it a centre for Ottoman trade with Italy and (after independence) Greece. By the late 19th century, the bazaar had more than a thousand shops. Inns – known by the Turkish word *han* – provided accommodation for different groups of traders: the buildings of the Elbasan Inn and the Monastery Inn have survived and were being restored at the time of writing. The Elbasan Inn (Hani i Elbasanit), was used as a basic hotel throughout the 1990s and 2000s and may reopen during the lifetime of this guidebook.

The centre of the Old Bazaar is a square, with cafés and souvenir shops around it and also in the cobbled streets leading off it. Kafé Komiteti, like its sister-bar in Tirana, is furnished and decorated entirely with original household items from communist days. It stocks a huge range of artisan raki and liqueurs – 140 different types! – and has three discrete areas, each with a different theme. The ground-floor bar has Illyria radio sets, wooden stools and marquetry on the walls. A second bar is laid out like a country house, with cushions and small tables. Upstairs has old suitcases serving as tables, a rare collection of crockery plates on the walls and, in a quirky touch, a toilet designed to look like a raki still. Kafé Kooperativa celebrates Albania's agricultural heritage, with tables and benches made from bales of straw, old-fashioned wood-burning braziers, and drinks such as mulled wine. Events take place in the square throughout the year, including the Spring Fair, beginning in the evening of 28 February; the annual Carnival, in early June; and the Korça Beer Festival in mid-August.

A few minutes' walk south from the Old Bazaar is the **Mirahori Mosque**, built in 1484 and thus one of the oldest mosques in Albania, although it was rebuilt in the late 18th century. Crossing the little park behind it will lead you out on to Boulevard Fan Noli, an attractive tree-lined boulevard that runs along the southern edge of the old quarter. If you have any energy left, turn right on to this boulevard and head uphill, past the National Museum of Medieval Art, to the **Birra Korça brewery**, founded in 1928. Guided tours of the brewery can be arranged when staff time permits; ask the security officers at the gatehouse.

St Mary's Church, Mborja
The village of Mborja, up beyond the brewery in the southern outskirts of Korça, was once the market town for the whole area, including Voskopoja and Vithkuqi – its name comes from the Greek *emporion*, meaning 'market'. Its little 14th-century church, known locally as Kisha e Ristozit ('Church of the Resurrection'), is a dignified and attractive building of local stone roofed with slates, like so many historic Orthodox churches in southern Albania. Unlike most of them, however, its marvellous frescoes have survived the ravages of time and of the atheism campaign.

The outer section of the church, the narthex, has a particularly enchanting series of frescoes, which begins with a disembodied hand holding a balance in which people are being weighed and found wanting. The unhappy-looking sinners are then whooshed down a chute into the jaws of a dragon, raped, or attacked by serpents. The inner part of the church (the naos) is tiny, with a beautiful dome; this is the original, cross-in-square church. It can be rather dark and a torch will be useful. The frescoes on the walls here show the Resurrection and assorted saints, but they have survived less well and the colours are not as vivid. The original icons, such as the breathtakingly beautiful St Michael, are in the National Museum of Medieval Art (pages 132–3).

To reach the church, bear left from the George Hotel, following the small sign for 'Ristozi 200m', and continue up the hill through the village until you see the church on the left. The villagers are used to foreign tourists and will help you to locate the key-holder. It takes about 40 minutes to walk from the town centre. Urban buses run up Boulevard Fan Noli as far as the George Hotel.

VOSKOPOJA

In the early 18th century, when the Industrial Revolution was just getting under way in Britain, Voskopoja was the largest city in the Balkans, bigger even than Athens or Sofia, with a population of about 35,000. It had the first printing press in the region, and an academy where artists were trained to create frescoes and icons for the churches in Voskopoja and elsewhere. Voskopoja itself had no fewer than 24 churches, two in each neighbourhood of the town, plus a basilica in each quarter. This past glory is remarkable. Towards the end of the 18th century, the city was plundered and burned several times, and it was completely supplanted in importance by the rapidly growing Korça. Today Voskopoja is a remote village, with a population of just a few hundred peasant farmers, mostly Vlach (page 19). Only seven churches have survived and some of these are in such disrepair that they are not open to the public.

One of the four basilicas was the Church of St Nicholas, or Shënkoll, which was built in 1726 at the height of Voskopoja's wealth and power. To find it, follow the sign up to the left as you enter the village from Korça, past the local council office. The church is usually kept locked, but the neighbours are used to foreigners trying to visit it and will go and look for the priest if you ask them. While you are waiting for him, you can admire the patterned brickwork of the exonarthex (portico) and the frescoes within it. These were painted by the brothers Kostandin and Athanas Zografi (page 133), whose work was in great demand throughout the Balkans. The bell tower was added later – originally there was another church, to the left as you look from the fence by the bell tower, which joined St Nicholas's to form a U-shape.

The interior frescoes, painted by David Selenicasi (from Vithkuqi), are in better repair than those outside, with beautiful rich colours. The iconostasis is original – the fire damage that can be seen on part of it was caused during World War II – but the icons that were once set in it are now in the National Museum of Medieval Art in Korça. The ornately carved throne was given to the faithful of Voskopoja from the episcopate of Durrësi in 1758, as can be seen from the inscription.

The basilica of St Thanas (Shën Athanas), built in 1724, is down the hill on the other side of the village; you will see its pale stone bell tower before you see the shingled roof of the church, tucked into the lee of a hillock. This technique of 'hiding' the church was more common in the 17th century, when it was a condition imposed by the Ottomans (this is also why the bell tower is often of more recent date than the body of the church). St Thanas's has a beautiful arcaded exonarthex with frescoes depicting scenes from the Apocalypse, painted by the Zografi brothers. Within, extending right around the walls of the naos, is an extended cycle of the martyrdoms of the saints, with lots of grisly detail.

St Mary of the Dormition (Shën Maria e Fjetjes) is one of the largest basilicas in Albania, holding up to a thousand worshippers; its size demonstrates how wealthy and powerful Voskopoja was at the time it was built (1699). The astonishing frescoes around its three-naved naos include a beautiful Pantocrator surrounded by saints, with the four evangelists at the four corners of the dome. There are more frescoes behind the iconostasis. There is a charge of 200 lek per person to visit these two churches.

High up in the forests above the village is the Monastery of St Prodhromi, the oldest building in Voskopoja. The church was built in 1632, with various wings of the monastery added later and now mostly ruined apart from a 20th-century section where the caretaker lives. The church is small, with a beautiful iconostasis; the entrance hall, or narthex, is reminiscent of a Bektashi *teqe* in its layout and furnishings. The monastery is signposted from the centre as 'St John the Forerunner'. The road up to it is in reasonable condition as far as the Akademia Hotel; unless you are in a 4x4 vehicle you should park there and walk the remaining few hundred metres.

Those with a particular interest in art and architecture will also want to visit the eight surviving churches in **Vithkuqi**, which once rivalled Voskopoja in the level of its development. Like Voskopoja, it was destroyed several times before it was finally supplanted by Korça.

GETTING THERE AND AWAY Both Voskopoja and Vithkuqi are about 25km from Korça; the drive takes about an hour each way. There are **buses**, but it is unlikely you will get there and back in the same day. If you do not want to stay overnight, you could agree a fare with a **taxi** driver to take you up there, wait, and bring you back to Korça.

WHERE TO STAY, EAT AND DRINK There are several small guesthouses in both villages, in addition to the Akademia Hotel listed here. The tourist office in Korça will be able to advise on these (page 131). The Akademia is very popular in the summer and it is advisable to book before making the journey up to Voskopoja.

🏠 **Akademia** (29 rooms, 11 chalets) Voskopoja; m 069 20 23 047; e info@ hotelakademia.al; w hotelakademia.al. The former 'Pioneers' Camp' above the village of Voskopoja, fully modernised; 2,286m above sea level; set in lovely gardens. English spoken. Good restaurant with traditional dishes; free Wi-Fi; bar, recreation centre, conference room, laundry service; hiking guides, horseriding & skiing can be arranged. Choice of chalets & rooms, all en suite with CH & TV. **$$**

PREHISTORIC SITES

The **Tumulus of Kamenica** (m *069 29 08 193, 069 26 87 009;* ⊕ *09.00–14.00 & 17.00–20.00 daily; 200 lek*) is one of the most significant prehistoric burial sites in the western Balkans. Three groups of graves have been excavated to date, with the remains of 420 humans in total. The earliest group dates from the late Bronze Age, the 12th or 11th century BC. The bodies were arranged within a circle 13m in diameter and covered by a tumulus (or barrow). During the Iron Age, the tumulus grew as more generations were buried in it. By the 7th century BC, the burial mound was 3m high. The people of Kamenica then began to bury their dead in new sites around the edges of the tumulus, sometimes surrounding the body with stones or even simple walls. These graves seem to have been family burials; DNA analysis of the skeletons in this group has shown that they were related to each other, whereas in the earlier tumulus there is no genetic connection. One of those buried was a woman who was at the start of the ninth month of her pregnancy – the skeleton of the foetus was still in her womb, meaning that she did not die in childbirth but of some illness. This is the only example of such a case found anywhere in Europe.

Unlike most prehistoric sites in Albania, Kamenica is very accessible to non-specialist visitors. The three excavated grave-groups can be viewed and part of the tumulus has been built back up, with earth, to its original height. The site museum has an excellent exhibition, in English and Albanian, which explains the history of the tumulus and the archaeological research that has been done there. A scale model of the site shows its various components. Replicas of some of the human remains and items found during excavation are also displayed. The site is easy to get to – it is only 8km from Korça, just off the main Korça–Erseka road. The turn-off is signposted for 'Tuma e Kamenicës', just before the village of Kamenica, and the minor road (less than 1km) is asphalted all the way to the site entrance. To get there by public transport, you can use any bus for Erseka, or beyond, and ask the driver to let you off in Kamenica.

The tumulus at **Rehova** (page 147) is the largest ever discovered in Albania, with nearly 300 graves. As well as the human remains, 700 pottery objects were excavated, including elegant double-handled jugs and rare double-cupped vessels. The findings have been published, in Albanian with English translation and full illustrations (*Tuma e Rehovës*, Skënder Aliu, Korça, 2012). The small museum in Rehova has an exhibition about this important site.

Another significant prehistoric site is the **Treni Cave** at the western tip of Lesser Lake Prespa (page 145). Excavations within the cave in the 1960s revealed that it was inhabited from the Neolithic period throughout the Bronze Age. On the cliff face opposite the cave, overhanging the lake, there is prehistoric rock art, a wonderful scene of hunters on horseback pursuing a deer. The entrance to the cave is sometimes protected by a gate; anyone who is especially keen to see inside should ask the staff of the Archaeological Museum in Korça (pages 133–5) to arrange access. There is no public transport to this site and some rough walking is involved. A reproduction of the rock art is displayed at the National Historical Museum in Tirana (pages 73–4).

Pogradeci lies on the southwestern shore of Lake Ohrid (called Ohër or Ohri in Albanian), a large (358km²), deep lake bisected by the international border between Albania and Macedonia. Ohrid is a tectonic lake, formed by movements in the earth's crust, and it has unique species of fish. It is fed by underground streams from Lake Prespa, about 10km away (pages 145–6). These streams bubble up in places to form attractive pools and backwaters – one of these is at Driloni, on the way to Macedonia, and another can be visited at Sveti Naum, just across the border (and, indeed, part of Albania until King Zog gifted it to Yugoslavia in 1925). Lake Ohrid's only outlet is the Black Drini River, which leaves it at Struga, on its northern tip, and flows through a corner of Macedonia before re-entering Albania.

The deepest parts of Lake Ohrid are nearly 300m, and below about 100m its temperature is a constant 6°C. Closer to the shore, however, the water warms up in summer to a very pleasant 20–21°C, and there are places to swim on both sides of the lake. The Macedonian side tends to be built up and busier, while the Albanian shore is quieter, although in high summer Pogradeci becomes quite lively.

Pogradeci's waste water is properly treated, not released straight into the lake, and so it is safe to swim there. There is a long stretch of sandy beach on the eastern side of town, towards the border. Further on in the same direction is Driloni, where the underground streams from Lake Prespa bubble to the surface. The restaurant at Driloni, surrounded by weeping willows, has tables and chairs set out by the pools formed by these springs, where you can sit with your drink and watch the swans go by.

The attractions of Pogradeci itself are pretty much limited to strolling around in the sunshine and eating fish, but it is also a good base for several interesting excursions (pages 143–5). The park along the lakeside has benches looking out on the water, and several attractive statues, including one of the poet Lasgush Poradeci. The author Mitrush Kuteli, extracts from whose stories are translated in this book, was also from Pogradeci.

GETTING THERE AND AWAY Pogradeci is only 4km from the Tushëmishti border crossing at the southern end of Lake Ohrid; it is about an hour's drive from Qafa e Thanë, southwest of Struga at the northern end of the lake. Qafa e Thanë is the main crossing between Albania and Macedonia; during daylight there are always **taxis and minibuses** waiting on the Albanian side. The Tushëmishti crossing can be reached on foot from the resort and hotel at Sveti Naum on the Macedonian side, by means of a path along the lakeshore. Transport on the Albanian side is not quite as reliable as at Qafa e Thanë; the earlier in the morning you get there the more chance you will have of finding a taxi waiting. If you plan to stay overnight in Pogradeci, you could telephone your hotel in advance and ask the management to send a taxi to come and meet you at the border. There are a couple of small hotels within walking distance of the border post on the Albanian side.

Frequent **buses** run between Tirana and Pogradeci, from early morning until early afternoon (later in the summer). They leave from the Southeast bus station, behind the Faculty of Economics [63 H6] and take less than 3 hours. From Korça, the journey takes about 45 minutes and the fare is 150 lek.

Pogradeci is well situated for several interesting cycle (or motorbike or 4x4) routes. From Maliqi, between Pogradeci and Korça, a minor road goes off to the west and follows the Devolli River until it flows into Lake Banja (page 118), just northwest of the small town of Gramshi (about 95km). From Gramshi, you could either continue north to Elbasani, or double back southwards, this time along the

The Southeast POGRADECI

5

River Tomorrica. An ancient track follows the Tomorrica upstream before curling around the base of the Tomorri Massif to Çorovoda, south of Berati (pages 127–8). Another interesting route, starting from either Pogradeci or Elbasani, is the road that links Librazhdi and Peshkopia (about 100km), which runs through very remote mountains and along the border with Macedonia. See pages 178–82 for more information about Peshkopia.

TOURIST INFORMATION The tourist information office (⏱ *09.00–17.00 Wed–Mon*) is in the piazza with the fountains, where the town hall is. It stocks a range of information leaflets and sells books, postcards and souvenirs. A useful street plan is posted outside the town hall. The municipality's website (**w** *bashkiapogradec.al*) has information, in Albanian only, about Pogradeci and nearby attractions.

⌂ WHERE TO STAY *Map, below*

⌂ **Royal** (25 rooms) Bd Rreshit Çollaku; ☎ 223 158/9; **m** 069 20 68 700; **e** hotel_royal08@yahoo.com; **f** Hotel royal pogradec. Right on the lakeside, fully modernised. Panoramic lift (lake views) to all floors; rooftop bar & restaurant with spectacular views; free Wi-Fi throughout; friendly, helpful staff, some English spoken. All rooms non-smoking, with nice en-suite bathroom, shower screens, hairdryer, some have bathtub; CH, AC, TV, bedside lights; most have lake view, some have good-sized balcony, furnished in summer. **$$**

⌂ **Enkelana** (100 rooms) Bd Rreshit Çollaku; ☎ 222 010; **m** 069 20 94 646, 069 40 52 956; **e** info@enkelanahotel.com; **w** enkelanahotel.com. Right on the lakeside, fully modernised. 2 lifts; restaurant, pizzeria, large terrace bar overlooking lake; free Wi-Fi throughout; souvenir shop. Direct access to beach; pedalos for hire; outdoor pool with separate section for children; sauna; conference room with simultaneous translation facilities. All rooms en suite with AC, LCD TV, fridge & small balcony, some with stunning views over the lake. **$**

✗ WHERE (AND WHAT) TO EAT AND DRINK *Map, below*

Lakes caused by plate tectonics are often home to species that do not occur elsewhere (Loch Ness is a tectonic lake, for example) and Lake Ohrid is no exception. Notably, it has two unique species of trout, both of which taste excellent. *Salmo letnica*, called *koran* in Albanian, has a delicate taste similar to that of sea trout; *Salmo ohridanus*

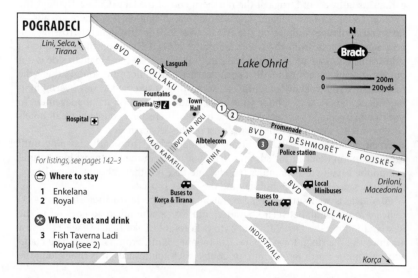

(*belushkë*) is smaller and tastes more like its cousin the rainbow trout. They are widely available in the restaurants around Lake Ohrid, but the populations in the lake are vulnerable to pollution and overfishing and so you will be doing the wild fish a favour if you eat the farmed ones.

One of the best places to eat *koran* is just before you get to Driloni from Pogradeci: a gravelled road off to the right leads to a fish farm (signposted 'Rritja e Koranit', ie: 'trout farm'), where you can choose your trout straight from the net and drink the restaurant's draught wine as you wait for it to be grilled. In town, there are several restaurants along Bulevardi Dëshmorët e Pojskës; a cheap-and-cheerful option is Fish Taverna Ladi (**$$**), just beyond the square. The best place for a formal dinner is currently the Royal Hotel (**$$$**).

EXCURSIONS FROM POGRADECI

Lini About 15 minutes' drive north of Pogradeci, just before the turn-off to the border crossing at Qafa e Thanë, is the village of Lini, on a promontory that forms a sheltered cove in Lake Ohrid. Above the village, on a bluff with lovely views of the lake and the Macedonian mountains, are the ruins of a 6th-century church. The walls have been partially restored so that the outline of the building can be seen – a single nave with an apse and two conches on either side, giving it a kind of five-leafed clover shape. Other buildings surround the church, including a deep cistern, brick-built and sealed with cement. The church and some other buildings are paved with fine mosaics. As usual in Albania, these are kept covered to protect them from the elements; at Lini, however, a small mosaic has been left covered with a tarpaulin that can be lifted up so that it can be seen. It shows two peacocks (or rather peahens) eating grapes that spring from a *kantharos*, a wine jug: wine is the symbol of the blood of Christ, while peacocks symbolise Paradise and everlasting life. It is a privilege to be able to see this beautiful mosaic; please do not forget to cover it up again before you leave the site.

Getting there and away To get to the church from the village, you can either climb the steps that begin opposite the mosque, or you can drive or cycle up the rough track that begins near the (modern) church. It takes about 20 minutes to walk; the last 50–100m are not drivable.

Where to stay
Motel B&B Lin (3 rooms) m 069 45 04 577.
Near the church; nicely furnished en-suite rooms, all slightly different; 2 dbls, 1 twin; shared terrace overlooking lake. Boat trips can be arranged. **$$**

Illyrian royal tombs The magnificent rock-hewn tombs at Selca, in the mountains to the west of Lake Ohrid, offer a rare insight into the funeral rites of Illyrian kings. Selca was first settled in the Bronze Age and became a royal residence in the 4th century BC. This was the territory of the Dassaretes, whose capital was the modern town of Ohrid, on the other side of the lake. They cut three tombs into the rock face for their kings, the earliest in the second half of the 4th century. It measures 6.5m by 4m, with an antechamber leading into the burial chamber, where a stone bed held the body of the deceased king. The other tombs are from the 3rd century. It is thought that one of these, a two-level tomb with Ionian 'columns' carved above the actual grave, may have held the remains of King Monun (page 87). This is because the bas-relief of a helmet that decorates the entrance is just like a real helmet, discovered in the

One of the few things people think they know about Albania is that it is covered in bunkers. As so often in this fast-changing country, what everyone knows is no longer the case.

In 1971, the Central Committee of the Albanian Party of Labour (as the ruling Communist Party was called) resolved to create a network of bunkers across the country. The building programme lasted from 1975 to 1983 and saw thousands of small single-person pillboxes sunk into the fields and hillsides, especially in strategic border areas. The exact number is not known; a figure that is often quoted is 173,000.

It is commonplace to sneer at the bunkers, but the military strategy which inspired them is solid. During World War II, the Albanian resistance fighters were generally best at mountain-based guerrilla warfare. They spent most of their time in the hills and came down to the plain only to carry out attacks. This modus operandi proved highly successful and it therefore made considerable sense to try to adapt it to the post-war situation in which Albania found itself.

The idea behind the bunkers was that they enabled this kind of mountain warfare to be conducted down on the plain. The small bunkers were laid out in lines radiating down from a large command bunker and had a line of sight to it. The large bunkers were permanently manned; the small ones were not. In the event of an invasion, every able-bodied male was expected to collect a gun and take up position in his assigned pillbox until ordered to leave it.

The commanders in the large bunkers had radio contact with their superiors, and from their positions high up on the hill they could control the road or valley along which the invaders would be coming. The men further down the hill could receive visual orders by looking through the slit on one side of their pillbox, and shoot the invaders through the other.

Those who consider it paranoid to think that your country is about to be invaded should remember that between 1947 and 1953 Britain and the USA did in fact attempt to infiltrate anti-communist agents into Albania. These attempts failed dismally; all the agents were captured almost as soon as they landed, and were either killed on the spot or executed after being tried as spies.

Until a decade ago, arrays of these small pillboxes, with their command bunkers above them, were very visible all over Albania. They were set 1–1.5m into the ground, a thick concrete casing over a steel framework, and were difficult for individual farmers to remove; they sometimes used them as outhouses or to store animal feed. Recently, however, enterprising Albanians have realised that the high-quality steel within them can be sold very profitably as scrap metal; explosives are used to break the concrete casing so that the metal can be extracted. There are now very few of these communist-era pillboxes left, although some of the larger ones are being preserved as tourist attractions. The Checkpoint installation in central Tirana (pages 81–2) includes a cross-sectioned pillbox that shows how they were constructed.

At the time of writing, it is still possible to see arrangements that display the strategy that lay behind their positioning on the hillside at the Bay of Palermo and around the junction for the border crossing at Qafa e Thanë, at the northern end of Lake Ohrid, among other places. Earlier bunkers can also be spotted, for example the long World War II bunkers at the turn-off to Apollonia (page 104).

Ohrid area during World War I and now in Berlin, which is inscribed with Monun's name. A little theatre beside the tombs, also carved out of the rock, may have been used during the funeral rites. The third tomb, which also has carved 'columns' at its entrance, is set a little apart; there are steps up to it and it is linked to the other two by a path. A fourth tomb, below the others, was built with stone blocks, some of them with chiselled decoration. The royal palace must have been on the summit of the hill above the tombs; excavation in this area continues. It is worth climbing at least part of the way up for the views. The Dassaretes chose a beautiful spot to lay their kings to rest.

The road is asphalted all the way to the village of Selca e Poshtme, leaving the highway at Uraka, just east of Prrënjasi; the last few kilometres beyond the village, up to the entrance to the site, are paved and can be tackled in any reasonably sturdy car. A path leads across a field and up to the tombs; it can be slippery in wet weather. There is a lovely Ottoman bridge (Ura e Golikut) on the way from Uraka to Selca, one of many built on the sites of much older bridges that formed part of the trade route which, in the 2nd century BC, became the Romans' Via Egnatia (page 8). Asphalting of the southern section of this road, via Dardhasi, is under consideration, which would create a very attractive alternative route between Korça and central Albania. A bus serves Selca e Poshtme from Pogradeci, a journey of just over an hour. The bus leaves Pogradeci around lunchtime and does not return until the following morning, but it would be a good option for those with tents.

THE PRESPA LAKES

The water that bubbles up so prettily at Drilon and Sveti Naum has travelled through about 10km of subterranean channels from another tectonic lake. Greater Lake Prespa is separated from Lake Ohrid by the Mali i Thatë Mountains. Mali i Thatë means 'the dry mountain', and it is so called because the limestone that forms it sucks Lake Prespa's water underground, leaving no visible rivers (this geological formation is called karst). The larger of the two Prespa Lakes, usually called simply 'Lake Prespa', has a surface area of 273km² and straddles the borders between Albania, Greece and Macedonia. The smaller, Lesser Lake Prespa, is only 45km², all but 6km² of which are in Greece. In 2000, the whole Prespa basin was designated as a Transboundary Park, the first cross-border protected area in the Balkans. The lakes are rich in wildlife and, in particular, are home to the largest population of Dalmatian pelicans (*Pelecanus crispus*) in the world.

Although it is quite close to Korça, the Albanian part of Greater Lake Prespa was, until recently, rather remote and difficult to reach, which means that the economy of the villages around the lakeshore is still based almost entirely on small-scale farming and fishing. The upgrading of the road over the hills from the highway has started to bring them some welcome income from tourism. Prespa is an ideal base for a few days of gentle hiking, birdwatching or just relaxing in the peaceful atmosphere; it is less than an hour's drive from Korça and so a day trip is perfectly feasible for those with their own (motorised) transport.

The main attraction is the island of Maligrad (meaning 'little town' in Macedonian, the native language of the villagers of the Prespa area). This small, uninhabited island rises steeply from the turquoise water of the lake. In the 14th century, people built a church here, within a natural rock shelter, and beautified it with frescoes outside and in. The church was too remote to attract the attention of the atheism campaigners (page 16) and so both it and its frescoes have survived, although the latter have been badly damaged by modern graffiti. As well as visiting the church, it is fairly straightforward to climb up to the summit of the island, a

5

tranquil spot covered with wild flowers and the remains of another, ruined, church. From the summit, there are good views of the snowy mountains on the western shore and of Lake Prespa's second island, Golemgrad ('big town'), which lies in Macedonian waters. A low spit of land at Maligrad's northwest has tiny beaches where you can swim when the weather is warm enough: Lake Prespa is 850m above sea level and the water is noticeably colder than Lake Ohrid, 150m lower. The boat trip out to the island is a good opportunity to see pelicans and pygmy cormorants (*Phalacrocorax pygmeus*) up close. The management of your hotel will be able to arrange a boat for you; the price depends on the number of people on the trip and its duration.

The point at which Lake Prespa drains into the karst is up at the northernmost corner of Albania's part of the lake, near the village of Gorica e Vogël. The cliffs around it are riddled with caves and sinkholes; broken reeds and other lake debris cluster around the outflow, providing sustenance to fish of all sizes. On the other side of the lake, the road ends just beyond Zaroshka, but there is a footpath beyond the (modern) church along the lakeshore and past a tiny chapel built into the rock face. Another, larger, cave church lies just across the border in Greece.

GETTING THERE AND AWAY The village best geared to visitors is Zaroshka, with hotels and restaurants. It is about 45 minutes' drive from Korça; the road is asphalted all the way. The administrative centre of the Prespa area is Liqenasi, served by a daily **bus** from Korça; it leaves Liqenasi at 07.00 and returns, from the local bus station in Korça, at 13.00. Otherwise, any bus from Korça to Bilishti will drop you at the petrol station ('*në karburant*') just before the village of Zëmblaku. Informal **taxis** wait at the petrol station for passengers to Liqenasi, Zaroshka or any of the other villages around the lake; the going rate is 1,000 lek. It is a very steep 17km from the petrol station to Liqenasi.

Zaroshka is about 30 minutes' drive from the Macedonian border at Stenje; the border crossing closes at night. Liqenasi has a health centre but there are no ATMs; bring sufficient cash from Korça or Bilishti.

 WHERE TO STAY, EAT AND DRINK Both hotels have good restaurants, busy at weekends, offering fresh fish, grilled meat, salads, and Macedonian wine at very reasonable prices.

Aleksandar (10 rooms) Zaroshka; **m** 068 25 49 759. On left just before entrance to village, in a stunning location overlooking the lake. Owners exceptionally kind & helpful; boat trips & other excursions can be arranged. Excellent restaurant ($$$); tables outside in garden with views of the lake & Maligrad Island. All rooms en suite with lake-view balcony. **$**

Ilo (6 rooms) Zaroshka; **m** 068 26 04 383 (Albanian number), +389 7666 7035 (Macedonian number). In the village, on the lakeshore. Boat trips can be arranged. All rooms en suite; 3 have balcony with lake view. **$**

THE GRAMOZ MOUNTAINS

The Gramoz range rises like a wall between Albania and Greece, with some of its summits over 2,500m high. These are serious mountains, with harsh weather conditions and a tough life for the people who live among them. Luckily for the visitor, a road runs along the Albanian side of the range, well surfaced for most of the way, which allows the spectacular scenery to be enjoyed in relative comfort. It is a good route for cyclists, although the narrow road means that you have to keep your wits about you. The gradients are much easier southbound, from Korça to Përmeti. There is public transport along the whole route: a bus leaves Korça for Gjirokastra at 06.00 (not Sundays) and for Përmeti at 13.00 (daily).

About 40km south of Korça is **Erseka**. At 900m above sea level, this is the highest town in Albania and the mountains that surround it give it a very alpine feel. It has a small Ethnographic Museum in the main square. Fans of Socialist Realist art will like the monument outside the museum, with its kilted warriors and the communist star still intact on the Albanian flag. The Inxhujo Hotel (🖰 *081 222 474*, **$**), in the square where the buses stop, has rooms, a restaurant and reasonable public toilets for customers.

In the mountains just above Erseka, the village of **Rehova** has a small museum, with information about the highly significant Rehova tumulus (page 140), and the church from which the iconostasis and several of the icons in the National Museum of Medieval Art were taken. Rehova is an attractive village in beautiful surroundings, but it is not an easy place to find one's way around. Anyone planning a special visit to see the museum should ask the staff at the Archaeological Museum in Korça (pages 133–5) to phone ahead and arrange for their Rehova colleague to meet you at the entrance to the village (the author wishes she had followed this advice). There are several guesthouses in Rehova – the tourist information office in Korça (page 131) can help with reservations, or there is an information panel at the entrance to the village – and it would make a good base for a few days' hiking.

Buses leave Korça for Erseka until around midday; some go from the main bus station opposite the Old Bazaar, while others wait near the town hall (see map, pages 134–5). You could also take one of the buses that continue through the Gramoz Mountains and tell the driver you want to get off in Erseka. The journey takes about an hour and the fare is 200 lek. There are usually taxis waiting where the buses stop in Erseka; it takes about 20 minutes to reach Rehova on foot, a very pleasant walk through lovely countryside.

It is about 100km from Erseka to Përmeti (pages 148–51). Beyond Erseka the road begins to climb, up startling hairpin bends, and the scenery becomes more and more dramatic. A statue by the roadside, of a partisan with a child, commemorates the **Massacre of Borova**: German reprisals for a partisan attack in 1943, after which the Wehrmacht returned to Borova and slaughtered over a hundred of the villagers, many of them burned alive inside the church. A second partisan statue surveys the valley, just beyond the village of Barmashi. The road rises again, through dense conifer and beech forests, which open out from time to time to reveal the towering mountains on either side. After another descent through more open country, another climb takes the road back over 1,000m, About 45km from Erseka, a turn-off leads to the little town of Leskoviku.

The next stretch of the main road is narrow and in poor condition. It is very slow going and, although the distance is further, it may take less time to drive down from Leskoviku to the border crossing into Greece (signposted for Tre Urat) and then back up to Çarçova. This detour should take no more than 45 minutes; the second section in particular is very pretty, following the Vjosa River as it enters Albania from its source in northern Greece.

The border crossing closes overnight, at 19.00 Albanian time (20.00 Greek time). If you get to Leskoviku too late to cross the border, simple accommodation (**$**) is available above the two restaurants on the street that becomes the road to the border: Jorgo (m *068 37 91 134*) and Leskoviku (m *069 27 30 716*). Jorgo serves huge portions of roast lamb or kid, salads and sweet local wine (**$$**). At the Çarçova junction is a shop and restaurant. A bus to Athens, via Tre Urat, passes Çarçova around 07.00 on Mondays and Fridays (it leaves Përmeti at 06.30; m *069 81 87 559, 068 23 86 048*).

🏠 **WHERE TO STAY, EAT AND DRINK** *Map, page 130*

🏠 **Farma Sotira** (5 chalets, 5 cabins) m 069 23 42 529; e info@farmasotira.com; w farmasotira.com. 27km from Erseka, 15km (30mins' drive) from Leskoviku, set in meadows fringed with fir & hazel woods; 1,100m above sea level. A working farm, with sheep, cattle, chickens & horses; also trout nursery; water from the farm's own spring. Guided hiking & riding excursions can be arranged; outdoor pool with separate shallow section for children; laundry facilities; English spoken; fast Wi-Fi throughout site. Excellent restaurant with open fire: home-reared lamb cooked in *saç* (Dutch oven), trout, *lakror* & other traditional dishes, all genuinely organic. B/fast inc with home-baked bread, honey & eggs from the farm. Campsite (**$**) with 3 charging points for mobile homes, space for tents, 5 wooden sgl-room cabins, with beds but no en-suite facilities (**$**); all sharing good, modern toilets & showers (1 of each for each sex). Each chalet sleeps up to 4 people in 2 rooms with nice en-suite bathrooms; heating & power points. **$$**

🏠 **Gërmenji Jorgo** (6 rooms) m 069 24 09 641. On the main road, 21km from Erseka, just beyond signposted turn-off for village of Gërmenji. Surrounded by glorious scenery; large terrace bar in garden; restaurant with traditional dishes; open fires in winter; Wi-Fi; laundry service. Camping possible; horseriding excursions can be arranged. All rooms have basic en-suite bathroom & balcony. **$**

PËRMETI *Telephone code: 0813*

Përmeti is a pleasant, clean little town in a lovely setting, surrounded by mountains and flanked by the River Vjosa. The journey to it, from both north and south, runs along the valley of this beautiful river, past dramatic gorges and waterfalls. The Vjosa rises in northern Greece as the Aoos and is one of the loveliest rivers in Albania, with crystalline, greenish-blue waters. Hill farmers lead their laden donkeys home across precarious wooden bridges and large birds of prey can be seen quite close at hand.

Përmeti was settled in prehistoric times, but the earliest traces of habitation are the remains of a medieval castle on the City Rock, which overlooks the gorge through which the Vjosa flows out of the town. In the course of World War II, Përmeti was burnt down no fewer than four times, by Italians and Germans; the 6th Partisan Brigade, led by Enver Hoxha and Mehmet Shehu (see box, page 83), was mustered here in 1943, and a large **memorial** to its fallen stands at the entrance to the town.

In 1944, the Congress of Përmeti elected the provisional government that took power following liberation later that year. It consolidated the exclusion of the non-communist forces from the country's future, annulled various decisions and agreements made by the pre-war monarchist government, and specifically banned King Zog from returning to Albania. The congress is commemorated with a fine Socialist Realist statue of a partisan, cast by the Përmeti sculptor Odhisë Paskali, which stands at the side of the main square. Përmeti is famous for its roses, which can be admired from late spring throughout the summer, and for its raki, which can be sampled at any time of year. It is also the home of *gliko*, a way of preserving fruit or walnuts in syrup, and of a budding Slow Food Consortium.

GETTING THERE AND AWAY There is a daily **bus** service between Përmeti and Korça; it leaves Përmeti at 07.00. The Gjirokastra–Korça service (daily except Sundays) can be boarded at the end of the bridge into Përmeti, where it passes between 08.00 and 08.30. The journey to Korça from Përmeti takes between 4 and

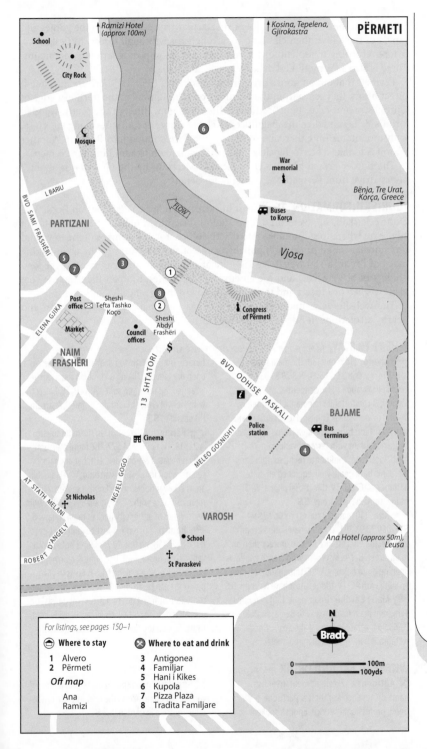

PËRMETI

↑ Ramizi Hotel
(approx 100m)

↑ Kosina, Tepelena,
Gjirokastra

School

City Rock

Mosque

L BARIU

BVD SAMI FRASHERI

PARTIZANI

War
memorial

Bënja, Tre Urat,
Korça, Greece →

FLOW

Buses
to Korça

Vjosa

5
7

3

1

8
2

Post
office ⊠

Sheshi
Tefta Tashko
Koço

Sheshi
Abdyl
Frashëri

Congress
of Përmeti

ELENA GJIKA

Market

Council
offices

NAIM
FRASHËRI

$

13 SHTATORI

BVD ODHISË PASKALI

BAJAME

ℹ

Cinema

MELEO GOSNISHTI

Police
station

Bus
terminus

4

NGJELI GOGO

AT STATH MELANI

St Nicholas

VAROSH

School

Ana Hotel (approx 50m),
Leusa

ROBERT D'ANGELY

St Paraskevi

N

Bradt

For listings, see pages 150–1

🏠 Where to stay

1 Alvero
2 Përmeti

Off map

Ana
Ramizi

😋 Where to eat and drink

3 Antigonea
4 Familjar
5 Hani i Kikes
6 Kupola
7 Pizza Plaza
8 Tradita Familjare

0 ▬▬▬▬ 100m
0 ▬▬▬▬ 100yds

The Southeast PËRMETI

5

149

5 hours and the fare is 600 lek. It is a spectacular trip, starting with the gorges and rapids of the Vjosa, then climbing on a rough road through forests to Leskoviku, before returning to asphalt for the run through the imposing Gramoz Mountains. There is also a Përmeti–Leskoviku bus daily at 12.30.

Përmeti is about an hour's drive from Gjirokastra (55km). There are infrequent direct **buses**; they leave from the terminus on the highway at the northern edge of Gjirokastra and take about 1½ hours. The route goes through the pretty, wooded Drinos Valley and then the magnificent Këlcyra Gorge. It continues along the Vjosa, with mountains on either side of the river, before coming into Përmeti. Another option is to take a bus to **Tepelena** and change there on to a minibus for Përmeti.

The border crossing at Tre Urat – called Mertzani by the Greeks – is about 2 hours' drive from Përmeti. See page 147 for details.

TOURIST INFORMATION The tourist information office (☏ *20015*) is on Boulevard Odhisë Paskali, opposite the police station. Friendly, English-speaking staff can advise on where to stay and what to do. The office stocks free maps of the town and brochures; a small museum highlights some of the traditions of the area. Hiking maps of Bredhi i Hotovës (page 153) are also available. Staff can contact the key-holders of St Paraskevi and the cinema (see opposite), to open them up for you; visits to *gliko* producers and to vineyards can also be arranged.

The website **w** visitpermet.org/permet has information about the town and nearby attractions in English and Albanian.

🏠 **WHERE TO STAY** *Map, page 149, unless otherwise stated*

🏠 **Alvero** (16 rooms) On the main square; ☏ 23514; **m** 068 23 39 508, 068 20 81 334; **e** vnikolla@yahoo.fr; **w** visitpermet.org/permet. Modern & comfortable; panoramic lift; friendly, helpful owners speak English, French & German; tours & fishing trips in the area can be arranged. Large restaurant with terrace overlooking river; fresh, local food; conference room, rooftop bar. All rooms have good, well-equipped en-suite bathroom, AC, LED TV, direct-dial phone, Wi-Fi, fridge; some have balcony. **$$**

🏠 **Ana** (10 rooms, 2 suites) **m** 069 28 94 536, 069 33 93 391; **e** hotelana@hotmail.com; **w** hotelana.eu. Entrance behind grocery shop on main street. Bar/b/fast room with French windows opening on to balcony; Wi-Fi throughout. All rooms en suite with AC, TV, fridge; most have balcony. **$$**

🏠 **Mali i Bardhë** [map, page 130] (9 rooms) 1km from main road on way to Bënja; **m** 068 21 63 964; **e** taseapostol@yahoo.com. Good restaurant with traditional menu; tables on terrace, fringed with 400-year-old plane trees; open fire indoors. Hiking & climbing tours can be arranged. All rooms en suite with CH, TV, balcony with view of either mountains or forest & stream; HB possible. **$$**

🏠 **Përmeti** (30 rooms) On the main square; ☏ 22611; **m** 069 78 34 572. The former 'Turizmi'; fully renovated & upgraded. Lift; bar on main square, good for people-watching; Wi-Fi in public areas & lower floors; some English spoken. All rooms en suite with AC, TV, good-sized dbl or twin beds, views of either City Rock or main square. **$$**

🏠 **Ramizi** (18 rooms) Just beyond the City Rock; ☏ 23858; **m** 068 20 73 826; **e** hotelramizi@yahoo.com. Restaurant, bar; wine & raki made on site; hiking & kayaking trips & visits to *gliko* producers can be arranged. Free Wi-Fi throughout; computer with fast internet access for guests' use. All rooms en suite with AC, TV, bedside light, shutters; 4 on top floor are wood-panelled attic rooms. **$$**

✗ **WHERE TO EAT AND DRINK** *Map, page 149*

✗ **Antigonea** Excellent meat, river fish, game dishes such as rabbit & partridge. Good, professional service, English spoken. **$$$**

✗ **Kupola** A good spot to break your journey if you are not going across the river into the town; tables outside in garden. **$$$**

✕ Tradita Familjare Large indoor restaurant, tables outside on main square; fairly standard menu of escalopes, chops & salads, some fish & game. $$$
✕ Familjar The standard menu of grilled meat & salads, nice interior with traditionally carved wood; handy for bus terminus. $$

✕ Hani i Kikes Friendly, welcoming atmosphere; traditional southern Albanian meals; good selection of wines. $$
✕ Pizza Plaza A lovely garden is hidden behind the unpromising café-like exterior on the street. Good pizza, also traditional Albanian dishes such as lamb's liver; English-speaking owner. $$

WHAT TO SEE AND DO Përmeti's setting is really beautiful. Behind the town rises the Dhëmbel mountain range, 2,050m high at its peak, and all around are other imposing mountains. The road access to the town is over the River Vjosa, which rushes through a dramatic gorge right next to the pavement. In summer, the local children swim and sunbathe on the shingle riverbanks. A huge boulder – the City Rock – sits by the gorge and can be climbed to enjoy the view of the river from the top; a metal staircase leads up the western face of the rock.

Most of Përmeti's buildings are modern, having been rebuilt after liberation in 1944. Two attractive old churches remain. **St Paraskevi** is a Greek saint who was martyred by decapitation; she is often shown in icons with one head on her shoulders and another in a bowl. Her name is the Greek word for Friday; in Albania, she and her churches are usually referred to as Shënepremtë, 'St Friday'. This St Friday was built in 1776, a long, low building with an attractive whitewashed exonarthex (a colonnaded porch). The roof is unusual: normally the roof of the narthex is lower than that over the nave, but here it is on a single level. Another interesting architectural feature is a channel, under the paved floor, which took water from the font out into the rainwater drain outside. The frescoes were painted in 1808, by Tërpo Zografi (page 133); they are lovely, but in sore need of conservation. Flooding in 1963 damaged the women's gallery so badly that, ever since, women have worshipped in the nave, although they sit separately from the men. The entrance door is modern, carved by a local craftsman to replace the original door that was destroyed during the atheism campaign (page 16).

St Nicholas (Shën Koll) is slightly older, built in 1757, and set in a peaceful garden, surrounded by cypresses and flowers. It is not usually possible to get inside, but in any case its interior was whitewashed in 1967.

Another interesting building is the **cinema**, built in the 1980s. It is possible to visit the projection box (ask at the tourist information office) and inspect the impressive projectors, made in China to a Soviet model, and other equipment. The walls are covered with stills from well-known Albanian films of the 1960s and 1970s; see page 24 for more about Albanian cinema in the communist period.

Every June, Përmeti hosts a **folk festival** in which traditional musicians come together from all over the Balkans. There is also a wine festival in the last week of May.

EXCURSIONS FROM PËRMETI
Historic churches The churches at Leusa and Kosina have outstanding frescoes and should be visited by anyone who is interested in Byzantine religious art. **Leusa** is only a couple of kilometres from Përmeti, a stiff uphill walk; the road is often in poor repair and a normal hire car is unlikely to be adequate. It is a large church, 23m long, built at the end of the 18th century. The paintings on the wall of the exonarthex have been damaged with graffiti, but there are some charming compositions among them, including a cute pelican. Inside, the frescoes on the narthex walls include gruesome scenes of sinners being tortured in various ways. A wooden staircase leads up to a screened gallery, with more frescoes. From here there is a good view of the

Abdyl, the oldest of the three famous Frashëri brothers, was born in 1839 and became a fairly senior civil servant in the Ottoman administration. In 1877, he was elected to represent Ioannina in the Ottoman parliament. By this time, he was already actively involved in the movement for Albanian autonomy. He set up a secret Albanian Committee, which submitted a memorandum to the Ottoman government in the spring of 1877; it called for the unification of the four Ottoman provinces (*vilayets*) into which the Albanian-speaking lands were divided, and for the establishment of Albanian schools. The memorandum met with no response.

Abdyl Frashëri gave the opening address at a meeting of Albanian nationalist leaders held in Prizreni in June 1878, which soon became known as the Prizren League. Most of the delegates at Prizreni were from Kosova or the Albanian highlands; Frashëri was one of only two from southern Albania. The meeting was timed to coincide with the Congress of Berlin, which had been convened by the European Powers – Britain, France, Austria-Hungary, Russia, Germany and Italy – to try to find a solution to the imminent disintegration of the Ottoman Empire and Russia's eagerness to fill the void left by it.

The 'solution', in the end, was the Treaty of Berlin, which returned Macedonia to Ottoman control, kept Serbia out of Kosova, handed Bosnia-Herzegovina over to Austrian administration, and gave part of Kosova to Montenegro. This last concession caused great resentment in Kosova, and radicalised the Prizren League. Abdyl Frashëri, who was Bektashi (page 22), used the network of the Bektashi order to rally support for Albanian autonomy among the Muslims of southern Albania, who were not affected by the Treaty of Berlin. As the Albanians' demands developed and became more radical, Abdyl Frashëri travelled around the capitals of Europe, lobbying on their behalf.

In early 1881, the Prizren League began to organise real resistance to Ottoman authority, capturing Prishtina and expelling the Ottoman administrators from the whole of Kosova. The empire belatedly realised the danger the League posed, and moved swiftly to suppress it. Abdyl Frashëri was captured and imprisoned, but the national awareness that the League had awakened could not be crushed so easily. He was released in 1886 on condition that he lived in Istanbul and took no part in political activity. His health was broken by his imprisonment and he died in 1892.

ceiling frescoes in the body of the church (the naos). Further frescoes decorate the walls of the naos; bats live in the vaults above it. The key is held by the family in the first house on the right off the track opposite the church gate.

Kosina Church is just off, and visible from, the main road towards Këlcyra, about halfway between the two towns. This beautiful little cross-in-square church, with its patterned brickwork, is typical of palaeo-Christian buildings of the 12th and 13th centuries. The fresco in the dome, of Christ Pantocrator surrounded by his saints, has survived reasonably well, but the whole church urgently needs conservation work. You can park in the village and walk the final 45m or so up to the church; ask locally for the key-holder.

Frashëri The village of Frashëri, where the illustrious brothers Abdyl, Naim and Sami Frashëri came from, is about 40km from Përmeti, high in the mountains beyond the Hotova Firs (Bredhi i Hotovës) National Park. It is a lovely drive (or cycle, for those with good leg muscles) through forests of fir and spruce that

The youngest of the three brothers, Sami Frashëri (1850–1904), edited an influential daily newspaper in Istanbul, which in 1878 published an article by Abdyl Frashëri outlining the demands of the Prizren League – a single *vilayet*, Albanian-speaking officials, elected local authorities and Albanian-language schools. Sami led the Albanian Committee of Istanbul, and went on to become the nationalist movement's chief propagandist. His essay entitled *What Albania has been, what it is, and what it will become* was effectively its manifesto. On the Albanian language, he wrote:

How can it be that Albanians do not have the right to write and read their language, when every nation has this right and nobody forbids it? Why are Albanians deprived of a right which every nation on earth has? Not to be able to write and learn their language, but to have foreign nations coming and opening schools in their languages?

After the crushing of the Prizren League, the emphasis of the nationalist movement shifted to cultural and linguistic demands. Cultural societies in Istanbul and Bucharest printed and distributed books in Albanian and raised funds for Albanian-medium schools (page 136). Naim Frashëri (1843–1900) was active in the Albanian Committee of Istanbul, but more importantly became one of the Albanian language's greatest poets. He wrote allegorical nationalistic works, such as *The Candle's Words* (*Fjalët e Qiririt*), and a paean of homesickness, *Livestock & Agriculture* (*Bagëti e Bujqësi*):

O Albania, my mother, while I am in exile
my heart has never forgotten your love.
When the lamb, wandering from the flock, hears its mother's soft voice,
it bleats two or three times and rushes off;
even if twenty or thirty people block its way
and frighten it, the lamb does not turn back, but goes through them like an arrow.
In the same way, my heart too leaves me here, where I am,
and hurries with longing to your lands.

open up from time to time to reveal towering mountains on all sides. The road is not asphalted, but it is in reasonable condition and a 4x4 is not required. There is no public transport; the turning off the main Përmeti–Këlcyra road, between Kosina and Piskova, is signposted for 'Bredhi i Hotovës' and the Bektashi *teqe* of Alipostivan. Note that some commercial maps of Albania show a completely fictitious route. The tourist information office in Përmeti can supply hiking maps of the trails around Bredhi i Hotovës.

In the 19th century, Frashëri was a sizeable place, with 22 distinct neighbourhoods. The village's most famous sons were the three brothers who contributed in different ways to Albania's Rilindja Kombëtare, the cultural movement that led ultimately to the country's independence. See box above for more about the Frashëri brothers. Their family home is now a museum, with interesting photographs and maps of the village and surrounding district as it was in the past. There are displays about the family and each of the three brothers, and paintings representing various events in which they played a part. Ask locally for admission.

THERMAL BATHS

Albania's thermal baths have been enjoyed since Roman times. In the 20th century, some of them were developed into spas – they are known generically by the Albanian word Llixhat (the indefinite form is Llixhe).

The first to have its waters scientifically tested was Park Nosi, in Llixhat e Elbasanit (page 118). The water here was first analysed in 1924, and the spa was built in 1932 by a businessman from Elbasani, Grigor Nosi (a brother of the politician Lef Nosi; pages 116–17). Detailed research into the chemical components of the water was conducted by a Czech scientist between 1932 and 1936; the main elements are sodium, magnesium, calcium and potassium. The spa treats a range of ailments, including rheumatism, circulatory problems and skin complaints such as eczema. The water is also said to aid fertility. The springs at Park Nosi rise from 13,000m below the surface and emerge at 56°C; the current administrator remembers, as a child, his grandfather Grigor Nosi boiling an egg for him in the thermal water. Nowadays, many other spa hotels have been built at Llixhat e Elbasanit, although some of them pump their water from underground, rather than allowing it to emerge naturally, as is supposed to be better for the conservation of its medicinal properties.

Another spa resort, built during the communist period, is near Peshkopia (page 182). The water here emerges, from three springs, at just above blood temperature (39–40°C); it comes from the same source, far underground, as Llixhat e Elbasanit and a similar (but much more expensive) spa across the Macedonian border in Kosovrasti. It is so full of sulphur that clients are not allowed to wear jewellery while bathing, because everything except gold will dissolve in it. The original spa here was built in 1964; the current building, with 50 individual bathing cubicles, was one of the last hurrahs of the communist period, inaugurated in 1990. The peak season is September and October, when 3,000 people come through the doors every day. Most people come for a course of treatment of five to seven days, increasing the length of time they soak in the water each day. Hot mud therapy is also available, said to be helpful in the treatment of gynaecological problems and scoliosis. The baths are kept open all year round, for drop-ins by local people or anyone who happens to be visiting Peshkopia. Full courses of treatment are offered from April to October.

The prices at these spas are astonishingly low by northern European standards. A 15-minute soak in a private cubicle costs 100 lek (less than €1). Medically trained staff, often with decades of experience, supervise the spa facilities at all times.

There are free thermal baths, open to the elements, in various places around the Albanian mountains. One of these is at Bënja, near Përmeti, a large open-air pool in a beautiful setting, fed by several thermal springs. (See opposite for details of how to get there.) Finally, there are numerous drinking-water springs, which are also said to have beneficial medical effects; these are often known as Uji i Ftohtë, the Albanian for 'cold water'. If you are making long-distance bus journeys in Albania, you will find that buses always stop at these famous spots so that passengers can fill their plastic bottles with this health-giving spring water.

Frashëri is a largely Bektashi village – indeed, the three famous brothers were Bektashi. The local *teqe*, built in 1781, was used as a school in the communist period. It is a single-storey, whitewashed building, with a *tyrbe* on the hillside above. It is indicative of the religious harmony that generally prevails in Albania that the caretaker of the *teqe* is a Christian.

There is no hotel in Frashëri; accommodation could probably be arranged with a local family, or you could ask to pitch your tent on their land. The road onward to Erseka is not suitable for cars, but it can be cycled. It takes the villagers 8–10 hours to walk. Hikers might alternatively head northwest to Çepani, in the district of Skrapari, and on to Çorovoda and Berati; page 128.

Bënja The thermal baths at Bënja are a popular day trip for the people of Përmeti. Below an elegant Ottoman bridge over the Lengarica River, the water from several thermal springs collects in a large pool, wide and deep enough to swim in. The water temperature of the springs is 23–32°C. The 3.7km canyon above the bridge is excellent for kayaking (at least unless plans resurface to dam the Lengarica for hydro-electric power); Outdoor Albania (page 29) can organise tailor-made tours here.

A minibus between Përmeti and Bënja operates in the summer, starting when enough local people want to go there (sometime in June) and continuing until summer turns to autumn. There is a café just before the bridge, where coffee, water and other drinks can be bought and which has a toilet for customers' use.

The Southeast PËRMETI

5

155

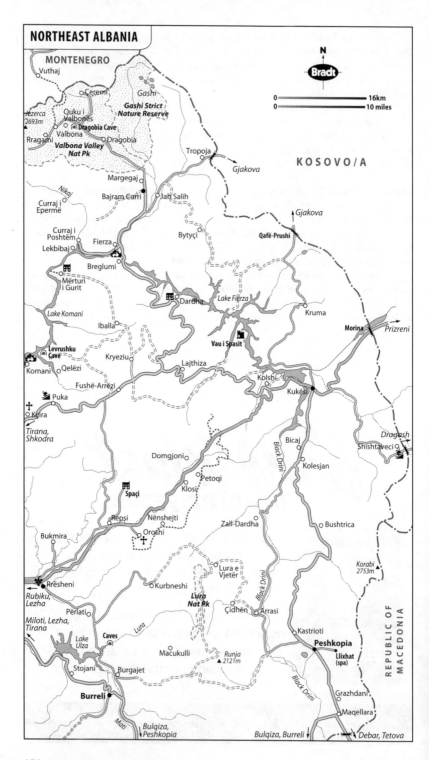

NORTHEAST ALBANIA

MONTENEGRO

Vuthaj

Çeremi

Gashi

Gashi Strict
Nature Reserve

Jezerca
2693m

Quku i
Valbonës

Dragobia Cave

Valbona

Dragobia

Rragami

Valbona Valley
Nat Pk

Tropoja

Gjakova

KOSOVO/A

Margegaj

Nikaj

Bajram Curri

Jah Salih

Gjakova

Curraj i
Epermë

Curraj i
Poshtëm

Bytyçi

Qafë-Prushi

Lekbibaj

Fierza

Breglumi

Mërturi
i Gurit

Dardha

Lake Fierza

Kruma

Lake Komani

Iballa

Morina

Prizreni

Levrushku
Cave

Vau i Spasit

Komani

Qelëzi

Kryeziu

Lajthiza

Kolshi

Fushë-Arrëzi

Kukësi

Puka

Kçira

Tirana,
Shkodra

Domgjoni

Bicaj

Black Drini

Dragash

Shishtaveci

Kolesjan

Petoqi

Spaçi

Klosi

Repsi

Nënshejti

Zall-Dardha

Bushtrica

Bukmira

Oroshi

Korabi
2753m

Rrësheni

Lura e
Vjetër

Black Drini

Rubiku,
Lezha

Kurbneshi

Lura
Nat Pk

Çidhën

Arrasi

Miloti, Lezha,
Tirana

Përlati

Kastrioti

REPUBLIC OF
MACEDONIA

Lake
Ulza

Caves

Macukulli

Lura

Runja
2121m

Peshkopia

Llixhat
(spa)

Stojani

Burgajet

Grazhdani

Burreli

Black Drini

Maqellara

Mati

Bulqiza,
Peshkopia

Bulqiza, Burreli

Debar, Tetova

0 ————— 16km
0 ————— 10 miles

6

The Northeast

MIRDITA   *Telephone code (Rrësheni): 0216*

The district of Mirdita is an enchanting blend of wild mountain scenery and centuries of unique religious and cultural history. The first of these unique features is the institution called the Captaincy, or Kapedania, a hereditary position that combined the roles of judiciary and head of state. The chiefs of all of Mirdita's clans accepted the authority of the Captain, not as first among equals, like the *bajraktarë* of the rest of highland Albania, but as their judicial authority and their head of state. Edith Durham (see box, pages 180–1) attended a council of the Mirdita clans in 1908 and took a famous photograph of the highlanders gathered, all armed to the teeth, on the lawns of St Paul's Church. The Captain resolved legal disputes according to the traditional Code, or Kanun (see box, pages 192–3) – the version used in Mirdita was the Code of Skanderbeg – and represented the region to the Ottoman authorities and, eventually, those of independent Albania. The Captaincy's palaces were in Mirdita's ancient capital, Oroshi.

Also in Oroshi was the seat of the Abbacy of Mirdita, with special Nullius status (the only one in Albania) that made it directly dependent on the Vatican, not on any of the archbishoprics covering the rest of Albania. Mirdita has always been fiercely independent and it managed to keep the Ottomans from establishing their authority over it, dealing with them instead as practically an autonomous state. Because of this resistance, almost the entire population of Mirdita is still Catholic. Most of its churches, including the Abbey at Oroshi, were burned to the ground during the atheism campaign of 1967 (page 16) and have been rebuilt since freedom of worship was restored in 1990.

There was some industrialisation during the communist period, most of it linked to the copper mines in the area. At its peak, the copper industry employed 5,000 people in Mirdita alone; there were small copper-processing plants all over the district, feeding into the main plant at Rubiku. From there, the copper was sent on to Shkodra to be further processed into wire and other industrial materials. The mines closed in the 1990s and the plants that processed the minerals now generally lie idle. Mirdita experienced very high emigration as a consequence of the lack of local employment but, thanks in part to the job opportunities created by tourism and other small-scale businesses, this trend is now beginning to reverse.

Until 2010, most of the district was difficult to get to; but the construction of the Durrësi–Kosova highway, which cuts straight through Mirdita, and improvements to minor roads have made formerly wild and remote places much more accessible. Hotel accommodation is limited, but it would be perfectly feasible for hikers or cyclists to base themselves in Rubiku or Rrësheni and explore the district from there. Those with tents could, of course, base themselves in whichever remote corner took their fancy; see page 44 for advice on wild camping in Albania.

GETTING THERE AND AWAY The **highway** connecting Kukësi (and Kosova) with the Adriatic port of Durrësi, Rruga e Kombit or 'the Road of the Nation', begins at the Miloti roundabout on the main north–south highway, about halfway between Tirana and Shkodra, and cuts pretty much due northeast, straight through Mirdita, with state-of-the-art tunnels blasted through any inconveniently located mountains. Cyclists can avoid almost all of the highway as far as Oroshi by crossing the Fani River just after the Miloti junction and then using the old roads that run more or less parallel to it.

There is good **public transport** to the district capital, Rrësheni, from Tirana and Lezha. In **Tirana**, buses leave from the North bus station [62 B2] from early morning until mid afternoon, usually on the hour; the journey takes about 1½ hours. From **Kukësi** (130km), any bus heading for Tirana could drop passengers at the turn-off for Rrësheni or Rubiku. Those with their own transport could also enter Mirdita from the district of Mati (pages 182–5), on the recently asphalted road from Burreli around the western tip of Lake Ulza.

With **bikes** or a **4x4** vehicle, an alternative route is the old road north to the district of Puka (pages 163–6), following the Fani i Madh River. Before the new highway this was the shortest, although not the quickest, way from Rrësheni to Kukësi; now all the traffic whizzes up and down the highway and this old road is almost deserted. The road surface is reasonable; it is a beautiful run of about 60km to Rrësheni from Fushë-Arrëzi, in Puka. This would make a very attractive little circuit around a fascinating part of highland Albania for those who do not have the time or inclination to venture further north. It is also possible to cross into Mirdita through the Lura National Park from Peshkopia; see page 162 for more information about this option.

⌂ WHERE TO STAY

⌂ **Marub** (19 rooms) Katundi i Vjetër, Rubiku; ☎028 450 013; m 068 20 77 424, 068 24 64 009; e info@hotelmarub.com, hotelmarub@yahoo. com; w hotelmarub.com. 2km from Rubiku, set in forested hills on the (asphalted) road to the village of Katundi i Vjetër. Modern alpine-style building, designed as a pilot project for sustainable tourism & to meet exacting environmental standards; beautiful views, ample car parking; biomass CH. Excellent restaurant using locally produced ingredients; bar; Wi-Fi. Guides & horses can be arranged for excursions in the area. Nicely furnished rooms, all en suite with water-saving shower, AC, satellite TV, fridge, ample power-points, bedside lights, balcony with mountain view. **$$**

⌂ **Arbëri** (7 rooms) Rrësheni; ☎23376; m 069 21 83 887. Opposite the cathedral, convenient for buses. Friendly management; excellent restaurant; bar with terrace above street. En-suite rooms. **$**

⌂ **Bujtina Jaku** (2 rooms) Katundi i Vjetër, Rubiku; m 068 64 39 608. Basic accommodation in village home in mountains above Rubiku (beyond the Marub Hotel), surrounded by forest. Veranda bar, simple restaurant. **$**

⌂ **Kaçorri** (23 rooms) Rrësheni; m 069 23 40 986. Conveniently located in the main square. Pleasant, helpful management; reliable water & electricity. Most rooms share the toilets & showers installed on each corridor; dbls have small balcony & wash/hand basin; trpls have TV & reasonable en-suite bathroom. **$**

✕ WHERE TO EAT AND DRINK

✕ **Eksklusiv** Rrësheni; ☎23375. Just off the main square, on the opposite side from the Kaçorri Hotel. Standard menu of *qofta* or steak with chips & salad; if given prior notice, they can also prepare locally caught trout. Excellent local wine, made from the indigenous Kallmet grape. **$$**

✕ **Europa** Rubiku. On the main street, on the right if coming from Tirana. Exceptionally good food inc, astonishingly, vegetarian dishes other than salad. Carnivores should (also) try the grilled pork. Excellent, locally produced, Arbëri Kallmet wine. **$$**

✕ Sofra Thkellës Përlati; **m** 068 47 71 640. About halfway between Rrësheni & Burreli (page 162). Superb traditional dishes: chargrilled meat & vegetables, homemade sausages, grilled vegetables. **$$**

WHAT TO SEE AND DO

Rubiku Rubiku is a pleasant little town, with well-maintained public spaces and a commendable absence of litter. Above it, prominent on a white crag, stands a beautiful old church.

Rubiku was one of four Benedictine foundations in Mirdita – the others were Ndërfani, Shalla and Oroshi (page 160). The church at Rubiku, St Saviour's (Kisha e Shelbuemit), was founded in 1166 and later transferred to the Franciscan order whose property it still is. There have of course been extensions and alterations made to the building over the centuries. In the 15th century, the oldest part of the church, above and behind the altar, was decorated with frescoes that, although damaged, still have the power to inspire those who worship here. The best way to be sure of being able to see inside the church is to go there on a Sunday or a major feast day. There are good views from the terrace behind the church. Both the church and the monastic buildings beside it were damaged during World War II, then allowed to fall into disrepair during the years of official atheism (page 16). The monastery is still in ruins; the church was reroofed and repaired in the 1990s and, later, the Stations of the Cross were installed along the road leading up to it.

Rrësheni The district capital, about 20 minutes' drive beyond Rubiku, is the only other town of any size in Mirdita. Rrësheni has a technical college, a Western Union office and, for those heading for the Lura Lakes, the last ATMs until Peshkopia. It is the main hub for public transport out to the rest of the district and for inter-city buses or minibuses to Lezha, Tirana and Shkodra. The bus terminus is on Rruga Shën Vinçenci i Paulit (St Vincent de Paul Street), near the cathedral.

Rrësheni has a small historical museum, a fascinating ethnographic collection and one of Albania's finest wine-producers. It is also worth visiting the cathedral – new in ecclesiastical terms as well as architectural because, before World War II, Mirdita's cathedral had been the Abbey at Oroshi. It was only in December 1996 that Rrësheni was made the seat of the diocese, covering not only Mirdita but also the neighbouring districts of Mati, Bulqiza and Dibra. Construction began almost immediately and continued in defiance of the destructive civil unrest that overwhelmed Albania at the beginning of 1997. The new cathedral was consecrated in 2001.

The ethnographic display is in the **Cultural Centre**, just off the main square. The traditional costumes of Mirdita are instantly recognisable because of the preponderance of red rather than the range of colours used elsewhere in highland Albania. The Cultural Centre has a display of more than 20 different types of costume, as well as a good collection of traditional musical instruments. It is also the home of the Mirdita Ensemble, nationally and internationally renowned performers of folk music and dance. The **historical museum** is at the other end of town, beside the Europa café. The displays illustrate the themes of Mirdita's development as a state, the importance of Catholicism and the region's ethnological heritage.

Kantina Arbëri, in the outskirts of Rrësheni, produces the Kallmet wine served in many restaurants in northern Albania and Tirana. Kallmet is an indigenous red-wine grape and Arbëri's are grown in Bukmira, in the hills to the north of Rrësheni. They also produce white wine from the Shesh i Bardhë grape, high-quality, cask-matured raki and – a recent trial – sparkling wine made using *méthode champenoise*. The house has a small wine-tasting room; booking is advisable (*Zona Industriale Mirditë;* ✎ *0216 22486;* m *069 20 57 553;* e *info@ kantina-arberi.com;* w *kantina-arberi.com*).

Oroshi The traditional capital of Mirdita, Oroshi was the seat of both its ecclesiastical and temporal powers: the Abbacy (Abacia), first mentioned in Vatican documents of 1703; and the Captaincy (Kapedania), Mirdita's unique system of government. The Captain was recognised by all other clan chiefs as the leader who could negotiate on Mirdita's behalf with foreign powers, such as the Ottoman authorities, and who was the last court of appeal in legal disputes, which were resolved according to the traditional Code (see box, pages 192–3). The Captaincy was a hereditary position, although it did not automatically pass to the eldest son (of course it was always a man; Mirdita was not *that* different from the rest of Albania!). The Captain and his household had two palaces at Oroshi, one of them right next to the Abbey.

The importance of Oroshi as a symbol of Mirdita's unity and resistance meant that aspiring oppressors have completely destroyed it no fewer than three times. The first was during a sustained assault by the Ottomans in the 1870s, described by Edith Durham (see box, pages 180–1) in *High Albania*. The church was then rebuilt by the energetic abbot Prend Doçi, who also successfully negotiated with the Vatican to be brought under the direct jurisdiction of the pope (as a 'territorial prelate' or 'prelate *nullius*'). This meant that, from that point on, the abbots of Oroshi would report directly to the Vatican, rather than via an archbishop – Oroshi was the only diocese in Albania that had this special Nullius status. The church and palace were burned down again during the Second Balkan War, then demolished by the Albanian government in 1967. The church that now stands on its historic site in Oroshi was built in 1994–95, using old photographs to create an exact replica of the building destroyed by the atheism campaigners. The individuals who represented Mirdita's traditional institutions were also eliminated by the communist government: Gjon Markgjonaj, the last Captain of Mirdita, led an insurrection against it and was killed in 1946; the Abbot of Oroshi, Monsignor Frano Gjini, was shot in 1948, one of dozens of Catholics executed in northern Albania who are now commemorated in Shkodra Cathedral (page 202).

The village of Oroshi, scattered across the hillside across from the church and the ruins of the palace, is now home to 20 families. It is served by two minibuses a day from **Repsi**, 7–8km away. Further up in the mountains is **Nënshejti**, a beautiful village with a 500-year-old church, set in magnificent scenery. It is 23km from Repsi, but the road is so bad that it takes at least 2 hours to get there. There is no public transport and a 4x4 vehicle is essential. There is no accommodation in Nënshejti at the time of writing, but it would be a wonderful place to camp.

Spaçi In 1968, the Albanian government decided to use the copper mine at Spaçi as a forced-labour camp for political prisoners. Over the next 24 years, thousands of men were imprisoned at Spaçi, behind three rings of barbed-wire fence that enclosed the whole 12ha of the mine. An unknown number died, sometimes of exhaustion and malnutrition, sometimes shot. Not all the bodies were returned to their families – the guards would take corpses across the river and bury them in unmarked graves on the hillside opposite. The author Fatos Lubonja, who spent 11 years in Spaçi, survived (just) and has written about his experience in a book translated into English as *Second Sentence* (I B Tauris, 2009). Spaçi was not the only forced-labour camp in Albania, but it was the only one that used exclusively political prisoners. There were also a few non-prisoners employed at Spaçi. Their job was to handle the explosives, which for obvious reasons were not made available to the prisoners. At any one time there was an average of 800 prisoners in the camp; when it closed, in 1991, 830 men were freed. They were kept, 30 to a room, in cells measuring 5m by 6m. The slightest breach of discipline could mean a stay in the isolation cell, where prisoners were left for days with no food or blankets, even in the sub-zero temperatures of winter.

This eerie place, in its bleak setting amid bare, harsh mountains, has been abandoned to the elements since 1991. Information panels in English have been installed around the site and work has begun to stabilise the buildings so that the the prison camp can be transformed into a museum, along the lines of Robben Island in South Africa. It is 14km from the highway; the road was upgraded in 2017. The camp is up the road signposted for Gurth-Spaç, not Kodër-Spaç.

Caves and *kulla* The easiest of Mirdita's **caves** to visit is the Vali's Cave (Shpella e Valit), near the district boundary with Mati (pages 182–5). (A *vali* was a provincial governor in the Ottoman administration.) The cave is 3–4km from the road and has stalagmites and stalactites. To its south, in Mati, is a cluster of three further caves. One of the longest of these is blocked with earth and it is thought that it may be connected with the Vali's Cave. The Marub Hotel near Rubiku (page 158) and Vila Bruçi in Burreli (page 184) can organise excursions to these caves.

There are also caves in the commune of Fani, in the far northeast of Mirdita. Fani is the most traditional part of Mirdita, due to being completely surrounded by high mountains (nearly 2,000m above sea level). Until a few years ago, it was almost impossible to get to. Now, though, the main village, **Klosi**, is right next to the new highway and slip roads have been built along it to provide access for the villagers. These include exits on either side at the entrance to the Kalimashi Tunnel, which is 5.6km long and cuts through the mountains to Kukësi district. Fani has 17 villages, many in spectacular settings, with traditional fortified houses (*kulla*; page 184) still occupied. One that can be reached in an ordinary car is **Petoqi**, 800m above sea level. The village of **Domgjoni** is less accessible, but has a 4th-century aqueduct system, a very unusual structure that provided water to the ancient settlement of Sukbukëra.

THE LURA LAKES

The Lura National Park covers 1,280ha of mountainous terrain around the Crown of Lura (Kurora e Lurës) Massif, which rises at its peak to 2,121m. The area was designated as a national park because of the beautiful lakes that lie within it, and a road into the park was constructed to give access to the seven largest. These lie in cirques 1,600–1,720m above sea level, surrounded by pine trees and wild flowers, with the mountains rising high above them. Each of the seven main lakes has a subtly different atmosphere. Several of them are covered in white and yellow water lilies, and huge dragonflies dart around them. Others have no flowers in them; the stillness of their water is dappled with the reflection of the surrounding trees.

The Lura Lakes were a popular destination for Albanian holidaymakers during the communist period and visitor numbers are now starting to pick up again. In the 1990s and 2000s, illegal logging within the park reached calamitous levels, destroying large swathes of pine forest and causing serious erosion by clear-felling on the hillsides.

Despite the logging companies' efforts, however, there is still quite a lot of forest left, and the lakes are lovely, tranquil places. The closest lakes to the village of Lura e Vjetër, about 1½ hours' drive from it, are Liqeni i Rrasave (Slate Lake) and Liqeni i Lopëve (Cattle Lake). Slate Lake is a pretty little tarn, with water lilies and reeds in the water, and beech trees growing around it. Cattle Lake is larger, and is overlooked by an impressively craggy hill. Around it are the remains of concrete steps and patios, which must have been built when Lura was a holiday resort. There is a path leading off the road to the right just before Slate Lake; it used to lead to another lake, but this was exploited for irrigation during the communist era and is now dry.

The next lake in the chain is Liqeni i Madh (Great Lake), which is divided into two sections by an artificial dyke. The main section is a large lake, surrounded by hills and trees, although these are marred by deforestation. Local children swim in this lake; less hardy adults might find the water a bit too cold. Great Lake is the highest of the main lakes, at 1,720m above sea level. Behind the dyke is a beautiful little lake, covered in water lilies, with a shady clearing under a couple of trees, which is an ideal spot for a picnic. Huge, electric-blue dragonflies live around this lake, which is considered as part of Great Lake.

The next two lakes along the road are Liqeni i Hotit (Hoti Lake) and Liqeni i Zi (Black Lake), so called because it is very deep. Black Lake is also very steep, and its sides are thickly forested with pines, although there is some deforestation further up the slopes.

It is 8.8km from Slate Lake to the last of the seven lakes, Liqeni i Luleve i Vogël (Little Flower Lake). The two Flower lakes (Liqeni i Luleve i Madh, Great Flower Lake, is the other) are in a part of the park where clear-felling has caused especially ugly scarring on the hillside and around the lakes themselves. They are remarkably beautiful lakes, particularly Little Flower Lake, whose surface is carpeted with yellow and white water lilies, but it is hard not to feel depressed – or outraged – by the environmental damage that surrounds them.

Most of the trees which were felled were mountain pines (*Pinus mugo*), although the national park is also recorded as having Macedonian pine (*Pinus peuce*), which is only found in this part of the Balkans. Its limited range gives it 'near-threatened' status. At lower levels are beech (*Fagus sylvatica*) and silver fir (*Abies alba*). There are roe deer, red squirrels, European brown hare, red foxes and polecats in the national park. Wolves, lynx, wild cats and brown bears used to live in the forests, although nowadays they have probably moved away to a quieter neighbourhood with fewer chainsaws. Golden eagles (*Aquila chrysaetos*) are readily spotted, from as low down as the hotel. Capercaillie (*Tetrao urogallus*) and rock partridge (*Alectoris graeca*) were formerly reported as breeding in the park, although no recent data are available.

GETTING THERE AND AWAY The best way to get to the Lura National Park, at the time of writing, is from the neighbouring districts of Mirdita or Mati (pages 182–5). The turn-off for Lura is at the village of Përlati, off the road that links Rrësheni and Burreli; it is a distance of about 50km, of which 20km are asphalted at the time of writing. It is hoped that the remainder will be asphalted within the lifetime of this guidebook. The journey takes about 2 hours. The main village in the national park is called **Lura e Vjetër**; once a day – possibly more in the summer, if there is demand – a **minibus** runs between the village and Rrësheni. This is currently the only way to reach the Lura Lakes by public transport.

The road from Peshkopia (pages 178–82) to Lura e Vjetër is at present even rougher than the road from Rrësheni. Work has begun on a new road which, if the original plans are followed, will cross below the southern end of the national park between Peshkopia and Burreli. This would then be the easiest way to get to the Lura Lakes.

GETTING AROUND THE PARK The road that runs roughly north–south through the national park is very bad – parts of it are more like a dry riverbed, with large stones and deeply rutted sections – and it is sometimes blocked completely with felled trees. A resilient and high-axled 4x4 vehicle is essential, unless you plan to move around on foot or on two wheels. A jeep with driver can be hired in Rrësheni (try asking at your hotel there), but not in Lura itself. The road is not passable in winter or after heavy rain.

If you are walking, there are short cuts up through the trees, although it is easy to lose the path and end up battling through the forest. You might consider hiring a local guide in the village – ask the hotel staff or the family you are staying with to find someone to show you the quickest way to the lakes.

The start of the route, however, is straightforward. From the Turizmi Lurë Hotel, head roughly southwest straight uphill. The walking is considerably more pleasant than along the stones and boulders of the road, over rough grass and past thickets of wild fruit – raspberries, blackberries, strawberries and blaeberries. The track rejoins the road at a flat, open area which would be a good place to camp overnight. It takes 30–40 minutes to reach this point from the hotel.

It is best to follow the road for the next stretch, until you come to a waterfall that runs under the road. A few metres after the waterfall, a clear path leaves the road to the right, and then rejoins it a couple of hundred metres before Cattle Lake. There are also large pipes leading downhill, and where these meet the road, their line can be followed as short-cuts.

Other possible campsites are around the main section of Great Lake and on the far side of Little Flower Lake. Caution should be exercised if logging is under way, as the trees are simply rolled down to the road from wherever they are felled. They are big logs and would have no difficulty whatsoever in sweeping a tent downhill with them.

WHERE TO STAY, EAT AND DRINK There are a couple of small hotels in Lura, one in the village of Lura e Vjetër, the other beside the road up to the lakes. Either of the two hotel proprietors can arrange transport for their guests from Rrësheni or from Tirana. It is also possible to find accommodation with local families in the village.

There are several places in the park where a tent could be pitched, in clearings in the steep, forested terrain; see above for some suggestions. If you plan to camp, you should bring adequate supplies of food and water with you. There are no shops in Lura e Vjetër, although it should be possible to buy basic foodstuffs such as bread and cheese from local families.

🏠 **Lura** (15 beds) m 068 21 87 497 (the owner, Hasan Hoti). In the village of Lura e Vjetër. All rooms en suite with TV & AC. B/fast inc. FB also possible. **$**

🏠 **Turizmi Lurë** (10 rooms) m 068 53 17 082 (the owner, Faik Buçi). About half an hour's walk from the village, in a magnificent setting at the entrance to the park, surrounded by trees & with wonderful views across the valley & the village below. Restaurant & bar. All rooms en suite with TV & AC. B/fast inc. FB also possible. **$**

PUKA *Telephone code (Puka town): 0212*

The district of Puka nestles in the corner formed by the spectacular lakes created by the hydro-electric damming of the Drini River. The old road from Shkodra to Kukësi, which more or less bisects Puka, follows much of the line of an ancient trade route along which the Romans built one of their great arterial roads, the Via Publica. This connected the Adriatic ports of Dyrrachium (now Durrësi) and Apollonia with Prizreni, Niš and, eventually, Odessa on the Black Sea. Traces of the Roman road can still be seen in Puka district. In the Ottoman period, the route became even more important: there was a customs post at **Vau i Spasit**, the ford by which travellers crossed the Drini from Puka to Hasi (page 174). Fortifications were built to protect the road at Qafa e Malit and at Vau i Spasit. These hundreds of years of Puka's history are reflected in the variety of its textiles as well as its castles, bridges and fortified houses. Ringed by mountains and fjord-like lakes, Puka also has magnificent scenery; and thanks to its good infrastructure, this scenery can be enjoyed in winter as well as summer. The town of Puka is 838m above sea level and, at the time of writing, it is the best place to ski in Albania; see page 166 for further information.

GETTING THERE AND AWAY The main road that cuts across the district of Puka makes much of its territory surprisingly accessible; and, happily for cyclists, the heavy traffic that used to congest it has now transferred on to the new Durrësi–Morina highway to the south.

There are **buses** and **minibuses** to the town of Puka from Tirana, Shkodra and Lezha. The buses from Tirana leave from the North bus station [62 B2], on the hour, from early morning until mid afternoon; the journey takes about 3½ hours. From the central square in Shkodra, the journey takes 1½–2 hours, depending on how often the minibus stops and for how long. In Puka, the buses wait in the main square near the HTP hotel.

With **bikes** or **4x4** vehicles, an alternative route into Puka is by the old road up from Mirdita (pages 157–61), following the Fani i Madhë River. The road is almost deserted, now that all the traffic uses the highway, and the surface is reasonable; it is a beautiful run of about 60km from Rrësheni in Mirdita to Fushë-Arrëzi in Puka.

WHERE TO STAY, EAT AND DRINK

Puka Town

🏠 **Hani i Përparim Laçit** (11 rooms) Lagja Laçaj, Puka; m 068 20 56 472; e perparim65@ yahoo.com. Hotel & guesthouse complex a few mins drive outside the town, near the ski piste also operated by the Laçi family. Welcoming & friendly; wonderful home cooking with local specialities; some English spoken; hiking, climbing & jeep excursions around the district can be arranged. 5 en-suite rooms in hotel above restaurant; guesthouse has 1 room en suite, others share showers & toilets. FB available. **$$**

🏠 **Hotel Turizëm Puka (HTP)** (33 rooms) Puka Qendër; ☎22586; m 067 20 70 304/6. The former 'Turizmi' hotel, privatised & completely refurbished; great location right in the town centre. Good restaurant with award-winning chef; popular bar serving Puka beer, brewed next door; lift; ample parking, Wi-Fi. Excursion guides can be arranged. All rooms with good en-suite facilities, hairdryer, TV, CH, phone; some have balcony. **$$**

Dardha

🏠 **Alpin** (6 rooms) On main road above Dardha village; m 068 55 09 598. Sympathetically designed modern chalet-style building; beautiful setting on edge of forest with views of Lake Fierza; landscaped gardens with trout pond & water features; restaurant offering local specialities. Motorboat available for lake excursions. All rooms en suite; 1 has balcony. **$$**

🏠 **Kunora** (4 rooms) On main road above Dardha village; m 068 23 13 943; e Albano-Uka@ hotmail.com. Beautiful location overlooking Lake Fierza, views on clear days to Bajram Curri & Kukësi. Renowned restaurant with traditional specialities, menus available in English & Italian; popular bar with selection of local drinks, inc cornelian cherry raki; private dining room with *sofra* (low, circular table), *oxhaku* (fireplace) & balcony. Boats available for lake excursions & fishing trips. Camping possible. Simple twin rooms, shared toilet & basic shower. **$**

WHAT TO SEE AND DO A good way to begin a visit to Puka district is by looking round the small **museum** in the town centre. It has an excellent exhibition of traditional costumes and other local textiles, richly embroidered with ancient designs. There is a small display of locally made musical instruments, *lahuta* and *sharki*, while the historical section gives an overview of the archaeology of the area, from prehistory through the Roman and Byzantine periods to the Middle Ages.

Most of Puka's historic churches were demolished in the late 1960s (see page 16 for more about the atheism campaign of those years). Some have been rebuilt since the restoration of freedom of worship; one of these is at **Kçira**, where the foundations of the destroyed church have been lovingly walled around and planted with herbs and flowers. The Catholic community of Kçira runs an interesting agricultural improvement programme, with experimental plantations of cereals, fruit and herbs. They are testing different kinds of crops, to see which do best in the local soil, and they dry herbs for use as medicinal infusions (see box, pages 6–7 for information about medicinal plants in Albania). They also keep pigs, which end up being turned into sausages, prosciutto and salami in the project's kitchens, and breed sheepdogs. Kçira is on the main road, 15 minutes' drive from Puka town; coming from there, the church is visible down a track to the right just after Kçira, indicated with a large cross at the junction.

Puka is famous for the quality and quantity of its ceps (*porçini*) and other fungi. Most of these are exported fresh to Italy; **Agropuka**, in Puka town, is spearheading an attempt to add value locally to these and other sought-after products. In modern dryers, they prepare ceps, fruit such as apple and persimmon, and herbal teas, which are then packaged in-house and sold locally and in Tirana, including in the airport duty-free shops. The factory outlet in Puka is an excellent place to stock up on these treats, whose great advantage for the traveller is that they are very light and unbreakable. Agropuka also sells fruit conserves and local honey. Finally, no visit to Puka town would be complete without sampling a beer from the town's very own brewery, next to the Hotel Turizëm Puka and with the same owners. The brewery produces an unfiltered version as well as the standard filtered beer.

A nice spot for a picnic, once you have bought all these goodies, is **Mrizi i Memajve**, signposted up a reasonable track off the main road about halfway between Puka and Fushë-Arrëzi. A *mriz* is a shady grove where livestock can shelter from the heat of the afternoon; Mrizi i Memajve is now used by the people of Puka for barbecues in summer. There are beautiful views of the surrounding mountains. It is also possible to camp here.

Puka district has many surviving fortified houses, or *kulla* (page 184). Some fine examples can be seen on the way to one of Puka's most exciting attractions: the Levrushku Cave (Shpella e Levrushkut), above Lake Komani. This cave was used as a hermitage and it has a tiny chapel at the entrance, built into the rock; for this reason, it is also known as **'the Christian's Cave'** (Shpella e Kaurrit). The exciting thing about it is that it can only be accessed from the lake; you clamber up the rock face from a small boat, as the hermits would have done, a 5–10m climb depending on the water level in the lake. At the entrance to the cave, in front of the rock chapel, the hermits built a wall with an embrasure, just like a fortified house. The interior of the main cave – 20m long – is divided into two levels, each with a balcony from which the inhabitants could keep an eye out for intruders. The Christian's Cave can be reached by boat from the dam at Komani, but a more interesting option is to hike (with a guide) from Qelëzi, an hour or so's drive up rough roads from Puka town. From Qelëzi, a path leads down to and then along the river which you will follow almost to the point where it joins Lake Komani. The path rises high above the river and provides lovely views of the mountains and of *kulla*, in clusters or standing alone. Two abandoned *kulla* can be explored just beyond the village of Levrushku, on either side of a smaller river (which you have to ford). Finally, you reach the place where the boatman will meet you and take you across the river and around into the lake, where the entrance to the Christian's Cave is marked by a high, tumbling waterfall. A whole day should be set aside for this excursion; it is one for which a guide is advisable, even for travellers who like to be very independent, because co-ordination with the boatman is essential and the path is not always clear.

Right on the other side of the district, on Lake Fierza, is **Dardha**. With two hotels above the village (page 164), this is an ideal base for a couple of days' hiking or boat trips on the lake. It is about 55km from Puka town, on the road to Fierza from where one can continue up to Tropoja or take the ferry down Lake Komani (pages 168–9) and back to the coast. The descent from here down to Fierza is very steep, with many hairpin bends; cycling in the opposite direction would be very hard work, possibly more than 2,000m ascent in total. There are old fortified houses in Dardha, one said to be 300 years old, right down on the lakeside. Near the top of the hill that leads down to the lake from the main road is a three-storey *kullë* whose owners can show you around. From the outside you can see the niche built into the wall of the guests' room; coffee and the implements to make it were kept here, so the head of the household could reach them easily from where he sat, to prepare and serve coffee for his guests. Below it is a *frëngji*, the embrasure from which unwanted visitors could be shot; the owners of the house have bricked it up to keep out draughts, but its shape is still clear. The owners do their best to maintain this fascinating old house, but the upkeep costs are very high and they would appreciate a small donation towards this.

In the dry weather of a normal summer, it would also be possible to get to Mërturi i Gurit, which has more than a dozen fortified houses, although only two of them are inhabited. A good base for hiking and exploring in summer, including to Mërturi, is **Iballa**, tucked into the centre of a ring of high mountains. There are no hotels or guesthouses in Iballa at the time of writing; local families may be able to offer simple accommodation.

WINTER SPORTS Puka is the best place to ski in Albania. It is easy to get to, it has good accommodation (page 164) and, in most years, there is snow from October to March, with over 1m in the winter months. Përparim Laçi (m *068 20 56 472*; e *perparim65@ yahoo.com*), who is a registered ski instructor with the Albanian Ski Federation, runs the small ski resort a few minutes' drive from the town centre. A piste has been cut through the forest, with a charming stone-built restaurant and small hotel at its foot. Skis can be hired and training can be provided for children aged five or over and adults. Ice skates are also available, for use on the nearby reservoir.

Përparim is also a mountaineer – he has climbed in the Himalayas – and can offer advice and guiding to climbers who wish to explore some of the peaks in Puka district or beyond.

TROPOJA

The district of Tropoja nestles in the top right-hand corner of Albania, cut off physically from the rest of the country by huge lakes and towering mountains. These geographical features, inconvenient though they are for the local people, offer the visitor the chance to see spectacular scenery in unspoiled surroundings rare in Europe. The highlights of any visit to Tropoja are the approach by boat up Lake Komani and excursions in the valley of the Valbona River. There are many mountain tracks for hillwalkers to enjoy, although you should exercise the same caution as you would in any other remote high mountain area – don't go alone, leave your planned route with someone you trust, don't assume your mobile phone will work, and so on.

Tropoja district takes its name from a village in its northeastern corner, which gives some indication of the disastrous effect on it of the Great Powers' decision (page 12) to deprive the newly independent Albania of what is now western Kosova. The district seems very far from Tirana, but it is very close and accessible to the Kosovar towns of Gjakova, Peja and Prizreni. There can scarcely be a single family in Tropoja that does not have relatives on the other side of the border: in Kosova, in Montenegro or in both. Yet during the communist period it was completely cut off from these trading centres, while for most of the first decade of democracy, sanctions against Yugoslavia closed the border once again. At the same time, the district was sidelined and starved of resources by successive governments, even when the president of Albania was Sali Berisha, a native of Tropoja village.

In these circumstances, smuggling and criminality flourished during the 1990s, and Tropoja gained a reputation for being violent and unsafe. In a kind of vicious circle, this meant it got even less money from central government and none at all from foreign donors, who were afraid to go there. A clampdown by central government during 2001–02 saw the security situation improve dramatically and, like elsewhere in Albania, Tropoja has also benefited from investment in roads and other infrastructure. Valbona in particular has become a thriving destination for Kosovar and international visitors.

GETTING THERE AND AWAY By far the best way to approach Tropoja from the south is on the **ferry** up Lake Komani, a world-class journey through outstanding fjord-like scenery. Details of this route can be found on pages 168–9. The only other feasible option from the south is the old road through Puka and across the bridge at Fierza (see opposite).

There are no roads into Tropoja from the west or the north. To reach the district by **road** from elsewhere in Albania normally requires crossing into and back out of neighbouring Kosova. The roads have all been upgraded and are in good condition. Border formalities are minimal for holders of most passports (indeed, practically non-existent for Albanian adults). Those driving foreign-registered cars into Kosova will be obliged to buy a minimum of 15 days' vehicle insurance, which at the time of writing costs €30.

There are two options by road via Kosova. The route served by public transport goes via Kukësi, Prizreni and Gjakova (page 174). Those with their own vehicles might consider the slightly shorter route (now also upgraded) via Kruma and the border crossing at Qafë-Prushi.

All **public transport** between Tirana and Bajram Curri, the administrative capital of Tropoja, goes via Gjakova, Prizreni and Kukësi. The fare for the whole journey is 1,000 lek; it takes about 5 hours. Buses leave Tirana's North bus station [62 B2] every 2 hours from 06.00 to 14.00. In the other direction, the first minibus leaves Bajram Curri for Tirana at 08.00 and departures continue until 14.00. Passengers can alight anywhere along the route; from Bajram Curri, it takes about 2½ hours to Kukësi and the fare is 500 lek. Minibuses from Gjakova to Bajram Curri leave frequently during the day and the journey takes about 1 hour. The one-way fare is 300 lek; if the driver is Kosovar, he will probably insist on being paid in euros. For transport between Bajram Curri and Valbona, see pages 171–2.

Properly equipped and prepared **hikers** have other options for getting to Tropoja. From Thethi, the popular hike over the Valbona Pass (1,817m) is covered on page 173 and the challenging alternatives, through the Nikaj Valley, on page 174. There

6

are no official border crossing points between Vermoshi (page 220) and the main road from Gjakova, but there are footpaths. One of these comes into Tropoja from the Montenegrin but Albanian-speaking district of Plava and links into the path down from the village of Çeremi to Valbona (page 173). The locals apparently do the journey between Çeremi and Vuthaj ('Vuthanjë' in Montenegrin) in 1 hour, but then Albanian villagers are pretty fast walkers. Hikers wishing to cross any of the international borders between Albania, Kosova and Montenegro should obtain permits in advance, to avoid problems at the exit border. See page 44 for details of how to obtain these permits.

WHERE TO STAY, EAT AND DRINK In the district capital, Bajram Curri, there is a good choice of hotels and a few restaurants (pages 170–1). Most visitors head quickly for Valbona, where there is a wide choice of accommodation, from boutique hotels to the family homes known as *hans*. There are *hans* elsewhere in the district too. For general advice on wild camping in Albania, see page 44.

LAKE KOMANI The journey along Lake Komani deserves to be one of the world's classic boat trips, up there with the *Hurtigrut* along the Norwegian coast or the ferry from Puerto Montt to Puerto Natales in Chile. Lake Komani is narrow and twisting, with sheer cliffs right down to the water in some stretches, complete with breathtakingly high waterfalls. It is part of a huge hydro-electric system constructed in the 1970s and 1980s but, unlike Lake Fierza further upstream, its topography was not much altered by flooding. In some places, the slopes are gentler and small clusters of houses can be seen. Here the people have terraced what little land is available, to pasture their livestock and grow maize and other crops. It must be a desperately harsh existence in these lakeside villages, where the only form of transport is a boat and where in bad weather you can be cut off completely from any shops, schools or medical care. Incredibly, some people apparently choose to live in even more remote spots, in the houses that can be spotted from time to time high up above the lake. Some of these houses are now abandoned, but others are still occupied, at least in the summertime, by hardy souls who work their land and build their haystacks as their ancestors did before them.

Thoughts of the hardship of these people's lives need not deter you from marvelling at the magnificent scenery. Because the lake follows the twisting line of the river on which it is based, the boat at times appears to be heading for an unbroken cliff face. At the last moment, as it begins to turn, the break in the rock appears and the continuation of the lake can be seen through the gorge ahead. In these narrow stretches, the steep rocks on either side of you seem even higher than they really are. The water is a deep jade colour, and the cliffs and trees climbing up above it are reflected in its intensity. In the less steep stretches, you can see the far-off summits of the Dinaric Alps, more than 2,500m high. Herons (*Ardea cinerea*) and pygmy cormorants (*Phalacrocorax pygmeus*) live around the lake, and golden eagles (*Aquila chrysaetos*) and chamois (*Rupicapra rupicapra*) can sometimes be seen up in the surrounding peaks.

Car ferries After a gap of three years, car ferries are now running again on Lake Komani, as well as passenger-only boats. Contact details for the main operators are on page 169. The journey takes about 2 hours.

The largest car ferry, the **Alpin**, leaves Fierza at 09.00 and returns there from Komani at noon, but only if it has sufficient reservations. In the peak summer months, it is fairly safe to assume that it will run; at other times of year, you should check before travelling to the lake. Rates vary according to vehicle size (motorbikes and saloon cars 3,000 lek, 4x4 vehicles 3,500 lek). A further 1,000 lek is payable per passenger. The ferry has a canopied upper deck from which to enjoy the spectacular views, a bar on the lower deck with a rather restricted range of drinks and snacks, indoor lounges (by reservation only) and adequate toilets.

The **Berisha** ferry, with space for ten cars, runs between 15 April and 30 October leaving Komani at 09.00 and returning there from Fierza at 13.00.

Passenger boats Pedestrians and cyclists have the additional option of one of the passenger boats. The traditional, year-round option, the *Dragobia*, leaves Fierza at 06.00 and begins the return trip from Komani at 09.00 (700 lek per person one way). The 'lake excursions' operated by **Mario Molla** are a more relaxed option, spending longer on the lake and stopping at a beach for a swim (May–October, €35, English spoken). In summer, Mario offers a daily pickup service from Shkodra, leaving at 08.00 to connect with his boat; he can also collect clients from Tirana airport.

The passenger boats leave Fierza not from the old ferry terminal, 3km beyond the town, but from a jetty on the other side of the bridge, called Breglumi ('The Riverbank'). Mechanical problems are a common occurrence with the passenger boats; they are not a good option for anyone whose time is tight. Boats can also be chartered for day trips on and around the lake.

Alpin m 068 801 27 31; e info@alpin.al; w alpin.al; f Trageti-Alpin
Dragobia and *Berisha* m 068 52 70 934, 069 68 00 748; e kontakt@komanilakeferry.com; w komanilakeferry.com, komanilake-explore.com

Mario Molla 026 373 003; m 068 20 22 686, (WhatsApp) 068 52 63 884, 068 63 74 712; e mariomolla@outlook.com, komanilake@hotmail.com; w komanilake.com; f KomaniLake

Getting there and away To get to Komani, the main road as far as Vau i Dejës is good; after the Komani turn-off, it is rather slow going for 22 mountainous kilometres, and you should allow at least 2 hours **by car** from Shkodra. Cars can be parked for the day or overnight beside the jetty at Komani. There is a small, basic hotel at the Komani jetty (Natyra; **$**) and a campsite beyond the tunnel (**$**). **Cyclists** should note that the tunnel leading to and from the jetty at Komani is badly lit and badly surfaced.

In the other direction, public minibuses run between Bajram Curri and Fierza in the mornings; the journey takes about half an hour. The going rate for a taxi from Valbona to Fierza is €30.

The operator of the *Berisha* and *Dragobia* ferries offers a **minibus** service, daily in summer, from Tirana and Shkodra, to connect with the car ferry and take passengers onwards to Valbona. From Tirana, the bus leaves from near the Zogu i Zi roundabout at 05.00 (€10 to Komani, €20 to Valbona); from Shkodra, the departure time is 06.30 (€5 to Komani, €15 to Valbona).

The most reliable and up-to-date source of information about the permutations of boats, ferries and buses, and all other aspects of travelling to or from Tropoja, is w journeytovalbona.com.

BAJRAM CURRI *Telephone code: 0213*

The administrative centre of Tropoja district, Bajram Curri was purpose-built under communism and named after one of the key figures in the liberation of Albania from Ottoman rule. Bajram Curri was in fact Kosovar, which brought him

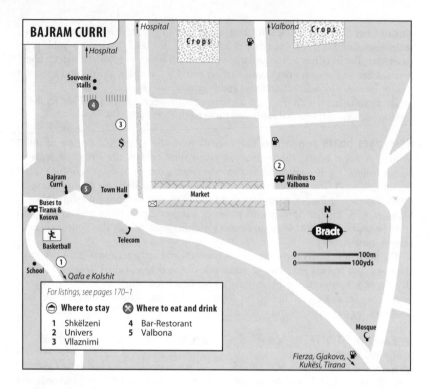

BAJRAM CURRI

↑Hospital
↑Hospital
↑Valbona
Crops
Crops

Souvenir stalls
④
③
$

Bajram Curri
⑤ Town Hall
Buses to Tirana & Kosova

Basketball

Telecom

① Qafa e Kolshit
School

② Minibus to Valbona
Market

N
Bradt

0 ————————100m
0 ————————100yds

Mosque

Fierza, Gjakova, Kukësi, Tirana

For listings, see pages 170–1

🏠 Where to stay   ✗ Where to eat and drink

1 Shkëlzeni   4 Bar-Restorant
2 Univers   5 Valbona
3 Vllaznimi

into conflict with Ahmed Zogu (later King Zog; page 12), for whom reunification with Kosova was not a priority. After two decades in and out of the leadership of Albania, he died in a cave near Dragobia in 1925, probably assassinated on Zog's orders. A large Socialist Realist statue of him looks down over the main square of the town named after him. The museum behind the statue was looted in 1997 and has been closed ever since.

🏠 Where to stay   *Map, above*

🏠 **Shkëlzeni** (36 rooms) Bajram Curri; **m** 068 35 97 178, 067 50 00 093; **e** hotel. shkelzeni@gmail.com; **f** Hotel Turizem Shkelzeni. The former 'Turizmi' hotel, completely renovated in 2017, now of a high standard; wheelchair-accessible throughout. Good restaurant (**$$$**), indoor & terrace bars; lift; Wi-Fi throughout; free parking; laundry service. All rooms good-sized & nicely furnished; good-sized en-suite bathrooms with rainshower, well-lit mirror, toiletries, hairdryer; some have bath tub as well as shower; flatscreen TV, AC, phone, minibar, some have balcony. **$$$–$$**

🏠 **Aste** [not mapped] (5 rooms, 3 more planned) Tropoja e Vjetër; **m** 068 58 27 445; **e** hello@asteguesthouse.com; **w** asteguesthouse. com. Beautifully furnished *han* in Old Tropoja, good

option for hikers. Living room with balcony; further balcony with views across Tropoja River; double-glazed & heated with wood stove. 1 bedroom en suite, 4 bedrooms share 2 bathrooms, all with new fittings & good shower. **$$**

🏠 **Vllaznimi** (19 rooms) Bajram Curri; **m** 068 20 79 060, 068 36 19 177. English spoken by some staff. Restaurant (**$$**) & lively, though very smoky, bar. All rooms en suite with TV, AC; 5 'superior' rooms have small balcony; nice, good-sized bathroom with shower; good-sized dbl bed or twins. **$$**

🏠 **Univers** (5 rooms) Bajram Curri; **m** 067 25 96 335, 067 25 96 366, 068 56 88 189. Above restaurant, Wi-Fi in public area. Twin rooms, all with basic en-suite bathroom, AC, TV. **$**

✕ Where to eat and drink *Map, opposite*

✕ Bar-Restorant (So called on sign above door) Behind the Vllaznimi Hotel. Serves good home-cooked Albanian dishes. $$

✕ Valbona Range of grilled & roast meat dishes at lunchtimes, salads & light meals at other times. $$

Other practicalities The town has the usual things you find in Albanian towns, such as grocery stores, ATMs, a post office, internet cafés, a hospital and a couple of large new mosques. Locally made souvenirs can be found in the kiosks of the small 'artisans' market'. Travellers heading onward to Valbona should note that there are no cash machines, Accident and Emergency facilities, or petrol stations beyond Bajram Curri. Nor are there any shops in the Valbona Valley; there is no shortage of food or drink, but hikers should stock up here on snacks, fruit, cigarettes, batteries, plasters and anything else that might be required. There is a small hardware store where the minibus for Valbona waits (see below).

There are no fixed-line telephones in the Valbona Valley. Once you are about 10 minutes out of Bajram Curri, the most reliable mobile-phone signal is Eagle (numbers beginning with 067). If you are using roaming on your home phone, you may need to change the settings manually so that it looks for Eagle first. Parts of the Valbona Valley have no mobile-phone coverage at all.

VALBONA The Valbona River is justly famous for its dramatic gorges and plunging waterfalls, as well as for the clarity and the beautiful, light-blue colour of its water. It rises on the slopes of Mount Jezerca (2,694m), which is the highest mountain wholly in Albania (Mount Korabi, near Peshkopia, is partly in Macedonia, although the summit is on the Albanian side of the border), and flows into the huge northern hydro-electric system at Fierza. The road runs alongside or above it for about 30km, up to Rragami, near its source, a few kilometres beyond the main village of Valbona (Valbona Qendër)

The river comes into view just before the road crosses it a couple of kilometres beyond Bajram Curri; if you are using your own transport it is worth stopping somewhere near the bridge, so that you can enjoy the view up and down the gorge. Dragobia is about halfway between Bajram Curri and the main village of Valbona; by this point, despite the magnificent scenery, cyclists may well be glad of a rest from the relentless uphill paths.

The path up to the **Dragobia Cave** (Shpella e Dragobisë), where Bajram Curri was killed in 1925 (page 170), starts on the other side of the river, a little further on towards Valbona. It is waymarked from the Rilindja Hotel (page 172); hiking maps are available from the hotel and from the guesthouses in Valbona.

As you approach the village of Valbona, the valley flattens out, and the river runs between meadows right through the village. Valbona was a thriving little resort until 1997, when it suffered in the civil unrest that engulfed Albania. In recent years, though, tourism has begun to flourish again and the village is quite lively in summer, with lots of visitors who come from Kosova for the day or the weekend, as well as a smaller number of foreign hikers.

Getting there and away A **minibus** operates from Valbona down to Bajram Curri in the mornings and back again in the afternoons; the one-way fare is 300 lek. It leaves Valbona punctually at 07.00, from the western end of the village, just down the hill from the Lamthi and Çardaku guesthouses (page 172); barring delays, it should be possible to connect with the Tirana minibus that leaves Bajram Curri at 08.00. The Valbona minibus usually leaves Bajram Curri again at about 14.30; it

6

picks up passengers outside a little shop just before the last petrol stations on the road out towards Valbona (see map, page 170). The road has been surfaced and widened as far as the main village of Valbona, although it tends to disintegrate in the winter. Beyond the main village, a drivable road goes as far as Rragami, bridging the river just beyond Fusha e Gjesë.

Where to stay, eat and drink

Hotels

Fusha e Gjesë (50 rooms) m 067 20 18 005; w fushaegjese.com. At the end of the asphalted road from Valbona, lovely setting, can be noisy at w/ends. Large restaurant with traditional dishes, bar, Wi-Fi, parking. Chalets with 1 dbl & 1 sgl bed, veranda, en-suite toilet & shower, wardrobe, heater. Sgl, dbl & trpl rooms, all en suite with AC, TV & balcony. **$$$**

Jezerca (8 rooms) Valbona Qendër; m 067 30 93 406. Stone-built traditional house, restaurant, Wi-Fi. Dorms & dbl rooms, sharing 4 modern bathrooms. Camping also possible (**$**). **$$**

Margjeka (9 rooms) Ziçi; m 067 33 82 162; e info@hotelmargjeka.al; w hotelmargjeka.al. More or less directly above Fusha e Gjesë, 500m uphill from the main road to Rragami. Restaurant with large terrace, beautiful views over the valley; open fire & TV in lobby; laundry service; German spoken; Wi-Fi in public areas & most rooms. All rooms en suite with CH; 2 family rooms (**$$$**), 7 twin or dbl. **$$**

Rezidenca (11 rooms) Quku i Valbonës; m 067 30 14 637; e alfred@journeytovalbona. com; w journeytovalbona.com. In settlement (also known as Quku i Dunishës) just off main road 3km before the main village of Valbona, coming from Bajram Curri; comfortable rooms in a traditional setting; same ownership as Rilindja, English spoken. Sitting room with sofas & open fire, restaurant, Wi-Fi, laundry service. Dbl & twin rooms, all nicely fitted out with CH, en-suite bathroom with good shower, private balcony with table & chairs. **$$**

Rilindja (5 rooms) Quku i Valbonës; m 067 30 14 637; e alfred@journeytovalbona. com; w journeytovalbona.com. Just off the main road on way up to Valbona; attractive wooden building set in landscaped garden & surrounded by magnificent mountains; large covered balcony looking on to the garden; English spoken. Excellent restaurant with international & local dishes. Hiking maps & brochures available, guides can be arranged. Campsite (**$**) with electric power-points & dedicated showers & toilets for campers. 2 twin rooms & 2 family rooms share good bathroom, 1 dbl en suite. **$$**

Tradita (5 chalets, 6 rooms) Valbona Qendër; m 067 33 80 014, 067 30 14 567; ⓕ Hotel.Tradita.Valbone. Restaurant. Chalets (**$$**), each with 1 dbl & 1 sgl plus 1 fold-up bed; AC; nice en-suite bathroom with shower. Rooms in stone-built farmhouse share 2 modern bathrooms; 2 dbl, 4 twin. **$–$$**

Guesthouses (han)

All prices are per person with b/fast (**$**); FB & HB options are also available.

Ilirjan Lamthi (12 beds) Rragami; m 069 25 22 486. 1 dorm, shared bathroom; home-cooked food, inc honey from Ilirjan's own bees.

Kol Gjoni (30 beds) Valbona, just beyond the main village; m 069 26 40 836. Some English spoken; a member of the family is the English teacher at the village school. Bar, restaurant with home-cooked food. Dbl, trpl & dorm rooms.

Lazër Çardaku (8 beds) Rragami; m 067 28 86 309, 069 23 11 499. Some English spoken; Lazër is a teacher at the village school. 2 rooms sharing modern bathroom; traditional, home-cooked food & homemade raki & wine; picnic lunches can be provided.

Mark Lamthi (16 beds) Rragami; m 069 25 03 941, 067 30 14 524. 1 twin room with beautiful carved wooden ceiling, 3 dorms, 2 shared bathrooms; camping also possible; home-cooked food.

What to see and do There are plenty of short **hikes** in the Valbona area, to lovely alpine meadows, mountain lakes and spectacular waterfalls. Hiking information is available at guesthouses in the village and at the Rilindja Hotel. The trout fishing in the Valbona River is generally excellent, and permits are not usually required for light, non-commercial fishing; the hotels and guesthouses may be able to provide rods. The path over the Valbona Pass, from Rragami to Thethi, has been waymarked and a guide is not necessary; see below for more about this increasingly popular hike. Waymarking has also been done around the Rilindja Hotel; for example, to the Dragobia Cave (page 171) and to Liqeni i Xhemës, a beautiful little lake hidden away among beech trees only a couple of hundred metres from the main road.

A longer waymarked hike – 2.4km from the main road – goes through the forests to **Çeremi**, a tiny traditional village right up on the border with Montenegro. There is also an asphalted road up to the village. For those who have hiked across the border into Albania (page 168), Çeremi is a good place to stop for lunch or for the night. **Berti's** (*4 beds;* m *067 22 74 913 – use SMS, no mobile signal in village;* **$**) offers a single dorm room with four single mattresses on the floor. Solar panels provide electricity and hot water, and there is a toilet and shower in separate cubicles. Camping is possible in a field behind the family house. Berti's mum prepares huge traditional lunches of home-produced ingredients. Some English is spoken.

For other hikes around the Valbona Valley, and certainly for longer expeditions, a local guide should be hired. The management of all the hotels and the families in all the guesthouses will be able to recommend a knowledgeable guide. For a day's guiding, the going rate is €50 a day; for an hour or so, around 1,000 lek. These guides are unlikely to speak much English. Horses can also be arranged. Outdoor Albania in Tirana (page 29) can organise hiking and climbing expeditions in the Valbona and Thethi areas.

Beyond the main village, a track across the (usually) dry bed of the Valbona River leads to the village-cluster of **Rragami**. There are several guesthouses here (see opposite). From here, you can continue on foot along the riverbed or return to the asphalted road and continue by car, over the new bridge, to the Fusha e Gjesë Hotel, where the asphalt ends. To drive any further requires a 4x4 vehicle (or two wheels). Users of less rugged cars can park at the hotel and walk the rest of the way to the hamlet of Gjelaj i Rragamit, where the drivable track ends. It is 9km from here to the Rilindja Hotel.

Gjelaj is a beautiful place, nestled right in the angle where the mountains meet, but it is a harsh environment to live in, with 2m of snow every winter and no community facilities at all. The village school closed in 2007, and so families with school-age children had no option but to move away or board their children with friends or relatives. In the summertime, though, when most visitors are here, there are plenty of people working their fields and tending their livestock. There are no shops or bars, but bread, cheese and raki can be bought from the villagers. Some of the local families provide simple accommodation (**$**), which can be booked online at w journeytovalbona.com. A scramble up through the woods above Gjelaj leads to a spectacular waterfall; the route is not obvious and it would be wise to hire a local guide.

From Gjelaj, an ancient path leads over the Valbona Pass to **Thethi**. This hike requires a good level of fitness and should not be attempted without adequate footwear and clothing. There is usually snow on the pass until the first week of June. The track has been waymarked and route-finding is straightforward. Horses or mules can be hired on either side of the pass to carry rucksacks or other equipment; ask at your guesthouse or hotel. See pages 217–18 for further information about this hike, the box on pages 216–17 for details of the plants, animals and birds that are present in these mountains, and page 212 for information about onward transport from Thethi to Shkodra.

For those who find the Valbona Pass a little too well trodden, an alternative route between Thethi and Valbona goes through the beautiful, wild country of the Nikaj Valley. Cut off from the rest of Tropoja by walls of mountains, the remote village of Curraj i Epermë is now uninhabited apart from three or four families who return for the summers. From Valbona, the easiest pass into the valley is Qafa e Kolshit, which can be reached by road from Bajram Curri; then you walk down to Bëtosha and up the river to Curraj i Epermë. There are also passes from Dragobia and Rragami, but they are more difficult. If you are coming to Tropoja by boat, you could get off at Lekbibaj and walk up to Peraj i Nikajt, from where a good, clear path leads over Qafa e Mrrethit (about 2 hours) and down to Curraj i Epermë. From there, it is a stiff hike over another gigantically high pass to Nderlysaj, down the Shala River from Thethi. Journey to Valbona has created the first reliable hiking map of these routes; see page 40 for details. There is no accommodation in Nikaj, although the families in Curraj i Epermë will look after you *in extremis*; wild camping is possible everywhere. Take enough food with you; there is plenty of wonderful spring water.

KUKËSI *Telephone code: 024*

The town of Kukësi is a pleasant but unremarkable town in a dramatic setting, surrounded by mountains and overlooking vast Lake Fierza, 72km long. This is the largest in a chain of three interconnecting lakes that generate most of Albania's electricity. The damming of Lake Fierza in 1978 created the Light of the Party hydro-electric plant but inundated several settlements, including the old town of Kukësi. The existing town was built to rehouse the people whose homes are now underwater and so it is entirely modern. In very dry years, when the water level in the lake is exceptionally low, the roofs of the old town appear above the surface and the old people go down to the lakeside to sit and look at their former homes.

While Kukësi is not a top tourist destination in itself, it is a convenient base from which to explore further afield: north to Tropoja, south to Peshkopia, west to Puka or Mirdita, or east to Prizreni and the rest of Kosova.

GETTING THERE AND AWAY
From Kosova Kukësi is only 42km from Prizreni, in southwestern Kosova, and **buses** ply frequently across the border, with the journey taking about half an hour. Border formalities are minimal, although non-Albanians have to show their passports. An alternative route from Kosova (or Tropoja) is from Gjakova (Đakovica, in Serbian) by the border crossing at Qafë-Prushi and via the district of Hasi. This road is now fully asphalted and it takes about an hour by car; using public transport would require a change of minibuses in Kruma (the district capital, usually also referred to as Hasi).

There are several **minibuses** a day between Kruma and Kukësi; the fare is 150 lek. This is a very interesting route with wonderful scenery – wild, desolate country, with traditional fortified houses (*kulla*) and beautiful views over Lake Fierza. The Jupa Hotel in Kruma offers simple accommodation (**$**) – three rooms, sharing a toilet and shower – and serves good fish and traditional Albanian food. Just off the main road at the junction for the village of Gjinaj, a simple wooden restaurant serves fresh *zander* (pike-perch) and grilled meat dishes. There are wonderful views from here of the confluence of the two Drini rivers.

From Tirana and the rest of Albania Kukësi is less than 3 hours' drive from Tirana. In Tirana, the **buses** leave from the North bus station [62 B2], more or less every 2 hours from 07.00 to 18.00.

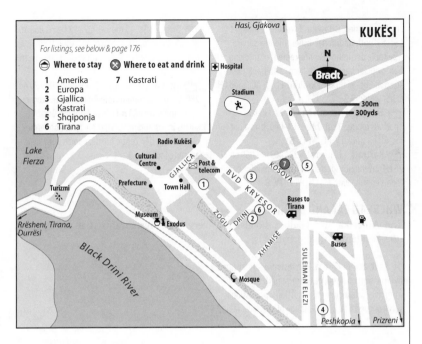

For listings, see below & page 176

KUKËSI

Hasi, Gjakova ↑

🏠 **Where to stay** ✕ **Where to eat and drink** ➕ Hospital

1 Amerika
2 Europa
3 Gjallica
4 Kastrati
5 Shqiponja
6 Tirana

7 Kastrati

Lake Fierza

Turizmi

Rrësheni, Tirana, Durrësi

Radio Kukësi

Cultural Centre

Prefecture

Town Hall

Post & telecom

Museum ✦ Exodus

Black Drini River

Mosque

Stadium

GJALLICA

BVD KRYESOR

ZOGU I DRINI

XHAMISE

KOSOVA

SULEIMAN ELEZI

Buses to Tirana

Buses

Peshkopia ↓   Prizreni ↓

0 ——— 300m
0 ——— 300yds

There are also **minibuses** to Kukësi from Rrësheni in Mirdita (page 158). From Bajram Curri (page 167), the buses to Kukësi (and Tirana) go via Kosova. The journey to Kukësi takes about 2½ hours; the through buses to Tirana drop passengers for Kukësi on the highway below the town, from where slightly rickety metal stairs lead up to town level. Negotiating these stairs with a large rucksack in heavy rain is an interesting experience. There is one bus a day between Peshkopia and Kukësi; it leaves Peshkopia at 07.30 and returns from Kukësi at noon.

The main bus terminus is along the street which runs from the eastern junction of the main boulevard down towards the lake (Rruga Suleiman Elezi). The best chance of obtaining information of any reliability about minibus departure times is to ask in the cafés here. The buses to Tirana wait on the boulevard itself, 100m or so around the corner from the main terminus, opposite the junction with the street down to the mosque (Rruga e Xhamisë). The map above shows these locations.

The civilian airport at Kukësi may become operational within the lifetime of this guidebook. Budget airlines are particularly interested in using this airport as an alternative to chronically fog-bound Prishtina.

WHERE TO STAY *Map, above*

🏠 **Amerika** (42 rooms) Lagjia 5; ☎ 223 278; m 068 20 37 874; e office@baramerika.com; w baramerika.com. Boutique hotel; professional, friendly service; English spoken; secure lift to all floors, operated with guest's key-card. Function suite, conference rooms, free Wi-Fi throughout. Generous cooked b/fast inc. Excellent restaurant (**$$$**; menu inc game & other specialities) & bar on ground floor; cocktail bar on top floor, beautiful

360° views of mountains & lake, accessed by panoramic lift. All rooms have well-finished en-suite bathrooms, TV, AC, ample power sockets, direct-dial phone, fridge, good curtains. **$$$**
🏠 **Gjallica** (22 rooms) Bd Kryesor; ☎ 222 527, 222 327; m 068 20 23 096/098/099; e hotelgjallica@gmail.com, info@hotelgjallica.al; w hotelgjallica.al. English spoken at reception; parking; conference facilities; boat trips on lake

can be arranged. B/fast inc. Excellent restaurant ($$$), with traditional dishes, friendly service, nice table decoration & enforcement of smoking ban; popular bar, separate from restaurant. Good-sized rooms, all en suite with Wi-Fi, TV, AC, good CH & hot water. $$

🏠 **Europa** (4 rooms) m 069 22 93 391. Spacious rooms: 1 sgl, 2 trpl, 1 4-bed; b/fast not inc. All en suite, TV, AC, Wi-Fi. $

🏠 **Kastrati** (15 rooms) 📞 224 403; m 069 68 17 762. Conveniently located for buses & minibuses. All rooms en suite with AC, CH, Wi-Fi, TV. $

🏠 **Shqiponja** (5 rooms) 📞 224 343; m 068 55 58 855. Quiet location; bar; no restaurant; Wi-Fi. All rooms have small en suite with shower; AC, electric radiator. $

🏠 **Tirana** (10 rooms) 📞 224 819; m 069 20 44 280; 🅕 Bar Restorant Hotel Tirana. On the corner of the main street. Wi-Fi; b/fast not inc. Good salads in restaurant ($$), some tables on terrace overlooking city-centre bustle. Rooms with basic en-suite facilities. $

✕ WHERE TO EAT AND DRINK *Map, page 175*

The Amerika and Gjallica hotels have very good restaurants that are open to non-residents. An alternative is:

✕ **Kastrati** Rr Kosova. Fish restaurant (identified by 'Fish' sign on street outside); superb fresh fish from river & lake, generous portions; professional service; good house wine, range of specialist raki. $$$

WHAT TO SEE AND DO

Municipal Museum The area around modern Kukësi has been settled since Neolithic times. The first people in the region for whom there is archaeological evidence lived at Kolshi (excavated in the 1970s) and were part of the Starçevo cultural community, the earliest settled farming society in the western Balkans (6000BC). Later, as in southeastern Albania, the people began to bury their dead in tumuli (barrows), such as those found at Çinamaku. No fewer than 80 tumuli were identified there, ranging in date from the 12th to the 7th centuries, then used again between the 4th and 2nd centuries BC, with the latest burials of all dating from the 1st century AD and even the early medieval period. Excavations at Çinamaku also uncovered Attic white-figure pottery (6th century BC) and coins minted by the Ardiaean king Genti (168–147BC).

The Romans built one of their great arterial roads through this region, to link the Roman port of Lissus (page 8) with the cities that are now called Prishtina and Niš. Romans settled in the Kukësi region too, but it was only in the 9th century that the town began to develop. Its location on the Drini River and on the Roman road made it an important link in the trading network between the Adriatic and the Danube.

The town museum (*free admission*) presents all this history through maps and artefacts, with most of the information translated into English. There is a section about the history of the town in the 20th century, including fascinating photos of Old Kukësi, now under the waters of Lake Fierza, and information about the flora and fauna of the district. Upstairs is a small ethnographic exhibition.

Exploring the town A walk around Kukësi takes an hour at most. The information panel in the piazza outside the museum is as good a place to begin as any. It has a map of the town and another of the surrounding region, with information about the main places of interest. The administrative buildings for the town and region are in the main square beyond.

The imposing tower beside the museum, overlooking the lake, is a monument to the exodus from Kosova during the 1998–99 war. Most of the 500,000 refugees who fled Kosova entered Albania at Kukësi, which – despite its own poverty and lack of infrastructure – somehow managed to cope not only with its Kosovar cousins but also with the hordes of foreign aid workers and journalists who descended on the town. The monument was erected by a group of grateful Kosovars in 2009, the tenth anniversary of the refugees' return to their homes (also via Kukësi) after NATO had driven out Slobodan Milošević's forces.

The town's lakeside promenade is a pleasant walk on a fine evening, when it fills with strolling families and couples. To the right are fine views of the lake; to the left is a park, with swings and other amusements for children. The Durrësi–Morina highway, which connects Kukësi and, beyond it, Kosova with the Adriatic Sea, runs below the promenade, along the lakeside. And towering above the town, lake and highway, Mount Gjallica rises to the southeast, 2,486m high.

Towards the end of the promenade, at the mosque, turn left to reach the main street, Boulevard Kryesor or (its new name, which nobody will know) Rruga Dituria. The buses for Tirana wait for passengers near this junction. Turning left on to Boulevard Kryesor, you will pass the Gjallica Hotel and come to the Radio Kukësi building, with a wonderful Socialist Realist bas-relief above its door. Turning left down Rruga Gjallica here brings you back to the main square, with the Cultural Centre, town hall and regional government building, or Prefecture.

The minor road up to the north, beside the Cultural Centre, leads through trees and above fields to the ruined shell of the former 'Turizmi' hotel, used as offices by international organisations during the war in Kosova and, since then, left to decay and crumble. From the other side of the ruins, there are marvellous views of Lake Fierza, the Black Drini coming into it from the south and the confluence of the White Drini just visible to the north. The White Drini rises near the Kosova–Montenegro border and flows down to Albania through Kosova; the Black Drini begins its overland life at the northern end of Lake Ohrid and flows through Macedonia before entering Albania to the south of Peshkopia. From here there is also a good view of the bridge over the Black Drini and the highway that continues to Rrësheni, Durrësi and Tirana.

The Black Drini (Drini i Zi)
The Black Drini runs through spectacular gorges, wild rocky mountains and pretty hillside villages, making for a magnificent drive or bike run. A new road, further to the east, is now the main route between Kukësi and Peshkopia and there is no longer any public transport on the Black Drini road. The old road is no longer maintained and a 4x4 vehicle is likely to be required.

From Kukësi, the road runs first through pretty woodland, with good views behind of the town and the lake, and past the airport (unused at the time of writing). The old and new roads separate at the village of Kolesjan, about 10km south of Kukësi. On the old road, the scenery now starts to become quite dramatic, with breathtaking views of the river far below and tributaries tumbling down towards it through willows and alders. There are clusters of houses fortified in the traditional style, using the slope of the hill to protect the back of the building, with small windows on the upper floors and none at all at ground level. Along the way, birds of prey hang on the thermals and spectacular white cliffs tower on the other side of the river.

Shishtaveci
Shishtaveci is the largest of a group of eight villages on the Shishtaveci Plateau, 31km southeast of Kukësi right on the border with Kosova. The plateau is over 2,000m above sea level at its highest point and, in the communist period, Shishtaveci,

with its natural ski-slope, was one of the country's ski resorts. In the summer, the countryside is beautiful. The road from Kukësi has recently been asphalted, all the way to the border crossing to Dragash (Kosova). A minibus leaves the village for Kukësi first thing in the morning and returns to Shishtaveci in the early afternoon. There are several guesthouses and a small hotel in the village; wild camping is also possible.

Hikers should exercise caution in this part of Albania and avoid straying off beaten tracks. This is because there may still be some unexploded ordnance remaining from the 1999 war in Kosova. The mines were laid by Kosovar fighters to stop the Serbs following them into Albanian territory; it is thought that all of them have now been cleared, but it is impossible to be certain that none has been missed. The northeastern border is the only part of Albania where landmines present even the most remote risk.

PESHKOPIA *Telephone code: 0218*

Peshkopia is set amid spectacular mountains that make it rather isolated from the rest of Albania. Like Tropoja (pages 166–7), it was cut off from its natural hinterland by the border drawn in 1913 and, like Tropoja, it suffered further from many years of neglect by the Albanian government. In recent years though, foreign investment and local enterprise have turned the town into a thriving and pleasant place. The district of which it is the administrative centre is called Dibër (or Dibra), and the town itself is also sometimes referred to by that name. This can lead to confusion, since the nearest town on the other side of the border is also called Dibër (or, in Macedonian, Debar). The key is to remember that only 100 years ago, before the drawing of the lines that have caused so much turmoil in the Balkans, it was all the same district. Many travellers use Peshkopia as a base from which to visit the Mavrovo National Park, only 26km away on the other side of the 1913 border, now in Macedonia.

GETTING THERE AND AWAY The road from the Albanian coastal plain to Peshkopia runs through spectacular scenery, above a precipitous river gorge, past Lake Ulza and through wild, rather bleak terrain dotted with fortified houses. After Burreli

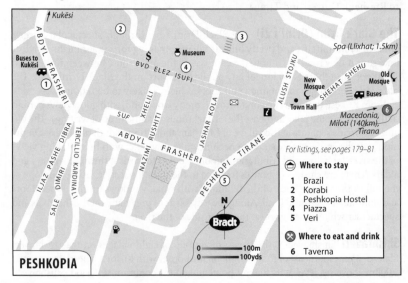

(pages 182–5), it continues to follow the lovely green Mati River upstream, before climbing over the watershed through forests of beech and conifers, with glimpses through them of the mountain peaks on either side.

It is 140km from the Miloti junction, on the coastal highway, to Peshkopia. However, this road is showing its age, especially compared with the new highway to its north, and the journey from Tirana will take between 4 and 5 hours. Construction work has begun on a new road, Rruga e Arbërit or 'the Arbëri Road', which will connect Macedonia with the Adriatic. If the original plans are followed, it will swing north of the existing road and no doubt improve Peshkopia's own transport links with Macedonia, as well as with Tirana and the coast.

Another new road, replacing the old road along the Black Drini River (page 177), links Peshkopia with Kukësi, via Kastrioti and Bushtrica. It is asphalted but mountainous – it apparently has no fewer than 760 bends – and the journey takes about 2 hours.

By public transport From Tirana, the **buses** for Peshkopia leave from the North bus station [62 B2], from early morning until mid afternoon. Note that buses advertised as going to 'Dibër' will take you to Peshkopia, not Macedonia! In Peshkopia, they terminate in and leave from the main square.

From neighbouring Macedonia, **minibuses** operate between Peshkopia and Dibra e Madhe (Debar) via Maqellarja, a bustling little transport hub about 13km from Peshkopia. If there is no direct bus at the time you want to travel, there are very frequent minibuses from Maqellarja to Peshkopia, taking about 30 minutes.

A daily **bus** service operates between Peshkopia and Kukësi; it takes just over 2 hours and the one-way fare is 800 lek. In Peshkopia, the bus departs from the bus park next to the Brazil Hotel. It leaves there between 07.00 and 07.30 and returns from the main bus terminus in Kukësi at noon.

By bike The new road between Kukësi and Peshkopia is very hard going on a bicycle. It has a good surface all the way, but the gradients are very tough – 15–20% in places. You should allow up to 8 hours on this route. A slightly easier alternative is the old road, which runs above the Black Drini River, another spectacularly beautiful route (see above).

Another route to and from Peshkopia for cyclists, bikers, or those with the use of a 4x4 vehicle, is the mostly unasphalted road to Librazhdi, about halfway between Elbasani and Lake Ohrid. This turns off the main Peshkopia–Bulqiza road, just after the village of Shupenza, and continues south for about 80km through remote mountain terrain, along the border with Macedonia.

WHERE TO STAY *Map, opposite*

Veri (48 rooms, 2 suites) ☎25090; m 069 20 98 186; e verihotel@gmail.com; f Bar-Restorant-Hotel Veri. New building with lift, good restaurant ($$$), bar, enclosed smokers' area; conference room; Wi-Fi. B/fast inc. Generously proportioned rooms, all with large, well-equipped en-suite bathroom, king-size bed, desk, bedside lights, flatscreen TV, AC. **$$$**

Piazza (20 rooms) Bd Elez Isufi; ☎24616; m 069 67 41 378; e info@hotelpiazza.al; w hotelpiazza.al. New building, great location on pedestrianised main street; free underground car park; free Wi-Fi throughout. Excellent restaurant ($$$), modern kitchen, all organic, good wine list; terrace bar. B/fast inc. Generously sized rooms, all with large en-suite bathroom, AC, flatscreen TV, desk, balcony. **$$**

Brazil (9 rooms) ☎23934; m 068 20 90 648. Next to the court (*pranë Gjykatës*), very handy for buses to Kukësi. Bar & restaurant; rooms of varying capacity, basic but clean. All rooms en suite with heater & TV. **$**

Korabi (60 rooms) Bd Elez Isufi; `22481; m 069 20 70 107, 068 20 70 107; f Bar-Restorant-Piceri-Hotel-Korabi (Turizmi). Refurbished communist-era hotel, central location. Good restaurant ($$$) with separate entrance; in summer, tables outside on lovely raised terrace. Free parking; conference room; laundry service; Wi-Fi; b/fast inc. All rooms en suite with AC, TV, balcony. **$**

Peshkopia Hostel (3 dorms, 2 private rooms) m 068 27 76 848, 068 31 33 451; w peshkopiahostel.com, outdooralbania-association.com/our-projects; f Peshkopia Backpacker Hostel. Renovated villa once used as accommodation for visiting communist leaders. Great location overlooking the town; huge garden with trees & hammocks; ample parking; Wi-Fi. 2 common rooms, 1 with fireplace; fully equipped kitchen; 2 bathrooms on each floor; towels & bed linen provided; b/fast inc. Camping possible. Tours organised, including to Lura & Mt Korabi. **$**

EDITH DURHAM

Edith Durham, like many other travellers to the Balkans, came to the region almost by accident. She was born in London in 1863, into a comfortably-off professional family. Her father was a distinguished surgeon, and her seven brothers and sisters later became eminent in their various professions. She herself studied fine art and exhibited twice at the Royal Academy. However, when her mother became ill in the 1890s, it fell to Edith, as the eldest daughter in the family, to abandon her artistic career and devote herself to her mother's care.

Understandably enough, she became depressed and ill herself – 'The future stretched before me in endless years of grey monotony, and escape seemed hopeless,' she wrote – and, in 1900, she was advised by her doctor to take two months' holiday every year, as a complete break from her duties as a carer. She decided to take a cruise, with a friend, down the Dalmatian coast from Trieste to Kotor, in Montenegro. From there, she followed Baedeker's advice to drive up to Cetinje, then the Montenegrin capital, in order to 'be able to say ever afterwards, "I have travelled in Montenegro"'. Durham was struck both by the picturesqueness of this tiny, mountainous princedom and by what she described as its 'impossibly feudal views'.

That first short trip to Cetinje and Podgorica, where she saw Albanians for the first time, had sown the seeds of a lifelong engagement with the Balkans. When she returned to London, she learned the Serbian language and studied Balkan history. In subsequent years, her travels grew increasingly adventurous; she visited Montenegro four times, travelled extensively in Serbia, and ventured into the Ottoman province of Kosova. In 1904, she published an account of these journeys, *Through the Lands of the Serb*. She hoped that her ethnographic studies of the region might help to solve the vexed question of Balkan borders, which continued to give rise to so much diplomatic intrigue and military skirmishes.

In 1903, she visited Albania, the least known of all the Balkan provinces and the only one without a sponsor in one of the Great Powers. She discovered a growing feeling of national unity among Albanians that belied their religious and cultural differences, and realised that Albanian national aspirations would need to be taken into account if the problems caused by the decline of the Ottoman Empire were to be adequately addressed. She returned to Albania in 1908 and embarked on a remarkable journey through the northern highlands. Very few foreign men had ever travelled in this remote and mountainous region; for a foreign woman to undertake such a journey was completely unprecedented. Durham recorded it in her book *High Albania*, a combination of travelogue,

✖ WHERE TO EAT AND DRINK   *Map, page 178*

The best restaurant in Peshkopia, at the time of writing, is that of the Piazza Hotel. The Veri and Korabi hotels also have good restaurants. All are open to non-residents. The **Taverna** café (**$$**), at the western end of the main square (closed in the evenings), offers traditional Albanian dishes, including the local speciality, *jufka*, a kind of fine pasta.

WHAT TO SEE AND DO

Municipal Museum   (*Bd Elez Isufi;* ◷ *08.00–16.00; free admission*) Peshkopia's museum is set back from the pedestrianised main street, just behind the Piazza Hotel. Its ground floor is devoted to the history of the Dibra region,

ethnographical observations and political reporting of the historical events that affected Albania during her stay.

In 1911, the Catholic clans of northern Albania, encouraged and armed by Montenegro, rebelled against Ottoman rule. The uprising did not last long – the clans were obliged to make terms with the Ottomans when Montenegro withdrew its support – but during and after it Edith Durham organised the provision of humanitarian aid from her base in Scutari (the Italian name for Shkodra). She distributed flour, roofing materials and money, and gave medical treatment to sick highlanders who would often travel for days to find her. She remained in Montenegro and Shkodra during the two Balkan Wars of 1912 and 1913, and described the events of the wars and her own experiences in *The Struggle for Scutari*.

Edith Durham was in Vlora when Greek troops occupied southern Albania in October 1914, and in Korça when it was taken the following year. She and a friend tried to save Korça by pleading on its behalf with the Council of Ambassadors in London; this involved their walking for three days across the mountains to Berati, the nearest place from where a telegram could be sent. After the war, she became the Secretary of the Anglo-Albanian Society, a pressure group of Members of Parliament and other promoters of Albanian interests. Her final visit to the country, in 1921, was cut short by illness, but during her stay she was greeted by cheering crowds and fêted by Albanian politicians. In Shkodra, delegations of clansmen came down from the mountains to welcome her.

Although she did not return to Albania after her 1921 trip, she continued to write about the Balkans. She was a council member of the Royal Anthropological Institute and wrote an ethnological study entitled *Some Tribal Origins, Laws & Customs of the Balkans* (published in 1928), as well as political-historical accounts of her travels such as *Twenty Years of Balkan Tangle* (1920). King Zog awarded her the Order of Skanderbeg and offered her a home in Albania. However, she remained in London, where she died in 1944.

Edith Durham is still revered in Albania, where she is sometimes referred to as 'The Highlanders' Queen' (Krajlica e Malësorëve; *krajlica* is an archaic word used in folk epics, and so the Albanian expression has a kind of fairy-tale sound to it). Streets still bear her name – sometimes they are the only streets that have signs – as do schools.

It is now very much easier to obtain copies of Edith Durham's books than it was before the advent of print-on-demand OCR reproductions (pages 280–3).

The Northeast   PESHKOPIA

6

including the years of resistance to Serbian occupation after Albania declared its independence in 1912. Elez Isufi, after whom the main street is named, was one of the leaders of these uprisings, which finally succeeded in driving out the Serbs in 1920. Isufi was also involved in the so-called 'democratic revolution' of 1924, which installed Fan Noli as prime minister until he was overthrown by Ahmed Zogu (page 12). The first floor has an exhibition of the traditional costumes and jewellery of Dibra, along with other ethnographic items such as agricultural and household implements.

Boulevard Elez Isufi is pedestrianised along most of its length. Fans of **Socialist Realist art** should visit the restaurant of the Hotel Korabi (page 180), where one of the walls has a wonderful mural of a highland wedding. An information panel opposite the town hall has maps of and information about attractions in the town and the surrounding area. A new mosque has been built at this end of the main street. The main square below is the terminus for most buses and the best place to find a taxi. Steps up from this square, between the new and old mosques, lead to the **old quarter**, with a few surviving Ottoman-era houses and, from the top, marvellous views over the town and of the mountains to the east.

Towards the end of October each year, Peshkopia hosts an important **festival of traditional music** (Oda Dibrane) from all over the Albanian-speaking world. It is difficult, although not impossible, to get tickets for Oda Dibrane, and it is essential to book accommodation in advance while it is on.

Llixhat e Peshkopisë Just outside Peshkopia is a well-known **spa complex**, 750m above sea level, known by the generic Albanian word for thermal springs: Llixhat (page 154). The three sulphurous springs that feed the Peshkopia spa have been exploited since the early 20th century, when two communal baths were built. The current building, opened in 1989, has 44 individual cubicles, a pool and rooms for mud treatment. The ground temperature of the water is 38–40°C.

Full courses of treatment are offered from April to October; the best time is September–October, when up to 3,000 people a day use the facilities. The spa stays open all year round; however, drop-in customers (⏲ 10.00–16.00; 100 lek) can soak for 10–15 minutes in a bathtub in one of the cubicles (bring your own towel). There are many hotels at the spa, open only in season, eg: Hotel Alpin (*45 rooms;* m *068 23 22 446; all rooms en suite with TV, FB;* **$**). Llixhat is 1.5km from Peshkopia – a good walk or a short taxi ride (200–300 lek) from the main square.

MATI *Telephone code (Burreli): 0217*

Mati was the home district of Ahmed Zogu, the clan chieftain who became King Zog (page 12), and it is full of history, fortified houses and caves. The district capital, Burreli, is only 36km from the main Tirana–Shkodra highway, on the road towards Peshkopia. There are several interesting places to visit in Mati and it is well worth a short detour, even if you do not have time to continue all the way to Peshkopia.

GETTING THERE AND AWAY The turn-off for Burreli and Peshkopia is signposted off the highway that links the Albanian coast with Kosova, the Rruga e Kombit or the 'Road of the Nation'. From the Miloti junction, on the coastal highway, the drive to Burreli takes about an hour through spectacular scenery (page 178).

From Peshkopia to Burreli is about 2 hours. Construction work has begun on a new road, Rruga e Arbërit or 'the Arbëri Road', which will connect Macedonia with

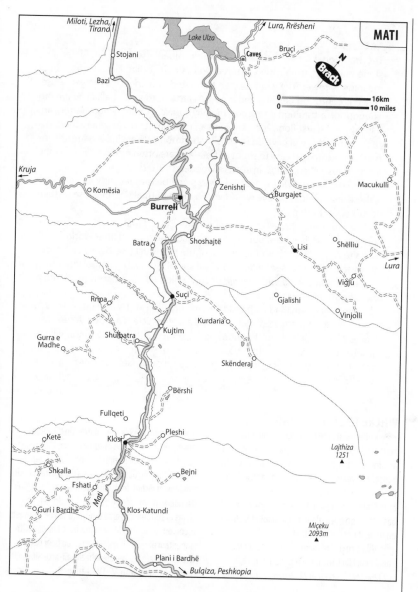

MATI

0 _____ 16km
0 _____ 10 miles

the Adriatic. If the original plans are followed, it will swing north of the existing road and will make the journey between Burreli and Peshkopia very much faster. For those with their own transport, an alternative route is from Kruja (pages 98–9) over the Shtama Pass (Qafa e Shtamës), about 50km. The road is asphalted, but there is no public transport and the pass is closed when there is snow.

Buses to Burreli from Tirana leave hourly from the North bus station [62 B2] from 07.00 to 17.00. The journey takes about 2½ hours, depending on the traffic in the outskirts of Tirana; the fare is 400 lek. From Peshkopia, the buses leave from the main square. Any bus for Tirana from Peshkopia can drop you off as it passes through Burreli. See page 185 for information about public transport around Mati.

The traditional family houses of northern Albania were highly defensible stone buildings, usually two or three storeys high, called *kulla*, whose literal meaning is 'tower'. The word is often translated into English as 'tower house', which is confusing because these houses are not towers at all. *Kulla* are big enough for a traditional extended family to live in; the living quarters are usually on the first floor, accessed with an external staircase; where there is a third storey, this will have been used for bedrooms. The windows are small – hard to fire into and easy to shoot out of – and are often protected with stone embrasures, called *frëngji*, instead of wooden shutters.

Mati has several well-preserved *kulla*, some built as recently as the 1930s – these later buildings have windows of a more normal size, because by then security was better.

The imposing cluster of *kulla* where the Zogu family lived, in Burgajet just across the river from Burreli, was razed to the ground after World War II. The site can be seen from the terrace of the Vila Bruçi (see below). An easily accessible place to see *kulla* is the village of Shulbatra (opposite) which has several fine *kulla* with *frëngji*, one of which has been converted into a guesthouse (Kulla Gjini).

Other villages in Mati with *kulla* are Guri i Bardhë and Macukulli. However, the roads up to them are very rough and a 4x4 vehicle is needed. A rural bus leaves Macukulli early in the morning for Burreli and returns to the village around lunchtime. It would probably be possible to find accommodation in one of the village homes, or of course one could camp (see page 44 for advice on wild camping).

WHERE TO STAY, EAT AND DRINK

Kulla Gjini (16 beds max) Shulbatra; m 068 53 03 481; e hotelmagra@live.com. Simple accommodation on 1st floor of traditional fortified house, 120 years old. 2 dorms with carved stone fireplaces, lounge area for guests with *sofra* (low, round table); wood-fired heating & hot water; basic toilet on guest floor, modern toilet & shower on ground floor within family home. **$**

Vila Bruçi (14 rooms) Lagja Drita, pranë Spitalit Poliklinik (near the hospital), Burreli; 23266, 22387; m 068 21 59 926; e vila-bruci@ hotmail.com; Vila Bruci Burrel. On the edge of town, wonderful views of surrounding countryside, quiet. Exceptionally helpful, friendly management; English spoken. Good restaurant (**$$$**), fresh trout, traditional dishes, local wine; terrace bar. Free Wi-Fi throughout; free secure parking; laundry service. Tours of surrounding area & beyond can be arranged. Generous b/fast inc. Most rooms have balcony with mountain or river views; those on top floor have wooden beams; some are wheelchair-accessible. All rooms en suite, with AC, TV, heating. **$**

BURRELI Burreli's main attraction is as a base for exploring the rest of Mati. The small **museum** (⏰ *mornings only Mon–Fri*) is worth a visit; the gunpowder machine is particularly interesting. Gunpowder was produced in Mati from Ottoman times until 1939, when Italy annexed Albania. The occupying forces closed down the gunpowder factories because they thought, probably quite correctly, that the Albanians might use the product to blow up Italian soldiers or strategic targets such as bridges. Aficionados of Socialist Realist art will like the murals in the main hall, one of them painted by Fatmir Haxhiu (1927–2001). The museum is open only on weekday mornings; the entrance is at the side of the building, not through the main gates where the local minibuses wait.

above   Gjirokastra became a UNESCO World Heritage Site in July 2005; its Ottoman bazaar is now home to artisans and souvenir shops (m50/D) pages 246–7

right   The 18th-century Gorica Bridge links two of UNESCO-listed Berati's museum zones (m50/S) pages 118–26

below   Iso-polyphony, a southern Albanian musical genre, is listed by UNESCO as part of Humanity's Intangible Cultural Heritage (SS) page 24

left	Southern Albania is studded with beautiful, neglected churches like this one at Kosina, near Përmeti (DD) page 152
below left	Albanian independence was declared in Vlora on 28 November 1912, and is commemorated with both this monument and a museum (GG) pages 265 & 267
below right	Kruja's attractively restored bazaar and buildings make the city an excellent place to get a feel for Albanian history and traditions (Pp/S) pages 98–102

above　Atmospheric Rozafa Castle has three layers of fortification, with the most secure section here, at its narrowest part (PJ/S) pages 195–7

right　The galleries around Durrësi's Roman amphitheatre contain a Byzantine chapel with a number of wall mosaics, the only examples of their kind ever to be found in Albania (SS) pages 93–4

below　Shkodra's Catholic Cathedral was designed and decorated by the city's foremost 19th-century artists (ES/S) pages 200–1 & 202

above   Traditional *qilime* — woven rugs — on sale at the bazaar in Kruja (WB/AWL) page 102

above left   The Albanian Orthodox Church is independent from other Orthodox authority and ordains its own bishops (SS) page 21

below left   The traditional kilt of southern Albania is known as a *fustanella* (DR/S)

below   A weaver at work in her house in Jagodini, near Elbasani (AL)

above   Driving in rural Albania means sharing the road with livestock; this is on the way to Thethi (MO/S) pages 212–13

right   The artisans' cooperative in Gjirokastra includes a stonemason's workshop (AL) page 241

below   Relaxing in the thermal waters at Bënja, near Përmeti (DZA/S) pages 154 & 155

above   The little town of Peshkopia is surrounded by spectacular mountains (GG) pages 178–82

below   The Vjosa River is spanned by precarious wooden bridges that provide picturesque crossing points for hikers (SS) page 147

bottom left The dramatic Mesi Bridge near Drishti is the longest Ottoman bridge in Albania, at 108m (AL) pages 202–3

bottom right The ancient city of Apollonia was a major port for many centuries, until the course of the Vjosa River shifted (WB/AWL) pages 105–7

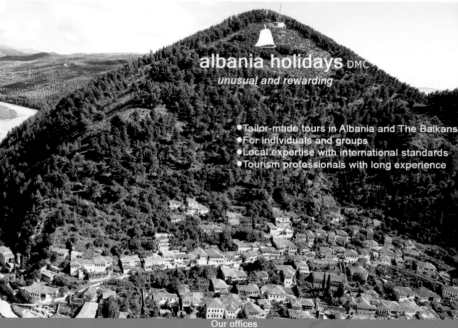

The other interesting sight in Burreli is the large statue of King Zog, just off to the side of the main square. The statue is modern, of course, since during the communist period it would have been completely out of the question to erect even a small bust of the exiled king.

SHULBATRA The village of Shulbatra, 10–15 minutes' drive from Burreli, is an easily accessible place to see *kulla*. It is also in a beautiful setting, above the Mati River (in summer, one can swim), with views of the mountains between Mati and Kruja (pages 98–102).

Shulbatra has several fine *kulla* with *frëngji* (see box, opposite). The best way to see inside one is to spend a night at **Kulla Gjini**, a family home now converted into a simple guesthouse. In the older part of this house, built 120 years ago, there is an inscription, carved into the stonework, in Ottoman Turkish (the family does not know what it means). The owner's grandfather built an extension in 1934 and carved his name, with the date, into the wall, as well as making sure to add built-in rifle holes. There are also stone fireplaces carved with stylised eagles.

To get there by public transport, you can take any minibus for Klosi, from the main bus terminus outside the museum in Burreli, and ask the driver to let you off at Ura e Shulbatrës ('the Shulbatra Bridge'). The turn-off can be identified from the large sign for 'Kulla Gjini'. From the main road, cross the bridge over the green Mati River and follow the asphalted road to the centre of the village. The asphalt ends here, although the road up to the guesthouse is just about drivable. It is better to park and explore the village on foot.

CAVES Another fascinating excursion in Mati is to a cluster of three caves in the north of the district, on the border with Mirdita (pages 157–61). Recent archaeological research has found evidence that one of these, the Neziri Cave, was inhabited in the Neolithic period.

The first of the caves, **Shpella e Blasit**, is 240m deep, through a short but very confined opening. Once you have wriggled through this rather scary tunnel, you emerge into a long, high cave, full of beautiful stalactites. The second, **Shpella e Keputës**, is also long, with thousands of sleeping bats; the end of this cave is blocked with earth, not bedrock as in Shpella e Blasit, and it is thought that it might ultimately link up with Shpella e Valit, across the district border in Mirdita. Finally, **Shpella e Nezirit** was home to those Stone Age people, who cooked and ate at the entrance to the cave. Nails in the floor of the cave show where the archaeologists measured out their trenches. Lake Ulza and the mountains of Kruja can be seen from the entrance to the cave, a good choice by the Neolithic inhabitants.

The hike up to the caves starts in the village of Bruçi, about half an hour's drive from Burreli, off the road to Rrësheni. The turn-off for Bruçi is at the petrol station in Uraka, 20km or so from Rrësheni and about 15km from Burreli. This main road is fully asphalted; after the turn-off, the asphalt continues for a while after Uraka and then peters out.

The hike takes about 2 hours, plus however long you spend in the caves and requires reasonable fitness and sensible shoes. A good torch is essential; a local guide is highly recommended. The owner of the hotel in Burreli (see opposite) is originally from Bruçi and can either organise a tour to the caves for you or contact one of their relatives in the village in advance, to meet you there. Alternatively, you can ask the staff in the café in Bruçi to contact a guide for you.

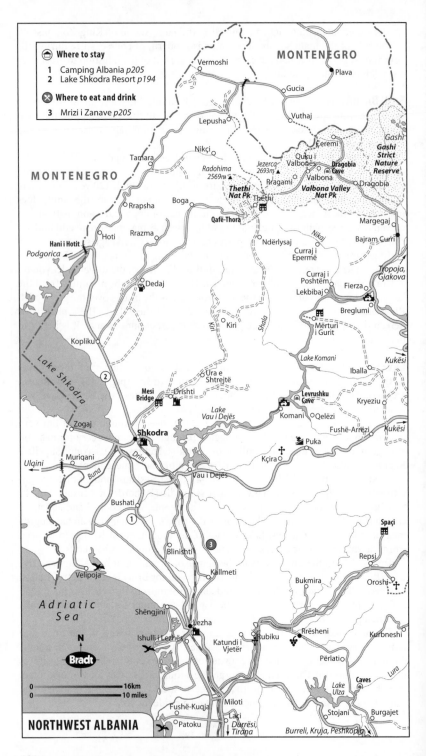

Where to stay
1 Camping Albania *p205*
2 Lake Shkodra Resort *p194*

Where to eat and drink
3 Mrizi i Zanave *p205*

MONTENEGRO

Vermoshi
Plava
Gucia
Vuthaj
Lepusha
Ceremi
Gashi
Gashi Strict Nature Reserve
Nikçi
Tamara
Quku i Valbonës
Jezerca 2693m
Dragobia Cave
Radohima 2569m
Bragami
Valbona
Dragobia
Thethi Nat Pk
Thethi
Valbona Valley Nat Pk
MONTENEGRO
Rrapsha
Boga
Margegaj
Qafë-Thora
Ndërlysaj
Nikaj
Bajram Curri
Hoti
Rrazma
Curraj i Epermë
Tropoja, Gjakova
Hani i Hotit
Podgorica
Curraj i Poshtëm
Fierza
Dedaj
Lekbibaj
Breglumi
Kiri
Kiri
Shala
Mërturi i Gurit
Kopliku
Lake Komani
Kukësi
Iballa
Ura e Shtrejtë
Kryeziu
Lake Shkodra
Mesi Bridge
Drishti
Levrushku Cave
Komani
Qelëzi
Fushë-Arrëzi
Kukësi
Zogaj
Lake Vau i Dejës
Shkodra
Puka
Ulqini
Muriqani
Drini
Kçira
Buna
Vau i Dejës
Spaçi
Bushati
Blinishti
Repsi
Bukmira
Oroshi
Velipoja
Adriatic Sea
Shëngjini
Kallmeti
N
Ishulli i Lezhës
Lezha
Rrësheni
Kurbneshi
Katundi i Vjetër
Rubiku
Përlati
Lura
Bradt
Caves
Lake Ulza
0 16km
0 10 miles
Fushë-Kuqja
Miloti
Stojani
Burgajet
Patoku
Laçi
Durrësi, Tirana
Burreli, Kruja, Peshkopia

NORTHWEST ALBANIA

7

The Northwest

SHKODRA   *Telephone code: 02*

Shkodra has been a highly significant city during most of its long history. It was the capital of the Illyrian state of the Ardiaeans from the 3rd century BC until the Roman conquest in 168BC. During the Ottoman occupation it was the seat of a semi-autonomous *pashalik* (see box, page 199) under the Bushati family, which at one point stretched east into what is now Kosova, and south as far as Berati. Shkodrans were prominent in the Albanian cultural and political renaissance (Rilindja Kombëtare) which led ultimately to independence from the Ottomans.

Italian influence has always been strong in Shkodra – the city was part of the Venetian Republic from 1396 until it was surrendered to the Ottomans, after a long siege, in 1479 (page 195). Almost all Shkodrans speak Italian, and donations from across the Adriatic fund much of the city's cultural, environmental and social welfare activity. Since the end of communist rule, though, there has been considerable immigration into the city from the surrounding highlands, and this has led to some friction between Shkodra's urban intellectuals and the highly conservative traditions of the mountain incomers.

Shkodra has one of Albania's best castles (which is saying a lot), attractive domestic architecture and several excellent museums: the archaeological display in the Historical Museum, the huge collection of 19th- and 20th-century photographs in the National Museum of Photography, the Cathedral's Diocesan Museum and the chilling Site of Witness and Memory. See pages 195–201 for further details of all these attractions.

Shkodra is a good base for excursions into the wild and beautiful Albanian Alps; see page 210 for information about how to get there. On the coast, there are important wetland habitats at Velipoja and Kune-Vaini, where many rare and attractive waterfowl and other birds can be observed. See pages 208–11 for further information about birdwatching in these reserves.

GETTING THERE AND AWAY
To/from Tirana   There are frequent **buses** from Tirana to Shkodra, running at least once an hour from 07.00 to 17.00. They leave from the North bus station [62 B2], take about 2 hours and cost 300 lek one-way. In Shkodra, the buses to Tirana depart from Sheshi Demokracia. They can be boarded or alighted from at almost any point along their route: for example, the bridge leading from the highway to Lezha, the junction at Miloti or the slip-road for the airport.

From Tirana **airport**, a right turn at the roundabout at the exit from the airport will lead you to the Fushë–Kruja junction of the main north–south highway, 2.8km from the airport. Unfortunately, there are no buses to Shkodra from the airport, at the time of writing. The Shkodra taxi drivers charge 1,000 lek per person to the airport, based on five paying passengers.

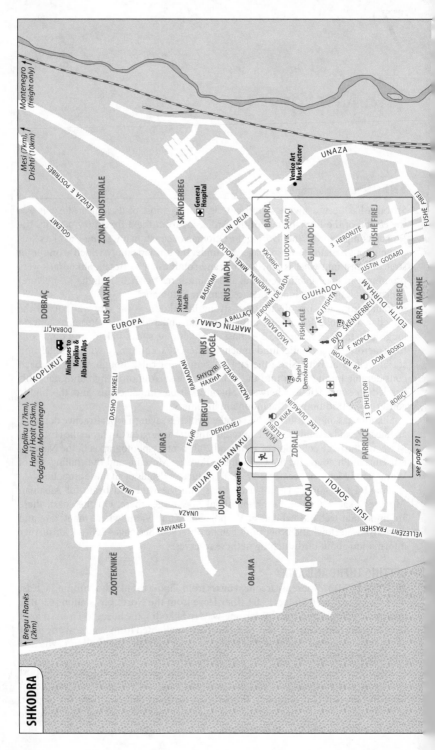

SHKODRA

188

Montenegro (freight only)

Mesi (7km), Drishti (10km)

Kopliku (17km), Hani i Hotit (35km), Podgorica, Montenegro

Bregu i Ranës (2km)

LEVIZJA E POSTRIBES

ZONA INDUSTRIALE

GOLEMIT

SKËNDERBEG

General Hospital

UNAZA

Venice Art Mask Factory

LIN DELIA

BADRA

DOBRAÇ

DOBRAÇIT

KOPLIKUT

Minibuses to Kopliku & Albanian Alps

RUS MAXHAR

EUROPA

BASHKIMI

KARDINAL MIKEL KOLIQI

RUS I MADH

Sheshi Rus i Madh

F SHIROKA

LUDOVIK SARAÇI

GJUHADOL

3 HERONJTË

FUSHË FIREJ

JUSTIN GODARD

DASHO SHKRELI

RAMADANI

MARTIN CAMAJ

BALLAÇI

RUS I VOGËL

SHYQYRI HAXHIA

NAZMI KRYEZIU

KARDINAL MIKEL

JERONIM DE RADA

VASO KADIA

FUSHË CELË

AT GJ FISHTA

GJUHADOL

EDITH DURHAM

SERREQ

ARRA MADHE

FUSHË FIREJ

KIRAS

FAHRI

DERGUT

DERVISHEJ

BUJAR BISHANAKU

DUDAS

Sports centre

ELVIRA ÇELEBIU

LEKE DUKAGJINI

ZDRALE

Sheshi Demokracia

28 NËNTORI

F NOPCA

BVD SKËNDERBEU

DOM BOSKO

13 DHJETORI

D

BORIÇI

PARRUCË

ZOOTEKNIKË

KARVANEJ

UNAZA

OBAJKA

NDOCAJ

ISUF SOKOLI

VËLLEZËRIT FRASHËRI

see page 191

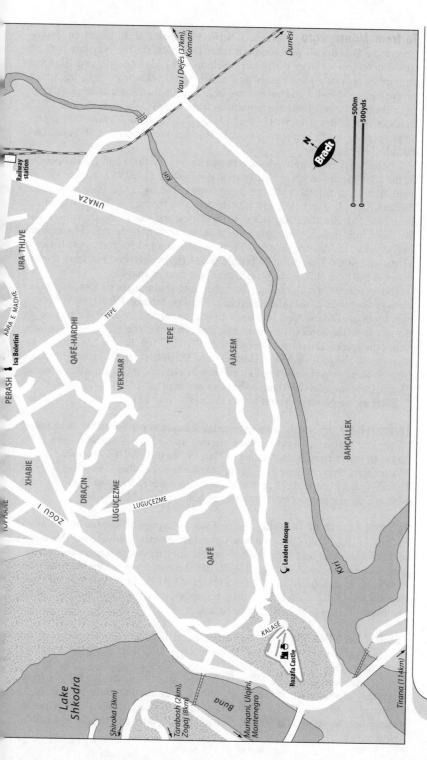

Lake Shkodra

Shiroka (3km)

Tarabosh (2km),
Zogaj (8km)

Muriqani, Ulqini,
Montenegro

Buna

KALASE
Rozafa Castle

Tirana (114km)

ℂ Leaden Mosque

QAFË

Kiri

BAHÇALLEK

LUGUÇEZME

LUGUÇEZME

DRAÇIN

VEKSHAR

TEPE

TEPE

AJASEM

QAFË-HARDHI

XHABIE

ZOGU I

TOPLANE

PERASH   Isa Boletini

ARRA E MADHE

URA THIJVE

UNAZA

Railway
station

Kiri

Vau i Dejës (37km),
Komani

Durrësi

Bradt

N

0   500m
0   500yds

To/from Montenegro Buses run between **Ulqini** (called Ulcinj in Serbo-Croat) and Shkodra all year round. It takes 1½ hours; the one-way fare is €6.50 (w *busticket4.me* or from the driver). Helpfully, the Montenegrin and Albanian authorities operate a joint border post at Muriqani, 14km from Shkodra, which saves time. In Shkodra, the buses leave from outside the Rozafa Hotel; in Ulqini, from the bus station. There are departures from Ulqini at 06.00, 07.00 and 13.15; buses leave Shkodra at 11.30, 15.00 and 16.00. Taxis also do this run; they charge €8 per person, or €25 for the whole car. In Shkodra, the drivers tout for passengers outside the Rozafa Hotel.

One bus a day runs via Shkodra and **Podgorica** between Kotor and Tirana operated by the Montenegrin company Old Town Travel (**** +382 32 520 495; w *kotortotirana.com*). The whole trip takes about 6 hours; between Shkodra and Podgorica, about 2 hours, depending on how long it takes to get across the border. The departure time from both Shkodra and Podgorica is 10.00 (Tirana and Kotor 2 hours earlier). The bus leaves from outside the Rozafa Hotel in Shkodra and from the main bus terminal in Podgorica. The one-way fare is €13 between Shkodra and Podgorica; €18 between Tirana and Kotor. Tickets can be bought online (w *busticket4.me*) or from the bus driver. A taxi from Shkodra to Podgorica airport costs around €35.

Those coming from Montenegro with their own transport, or on foot, might also consider the border crossing between Gucia (Gusinje, in Serbo-Croat) and Vermoshi, high up in the Dinaric Alps. It is open all year round and the road is asphalted all the way from the border. A minibus operates every morning except Sundays from Vermoshi (pages 220–1) to Kopliku and Shkodra. See Bradt's *Montenegro* for information about Gucia, Vuthaj (Vusanje) and the district capital, Plava. Minibuses from Shkodra to Vermoshi, Kopliku and other destinations to the north, including Thethi, leave from Rus Maxhar, in the city's northern suburbs.

There are no passenger **trains** across the border with Montenegro.

To/from Italy Information about entering Albania by private yacht can be found on page 32. For lesser mortals, there are two ways to get to Shkodra from Italy: one is to take a ferry from Ancona or Bari to Bar (called Tivari in Albanian) in Montenegro, then continue via Ulqini, 26km away. The other is to take a ferry to Durrësi (page 91) and drive up the highway from there. The road is good all the way; in a car, the journey takes just over an hour, by bus a little more.

To/from Kosova or Tropoja The best way to approach Shkodra from Kosova or Tropoja (pages 166–7) is on a boat down Lake Komani from Fierza. This is one of the world's great boat trips, through breathtaking mountain scenery and narrow gorges, and is described on pages 168–9. The alternative is to use the old road from Kukësi, via the beautiful district of Puka (pages 163–4). Public transport uses the new highway from Kukësi; any bus will drop passengers off at the Miloti junction, where northbound buses to Shkodra can be hailed.

TOURIST INFORMATION An information panel outside the terrace-bar of the Rozafa Hotel has maps of and information about attractions in the town and the surrounding area.

The local authorities in Shkodra rename streets constantly. Most people, when they use any street names at all, still use the old, communist-era names. As elsewhere in Albania, Shkodrans are more likely to give directions with reference to neighbourhoods and landmarks. The **municipal police** are friendly and helpful to lost tourists.

7

SHKODRA
City centre

Stadium

Where to stay
1 @Home Hostel
2 Colosseo
3 Grand Hotel Europa
4 Kaduku
5 Mi Casa Es Tu Casa
6 Red Bricks
7 Rozafa
8 Tradita

Where to eat and drink
9 ArtiZanave
10 Piazza Park
11 Rozafa
12 San Francisco
   Tradita (see tr)
13 Vila Bekteshi

For listings, see pages 192–4

RUSI MADH

BADRA

GJUHADOL

SERREQ

PARRUCË

ZDRALE

Railway station
(approx 500m)

National Museum of Photography Marubi

FUSHË ÇELË

Stigmatine Sisters

Cathedral

Diocesan Museum

GEREJ

Site of Witness & Memory

St Francis

Orthodox

Partisans

Ebu Bekr

Mother Teresa

Luigj Gurakuqi

Albtelecom

Post office

Cinema

PALOK KURTI

Migjeni Theatre

Radio Shkodra

Sheshi Demokracia
Fountain

Hospital

2nd April

University

City Hall

Rozafa TV

Court

Prefecture

Fountain

Historical Museum

Beach

250m
250yds

0
0

N

Tirana, Shiroka, Ulqini

Street names:
EVLIJA ÇELEBIU
OSO KUKA
LEKE DUKAGJIN
QEMAL DRAÇINI
KONGRESI I MANASTIRIT
DR SELAUDIN BEKTESHI
BUJAR BISHANAKU
VASO KADIA
JERONIM DE RADA
KARDINAL MIKEL KOLIQI
FASH
FILIP SHIROKA
LUDOVIK SARAÇI
MARIN BEÇIKEMI
JUSTIN GODARD
EDITH DURHAM
GURAKUQEVE
MUJGESHAVE
AT GJERGJ FISHTA
AT SHTJEFËN GJEÇOVI
BOULEVARD SKËNDERBEU
JISUTIEVE
NENTORI
28
FRANC
NOPCA
DOM BOSKO
HASAN RIZA PASHA
IDMONEND
KOLE
TEUTA
WILSON
DHJETORI
13
DAUT
BORIÇI
ZOGU I
LIDHJA E PRIZRENIT
ISUE SOKOLI
BERDICEJ

Many agencies now organise hiking in the Albanian Alps; see page 29 for information about specialist hiking companies.

WHERE TO STAY *Map, page 191, unless otherwise stated*

Colosseo (41 rooms) Rr Kolë Idromeno; 224 7513/4; m 068 20 07 751; e info@colosseohotel.com; w colosseohotel.com. Centrally located in pedestrian street, opposite mosque (light sleepers beware combination of late-night music & early-morning call to prayer). English spoken; lift; free parking; indoor pool, gym, sauna (extra charge). Good, long-established restaurant offering Albanian & Italian dishes, separate entrance; bar on top floor with great city views. Good Wi-Fi throughout; business facilities available. Large well-fitted rooms, all with stylish en-suite bathroom; AC, bedside light, safe, minibar, hairdryer, flatscreen TV, desk, phone, good mirrors, thick curtains; some have balcony. **$$$$**

Grand Hotel Europa (50 rooms) Sh 2 Prilli; 224 1211, 224 6381; m 069 20 68 492; e info@europagrandhotel.com; w europagrandhotel.com. English spoken. Restaurant with international & Albanian cuisine; lobby bar & cocktail bar. Lift, free parking, laundry service; outdoor pool, garden; gym, sauna, Turkish bath, spa (extra charge);

BLOOD FEUD

Blood feud is an ancient mechanism for resolving serious conflicts between clans or other social groupings. It has been (and still is) used in many cultures, but rarely has it achieved the degree of formal codification as it did in Albania. The codes that govern blood feud and other matters of clan administration were transmitted orally until recent times, and are known by the Turkish (from Arabic) word for 'law', Kanun. There were several versions of these codes in different parts of highland Albania; the best known are those of Lekë Dukagjin and of Skanderbeg. The latter, of course, is Albania's national hero, the chieftain who united all the northern clans against the Ottoman invaders in the 15th century (see box, pages 206–7, for more about Skanderbeg). The Dukagjins were another of the powerful clans of medieval Albania, and the Lekë concerned is thought to have been the clan chief in the 15th century, although many of the laws in his Kanun must date from earlier times.

The Kanun regulated all aspects of life in the northern clans, including marriage, property and taxes. It also attempted to regulate the practice of revenge killing, or *gjakmarrja* ('blood-taking'), by setting out ways in which feuds between clans could be reconciled. In a society governed by revenge, if a member of your clan is killed by a member of a rival clan, you are duty bound to avenge that killing. The family of the man you kill (in such societies, women and children do not count) is then obliged to kill either you or – if that proves impossible – one of your close male relatives. It is perfectly obvious that if no mechanism is found for stopping this cycle, your clan and that of your enemy will both die out.

The Kanun way to end a blood feud was *besa*, an Albanian word that means many things ranging from 'word of honour' (its usual modern meaning), through 'sacred oath', to its Kanun meaning of a truce between clans. Besa could be cemented with a marriage between the two families concerned, or by the payment of a tribute, or not at all, since the word itself was enough – but it was not necessarily permanent and, if the feud revived, the male members of the families involved would begin the cycle again. The lock-in tower in Thethi (pages 214–15) is a reminder of the devastating effect that blood feud had on northern Albanian families.

The communist government managed to suppress blood feud fairly thoroughly, presumably through the same mechanisms of fear and suspicion casino; in-house travel agency, business centre, ATM, free Wi-Fi throughout. Suites, dbl & twin, all en suite with hairdryer, direct-dial phone, flatscreen TV, AC, safe. **$$$$**

🏠 **Rozafa** (44 rooms, will have 77) Rr Teuta; 📞224 2767; m 067 40 29 369; e info@ hotelrozafa.al; w hotelrozafa.al. Former Turizmi hotel, 4 floors completely renovated in 2016, 3 remaining floors will follow; superb central location. English spoken at reception; lifts, free parking; restaurant, bar, Wi-Fi. All rooms en suite, some with bathtub as well as shower; minibar, flatscreen TV, AC with temperature control, desk, hairdryer; some have balcony with panoramic city views. **$$$**

🏠 **Tradita** (12 rooms) Rr Edith Durham 4; 📞224 0537; m 068 20 86 056, 068 62 63 770; e info@traditagt.com; w traditagt.com. A 17th-century, stone-built house in the Shkodran style; owner's collection of traditional costumes, musical instruments, household implements & art on display throughout public areas; cultural events organised. Lively bar with good selection of raki; excellent restaurant serving northern Albanian specialities. Friendly, welcoming staff; English spoken. Free secure parking, free Wi-Fi throughout, free bike use; laundry service. Bedrooms in modern annexe overlooking attractive central courtyard garden, all en suite with free Wi-Fi & fridge. **$$$**

which it used to suppress activities such as listening to the BBC World Service. In the 1990s, however, blood feud re-emerged and has once more become a serious problem, although foreigners are extremely unlikely to be even tangentially affected. Feuds have been revived from several generations back, and because there is now freedom of movement, the young men who are at risk have left their mountain villages for Albanian cities, for Italy or Greece, or for further-flung destinations. Unfortunately, freedom of movement also means that the feud can follow them, thus spreading the problem from the highlands into the poor suburbs of the big cities.

Shkodra has been particularly badly affected by blood feud, with certain streets in the city functioning effectively as a 'lock-in neighbourhood', populated by people who have fled their villages and who allow no stranger to enter, lest he bring death to one of the families there. Having an enclave like this means that the men need not be confined to their houses, but can at least walk up and down the street and drink coffee with their neighbours. The women, of course, fulfil the same role as they would in the village, except they can buy food in the market instead of ploughing the fields on their own. There is even a 'lock-in apartment building' in the centre of Tirana.

The traditional codes exclude women and children from revenge killing. However, because they were maintained orally, by the elders of each clan or village, there was nobody left to interpret them according to the ancient custom when they were revived after 50 years of suppression. Since the resurgence of blood feud in the 1990s, therefore, it has taken on quite anarchic aspects. Young boys are prevented from attending school because they might be the target of a blood feud, and the old besa systems of feud reconciliation have almost completely broken down. The botched land privatisation of the early 1990s has not helped; the majority of revenge killing cycles nowadays are started over disputes about property or water rights.

One group that offers advice to families involved in blood feud and helps with reconciliation, when this is possible, is the Diocesan Commission in Albania of the Catholic organisation Justice & Peace (*Sh Papa Gjon Pali II*; 📞 *022 248 795*; e *p&dshkod@albnet.net*; w *kishakatolikeshkoder.com*).

🏠 **Kaduku** (15 rooms) Rr Studenti 84/1, Sh Demokracia; ☎242 216; m 069 25 51 230; e info@hotel-kaduku.com; w hotel-kaduku.com. Good location, just off the central square, but quiet because set back from the street (signposted). Friendly, very helpful staff; English spoken; luggage storage possible. Free parking; free bike use; restaurant with some traditional dishes. Substantial b/fast inc. Range of room sizes, all en suite with hairdryer, AC, CH, flatscreen TV, free Wi-Fi. **$$**

🏠 **Red Bricks** (14 rooms) Rr Studenti, Sh Demokracia; ☎290 0888, 157 0035; m 067 52 42 200, 069 89 43 200; e info@theredbricks-al.com; w theredbricks-al.com. Centrally located; English spoken; lift; business facilities; parking. Indoor & outdoor bars; free Wi-Fi & cabled broadband. B/fast inc. All rooms have en-suite bathroom with scales, hairdryer, shower with screen & alarm; plus AC, big flatscreen TV, safe, daybed, iron, minibar, mineral water inc, tea- & coffee-making facilities. **$$**

🏠 **@Home Hostel** (2 dorms, 2 rooms) Rr Franc Baron Nopca 17; m 069 86 70 887; e info@athomehostelshkoder.com; w athomehostelshkoder.com. Kitchen with wood-burning stove, electric & gas hobs, 2 fridge-freezers; lounge; courtyard & garden. Free parking, free Wi-Fi; lockers; laundry service; bike hire. Tours arranged. B/fast inc.1 twin en suite, 1 twin with adjoining bathroom, 2 dorms of 4 & 6 beds, each with own bathroom. **$**

🏠 **Mi Casa Es Tu Casa** (30 beds) Bd Skënderbeu; m 069 38 12 054; e hostelshkoder@gmail.com; w micasaestucasa.it. Old Shkodran house (photographed by Marubi in 1912), lovely garden with fruit trees & tortoises, comfortable veranda; English spoken. Beware of the dog! Bike hire; kitchen; big sitting room; bar; washing machine; free Wi-Fi; sheets & towels provided. Bike & horseriding tours arranged. Camping possible in garden; separate shower & toilet for campers. Studio apt with en-suite bathroom & kitchen (**$$**). Dbl room (**$$**) & dorms share toilets & showers. **$**

🏠 **Lake Shkodra Resort** [map, page 186] Vraka; ✪ 42° 08′ 30.2″ N 19° 27′ 93.8″ E; m 069 27 50 337, 067 41 17 947; e faye@lakeshkodraresort.com; w lakeshkodraresort.com. Campsite on the lakeside, about halfway between Kopliku & Shkodra; signposted from highway. Bike & kayak hire, fishing, sandy beach. Free Wi-Fi; laundry service; ample showers & toilets; lakeside restaurant & bar. Glamping tents available (**$$**); also 2-bedroom chalet, sleeps 4 (**$$$$**). **$**

✗ WHERE TO EAT AND DRINK *Map, page 191*

The local speciality is carp (*krap*) from Lake Shkodra, although it is not always available. It is easier to find in the restaurants on the lakeshore, on the other side of the Buna River; the closest are just before the old bridge (eg: the Beer Garden), or there is public transport to Shiroka and Zogaj (bus stop opposite the Rozafa Hotel).

✗ **Piazza Park** Sh Nënë Tereza. Upmarket pizza, pasta, salads, etc. Tables outside on large terrace in summer. **$$$**

✗ **Rozafa** Rr Marin Beçikemi; m 068 60 15 026. Across from cathedral; tables outside in summer; friendly service. Seafood, excellent pasta, risotto, pizza. **$$$**

✗ **San Francisco** Rr Kolë Idromeno. English spoken & English menu; big terrace on 1st floor, overlooking pedestrian street. Meat, seafood, carp, pasta, good pizza. **$$$**

✗ **Tradita** Rr Edith Durham 4; ☎240 537; m 068 20 86 056. It is well worth eating here even if you are not staying at the hotel. Restaurant in 17th-century stone-built house, open hearth where meat is grilled, excellent menu with local specialities inc game, wild fungi & forest fruits in season. Some English spoken; service can be rather slow. Interesting exhibition of traditional costumes & other items at entrance. **$$$**

✗ **Vila Bekteshi** Rr Hasan Riza Pasha; ☎240 799; m 069 28 67 445, 066 66 63 558. Near the Orthodox church; also known as 'Çoçja'. Tables outside in internal courtyard & upstairs in formal dining room. Good service, some English spoken. Italian-inspired menu, excellent meat dishes, pizzas good even by high Albanian standards. Locally brewed beer on draught; good house wine. **$$$–$$**

✗ **ArtiZanave** Rr Berdicej, Gjuhadol. Social enterprise, community-run restaurant; part of Slow Food movement. Simple, tasty salads & grilled meat. **$$**

WHAT TO SEE AND DO

Rozafa Castle (⏲ *09.00–14.00 Tue–Sun; 200 lek*) Shkodra's castle stands above the confluence of its three rivers, the Drini, the Kiri and the Buna, and thus controls all but the northern approach to the city. It is an excellent place for a castle and has been fortified since Illyrian times, when the Ardiaean queen Teuta launched her attacks on the Romans from it (page 8). Traces of the Illyrian walls, constructed of large stones with no mortar, can still be seen at the entrance to the castle.

Most of what remains is Venetian and Ottoman. The outer walls follow the line of the hill; within, successive lines of fortification create three distinct areas, of which the most secure and easily defensible is the section at the narrowest part. The views from the citadel are wonderful, across Lake Shkodra to Montenegro, out to the Adriatic, and down towards Lezha.

Rozafa Castle was twice besieged by Ottoman armies. When it finally surrendered in January 1479, it was only after a lengthy blockade, supervised for a time by Sultan Mehmed II in person, had brought Venice to the realisation that it had no choice but to make peace. Rozafa was the last fortress in Albania to fall to the Ottomans. Two-and-a-half thousand Shkodrans chose to leave under the terms of the surrender and were granted pensions by Venice. The new rulers continued to use the castle as a military and administrative centre; it was the vizier's residence and, from 1840, was the capital of the whole northern Albanian province (*vilayet*). It was last used for military purposes in 1913, when it operated as the Ottoman command centre during yet another siege, this time by Montenegrins.

You enter through the vaulted barbican gate to the first courtyard. A trickle of lime down the wall of this courtyard marks where people believe the eponymous Rozafa was walled up alive to guarantee the strength of the walls (see box, pages 196–7). Women still gather here to acknowledge Rozafa's sacrifice and to pray for their own fertility. The second enclosure was the main living area, with the barracks, stores and prison; the latter was in use until the early 20th century. The **ruined church** on your right was once Shkodra's cathedral, a 13th-century building that remained in use even after the Ottoman occupation, until it was converted into a

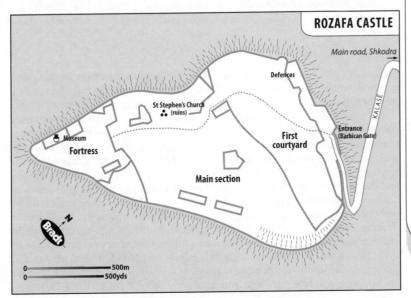

From Mitrush Kuteli's Old Albanian Tales

On top of Valdanuz Hill, three brothers were working. They were building a castle. The wall which they built by day collapsed by night, so they were never able to get it any higher.

Along there came a good old man. 'May your work go well, you three brothers!'

'May you go well, too, good old man. But where do you see anything going well with us? By day we work, by night it falls down. Might you be able to give us some advice? What can we do to keep the walls standing?'

'I know,' said the old man, 'but it would be impious to tell you.'

'On our heads be it, because we want this castle to stay standing.'

The good old man pondered and said, 'Are you married, my brave lads? Do all three of you have girls?'

'We are married,' they replied. 'All three of us have our girls. So tell us, then, what to do to keep this castle standing.'

'If you want to keep it up, bind yourselves by a solemn oath; do not tell your girls, do not discuss at home what I am about to tell you. Whichever one of the sisters-in-law comes tomorrow with your meal, take her and wall her up alive in the castle wall. Then you will see how the wall will take hold and will remain for ever and a day.'

So spoke the old man, and he left: one moment he was there, the next he was gone.

Alas! The eldest brother broke his solemn word. He discussed it at home, he told his own wife just as it was, he told her not to go there the next day. The middle brother also broke his solemn word: he told everything to his own wife. Only the youngest kept his solemn word: he did not discuss it at home, he did not tell his own wife.

In the morning, the three of them got up early and went to work. Sledgehammers struck, stones split, hearts beat, the walls grew higher.

In the house, the lads' mother knew nothing. She said to the eldest wife, 'My dear, the workmen want bread and water; they want a flask of wine.'

The eldest wife replied, 'On my honour, mother, today I cannot go, because I am ill.'

mosque in 1869. The circular, chimney-like structures here and there are the access points for water cisterns, constructed in the 15th century and fed by pipes running into them from all over the castle.

The third section was the real fortress, with underground stairways and tunnels connecting to different parts of the citadel. Some of the entrances to these secret passageways can still be seen, although the tunnels themselves are not open. The well is original; it was stolen in the civil unrest of 1997 and reappeared mysteriously ten years later. The three-storey Venetian building at the end of the third courtyard was the garrison commander's residence in the 14th and 15th centuries and now houses the **museum** (*150 lek*). This covers not only the history of the castle but also of the surrounding area. It is perhaps the only museum in Albania that is designed to be accessible to blind visitors, with information in Braille (in Albanian and English) and tactile displays. The exhibition includes a 3rd- or 4th-century mosaic, discovered at the foot of the castle hill; this is the only mosaic ever found in northern Albania. There is stonework from this castle – including a Venetian lion that may once have been over the entrance gate – and from the nearby castle of Drishti (page 203); coins

The mother turned and said to the middle wife: 'My dear, the workmen want bread and water; they want a flask of wine.'

'On my honour, mother, today I cannot go, because I am going to visit my parents.'

The lads' mother turned to the youngest wife. 'My dear ...'

The youngest wife leapt to her feet: 'Honoured mother, what is your command?'

'The workmen want bread and water; they want a flask of wine.'

'On my honour, mother, as for myself, I have my little son. I am afraid he will want my breast and he will cry.'

'On you go, we will take care of the boy, we won't let him cry,' said her sisters-in-law.

The young wife, the good wife, got up, she took bread and water, she took the flask of wine, she kissed her son on both cheeks and set off. She climbed up Valdanuz Hill, towards the place where her husband and her two brothers-in-law were working.

'May your work go well, workmen!'

But what was this? Their sledgehammers stopped striking, but their hearts beat harder and harder. Their faces grew pale. When the youngest saw his wife, he cast the hammer from his hand, he cursed the stone and the wall. His wife said, 'What is the matter, my lord? Why do you curse the stone and the wall?'

The oldest brother broke in: 'It was a black day when you were born, sister-in-law. We have given our word to wall you up alive in the castle wall.'

'Oh my brothers-in-law, may you prosper! But I have one request for you: when you wall me up, leave my right eye free, leave my right hand free, leave my right foot free, leave my right breast free. For my son is little. When he starts to cry, with one eye I shall look at him, with one hand I shall caress him, with one foot I shall rock his cradle, and with one breast I will feed him. May my breast turn to stone, may the castle endure, may my son grow up brave and strong, may he become king and rule!'

They took the young wife and walled her up in the foundations of the castle. And the walls grew higher, they did not collapse as before. But at their foot, the stones are damp and mossy to this day, because the mother's tears still fall for her son.

from various periods, including some minted in Shkodra by the Nemanjić dynasty of medieval Montenegro, and others with the symbol of the Balsha family, the feudal power in northern Albania in the 13th to 15th centuries; and copies of documents including a map from 1600, the Statute of the city of Shkodra, written – in Latin and Dalmatian – in 1346 and discovered in Venice in 2002, and interesting political cartoons from the early 20th century. Next to the museum is an atmospheric **restaurant**, which has excellent views from the balcony to its rear.

From the castle walls, you can see the **Leaden Mosque** on the floodplain below, an 18th-century building in classical Ottoman style. It was the first mosque to reopen after freedom of religion was restored in 1990. However, problems with flooding then forced it to close for many years. It reopened in 2016 and the imam, who lives nearby, is happy to show visitors around his beautiful mosque (he does not, however, speak English).

It is a long way to the castle from the centre of town, and a stiff climb up from the main road; if you do not have your own transport, you could take a taxi up and walk back down to catch a bus back into town.

Historical Museum (*Rr Oso Kuka 12;* ☎ *243 213;* ⏱ *09.00–15.00 Mon–Fri, groups at other times by arrangement 1 day ahead; 150 lek*) The house of Oso Kuka, who died defending Shkodra against Montenegrin attackers in 1861, is now home to the town's Historical Museum, and provides an opportunity to see traditional domestic architecture. From the street, a Shkodran house is just a windowless wall with a thick wooden door; once through this door, you find yourself either in a narrow entrance hall or, as in the case of Oso Kuka's house, in a courtyard, with the house in the centre, far away from the surrounding walls. The courtyard always had a well and this one has two: the original, from when the house was built in 1840, and a Venetian well from the 15th century. Various large items recovered from the castle or found elsewhere in the area are displayed in the courtyard and in the garden behind the house. One of the most interesting is an Ottoman coat of arms, intricately carved in stone, which dates from the late 19th century and was found in the castle.

The archaeological collection is exhibited on the ground floor of the house, which – like traditional houses all over Albania – was originally used for storage or workshops. The archaeological display could do with better labelling, but there are some interesting items. The prehistory section includes finds from the Mesolithic site at the Gajtan Cave; Bronze Age goods from Mycenae and the Celtic world, which demonstrate the extent to which Shkodra was then trading with other civilisations; and a cute 'family' of terracotta figurines, discovered in a burial mound. The museum has a good collection of coins and medals, including a rare *denarius* bearing the head of Brutus, Julius Caesar's rival, and coins struck in Shkodra in the 2nd century BC, during the reign of the last Illyrian king, Genthios; these bear on their reverse a *liburnis* – a small, fast ship – like that on the modern 20-lek coin.

In the days when this house was lived in, the living quarters were on the first floor, reached by a flight of wooden stairs up to a large wooden landing, with doors leading off it to the rooms within. One of these rooms, the *oda e miqve* or guest room, now houses the museum's ethnography collection. Beautifully carved wood decorates the walls, and the room is overlooked by a gallery, where the women of the house could sit while their menfolk were entertaining guests. The hosts and their guests sat on either side of the huge stucco chimney, made in a style unique to Shkodra. Traditional costumes are displayed in glass cases in this room: those worn by Muslim and Catholic men and women in the city, alongside the outfits characteristic of Shkodra's mountainous hinterland.

The last communist President of Albania, Ramiz Alia, was born in this house while his parents were renting it; Shkodrans, including some taxi drivers, still refer to it as *Shpia (Shtëpia) e Ramizit*, 'Ramiz (Alia)'s house'.

National Museum of Photography Marubi (*Muzeu Kombëtar i Fotografisë Marubi; Rr Kol Idromeno;* ☎ *240 0500;* e *info@marubi.gov.al;* ⏱ *09.00–14.00 & 15.00–18.00 Tue–Sun; 700 lek*) The Marubi photographic archive (Fototeka) is a marvellous record of historical events and ordinary people in northern Albania. In 2016, it relocated to a newly renovated museum on Shkodra's main pedestrian street, where high-quality prints, glass negatives and photographic equipment are now displayed in airy, light exhibition rooms.

The earliest of the photographs in the collection were taken by Pietro Marubbi (1834–1903), an Italian Garibaldist who came to Shkodra as a political refugee and albanicised his name to become Pjetër Marubi. The very first photograph ever taken in Albania is here, a portrait of a Shkodran man made by Marubi himself in

1858. One of his students was Kolë Idromeno (1860–1939), who took his first art lessons in Marubi's studio and went on to become one of Albania's most eminent painters. Idromeno's work as a photographer is less well known, as is the fact that he was responsible for screening the first film ever shown in Albania, in 1912. Idromeno painted the ceiling of Shkodra Cathedral, while Marubi painted frescoes on its walls.

Pjetër Marubi had no children of his own, so he adopted his gardener's sons and trained them in photography. The elder boy died tragically young, of TB; the younger, Kel (1860–1940), followed in his adoptive father's footsteps and, by the end of the 1920s, had been appointed as King Zog's official photographer.

Kel's son Gegë (1907–84) also trained as a photographer. During the communist period, the Marubi studio was incorporated into the Kooperativa e Artizanatit Shtetëror, the 'State Cooperative of Creative Artists'. The studio filmed and photographed staged 'prisoner escapes' and 'weapon caches' for Albania's secret police, the Sigurimi (page 80), which helped to justify executions and imprisonment

THE BUSHATI DYNASTY

By the 17th century, the gradual weakening of Ottoman authority over the empire's peripheral areas led, in Albania, to the rise of feudal lords known as *beys* or *pashas*, all anxious to control as much territory (and therefore revenues) as possible – the territory controlled by each pasha was called a *pashalik*. The rivalry between the pashas gave rise to wars and, ultimately, to a period of anarchy. This was brought to an end, in the middle of the 18th century, by the emergence of two powerful pashas, one in northern Albania and one in the south, who managed to gain control of almost all the small pashaliks and merge them into two huge ones. The southern pashalik was ruled by Ali Pasha Tepelena, about whom there is more information in the box on pages 254–5.

The northern pashalik was created in 1757 by Mehmet Bey Bushati (the surname is alternatively spelt 'Bushatlli'). It was Mehmet Bushati who, in 1773, built the Leaden Mosque, below Rozafa Castle (page 197). His ambitious son, Kara Mahmoud Bushati, extended the territory of the pashalik of Shkodra east to what is now Kosova and south as far as Berati, the border with Ali Pasha Tepelena's territory. In 1785, Kara Mahmoud invaded Montenegro and captured the pirate stronghold of Ulqini. The Ottoman authorities besieged his troops in Rozafa Castle for three months in 1787, but Kara Mahmoud managed to secure an imperial pardon by threatening to switch his allegiance to Austria-Hungary. Like his southern counterpart Ali Pasha, however, he ended up overstretching Ottoman tolerance. When he launched a second attack on Montenegro in 1796, he was defeated and – again, like Ali Pasha – beheaded. The Ottoman authorities appointed his brother Ibrahim Pasha as the governor of Shkodra, which, thanks to Kara Mahmoud's policies, had become an important trading centre.

The pashalik remained under the control of the Bushati family, effectively autonomous until 1830, when Sultan Mahmoud II determined to break the independence of the Albanians. Another siege of Rozafa ended in the surrender of the Bushatis and the end of the pashalik of Shkodra. This did not mean the end of the family's influence, though, and nor did it do much to improve the porte's control of its restless Albanian subjects.

of the regime's political opponents. In 1970, Gegë Marubi donated his family's archive to the state, which remains responsible for its conservation. The collection also includes work by other Albanian photographers.

The exhibition displays fascinating images of people and places in the northern highlands, views of the cities of Durrësi and Shkodra in Ottoman times, interwar portraits of ordinary Shkodrans and of prominent men and women, including Edith Durham (see box, pages 180–1), and the photographic record of many historic events, from as far back as 1878. There are examples of early photographic equipment and a mock-up of Pjetër Marubi's studio, where the great and the good of Shkodra vied to have their portraits taken.

The permanent exhibition is on the first floor of the museum, while the ground floor hosts temporary exhibitions. All the labelling is in English and Albanian. At least an hour should be allowed to look around the whole museum. There is also a short video, with soundtrack in English or Albanian, which explains more about the context in which some of the early photographs were taken, and a small library of books about photography.

The Marubi archive holds nearly half a million glass-plate negatives and films. About 100,000 of the photographs have been digitalised in high resolution. Some of them can be seen in the Marubi Virtual Museum (w *marubi.gov.al*).

Site of Witness and Memory (*Vendi i Dëshmisë dhe Kujtesës; Bd Skënderbeu;* ⊕ *09.00–14.30 Mon–Fri, 09.30–12.30 Sat–Sun; 150 lek*) From 1946 to 1991, a rather unassuming 19th-century house on Shkodra's main boulevard became the regional headquarters of the Ministry of Internal Affairs. This innocuous name belies the political persecution and terror that emanated from this building for 45 years. The storerooms of the former Franciscan seminary were transformed into detention cells and interrogation rooms for the Sigurimi, communist Albania's secret police. Thousands of people passed through these cells before they were sentenced; they were then either executed or sent on to other prisons or prison camps such as Spaçi (pages 160–1).

Now the building has been transformed again, this time into a museum that commemorates those who suffered there. Panels in English and Albanian explain various aspects of Albanian communism, including the destruction of religious buildings, the anti-communist uprisings in northern Albania, and the public trials that took place in buildings around Shkodra. The events are brought to life through photos, documents, press cuttings and personal items belonging to prisoners. Finally, a walk of 50m leads to the corridor of prison cells, 29 of them plus a reconstructed interrogation room (or rather, torture chamber).

The purpose behind the Site of Witness and Memory is to provide an opportunity for Albanians to understand and learn from their past. It is a welcome by-product that it also helps non-Albanians to learn about this terrifying period of the country's history. It takes at least an hour to give the exhibition the attention it deserves. The admission charge includes an information booklet in Albanian and English.

Diocesan Museum (*Muzeu Dioqezan; Sh Gjon Pali II;* m *067 55 52 076;* e *muzeudioqesansp@gmail.com;* w *kishakatolikeshkoder.com;* ⊕ *09.00–13.00 Mon–Sat, summer also 15.00–17.00 Mon–Fri; free admission*) Shkodra is the centre of Albanian Catholicism, the seat of the archdiocese of Shkodra and Pulti. The current archbishop, Angelo Massafra, is from the Albanian-speaking Arbëresh community of southern Italy.

St Stephen's Cathedral was built in 1858, to replace the cathedral in Rozafa Castle which had been closed by the Ottoman authorities and converted into a mosque. The Russian tsar, Alexander Nevsky, helped to fund its construction and Shkodra's leading artists of the time designed and decorated it.

Slightly hidden behind the cathedral, in its former sacristy, the Diocesan Museum provides fascinating insights into the history of Catholicism in northern Albania, from its earliest traces in the 12th century. The exhibition is organised thematically, starting with archaeological finds from medieval monasteries and religious medallions. Documents, maps and photographs help to put the items on display into their proper context.

In 1946, the country's new Communist government closed all Catholic schools and confiscated the buildings. In 1967, matters became even worse for Albania's Catholics (and those of other religions) when the government declared the world's first atheist state (page 16). Churches and mosques were demolished or used for secular purposes; St Stephen's Cathedral was converted into a sports hall and used for basketball and volleyball matches. Priests and imams were imprisoned or executed. The Diocesan Museum displays astonishing items such as a secret, handwritten baptismal certificate, hand-carved rosaries and a miniature 'Mass kit'. The latter has everything needed to celebrate a clandestine Mass, including a model of a bishop, all kept hidden in a little wooden chest under the floorboards of the home of its owners. A beautiful wooden statue of the Franciscan saint Rocco, dated to the 16th or 17th century, was hidden within the wall of another family's home to protect it from the atheism campaigners.

Shkodra was chosen as the location for the national Atheism Museum, which began as a temporary exhibition in 1967 and displayed relics and artefacts looted from closed or demolished religious buildings. Some of the church bells on display in the Diocesan Museum – at the foot of the bell tower, in fact – were recovered from the Atheism Museum after it closed in 1982.

Venice Art Mask Factory (*Rr Lin Delia;* m *068 20 47 291;* e *edmondangoni@ gmail.com;* ⊕ *Mon–Sat by arrangement*) In an intriguing twist on the historic links between the two cities (page 187), many of the masks worn by revellers at the Venice Carnival are produced in a factory on the outskirts of Shkodra. They are handmade with papier-mâché (*cartapesta* in Italian): sheets of paper are soaked in glue and layered over a mould to make the basis of the mask. Once it is dry, it is then painted, decorated with sequins, gold leaf, lace and feathers, and finally varnished to give it an antique look – the whole process has 15 stages. Visitors can watch the masks being made and admire the finished products in the factory showroom.

A walk around town Although Shkodra is a large and rather straggly town, the historic centre is quite compact and easy to walk around. The circuit described here should not take much more than an hour, excluding time to look around. Alternatively, do as the Shkodrans do, and cycle. Several hotels and hostels provide bikes for their guests.

The main **Mosque** is as good a place to start as any, since it occupies practically a whole block of the town centre and is impossible to miss. The original mosque on this site had been destroyed in an earthquake in 1905 and was rebuilt by the Ottoman authorities in 1910; it was then known as the Ebu Bekr Mosque. Its beautifully engraved minarets and copper roofs were not enough to save it from the atheism campaigners, however: the mosque was razed to the ground in the late 1960s, the graves in its gardens were levelled and olive trees were planted over them. It was rebuilt in 1995, with funding from the Saudi El-Zamil family.

Behind the mosque, in the large garden that surrounds it, is a rather weather-beaten and neglected partisan monument.

Leaving the mosque grounds, turn left out of the gate and then left again towards the road junction called Mother Teresa Square, with a recent statue of the nun herself, outside the Albtelecom building. Albania claims **Mother Teresa** (1910–97) as its own – although she was born in Macedonia – thanks to her father's Mirdita origin. Shkodra, with its large Catholic community, is especially proud of her; on Mother Teresa Day in October, the people decorate the statue with flowers. Across the junction, with his hands in his pockets, is **Luigj Gurakuqi** (1879–1925), one of Shkodra's most illustrious sons, who served Albania in various capacities including as Minister of Education in the independent country's first government.

The statue of Gurakuqi stands on the spot that was graced by a bust of Stalin until January 1990. Following the street to Gurakuqi's left will lead you to the **2nd of April Monument**. This commemorates the date in 1991 when Shkodran students and others demonstrated in protest against the result of the elections two days earlier, which had been won by the Albanian Party of Labour (the name of the Communist Party, which had governed Albania since 1944). Security forces opened fire on the demonstrators and four students were killed.

From the 2nd of April Monument, a short cut across the grounds of the Grand Hotel Europa will bring you to some attractive 19th-century governmental buildings: the Prefecture, pretty much straight ahead of you, and the City Hall round to the left. Following this street beyond the City Hall will bring you back to Mother Teresa Square.

Now cross the main road to the pedestrian street named after Shkodran painter Kolë Idromeno. It is full of cafés, restaurants and souvenir shops, many of them in restored 19th-century houses. Towards the end of the pedestrianised area, a street down to the right, Rruga Gjuhadol, will bring you out at Sheshi Gjon Pali II ('John Paul II Square') and the **Catholic Cathedral**. Its construction began in 1858, with special permission from the Ottoman authorities; the wooden ceiling was designed by Kolë Idromeno and Pjetër Marubi (pages 198–9) painted its walls with frescoes. The cathedral was reconsecrated in 1991 at a mass attended by, among many others, Mother Teresa. To the left of the altar is a display of photographs commemorating the dozens of Albanian Catholics – priests and lay people – who were executed during the communist regime. The bell tower, designed by Kolë Idromeno and his father Arsen, was demolished in 1968 and rebuilt in 1999.

Returning to the centre by a slightly different route, turning off Rruga Gjuhadol on to Rruga At Gjergj Fishta, will take you past the Franciscan convent and church, with its lovely vaulted ceiling, and back to the start of the pedestrian street.

Drishti and the Mesi Bridge

About 7km upstream from Shkodra, on the Kiri River that rises far up in the mountains that surround Thethi, is a spectacular Ottoman bridge called Ura e Mesit, or the **Mesi Bridge**. There are lots of old bridges in Albania called Ura e Mesit, which just means 'the Bridge in the Middle' – that is, the place where people from communities on opposite sides of the river met and traded. This particular bridge was built in 1868 by Mehmet Pasha Bushati, a member of the family which administered northwestern Albania on behalf of the Ottoman authorities. At 108m long, it is the longest Ottoman bridge in Albania, with 13 arches, and it is the only one with a curve. It was built for the transport of timber down from the mountains to the Buna River and on to Ulqini, which at the time was Shkodra's main port. Until 1965, when the modern bridge next to it was built, it was the only substantial bridge across the Kiri upriver of Shkodra itself. But

Mehmet Pasha built his bridge at a crossing that had been used for many centuries before him, a link in a much older route connecting Shkodra with Drishti.

Drishti – or, as it was known at the height of its power, Drivasto – had an importance in the past which is hard to imagine nowadays. A fortress was built there in late antiquity; it was the seat of a bishopric until the end of the 9th century, and the citadel whose ruins can still be seen dates from the 14th century. Rozafa Castle outside Shkodra is clearly visible from the citadel; Drishti and Rozafa were both important links in the chain of communication by beacon, used by Skanderbeg (see box, pages 206–7) and no doubt by earlier lords. In 1396, Drivasto was acquired by the Venetian Republic; the well that can still be seen, surrounded by a ramshackle wall, is thought to be Venetian, from the mid 15th century. By then, around 100 families lived in the town. But in 1478, during the final siege of Shkodra, the houses within the castle walls and the fields below it were destroyed by Ottoman troops, as part of their strategy of starving out the city's defenders. Edith Durham (see box, pages 180–1) visited Drishti in 1908 and was entertained in the imposing house of the head of the village, the one with the covered balcony (*çardak*), on your right as you come through the castle walls from the main road. The house had two entrances, each with its own flight of stone stairs, one for men and the other for women; the front steps are ruined now, but the back flight is still visible.

The road is in reasonable condition as far as the castle entrance, although a 4x4 would probably be needed in wet weather. Minibuses ply several times a day between Shkodra and Mesi, where the bridge is. From Mesi, a minibus runs early every school-day morning and then again at lunchtime to the school in the modern village of Drishti, below the castle; it takes the school teachers to work and brings them back again, but they will probably be prepared to squeeze up and make room for one or two foreign tourists, if necessary. It is quite a long way from the village up to the castle, but if you are on foot you can use the cobbled path that leads up to the main gate – the entrance on the other side of the castle from the gate where the asphalt road passes.

LEZHA *Telephone code: 0215*

Albanians are always very keen for foreigners to visit Lezha, because it is where their national hero Skanderbeg, or Gjergj Kastrioti, brought the Albanian clan chieftains together to swallow their differences and unite against the Ottoman threat. When Skanderbeg died in 1468, after 24 years successfully resisting the Ottomans, he was buried in Lezha's cathedral.

Lezha has Illyrian fortifications, including the citadel above the town, which can be visited. During the Roman period, it was called Lissus and was an important river port. In 48BC, Mark Antony landed at what is now Shëngjini (then called Nymphaeum) on his way to link up with Julius Caesar in their campaign against Pompey. Lezha was part of the Venetian Republic for most of the 15th century, and in this period the town – by then called Alessio – and its port thrived. In the Ottoman period Lezha, like Durrësi and other Adriatic-facing Albanian towns, fell into decline, and it did not really begin to recover until Italy's economic and political influence began to grow in the 1930s.

Shëngjini, known in Italian as San Giovanni di Medua, is the second-largest port in Albania, after Durrësi. To the south of the port, a beautiful sandy beach stretches for several miles to the Merxhani Lagoon, part of the wetlands that make up the Kune-Vaini Nature Reserve. In the summer months, this resort is a very popular destination for Albanian-speaking tourists, and it can become rather busy, although it is less crowded than the beaches further south at Durrësi.

The Kune-Vaini reserve straddles both sides of the Drini River, and offers magnificent birdwatching opportunities (pages 208–11). It is within easy reach of both Shëngjini and Lezha, either of which would make an ideal base for day trips into the reserve.

GETTING THERE AND AWAY The highway between Lezha and Shkodra has been fully upgraded, and the two towns are now less than an hour's drive apart. Alternatively, it is perfectly feasible to visit Lezha on a day trip from Tirana, also about an hour away.

Buses ply the route constantly until at least 17.00. They leave Tirana from the North bus station [62 B2] and Shkodra from Sheshi Demokracia. If there is no transport specifically for Lezha at the time you want to travel, you can catch any bus up or down the coastal highway and get off at the Lezha junction; from there, it is a 5-minute walk across the bridge into the centre of Lezha. In Lezha, the bus station is on Bulevardi Gjergj Fishta.

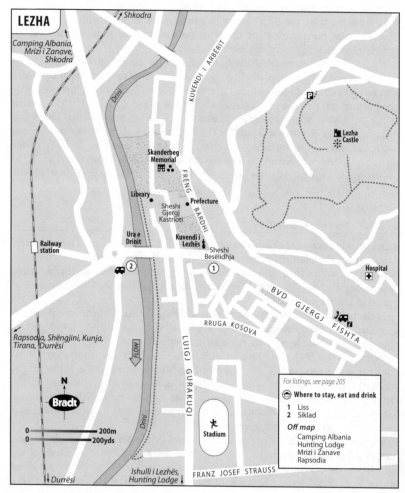

There are frequent **minibuses** to Shëngjini from Lezha. In July and August, there are also minibuses from Shkodra directly to Shëngjini, leaving in the morning and returning in the afternoon. There is no public transport to the Vaini area of the nature reserve, but a 4x4 is not required and any Lezha taxi driver could take you.

🏠 WHERE TO STAY *Map, opposite, unless otherwise stated*

🏠 **Liss** (21 rooms, 2 suites) Sheshi Besëlidhja; ☎24700; m 067 20 09 841, 069 66 90 799; e hotel-liss@uldedajgroup.al; w hotelliss.al. The former 'Turizmi', right in the centre of town, completely renovated. Comfortable, well run, some English spoken. Good restaurant, popular bar, terrace; free parking, free Wi-Fi; laundry service. All rooms en suite with hairdryer, TV, AC, phone, minibar. **$$$**

🏠 **Siklad** (14 rooms) Pranë urës së Drinit; ☎22333; m 068 20 33 445, 069 25 91 848. At the bridge from the highway into town; restaurant on ground floor; friendly management; free parking, free Wi-Fi throughout. B/fast inc. All rooms en suite with good shower, hairdryer, flatscreen TV, AC. **$$**

🏠 **Camping Albania** [map, page 186] Barbullushi ✪ 41° 55' 25.9" N 19° 32' 30.7" E; m 067 38 07 207, 067 38 18 092; e info@camping-albania.eu; w camping-albania.eu. Just beyond Bushati; signposted off the highway, roughly halfway between Lezha & Shkodra. Dutch-run, western European standards, English spoken; pitches for up to 50 mobile homes & tents; ample showers & toilets; laundry service. A few simple guest rooms, some en suite (**$$–$**) are also available. On-site restaurant, large outdoor pool with spring water, free Wi-Fi throughout site. **$**

✗ WHERE TO EAT AND DRINK *Map, opposite*

The restaurant at the Liss Hotel is the best place to eat in Lezha itself, with an Italian-inspired menu of pasta, pizza, escalopes and grilled meat (**$$$–$$**). Weather permitting, the sunken garden outside the restaurant is a very pleasant place to eat or drink, with the tables arranged around a fountain. In Shëngjini, there are good, cheap fish restaurants (**$$$**) near the entrance to the port.

The wider Lezha area has several excellent restaurants and is becoming a culinary destination in its own right. Visitors who are interested in gastronomy should try to sample at least one of the restaurants listed here.

✗ **Rapsodia** On the Shëngjini road, about 4km out of Lezha; m 068 29 47 771; e info@hotelrapsodia.com; w hotelrapsodia.com. A fairly formal restaurant with excellent antipasti & fish, as well as Italian-influenced meat dishes. Once a month, the chef prepares a special gastronomic menu, sometimes cooking with flowers, sometimes reversing the order of courses; phone for details. 9 en-suite guest rooms also available (**$$**). **$$$$$**

✗ **Hunting Lodge** (Hoteli e Gjuetisë) Ishulli i Lezhës; m 069 21 70 898. Built in the 1930s by Mussolini's son-in-law, Count Galeazzo Ciano, who also served as Fascist Italy's foreign minister; used by party functionaries during the communist period & ransacked by rioters in 1997; reopened after refurbishment in 2003. Specialises in traditional Albanian cuisine, inc excellent fresh fish; a good choice for a leisurely lunch after a long morning's birdwatching in the Vaini marshlands.

Also has basic guest rooms (**$**), but the hotel part of the building is in poor repair. **$$$**

✗ **Mrizi i Zanave** [map, page 186] Fishta, Blinishti; m 069 21 08 032; e info@mrizizanave.com; w mrizizanave.com. Beautiful setting in the countryside northeast of Lezha, in the birthplace of the priest & Gheg poet Gjergj Fishta (the restaurant takes its name from the title of his masterpiece). Part of the Slow Food Convivium; uses local ingredients, some from its own farm, to prepare perfectly grilled meat, exquisite salads, unusual side dishes & desserts. The good house wine is also locally produced. In summer, tables outside on shady terraces. English spoken. The owners' environmental commitment extends to having installed a solar-powered flour mill. Blinishti is signposted off the main Lezha–Shkodra highway; homemade signs direct you to Mrizi i Zanave; phone the restaurant if lost. **$$$**

WHAT TO SEE AND DO

Skanderbeg Memorial (🕐 09.00–13.00 & 15.00–18.00 Tue–Sun; 100 lek) Lezha's main claim to fame is as the place where Albania's national hero, Skanderbeg (see box below), united the country's feuding clan chiefs against Ottoman attack, and where he was buried after 24 years of resistance. There is a monument to the gathering of the clan chiefs – known in Albanian as Kuvendi i Lezhës, the Assembly of Lezha – at the corner of Sheshi Besëlidhja ('Pledge-bond' Square), as you enter Lezha over the bridge from the highway.

When Skanderbeg died, in January 1468, he was buried in St Nicholas's Cathedral in Lezha. His death marked the beginning of the end for the Albanian resistance, and when the Ottomans occupied Lezha, they ransacked Skanderbeg's tomb and converted the cathedral into a mosque. Between 1880 and 1905, the site was used by the local Bektashi community (page 22) as a *tyrbe*, or shrine;

SKANDERBEG

Albania's national hero was born Gjergj (George) Kastrioti, the son of a powerful Albanian chieftain who controlled a large swathe of what is now northern Albania from his citadel at Kruja. When the Ottomans advanced towards Kruja in 1433, Gjergj's father struck a deal with them to be allowed to continue ruling his lands as a vassal – this was not untypical of the decentralised way in which the Ottoman Empire administered Albania in later years too. As part of the deal, Gjergj was sent to be brought up in the sultan's court, where he was trained as a soldier and given the name Skënder (Alexander), with the honorific ending 'beg' (or 'bey').

In 1443, the Ottomans suffered a serious defeat at Niš, in Serbia. Skanderbeg seized the moment and raised his family's standard – the double-headed eagle on a red background which is the national flag of modern Albania – from the castle at Kruja. The exact circumstances in which he did so are unclear, but the traditional version is that he and his men deserted the Ottoman army at Niš and rode from there to Kruja, where Skanderbeg tricked the Ottoman guards into letting him into the citadel.

He then achieved the feat that has given him his place in history. The Albanian clans, like their Scottish counterparts of the same period, spent most of their time fighting each other, which made them easy prey for better-organised invaders. Skanderbeg managed to gather all the clan chiefs together, in Lezha, on 2 March 1444, and made them undertake to put their differences aside. A solemn undertaking of this sort is known in Albanian as *besa*, an expression that is still widely used in modern times to mean something like 'word of honour'. The agreement of the besa at Lezha is called *besëlidhja* in Albanian, and has given its name to the town's main square.

The Lezha besa allowed the clans to concentrate on fighting the invaders, and they held them at bay for an astonishing 34 years. Kruja came under siege in 1449–50, and many died before the Ottoman forces withdrew. The sultan, Murad II, died soon after the retreat from Kruja. His successor Mehmed II turned his attention to Constantinople, and it was not until he had conquered that city that he returned to Albania. Meanwhile, Skanderbeg tried to rally support for his beleaguered country from other European nations, but his diplomatic initiatives brought little success. In 1466, the Ottoman army returned to Kruja; Skanderbeg sought military assistance from Naples, which enabled him to break the siege the following year.

Skanderbeg died of malaria in Lezha in 1468, leaving only a son who was too young to take over his father's command; yet the besa held and the clans stayed united against the Ottomans. Kruja finally fell in 1478. The last citadel to be lost

---

Bektashis believe that the young Gjergj Kastrioti converted to Bektashism while he was in Constantinople. For the quincentenary of Skanderbeg's death, shortly after Albania had been declared the world's first atheist state, the mosque was requisitioned, its minaret was removed and Lezha's former cathedral became a shrine to Skanderbeg.

The Skanderbeg Memorial is protected by a modern pillared structure that surrounds and roofs the ruined cathedral. As you pass through the carved wooden doors into the cathedral, there is a bronze bust of the hero directly ahead of you. Behind it, on a red mosaic background, is the double-headed eagle which was Skanderbeg's flag and is now the national flag of Albania. Below the bust are replicas of his sword and his helmet topped with a roebuck's head; the 15th-century originals are in the New Imperial Palace (Neue Burg) in Vienna, part of the Kunsthistorisches Museum's Arms and Armour Collection. On each of the side walls hang shields, each

was Rozafa Castle in Shkodra (pages 195–7), the following year. Folk legend has it that Skanderbeg's son led a group of Albanians across the Adriatic to settle in southern Italy. To this day there are villages there in which an archaic form of Albanian is spoken; the dialect, and the people who speak it, are called Arbëresh.

The year after the Ottomans had taken Shkodra, they crossed the Adriatic and captured the castle of Otranto. They were unable to hold it for more than a few months, thanks in part to a revolt in Albania that occupied their troops there, and under the next sultan, Bayezid II, they gave up on their plans to expand their conquests westwards beyond the Balkans. It is often said that had it not been for János Hunyadi, the Turks would have taken Vienna and the political fault-lines of Europe would have been hundreds of miles further north than they are. Less attention has been given to the possibility that without Skanderbeg and the Albanian resistance, much of what is now Italy would have fallen, and the fault-lines would have been several hundred miles further west.

THE DEATH OF SKANDERBEG

They brought [Skanderbeg] his son – small and tender, with long golden hair. Skanderbeg took him in his arms and said: 'Oh, my little flower, who has bloomed amid the surge of battle; oh, flower of my broken heart! When I die, my comrades will continue the war. And if it turns out that you are not big enough to hold and wield a sword, take care that the Turks do not imprison you alive and lock the door. I know the Turks well. They try to distort a man's spirit, to turn him against himself and his clan, to make him an oppressor of his own land. And then honour is blanketed in disgrace.

And so, if you see that you are in trouble, take your mother and three ships, the best we have, and set off across the sea. Then, when you grow up, come back to your land and carry on my struggle. I say this to you not to save you from death, but to save the clan from defilement; because defilement is worse than death.

When you reach that pebbly beach over there, you will see a shady, mournful cypress. There, to the trunk of that cypress, tie my horse; and above the horse, raise my flag so that it ripples; and under the flag, tie my sword. When the sea breeze blows, my horse will whinny, the flag will flutter and my sword will resound under the shady cypress. The Turks will hear it. They will be afraid of the death which my sword brings, and they will not dare to throw themselves into battle.

From Mitrush Kuteli's Old Albanian Tales

representing one of the battles he waged against the invaders. On the back wall of the cathedral, a fragment of fresco has survived from the 15th century.

Recent excavations have revealed a 12th-century baptistery just next to the memorial, which shows that there was a church on this site long before the cathedral was built. In the surrounding park, remains of Illyrian and Roman fortifications can be seen, which once extended all the way up the hill to the citadel.

Lezha Castle (⊕ *09.00–noon & 15.00–20.00 daily; 100 lek*) Lezha was one of the links in the chain of castles used by Skanderbeg to communicate information up and down the country; a beacon lit here can be seen from Rozafa Castle, 45km to the north, and at Kruja, 54km south. In dry weather it is possible to drive up to the castle in any reasonably robust car; when the track is wet, a 4x4 will be needed. It is a pleasant, though steepish, walk of 30–45 minutes, with good views of the Drini Delta on the way and, of course, from the castle itself, at the top. There is another well-preserved section of the ancient wall about halfway up.

The interior of the citadel is very interesting, especially if you have previously visited Rozafa. Like its bigger and better-preserved neighbour, Lezha Castle has a church that was converted into a mosque, a cistern for storing rainwater, and a dungeon, complete with air hole so that the unfortunate prisoners could breathe. The citadel was first fortified in the 4th century BC; the surviving buildings and the watchtowers are medieval, built between the 15th and 17th centuries. A helpful information panel has been installed near the entrance to the castle, with a timeline and information about the main buildings within.

ZadrimArt (m *068 28 28 582;* 🛇 *ZadrimArt-Krajen Lezh*) The ZadrimArt workshop creates and sells beautiful ceramics. It was set up by the priest of this Catholic district, Zadrima, to generate employment for the villagers so that they would not have to leave the area in search of work in Tirana or Italy. They will show you the whole process, from treating the clay, forming the items on the potter's wheel, painting them with traditional or modern designs and, finally, firing them. Then you can browse in the sale-room for bowls, jugs, plates and smaller souvenirs. Examples of the workshop's products are shown on its Facebook page. The staff will wrap your purchases carefully, so that you have a chance of getting them home in one piece. ZadrimArt is a 10-minute drive from Mrizi i Zanave (page 205); ask at the restaurant for directions.

Beaches The beach at Shëngjini is lovely to walk along, but the water is often rather murky, probably because the port is so close. It becomes very crowded in the peak summer months. The water is cleaner and the beach quieter further along the bay towards the nature reserve at Kunja.

To the northwest, almost at the border with Montenegro, is another popular beach resort, Velipoja. There are many hotels at Velipoja (**$$$–$$**), although not all of them stay open throughout the year. Minibuses go to Velipoja from Shkodra.

BIRDWATCHING IN THE NORTHERN ALBANIAN WETLANDS The wetlands

surrounding the mouths of the Buna and Drini rivers are of international importance to waterfowl. Some 700ha at Velipoja, on the left bank of the Buna's outlet to the sea, and 2,300ha around the Drini Delta – the Kune-Vaini Nature Reserve – have been designated as protected, mostly under IUCN Category IV ('a protected area managed mainly for conservation through management intervention'). Both reserves are easy to get to and have good accommodation nearby, making them ideal destinations for ornithologists. It should be noted, however, that the development of beach tourism in Velipoja and Shëngjini has already begun to affect the protected areas. This is a particular problem in the Kunja area, to the north of the River Drini, where the beach extends from Shëngjini all the way to the island of Kunja e Vogël, at the end of the Merxhani Lagoon.

There are now several restaurants and hotels within the nature reserve itself. The Vaini part of the reserve is less developed, and is likely to be a more fruitful destination for birdwatchers. Room rates in Shëngjini increase substantially in July and August, when all the hotels there are likely to be fully booked several weeks in advance.

The habitats The Velipoja area begins on the Albanian side of the River Buna, where a large expanse of inland marshes and reed beds make up the Dumi Marsh (Këneta e Dumit). A forest of broad-leaved deciduous woodland stretches along to a sandy beach, with dunes and small pools. At the eastern end of the beach is a large, shallow coastal lagoon – the Viluni Lagoon (Laguna e Vilunit), about 300ha – at the foot of rocky and forested mountains. These hills continue down the coast to Shëngjini and the start of the Drini Delta.

The Drini is Albania's longest river, and where it meets the sea it has created a complex of relatively intact coastal lakes, marshes and forests covering many square kilometres. Brackish lagoons, sandbars and beaches, marshes, reed beds and woodland areas combine to make a very varied environment, which extends south to the mouth of the River Mati and beyond. Some of the woodland is broad-leaved, while some is planted pine; much of the forest has been destroyed by indiscriminate tree felling. The surrounding area is cultivated (Lezha is famous for its watermelons) and was networked with an extensive system of dykes, dams, ditches and channels, although since the fall of communism these have not been well maintained and the marshes are beginning to reclaim the land in some places.

The birds Velipoja and Kune-Vaini are important sites for wintering waterfowl and for migratory waterbirds. No fewer than 8,000 individuals were recorded in a 1993 census at Velipoja, and 17,000 individuals at Kune-Vaini in January 1995. Species that nest in the Drini Delta area include spoonbills (*Platalea leucorodia*), cormorants (*Phalacrocorax carbo* and *P. pygmeus*), various herons and egrets, and grebes (Podicipedidae). Among the waterfowl that winter there are the red-crested pochard (*Netta rufina*), goldeneye (*Bucephala clangula*), shelduck (*Tadorna tadorna*), teal (*Anas crecca*), wigeon (*A. penelope*) and pintail (*A. acuta*). The 'near-threatened' ferruginous duck or white-eyed pochard (*Aythya nyroca*) may also visit.

Herons, spoonbills and pygmy cormorants used to breed inside the Velipoja reserve, close to the mouth of the Buna, but they moved across to an island on the Montenegrin side of the river in the 1990s, probably because they were being disturbed by illegal activities such as poaching and woodcutting. They still feed on the Albanian side and if the park's protected status is properly enforced it may be possible for the breeding colony to re-establish.

Around the Mati Delta is a third nature reserve, Fushë-Kuqja–Patoku. It is also an important site for migratory and wintering waders, including the slender-billed curlew (*Numenius tenuirostris*), which is globally endangered and very rarely seen in Europe. Pied avocets (*Recurvirostra avosetta*) winter at Patoku and there was formerly a small breeding colony of Dalmatian pelicans (*Pelecanus crispus*) on one of the islands.

PHALACROCORAX CARBO The **great cormorant** is a black, long-bodied, long-necked waterbird. It swims and dives for fish, and may perch on rocks and in dead trees. It characteristically stands with its wings outstretched, to dry them. In spring it has white feathers on its head and neck, and bold white patches on its flanks.

PHALACROCORAX PYGMEUS The 'near-threatened' **pygmy cormorant** is about half the size of *P. carbo*, but otherwise looks similar. It nests in trees, preferably willow (*Salix*), and feeds in reed beds and in the transition zones between reed beds and open waters. Pygmy cormorants occasionally forage together in flocks. It is thought that they may drive shoals of fish towards the edge of reed beds, in order to catch them more easily.

ARDEOLA RALLOIDES The **squacco heron** is a beautiful small heron and, like the other herons described here, most winter in Africa. The breeding plumage is mainly golden, with long brown streaked nape plumes and a greenish-blue bill, but in flight it is surprisingly white. It is rather shy and often solitary, feeding either by 'standing and waiting' or walking slowly along.

EGRETTA GARZETTA **Little egrets** are white, medium-sized herons, with black legs and bright yellow feet, and in the breeding season have long white nape plumes. They are sociable, often boisterous, birds and nest with other herons in trees. They feed mostly on fish and small shore-dwelling animals.

NYCTICORAX NYCTICORAX The black-crowned **night heron** is the size of the little egret, but stockier. Adults are a soft grey colour, with a black back and crown, and white head plumes in spring. Young birds are brown-buff and spotted. The legs are raspberry-pink at the start of the breeding period and yellowish the rest of the

THE ALBANIAN ALPS

The mountain range that forms the border between Albania and Montenegro is known variously as the Albanian Alps, the Dinaric Alps, the Accursed Mountains or, more usually in everyday Albanian parlance, just 'the Highlands' (Malësia). The eastern part of the highlands is covered on pages 166–74. This section covers the western part, Malësia e Madhe or 'the Big Highlands'.

By **public transport**, the usual system of rural buses applies (page 42): the driver leaves the village early in the morning and then returns to the village around lunchtime. The exception to this rule is Thethi. Buses and minibuses to the highland villages leave Shkodra from the northern suburb of Rus Maxhar (see map, pages 188–9). It is always worth checking in the morning whether the bus you want has in fact come to Shkodra that day. Sometimes they only go as far as Kopliku, a small town 17km north of Shkodra. There are frequent buses from Shkodra to Kopliku, also from Rus Maxhar. The shopkeepers around the street in Kopliku where the minibuses wait are very helpful and will try to find out for you what time the bus you want is likely to depart.

Kopliku has the last ATMs that you will see before your return from the highlands. It is essential to carry sufficient cash for your trip; credit cards cannot year. It rests by day in clumps of trees or bushes and is easiest to see at dusk, when it flies around and feeds.

PLATALEA LEUCORODIA **Spoonbills** are white, but much larger than little egrets. They have long, broad, spatulate bills, which make them unmistakable. They feed with a graceful side-to-side sweeping action, catching small aquatic animals. In the breeding season, adults have a yellow patch round their necks and a bushy crest at the back of the neck.

PLEGADIS FALCINELLUS The **glossy ibis** is the size of a little egret but very dark, and with a long, down-curved bill. The rich chestnut plumage has beautiful green and purple highlights. It is quite common in southeastern Europe, although its numbers are declining. Glossy ibis eat small water-dwelling animals and, like spoonbills, they fly with their necks stretched out, often in single file.

AQUILA CLANGA The **spotted eagle** is a medium-sized eagle (wingspan 1.53–1.77m), with dark brown plumage and slightly paler flight feathers. Juveniles have rows of white spots along the upper wing. It occurs in lowland forests near wetlands, where it nests in tall trees, and feeds on small mammals, waterbirds, frogs and snakes. Its global population is decreasing as a result of extensive habitat loss and persistent persecution, and it is classified as 'vulnerable'. BirdLife International estimates that there are no more than 900 pairs remaining in Europe, with only small numbers wintering in southern Europe.

HALIAEETUS ALBICILLA **White-tailed eagles**, also known as sea eagles, are huge birds (wingspan 1.90–2.40m), classified as 'near-threatened'. The adults are easily identified from their white tails and large yellow bills. However, it takes about five years for adult plumage to be acquired and immature birds can be confused with other eagles.

be used anywhere in the Albanian Alps. Nor are there any landline telephones beyond Kopliku.

The best map of this area, *Vermoshi: Tamarë, Razma, Thethi*, is produced by Huber Kartographie GmBH (page 40). If you are hiking to Thethi from Valbona (pages 171–4), you could also (or alternatively) buy Journey to Valbona's *Qafa e Valbonës* map, one of its series of excellent little hiking guides. This one shows the route over the Valbona Pass, with hiking notes, and around the main settlement of Thethi, including a useful map of the village itself.

THETHI About 50km northeast of Kopliku, at the head of the Shala River, lies the national park named after its largest settlement, the village of Thethi. The area was a tourist resort during (and, indeed, before) the communist period and its attractive, traditional features were accordingly maintained, while in other parts of highland Albania they were destroyed either deliberately or through neglect. Edith Durham (see box, pages 180–1) visited Thethi in 1908, and described her stay there in her book *High Albania*. 'Life at Thethi was of absorbing interest,' she wrote. 'I forgot all about the rest of the world, and ... there seemed no reason why I should ever return.' The modern visitor's reaction is likely to be similar.

There are 200 houses scattered across the valley, although only a handful of families live there all year round. Most people spend the winter in either Shkodra or Kopliku, and return to Thethi in April or May, for the start of the tourist season; they leave again in September or October, before the harsh winter weather sets in. The traditional houses are built of stone, and roofed with shingles (wooden tiles). They were designed to be easily defensible – these mountains were once the heart of blood-feud territory (see box, pages 192–3) and every family needed to be able to defend its menfolk against revenge. A traditional house of this kind is now the village museum. Of especial interest is the 'lock-in tower' (*kulla e ngujimit*), the only one remaining of its kind that is easily accessible to visitors. The beautiful little church dates from 1892. See below for details of these buildings; they are all in the main settlement and can easily be visited during a day trip. A longer stay in Thethi will allow you to explore further afield and see some of the beautiful natural phenomena in the park. There are also many longer treks for the fit and well equipped, including the popular hike across the Valbona Pass to Tropoja.

Getting there and away The main road to Thethi is clearly signposted from the highway north from Kopliku to the border with Montenegro. Just over an hour from Shkodra is the village of Boga, which was photographed by Marubi in the late 19th century (pages 198–9). Boga has guesthouses and a campsite; given the relentless climb that lies ahead, these may be especially appealing to those intending to cycle to Thethi. A series of increasingly steep and alarming hairpin bends leads up to the pass, Qafë-Thora, 1,775m above sea level. The road is asphalted as far as the summit, but not (at the time of writing) beyond it. The views on the way are outstanding on a clear day, with towering mountain peaks on either side. There is a viewpoint at the pass and a café nearby.

The 15km from the pass to the main settlement of Thethi (known as *Qendër*, 'Centre') are equally steep and switchbacked, and the road is rough. A 4x4 vehicle is preferable, although in dry weather it is possible to make the trip, with caution, in a reasonably robust car. About 20 minutes' drive beyond the pass, a dignified stone memorial to Edith Durham looks down over the village she found so fascinating. It takes about 3 hours to drive from Shkodra to the main settlement of Thethi.

If you do not have your own transport, the most convenient option is one of the many **jeeps** that take passengers to and from Thethi in the summer. Your hotel or hostel in Shkodra (or Thethi) should be able to find a driver for you. Typically, they take three or four passengers and charge €10 a head each way; the driver will usually collect you from your accommodation in the morning. A **minibus** runs up to Thethi and back to Shkodra every day in summer. It leaves at around 07.00 from Rus Maxhar, in the northern outskirts of Shkodra (see map, pages 188–9), and returns from Thethi between noon and 14.00; the fare is also €10 each way. It is best to reserve a seat in advance; your hotel or guesthouse can help you with this.

Outside July and August, getting to or from Thethi without your own transport will be more difficult. It may be possible to hitchhike; expect to pay something towards the driver's fuel. There are daily minibuses to Boga from Kopliku or Shkodra. To walk to or from Boga, the footpath called the Sheep Track (pages 216–17) is a much shorter route than the road; it takes the locals 6 hours. There are half-a-dozen places to stay overnight in Boga (eg: *Boga Alpine Resort;* m *067 37 06 462;* w *bogaalpine.com;* **$$–$**).

All but the hardiest cyclists will find the 25km from Boga to Thethi quite challenging, with gradients averaging about 10%. In particular the unasphalted stretch between Qafë-Thora and Thethi would be very rough going on a bike.

Snow and ice close Qafë-Thora for between four and six months every year. The only way out of Thethi then is south, along the Shala and Kiri rivers, to approach Shkodra from Drishti and Mesi (pages 202–3). This road is unasphalted and the local people rarely use it except in emergencies. Those who spend the winter in Thethi stock up on essentials before winter sets in. However, if you are travelling in your own 4x4 vehicle or by bike, you could return from Thethi by this route, by way of variety. It is about 130km back to Shkodra.

For information about walking into or out of Thethi, see pages 216–18.

Where to stay, and other practicalities

There is plenty of accommodation all over Thethi. Long acquainted with the requirements of western European tourists, the guesthouses have modern bathroom facilities, now often ensuite, and warm, comfortable beds. Many are registered with w booking.com or other international websites. Some are also listed, along with suggestions for hikes, on w albanian-mountains.com. There is always constant running water, often from the house's own spring, but the electricity supply is sometimes interrupted. Some guesthouses have solar PV panels.

Bed-and-breakfast, full- and half-board options are usually offered. Meals consist of traditional northern Albanian dishes, with vegetarian options available. Packed lunches can easily be arranged if you want to spend the day hiking. Campers can order meals at the guesthouse adjoining their campsite, or eat in one of the restaurants in the village (eg: Shpella or Zorgji). Food to cook yourself cannot be bought in Thethi.

The health centre, next to the school, is not staffed full-time; you should bring any essential medicines with you. There is good mobile-phone coverage in the main settlement, but not everywhere in the national park.

Harusha (13 rooms) Qendër; m 069 27 70 294, 068 58 33 476; e welcome@guesthousethethi. com; www.guesthousethethi.com; f Guest House Harusha. Just across the bridge at the entrance to the main settlement; convenient for hiking to Valbona. Open all year round (the family winters in Thethi). Some English spoken; free Wi-Fi. Campsite & parking for campervans with 4 dedicated showers & toilets; can be noisy. Various sizes of rooms; 8 dbls & some others ensuite. **$$$**

Çarku (19 beds) Gjeçaj; m 069 31 64 211, 068 36 44 788. On the right-hand side of the road as you come down into Thethi from Qafë-Thora, high above the main settlement. Some English spoken. Meals can be taken on terrace; beautiful views across Shala Valley to mountains towards Valbona. 1 dbl ensuite, other rooms share 2 bathrooms. **$$**

Shpella (12 rooms) Qendër; m 069 37 74 851; e shpella.family@googlemail.com; f Thethi Shpella Guesthouse. Centrally located below 'lock-in tower'; English spoken. Qualified hiking guide in family; 4x4 available for excursions; airport pickup possible from Tirana or Podgorica; all-in packages

available with sister-hotel in Shkodra (€50pp). Restaurant (open to public) with tables in garden; free Wi-Fi. Campsite with dedicated shower & toilet indoors. Rooms of various sizes; 10 en suite, 2 share bathroom. B/fast inc. **$$**

Zorgji (7 rooms) Qendër; m 068 23 19 610; e pellumbkola@gmail.com. Split location: 2 en-suite trpls above restaurant, centrally located next door to school; 5 en-suite rooms of varying sizes in traditional stone-built house on hillside above (vehicle & foot access; camping possible. Some English spoken. Restaurant & bar (open to public) with tables in large garden; free Wi-Fi. B/fast inc. **$$**

Dedë Nika (20 beds) Ndërlysaj; m 069 33 46 423. Conveniently located if approaching Thethi from the south or from Curraj i Epermë (page 174). **$**

Rupa (7 rooms) Qendër; ☎ (in Shkodra) 022 244 077; m 068 20 03 393; e rorupaog@ yahoo.com. Centrally located between school & church; some English spoken; free Wi-Fi. Camping possible. Various sizes of rooms; 3 ensuite, 4 sharing 2 bathrooms. **$**

What to see and do The road into Thethi from Qafë-Thora winds down through beech forest, passing meadows, farmhouses and the lovely Gjeçaj Waterfall, which tumbles from its cliff only metres from the road. The main sights in the village (Qendër) are down to the right across the bridge; an information panel with a map of the national park has been installed at the junction here. Wooden signs direct visitors to the places of interest.

The first of the village's public buildings you come to is the **school**, with a memorial stone outside to John Holmes of the Balkans Peace Park Project (see box, page 219), which did so much over the years to support sustainable tourism in Thethi. Adjoining the school is the health centre, the building where Albania's mountaineering community held its first ever event, in 1956.

Thethi is a Catholic village; the Ottomans left these remote mountain settlements largely to their own devices and the people had no reason to convert to Islam (see page 10 for the reasons why some did elsewhere). The village **church**, built in 1892, was restored and reroofed in 2005–06 thanks to donations from 'the children of Thethi' in the United States. Edith Durham was welcomed to Thethi in 1908 by the Franciscan priest of this church: 'a solid, shingle-roofed building, with a bell-tower.' A footpath leads from the church, across fields and up a stony track, to the stone-built house that is now Thethi's **Museum** (*200 lek*). This was the house of Lulash Keqi, which Rose Wilder Lane (Laura Ingalls Wilder's daughter) visited in 1921 and which she describes in *The Peaks of Shala*. Like all traditional houses in Albania, the ground floor was used for livestock, workshops and storage; the living quarters were on the first floor. This being the warlike highlands, the rooms on this floor were carefully designed to be defended against attackers, with rifle loop-holes on all sides and, at the corners, the elaborate *frëngji*, embrasures with rests for the gunmen's elbows, and an outer grille of stone. The chute built into another wall was used for slops etc, while the men were 'in blood' – that is, when they were involved in a vendetta – and unable to leave the house. There are a few household items on display, but the main interest here is the building itself.

Perhaps the most interesting building in the village is the **lock-in tower** (*kulla e ngujimit; 150 lek*), which is said to be 400 years old. This highly defensible building was used, until as recently as the 1920s, whenever a Thethi man had committed murder and was therefore subject to blood-feud. The killer was allowed a fortnight's grace, incarcerated in the tower, while the village elders negotiated with the wronged family to try to reconcile the feud. Apart from the heavy door, which opens straight on to the bedrock on which the tower was built, there are no openings at all on the ground floor. As long as negotiations were under way, the murderer was protected from reprisals by gunmen on the upper floor, where *frëngji* can still be seen on each wall. If the feud conciliators (*pajtimtarë*) were successful, the man was set free to fulfil his side of the bargain, often by marrying a daughter of his victim. If not, he was released from the tower to seek his own solution, either fleeing the district or being killed in turn by his victim's family.

In the past, every village in northern Albania had a lock-in tower like this. King Zog (page 12) had many of them destroyed as part of his campaign to modernise the country (and, conveniently, to punish the Catholic clans that opposed him). In the communist period, those that remained were either used for storage, until they collapsed through lack of maintenance, or were deliberately dismantled and the stone reused for other buildings. Only a few now remain, in very remote parts of the high mountains. They are all designated as Cultural Monuments now, but the preservation and restoration of this tower is thanks to Thethi's history as a magnet for visitors since the days of Edith Durham. The roof was repaired and the building conserved in 2007, with Dutch funding. Photographs of famous *pajtimtarë* decorate the walls on the first floor; they include Sokol Koçeku, grandfather of the current owner. Mr Mark Koçeku also runs a guesthouse next door (w thethiguesthouse.com; **$$**).

From the tower, it is a short drive or an easy walk to the Grunas Canyon, a spectacular gorge 2km long and 60m deep, crossed high above by the Gërla Bridge. Anyone who likes waterfalls and can manage a little scrambling should visit the **Grunas Waterfall**. It plunges 25m into a deep pool of ice-cold water. Smaller waterfalls and rapids rush the stream down from this pool to meet the Shala River. You can walk up to the waterfall from the canyon or from the lock-in tower, following a footpath until you see the waterfall up on the left. In 2007, archaeologists discovered a large Bronze Age site near the Grunas Canyon.

Some 3 or 4km further along the road, at the settlement of Ndërlysaj, the force of the river has carved spectacular formations out of the rocks. A wooden bridge enables visitors to get a good look at these falls. There are natural pools that are good for swimming, although the water is very cold even in summer.

Hiking in the national park The most popular hiking routes around Thethi have now been waymarked. However, it is essential to bear in mind that, away from the scattering of settlements which make up the village, the area is very sparsely populated and there are no friendly mountain rescue helicopters. Minor accidents such as sprained ankles acquire much greater significance when the nearest help is 4 hours' limp away and, although there is mobile-phone coverage in the main settlement (Qendër), it cannot be relied upon elsewhere in the national park. For anything beyond a short stroll around the centre or along the road, suitable footwear and a good map are essential. Less experienced hikers may prefer to hire a guide; the family running your guesthouse will be able to find one for you. For a full day's guiding, you should expect to pay around €50.

In the mountains, **ornithologists** should look out for the beautiful and graceful bee-eater (*Merops apiaster*), the green and great-spotted woodpeckers (*Picus viridis* and *Dendrocopus major*), the rock partridge (*Alectoris graeca*), the hoopoe (*Upupa epops*), with its exotic-looking crest, the capercaillie (*Tetrao urogallus*), and the *balkanica* race of the shore lark (*Eremophila alpestris*), which has a warm pink nape and pale yellow facial markings, as well as its characteristic black horns.

Little herpetological mapping has been done in Albania, but **snakes** that definitely reside in Thethi are the venomous nose-horned viper (*Vipera ammodytes*) and the harmless smooth snake (*Coronella austriaca*). There are fire salamanders (*Salamandra salamandra*) and alpine salamanders (*Salamandra atra*), which like to come out when it rains; the nose-horned vipers like eating them, so they come out in the rain too. There are yellow-bellied toads (*Bombina variegata*), tree frogs (*Hyla arborea*) and agile frogs (*Rana dalmatina*). Hermann's tortoise (*Testudo hermanii*) is also present in the area. (Thanks to Joost Smets for this information.)

The Shala River rises high up above Thethi, in the karst of Mount Arapi (2,217m), the cliff that towers over the Thethi Valley from the north, and it flows pretty much north to south until it meets Lake Komani (pages 168–9). It emerges above ground just before the settlement of **Okoli**, in a number of little springs surrounded by beech trees, and there are several nice picnic spots in the vicinity. To get to Okoli from the main village of Thethi, turn left instead of right after you have crossed the bridge near the school, and keep going along the road. If you are staying up above the village, on the way down from Qafë-Thora, you can cut across the hillside, through woods and meadows, and come down to Okoli from the west. As you approach the village from this direction, you pass some World War II bunkers, of quite different design from the Communist-era pillboxes.

Climbing up the eastern flank of Mount Arapi, the path continues up to **Qafa e Pejës** (the Peja Pass), 1,700m high, which used to link Thethi with the Montenegrin towns of Gusinje (Gucia, in Albanian) and Plava. To cross the international border on foot between Albania, Kosova and Montenegro, advance permits are needed; see page 44 for advice on obtaining these. There are interesting caves on Mount Arapi, pretty much due north from Okoli, and others above the alpine meadows called Fusha e Dënellit, on the other side of Thethi. Details of these routes can be found in the *Vermoshi: Tamarë, Razma, Thethi* map (page 40). The paths are not always easy to identify, however, and the use of a guide is highly recommended.

Further up the main road out of Thethi, a footpath called Shtegu i Dhenve ('the Sheep Track') leads up to a pass at 1,830m and onward to Boga (at least 6 hours' walk). On a clear day there are excellent views from here over the Boga Valley as

FLORA AND FAUNA IN THE ALBANIAN ALPS   *Catherine Bohne*

The Malësia is a naturalist's dream. The convergence of the central European alpine climate with the Mediterranean produces the richest flora in Europe, with an estimated minimum of 3,200 naturally occurring species of higher plants (compare this with the 1,500 native species of the British Isles). With 14 species of wild thyme, six different mints, lavender and rosemary and 16 different members of the Sage genus, a walk in the highlands simply *smells* good.

Begin with staring at what's under your feet: the limestone rock from which the mountains are formed. Some 50–100 million years old, the mountains were forced upwards when Africa hit Europe (in summary) and so everything around you is formed of sedimentary limestone, which was originally coral on the bottom of a large, shallow inland sea. This same limestone and its tendency to dissolve in strange patterns both above and below ground gives rise to the karst geology, characterised by underground rivers, excellent drainage (not so exciting to you perhaps, but thrilling to the plants) and many, many caves. There should also, of course, be many fossils.

As you stand and stare across a valley, the further peaks and rocky outcrops may appear barren, but closer inspection reveals them to be a riot of tiny gem-like plants, such as alpine succulents, Saxifrage, Sempervivums, Silenes and Sedums (to mention only things beginning with 's'). Moving down from the peaks, you find the grassy meadows of the Bjeshkët ('alps'), an absolutely dizzy fit of flowers from May to July. Here you will find the endemic Albanian lily (*Lilium albanicum*), as well as fritillaries, several species of orchids, and some of the 32 species of *campanula* (bellflowers) on record. Dianthus (22 species of pinks), flowering peas and Lathyrus (up to 26 species), Geranium (also a possible 26) and let's not forget up to 60 species of clover. And these are just a handful of the things it's *easy* to see.

If you can tear your eyes away from all this, you might look up to spot a golden eagle (*Aquila chrysaetos*) soaring majestically (or dropping a baby goat from a great height to stun it for lunch). Luckily for the eagles, the heights are also hopping with a large population of chamois (*Rupicapra rupicapra*); watching one casually run straight down a seemingly vertical cliff is a heart-stopping thrill not to be missed.

Descending further, these frequently vertical meadows and rock faces will intersect with marginally more gentle slopes formed by millennia of piled rock debris, now blanketed most often with beech forest (*Fagus sylvatica*). Besides being straight out of Grimms' Fairy Tales, these forests also shelter what may well

well as back down across the Shala Valley. Before the road over Qafë-Thora was built in the 1930s, this was the only way for the people of Thethi to get to Boga; instead, their natural links were with Shkodra, using the route along the Shala and Kiri rivers, and with the village of Rragami in the neighbouring district of Tropoja.

Hiking from Thethi to Valbona An ancient track runs between Thethi and Rragami across the Valbona Pass, over 1,800m above sea level; most winters, the pass is snowbound until May or even early June. The track has been waymarked and, in summer, it is quite straightforward to find the way. However, the hike requires a reasonable level of fitness and should not be attempted without adequate footwear and clothing. Horses can be hired in Thethi or Valbona to carry rucksacks; enquire at your guesthouse. The going rate for a horse, with a human to manage it, is €50; each horse can take up to 60 kilos of luggage. Depending on how fit you are and how much kit you are carrying, it takes 4–5 hours to reach the Valbona Pass,

be the largest population of *Ursus arctos* – brown bear – left in Europe. Although they will avoid you assiduously, sightings are still frequent and signs of their passing – footprints, scratched trees and droppings – are easy to spot. Other large animals you might see signs of include wild boar (*Sus scrofa*) and, of course, no fairy-tale woods would be complete without ... wolves (*Canis lupus*). There are an estimated 400 wolves in these mountains, making this the largest population in Europe. While hard to spot in the summer, when they move up to the meadows to follow the flocks of sheep and goats, in winter they are extremely prevalent, their tracks are easy to follow (particularly as they circle the houses at night) and an enthusiastic observer can begin to recognise the tracks of individual wolves. Things you are almost guaranteed not to see a sign of, but might like to know are around, include the wild cat (*Felis sylvestris*) and the very rare Balkan lynx (*Lynx lynx*). The Balkan Lynx Recovery Programme, which involves Albanian and international biologists, has been using camera traps since 2008, in an effort to monitor the movements of lynx and other wildlife in the Albanian highlands.

Also lurking in the forest are another plethora of rare (elsewhere) and beautiful plants of which the most notable is the *Ramonda serbica*, a sort of Balkan version of an African violet. Badgers (*Meles meles*) make a racket snuffling through the undergrowth, and a rainy day will bring out hordes of fire salamanders (*Salamandra salamandra*). Once down by the riverbanks, strolling through stands of silvery willows, you can look for the round webbed tracks of the common otter (*Lutra lutra*) and peer into eddy pools for the highly prized local trout. Smaller animals you might encounter without ever straying from your hotel or guesthouse include such pleasures as red foxes (*Vulpes vulpes*), the incredibly cute fat dormouse (*Glis glis*) and the noble eastern hedgehog (*Erinaceus concolor*).

All of this of course only touches on a fraction of what's actually here to be seen. Not mentioned yet are such joys as beetles, butterflies, the oddly friendly grasshoppers (pink ones as well as green!), snakes, vipers, cuckoos, woodpeckers – the list goes on and on.

Finally, a word of encouragement. One of the main reasons for this richness is the historical isolation and economic neglect of the area. As this changes, these precious populations will come under threat. The interest and enthusiasm of visitors will be invaluable to the future survival of this last remaining corner of wild Europe.

The Northwest   THE ALBANIAN ALPS

7

and then another 2–3 hours down to Rragami. Obviously this hike can also be done in the opposite direction, from Rragami to Thethi; it simply comes down to how you choose to organise the rest of your trip.

The path out of Thethi leads fairly gently uphill from the Shala River to meet the very rough vehicle track (difficult even with 4x4) to the settlement of **Gjelaj.** The first of three cafés on the route, just above Gjelaj, is a good opportunity for a breather before a very steep section through beech forest; it is possible to camp at this café.

About an hour beyond Gjelaj, a spring just before the end of the forest is the next place where water bottles can be replenished. Then you emerge on to a beautiful alpine meadow, carpeted with lavender, clover of different colours and little orchids. All these flowers, of course, mean lots of butterflies: blues, arguses and tortoiseshells, among others. Several very rare butterflies can be found in the Albanian highlands, including the apollo (*Parnassius apollo*), large blue and Alcon large blue (*Maculinea arion* and *Maculinea alcon*).

The meadows give way to more beech forest, with patches of tiny, tart wild strawberries. A second café stands in a clearing; camping is also possible here (m *068 52 35 920*). Members of the family who live here (except in winter) sell cold drinks and slices of the northern Albanian dish called *fli*, layers of filo pastry and butter which might have been invented as a hiking snack. The toilets are impeccable, with running water, soap, clean towel and mirror. This is the last chance to fill water bottles until far down on the other side of the pass.

It takes about an hour from the café to the Valbona Pass. At the top, there are magnificent views across the valley to Qafë-Thora and Qafa e Pejës, and down into Thethi and towards the source of the Shala. However, it is a bleak spot and often very windy. The path down on the other side is steep and feels as if it is going in the wrong direction (it isn't). It will be with relief that you find yourself at the third and last of the trail-side cafés, Kafe Simoni, at the source of the Valbona River. Another steep slog downhill brings you to Gjelaj i Rragamit, the twin settlement of Gjelaj i Thethit where the hike began. As on the other side, there is a rough track to this settlement, useable by 4x4 vehicles. It is 3km from here to the asphalted road and the restaurant at Fushë e Gjesë. See pages 171–3 for information about Rragami and onward travel to Valbona and Bajram Curri.

RRAZMA Like Thethi, Rrazma became a tourist destination in the 1930s. It never took off in quite the same way, however, and has only recently begun to redevelop its tourism potential. It would be a good base for hiking, especially for those who do not have the time or the inclination to venture further into the mountains to Thethi or Vermoshi. Rrazma is much closer to Shkodra and the road is good all the way. There is a range of accommodation and a good choice of places to eat, although the village does close down to some extent outside the peak summer months. In the winter, cross-country skiing is possible, although there is no piste.

Where to stay

Natyral Rrazma Resort (26 rooms) m 068 60 45 455/7; e info@natyralrazmaresort. com; w natyralrazmaresort.com. Modern building in traditional style; English spoken at reception; indifferent restaurant ($$$$); bar; 25m indoor, heated swimming pool, sauna, cinema, computer in lounge with internet for guests' use; skis available. All rooms non-smoking, nicely decorated, with flatscreen TV, minibar, AC, CH; well equipped but rather small ensuite bathroom, some have bathtub, others only shower. 3 rooms have balcony, 1 suite has large terrace, all with mountain views. Cash only. **$$$$**

Tigri m 068 30 11 010. Clean & friendly. Rooms en suite with TV. **$$**

Since 1999, a group of international and local organisations and individuals have been working within the Balkans Peace Park Project (B3P) to establish a cross-border park that would straddle the highlands of northern Albania, southern Montenegro and western Kosova.

There are more than 600 environmentally protected areas in the world that straddle international boundaries; one of them can be found at the other end of Albania, encompassing the two Prespa Lakes shared by Albania, Greece and Macedonia. About 25 of these cross-border parks are specifically dedicated as 'Peace Parks', symbols of peace and co-operation between countries where sometimes there has been serious conflict. One of the first was the Morokulien Peace Park between Norway and Sweden, set up in 1914. B3P is one of about 400 cross-border projects in the European Green Belt, an initiative of the International Union for Conservation of Nature (IUCN), which runs the length of the old 'Iron Curtain', from Finland to the southeastern Balkans.

The mountains and valleys in the area proposed for the Balkans Peace Park are home to people who have retained their traditional lifestyles to an extent that is unusual in Europe, and are a habitat for exceptional flora and fauna. But the lack of economic opportunity has led to environmental threats, such as illegal logging, and the cultural threat of depopulation as people move to the cities for work. B3P's vision is of a Peace Park where communities from all three countries working together to protect their environment, stimulate local employment and promote sustainable tourism in the region. In Albania, the Peace Park boundaries would cover Kelmendi, the Valbona Valley and Shala, the area that includes Thethi. Its partner organisation, B3P-Albania, is registered as a non-profit organisation in Shkodra.

B3P's earliest initiatives were to support walking, bike and horse treks, researching old and new routes in the proposed Peace Park area and working to help open up cross-border tracks. It has sponsored and organised international conferences, facilitated several significant academic studies in the region, and established regular exchange visits between the communities in the area and the Yorkshire Dales National Park in England. From 2008 to 2015, it ran an annual summer programme in the former village school in Thethi, bringing together Albanian teachers and foreign volunteers. The summer programmes later expanded across northern Albania and into Kosova and Montenegro. Adults as well as schoolchildren had the opportunity to learn skills that help their community to survive: English, so that they can communicate with foreign tourists; marketable arts and crafts; and agricultural techniques such as permaculture.

More information about B3P's activities can be found on its website (w *balkanspeacepark.org*).

✕ **Where to eat and drink** There are several restaurants around Rrazma, serving everything from traditional northern Albanian dishes to pizza. They are a better (and less expensive) option than the restaurant in the Natyral Rrazma Resort, which – although beautifully designed, with traditional open fireplace and attractive art on the walls – offers very average Italian cuisine, imported wine only and slow, erratic service.

The Northwest   THE ALBANIAN ALPS

7

KELMENDI The district of Kelmendi is Albania's northernmost extreme, a finger of territory poking up into Montenegro. The main villages are Tamara (the administrative centre), Lepusha and Vermoshi – each of them a scattering of stone-built houses surrounded by magnificent mountains. Some of these houses have been kitted out as guesthouses, from where day hikes and longer expeditions can be undertaken. The local produce is delicious – fish from the rivers, lamb and pork from the families' own livestock, cream cheese and yoghurt, fruit conserves and syrups, and plum raki.

Tamara has shops, a post office and cafés; the Prodhimë të Kelmendit shop stocks a range of local foodstuffs, including honey, raki, different kinds of jam and fruit syrup and mountain tea (çaj mali). The tourist information office also sells local produce. In Vermoshi, there is a café and a little shop that sells household goods, fruit and groceries, beer and cigarettes. The Albanian mobile-phone networks are rather intermittent beyond Tamara; a Montenegrin signal can be picked up in some spots. Lepusha and Vermoshi both have internet connections.

Getting there and away The sole road linking Kelmendi with the rest of Albania runs up the spectacular, rugged valley of the Cemi River; it is now asphalted all the way to Vermoshi, which has cut the journey time to less than 2 hours from Shkodra.

A minibus runs from Shkodra up the valley to Vermoshi every day except Sundays. It leaves from behind the Malësia e Madhe Restaurant at Rus Maxhar (see map, pages 188–9) at about 13.30; however, you should check in the morning whether or not the driver has definitely come down that day. The fare to Vermoshi is 700 lek. For Lepusha, you should ask to be dropped off at the Bordoleçi Pass (Qafa e Bordoleçit), on the main road just above the village. Another minibus serves the route between Shkodra and Tamara. It also leaves Shkodra around 13.30; the fare to Tamara is 400 lek.

From **Montenegro**, a road leads up to the border crossing from the village of Gucia (called Gusinje in Serbo-Croat), in the district of Plava. (See Bradt's *Montenegro* for further information about accommodation and transport options there.) There is no public transport on the Albanian side; it is about 3km from the border to the main road. The border crossing is open all year round and, in winter, snow is usually cleared fairly quickly from the main road.

In summer, it is possible to hike to Lepusha from Thethi (pages 211–18), a two-day trip; there are guesthouses in Nikçi (eg: *Prekë Isufi;* m *069 52 85 003*) where the journey can be broken. The *Vermoshi: Tamarë, Razma, Thethi* map (page 40) gives details of this route, and other suggested hikes in the area. The passes are usually blocked with snow until at least May.

Tourist information (m *069 47 24 658;* f *Kelmend-Shkrel;* ⊕ *09.00–18.00*) The Italian-funded tourist information office in Tamara stocks a range of useful leaflets and maps, sells guidebooks (including the hiking map mentioned above) and local foodstuffs. The helpful, enthusiastic staff can advise on accommodation throughout Kelmendi and assist with making reservations.

🏠 **Where to stay, eat and drink** There are family-run guesthouses throughout Kelmendi, providing simple accommodation with shared toilet and shower facilities. The website w kelmend-shkrel.org has information, in English as well as Albanian and Italian, about several options. The daily rate for full board is around €25 per person; some guesthouses also offer half-board or bed and breakfast.

Some of the houses in Vermoshi are across the river from the main road; when the river is low you can ford it in a car, but otherwise there is only a footbridge. The family you are staying with will help you with your luggage if required.

🏠 **Gjergj Frani** (20 beds) Vermoshi; m 066 66 69 022, +382 69 53 06 03 (Montenegro). Up a track off main road just before Vermoshi; 10 rooms of varying sizes; kitchen; dining room; washing machine; large covered terrace; garden with gazebos. Hiking guides with English & other languages can be arranged.

🏠 **Kafe Natyra** (30 beds) Vermoshi; m +382 69 52 61 18 (Montenegro). Just off main road; 5 rooms in family house, large dorm & 1 twin in new wood-panelled building. Restaurant in tree house in huge cherry tree; all food home produced; outdoor pool with shallow section for children; orchard. Wi-Fi. Camping also possible (**$**).

🏠 **Leonard Lumaj** (7 beds) Vermoshi; m 069 30 30 733. Guesthouse separate from family home, across the river from the road. Modern bathroom, fully equipped kitchen, large sitting room. Wi-Fi in family home. Mr Lumaj operates the minibus to Shkodra, making this a convenient option if that is how you are getting to Vermoshi. Ground-floor dorm with 4 beds. 1 dbl, & 1 dbl & sgl upstairs.

🏠 **Lepusha** (8 beds) Lepusha; m 069 99 35 806, +382 69 27 79 72 (Montenegro); e zef. nilaj@gmail.com; f Bujtina Lepushe Page. Signposted from the main road, asphalted to gate & beyond; landscaped garden; campsite on raised terrace among fruit trees; Wi-Fi. 3 rooms (1 wood-panelled dorm, 1 sgl, 1 twin) sharing large modern bathroom.

🏠 **Maja e Trojanit** (9 beds) Budaçi; m 069 45 19 116. About halfway between border turn-off & Qafa e Bordoleçit. 3 rooms (2 dorms, 1 dbl) sharing 1 shower & toilet; kitchen.

🏠 **Prelë & Mariana Vuktilaj** (28 beds) Vermoshi; m +382 69 55 24 35 (Montenegro); e antonjo_vuktilaj@hotmail.com; can be booked on w booking.com. Across the river from the road. 7 rooms, 3 dorms & 4 dbls, sharing 5 modern bathrooms; dining room with TV; balcony running the length of the house; mini museum of traditional implements & costumes; courtyard with seating & views out across valley. Horseriding can be arranged; Mr Vuktilaj can lead hiking & climbing trips.

7

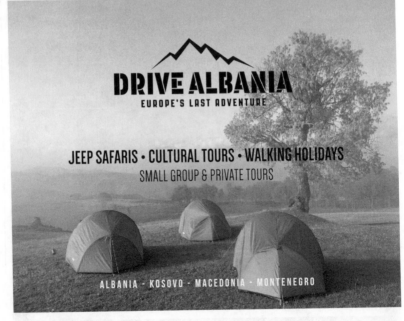

8

The Southwest

SARANDA *Telephone code: 0852*

Southwestern Albania has many unmissable attractions: the wonderful archaeological site and national park at Butrint; the imposing Ottoman city of Gjirokastra; the beautiful beaches and crystalline waters of the Riviera. Sadly, though, Saranda – the point of entry to Albania for many foreign visitors – is no longer the attractive little port it once was. Thousands of people make the trip across the Corfu Channel every summer, most of them taking advantage of the day trips to Butrint organised by tour operators and the ferry companies on Corfu. It is a pity that their first encounter with Albania is the unappealing concrete jungle that Saranda has become. Nonetheless, it is still the most practicable base from which to visit the beautiful and interesting places in its vicinity.

Saranda has an excellent climate, averaging around 290 sunny days a year, with pleasantly warm temperatures rarely exceeding 30°C. Some of the hotels have outdoor pools, generally open only in the peak summer months, while some are linked to one or other of the beach resorts along the coast towards Butrint. The beach in the town is a pleasant enough place to catch a few rays in between sightseeing. If a day at the beach is what you are after, though, it is better to head south to Ksamili (page 236) or north to the Albanian Riviera (pages 253–9).

The Greek name for the town – Ayia Saranda, 'forty saints', from which the Albanian name comes – springs from a legend of 40 Christian legionaries who were put to death here in AD320. A pilgrimage church dedicated to the 40 saints was built on a hill behind modern Saranda in the 5th century, rebuilt in the early 9th century and, unfortunately, used as a base by German troops during the Battle for the Liberation of Saranda in 1944 – unfortunate, because it led to the church's destruction by British bombers. The neighbouring hill of Lëkurësi is the site of an early 19th-century castle, one of many built by Ali Pasha Tepelena (see box, pages 254–5), which has been converted into a popular restaurant and bar. From the terraces of the restaurant there are magnificent views over the Ksamili Peninsula to the Butrint Lagoon and across to Corfu. Some damaged frescoes can still be seen in the remains of the garrison church.

GETTING THERE AND AWAY

By sea Daily **hydrofoils** connect the towns of Saranda and Corfu all year round. See page 226 for contact details for the operators. In peak season (July–mid-September), there are at least six crossings a day in each direction; the first departures from both Corfu and Saranda are at 09.00. The shoulder months have four sailings a day; off-season (October–early May), there are daily departures from Corfu at 09.00 and from Saranda at 10.00 and 13.00. The journey by hydrofoil takes about 40 minutes. The one-way fare is €18–19 off-season, €20–23.80 in July and August. There are also **car ferries**; see operators' websites for details.

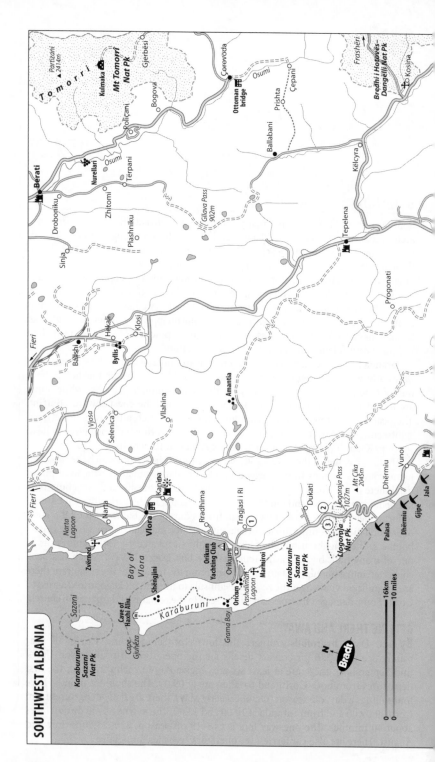

SOUTHWEST ALBANIA

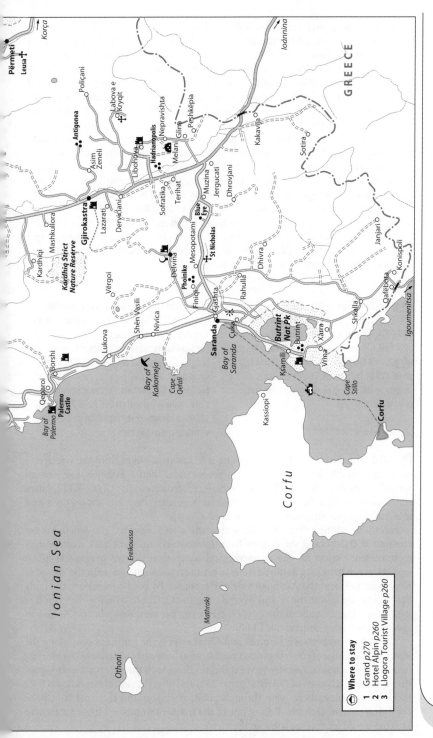

GREECE

↑ Korça

Përmeti
Leusa

Poliçani

Labova e
Kryqit

Antigonea

Asim
Zeneli

Libohova

Hadrianopolis
Melan
Glinë

Nepravishta

Peshkëpia

Kakavija

Iodnnina ↑

Sotira

Gjirokastra

Lazarati

Deryiçiani

Sofratika

Terihat

Muzina

Jergucati

Dhrovjani

Mashkullora

Kardhiqi

Kaldhiq Strict
Nature Reserve

Vërgoi

Blue
Eye

Mesopotami

St Nicholas

Belvina

Phoinikë

Finiq

Gjashtë

Rahullë

Dhivra

Janjari

Konispoli

Shën Vasili

Nivica

Saranda
Çukë

Bay of
Saranda

Butrint Nat Pk

Butrint

Xarra

Vrina

Shkalla

Qafëbota

Igoumenitsa ↑

Lukova

Borshi

Bay of
Kakomeja

Cape
Qefali

Ksamili

Cape
Stillo

Corfu

Qeparoi

Palermo
Castle

Bay of
Palermo

Kassiopi

Corfu

Ionian Sea

Ereikoussa

Mathraki

Othoni

ⓘ Where to stay

1 Grand *p270*
2 Hotel Alpin *p260*
3 Llogora Tourist Village *p260*

225

The hydrofoils and ferries to Albania leave from the far end of the main port in Corfu town, where the cruise ships berth. Tickets must be purchased before boarding, from one of the ticket agencies near the entrance to the port. Economical **hotels ($$$)** for an overnight stay in Corfu include Atlantis (\ +30 266 103 5560; w atlantis-hotel-corfu.com), convenient for the seaport, and Bretagne (\ +30 266 103 0724; w hotelbretagne.gr), within walking distance of the airport. Corfu city buses operate hourly between the airport and the seaport (w corfucitybus.com).

Passport control in Saranda is usually swift and efficient. The centre of Saranda is 10 minutes' walk from the passenger terminal and the bus terminus is about 15 minutes away. Yellow, licensed taxis wait just beyond the barrier at the entrance to the port. Several agencies offer **car hire** (page 41), all clustered around the exit from the port on Rruga Mit'hat Hoxha. Saloons and 4x4 vehicles are available.

Several companies operate one-day tours to Albania from Corfu. The day trips usually comprise a visit to Butrint, a restaurant lunch and some free time in Saranda. In summer, Finikas also operates a hydrofoil between Corfu and Himara (pages 257–9), excursions by boat from Saranda, and bus tours to Butrint, Gjirokastra and Parga; consult its website for details.

Ferries

Finikas Lines \0852 26057 (Saranda), +30 266 103 8690 (Corfu); m 069 20 73 711, 067 20 22 004; S finikaslines; e info@finikas-lines. com, finikaslines@yahoo.com; w finikas-lines.com

Sarris Cruises \0852 24751 (Saranda); m 069 20 81 182, 069 20 91 699; S Sarris. Albania; e info@sarris.al, pilo.gllava@hotmail. com; w sarris.al

Car hire

Finikas Lines \0852 26057 (Saranda), m 069 20 73 711, 067 20 22 004; e info@finikas-lines.com; w finikas-lines.com

Sipa Tours (also has branch at Orikum Yachting Club) \0852 26675; m 068 20 35 250; w sipatours.com

Tirana Car Rentals (also has branches in Vlora, Tirana & Durrësi) m 068 20 39 787, 068 40 30 505; e saranda.port@tirana-car-rentals.com; w tirana-car-rentals.com

By land
The traditional border crossing is at **Kakavija**, 60km from the Greek city of Ioannina and 9.5km from the turn-off for Saranda. There are daily bus services to Saranda from Athens and other Greek cities. Alternatively, the Greek KTEL buses run several times a day up to the border at Kakavija; there are always taxis and minibuses on the Albanian side of the border.

For those coming from Greece with their own transport, the small border crossing at **Qafëbota**, a short drive from Igoumenitsa on the Greek mainland, is a convenient option for the archaeological complex at Butrint (pages 231–6). It would be worth making a short detour to see the traditional houses in the village of Konispoli, just over the Albanian side of the border. By public transport, the daily buses between Igoumenitsa and Saranda use the Qafëbota crossing. Konispoli is within walking distance of the border; buses run between Saranda and Konispoli several times a day, until about 14.00.

The main road between Saranda and **Gjirokastra** is the southern one, along the Bistrica River. Buses (*300 lek*) ply this road until at least early afternoon; the journey takes about 1¼ hours. An alternative route, for those with their own transport, goes through the small town of Delvina (pages 238) and offers beautiful views down over the Bistrica Valley; there is no through public transport and the road is in poor condition beyond Delvina. Taking one of the frequent minibuses from Saranda to Delvina would let you see some of the views.

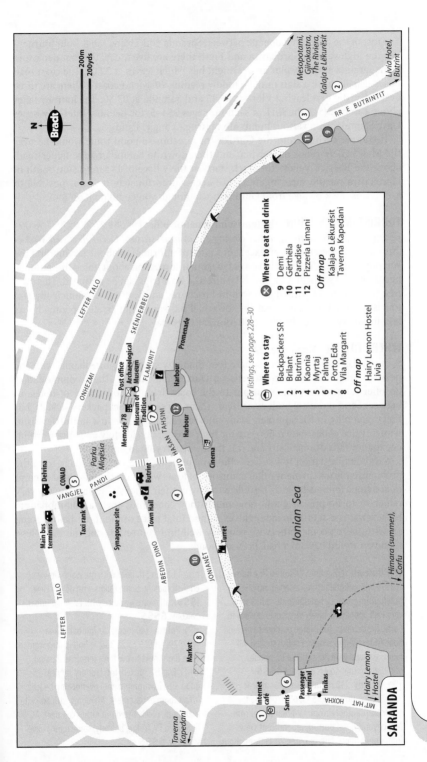

SARANDA

0 ────── 200m
0 ────── 200yds

N

Bradt

Mesopotami,
Girokastra,
The Riviera,
Kalaja e Lëkurësit

Livia Hotel,
Butrint

RR E BUTRINTIT

LEFTER TALO

ONHEZMI

SKËNDERBEU

Post office
Archaeological
Museum

Memorje 78
Museum of
Tradition

FLAMURIT

BYO HASAN TAHSINI

Promenade

Harbour

Harbour

Cinema

Turret

Parku
Miqësia

Synagogue site

PANDI

VANGJEL

CONAD

Delvina

Main bus
terminus

Taxi rank

LEFTER
TALO

ABEDIN DINO

JONIANET

Town Hall

Butrint

Market

Internet
café

Sarris

Passenger
terminal

Finikas

MIT HAT.

HOXHA

Hairy Lemon
Hostel

Taverna
Kapedani

Himara (summer),
Corfu

Ionian Sea

For listings, see pages 228–30

Where to stay
1 Backpackers SR
2 Brilant
3 Butrinti
4 Kaonia
5 Myrtaj
6 Palma
7 Porto Eda
8 Vila Margarit

Off map
Hairy Lemon Hostel
Livia

Where to eat and drink
9   Demi
10 Gërthëla
11 Paradise
12 Pizzeria Limani

Off map
Kalaja e Lëkurësit
Taverna Kapedani

Most of the buses that operate between Saranda and Tirana (an 8-hour journey) use the highway via Gjirokastra and Fieri; there are five a day, the first departure from Saranda at 05.00, plus an overnight bus which leaves at 22.00. The **coast road** buses usually have a sign in the window reading *Bregdeti* ('coast'); there are three every day, the first leaving Vlora at 06.45 and Saranda at 05.30. The journey takes about 4 hours. (See the *Riviera* section, pages 254–5, for details.) Inter-city buses leave Saranda from various points along Rruga Vangjel Pandi.

If you are **cycling** from the Gjirokastra direction, a good route would be over the Mali i Gjerë range to Delvina, and then down to Saranda by the upper road, above the Bistrica Valley. The track starts at the village of Lazarati, 5km south of Gjirokastra on the main highway to Greece; unfortunately it is not possible to access this track by bike from Gjirokastra, although you could do it on foot.

TOURIST INFORMATION The **tourist information office** (m *069 27 91 052;* ⊕ *08.00– midnight in high summer, earlier closing out of peak season, Dec–Feb closed Wed & Thu*) on the promenade is an excellent source of information about Saranda and the surrounding area. The staff have a database of information about hotels, restaurants, bus times and so forth. Car hire, bike hire and boat trips can be arranged. There are free town plans of Saranda, as well as brochures and leaflets. A municipally run tourist information kiosk near the town hall has somewhat erratic opening hours but, in theory, is open 08.00–16.00 Monday to Friday.

WHERE TO STAY *Map, page 227*

Saranda has more hotels per square foot than anywhere else in Albania, with the possible exception of the coast between Durrësi and Kavaja. The accommodation on offer ranges from the luxurious to the basic, with a good choice of hotels in between, and more are built every year. There are several backpackers' hostels, but they open only in the summer. Many mid-range hotels also close in the depths of winter. Price codes shown here are for high season; outside July and August room occupancy falls dramatically and it is then worth trying to haggle.

Saranda bus station is – so far – the only place in Albania that suffers from the problem, common in many other countries, of touts who meet the buses and attempt to convince foreign-looking travellers to stay in their 'hotels'. They are usually very reluctant to be precise about how much they charge for their accommodation; however, it is essential to agree the exact and final price of the room before going off with these people, otherwise you may well find yourself paying more, for less, than you would have in a real, licensed hotel.

Butrinti (78 rooms, 24 suites) Rr e Butrintit; ☏25593–6; e hotelbutrinti.reservation@ hotelbutrinti.com; w hotelbutrinti.com. 5 stars, very well appointed, lovely views over the bay to Corfu. Restaurants, bars, large outdoor swimming pool, fitness centre, sauna. English spoken. All rooms en suite with AC, satellite TV, phone, minibar, internet access & safe. **$$$$$**

Brilant (18 rooms, 2 suites) Lagja 1; ☏26262; m 069 20 53 533, 069 20 57 354; e info@brilanthotel.com; w brilanthotel.com. Just beyond Hotel Butrint, magnificent views from upper floors. Lift, bar, free Wi-Fi throughout,

b/fast bar on 5th floor with great sea views; English spoken. Some rooms with no sea view (**$$$**); all rooms en suite with TV, AC, minibar, balcony. **$$$$**

Palma (40 rooms) Rr Mit'hat Hoxha; ☏22929; m 069 65 28 336; e hotelpalma@gmail. com. Right next to the ferry terminal. Parking, Wi-Fi, English spoken; lift; laundry service; good-sized swimming pool overlooking beach; b/fast room in basement. All rooms with en-suite bathroom, nicely fitted but rather compact; AC, flatscreen TV, fridge, balcony; some rooms have sea view. **$$$$**

Porto Eda (24 rooms, 1 suite) Bd Hasan Tahsini; m 069 72 33 180; e portoeda@gmail. com, info@portoeda.com; w portoeda.com. Centrally located, on promenade opposite little harbour. Lift; bar; free parking; English spoken at reception. Generous b/fast inc, in lounge with newspapers & books. All rooms have well-designed en-suite bathroom with hairdryer & shower screen; AC, minibar, TV, safe, clock-radio, coffee- & tea-making facilities, direct-dial phone, balcony with sea view. **$$$$**

Kaonia (24 rooms) Rr Jonianët; 22600; m 067 20 54 944; e kaoniahotel@yahoo.com, dgjoni@bkt.com.al; ☐ Hotel Kaonia. On the promenade a few mins' walk from the town centre. Bar with terrace, lift, free parking, Wi-Fi in public areas. All rooms en suite with AC, flatscreen TV & balcony; some have sea view. **$$$**

Livia (11 rooms, 1 suite) Butrint; 0891 22040; m 067 34 77 077; e info@hotel-livia. com; w hotel-livia.com. 90m from entrance to Butrint site. Good restaurant serving fresh fish (**$$$$**), tables in peaceful garden overlooking Vivari Channel. Free parking, free Wi-Fi throughout. Suite has huge private terrace (**$$$$**). All rooms en suite with AC, flatscreen TV, hairdryer, iron, mosquito net, fridge, balcony. **$$$**

Myrtaj (14 rooms) Rr Onhezmi; 24411; m 069 20 93 990. Opposite the taxi rank & inter-city buses; can be rather noisy early in the morning. All rooms en suite with AC & TV; some have balcony with sea view. **$$**

Vila Margarit (12 rooms) Rr Jonianët; m 069 31 88 696; ☐ Vila Margarit Sarande – Albania. Next to fruit & veg market, handy for ferries & for seafront; English spoken, helpful management. Free parking, free Wi-Fi throughout; bar; terrace. All rooms en suite, nicely decorated, with AC, TV, fridge, bedside light, small balcony; some have sea view. **$$**

Backpackers SR (14 beds) Rr Mit'hat Hoxha 10; m 069 43 45 426; w backpackerssr.hostel. com. Good location near port terminal. Kitchen with fridge & cooker; washing machine; luggage storage; lockers; lift. Free Wi-Fi & bedlinen; 3 dorms, all with balcony with sea view. B/fast inc. **$**

Hairy Lemon Hostel (18 beds) Rr e Arbërit, Lagja Kodër; m 069 88 99 196; e saranda@ hairylemonhostel.com; w hairylemonhostel.com. Quite far from the town centre; 20m from sea. Fully equipped kitchen; barbecue facilities; washing machine, lift, luggage storage, lockers. Free Wi-Fi & bed linen. B/fast inc. Useful information about buses on website. **$**

✖ WHERE TO EAT AND DRINK *Map, page 227*

Almost all of Saranda's restaurants serve pretty much the same things at roughly the same prices: fish, seafood, pastas, risottos and wood-fired pizzas. Sea bream and sea bass will be farmed unless the menu specifies otherwise. Mussels, the local speciality, have been farmed in the Butrint Lagoon since the 1960s. The promenade restaurants are, as one would expect, more expensive than those in the town centre. Out of season, many restaurants tend to close quite early in the evening (or altogether). Those listed here are normally open all year round.

✖ **Gërthëla** Rr Jonianët; m 069 28 54 281. An exclusively fish menu, mostly wild, inc less well-known varieties as well as the usual sea bass & sea bream. Nice sea-themed décor; professional service; pleasant atmosphere. **$$$$$**

✖ **Paradise** Rr e Butrintit. At the far eastern end of the promenade, suspended over the water on stilts; also known as Ylli's. A bit pricier than elsewhere, but lots of people think the view is worth it. Good range of fish & seafood, professional service. **$$$$$**

✖ **Demi** Rr e Butrintit. Big covered terrace built out over the sea, just beyond the Hotel Butrinti

on the way out of town. Fresh fish, various mussel dishes, seafood risotto & pasta. Also has hotel rooms (**$$$$$**). **$$$$**

✖ **Kalaja e Lëkurësit** Behind the town, just off the main road (signposted); 25533. Built on the ruins of an Ottoman castle; fabulous views right down the Butrint Lagoon & up the coast to the north of Saranda. Traditional southern Albanian dishes. Open-air concerts in summer. **$$$$**

✖ **Pizzeria Limani** Bd Hasan Tahsini. A lovely setting on the town harbour, in among the little boats & looking out across the bay. The usual menu, including fish, not just pizza. **$$$**

✗ Taverna Kapedani Rr Idriz Alidhima. Just before the football stadium, on the other side of the street, past Carrefour supermarket. Superb fresh fish, good house wine, excellent value. Menu translated into English. **$$$**

OTHER PRACTICALITIES The tourist information kiosk (page 228) doubles as a **bookshop**, with a wide selection of publications in Albanian, English and other languages – including (usually) this guidebook. There are also children's books and games. In summer, foreign newspapers are available from 09.00. Postcards and stamps can be bought and the cards can be posted on the spot. Credit cards are accepted during the summer.

The **post office** (⊕ *08.00–20.00 daily*), just up from the little harbour, provides free internet access at a reasonable speed.

WHAT TO SEE AND DO Saranda is an ancient town, first settled in the 4th century BC by the Chaonians (page 236), who called it Onchesmus. Cicero mentions it as a convenient harbour with a favourable prevailing wind. It was never a Roman colony, but it must have been reasonably prosperous in the 2nd and 3rd centuries AD, since mosaics from that period have been found at various sites in the town.

In the 4th century AD, Onchesmus was fortified with a roughly semicircular wall, about 850m long and 6m high. These fortifications were further strengthened with turrets and, in one of these, coins were found that date the tower's useful life to the period from AD334 to AD578. The remains of one of the **turrets** can be seen on the town beach. The waterfront itself was not fortified, presumably because it could be defended from the sea, so this tower marks where the wall ended. The British artist and poet Edward Lear sketched the city walls in 1857, when they were practically intact. Even into the 1990s, it was still possible to see stretches of the fortifications. The relentless pace of new building in Saranda since then has destroyed almost all of them and only a couple of small sections remain.

The **Museum of Tradition** (*Muzeu i Traditës;* ⊕ *summer 09.00–14.00 & 19.00–22.00 Mon–Fri, 19.00–22.00 Sat–Sun, winter 09.00–14.00; 100 lek, also giving admission to Archaeological Museum*), on the promenade, is an excellent place to learn about Saranda's history. The exhibition begins with a reproduction of Lear's sketch and a 1930 photograph from roughly the same vantage point, by which time only eight of the 20 original watchtowers survived. More photographs from the 1930s show the Forty Saints Church before its destruction in World War II. Nothing of the original church remains above ground, although it is possible to visit the crypt (enquire at the tourist information office) which has some surviving frescoes.

The exhibition continues with very interesting photographs of Saranda between the wars. The town was built on a grid system in the 1930s; the buildings were deliberately kept low-rise so that the whole town could be seen from the sea, rising like the seats of a theatre. A collection of ethnographic objects illustrates everyday life during this period. Upstairs, textiles and musical instruments are displayed alongside photographs of people producing and playing them. The final room of the exhibition gives a fascinating glimpse into life in the 1960s and 1970s, in the town and the surrounding area, through more photographs and household utensils.

A whole corner opposite the main square has been excavated to reveal the remains of a 5th-century **synagogue complex**, with a mosaic floor depicting Jewish symbols such as a menorah (candelabrum) and a ram's horn. Earlier mosaics on the same site appear to have formed the floor of a Roman villa. Towards the end of its life in the last quarter of the 6th century, part of the synagogue was converted into a Christian church and a third layer of mosaics was laid. The panel at the entrance to the site is very informative, with a helpful map; photographs are displayed of the menorah mosaic, which is usually kept covered to protect it from the elements.

Another of Saranda's mosaics can be seen in the **Archaeological Museum** (*Rr e Flamurit;* ⊕ *summer 09.00–14.00 & 16.00–21.00 daily; 100 lek also giving admission to Museum of Tradition*). This mosaic was discovered in the 1960s, during building work at the neighbouring post office, and the museum was built specifically to protect it. It has been dated to the 6th century AD and is thought to have been the floor of a basilica. The museum also has a small display of photographs and information about the archaeological and historical sites in the Saranda area, including Butrint, of course, but also Phoinike and the Islamic buildings around Delvina (page 238).

One aspect of Saranda's communist history can be seen opposite the post office on Rruga e Flamurit: **Memorje 78**, a concrete pillbox, half-excavated so that you can look through a grille into its interior. Inside, there is an information panel with photographs of different types of bunker (page 144) and diagrams of their design.

Boats can be hired for day trips at the little harbour (eg: the 'Ajla'; m *069 64 46 410*). They set off between 09.00 and 10.00 each day; the tourist information office at the harbour can advise. These excursions typically include one or more of the nearby beaches to which there is no road access; the boatmen leave when they have enough passengers to make it worth their while. The going rate is 5,000 lek per passenger.

BUTRINT

The ancient city of Butrint, one of UNESCO's World Heritage Sites, is far and away the most visited archaeological site in Albania, with visible remains spanning two-and-a-half millennia – from the first settlers in the late 6th or early 5th century BC to Ali Pasha Tepelena (see box, pages 254–5) at the beginning of the 19th century AD. Then the site became overgrown and half-forgotten, visited only by the occasional artist (including the British nonsense poet Edward Lear), until 1928, when the Italian Archaeological Mission, led until his death by Luigi Maria Ugolini, began to uncover the city's hidden treasures. After World War II, Butrint was once again abandoned and forgotten until the Albanian Centre for Archaeology began excavating there in 1956. Archaeological research has continued at the site ever since.

Informative and well-presented panels guide the visitor through the city; the small museum, on what was once the acropolis, illustrates Butrint's history through beautiful artefacts; further interesting sites lie across the Vivari Channel, which connects Lake Butrint with the sea, and can be visited on foot or by boat. There is so much to see in and around Butrint that anyone with more than a fleeting interest in history or archaeology could easily spend a whole day (or more) there. Anything less than 3 hours is likely to feel rather rushed and unsatisfactory.

An information leaflet, with a map of the site, is available at the ticket office at the entrance to the site. To find out about the site before your visit, the official website (w *butrint.al*) has information about its archaeological monuments and environmental importance. More academic information can be found on the website of the Butrint Foundation (w *butrintfoundation.co.uk*), a charitable trust set up in 1993 to save Butrint from the neglect and looting that threatened its survival at the time. The Butrint Foundation's excellent publications can be ordered from this website and are also often on sale in the courtyard outside the Butrint museum.

GETTING THERE AND AWAY The ancient city of Butrint is about half an hour's drive from Saranda, 24km on a good asphalted road that runs alongside Lake Butrint and

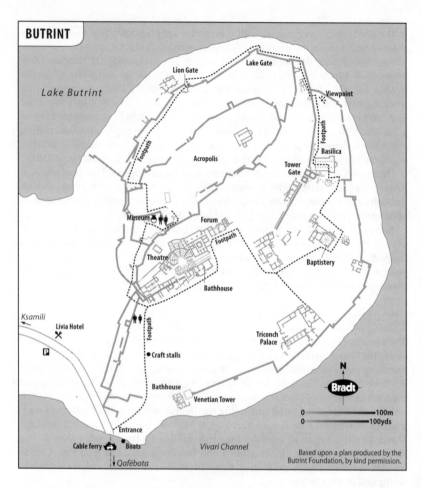

BUTRINT

Lake Butrint

Lake Gate
Lion Gate
Viewpoint
Footpath
Acropolis
Basilica
Tower Gate
Footpath
Museum
Forum
Footpath
Theatre
Baptistery
Bathhouse
Ksamili
Livia Hotel
Footpath
Triconch Palace
Craft stalls
N
Bradt
Bathhouse
0 — 100m
0 — 100yds
Venetian Tower
Entrance
Cable ferry Boats
Vivari Channel
Based upon a plan produced by the
Butrint Foundation, by kind permission.
Qafëbota

through the village of Ksamili. Cyclists might prefer to use the back road, along the eastern shore of the Butrint Lagoon, which has much less traffic and lets you approach the site on the cable ferry (page 235).

Buses between Saranda and Butrint leave hourly in each direction until 18.30; the one-way fare is 100 lek. In Saranda, there are bus stops at the junction of Rruga Mit'hat Hoxha and Rruga Jonianët; opposite the synagogue and basilica site; and opposite the Butrinti Hotel. The last bus back to Saranda from Butrint leaves at 19.30. Any Saranda **taxi** will do the run; you should agree the fare before setting off. Either you could negotiate a charge for extra waiting time with the driver or, if you have a mobile phone, you could arrange to call him when you are ready to be collected. The town's main taxi rank is on the corner of the central park in Saranda, opposite the CONAD supermarket.

Butrint can also be reached from the other direction, the border crossing from Greece at Qafëbota; see page 226 for details of this route.

In the tourist season, Butrint becomes very busy; thousands of visitors pass through the site on the peak days. If you can be flexible with your time, it is better to visit either first thing in the morning, before the tour groups arrive from Corfu, or later in the afternoon, when they have left.

GETTING AROUND AND OTHER PRACTICALITIES A reasonably surfaced path leads around the site. Most of it is fairly flat, apart from a slight climb up to the viewpoint for the aqueduct (page 234) and back down to the Lake and Lion gates. However, the museum is on the city's acropolis, on the summit of the hill above the monumental centre. The usual access to it is through the Lion Gate and up several flights of steps, with intermittent handrails. Visitors with limited mobility may find it easier to use the steps to the west of the theatre.

A toilet block has been installed near the entrance to the ancient agora, but it is sometimes closed. The only reliable toilets within Butrint are on the acropolis. The Livia Hotel, a few minutes' walk from the site entrance, serves meals ($$$$) and drinks, and obviously has toilets for customer use.

You should be sure to have enough drinking water with you, especially in high summer when it can become extremely hot. There is nowhere to buy water within the site. You may also wish to stock up on insect repellent; Butrint is low-lying and surrounded by water, ideal territory for mosquitoes and other biting insects.

A bookstall outside the museum sells publications, in a range of languages, about Butrint and other archaeological sites in Albania. In the tourist season, craft stalls near the ticket office sell souvenirs such as handmade mosaic decorations, woodcarvings, textiles and jewellery.

For boat trips to Diaporit and Ali Pasha's Castle, see page 236. Plays are staged in the Butrint theatre, notably during an international drama festival that is held every summer, Butrinti 2000. Details of each year's performances are on the festival's website (w *butrinti2000.com*); the tourist office in Saranda (page 228) should also have information about this.

THE CITY (⏲ *08.00–sunset daily; museum* ⏲ *08.00–16.00; 700 lek for non-Albanians, inc museum admission*) Butrint is first mentioned in the 6th century BC as a harbour; its location at almost the narrowest point of the Straits of Corfu made it a strategic crossroads between the Ionian islands, particularly Corfu itself, and the wealthy trading cities of Epirus. Pottery from the 7th and 6th centuries BC has been found on the acropolis hill, but any traces of such an early settlement were built over in antiquity.

In the 5th century and into the 4th century BC, Butrint was effectively part of Corcyra (Corfu), the Corinthian colony across the Straits. Later, the city became integrated into the Epirote Alliance, as part of the Chaonian territory whose capital was Phoinike (pages 236–7). In 167BC, Rome's wars with Macedonia came to an end with the final victory for Rome, and Butrint, like the rest of Epirus, became part of a Roman-administered province.

The earliest building below the acropolis was a **sanctuary** to the god of medicine, Asclepius, in what developed into the city's monumental centre. In the 4th century BC, or slightly later, a **defensive wall**, with imposing gates at regular intervals, was built around the expanding lower city – a stretch of this, with large irregularly shaped blocks, can still be seen as you enter this area. Worshippers came to the sanctuary to be healed and, to meet their other needs, various other buildings were erected: a temple, in front of the shrine; a hostel for pilgrims or priests to stay – the so-called Peristyle Building; and, between them, a **theatre**, built with donations made to the god. An inscription on the theatre seats dates its construction to the early 2nd century BC, although this was almost certainly an extension of an earlier, simpler theatre. To the side of the walkway leading into the theatre, inscribed blocks form part of the wall; these record the freeing of slaves, more than 500 of them, between 163BC and 44BC. Behind the Peristyle Building, a long portico (a stoa) once ran, with a well set into the hillside within it; the ropes that hauled water from this well over the centuries have worn deep grooves into its marble door.

Wealthy Romans – including Cicero's friend Atticus – had been buying up land at Butrint throughout the 1st century BC, and in 44BC the city became a Roman colony. The official language became Latin and Butrint began to mint coins. In the city centre, the old Hellenistic agora (market) was remodelled and turned into a Roman forum. During Ugolini's excavation of the theatre, several statues were found within it, including three portrait heads of the emperor Augustus, his wife Livia and his general Agrippa, which have been dated to 27–12BC. Agrippa is in the National Archaeological Museum in Tirana; Augustus and his wife are displayed in the Butrint Museum (the head of Livia, looted in the 1990s, was recovered in 2000). Shops sprang up around the forum and a bathhouse was built next to it, paved with a black-and-white mosaic. The mosaic, like all the mosaics at Butrint, is kept covered to protect it; the hypocaust with which the baths were heated has been partly reconstructed. To feed the baths and fountains with water, Roman engineers constructed an **aqueduct** to bring water from springs 4km away across the Vrina Plain, near the modern village of Xarra. Some of the piers that carried the aqueduct can still be seen, looking across the water towards Xarra from a viewpoint on the path around the site. The aqueduct was extended into the city in the 1st century AD and piers from that extension survive near the Great Basilica.

In the 1st century AD, the city spread across the Vivari Channel and a whole new suburb began to develop on the Vrina Plain. In the old lower city, the theatre was expanded, with a new stage and seating for 2,000 or so spectators, and more bathhouses were built. The city continued to grow and its wealthiest citizens commissioned prestigious villas on both sides of the Channel. One of these, at Diaporit on the eastern shore of Lake Butrint, can be visited by boat (page 236). Another lies southwest of the monumental centre; when it was first constructed, it was a traditional Roman villa, with elegant, mosaic-floored rooms arranged around a central courtyard. It is known as the **Triconch Palace** because, around AD420, it was expanded into a much more substantial building that included a dining room (*triclinium*) with three scalloped niches. The palace even had its own water gate, by which visitors arriving by boat could enter the building straight from the water's edge. Strangely, in view of all the work that had been done to create this beautiful residence, it was abandoned shortly before it was completed; carved window frames had been installed but the floors were never paved and the walls were left unpainted. The most likely reason is that the rising water table brought construction to a halt.

Perhaps as a way of coping with seasonal changes in the water table, the people of Butrint now began to build their houses of perishable timber. The city was not plunged into poverty – far from it, as archaeological finds, including many coins (which are datable), attest – but from the 6th century onward, the only stone buildings were Christian structures. The most important of these are the **Great Basilica** and the associated, though not adjacent, **Baptistery**. The latter was the largest baptistery east of Rome, apart from Hagia Sofia in Constantinople (now Istanbul). Unfortunately for the visitor, its magnificent mosaic floor is kept covered with sand and plastic sheeting, the only cost-effective way to protect it from the elements. Happily, however, a photographic reproduction of the mosaic is displayed in the Butrint Museum. The baptistery's design is as symbolic as the mosaic's, with two concentric rings of eight granite columns (eight being the symbol of salvation and eternal life) and seven concentric bands in the mosaic that culminate in the eighth circle of the font. The fountain set into the wall, directly opposite the entrance and thus forming the other end of the building's principal axis, is almost unique in a baptistery and must represent the Fountain of Life referred to in Genesis. The mosaic, too, is full of Christian symbolism: cockerels, which represent rebirth and resurrection; birds and fish representing the faithful; and two large compositions on the principal axis, showing drinking peacocks (symbols of Paradise) and stags (symbolising the faithful who thirst after God).

Some of the motifs in the baptistery mosaic were also used in the Great Basilica; these similarities allow both buildings to be dated to the second quarter of the 6th century. The Basilica is huge, 31.7m long and 23.7m across, and is dominated by a pentagonal apse with arched windows; two of the original large windows were blocked in, and the middle one replaced, when the basilica was refurbished in the 13th century.

Not long after these magnificent Christian monuments were erected, Butrint's fortunes took a turn for the worse. In the 6th century, a new city wall was quickly built around the lowest-lying parts of the peninsula, obviously to defend the city from attackers. A further refortification took place in the 13th century and a new castle was built on the acropolis; reconstructed in the 1930s, this castle now houses the Butrint Museum. These walls were conserved just a few years ago and a path has been cleared around much of their length, so that visitors with a little more time at their disposal can explore this aspect of the site. The Venetian Republic purchased Butrint, along with Corfu, in 1386 and built the tower at the entrance to the site (now used as offices for the archaeologists and other staff of the national park), the triangular fortress on the other side of the Vivari Channel and, probably, the fortress at the mouth of the channel that is known as **Ali Pasha's Castle**. All these fortifications hark back to the first defensive wall, built in the 4th century BC. The path around the site and up to the museum passes three of the gates in this wall: the main entrance to the city, Tower Gate, near the baptistery; the Lake Gate, which Ugolini called the Scaean Gate, after the *Aeneid*; and the Lion Gate, so called from the carved lintel of a lion sinking its teeth into a bull's neck, which was placed there long after the gate was first constructed. The carving is typical of Greek archaic art of the 6th century; it is thought that this relief may have come from a building associated with the sanctuary on the acropolis.

BEYOND THE CITY The triangular fortress and the remains of the aqueduct, across the Vivari Channel, are easy to visit on foot. A delightfully old-fashioned cable ferry plies to and fro across the channel; the charges range from €0.50 for foot passengers, through €1 for cycles and €3 for saloon cars, to €10 for mobile homes. The gate into the triangular fortress is in the wall furthest from the ferry jetty – the southern side. Within the walls is a courtyard, in the centre of which is a circular building (perhaps a *hamam*, or steam bath, added later by the Ottomans). The western wall contains several small vaulted chambers, probably originally used as gunpowder magazines, workshops or stores. In the southwestern corner is an unusually shaped tower; there are good views of the city of Butrint from its upper floor and from the fortress battlements.

To reach the piers of the Roman aqueduct, continue along the edge of the Vivari Channel until you reach the fish traps and the building beside them, where there are beehives. Cross the little bridge there, and head slightly inland along a track that leads to an excavated area of the Roman suburb on the Vrina Plain. By the 2nd century AD, this included villas and a public bathhouse, with a large cistern that was supplied with water from the aqueduct. If you look along the wall of the cistern, you will see the bases of the aqueduct piers in a line running towards Xarra, the village on the hill. It is about 15 minutes' walk from here back to the cable ferry.

Ali Pasha's Castle is on a little island at the edge of the marshes and can only be reached by boat. The trip out to the fortress meanders through the wetlands, with good opportunities to see waterbirds, and offers an entirely different perspective of the Butrint area. The fortress itself is beautifully constructed and is well worth exploring. The directorate of the Butrint site plans to install an exhibition within the fortress, which will illustrate aspects of Ali Pasha's life (see box, pages 254–5) and of the surrounding geography.

The expansion of Butrint in the 1st century AD meant new building not only on the Vrina Plain, but also at Diaporit, on the eastern shore of Lake Butrint. A large villa has been excavated here, with a bath complex, a peristyle and a mosaic-floored *triclinium*. The boatmen who hang around the entrance to the city can take you out to Ali Pasha's Castle or Diaporit.

There are clear views from the Saranda–Corfu ferry (page 223) of the entrance to the Vivari Channel – with Ali Pasha's Castle, the triangular fortress and the reconstructed Butrint Castle – which give a very good idea of the geography of the channel and the city.

In 2000, as part of the Albanian government's efforts to protect Butrint, the archaeological site and the surrounding area were given national park status. The park now extends for 86km² and, in addition to its archaeological significance, has a wide variety of animal habitats and great biodiversity. It is listed as a Wetlands Site of International Importance, under the Ramsar Convention. The directorate of the national park hopes to develop trails around the park, of varying distances and levels of difficulty. The staff at the site ticket office may be able to advise on this.

AROUND SARANDA

Ksamili Until a decade or so ago, Ksamili, 17km south of Saranda on the road to Butrint, was a charming hamlet, with a few dozen houses, a lovely little sandy beach and one restaurant. Then, like many other formerly idyllic spots on the Albanian coast, a frenzy of building overwhelmed it. It is now full of hotels and holiday apartments that sit empty for nine or ten months of the year. If you can find your way through them, however, Ksamili is a nice place to stop for a swim or a meal on the way to or from Butrint, especially outside the peak tourist season.

As well as fresh fish and seafood, the **Rilinda Restaurant** (**$$$**) has the best location, opposite one of the islands that close off and protect Ksamili Bay; the restaurant runs a bar on the island during the summer, to which you can swim or take a pedalo or rowing boat. To find the Rilinda using public transport from Saranda, get off the bus at the first of the two stops in Ksamili and head right until you reach the sea.

Phoinike The ancient city of Phoinike was the capital of Chaonia, one of the three largest states (*koina*) in the Federation of Epirus. It was built on a hill that controlled the valley between Butrint to its south and the mountains that run into the Ionian Sea, to its north. It is first mentioned, in Greek sources, in 330BC; the walls surrounding it were built at the end of the 4th century BC and the beginning of the 3rd, with the huge polygonal stones common to Epirote cities (there are stretches of similar walls at Butrint). The middle of the 3rd century BC was the high point of Phoinike's power. The city became the capital (or one of the capitals) of Epirus in 232BC and minted its own coins. In 205BC, it was here that the peace treaty was signed that ended the First Macedonian War: the Peace of Phoinike.

The buildings on the acropolis are rather difficult to make sense of, because there are many layers built one above another, in periods ranging from the 4th century BC to the 4th century AD. The buildings around the edge of the acropolis were shops; in times of war, these were used to shelter citizens who lived outside the protective walls. Easier to understand is the theatre, built into the slope of the hill in a magnificent setting. It is much later than the main buildings on the acropolis, dating from the 2nd and 3rd centuries AD; it has not been fully excavated but is thought to have had a capacity of 12,000 spectators. The views from the acropolis and the theatre are superb; the Butrint Lagoon can be seen quite clearly, as can the southernmost villages of the Albanian Riviera.

The modern village of Finiqi is on a minor road that links the Saranda–Delvina road and the main Saranda–Gjirokastra road. From the village, an asphalted road leads up to the entrance to the site; it is steep, but a 4x4 is certainly not required. There is also a footpath up from the village, which is a 30–45-minute walk. Getting to Phoinike by public transport is difficult; all but the most budget-conscious will hire a taxi in Saranda for the round trip. There is one bus a day to Finiqi, but it leaves Saranda at lunchtime and does not return until the following morning. The village is a couple of kilometres from the main Saranda–Gjirokastra road.

There is little interpretation at the site, but the Regional Directorate for National Culture in Saranda produced a helpful leaflet some years ago; the tourist information office may have copies. The academic database w fastionline.org has information about the excavations at Phoinike between 2001 and 2009, led by the University of Bologna and the Albanian Institute of Archaeology.

St Nicholas's Church, Mesopotami
The Church of St Nicholas (Kisha e Shënkollit) stands, surrounded by cypresses, on a hillock just outside the village of Mesopotami. It was built in the 11th century on the site of an earlier church – indeed, some of the limestone blocks used in its construction came from an even older building, perhaps in the nearby city of Phoinike. Some of these blocks, which make up part of the rear wall of the church, bear curious carvings that are thought to pre-date the arrival of Christianity here: an eagle, a lion, a dragon and an even weirder mythical creature, apparently strangling itself with its own tail. Inside the church, the central pillar is constructed around a stone column. Some frescoes survive behind the altar.

It is easy to get to St Nicholas's by public transport, using one of the many buses and minibuses that run between Saranda and Gjirokastra. Coming from Saranda, you should alight just beyond Mesopotami, where a sign reading '300m, Manastir' (Albanian for 'monastery') indicates a track up to the right. In theory, a caretaker should be on duty every morning; in practice, the site is often deserted apart from lizards and goats.

The Blue Eye
(*100 lek/car, 50 lek/person*) The Blue Eye (Syri i Kaltër) is an unusual underwater spring, set in shady woods 2km off the main road between Gjirokastra and Saranda. The water bubbles up through a deep pool, making a curious circular shape, deep blue at its centre and almost electric blue around the edges, like the pupil and iris of an eye. The rocks from which the spring rises are more than 45m below the surface and the pool has never been fully explored.

The Blue Eye is a pretty spot, with oak trees fringing the pool and flowers growing on the banks. It is surrounded by woodland and by streams and pools that flow from the spring. In the old days the area was reserved for the party elite to hunt and fish in, and ordinary Albanians were banned, which is usually a good indicator of how nice a place is.

The Blue Eye is 2km from the turn-off, indicated by a large brown 'tourist attraction' sign, after the Bistrica hydro-electric plant and just before the road begins to climb up to the Muzina Pass (22km from Saranda). Only the first stretch of the road is asphalted, but it is not in bad condition by Albanian standards. A path leads through the trees from the car park to the Blue Eye. There are several cafés around the park, with reasonable toilets.

Islamic historical buildings, Delvina Two very significant Islamic sites can be visited either with one's own transport or by taxi from Delvina, a small town about 20km from Saranda, high in the hills above the Bistrica Valley. The **Rusan Mosque** was mentioned by the 17th-century Turkish traveller Evliya Çelebi; its architecture is especially interesting, with several different levels of roof. Slim, agile visitors can climb the tightly winding stairs to the top of the minaret, where these can be seen more clearly. The hexagonal buildings nearby, whose tiled roofs look so attractive from above, are of later date, from when the site was used as a Bektashi *teqe* (page 22); one of them contains the graves of several Bektashi *babas*. The mosque's beautiful ceiling, inscribed with verses from the Koran, can be admired more closely from the gallery.

On the other side of Delvina is the recently restored **Xhermëhalla Islamic Complex**. The buildings within it include a mosque, a ruined *madrasa*, or Islamic school, a bathhouse and several Bektashi *tyrbe*s, as at Rusan. During restoration work, a hitherto unknown fountain was revealed, below the entrance to the mosque and *madrasa*; this was where the faithful washed before entering the mosque to pray. There are good views from Xhermëhalla of the ruins of the Byzantine **Delvina Castle**, perched imposingly on a crag. It is possible to hike up to the castle, but there is not much to see once you get there apart, of course, from the views.

Both the Rusan Mosque and the Xhermëhalla Islamic Complex are very close to Delvina: only 5 or 10 minutes' drive. Simple accommodation is available in Delvina at the Shameti Hotel (\ *0815 22380;* **$**), centrally located with good views from the terraces on the upper floors.

GJIROKASTRA *Telephone code: 084*

The austere and beautiful town of Gjirokastra began to spread downhill from its castle in the 13th century. The castle still broods on its hill, overlooking the whole city and the river valley below. From that vantage point, the grey stone of the houses below and the grey slates of their roofs blend into the hillside, distinguished from it only by their whitewashed walls. Gjirokastra's architecture and haunting atmosphere are described by one of the city's most famous sons:

> This was a surprising city, which seemed to have come out of the valley unexpectedly, one winter's night, like a prehistoric being, and clambered up with difficulty, stitching itself on to the side of the mountain. Everything in this city was old and made of stone, from the streets and fountains right up to the roofs of its big houses, a century old, which were covered with stone tiles the colour of ash, like so many huge carapaces. It was difficult to believe that under these hard shells the soft flesh of life thrived and was renewed.
>
> Ismail Kadare, *Kronikë në gur (Chronicle in Stone)*, Onufri, 2000

Gjirokastra first enters history in 1336, in the memoirs of John Cantacuzenus. He was the son of the governor of the Morea, the Byzantine province in the Greek Peloponnese, and would later become Emperor John VI Cantacuzenus. In the 15th century, it was besieged and then captured by the Ottomans, but unlike many other hitherto important Albanian towns, Gjirokastra flourished under its new rulers. It was the administrative centre of a province (*sanjak*) covering what is now central and southern Albania, and it became a major trading centre.

By the 17th century, the city had 2,000 houses, and the bazaar was constructed at this time. It was subsequently destroyed by fire, and the shops and other buildings that remain in the old bazaar area, Qafa e Pazarit, date from the early 20th century. Most of the large traditional houses (pages 245–9) were built in the first half of the 19th century.

In the 20th century, Gjirokastra produced two particularly well-known sons. **Enver Hoxha** (see box, page 83) was one of the leaders of the partisan resistance in World War II and went on to run Albania for 41 years, until his death in April 1985. The site of the house where he was born in 1908 is now the Ethnographic Museum, and a good example of Gjirokastra traditional architecture. **Ismail Kadare** (see box, page 246) is the only Albanian writer who is at all well known in the English-speaking world; he stayed in Albania until late 1990, at which point he left the country for France where he still spends most of his time. Other local heroes are Çerçiz Topulli, who led an uprising against the Ottomans in 1908 and whose statue stands in the square named after him, and the two young women who are commemorated with a monument in the same square, Bule Naipi and Persefoni Kokëdhima, hanged by the Germans on suspicion of being partisans.

Gjirokastra became a UNESCO World Heritage Site in July 2005. It had been awarded the status of a 'museum-city' by the Albanian government in 1961, which gave legal protection to its architectural heritage and kept new building out of the historic centre. Thanks to this, and no doubt also to its steep cobbled streets, the town has retained its charming atmosphere.

It was a steep city, perhaps the steepest in the world, which had broken all the laws of town planning. Because of its steepness, it would come about that at the roof-level of one house you would find the foundations of another; and certainly this was the only place in the world where if a passer-by fell, instead of sliding into a roadside ditch, he might end up on the roof of a tall house. This is something which drunkards knew better than anyone.

It really was a very surprising city. You could be going along the street and, if you wanted, you could stretch out your arm a bit and put your hat on top of a minaret. Many things here were unbelievable, and a lot was dream-like.

Ismail Kadare, *Kronikë në gur* (*Chronicle in Stone*), Onufri, 2000

GETTING THERE AND AWAY There are various ways to get to Gjirokastra from **Greece**. The daily **bus** service from Ioannina, 90km away, leaves at 06.00 from just outside the main bus station. Alternatively, Greek KTEL buses run several times a day up to the border at Kakavija; taxis and buses wait on the Albanian side of the border to run people the 30km up to Gjirokastra. The buses are scheduled to leave Kakavija at 07.30, 10.30, 14.00 and 16.30. To get to them, you have to walk across the border and uphill, past all the taxi drivers, to the petrol station; youthful porters hang around on the Albanian side to transport heavy luggage. There are also buses to Gjirokastra from Thessaloniki and Athens.

Buses ply between **Saranda** and Gjirokastra every hour or so, from 05.00 until 14.00; the fare is 300 lek. The journey takes about 1½ hours, on a good asphalt road along the Bistrica River and then over the Muzina Pass into the Drinos Valley. If you have your own transport, the alternative route through the town of Delvina offers good views across the Bistrica Valley, although east of Delvina the road is in poor condition. Mountain bikers might consider the track across

8

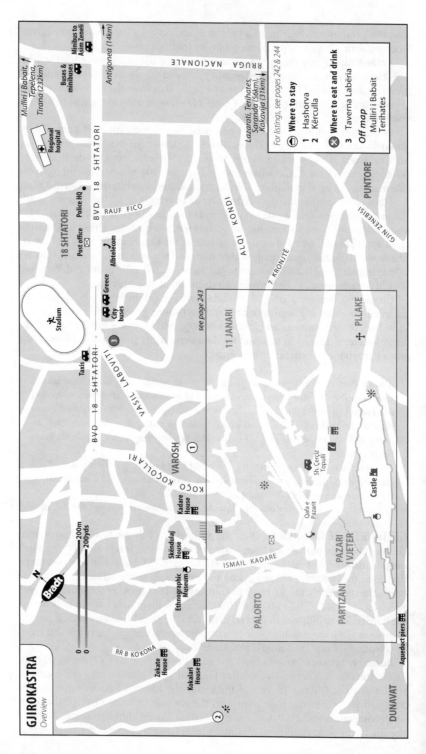

GJIROKASTRA
Overview

Zekate House
Kokalari House
RR B KOKONA

Ethnographic Museum
Skëndulaj House
Kadare House

KOÇO KOKOLARI
VAROSH

BVD 18 SHTATORI
VASIL LABOVITI

Taxis

Stadium

City buses
Greece
Albtelecom

Post office
18 SHTATORI
RAUF FICO
Police HQ
BVD 18 SHTATORI

Regional hospital

Mullini i Babait, Tepelena, Tirana (232km)
Buses & minibuses
Minibus to Asim Zeneli

Antigonea (14km)

Antigonea
RRUGA NACIONALE

Lazarati, Terihates, Saranda (56km), Kokavija (31km)

N
Bradt

0 ——— 200m
0 ——— 200yds

ISMAIL KADARE
PALORTO
PARTIZANI
DUNAVAT
Aqueduct piers
PAZARI I VJETER
Qafa e Pazarit
Sh. Cërciz Topulli
Castle
11 JANARI
7 KRONJTË
ALQI KONDI
GJIN ZENEBISI
PUNTORE
PLLAKE

see page 243

For listings, see pages 242 & 244
ⓘ **Where to stay**
1 Hashorva
2 Kërculla
✗ **Where to eat and drink**
3 Taverna Labëria
Off map
Mullini i Babait
Terihates

240

the Mali i Gjerë range from Delvina to the village of Lazarati, a few kilometres south of Gjirokastra.

From **Tirana**, the buses to Gjirokastra leave from the Shqiponja bus station [62 A1], from early morning until early afternoon. They take between 4 and 5 hours. A bus runs every day except Sundays between Gjirokastra and Korça; it leaves Gjirokastra at 07.00. (Pages 146–8 has more information about this long but beautiful journey through the magnificent scenery of the Gramoz Mountains.) There are buses in the mornings between Gjirokastra and **Përmeti**; later in the day, you will need to change in Tepelena.

Gjirokastra's main bus terminus is beside the highway, in the northern outskirts of town. The buses to Greece leave from a stop on Boulevard 18 Shtatori, opposite the stadium.

GETTING AROUND Buses cannot drive up into the old town, but there are always taxis waiting to ferry people up from the bus terminus. Any bus coming from Saranda or Kakavija will drop passengers off at the foot of the hill going up to the old town. It is a very long, steep climb on foot. City buses ply between Boulevard 18 Shtatori and Sheshi Çerçiz Topulli, via the highway and this junction, with a flat fare of 30 lek. In the old town, there is a taxi rank in Sheshi Çerçiz Topulli.

People in Gjirokastra, like everywhere else in Albania, navigate by neighbourhoods (*lagja*) or landmarks. Those who are driving themselves should note that, in the old town, most streets are very narrow and steep; indeed, some are flights of steps. For pedestrians, these are useful short cuts between the old and new towns; driving a vehicle requires deep local knowledge and impeccable hill starts.

TOURIST INFORMATION The tourist information kiosk is on Sheshi Çerçiz Topulli (⊕ 08.00–16.00 Mon–Fri, 10.00–14.00 Sat). A map of the old town is posted at the western end of Sheshi Çerçiz Topulli, next to the statue of Bule and Persefoni. A couple of the shops on Qafa e Pazarit (eg: AlbTour) provide tour-guiding services, in English and other languages, and sell guidebooks (including this one). The website of the Gjirokastra Conservation and Development Organisation (GCDO; w *gjirokastra.org*) has a wealth of information about the city, in English and Albanian. GCDO supports the **artisans** whose workshops are around Qafa e Pazarit and on Rruga e Kalasë ('Castle Street'). They include lacemakers, a woodcarver and a stonemason, who make exquisite pieces of art as well as small souvenirs.

Caravan Travel organises excursions on horseback, with English-speaking guides, to places of interest in the Gjirokastra area. For experienced riders, the highlight is a week-long tour along the old trading routes in the Zagoria and Pogoni mountains, with visits to Labova e Kryqit (page 252) and other beautiful churches, and finishing at Antigonea (pages 249–50). Bespoke tours can also be arranged. See page 29 for contact details.

🏠 **WHERE TO STAY** *Map, page 243, unless otherwise stated*

🏠 **Argjiro** (30 rooms, will be 49) Rr Gjin Zenebisi; ☎ 267 022; m 069 57 06 315; e hotelargjiro@gmail.com, reservation@hotelargjiro.al; w hotelargjiro.al. Central location; 1885 building used as hotel in communist era, completely rebuilt in 2016; additional rooms should be renovated by 2018. Lift; b/fast room (evening meals can also be arranged); indoor &

terrace bars; conference room; laundry service. Wi-Fi, parking, good English spoken. All rooms en suite, some with bathtub; AC, flatscreen TV, phone, bedside light; some have balcony. **$$$**

🏠 **Kalemi 2** (14 rooms, 2 suites) Rr Alqi Kondi, Qafa e Pazarit; ☎ 266 010; m 068 22 34 373, 068 40 11 413; e info@kalemihotels.com; w kalemihotels.com. Sympathetic restoration of a beautiful Category 2 house (page 247), reroofed in slate; each room has a hand-carved wooden ceiling in a different design. B/fast room, laundry service, good English spoken; Wi-Fi, parking; magnificent views of castle from upper floors & terrace. Lavish b/fast inc. All rooms en suite with LCD TV, AC, desk, fridge; suites have bathtub as well as shower. 2 rooms on ground floor **$$**; all others on upper floors with views. **$$$**

🏠 **Kërculla** [map, page 240] (10 rooms, 2 suites) Rr Bashkim Kokona; **m** 069 44 10 222; 🇫 Kerculla Resort. A new building in traditional style, in amazing mountaintop setting above the city. Big restaurant on ground floor; more intimate dining room upstairs, with open fire; bar. 2 large terraces; large outdoor pool with views of city & mountains; BBQ; children's play area. Business facilities; laundry service. Wi-Fi, ample parking. Suites in separate building nearby. Rooms beautifully finished, each with a different pattern of stone; all en suite & with balcony (more views), plus flatscreen TV, AC, heating, phone, minibar, safe. **$$$**

🏠 **Çajupi** (34 rooms) Sh Çerçiz Topulli; **** 269 010; **m** 067 26 43 431, 068 20 54 962; **e** info@cajupi.com; **w** cajupi.com. English spoken at reception. Restaurant on top floor with good menu & views; bar with traditional décor; lift to all floors; Wi-Fi throughout. All rooms en suite (some also have bathtub), with AC, flatscreen TV; some have small balcony & city view, others overlook forest on castle hill. **$$**

🏠 **Kalemi 1** (15 rooms) Lagja Palorto; **** 266 010; **m** 068 22 34 373, 068 40 11 413; **e** info@kalemihotels.com; **w** kalemihotels.com. A traditional Gjirokastra house, lovingly restored by the owner; 1 dbl room has a beautiful carved ceiling. Magnificent views of the city & the castle from the balconies on the upper floors. Bar; Wi-Fi, parking; good English spoken. Lavish b/fast with fresh bread inc. All rooms en suite (some have

bathtub, as well as shower), with TV, CH; some also AC. **$$**

🏠 **Kodra** (12 rooms, 1 suite) Rr Alqi Kondi; **** 262 115; **m** 069 40 62 661, 069 69 48 718; **e** info@hotelkodra.com; **w** hotelkodra.com. Built into the base of the platform which, until 1991, supported a huge statue of Enver Hoxha. Good restaurant (**$$$**) with traditional décor; Wi-Fi throughout; parking; laundry service; direct access to terrace bar above hotel with great views; English spoken. All rooms en suite with TV, AC. **$$**

🏠 **Kotoni** (7 rooms) Lagja Palorto; **m** 069 27 69 814; **e** eda.golemi@gmail.com. Traditional house with views of castle & old town. Rooms have original features such as carved ceilings. B/fast room & terrace restaurant; English spoken. All rooms en suite with flatscreen TV, AC, Wi-Fi. **$$**

🏠 **Babameto House & Hostel** (6 rooms) Lagja Pazari i Vjetër; **** 262 090; **m** 069 36 55 915, 069 23 73 093; **e** info@gjirokastra.org; **w** hostelbabameto.beep.com. A historic 19th-century Gjirokastra house, fully restored. Kitchen, bar, Wi-Fi, lockers, ironing board; towels & sheets provided. Conference room, traditionally furnished sitting room, courtyard. Bike hire available. 2 rooms en suite, with balcony; 2 dorms sharing showers & toilets. **$**

🏠 **Hashorva** [map, page 240] (3 rooms) Lagja Varosh; **** 262 314; **m** 069 35 62 098; **e** hotelhashorva@yahoo.com. A traditional Gjirokastra house, partially modernised; bedrooms have carved wooden doors & other traditional architectural features; pleasant garden. Parking, Wi-Fi, laundry service. 2 twin rooms share a large, simple bathroom, 1 dbl room is en suite. **$**

🏠 **Sopoti** (17 rooms) Centrally located, just off Sh Çerçiz Topulli; reservations through **w** hostelworld.com. Bar; laundry service. Good-sized sgl, dbl & trpl rooms, sharing basic washing & toilet facilities. **$**

✖ WHERE TO EAT AND DRINK *Map, opposite, unless otherwise stated*

Gjirokastra is proud of its traditional dishes and several restaurants offer them (see listing below). *Pashaqoftë* is soup with small meatballs; *qifqi* are little rice patties, fried in olive oil; *sarma* are stuffed vine-leaves, like the Greek *dolmades*; *shapkat* is a kind of pie with spinach; and *tigani* is pan-fried pork with onions. *Oshaf* is a dessert made with sheep's milk and dried figs.

✖ **Kujtimi** Qafa e Pazarit. Good salads, traditional Gjirokastra dishes such as *qifqi*, plus whatever is available & fresh – fish, mussels, frogs' legs. Most tables outside on the lovely vine-shaded terrace. **$$$**

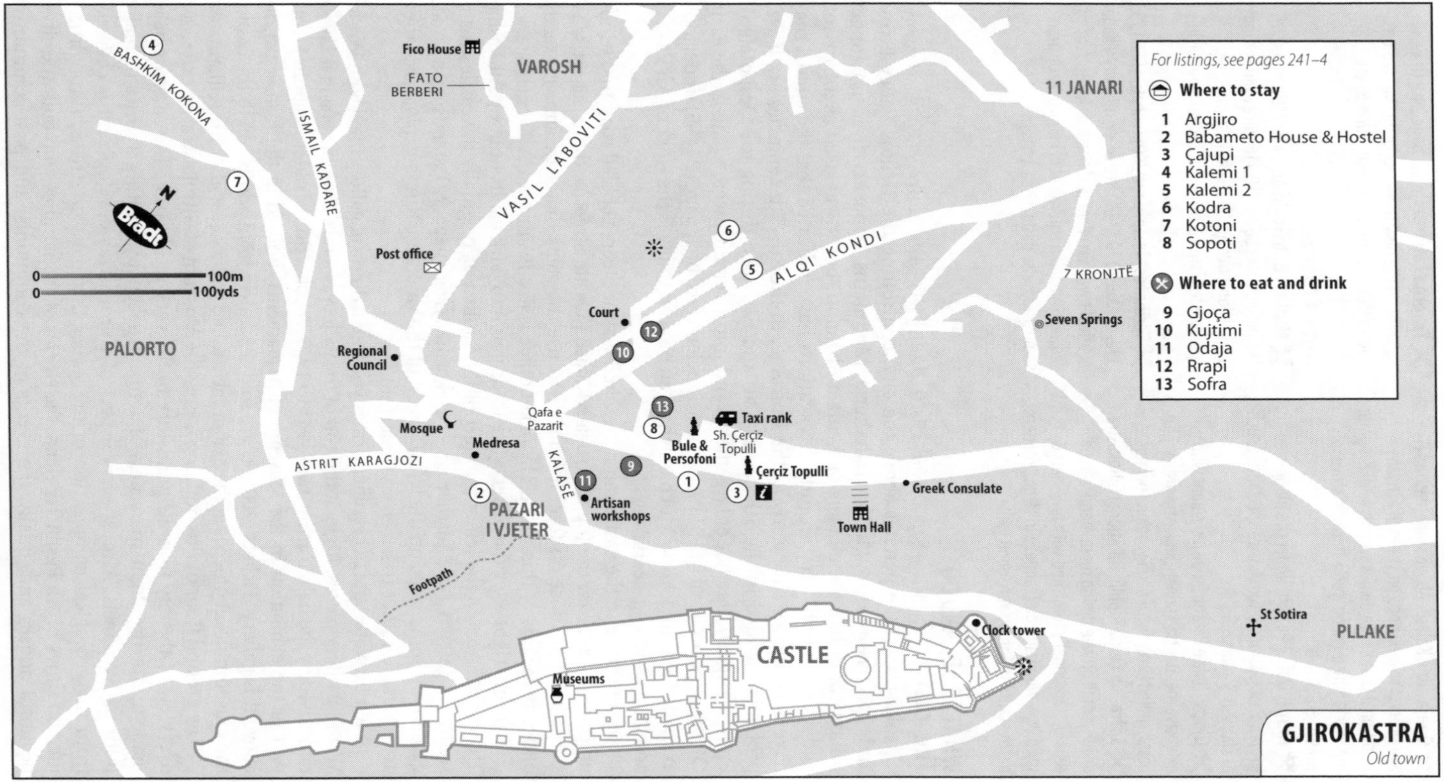

GJIROKASTRA
Old town
For listings, see pages 241–4
Where to stay
1 Argjiro
2 Babameto House & Hostel
3 Çajupi
4 Kalemi 1
5 Kalemi 2
6 Kodra
7 Kotoni
8 Sopoti
Where to eat and drink
9 Gjoça
10 Kujtimi
11 Odaja
12 Rrapi
13 Sofra
BASHKIM KOKONA
ISMAIL KADARE
VASIL LABOVITI
ALQI KONDI
ASTRIT KARAGJOZI
KALASË
7 KRONJTË
11 JANARI
Fico House
FATO BERBERI
VAROSH
PALORTO
PAZARI I VJETER
PLLAKE
Post office
Court
Regional Council
Mosque
Medresa
Qafa e Pazarit
Taxi rank
Sh. Çerçiz Topulli
Bule & Persofoni
Çerçiz Topulli
Artisan workshops
Town Hall
Greek Consulate
Seven Springs
Footpath
CASTLE
Museums
Clock tower
St Sotira
0 100m
0 100yds
Bradt
N

✘ Odaja Rr e Kalasë. Above stonemason's & woodcarver's workshops on street of artisans. Traditional Gjirokastra dishes such as *qifqi* & *tigani*; friendly family owners; wood-burning stove in winter. $$$

✘ Rrapi Qafa e Pazarit, under the plane-tree (*rrapi*). Pasta, salads & Gjirokastra specialities such as *shapkat* & *sarma*. $$$

✘ Gjoça Qafa e Pazarit. Small restaurant with extensive menu – traditional Gjirokastra dishes, plus pasta, grilled lamb, fish. Friendly, helpful owners. $$

✘ Sofra Sh Çerçiz Topulli. Traditional Gjirokastra dishes; small private dining room, hand-carved ceiling, traditionally furnished with low seats & *sofra* (low wooden table), annexe to larger, modern bar/restaurant. Family-run, good value. $$

✘ Taverna Labëria [map, page 240] Rr Vasil Laboviti, in the new town, opposite the stadium. Specialises in chargrilled meat, innards, etc. $$

Out of town

✘ Mulliri i Babait [map, page 240] Mashkullora; m 069 24 10 416. Nice rural setting, a few kilometres north of Gjirokastra. Serves spit-roasted lamb & other traditional meat dishes. $$$

✘ Terihates [map, page 240] Terihat; 0884 231 390; m 069 20 79 874/5. In a Greek-minority village south of town. Excellent traditional dishes such as *kukurec* (Albanian equivalent of haggis) made from lamb or kid; also pasta, pizza, etc. $$

WHAT TO SEE AND DO

The castle (⊕ *May–Sep 09.00–19.00 daily, Oct–Apr closes earlier; 200 lek*) Gjirokastra's castle perches above the city, controlling the Drinos Valley below and the passes through the Lunxhëria Mountains opposite. It is no longer inhabited, unlike the citadels of Kruja and Berati, but it was used as a garrison and a prison until very recently. Excavations have indicated that the citadel may have been inhabited as early as the Iron Age, in the 8th–7th centuries BC; it was probably fortified in the 5th century BC and extended during the Despotate of Epirus (page 9). Further enlargements and improvements were made in the early Ottoman period and in 1811 Ali Pasha Tepelena (see box, pages 254–5) undertook extensive building work. Much of what can be seen today is the work of Ali Pasha's architects and engineers.

The entrance to the castle can be reached via the steep, cobbled road that winds up the hillside from the top of Rruga e Kalasë ('Castle Street'), where the artisans' shops are. For those on foot, it is faster to use the steps that start almost exactly opposite the end of this street. The ticket office is just inside the castle entrance.

Turning right after the ticket office leads you into dark vaults built by Ali Pasha. The high tunnel to the left at the start of the vaults was originally the castle's main southern gate. A little further on, a Bektashi *tyrbe* (page 22) stands in a small garden, up some steps on the left. The rest of the vaults are fun to explore, but they are unlit and rather treacherous underfoot.

A left turn after the ticket office brings you into a dimly lit gallery lined with World War II artillery pieces. Right at the end of the gallery is a rare example of a Fiat L6/40 tank, used by the Italian army from 1941 to 1943. A collection of older weapons forms part of the exhibition in the **Museum of Armaments**, housed in the former prison above this gallery. Tickets (*200 lek*) are sold separately from admission to the castle; the museum ticket office is at the exit of the vaulted gallery, just after the Italian tank.

The ground floor of this building is now the **Museum of Gjirokastra**, an extensive overview of the city from its prehistory to the very recent past. The curators have made up for the slight sparseness of actual artefacts by creating a series of really informative panels. Almost every aspect of Gjirokastra's development is covered, from the geological composition of the stones that pave its streets, through the life and times of Ali Pasha Tepelena, the stories of the families who built the city's beautiful houses and, finally, the events of the communist and post-communist periods. There are even some women featured, notably the writer Musine Kokalari (1917–83), imprisoned and persecuted by the communist authorities, and 'Gjirokastra's first feminist', Urani Rumbo (1895–1936). The exhibition is so extensive that any visitor with more than a passing interest in the city will want to spend at least an hour looking around – ideally longer.

The **prison** was built in 1929 to accommodate King Zog's enemies, and then used enthusiastically by the Wehrmacht during World War II; in the summer of 1944, the Germans were holding 500 prisoners in the 50 cells here. The prison remained in use until 1968, when the first National Folk Festival took place in Gjirokastra Castle and it was felt that political prisoners were not entirely compatible with this happy event. It was transformed into the Museum of Armaments, which opened in 1971. The exhibition begins with the post-1912 struggles by people in different parts of Albania to consolidate their independence, notably the 'Vlora War' of 1920 against Italian occupation. However, the museum focuses mainly on World War II, with armaments taken from Italian or German troops and some British weapons that were supplied to the partisans by the Special Operations Executive (SOE; see boxes, pages 13–15). After touring the exhibition, the guide will take you to see some of the prison cells: a chilling experience. A gruesome display case at the end of this section contains the clothes worn by Bule and Persefoni, the young women hanged by the Germans in 1944.

It will be with some relief that you emerge from the gallery on to a small terrace. In the corner sits a two-seater jet that the communist regime claimed was an American spy plane, forced down in 1957. The US air force's version of events is that the pilot, Major Howard Curran, 'strayed' into Albanian airspace during a routine flight to Naples from a US base in southern France and was forced to land by Albanian MIGs. Major Curran was released after being held for a couple of weeks; his plane, however, stayed where it was, at Rinas airport, before the Albanian government decided that it should be displayed in Gjirokastra. Beyond the plane, a path leads into an open area, largely taken up with the staging for the folk music festival which takes place here at rather random intervals (the most recent was held in May 2015). Another Bektashi *tyrbe* nestles against the castle wall, behind the staging.

Beyond the stage is the **clock tower**, another of Ali Pasha's improvements to the castle, although it was heavily restored in the 1980s. Below it, the structure of a very old church – possibly dating back to the Byzantine phase of fortification – has recently been identified. A viewpoint at the eastern extreme of the castle offers panoramic views of the Drinos Valley and the Lunxhëria Mountains beyond. A rather worn panel indicates the position of various points of interest, including Antigonea (pages 249–50).

In addition to the vaults, the clock tower and other improvements, Ali Pasha also built an **aqueduct**, which brought water from springs on Mount Sopoti, 10km away, to huge cisterns under the central area of the castle. The aqueduct was demolished in 1932, unfortunately; the bases of three of its piers still stand at the southwestern tip of the castle, a few minutes' walk from the entrance towards the neighbourhood of Dunavat. You can return to the city through the tunnel *under* the castle, reasonably well lit and beautifully restored, after decades of neglect.

Gjirokastra dwelling houses

Although based on standard Ottoman architectural principles, the beautiful 19th-century houses of Gjirokastra are unique. Berati's houses are lovely too, but their structure is different and the topography of the town makes them seem more uniform. In Gjirokastra, no traditional house is quite like another, although they have been classified according to certain design characteristics such as the number of wings that they have.

Many of the best examples of Gjirokastra domestic architecture were built in the first three decades of the 19th century. The Pazari i Vjetër (Old Bazaar) quarter, for example, dates mostly from around 1830. The houses are characterised by their defensively designed lower floors, with narrow entranceways and small windows set high in the wall. The entrance arches (*qemeret*) are made of dressed stone, often

ISMAIL KADARE

The Albanian writer who is best known outside the Albanian-speaking world is Ismail Kadare (the stress is on the last vowel of both his names), who was born in Gjirokastra in 1936. He studied literature at the University of Tirana and went on to study at the Gorky Institute in Moscow. He returned to Albania after the break with the Soviet Union in 1961 and worked as a journalist, as well as publishing a volume of poetry. His first novel, *The General of the Dead Army*, was written between 1962 and 1966, and brought him immediate renown. It was later made into a film, in which Marcello Mastroianni played the eponymous general, seeking the remains of Italian soldiers fallen during the Fascist occupation of Albania.

Following the success of his first novel, Kadare became the editor of the Albanian literary review *Les Lettres Albanaises*, and went on to write over a dozen novels, as well as short stories and essays. Many of his works are heavily allegorical and it is difficult for non-Albanians to grasp the layers of meaning in them; his novels *The Monster* (banned in Albania for 25 years) and *The Palace of Dreams*, and the work of literary criticism *Aeschylus*, are examples of these rather obscure, but ultimately rewarding, works. Some of his other novels, on the other hand, are much more accessible to the foreign reader and give very interesting insights into aspects of Albanian daily life in the latter half of the 20th century. *Chronicle in Stone*, about growing up in Gjirokastra, and *Broken April*, about the revenge culture of the northern highlands, are good to start with. *The Concert* sheds some light on Albania's break with China (page 16) and how it affected Albanian professionals. *The Castle* is about Albania's resistance to the Ottoman invasion – the eponymous castle is Skanderbeg's seat at Kruja. The more recent (2003) works *Agamemnon's Daughter* and *The Successor* are fictionalised accounts of the fall from grace of Mehmet Shehu, Albania's prime minister from 1954 to 1981.

Ismail Kadare was allowed to travel widely by the communist government, and he could have defected from Albania on several occasions, but he chose not to. He was one of a group of writers and other influential people who lobbied for cultural liberalisation in the late 1980s. Towards the end of 1990, when communist regimes had collapsed all over central and eastern Europe, and it was obvious that even in Albania the end could not be far off, he left the country and obtained political asylum in France, where he still spends much of his time. Many young Albanians who took part in the struggle for democracy were hurt and baffled by what they saw as Kadare's abandonment of them. His 1991 book *Albanian Spring* (out of print in its English translation) outlined his reasons for leaving the country but, like much of Albania's recent history, it remains a very controversial matter.

Kadare is frequently mentioned as a contender for the Nobel Prize for Literature. In 2005, he was awarded the inaugural Man Booker International Prize and, in 2016, the French Legion of Honour.

worked with great skill and refinement, and engraved with images of animals or birds; their wooden doors are also decorated with carvings. The ground floor of the house was traditionally used for storage and had a cistern (*stera*) into which rainwater was piped from the roof. The size of the cistern was an indicator of the status of the family that owned the house. The roofs themselves are of grey stone slates, supported on a wooden frame.

The living quarters, as is usual in Albanian vernacular architecture, are on the upper floors. In Gjirokastra there are usually two or three floors in total, with a few four-storey houses. Some of the houses are simple vertical structures; a widespread variant has a single wing added to this central structure, while the wealthiest families built houses with two wings. The Zekate house, right up at the top of the Palorto quarter and visible from many vantage points in the old town, is an outstanding example of the latter style.

Internally, each house is laid out in a way that reflects the family structure of the time. The main room was the 'winter room' (*dimërorja*), also called the 'fire room' (*dhoma e zjarrit*), with an ornate fireplace (*oxhaku*) that decorated the room as well as warming it. The number of chimneys and windows was another status symbol for Gjirokastra's wealthy families. One or more living rooms were used by family members for day-to-day activities. Guests were received in a separate room (*oda e miqve*), which was always the most beautifully decorated in the house. The walls were sometimes adorned with frescoes, and the ceiling was often of carved and sculpted wood. Reception rooms often had a wooden gallery – sometimes closed, sometimes open – where the women of the household could keep an eye on proceedings; this was especially useful when the men below were discussing the possible betrothal of their children. The rooms were linked by wide corridors and covered balconies (*nëndivani* and *divani i sipërm*), which were also used as living areas in hot weather. Three-storey houses with double wings also had open balconies set between the two wings.

On paper the traditional houses of Gjirokastra enjoy quite strict legal protection. Fifty-one of them have Category 1 listing, meaning that no external modifications are permitted; over 350 others are listed in Category 2, where some modification is allowed as long as the façade is not altered. In practice, however, these beautiful buildings are at great risk from neglect, abandonment and fire. Some were wrecked in the civil unrest of 1997, the family house of the writer Ismail Kadare was badly damaged in a fire in 1999, and every year more traditional houses are lost to collapse. Illegal building work also takes place within the supposedly protected Museum Zone of the town.

Traditional houses can be found throughout the old town, especially in the Partizani, Dunavat and Palorto neighbourhoods. Some have been converted into hotels – see pages 241–2 for details. Many others are unoccupied and can only be seen from the outside. Two original houses which have been restored and can be visited are described on pages 248–9; others may well open to the public in due course.

The **Kadare house** (*Rr Fato Berberi 16; 200 lek*) has now been rebuilt and opened to the public. This is where Ismail Kadare (see box, opposite) was born, to a professional family (his grandfather was a judge) and where, in his early teens, he wrote his first story. The ground floor and basement have been painstakingly reconstructed, funded by UNESCO and the Albanian state, and you can see the rainwater cistern, the pantry and the beautiful external staircase. Photographs illustrate the reconstruction process. The first floor has been completely rebuilt, but it gives an impression of how the living space was distributed. Some original items which belonged to the family are on display, including an intricately decorated wooden chest.

The Kadare house is not at all easy to find. The easiest route is to head downhill from the square where the Regional Council is, past the post office; Rruga Fato Berberi is a small, winding street to the left. The first imposing traditional house on this street is the colourful **Fico house**; the Kadare house is a little further, on the other side of the same street.

Another reconstructed traditional house is now the **Ethnographic Museum** (⊕ *09.00–19.00 daily; 200 lek*), on the site of the house where Enver Hoxha was born. The original building was destroyed by fire in the 1960s and it was rebuilt as a showcase for the classic features of a traditional Gjirokastra house. The museum contains many interesting items from daily household life and has (old) maquettes of three types of traditional architecture, including the Zekate house (see below).

The nearby **Skëndulaj house** (⊕ *09.00–19.00 daily; 200 lek*), built originally around 1700 and partly rebuilt in 1827, was formerly the Ethnographic Museum. It was confiscated in 1984 from the family who had lived in it for generations; they recovered it in 1992 and have restored it beautifully. The external architecture of this house has a couple of unusual features: lines of chestnut wood set into the wall every metre, to strengthen it, and a window and slit in the corner of the building through which the cistern could be cleaned and its water level checked. The cistern has a capacity of 130,000 litres and is piped into the house through a tap. One wall of the cistern is also the wall of the pantry; an ingenious method of keeping food cool. Another interesting architectural feature is the underground shelter, a vaulted cellar; on the floors above it are kitchens whose ceilings are also vaulted, making the whole structure incredibly strong. Many of the household implements displayed in the kitchens – the coffee-roaster, for example – were used by the family until just a decade or so ago.

The Skëndulaj house has 64 windows, nine chimneys and six toilets (long-drop toilets, admittedly, but nonetheless quite impressive for the early 19th century). Some of the reception rooms also have an en-suite steam room (*hamam*), as well as galleries (*mafil*) and cupboards for storing bedding (*musandra*). The *divan*, or covered balcony, overlooks the city and connects with every room on that floor. It has a raised platform on which the mother of the household would sit in the mornings with her daughters-in-law to share out the day's tasks. The most elaborately decorated room, the *oda e miqve*, has no fewer than 15 windows, some with stained-glass lozenges. The frescoes on the fireplace, which are original, are full of symbolism: pomegranates and pomegranate flowers are believed to bring luck to your children, while candles symbolise the development of the family. The *mafil* was enclosed in glass in 1985, after the house had been requisitioned by the government; originally it had a wooden grille like the galleries in the other rooms. The *oda e miqve* was used for betrothal ceremonies, which would take place in the raised part of the room. The ceiling above this part of the room has two ceiling roses, rather than the usual single rose, to symbolise that two people will now live under the same roof.

The **Zekate house**, an imposing double-winged house at the top of Palorto, was built in 1810 by one of Ali Pasha Tepelena's administrators, Beqir Zeko. The tall arches of the entranceway support the weight of the upper rooms. On the ground floor, to the right of the entrance, is the large rainwater cistern; the family's status is further displayed by the stained-glass windows, elaborate fireplaces and carved wooden ceilings. The reception rooms have wooden galleries and *musandra*. The winter rooms have adjacent toilets and steam rooms (*hamam*). The top, third, floor is astonishing: the summer *divan* has spectacular views, particularly from the dais in the corner where the head of the household would sit with his most important guests. Finally, the remarkable reception room on this floor has beautiful frescoes on the walls and fireplace; an elaborate gallery and *musandra* over the entrance to the *oda* and its en-suite toilet; a magnificent carved and gilded ceiling; painted doors and coloured-glass windows. The Zekate house was restored in 2005. It does not have set opening hours, but the elderly couple who own it live next door and are usually somewhere around; admission is 200 lek.

Town hall air-raid shelter
(⊕ *summer 08.00–20.00 daily, winter 09.00–14.00 Mon–Fri, 09.00–17.00 Sat, 09.00–15.00 Sun*) During the communist years, when town halls across Albania were known as 'Executive Committees', air-raid shelters were built under them so that the Committee Members and staff could continue to administer their town in the event of enemy bombardment. It is said that the shelters under the Executive Committee of Tirana, which nowadays houses the administration of the Albanian Parliament and other national institutions, were connected to Enver Hoxha's villa in 'The Block' (page 82).

The city of Gjirokastra was no exception. Its air-raid shelter, now open to the public, is in fact a huge labyrinth of underground corridors with small offices opening off them. Many of the offices still have the signs on their doors indicating which department or functionary would have worked within; even the telephone switchboard operators would have relocated down to the bunker. The functionaries would have slept, as well as worked, in their little windowless offices. In the centre of the labyrinth is a large meeting hall, beyond which are the offices of the party officials who made up the Executive Committee itself. Private stairways (now blocked-up) led down to this VIPs' corridor from their offices above ground. The whole structure was designed to resist the impact of missiles of up to six tonnes; exploring the complex gives a unique insight into the Hoxha regime's permanent state of alert for enemy attack. Maps at the entrance show the entire network of tunnels under the city.

The Seven Springs (7 Krojët)
Part of a Muslim's preparation for prayer involves purification by washing, which means that running water can be found in or near every mosque. Gjirokastra's 'Seven Springs' were built into the foundations of a 17th-century mosque. The mosque was destroyed in 1967 (page 16), but the springs have survived and some are still in use. An inscription in Ottoman Turkish above the main fountain includes the line 'The one who built the pool shall be happy.' Across the stream is a bathhouse, or *hamam*, unfortunately not open to visitors.

Antigonea
(w *antigonea.com;* ⊕ *08.00–16.00 Mon–Fri, 09.00–15.00 Sat–Sun; 200 lek*) In 295BC, the king of the Molossians, one of the three main tribes of Epirus, founded a city and named it after his wife, a princess of both the Macedonian and Egyptian royal families. The Molossian king was Pyrrhus, whose later battles against expansionist Rome would come to be known as 'Pyrrhic victories'; his wife's name was Antigone and the new city was called Antigonea.

For more than a hundred years, Antigonea was a major economic and cultural centre. Then, after Rome's victory in the Third Macedonian War (171–168BC), Epirus was unfortunate enough to be on the route of the victorious army's return home. Even though the Epirote state had not been involved in that phase of the war, 70 of its cities were sacked and 150,000 of its citizens were taken to Rome as slaves. Antigonea's neatly planned streets and luxurious houses were reduced to rubble and its walls reduced in height.

In a beautiful and highly strategic setting, on a mountainside overlooking the Drinos Valley opposite Gjirokastra, Antigonea is one of the few archaeological sites in Albania which has been extensively excavated and has good interpretative materials for the non-specialist visitor. Well-designed information panels, placed at various significant points throughout the site, explain the history and function of the buildings.

The main things to see are the remaining sections of the city's fortifications and the remains of several impressive buildings. The best stretches of the city walls are those around the acropolis, near the site entrance, and right at the other, southern end, where you can see how the Romans destroyed the main gate to the city and pushed over the top of the wall. Near this gatehouse are the remains of a stoa (a covered walkway), which is a very clear example of the Epirote dry-stone building technique, using large polygonal stones.

The path through the city takes the visitor past a group of houses. It was while one of these houses was being excavated, in 1968, that the site was identified as Antigonea, thanks to the discovery of 14 bronze *tesserae* imprinted with the name of the city; these are thought to have been voting tokens, used in the city's decision-making processes. The path continues down some steps to the so-called House of the Peristyle, with its colonnade that would have surrounded a garden or courtyard in the interior of the house. Note the large stone nearby with differently sized holes in it; this was for measuring out accurate quantities of various types of foodstuff such as oil, flour and so forth – the Molossians' Trading Standards Authority.

The city's main street ran north–south from the acropolis to the main gate; part of it can be seen below the House of the Peristyle, while excavations in 2013 revealed another section further to the south. In what was the centre of the city – the agora – another stoa, nearly 60m long and double-storeyed, was built up on an artificial terrace, above the line of the hill, so that it had spectacular views and could be seen from far around. Houses and workshops were built on a grid pattern around the agora, some of them with imposing columns that can still be seen. Almost at the end of the site is a palaeochristian basilica, triconch in shape and with mosaic floors (normally kept covered, unfortunately), from around AD500.

A useful leaflet with a map of the site and information about the main buildings and fortifications is included in the admission fee. The website gives brief information about the site, in English, and about other things to see in the area. It takes about half an hour to get to Antigonea by car from Gjirokastra; the road is signposted, for 'Parku Arkeologjik Antigone', from the main highway, near the bus terminus. The road is asphalted all the way to the site entrance and there is ample parking there. It is a lovely drive, through beautiful scenery and past several traditional villages with attractive Byzantine churches. It is also possible to hike up to Antigonea; it takes about 1½ hours. The footpath starts at the Archaeological Park's office, in the village of Asim Zeneli, and leads over the hills to the archaeological site, emerging behind the site office and the old fountain.

Hadrianopolis In 1970, a landslide revealed the remains of a classical theatre in the Drinos Valley, south of Gjirokastra, and academics were baffled as to what it was doing there. Ancient sources mentioned a city, built during the Emperor Hadrian's reign (AD117–38) and called Hadrianopolis after him, and located it somewhere between Apollonia and Butrint; but surely this theatre in the middle of nowhere could not possibly have anything to do with a city? It was not until 2002, when the site of the theatre was drained and some of the area around it was excavated, that the first archaeologists began to realise that they really were looking at a city. They had, after all, discovered Hadrianopolis.

The lovely little theatre retains many of its original features – the entrances to the first and second rows of seating, the stage with its entrances for the actors and, below it, for the prompters, and the paved *orchestra*. Performances are occasionally staged in the theatre nowadays. Beyond the theatre, a beautiful stretch of wall, in a herringbone pattern, is part of the forum; there are hypocausts here, too, showing where the bathhouse was. Other buildings that have been excavated include part of the wall that surrounded the city, an ancient cemetery outside that wall and two temples. Hadrianopolis seems to have gone into some decline in the 3rd century, but the settlement survived into the 6th century. Its name lives on in the modern Albanian 'Dropulli', the collective name for the villages that flank the river between Gjirokastra and the Greek border.

The site, unattended, is about a kilometre up a rough track from the village of Sofratika, just off the highway to Greece. Minibuses serve Sofratika from Gjirokastra; it would be an easy walk to the site from the village, or from the junction on the highway.

LIBOHOVA *Telephone code: 0881*

The small town of Libohova, in the Bureto Mountains on the other side of the Drinos Valley from Gjirokastra, would make an excellent base for a couple of days' hiking and sightseeing. It is easy to get to, has good accommodation, and there are several interesting things to do in and around the town. These include an early 19th-century fortress, a historic Bektashi *teqe* and an outstanding 6th-century church.

GETTING THERE AND AROUND There are **buses** to Libohova from Gjirokastra every morning. The journey by car takes less than an hour; the bus takes a bit longer. Getting *around* the area is another matter. To get to most of the places mentioned here, unless you have your own vehicle, you would need to negotiate a price with a Libohova taxi driver. Bikes would be ideal, as long as your thigh muscles are in good shape.

WHERE TO STAY, EAT AND DRINK The Hotel Libohova on the town square (*4 rooms;* m *069 54 64 605;* f *Bar Restorant Hotel "Libohova"; all rooms en suite with TV & AC;* **$$**) is comfortable but rather small. If it is full, the 'Turizmi' (the communist-era hotel) on the other side of the square is more basic but much larger, and will almost certainly have rooms. Both have lovely views out over the Drinos Valley.

The owner of the Hotel Libohova also runs the terrace restaurant (**$$$**) under the plane tree in the square. The salad ingredients are locally produced and delicious, as is the cheese which is processed at a factory at the foot of the hill.

WHAT TO SEE AND DO The main square in Libohova is dominated by the huge plane tree in its corner. This tree is said to be the largest of its kind (*Platanus orientalis*) in the Balkans, and to be 500 years old. It is 25–30m high and its branches extend for several metres in all directions. The terrace restaurant below it is made even cooler by the water that is channelled straight from the spring and past the tables. The views from the square across the Drinos Valley are spectacular on a clear day.

In the 19th century, Libohova was a much larger town than it is today, and the feudal landowners – the Libohova family – enhanced its importance through some clever diplomacy, marrying into the family of Ali Pasha Tepelena (see box, pages 254–5). This was a smart move that gave the town the protection of the most powerful man in southern Albania at the time and allowed it to prosper. Ali Pasha's sister, Shanishaja, is buried in the Libohova family's own graveyard, which is 5 minutes' walk from the town square, up past a Bektashi *tyrbe* and then down towards the stream. Unfortunately the graveyard has been neglected for many years and is very overgrown – you should ask someone to show you where it is, since if you try to follow directions you will probably walk right past it. It is no longer possible to tell which of the graves is Shanishaja's.

Ali Pasha's other legacy to Libohova was its fortress, the west wall of which can be seen from the road as you drive into the town. The entrance to the fortress is through someone's backyard (the owners seem to have no objection to tourists blundering through their property), downhill from the main square. There is nothing left of the interior of the fort itself, apart from some bricked-up archways, but the walls are very imposing – smooth blocks of grey stone about 2m thick in places.

Labova e Kryqit (*200 lek*) The parishioners of Labova e Kryqit ('Labova of the Cross') say that the construction of their church was ordered by the Emperor Justinian (AD527–65), who donated a fragment of the Holy Cross to the church and was married in it. The building that stands here today, however, is much later, perhaps 13th century. Dedicated to the Birth of Mary, it is built with the red bricks, laid in patterns, which are so characteristic of early churches in Albania, and it is roofed with the grey slates that give Gjirokastra its beautiful austerity. An even later exonarthex (portico) runs the length of the front wall.

Inside the church is a magnificent iconostasis of ornately carved and gilded wood, dating from 1805 and decorated with dragons and eagles. On each side of the iconostasis, and behind it, are beautiful frescoes, and on the arch behind the throne are images that blend the pagan beliefs of the people with Christian symbolism. More frescoes decorate the walls of the nave. The works of art in the church have been conserved and restored and, when the restorers removed one of the icons for treatment, they found a much older icon (possibly 16th century) hidden underneath it and now displayed beside it – a crowned figure representing, so the story goes, the Emperor Justinian himself. Another icon shows St Paraskevi, martyred in the 2nd century, with her head in a bowl (and a second head, still attached to her neck).

Subsidence over the centuries has made the cupola lean very noticeably, and the building has had to be reinforced on several occasions; an inscription indicates that such reinforcement was carried out in 1783, but it has continued into modern times. Some of the reinforcement work can be examined in the gallery of the church and the bell tower.

The church is set in a walled garden, and both the garden gate and the church itself are kept locked. The family that holds the key lives nearby; the telephone number may be posted on the gate, or you can ask anyone in the village to find them to let you in.

This beautiful church can be reached by bus from Gjirokastra – there are two buses every morning – or by private car or taxi from there or from Libohova. Labova e Kryqit is about an hour's drive from the main north–south highway. The last half hour is mostly unpaved. There is a public fountain and a café in the square.

The *teqe* at Melani As you come down the hill from Libohova towards the highway, a minor road off to your left leads to one of the holiest sites of Bektashism, the *teqe* at Melani. Built in the early 19th century, it occupies a splendid site, high on an isolated hill commanding glorious views of the Drinos Valley. Traces of fortification can be seen lower down around the hill, parts of which date back to the 4th century BC.

The *teqe* is a large building in which the faith's followers study, pray, meditate and listen to the teaching of the *baba* (father). The building is not always open, and the best time to visit is on one of the Bektashi holy days, when hundreds of believers make their way to Melani. These are social as well as religious occasions; people come with their family and friends, and bring picnics that they enjoy under the poplar trees which surround the *teqe*. There is a *tyrbe* (shrine) in front of the *teqe*, the burial place of one of the early *babas* there. You should remove your shoes before entering either the *tyrbe* or the *teqe* itself, and avoid stepping on the threshold.

The Melani *teqe* was damaged and looted during the atheism campaign of the late 1960s. When freedom of worship was restored, local believers collected money and materials and rebuilt the *teqe* with their own hands, sleeping in turns there every night to make sure their work was not vandalised. Many of those who helped with the restoration were from Lazarati, a Bektashi village a couple of miles south of Gjirokastra.

TEPELENA   *Telephone code: 0814*

Tepelena was the home town and secondary residence of Ali Pasha Tepelena, who was Governor of Ioannina from 1788 to 1822. Ioannina, now in northern Greece, was at the time the capital of the administrative district (*sanjak*) that covered much of southern Albania. Ali Pasha rebuilt the castle in Tepelena and then made it his secondary residence, after Ioannina itself. See the box on pages 254–5 for more information about Ali Pasha and his sticky end.

From the main square, where there is a large bronze statue of a reclining Ali Pasha, the castle is a few minutes' walk along Rruga Ali Pasha Tepelena. Its massive walls encircle an area of 4–5ha, dominating the valley of the Vjosa River below. The castle is still inhabited and there is no charge to visit it. A bar has been set up on the roof of one of the towers, from where there is a good view of the river valley and the bridge over the Vjosa, whose foundations are those built by Ali Pasha Tepelena.

GETTING THERE AND AWAY Tepelena is 30 minutes away from Gjirokastra and is linked with it by frequent **buses** and **minibuses**. It would also be an easy day trip from Përmeti (pages 148–51). From the north, in addition to the buses and minibuses specifically for Tepelena, which go to the main square, it is also possible to alight from any vehicle heading for Gjirokastra or Përmeti. These stop on the main road below Tepelena; it is quite a stiff climb up from there to the town centre, but there are always taxis waiting where the buses stop.

THE RIVIERA

To the north of Saranda is a stretch of coast known as the Albanian Riviera, which is one of the most beautiful in the whole Ionian Sea. In any other country, it would have been completely swamped with high-rise hotels in the 1970s. There are not many good consequences of Albania's isolation and poverty under communism, but this unspoilt coastline was one. However, the country is making up for lost time by developing these lovely beaches as fast as it possibly can. Almost every little bay now has an access road, with cafés and restaurants on the beach. There are hotels and rooms to let in every village along the coast road and temporary, summer-only campsites at many of the beaches. Prices increase dramatically in summer, when the demand for good hotel rooms far outstrips the supply, and it is advisable to reserve accommodation in advance. It is essential to carry sufficient cash. Few of the hotels on the Riviera accept credit cards and the only ATMs are in Himara (pages 257–9).

The road out of Saranda begins inland and runs along the landward side of the mountains until the village of Shën Vasili (the site of a prison camp in the communist period, then called Përparimi – 'Progress'). After Shën Vasili, the road begins to climb gradually above the deeply indented bays and the view from the road above is unforgettable. Rivulets run from the mountains and lose themselves in the fine sand of the beaches. The hillsides are full of olive groves, planted on terraces that were cut by detachments of students from Tirana at around the same time as the villages of the Greek coasts were being covered in concrete.

GETTING THERE AND AWAY The journey from **Saranda** to Vlora takes about 4 hours by car; the road is well surfaced, but narrow and steep over the Llogoraja Pass. There are four coast-road **buses** every day; they usually display a sign on the dashboard reading *Bregdeti* ('coast'), to differentiate them from the buses that go via Tepelena

ALI PASHA TEPELENA

By the middle of the 17th century, the old system of provincial government in the Ottoman Empire had broken down. No longer did the governors of *vilayets* and *sanjaks* (provinces) work their way up through the ranks of the imperial administration. Instead, increasingly, they were appointed directly by the palace or by other great households; by 1630, only about a quarter of *sanjak* governors and governors-general had previous experience of provincial government. Rapid turnover in the administration also became common, with more than half of the governors-general in 1630 staying in their posts for less than a year.

In Albania, one outcome of these changes was the emergence of near-autonomous local rulers who were known as *pashas*. It was in the *pasha's* interest to expand the territory he controlled – his *pashalik* – whether by war or payment, because the larger it was, the greater his income and power. Towards the end of the 18th century, practically all of these small *pashaliks* had come under the control of two powerful *pashas*, one in southern Albania and the other in the north. See page 199 for information about the northern *pashalik*, whose capital was Shkodra.

The southern *pashalik* was centred on the city of Ioannina, which is now in northern Greece but at the time was in the same administrative region as much of southern Albania. In 1788, the sultan appointed as Governor of Ioannina a man from Tepelena called Ali. He had started his career as a brigand, and used his knowledge of other robber bands to curry favour with the sultan (ie: he shopped his friends), who rewarded him first with a small *pashalik* and then with Ioannina.

From there, Ali Pasha Tepelena used a combination of skilful diplomacy and ruthless violence to extend his authority throughout southern Albania and a large part of the Greek mainland. This was the period of Napoleon's expansions into Italy and Dalmatia, and Ali Pasha played the French and the British off against each other, consolidating his own power as he did so. In 1809, he captured Berati, and then Vlora and Gjirokastra. In that same year, Lord Byron visited Ali Pasha's court at Tepelena and described him in a letter to his mother:

His highness is 60 years old, very fat, and not tall, but with a fine face, light blue eyes, and a white beard; his manner is very kind, and at the same time he possesses that dignity which I find universal amongst the Turks. He has the appearance of anything but his real character, for he is a remorseless tyrant, guilty of the most horrible cruelties, very brave, and so good a general that they call him the Mahometan Buonaparte.

Throughout the territory that Ali Pasha controlled, he built castles, aqueducts, bridges and mosques, many of which can still be seen. He was interested in and Gjirokastra. The first bus of the day leaves Saranda at 06.00 and continues to Tirana; after this, there are departures for Vlora at 11.30, 13.00 and 14.30. In the other direction, from Vlora to Saranda, there are departures at 06.45, 07.00 and 08.30; the bus from Tirana can be boarded on its way through Vlora, at around 10.00. Buses also run every day from Vlora to Himara (page 258) and Qeparoi.

Any bus will let you off in any of the small towns on its route, or at the road-ends for the beaches or the castles. Similarly, you can get *on* a bus anywhere along its route; ask locally for the time it is expected where you are. It is unwise to rely 100% on the last bus of the day, especially in summer when they are often full and you may be left stranded at the roadside, without alternative transport.

learning about new construction techniques, and hired European architects and builders to work for him. He converted to Bektashism (page 22) in about 1810, around the time when it was taking hold in Albania. His conversion allowed the Bektashi *babas* to preach more freely and to establish *teqes* throughout the territory under his rule.

By 1820, the huge area that he controlled was beginning to alarm the imperial authorities. He was dismissed as governor and ordered to hand his *pashaliks* back to the sultan's authorities. In a last audacious move, Ali Pasha then threw in his lot with a Greek revolutionary organisation. This was the last straw for the Ottomans. They besieged his castle at Ioannina and, after 17 months, in January 1822, he was killed and beheaded. His head was sent to Istanbul and his body was buried in Ioannina, next to that of his wife Emine.

AN ALI PASHA TOUR It would be relatively easy to self-assemble a short Ali Pasha tour, starting from either Ioannina or Corfu. Ioannina Castle houses Ali Pasha and Emine's tomb, next to the Fatih Mosque that he rebuilt in 1795. You can also look at the double-walled fortifications that his European engineers built. From Ioannina it is a short bus journey across the border to Gjirokastra, where Ali Pasha extended the fortifications and built a 10km-long aqueduct (demolished in 1932, sadly, although some traces are still visible).

Two impressive castles built for Ali Pasha, at his home town of Tepelena and at Libohova, are within easy reach of Gjirokastra and could be visited from there on day trips. See pages 251–3 for information about these towns and their castles.

At Butrint, on an island at the mouth of the Vivari Channel, which connects the Butrint Lagoon with the Corfu Channel, is a small fortress that Ali Pasha is said to have built in 1814, in response to Britain's capture of Corfu and the other Ionian islands. This castle can be visited by boat from Butrint; while you are there anyway, it would be perverse not to visit the main Butrint site, which is packed with wonderful things (pages 231–6). Another Ali Pasha fortress stands at Porto Palermo, less than 2 hours north of Saranda up the beautiful coast road (page 256).

Fairly frequent buses link Ioannina with Igoumenitsa, just across the strait from Corfu. Ferries and hydrofoils run every day from Corfu to Saranda (page 223). There are direct buses from Ioannina to Gjirokastra (page 239). If you have your own transport, you could return to Ioannina directly from Tepelena, via Përmeti and the Tre Urat border crossing (page 147).

The coast road is a lovely route for **cyclists**. There are some very steep stretches, but the magnificent scenery is a good excuse to stop for lots of rests. The Riviera buses will take bikes, if the gradients get too much; the appeal of this option is likely to grow as the Llogoraja Pass (pages 259–60) draws closer. Drivers are usually courteous to cyclists, but caution is required; cycling after dark is certainly not advisable. It is about 140km from Saranda to Vlora.

BORSHI Just before the village of Borshi, just over an hour from Saranda, a minor road up to the right leads up to **Borshi Castle**, sometimes also referred to as Sopoti Castle. The first written reference to it is in 1258 and the hill on which it stands was already fortified by the 4th century BC. However, what can be seen today dates from the 18th century. The mosque just within the entrance was built at that time; the painted ceiling and walls must have been beautiful when the fresco was in better condition. The whole castle is rather neglected and overgrown, but the views from it are spectacular, out across the Ionian Sea to Corfu in one direction and, in the other, towards the mountains that run the length of the Riviera. There is a paved footpath up from the car park to just short of the castle entrance, with stone benches on which to rest and enjoy the views. If you are on foot, the best place to start is the Ujvara Restaurant; ask the waiters to show you the short cut up to the road. It takes about half an hour to walk up to the castle entrance from the restaurant. The Ujvara is a lovely place to stop for a meal (**$$$**) or a drink, with its tables arranged on terraces surrounded by waterfalls (the eponymous *ujvara*); the service is friendly and some English is spoken.

BAY OF PALERMO After Borshi, the road drops down to the coast and rounds the Bay of Palermo, where Ali Pasha Tepelena (see box, pages 254–5) built one of his imposing fortresses on what is practically an island: a promontory connected to the mainland by a narrow – and easily defensible – causeway. The promontory closes off part of the bay to create a sheltered harbour, still used today by local fishermen, and a pleasant pebbly beach. Cars can be parked either at the restaurant on the main road – a good place, with its shady terrace and impeccable toilets, for a drink or meal after your visit – or just beyond the causeway, beside a restored church (said to have been built by Ali Pasha for one of his wives, a Christian) and ruined 20th-century buildings, whose superb communist-era slogans are still visible under the more recent graffiti. It is a few minutes' walk up a rough track to the **castle** (*100 lek*). An information board has been installed at the start of the track, with helpful plans of the fortress and a brief history of it in English and Albanian. There is another board with plans as you enter the fortress.

The interior of the castle consists of a huge vaulted chamber with archways leading off it into smaller rooms and dark tunnels (a torch is essential), well worth exploring thoroughly. A stone staircase leads up to the battlements, from where part of the outer walls can be reached. The views are stunning. The islands that can be seen in the distance are Greek territory, lying off the northwest of Corfu. Not surprisingly, there are dense arrays of bunkers (see box, page 144) on the hillside overlooking the bay. The fortress itself was used as a military depot during the Italian occupation, and probably afterwards, too. From the castle (and at certain points along the road) you can see a huge tunnel blasted into the cliffs on the northern side of the bay. This was built as a shelter for the submarines that the Soviet Union based in the Adriatic from the late 1950s. When Albania broke off relations and sided with China (page 16), the USSR reluctantly left most of the submarines behind.

HIMARA *Telephone code: 0393*

Himara is the largest town between Saranda and Vlora, with a high school, district hospital, ATMs and so forth. Most of the inhabitants are ethnically Greek, and the whole area suffered large-scale emigration when Albania's borders opened in the early 1990s, as people rushed south to seek work in Greece. Greater stability in Albania and the economic opportunities provided by tourism are beginning to reverse this trend, and Himara is now an attractive little resort with good hotels and restaurants. If you find Saranda overdeveloped, this is the place to come. The standard of service is better than at some other resorts on the Riviera, and the local people are friendly and helpful.

The swimming in Himara is excellent, with clear blue water that stays warm until late in the year. Non-swimmers, however, should note that the beach slopes very sharply into the sea, unlike the gentle Adriatic coast further north. There is no longer much of a beach left in the town centre, where most of it has been replaced with a vast expanse of promenade, but the terraces of the bars and restaurants behind it are pleasant spots to sit and admire the sea. The beach just to the south of the town, called Potami, is pebbles, but the hotels there provide sun-loungers and the sea is crystalline. Quieter beaches nearby include Livadhja to the north, 25 minutes' walk beyond the football pitch, and Llamani, a beautiful cove 10 minutes' drive south.

Excavation in the cave of **Spile** (which means 'cave' in Greek, the mother tongue of most of the local people) revealed evidence of habitation in the Neolithic period. The cave is right next to the main road as it meets the promenade. The gate is

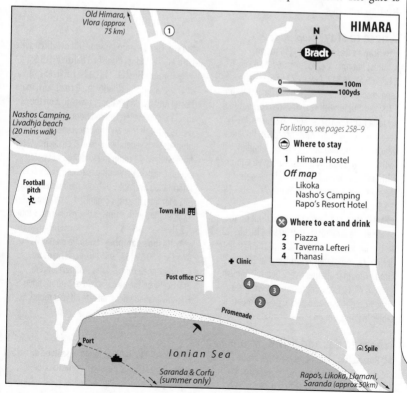

locked; when there is someone there to open it, admission is 100 lek. **Old Himara**, above the modern town, is often referred to as the 'castle of Himara' and, in the 5th–4th centuries BC, when Himara was part of Chaonia (page 236) it really was fortified. Procopius of Caesarea, in the 6th century AD, mentions it as one of the fortresses rebuilt by Justinian. It now has an astonishing number of churches in various stages of dilapidation, some with beautiful frescoes. It is a pleasant and scenic walk of 30–45 minutes from Spile to Old Himara.

In Greek, *potami* means 'rivers', and the springs at Potami are still the source of all of Himara's drinking water. The derelict pumping station behind the Likoka Hotel was built in the 1960s to irrigate the citrus trees and olives on the terraced land above the town.

Getting there and away The road between Saranda and Vlora is asphalted and in good condition all the way. Himara is almost exactly halfway and the journey from either direction takes about 2 hours. See pages 254–5 for details of public transport on the coast road. There is also a daily departure from Tirana to Qeparoi, via Himara, at about midday and, in summer only, another at 17.00. Direct buses link Himara with Athens and other Greek cities.

A hydrofoil service between Corfu and Himara started in the summer of 2017. Operated by **Finikas Lines** (w *finikas-lines.com*; see page 226 for further details), it runs on Mondays, Thursdays and Saturdays. The one-way adult fare was €39. There is no guarantee, of course, that this level of service will be maintained in future, but it is a lovely way to approach Himara, with magnificent views of the southern Riviera beaches.

🏠 **Where to stay** *Map, page 257*

🏠 **Rapo's Resort Hotel** (48 rooms, 3 suites) Potami; 📞22857; m 069 20 62 842, 069 62 26 312, 069 89 73 986; e info@ raposresorthotel.com; w raposresorthotel.com. Lifts; restaurant with sea-view terrace; outdoor pizzeria in gardens; bar. English spoken; Wi-Fi; secure parking; credit cards accepted. Private beach, 2 swimming pools (1 big, 1 smaller). All rooms en suite, nicely furnished & well equipped with balcony, hairdryer, iron, minibar, safe, internet access, direct-dial phone, AC, cable TV. **$$$$$**

🏠 **Likoka** (14 rooms) Potami, right on the beach at the far end; m 069 20 91 419, 069 22 11 484; e likokaanastas@gmail.com. The first hotel in Himara, completely refurbished in 2014, still family-run; management very helpful; English spoken; Wi-Fi. Excellent restaurant with fresh locally caught fish; also pasta, salads, meat; tables inside & out on raised veranda overlooking the sea. One 2-bedroom suite. All rooms en suite with AC, TV, fridge, furnished balcony. **$$$**

🏠 **Himara Hostel** (18 beds) m 069 51 71 901; e wehadsomuchfun@gmail.com; 📘 Himara Hostel Albania. In the upper town, just off the main road to the left coming from Vlora. Lovely courtyard with fruit & citrus trees; spacious grounds with vegetable garden & chickens; water from well. Wi-Fi; computer with internet access; equipped kitchen, washing machine; maps & local information available. Outdoor bar in evenings; bikes for hire; day trips organised. 2 dbls en suite; 1 dbl sharing with dorms; 3 dorms sharing 3 toilets & 2 showers. **$$–$**

🏠 **Nasho's Camping** Livadhja m 069 75 87 833, +30 69 4532 0562 (Greece); e ouzeri. nashos@gmail.com; 📘 nashos.meze.ouzeri. Practically on the beach; good restaurant open. Friendly management, on-site all year round. **$**

✖ **Where to eat and drink** *Map, page 257*

✖ **Piazza** On seafront promenade; m 069 25 47 365, 067 39 18 997; e piazzahimare@gmail.com. Tables outside on terrace with sea view; nicely decorated indoors. Wide range of seafood dishes; pasta & pizza; huge portions; home-produced wine; good service, English menus, English spoken,

258

free Wi-Fi for customers. Also has 3 hotel rooms & 2 apts (**$$**). **$$$**

✗ Taverna Lefteri On pedestrian street parallel to the promenade. Fish & seafood as well as grilled meat, pasta & traditional dishes such as *mish turli*

(page 47). Informal atmosphere, good house wine. **$$$**

✗ Thanasi On pedestrianised street parallel to promenade. A good bakery, with the usual range of bread & buns, plus excellent *byrek*. **$**

THE NORTHERN RIVIERA North of Himara, the marvellous scenery continues, with dramatic mountains rising up from the coast and the deep blue sea shimmering in the sunlight. The road goes through the pretty villages of Vunoi and Dhërmiu; below them, and below the road, are lovely beaches, with fine, clean sand, transparent blue sea, plenty of accommodation and lively nightlife in the summer. Jala Beach is 5km from the main road, just before the first houses in Vunoi; Dhërmiu Beach, sometimes known by its Greek name, Dhrimadhes, is 1.5km from the road. Both beaches are clearly signposted and both roads are well surfaced. There is no public transport to the beaches; those travelling by bus should ask to be let off at 'Plazh' ('beach') and then walk, or try to hitchhike, down the hill.

A few kilometres beyond Dhërmiu, the road begins to climb towards the Llogoraja Pass. On the right, perched on the hillside, is the village of Palasa. To the left is Palasa Beach, where in 48BC Julius Caesar landed from Brundisium (now Brindisi), in pursuit of his rival Pompey (page 8). This is the northernmost beach on the Riviera, part sand, part pebble, and with wild flowers and oregano growing in the scrub behind the beach. Caesar led his legions from here over the Llogoraja Pass to Oricum; you can follow in their footsteps, more or less, although the paths are not at all clear. It would be easier in reverse, from Llogoraja; see below.

It is about 3.5km from the highway to the start of Palasa Beach. A short climb from the end of the beach leads to a series of huge tunnels blasted into the hillside facing the sea, their communist-era instructions still visible.

Where to stay, eat and drink There are many hotels and private rooms at both Jala and Dhërmiu beaches. Temporary **campsites** open during the summer at these and most other beaches on the Riviera; some are quite luxurious and offer the option of renting a furnished tent, rather than pitching your own. Many hotels and guesthouses on the Riviera beaches can be reserved through the usual international booking websites or the Tirana-based Albania Holidays (w *albania-hotel.com*; see page 28 for other contact details). Out of season, many guesthouses and hotels close. In July and August, it would be wise to reserve accommodation in advance if you are keen to stay at a specific resort.

🏠 **Shkolla Vuno** (3 dorms) Vunoi; m 068 40 63 835; e shkollavuno@hotmail.com; w tiranahostel.com; ⏰ Jun–Sep. An initiative of the Outdoor Albania Association (page 54), this backpackers' hostel is a repurposing of the old village school, which closed in 2011 due to the declining school-age population. Well-equipped kitchen; b/fast inc; tables, benches & hammocks in courtyard; outdoor showers with solar-heated water; toilet block; camping in olive grove. English spoken. Visitors can participate in activities to benefit the local community: clearing up litter, clearing paths, or repairing buildings. Hiking to Jala & Gjipe beaches or into mountains; kayaks available to rent. **$**

LLOGORAJA The hairpin bends ahead of Palasa lead to the Llogoraja Pass, over 1,000m above sea level. A tourist information kiosk and viewpoint are in a lay-by on the left as the road climbs above the beaches. To your right are the bare peaks of the Çika Mountains, 2,045m at their highest point, with pines and firs shrouding the hillside below them. To your left the cliffs drop almost sheer into the Ionian Sea, as wine-dark as it was when Odysseus sailed it. The whole area around the top of the pass – over 1,000ha – is designated as a national park. It is rich in wildlife (roe deer, foxes, squirrels, wild boar and wolves are common) and would make an excellent base for a few days' hiking. Hang-gliding from the clifftops out over the sea can be arranged (enquire at your hotel).

A short hike that requires no more than reasonable fitness and sensible shoes is to Caesar's Pass (Qafa e Çezarit), where Julius Caesar is thought to have led his legions over the mountains from their landing at Palasa. The (unmarked) path leads up from the right-hand side of the road, roughly opposite Sofo's restaurant. The walk through the pinewoods takes 20–30 minutes, before you emerge on to more open ground and a viewpoint, with stunning views of the tip of the Karaburuni Peninsula and the start of the Adriatic.

A good circular hike goes up to Qafa e Thellë ('the Deep Pass'), along the ridge to the phone masts, then down to the top of the pass. The path starts from an obvious point between the Iliria Restaurant and the Hotel Alpin; it has been paved and is generally in reasonable condition, although sensible footwear should obviously be worn. It is possible to hike over Qafa e Thellë to the start of the Karaburuni Peninsula and Caesar's landfall at Palasa, but the paths on the other side of the mountain are difficult and unclear; a local guide should be hired.

There is no public transport specifically to Llogoraja, but several buses and minibuses a day run between Vlora and Himara, Qeparoi or Saranda; see page 255 for further details. If you do not plan to stay overnight, you should ascertain on arrival the expected time of the last bus on which you can return or continue onward.

🏠 Where to stay, eat and drink *Map, pages 224–5*

There are several hotels within the national park, interspersed with restaurants all offering the same specialities of spit-roasted lamb and kid. Both hotels listed here have good restaurants.

🏠 **Llogora Tourist Village** (22 rooms, 3 suites, 16 chalets) ✆ 033 225 790; m 069 33 44 400; e info@llogora.com; w llogora.com. Set in over 1ha of beautiful grounds on the edge of the forest, with deer wandering freely. Restaurant with international menu & traditional dishes; bar, tennis court, indoor pool, gym, children's play area; babysitting service. Some English spoken; Wi-Fi in public areas. Guided treks, hang-gliding & jeep excursions can be arranged. Each chalet has 1 dbl & 1 twin bedroom, living room with TV, CH, fridge, bathroom with shower, furnished veranda angled away from the chalet next door. Hotel rooms all en suite with TV, CH, good-sized balcony, bedside lights. **$$$**

🏠 **Hotel Alpin** (20 rooms) m 069 20 55 936, 069 23 90 561; e info@hotelalpin-al.net; can be booked through w albania-hotel.com. Helpful English-speaking management; hiking guides can be arranged; good restaurant, tables outside on large veranda in summer; no Wi-Fi. All rooms en suite with satellite TV, CH, fridge; some have balcony with views over national park. **$$**

VLORA *Telephone code: 033*

The Bay of Vlora is where the Adriatic and Ionian seas divide, and the city has a real southern Mediterranean feel to it. It has a long history, but its main claim to fame is as the place where Albanian independence was proclaimed in 1912. Vlora has three very different museums and is a good base for several interesting excursions. Its geographical position – roughly midway between Tirana and Saranda, and only 75km from Italy – and good transport links make it a convenient entry point into Albania.

Then known as Aulon, the town existed in antiquity – the Roman poet Martial, who wrote in the late 1st and early 2nd centuries AD, refers to it (in Epigram XIII. CXXV) as producing fine wool and wine; true to form, he says he'd rather have the wine. By the 4th century AD it is mentioned frequently as a landing port from the Italian ports of Otranto and Brindisi and, especially, as a stopping-off point on the road between Apollonia and Butrint (pages 105–7 and 231–6). During the reign of the Emperor Justinian (AD527–65), it was one of the eight largest cities in the province of New Epirus and was the seat of a bishopric. It was taken by the Normans in 1081 and went on to suffer the same fate as Albania's other coastal cities, changing hands several times over the centuries. Vlora has always been a particularly attractive prize, because Sazani Island, in the Bay of Vlora, controls maritime access to the Adriatic.

It was the first Adriatic port to fall to the Ottomans, in 1417. Ali Pasha Tepelena (see box, pages 254–5) took it in 1810 and held it until he was captured and killed in 1822. On 28 November 1912, delegates from all over Albania met in Vlora and declared their country's independence from the Ottoman Empire. Unfortunately for the provisional government and its prime minister, Ismail Qemali, achieving independence was not quite as simple a matter as announcing it. Vlora and – of course – Sazani were occupied by Italy in 1914, and it was 1920 before the Italians could be dislodged. Indeed, Albania's sovereignty over Sazani was not wholly secure until after World War II.

Vlora's recent past has been equally turbulent. In March 1991, while most of the world was concentrating on the Gulf War, 20,000 or so young Albanians commandeered ships in the harbours of Vlora and Durrësi and took them to Brindisi (page 17). In February 1997, riots in Vlora against failed pyramid-saving schemes developed into a civil uprising that engulfed the whole country and destabilised it for many months. At the same time, Vlora's proximity to southern Italy made it a natural base for Mafia-type operations, and it became the centre of an international network of clandestine emigration and the trafficking of women. For a few years, until a clampdown in 2002, it was effectively under the control of armed gangs. Vlora and the surrounding beaches are now safe and visitors need have no special concerns.

GETTING THERE AND AWAY

By sea Car ferries run daily between Vlora and the Italian port of Brindisi throughout the year, excluding Sundays in low season. They leave Brindisi at around 23.30 every night and dock in Vlora at about 07.00 the following morning. The return journey to Brindisi is faster; the ferries leave Vlora at around 13.00 and arrive at about 18.30. A range of cabin accommodation is available. The one-way passenger fare in deck class ranges from €50 in low season to €70 in high season, plus embarkation taxes; return fares booked at the same time are reduced. Fares, schedules and online bookings are available on the Italian ferry websites w traghetti. it and w traghettiamo.it.

By land New bypasses are being built around the cities of Vlora and Fieri (construction still ongoing in 2017), which together will cut at least an hour off the journey time between Saranda and Tirana. At the time of writing, the journey to Vlora from Tirana takes about 2½ hours and from Saranda about 4 hours.

There are frequent buses to and from **Tirana**, from early in the morning until mid afternoon. In Tirana, they leave from the Shqiponja bus station [62 A1]; in Vlora, the terminus is near the railway station, 10 minutes' walk from the city centre.

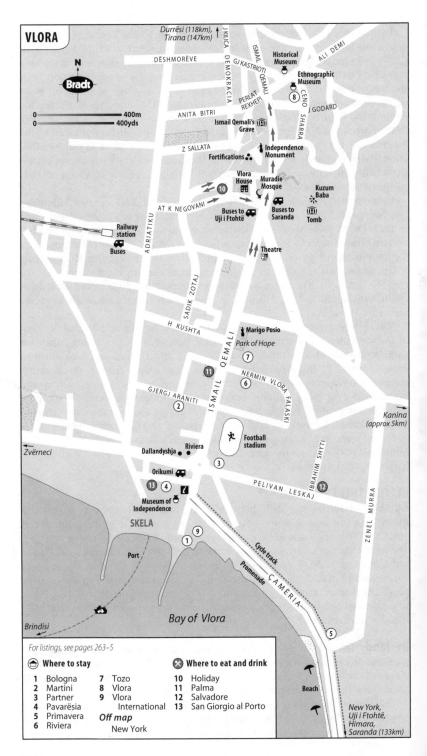

VLORA

N

Bradt

0 ————— 400m
0 ————— 400yds

Durrësi (118km),
Tirana (147km)

DËSHMORËVE

J KILICA

GJ KASTRIOTI

ISMAIL QEMALI

ALI DEMI

Historical Museum

Ethnographic Museum

⑧

CENO SHARRA

J GODARD

PERLAT REXHEPI

ANITA BITRI

Z SALLATA

Ismail Qemali's Grave

Independence Monument

Fortifications

Vlora House

Muradie Mosque

Kuzum Baba

⑩

Buses to Uji i Ftohtë

Buses to Saranda

Tomb

AT K NEGOVANI

ADRIATIKU

Railway station

Buses

SADIK ZOTAJ

Theatre

H KUSHTA

ISMAIL QEMALI

Marigo Posio

Park of Hope

⑦

⑪

NERMIN VLORA FALASKI

⑥

GJERGJ ARANITI

②

Kanina
(approx 5km)

Zvërneci

Dallandyshja

Riviera

Football stadium

③

IBRAHIM SHYTI

Orikumi

⑬ ④

ℹ

PELIVAN LESKAJ

⑫

ZENEL MURRA

Museum of Independence

SKELA

⑨

Port

①

Cycle track

Promenade

ÇAMERIA

⑤

Brindisi

Bay of Vlora

New York,
Uji i Ftohtë,
Himara,
Saranda (133km)

Beach

For listings, see pages 263–5

🛏 **Where to stay**

1 Bologna
2 Martini
3 Partner
4 Pavarësia
5 Primavera
6 Riviera
7 Tozo
8 Vlora
9 Vlora International

Off map
New York

✴ **Where to eat and drink**

10 Holiday
11 Palma
12 Salvadore
13 San Giorgio al Porto

The fare is 500 lek. There are also buses in the mornings to and from all other major towns in southern and central Albania.

The road between **Saranda** and Vlora is well surfaced, but narrow and steep over the Llogoraja Pass. There are three buses every day, plus a through bus to Tirana and services to Vlora from Himara and other towns on the Riviera (pages 254–5). There are frequent minibuses up and down the coast as far as Rradhima and Orikumi until lunchtime (later in the summer). All the coastal services leave from the bus stop opposite the Riviera shopping centre (Qendra Riviera).

GETTING AROUND Vlora is a large city, and the distances between the sights in the centre, the port and the beaches are too great for all but the most enthusiastic walker. There are plenty of taxis, which can either be flagged down in the street or found at the many taxi ranks throughout the town. Urban buses are frequent, with a flat fare of 30 lek. The most useful route for the visitor is the 'Uji i Ftohtë' bus, a frequent service that leaves from a bus stop behind the Muradie Mosque (*xhamia*) and runs down the Boulevard past Skela (the port) and along the promenade, as far as the Uji i Ftohtë post office. The hotels in Uji i Ftohtë are further on from here, but there are always taxis waiting where the bus terminates. The buses get very crowded and the only way to be sure of a seat is by boarding at the terminus at one or other end of the route.

TOURIST INFORMATION A tourist information kiosk at Skela (the port), open only in summer, has helpful, English-speaking staff who can advise on what to see and how to get around the city and the surrounding area. They have free maps of Vlora and of the Albanian Riviera, brochures about the various attractions, and up-to-date information about bus times. Any travel agency in Vlora (eg: *Dallandyshja Travel, in the Riviera shopping centre;* ☏ *222 222;* m *068 20 05 319*) can provide timetable information about, and tickets for, all ferry departures, from Saranda and Durrësi as well as from Vlora. They can also arrange tours of the area and excursions by boat to the Karaburuni Peninsula (pages 269–70). Some hotels in Vlora also offer excursions to Karaburuni.

The website of the Municipality of Vlora (w *bashkiavlore.org*) has extensive information, in Albanian, about things to do and places to visit in the area.

WHERE TO STAY *Map, opposite*
Choosing where to stay in Vlora really comes down to what you want to do while you are there. The hotels in the centre are handy for museums and public transport; those at Skela and the beaches often have lovely sea views. Most of the city beach has now been replaced with a huge promenade and newly planted trees. Those with their own transport might prefer to head further down the coast, to one of the many hotels that line the Bay of Vlora. Substantial reductions in room rates can often be negotiated outside the peak tourist season of July and August.

Town centre

🏠 **Partner** (57 rooms) Rr Pelivan Leskaj; ☏ 408 282; m 069 40 78 108; e reservation@hotelpartner. al; w hotelpartner.al. English spoken; lift; restaurant; bar; spa; free Wi-Fi. Business facilities; laundry service; car hire; parking; safe at reception. B/fast inc. Some rooms have sea view. Good-sized rooms, all with large en-suite bathroom, some with bathtub;

good lighting, hairdryer, AC, flatscreen TV, bedside lights, thick curtains, fridge, direct-dial phone. **$$$**

🏠 **Martini** (20 rooms) Rr Gjergj Araniti; ☏ 224 017; m 069 20 83 049, 069 20 38 877; e hotel_martini@hotmail.com; ⨍ hotelmartinivlore. Signposted at the corner of the main boulevard with Rr Gj Araniti. English spoken; good Wi-Fi throughout; nicely

decorated with original art. Free parking; friendly management. Generous b/fast inc. All rooms en suite with AC, flatscreen TV, fridge, bedside lights; most have balcony. **$$**

🏠 **Riviera** (14 rooms) Rr Nermin Vlora, pranë Shkollës Industriale; 📞408 212; m 069 38 96 622, 069 62 25 202; e hotel.riviera@yahoo.com. Restaurant; some English spoken at reception. All rooms en suite with twin beds, AC, TV. **$$**

🏠 **Tozo** (15 rooms) Bd Ismail Qemali; 📞223 819; m 069 85 67 520. Set back from boulevard behind the little Park of Hope. Restaurant, terrace bar; parking; Wi-Fi; professional management. All rooms en suite, showing their age a bit, with AC, TV, good curtains; some have balcony. **$$**

🏠 **Vlora** (15 rooms) Rr Justin Godard; m 069 33 43 947. Restaurant, comfortable 1st-floor bar with large terrace overlooking Independence Monument; lift; some English spoken. Good-sized rooms, all en suite with LCD TV, AC, Wi-Fi, balcony, fridge. **$$**

Seaside

🏠 **New York** (85 rooms) Uji i Ftohtë; 📞406 648/9; m 068 40 13 306, 069 21 71 363; e info@ hotelnewyork.al; w hotelnewyork.al. Just before the Uji i Ftohtë tunnel (old coast road). Professional, helpful staff; good English spoken at reception. Restaurant with sea view; poolside pizzeria & grill; popular bar with terrace; business centre, conference facilities. Wi-Fi throughout (inc on beach!); lift; laundry service; free secure parking. Garden, children's play area, terrace. Outdoor pool, tiny private beach below restaurant. Most rooms have balcony, many have magnificent sea views. All rooms en suite with AC, safe, flatscreen TV, minibar, direct-dial phone, desk, drying-rack for beachwear. **$$$**

🏠 **Vlora International** (60 rooms, 6 suites, 6 apts) Skela, Lagja Pavarësia; 📞424 408; m 069 20 70 838; e hotel@vlora-international.com; w vlora-international.com. English spoken. Wi-Fi, parking, restaurant, bars, terrace; lift; conference rooms, business facilities. Indoor pool, hot tub, spa. Good-sized rooms, some with balcony, all have good-sized en-suite bathroom, AC, LCD TV, safe, phone, fridge, bedside lights. **$$$**

🏠 **Bologna** (40 rooms) Skela, Lagja Pavarësia; 📞409 600; m 069 73 01 015; e hbvlora@gmail. com; 📘 Bologna hotel. Contemporary boutique hotel in fabulous setting right on the sea front; large terrace bar & good restaurant overlooking sea; stylish reception area; parking; conference room; lift; Wi-Fi. Cooked b/fast inc. Generously proportioned, beautifully designed rooms, all with nice en-suite bathroom, AC, flatscreen TV, minibar & balcony; most have great views across the Bay of Vlora. **$$**

🏠 **Pavarësia** (36 rooms, 2 suites) Rr Kosova, Lagja Pavarësia; 📞430 940; m 068 20 65 440/1; e info@hotelpavaresiavlore.com; w hotelpavaresiavlore.com. Lift; restaurant & bar; English spoken; friendly, helpful staff; local honey & jam at b/fast. Nicely designed rooms, all en suite with balcony, AC, Wi-Fi, TV. **$$**

🏠 **Primavera** (18 rooms) Rr Çamëria; 📞229 664; m 069 20 65 610; e info@hotel-primavera. al; 📘 Hotel primavera vlore. Just off promenade, on side street opposite Naval School. Friendly management; restaurant (**$$$**) & bar open to guests until late. Free Wi-Fi & parking. All rooms en suite with AC, flatscreen TV, balcony, drying-rack for beachwear; some have sea view. **$$**

✖ WHERE TO EAT AND DRINK *Map, page 262*

Almost all Vlora's restaurants have similar, Italian-influenced menus: pasta, risotto, veal escalopes, plus – as you would expect on the coast – grilled fish and seafood.

✖ **San Giorgio al Porto** Lagja Pavarësia; 📞403 422; 📘 Ristorante "san giorgio" vlore,albania. In basement, across street from university, just beyond Pavarësia Hotel. Formal dining; professional service. Excellent seafood & fish, proper Italian risotto, interesting salads & vegetables; all nicely presented. **$$$$**

✖ **Holiday** Across from mosque; Tables outside in lovely sheltered gardens; grilled meat, pizzas & salads. Also nice for coffee or beer. **$$$**

✖ **Palma** (also known as 2 Palmat) Bd Ismail Qemali. Excellent pizzas, pasta, fish; speciality seafood pizza includes mussels & prawns baked in shells on pizza. Good service, tables outside in large shaded garden; lively atmosphere. **$$$**

✕ Salvadore Rr Pelivan Leskaj; ☏ 408 808; m 069 87 51 441; ⊕ noon–16.00 & 19.00– late. Large restaurant above fish wholesalers; signposted from the corners of Bd Ismail Qemali & Rr Çamëria. Nicely decorated, with 1st-class toilets; English spoken. Superbly fresh fish & seafood; good value. $$$

WHAT TO SEE AND DO

Museum of Independence (*Muzeu Pavarësia; Rr Ismail Qemali, Skela;* ⊕ *09.00–17.00 Tue–Sat; 10.00–14.00 Sun; 100 lek*) When the First Balkan War started in October 1912 (pages 11–12), the Albanians realised that, if they did not obtain independence from the Ottoman Empire, their territory would be swallowed up by their Balkan neighbours. Ismail Qemali (1844–1919), one of 26 Albanians elected to the Ottoman Parliament after the Young Turk revolution of 1908, travelled to Vienna and Budapest to obtain diplomatic support for Albanian independence.

On his return to Durrësi, he found that Serbian troops were approaching the Adriatic, and he made his way across the treacherous marshes (now long since drained) of the Myzeqeja Plain to the relative safety of Vlora. It was thus that on 28 November 1912, Albanian independence was proclaimed in Vlora and Skanderbeg's ancient emblem, the double-headed black eagle, was raised at the spot that is now called Flag Square (Sheshi i Flamurit). Albania's first government, led by Ismail Qemali, set up its headquarters in the only building available, the former quarantine hospital in the port. This modestly sized villa is now the Museum of Independence.

The most interesting thing about the museum, for the majority of non-Albanians, is that several of the rooms have been kept as they were when they were used by those first ministers. Ismail Qemali's chair is still there behind his desk, and his bookcase still has books in it. On the long table in the Cabinet Room is the pen with which official documents were signed, and next to it, the government seal with its double-headed eagle symbol. Photographs of each of the first ministers hang on the wall; there are many other interesting photographs and paintings on display throughout the museum.

Ethnographic Museum (*Rr Ceno Sharra;* m *069 54 36 974;* ⊕ *09.00–16.00 Tue–Sat; 09.00–14.00 Sun; 100 lek*) The Ethnographic Museum in Vlora is located in the house where, in 1908, the Labëria Patriotic Club was set up. Towards the end of the 19th century, after the crushing of the Prizren League, the Albanian nationalist movement switched its focus from political demands to cultural campaigning. 'Patriotic clubs' were set up in towns around Albania and in other Ottoman cities with a significant Albanian population, including Istanbul itself, where it was called the 'Albanian Committee'. The Labëria Patriotic Club was named after the region of which Vlora is the main town. It provided evening classes to people who wanted to learn how to read and write in Albanian, their mother tongue – no fewer than 50 Vloran women registered for these classes, and one of their teachers was Marigo Posio (page 267).

The signs to the museum around the city centre refer to it in English as 'House of Labëria Club'. However, the collection on display mainly consists of ethnographic objects and traditional costumes. The first room on the ground floor contains household items such as wooden milk-churns and copper trays. The room on its left is devoted to agriculture; in addition to examples of agricultural implements, including a tobacco-cutting machine, it has a meticulous scale-model of a farmstead, showing the separate buildings for family and guests, little models of livestock, and even tiny hanks of tobacco drying under the eaves.

The room on the right acknowledges Vlora's role as a fishing town. The centrepiece is a boat carved about 30 years ago from a single tree trunk, an ancient technique that was still in use until very recently. Larger versions of the nets on display are still used – the circular net is cast from the boat over a shoal, and the fishermen move the mast up and down to lure the fish into the centre of the net, so that as many as possible are trapped before they pull it in. The long trap and the multi-pronged fork hung on the walls are used to catch eels in the lagoons of Narta and Pashaliman; the eel trap has two layers of mesh and, as the eel swims in, the pressure of its head tightens the inner layer so that it cannot escape. Of course these ingenious techniques are rather bad news for eels and fish, but they are a lot better than dynamite, which in the 1990s replaced traditional fishing methods along much of the Albanian coast. An annexe on the ground floor has a small but interesting exhibition of Communist-era household items, with everything from paintings to china raki sets.

Upstairs, the 'men's room' of the house was where (male) guests were entertained, and some of the original furniture can be seen there, including a tray for serving raki and a *sofër* – a low, circular dining table – inscribed with the owner's name in the Greek alphabet and the date 1896. Guests sat in order of age on the cushioned seats around the walls; the host sat on the left of the fireplace and his most distant relative sat on its right.

The 'women's room', across the hallway, has some interesting examples of traditional Vloran costumes – as women grew older, they wore darker and darker shades of cloth – and dowry chests. The old tradition was that every bride had an Albanian flag and an embroidery of Skanderbeg (see box, pages 206–7) in her dowry chest, and some of these are exhibited, too. Finally, the 'work-room' has as its centrepiece a genuine loom, with examples of traditional carpets and *qilime* (rugs).

Historical Museum (*Rr Perlat Rexhepi*; ⊕ *09.00–16.00 Tue–Sat; 09.00–14.00 Sun; 100 lek*) Located in what was once Vlora's town hall, the Historical Museum is a good place to find out about the archaeology and history of the whole area.

On the left of the entrance is the museum's collection of Neolithic and Bronze Age artefacts. Maps and photographs on the walls explain the most significant sites for each period. There are finds from the Bronze Age tumulus at Vajza and from the ancient city of Amantia. Amphorae and other items retrieved from recent underwater excavations are also displayed in this room. The city of Vlora has seen little excavation, because it has been continuously inhabited throughout its history, but fragments of Roman artefacts are constantly unearthed whenever a building contractor or utility company digs more than a couple of metres down. Some of these casual finds are displayed in a case near the door.

Across the hallway, the second room has scale-models of traditional houses and of the 12th-century church of Marmiroi (page 271), bells from Venetian clock towers, and inscriptions from mosques, churches and – rare in Albania – a Jewish gravestone inscribed in Hebrew. Vlora's status as a major trading centre meant that it had a large Jewish population during the Ottoman period, but few traces of this thriving community have survived. A lovely, though headless, statue of Artemis/Diana, goddess of the hunt, with her dog by her side, was excavated by Luigi Ugolini, the Italian who led the first excavations of Butrint (pages 231–6). Recent acquisitions have come to the museum from the Vlora family, descendants of wealthy 19th-century landowners whose best-known scion was the politician and writer Eqrem Bey Vlora (1885–1964). When the family was renovating its ancestral property in the city – the beautiful house which can be seen, through its gates, between the Muradie Mosque and the Independence Monument – they donated a number of pieces to the Historical Museum. These include a Roman head of Dionysus and a 19th-century marble carving of a child's head.

Exploring Vlora Like most of Albania, Vlora has experienced a lot of new building in the past 20 years, and viewing the city from above is a good way to make sense of its geography. **Kuzum Baba** was a Bektashi cleric, whose *tyrbe* (tomb) is on the summit of the hill above the Muradie Mosque. Steps from Boulevard Ismail Qemali, across the road from the mosque, lead to a statue of Dede Ahmed Myftar, who was the leader of the world Bektashi community from 1947–80 (see page 22 for more about Bektashism). You can continue from here on foot to the top of the hill, where the Bektashis' regional headquarters is housed, in an attractive yellow and green building set in peaceful gardens. Outside, a paved ramp leads to Kuzum Baba's tyrbe, with a shrine beside it full of lit candles. The large terrace of the restaurant here (or, if you are feeling brave, its roof) offers the best viewpoint, over the whole city and beyond, to Karaburuni, Sazani, Zvërneci and Narta. It is also possible to drive up to the restaurant from the other side of the hill.

The building where the flag was first raised was badly damaged while the city was being bombarded by Greece in December 1912, and it was knocked down in 1932. The area cleared by this demolition has been kept as a large open space and is called Flag Square, or Independence Square. Dominating the square is the Independence Monument, an imposing bronze cast in the Socialist Realist style. Around its base stand various key figures in the independence movement, including Ismail Qemali and the Kosovar hero Isa Boletini; above them, on a rock, a flag-bearer makes ready to hoist the double-headed eagle of Albania. Vlora's football team is called Flamurtari ('the Flag-bearer') in honour of the anonymous patriot who first raised the flag of independence. Beside the monument, near where the demolished house once stood, the Albanian flag flies from a small column. Ismail Qemali himself is buried, beneath a Socialist Realist statue of a warrior, in the park behind this column.

At the southern end of the park is a short stretch of wall, whose foundations may date back to the 4th century AD, with 6th-century additions in brickwork. These ancient fortifications were rebuilt and extended in the 16th century, with eight towers forming an octagon. This refortification was one element of major building work in Vlora ordered by Suleiman I, the Magnificent (Sultan from 1520 to 1566), to secure Ottoman trade to and from the port. Exiting the park by the side street which runs between the Holiday restaurant and the Vlora family's house will bring you to another building project of the same time: the beautifully proportioned Muradie Mosque, with its elegant minaret of carved stone. It is thought to have been designed by the great architect Sinan (1489–1588). He built mosques, bathhouses, bridges and *hans* (inns) throughout the empire, and is considered to be one of the founders of Ottoman architecture. The minimalist decoration within consists of elegant plasterwork fluting and Koranic calligraphy on the ceiling dome.

If you continue down the main road, towards the port, you will pass the theatre. A hundred metres or so further, in a small park (the Park of Hope) on the same side of the street, is an attractive bust of Marigo Posio. She was born in 1878 and brought up in Korça, where she married and became involved in the nationalist movement. She and her husband attracted the attention of the Ottoman authorities, and moved to Vlora to shake them off. When the Labëria Patriotic Club was founded in 1908 (page 265), Marigo Posio taught Albanian literacy at the night school there, under the outward guise of giving embroidery classes. Her real contribution to the art of embroidery, however, was the double-headed eagle on the flag that was raised in Vlora on 28 November 1912 – a painting of her embroidering the Albanian flag hangs at the top of the stairs in the Museum of Independence (page 265). The original flag was handed down by Ismail Qemali to one of his many sons, and is now lost. Marigo Posio died in 1932 and was buried between two olive trees on the island of Zvërneci.

Around Vlora Those with their own transport (including bicycles) will find it easy to explore a little further afield.

Kanina Castle is about 5km from the city centre; neatly paved steps lead up to the castle from the car park. Kanina was the seat of a bishopric in the 12th century and changed hands several times during the slow collapse of the Byzantine Empire (pages 9–10), until it fell to the Ottomans in 1417. It was used as an Italian garrison during World War II and then, in the communist period, it was a surveillance centre for the Albanian air force. On a clear day, there are wonderful views over the city and out to Karaburuni and Sazani in the west; northwards to the Narta Lagoon and Zvërneci; and across the Vjosa River towards the mountains of Mallakastra in the east.

The **Narta Lagoon** is one of a string of brackish lagoons along the Albanian coast; see pages 208–11 for information about birdwatching in these valuable habitats. Narta has been exploited for its salt since Roman times – the salt-works on its eastern side, now operated by an Italian company, are clearly visible from the highway between Vlora and Fieri.

HIKING ON KARABURINI   *With thanks to Eva de Hullu and Joost Smets*

The Karaburuni Peninsula offers a fantastic opportunity to hike in one of the wildest parts of Albania. There are two ways to get to Karaburuni: by sea or on foot. Outside the tourist season, when you could buy drinks and snacks at the pop-up bars on the beaches, you will have to bring all your own food and – more importantly – drinking water with you. This means that the best way to approach the peninsula is by boat, from either Rradhima or Vlora (see page 270 for details). This would make it possible to hike back out within a day, if you do not want to camp there overnight. Otherwise, it might be possible to hire a donkey or mule in Orikumi to carry your supplies. You could also try hiding some bottles of water in the bushes halfway along the peninsula, to collect on your way back.

A dirt track, which looks as if only the sturdiest of military vehicles would survive it, links the Pashaliman base with what remains of **Shëngjini**. Still marked as a village on some maps of Albania, Shëngjini was a military base during the communist period. All the buildings were deliberately demolished, leaving only remnants of walls and a strikingly dense concentration of bunkers of various shapes and sizes. The 'bunker strategy' described in the box on page 144 can be seen clearly here, with large bunkers watching out over the shores dotted with smaller ones. Bunkers that contained heavier weaponry look out over the bay and Sazani. Their inner walls once carried instructions – now roughly painted over – on how to operate the weapons.

Before reaching Shëngjini, you walk through a smaller deserted military post. The pier leading from these barracks into the sea is now a popular picnic spot for Albanians. Around the military buildings are fig trees, perhaps planted by soldiers decades ago – a welcome treat, with their sweet fragrance, in this harsh environment. If you are planning to stay overnight, the ruins of Shëngjini would

At the southern tip of the lagoon is the island of **Zvërneci**, with its church and monastic buildings, which, by tradition, was the last resting place of Vlora's most illustrious sons and daughters – Marigo Posio is one of those buried here. The monastery was once home to a community of Orthodox monks; after 1967, it was used as an internment camp for political prisoners. The buildings have now been restored and a footbridge has been built to link the island with the mainland. Behind the church, steps lead up to the peaceful woods which cover the rest of the island.

To get to Zvërneci from Vlora, leave Skela (the port) by the main road west, through unprepossessing industrial outskirts and then a forest of pines and firs which shelters a long sandy beach. Beyond the forest lies the village of Zvërneci and, about half a mile beyond that, a small car park and the footbridge to the island. There is no public transport to the island; it takes about 2 hours to walk from Skela.

KARABURUNI The northern tip of the Karaburuni Peninsula, Kepi i Gjuhëzës, is where the Adriatic and Ionian seas meet. The peninsula, which closes off the Bay of Vlora to the south, was a closed military zone during the whole of the communist period. There is still no vehicular access; the only ways on to Karaburuni are from the sea or on foot (see box below). In recent years, it has become a popular destination for holidaymakers staying in Vlora and the resorts around the bay; between mid-June and mid-September, several companies run scheduled day trips to the beaches on the eastern shore. 'Pop-up' restaurants operate at these beaches in summer.

be a suitable spot to pitch your tent; just 100m beyond them, alternatively, is a rare field of something vaguely resembling grass – most of Karaburuni is covered with trees or thorn-bushes. There are many butterflies and other insects.

About 30km from Orikumi (it looks shorter on maps, but the road keeps turning in discouraging bends) and 5–6km beyond Shëngjini, the Karaburuni Peninsula reaches its most remote point. The track passes high above Haxhi Aliu's Cave, at sea level; the steep cliffs mean the cave cannot be reached from above. At the cape, artificial caves overlook the narrow strait between Karaburuni and Sazani. Inside, posters explain how to set landmines, how to tell various chemical weapons apart and how to make a built-up area safe following a gas attack. Red-painted quotations by Enver Hoxha still grace the walls. Strange white flowers grow all around, 1.5m high, with huge red bulbs.

As you walk off the peninsula, a few kilometres before the Pashaliman base comes into view, you will come to some fishermen's huts. The fishermen will look perplexed to see somebody approaching from the west, but once they have restrained their dogs they will be glad to fill your empty bottles with water.

It is trickier than it seems to leave Karaburuni without walking into the naval base by mistake. After the fishermen's huts, you come to some military buildings. Beyond these, it looks at first as if you're walking straight into the base; however, this is the correct track for avoiding it. You descend nearly to sea level, past more buildings, and then turn right, slightly uphill, keeping the barbed wire to your left. A bend in the road will lead you slightly above the military base and around Pashaliman Lagoon. The detour around the lagoon adds at least 5km to the walk, but it is far quicker in the long run than being arrested and interrogated for trespassing on the base.

The day trips leave from the port in Vlora and from the harbour at Rradhima. The travel agencies in Vlora can book them for you (page 263), or you can pay on the day. They leave Vlora port (Skela) at 10.00 and return around 18.00, charging 2,000 lek per person. The boats from Rradhima are smaller and do not have formal schedules – just turn up at the harbour around 09.00 and ask around.

As well as the peninsula, the boat trips usually give passengers a chance to see Sazani island, which is still a military base but may be opened up to visitors during the lifetime of this guidebook. On Karaburuni itself, they take you into the **Cave of Haxhi Aliu,** the longest sea cave in Albania. Haxhi Aliu was an 18th-century pirate from Ulqini (now in Montenegro) and this cave, 100m long and with an internal lake, was one of his hideouts.

Another cave, at **Grama**, on the western (Ionian) shore of the peninsula, was used during World War II as a base by the southern mission of SOE (Special Operations Executive; see boxes, pages 13–15). Code-named 'Sea Elephant', it was chosen not only for its extreme remoteness, but also because it was larger (and, one hopes, had fewer lice and scorpions) than the mission's previous base on the peninsula, code-named 'Seaview'. The cliff face at Grama has thousands of inscriptions, carved into it over the centuries by passing sailors, soldiers and merchants – the earliest are said to date from the 3rd century BC. There is a tiny beach, ringed by cliffs, where some of the day trips take passengers.

It is possible to **kayak** from Orikumi or Rradhima to Karaburuni, but the currents are strong and the winds unpredictable. Only experienced sea kayakers should contemplate this option. Outdoor Albania (page 29) can give advice and arrange kayak hire if required.

For those wishing to **hike** in the wilderness of Karaburuni, accessing the peninsula from the sea is a much easier option than on foot: hiking in from Orikumi means a lengthy detour around the Pashaliman Lagoon to avoid the naval base (see box, pages 268–9). Alternative routes follow in the footsteps of the SOE agents over the mountains of Llogoraja (pages 259–60), but the paths are difficult and unclear; they should not be attempted without an experienced local guide. Going in and out by boat would also solve the problem of carrying sufficient water – there are no springs on the peninsula itself – because you could bring some in on the boat and replenish your stocks as required at one of the beachside restaurants.

ORIKUMI   *Telephone code: 0391*

The old road, soon to be replaced for most purposes by the Vlora Bypass, hugs the Bay of Vlora, with the Karaburuni Peninsula and the island of Sazani, 9km offshore, closing the bay off to the west. A string of hotels lines the coast; almost every little cove has its own hotel. Rradhima has several good restaurants, offering fish and traditional southern Albanian dishes, as well as a little harbour from where day trips depart for Karaburuni (see above). The village of Tragjasi, with its well-appointed **Grand Hotel** [map, pages 224–5] (*21 rooms;* \ *0391 22039;* m *068 20 35 447, 069 64 34 802;* f *Grand Hotel Tragjasi;* **$$$$**), sits in the hills above the southern end of the bay, about 3km from the junction with the main road. This is Tragjasi i Ri ('New Tragjasi'), built to replace the old village that was burned to the ground by German troops in 1944, to punish the villagers for the presence of an SOE mission there. Just beyond the turn-off for Tragjasi, 18km from Vlora, is the small resort town of Orikumi, with its long pebble beach. Minibuses run frequently between Vlora and Orikumi until early afternoon – later in the summer. The journey takes about half an hour and the fare is 100 lek. Veip Isaraj's restaurant in Orikumi serves good fish and generous salads (**$$$**).

What to see and do Just outside Orikumi, where the Karaburuni Peninsula begins to curl up to the north, the church of **Marmiroi** perches on a hillock amid the marshes. This 13th-century church has three lovely frescoes: a Virgin with Child, John the Evangelist and (somewhat restored) St Michael. Its high cupola can be seen from far off, but it is a little tricky to get to because of the reed beds that surround it. There is a footpath from the edge of town – cross the irrigation canal and follow the path around the reed beds until you come to a solid path through the reeds. Alternatively, a rough vehicle track leads off from the beachfront just before the entrance to the naval base; it does not go all the way to the church, so you will need to find your own way around the reed beds to the solid path.

Within the naval base is the archaeological site of **Oricum**. This ancient city was founded in the 6th century BC by colonists from the Greek island of Euboea. It developed into an important trading post thanks to its geographical position and excellent harbour, protected by the peninsula that the Greeks called Acroceraunia, 'the thunder-riven heights', and the Ottomans named Karaburun, 'the black cape'. By the 3rd century BC, Oricum was minting its own coins and building a theatre for the entertainment of its citizens. Philip V of Macedon occupied it for a while during the First Macedonian War (214–205BC); later, during the Roman Civil War, it quickly surrendered to Julius Caesar after he landed with his troops at Palasa, on the other side of the Llogoraja Pass (pages 259–60).

The original theatre was replaced in the 1st century AD, but its Hellenistic layout was retained and some of the stones were re-used. This is the little theatre that can be seen today, whose capacity would have been around 400 spectators. Stone staircases led down to it from the acropolis, with shops and houses on either side of the steps. A beautiful flight of 27 steps, complete with a drainage channel carved into the rock on one side of the flight, has been excavated near the theatre; there are ten similar staircases around the city, running parallel to each other. Another can be seen near the entrance to the site, the so-called 'Western Staircase' (Shkalla Perendimore; signposted). Three deep wells have also been discovered, but there is no longer any water in them. The sea has advanced and retreated over the centuries and much of the ancient city is under the waters of the lagoon. This is what the Ottomans called Pashaliman, 'the Pasha's harbour', and the lagoon still bears this name, as does the Albanian navy base within which Oricum is located.

Although it is in a military area, the archaeological site is open to the public (*200 lek*). Technically, visitors should request an entry permit in advance from the Regional Directorate of National Culture in Vlora (**m** *069 75 70 368;* **e** *drkkvlore@ yahoo.com*). In practice, however, it is usually possible for individual visitors to persuade the guards on the gate to allow access. You must travel in a vehicle, not on foot, and be accompanied; one of the guides is usually at (or near) the entrance gate to the base from about 09.00 until about lunchtime on weekdays. Not all the guides have their own cars; if necessary, they will arrange a taxi.

The Southwest VLORA

8

Appendix 1

LANGUAGE

THE ALPHABET Although the Albanian alphabet has a large number of letters (36), each consonant is always pronounced in exactly the same way, whatever its position within a word. A few of them do not have exact equivalents in English and, for these cases, approximations are given in the list below. Vowels can be long or short but, with one exception, they are very easy to pronounce.

The only vowel which might cause difficulty is ë, which represents the sound which philologists call '*schwa*'. It is the vowel sound a native English-speaker makes in the second syllable of the word 'understand'; a native French-speaker makes the same sound in the first word of '*je comprends*'. For speakers of Slavic languages, it is like a vocalic 'r' without the 'r' sound (like the semivowel in the Serbo-Croat word '*trg*'). There are two problems with ë. One is that at the end of a word it is scarcely pronounced at all, but it can affect the length of the vowel in the previous syllable. The other is that, unlike most Indo-European languages, the *schwa* in Albanian can be stressed; this is hard for non-native-speakers to get right, because we are used to *schwas* snuggling in between consonants without anybody noticing they are there.

Fortunately, it is so unusual for any foreigner to be able to string together more than a few Albanian words that any slight mispronunciation of ë or anything else is invariably overlooked in the torrent of congratulations.

PRONUNCIATION

A as in cut or cart
B as in big
C as the 'zz' in pizza
Ç as in church
D as in dog
Dh the 'th' in that
E as in get or as in say
Ë as in 'the' in 'the cat sat on the mat'
G as in gold (always hard)
Gj – the 'du' in 'endure' is an approximation
I as in hit or meet
J the 'y' in year (not jam)
K as in kite
L as in log
Ll – a double 'l' sound, a bit like a Russian or Serbo-Croat 'dark' L
M as in mat
N as in not

Nj the 'ni' in union
O as in hot or thought
P as in pat
Q – the 'tu' in 'mature' is an approximation
R as in road
Rr – a trilled double 'r'
S as in sun
Sh as in shine
T as in tin
Th as in thick
U as in bush or moon
V as in vote
X the 'ds' in kids
Xh as in judge
Y – the French sound in 'tu' or the German 'ü' as in 'dünn'
Z as in zoo
Zh – the 's' in pleasure

DEFINITE AND INDEFINITE ARTICLES In Albanian, the definite article ('the' in English) does not (normally) go before the word it defines but is suffixed to it. Thus, 'the Boulevard' is '*Bulevardi*', while any old 'boulevard' is '*bulevard*'. This feature is not unique to Albanian – it is found, for example, in Swedish and Romanian. Different prepositions, as well as taking different cases of the noun, also require either the definite or the indefinite form. This is not something which the visitor need worry about unduly, except to be aware that the rules apply to place names as well as to every other noun.

When they are speaking English or another foreign language, Albanians tend to use the definite form of place names – that is, they will refer to 'Gjirokastra' rather than 'Gjirokastër', and 'Kukësi' rather than 'Kukës'. When they speak Albanian, of course, they use whichever form of the word is grammatically appropriate, but most other languages do not have the grammatical framework which allows them to do that. This book therefore uses the definite form of all place names except for Butrint, which is so consistently called this in every English-language publication that it would be confusing to refer to it here as 'Butrinti'.

However, on road signs, bus signs, railway timetables and the like, the destination will always appear in the indefinite form. This is because it is invisibly governed by the preposition *në*, meaning 'to' or 'in', which must be followed by the indefinite. So, for example, the buses run *nga Tirana në Durrës* ('from Tirana to Durrësi') and then return *nga Durrësi në Tiranë* ('from Durrësi to Tirana'). All Albanian-produced maps, and most foreign-produced ones, too, consistently use the indefinite form. In many cases the difference is quite small and it is easy to tell which place is meant. Some which are not so obvious are listed at the end of this Appendix.

PHRASEBOOKS AND LANGUAGE COURSES The best phrasebook available commercially outside Albania is the *Albanian–English, English–Albanian Dictionary & Phrasebook*, by Ramazan Hysa, published in 2000 by Hippocrene Books.

Albanian grammar is difficult, and moving beyond simple phrases requires serious study. *Colloquial Albanian*, by Isa Zymberi, is the best book that is readily available in the UK and North America, although its idiom tends towards the Kosovar. It can be purchased with or without the accompanying CD (which is even more Kosovar). Other language course books can be purchased in Tirana.

WORDS AND PHRASES
Essentials

Good morning	*Mirëmengjesi* (until about 11.00)
Good afternoon	*Mirëdita* (until about 16.00 or 17.00)
Good evening	*Mirëmbrëma*
Good night	*Natën e mire* (when leaving people at the end of the evening)
Hello	*Përshëndetje*
Goodbye	*Mirupafshim*
What is your name?	*Si e keni emrin?*
My name is …	*Emri im është …*
Where are you from?	*Nga jeni?*
I am from …	*Jam nga …* [see town and country names in the next section, and use the definite form]
How are you?	*Si jeni?*
Pleased to meet you	*Gëzohem*
Thank you	*Faleminderit*
Please	*Ju lutem*
Don't mention it	*S'ka gjë*

A1

Excuse me	Me falni
Cheers!	Gëzuar!
Yes	Po
No	Jo
I am looking for …	Po kërkoj …
I don't understand	S'kuptoj
Slowly, please!	Avash, ju lutem!
Do you understand me?	A me kuptoni?

Questions

how?	si?	when?	kur?
what [is …]?	çfarë [është …]?	why?	pse?
where?	ku?	who?	kush?
which?	i cili/e cila?	how much?	sa?

Numbers

1	një	11	njëmbëdhjetë
2	dy	12	dymbëdhjetë
3	tre	13	trembëdhjetë [etc]
4	katër	20	njëzet
5	pesë	21	njëzetenjë
6	gjashtë	30	tridhjetë
7	shtatë	40	dyzet
8	tetë	50	pesëdhjetë
9	nëntë	100	(një) qind
10	dhjetë	1,000	(një) mijë

Time

What time is it?	Sa është ora?
It's …	Ora është …
am/pm	paraditës/mbasditës
today	sot
tomorrow	nesër
yesterday	dje
(the) morning	mëngjesi
(the) evening	darka

Days of the week

Monday	e hënë	Friday	e premtë
Tuesday	e martë	Saturday	e shtunë
Wednesday	e merkurë	Sunday	e dielë
Thursday	e enjtë		

Months of the year

January	Janar	July	Korrik
February	Shkurt	August	Gusht
March	Mars	September	Shtator
April	Prill	October	Tetor
May	Maj	November	Nëntor
June	Qershor	December	Dhjetor

Getting around
Public transport

Ticket (single/return)	*biletë (vajtja/vajtja e ardhja)*
I want to go to …	*Dua të shkoj në …* [and use indefinite form]
How much is the ticket?	*Sa kushton bileta?*
What time does it leave?	*Në çfarë orë niset?*
What time is it (now)?	*Sa është ora?*

from	*nga*	plane	*avion*
to	*në*	ferry	*traget*
bus station	*agjencia (e udhëtarëve)*	car	*makinë*
railway station	*stacioni i trenit*	taxi	*taksi*
airport	*aeroporti*	arrival	*mbërritja*
port	*porti, skela*	departure	*nisja*
bus	*autobus*	here	*këtu*
minibus	*furgon* or *kombi*	there	*atje*
train	*tren*	Bon voyage!	*Rrugë të mbarë!*

Self-drive

Is this the way to … ?	*Kjo është rruga për në …* [and then use indefinite form]?
Where is there a petrol station?	*Ku ka pikë karburanti?*
Please fill up the tank	*Të lutem mbushe plot serbatorin*
I'd like … litres	*Do desha … litra*
diesel	*naftë*
leaded petrol	*benzinë me plumb*
unleaded petrol	*benzinë pa plumb*
I have broken down	*kam pësuar defekt*

Road signs

Give way	*Jep përparësinë*	Exit	*Dalje*
Danger	*Rrezik*	Detour	*Rrugë e tërthortë*
Entry	*Hyrje*	One way	*Rrugë një kalimshe*
No entry	*Nuk lejohet hyrja*	Keep clear	*Mos zij rrugën*

Directions

Where is … ?	*Ku është … ?*	north/south	*veri/jug*
	[then use definite form]?	east/west	*lindje/perëndim*
straight on	*drejt*	opposite	*përballë*
left	*majtas*	behind	*prapa*
right	*djathtas*	in front of	*para*
… at the traffic lights	*… në semaforë*	near	*afër*
… at the roundabout	*… në rrumbullakë*		

Signs

Entrance	*Hyrja*
Exit	*Dalja*
Open	*Hapur*
Closed	*Mbyllur*
Ladies (toilet)	*Gra(të)*
Gents (toilet)	*Burra(t)*
Information	*Informacion*

Accommodation

Where is the XX hotel?	*Ku gjendet hoteli XX?*
Please show it to me on the map	*Ju lutem ma tregoni në hartë*
Do you have a ... room?	*A keni një dhomë ...?*
... single ... (room)	*... teke*
... twin ...	*... dyshe*
... triple ...	*... treshe*
... double ...	*... dopio/matrimonial*
... with an ensuite bathroom?	*... me banjë brenda?*
How much per night?/per person?	*Sa kushton nata?/veta?*
Where is the bathroom?	*Ku është banjo?*
Is there water?	*A ka uji?*
Is there electricity?	*A ka drita?*
Is breakfast included?	*E përfshihet mëngjesi?*
I'm leaving today	*Sot largohem*

Food

Do you have a table for X people?	*A keni tavolinë për X veta?*
I don't eat meat	*Nuk ha mish*
I don't eat fish	*Nuk ha peshk*
I don't eat dairy products	*Nuk ha bulmet*
[Please] bring me a ...	*me sillni një ...*
fork	*pirun*
knife	*thikë*
spoon	*lugë*
May I have the bill?	*Më bëni llogarinë?*

bread	*bukë*	meat	*mish*
butter	*gjalpë*	lamb	*... qengji*
cheese	*djathë*	veal	*... viçi*
olive oil	*vaj ulliri*	pork	*... derri*
pepper (ground)	*piper*	suckling pig	*... gici*
salt	*kripë*	kid	*... keci*
sugar	*sheqer*	chicken	*... pulë*
ice cream	*akullorë*		

Drinks

water	*uji*	tea	*çaj*
still mineral water	*uji mineral pa gaz*	coffee	*kafe*
sparkling water	*uji me gaz*	espresso	*kafe ekspres*
ice	*akull*	Turkish coffee	*kafe turke*
milk	*qumësht*	beer	*birrë*
fruit juice	*lëng frutash*	wine	*verë*

Shopping

I'd like to buy it	*Dua ta blejë*
How much is it?	*Sa kushton?*
I don't like it	*Nuk me pëlqen*
I'm only looking	*Po shikoj*
It's too/very expensive	*është shumë e shtrenjtë/ është shumë i shtrenjtë*
It's cheap	*është i lirë/është e lirë*

I'll take it	*Do ta merr*
I'd like more	*Dua më shumë*
I'd like less	*Dua më pak*
I'd like a smaller one	*Dua një më të vogël*
I'd like a bigger one	*Dua një më të madh*

Where is ... ? / *Ku është ... ?*

... the bank	*... banka*
... the post office	*... posta*
... the church	*... kisha*
... the mosque	*... xhamia*
... the embassy	*... ambasada*
... the exchange office	*... zyra këmbimi*
... the telephone centre	*... Telekomi*
... the museum	*... muzeu*
... the archaeological museum	*... muzeu arkeologjik*
... the ethnographic museum	*... muzeu etnografik*
... the historical museum	*... muzeu historik*
... the art gallery	*... galeria e arteve*
... the castle/fortress	*... kalaja*

Emergencies

A&E clinic	*Urgjenca*
Please help me	*Ju lutem më ndihmoni*
Call a doctor	*Thërrohuni mjekun*
There's been an accident	*Ka pasur një fatkeqësi*
I'm lost	*Jam e/i humbur*
Go away!	*Iku!* (although the author's experience is that the annoying person is more likely to go away if s/he is addressed in a language which is not Albanian)
police	*polici(a)*
policeman	*polic(i)*
fire brigade	*zjarrfikësit*
ambulance	*autoambulancë*
thief	*hajdut*
hospital	*spital*
I am ill	*Jam i sëmurë* (if the speaker is male); *Jam e sëmurë* (if the speaker is female)

Health

diarrhoea	*diarrea*	asthma	*astmë*
nausea	*krupa*	epilepsy	*sëmundja e tokës/ sëmundja e hënës*
(a) doctor	*mjek*		
(a) prescription	*recetë*	diabetes	*sëmundja e sheqerit*
(a) pharmacy	*farmaci*	I'm allergic	*Jam alergjik*
painkiller	*analgjesik*	... to penicillin	*... penicilinës*
antibiotic	*antibiotik*	... to peanuts	*... kikirikesh*
antiseptic	*antiseptik*	... to bee-stings	*... thumbëve bletësh*
condom	*prezervativ*		
contraceptive	*mjet kontraceptiv*		
suntan lotion	*krem dielli*		

Other

I want to make a phone call	*Dua të bëj një telefonatë*
I do not understand	*Nuk kuptoj*
I do not speak Albanian	*Nuk flas shqip*
Do you speak English?	*A flisni anglisht?*
... French?	*... frengjisht?*
... Italian?	*... italisht?*
... Russian?	*... rusisht?*
OK	*Në rregull*
Of course	*Patjetër*

Adjectives (all in singular indefinite form)

beautiful	*i/e bukur*	hot	*i/e ngrohtë*
old	*i/e vjetër*	cold	*i/e ftohtë*
new	*e re/i ri*	difficult	*i/e vështirë*
good	*i/e mirë*	easy	*i/e lehtë*
bad	*i/e keq*	far	*larg*
early (in the day)	*herët*	near	*afër*
late (in the day)	*vonë*		

SOME PLACE NAMES IN ALBANIA

Definite	Indefinite	Italian	Greek (transliterated)
Shqipëria	**Në Shqipëri**	**Albania**	**Alvania**
Dhërmiu	Dhërmi		Dhrimadhes
Dibra	Dibër		
Durrësi	Durrës	Durazzo	Dhirrachion
Gjirokastra	Gjirokastër		Argirokastron
Himara	Himarë		Cheimarra or Chimara
Korça	Korçë		Koritsa
Ksamili	Ksamil		Eksamilion
Lezha	Lezhë	Alessio	
Llixhat	Llixhe		
Llogoraja	Llogara		
Saranda	Sarandë	Santi Quaranta	Agii Saranda
Shëngjini	Shëngjin	San Giovanni	
Shkodra	Shkodër	Scutari	
Tirana	Tiranë	Tirana	Tirana
Vlora	Vlorë	Valona	Avlona

SOME PLACE NAMES IN GREECE

Definite	Indefinite	English	Greek (transliterated)
Greqia	**(Në) Greqi**	**Greece**	**Ellas**
Athina	Athinë	Athens	Athina
Janina	Janinë	Ioannina	Ioannina
Korfuzi	Korfuz	Corfu	Kerkira
Kosturi	Kostur	Kastoria	Kastoria
Selaniku	Selanik	Thessalonica or Salonica	Thessaloniki

SOME OTHER USEFUL PLACE NAMES
English
Europe

England
Great Britain
Edinburgh
Ireland
Northern Ireland
London
United Kingdom
Republic of Ireland
Scotland
Wales

Albanian
Evropa

Anglia
Britania e Madhe
Edimburgu
Irlanda
Irlanda e Veriut
Londra
Mbretëria e Bashkuar
Republika e Irlandës
Skocia
Uellsi

The World

Australia
Canada
New York
Istanbul
Skopje
USA
New Zealand

Bota

Australia
Kanadaja
Njujorku
Stambolli
Shkupi
Shtetet e Bashkuara të Amerikës
Zelanda e Re

SEND US YOUR SNAPS!

We'd love to follow your adventures using our *Albania* guide – why not send us your photos and stories via Twitter (🐦 *@BradtGuides*) and Instagram (📷 *@bradtguides*) using the hashtag #Albania. Alternatively, you can upload your photos directly to the gallery on the Albania destination page via our website (w *bradtguides.com/albania*).

Appendix 2

FURTHER INFORMATION

BOOKS London company I B Tauris is the most significant publisher of works about Albania in English. It is worth checking their website (**W** *ibtauris.com*) from time to time to see if they have published anything new which interests you.

General history

Ceka, Neritan *The Illyrians to the Albanians* Migjeni, 2005. An authoritative and fascinating account of the ancient history of this ancient land.

Crampton, R J *The Balkans Since the Second World War* Longman, 2002. A readable introduction to a complicated area and a complicated history, covering Albania, Bulgaria, Romania and Yugoslavia, as well as Greece.

Durham, Edith *Burden of the Balkans*, 1905; available from various print-on-demand publishers. The history of the Balkans through Edith Durham's rather partisan eyes; at least you know which side she's on!

Durham, Edith *Twenty Years of Balkan Tangle* George Allen & Unwin, 1920; available from various print-on-demand publishers. Edith Durham's account of the historical developments in the Balkans during the disintegration of the Ottoman Empire, many of which she witnessed or even participated in.

Imber, Colin *The Ottoman Empire 1300–1650* Palgrave Macmillan, 2002. An excellent general history of the rise of the Ottoman Empire, with interesting chapters on its administration and military structure.

Malcolm, Noel *Kosovo: A Short History* Macmillan, 1998. Explains the later Ottoman period better than anyone else; also good on the political aspects of the Albanian nationalist movement.

Norwich, John Julius *Byzantium: The Decline & Fall* Penguin, 1996. The third and final instalment of Lord Norwich's accessible and reliable history of the Byzantine Empire, covering the confusing period when most of Albania changed hands several times. The family trees are invaluable; the bibliography is good, too.

Pettifer, James *The Kosova Liberation Army* Hurst & Co., 2012. A history of the KLA from 1948 to 2001, written by a defence specialist and Balkans expert. Mostly about Kosova, obviously, but also gives fascinating insights into Albanian military theory and the fevered atmosphere of Tirana in 1998–2000.

Vickers, Miranda *The Albanians: A Modern History* I B Tauris, reprinted 2001. Detailed, reliably researched and well written. An excellent guide to Albania's complicated history in the 20th century, and an indispensable companion for anyone trying to understand why Albania is the way it is now.

Vickers, Miranda and Pettifer, James *Albania: From Anarchy to a Modern Identity* Hurst & Co, 2nd edition, 1999. Good account of the transitional period from the late 1980s to 1996.

Vickers, Miranda and Pettifer, James *The Albanian Question: Reshaping the Balkans* I B Tauris, 2007. A carefully researched and riveting account of the last decades' events in the Albanian-speaking lands, including the pyramid-scheme riots in 1997 and the attempted coup in 1998, as well as the Kosova War and refugee crisis.

Winnifrith, T J *Badlands – Borderlands* Gerald Duckworth & Co, 2002 (out of print). Disentangles the confusing history and complicated heritage of southern Albania.

Winnifrith, T J *Tribes & Brigands in the Balkans*, I B Tauris, 2012. The first comprehensive history of northern Albania; unfortunately already out of print.

World War II

Bailey, Roderick *Smoke without Fire? Albania, SOE & the Communist Conspiracy Theory* in S Schwandner-Sievers and B Fischer (eds) *Albanian Identities: Myth, Narrative and Politics* Hurst & Co (New York), 2002

Bailey, Roderick *The Wildest Province: SOE in the Land of the Eagle* Jonathan Cape, 2008. The definitive account of what SOE did in Albania, based on recently declassified records and interviews with survivors.

Bethell, Nicholas *Betrayed* Random House, 1985. An account of the British and US attempts to infiltrate saboteurs into Albania between 1949 and 1953.

Fischer, Bernd J *Albania at War 1939–1945* Hurst & Co, 1999. The only modern academic history of Albania from the Italian invasion of 1939 to the end of World War II.

Foot, M R D *SOE: The Special Operations Executive 1940–46* Greenwood Press, 1984. Includes SOE's work in Albania.

Mangerich, Agnes Jensen, with Rosemary L Neidel and Evelyn M Monahan *Albanian Escape: The True Story of US Army Nurses Behind Enemy Lines* University Press of Kentucky, 2006. A stranded American nurse's account of occupied Albania.

Shehu, Mehmet *La Bataille pour la Libération de Tirana* Editions Naim Frashëri (Tirana). Detailed account of the Battle for the Liberation of Tirana in 1944, written by one of the participants. Hard to obtain, may be available in the UK through inter-library loan.

Memoirs by SOE agents See boxes, pages 13–15.

Amery, Julian *Approach March: A Venture in Autobiography* Hutchinson, 1973

Amery, Julian *Sons of the Eagle: A Study in Guerilla War* Macmillan, 1948

Davies, Edmund F *Illyrian Adventure: The Story of the British Military Mission in Enemy-Occupied Albania* Bodley Head, 1952

Glen, Alexander *Footholds Against a Whirlwind* Hutchinson, 1975

Hibbert, Reginald *Albania's National Liberation Struggle: The Bitter Victory* Pinter, 1991

Kemp, Peter *No Colours, No Crest* Cassell, 1958

Kemp, Peter *The Thorns of Memory* Sinclair-Stevenson, 1990

Oakley-Hill, D R *An Englishman in Albania* I B Tauris, 2004

Smiley, David *Albanian Assignment* Chatto & Windus, 1984

Historical background

Achtermeier, William O *The Turkish Connection: The Saga of the Peabody-Martini Rifle* in *Man at Arms Magazine* Vol 1, No 2, 1979

Dumas, Alexandre (père) *Ali-Pacha* in *Causes Célèbres* Veuve Dondey-Dupré, 1840. Romanticised but fun version of Ali Pasha Tepelena's career. Available as an ebook in English translation for Kindle (**w** *amazon.co.uk*). The French original has been digitised by Google.

Durham, Edith *Albania & the Albanians* I B Tauris, 2004. An edition, by Bejtullah Destani, of Edith Durham's articles and letters, most of them unavailable for over 60 years. A fascinating historical document.

Fleming, K E *The Muslim Bonaparte: Diplomacy & Orientalism in Ali Pasha's Greece* Princeton University Press, 1999. Critical biography of Ali Pasha Tepelena. Can be ordered through the publisher's website (**w** *pup.princeton.edu*).

A2

Lubonja, Fatos *Second Sentence: Inside the Albanian Gulag* I B Tauris, 2009. A memoir of life as a prisoner in the forced labour camp of Spaçi (pages 160–1). Harrowing but essential reading.

Pettifer, James (ed) *Albania and the Balkans* Elbow Publishing, 2013. Essays in honour of Sir Reginald Hibbert, the SOE agent and (later) diplomat. Ambitious in scope, will have something to interest almost everyone.

Rees, Neil *A Royal Exile* Studge Publications, 2010. Published to mark the 70th anniversary of the exiled King Zog's arrival in England. Oral and archive history of the 'royal' family's six-year stay in the Thames Valley and Chilterns.

Tomes, Jason *King Zog* Sutton Publishing, 2003. Biography of Ahmet Zogu, who crowned himself King of the Albanians in 1928. Power struggles, intrigues, pistol fights and assassinations.

Cultural background

Allcock, John and Young, Antonia *Black Lambs & Grey Falcons* Berghahn Books, 2000. A collection of essays about women travellers in the Balkans, including Edith Durham, Margaret Hasluck and Rose Wilder Lane.

De Waal, Clarissa *Albania: Portrait of a Country in Transition* I B Tauris, 2013. A wealth of information and unique observation drawn from the author's anthropological fieldwork in rural Albania since the 1990s.

Hasluck, Margaret, edited by Robert Elsie *The Hasluck Collection of Albanian Folktales* CreateSpace Independent Publishing Platform, 2015. Some 115 folktales collected and translated into English by Hasluck and her friend Lef Nosi (see box, pages 116–17).

Hasluck, Margaret *The Unwritten Law in Albania* Cambridge University Press, 2015. Hasluck's posthumous masterwork, a comprehensive study of the legal system among the mountain clans, including blood feud (see box, pages 192–3). Engagingly written, with many insights into daily life in the Albanian mountains.

Kadare, Ismail. Almost anything by this great Albanian writer gives an insight into the culture and history of the country. *Broken April* and *Chronicle in Stone* are especially illuminating on the north and on Gjirokastra, respectively. His novel *The Successor* is a fictionalised account of the mysterious death of Mehmet Shehu, and is worth reading for that reason although it is not one of his best works. It and some of his other novels, translated into English from the French versions, are published by Canongate. Affordable paperbacks of the Albanian–French translations are published in the *Livre de Poche* series.

Kanun of Lekë Dukagjin. It is difficult to find good translations of the *Kanun*. The best is a parallel edition, with Albanian on one page and the English version opposite, published in the US by Gjonlekaj Publishing Co (1989). The International Bookshop in Tirana's Skanderbeg Square stocks it, but outside Albania it is hard to obtain.

Various authors *Albania: A Patrimony of European Values* Tirana, 2001. A useful overview of aspects of Albanian culture such as literature, fine art and music. On sale in Tirana bookshops.

Young, Antonia *Albania: World Bibliographical Series* ABC-Clio, 1997. A bibliographic guide to cultural and historical aspects of Albania. Out of print, but may be available in reference libraries.

Young, Antonia *Women Who Become Men* Berghahn Books, 2000. Interviews with some of northern Albania's 'sworn virgins', a fascinating insight into this dying tradition.

Zymberi, Isa *Colloquial Albanian* Routledge, 1991. Language course which gives a thorough grounding in Albanian grammar.

Travel writing

Carver, Robert *The Accursed Mountains* Flamingo, 1999. Sensationalist and negative account of travelling in Albania and meeting Albanians, none of whom the author appears to like. Albania was not like this in 1996, when he was there, and it is not like this now.

Cusack, Dymphna *Illyria Reborn* William Heinemann Ltd, 1966. An uncritical but fascinating glimpse of communist Albania before the atheism campaign – she hears church bells ringing and *muezzins* calling the faithful to prayer, and describes Tirana as being full of minarets. Her encounters with ordinary Albanians are described in a delightfully positive light.

Durham, Edith *High Albania* Edward Arnold, 1909; available from various print-on-demand publishers. Classic and enthralling account of travels in northern Albania in the early 20th century.

Hanbury-Tenison, Robin *Land of Eagles: Riding Through Europe's Forgotten Country* I B Tauris, 2014. An account of the journey on horseback by the author and his wife, from the far north to the far south of Albania, peppered with adventure and mishap, discovery and unexpected encounters.

Lane, Rose Wilder and Dore Boylston, Helen *Travels with Zenobia: Paris to Albania by Model T Ford* University of Missouri Press, 1983 (out of print). The authors – one the daughter of Laura Ingalls Wilder, the other the creator of the Sue Barton novels – drove across Europe to Albania in 1926.

Lear, Edward *Edward Lear in Albania – Journals of a Landscape Painter in the Balkans* I B Tauris, 2008. Lear, famous for his nonsense poetry, was a professional artist, who visited Albania in 1848 and 1857, and made a large number of drawings and watercolours of Butrint, Berati and elsewhere. This welcome reissue of his detailed and humorous journal of his 1848 trip is illustrated with some of his own sketches and paintings.

Ward, Philip *Albania* Oleander Press, 1983 (out of print). A rare record of a visit to communist Albania.

Guidebooks

Ceka, Neritan *Apollonia: History & Monuments* Migjeni, 2001. Scholarly guide to the archaeology and history of Apollonia, an invaluable companion to the site. On sale in Tirana and in Albanian museum bookshops.

Ceka, Neritan *Buthrotum: History & Monuments* Migjeni, 2006. Scholarly guide to the archaeology of Butrint. On sale in Tirana and in Albanian museum bookshops.

Ceka, Neritan and Muçaj, Skënder *Byllis: History & Monuments* Migjeni, 2004. Scholarly guide to the history and buildings of Byllis; has photographs of the Byllis mosaics, usually kept covered. On sale in Tirana and in Albanian museum bookshops.

Gilkes, Oliver *Albania: An Archaeological Guide* I B Tauris, 2012. Detailed notes on archaeological sites, large and small, throughout Albania, especially strong on the southwest of the country. Includes many site plans and very useful advice on access.

Gilkes, Oliver et al *Gjirokastra: the essential guide* Gjirokastra Conservation and Development Organization, 2009. A pocket guide to the city of Gjirokastra and the surrounding region. Small but full of information about the places to visit, some with site plans, and illustrated with modern and historic photographs.

Hansen, Inge Lyse (series editor) *Hellenistic Butrint*, *The Butrint Baptistery and its Mosaics*, *The Rise and Fall of Byzantine Butrint* and *Venetian Butrint* Butrint Foundation, 2007–2009. An indispensable series of archaeological guides to the whole of the Butrint site, in English and Albanian. Scholarly and beautifully illustrated.

Other Balkan country guidebooks For a full list of Bradt's Balkan country and other Europe guides, visit **w** bradtguides.com/shop.

Abraham, Rudolf and Evans, Thammy *Croatia: Istria, with Rijeka and the Slovenian Adriatic* (2nd edition) Bradt Travel Guides, 2017

Bostock, Andrew *Greece: The Peloponnese, with Athens, Delphi and Kythira* (3rd edition) Bradt Travel Guides, 2016

Clancy, Tim *Bosnia & Herzegovina* (5th edition) Bradt Travel Guides, 2017

Clancy, Tim *Via Dinarica: Hiking the White Trail in Bosnia & Herzegovina* Bradt Travel Guides, 2018

Evans, Thammy *Macedonia* (5th edition) Bradt Travel Guides, 2015

Knaus, Verena and Warrander, Gail *Kosovo* (3rd edition) Bradt Travel Guides, 2017

Letcher, Piers with Abraham, Rudolf *Croatia* (6th edition) Bradt Travel Guides, 2016

Mitchell, Laurence *Serbia* (5th edition) Bradt Travel Guides, 2017

Rellie, Annalisa *Montenegro* (5th edition) Bradt Travel Guides, 2015

WEBSITES
Travel information

W **punetejashtme.gov.al** The website of the Albanian Ministry of Foreign Affairs has information (in English) about entering Albania, the contact details for Albanian embassies throughout the world, and information about the Ministry's activities.

W **tirana-airport.com** The official website of Tirana International Airport, hosting a wealth of useful information, including a full list, with contact details, of airlines that operate scheduled flights into Tirana, information about onward travel, and real-time arrivals and departures.

Tourist information

W **albania-holidays.com** Offers tours throughout the country, city tours of Tirana and bespoke arrangements. Hotel reservations can be made through its sister website W **albania-hotel.com**.

W **albaniantourism.com** The Albanian Ministry of Tourism's website has information about archaeological and historical sites, cultural events and museums. Also contact information for selected hotels across the country, though these cannot be booked through the site.

W **hostelworld.com** Reservation site for several Albanian hotels as well as hostels.

W **outdooralbania.com** Outdoor Albania specialises in tours to the Albanian outdoors. Offers a range of hiking tours in the Albanian Alps and Tomorri Massif; kayaking and rafting trips; and one-day walks and hikes in Tirana and the surrounding mountains.

General background

W **albania.usembassy.gov/index.html** Information about the United States's activities in and policy towards Albania.

W **balkanspeacepark.org** A network of academics, artists, environmental activists and local people living and working in the valleys and villages of northern Albania, Montenegro and Kosova. See page 219 for more about B3P.

W **https://cia.gov/library/publications/the-world-factbook/geos/al.html** The CIA factbook on Albania, with a reasonably up-to-date summary of recent history and the Agency's assessment of the current state of affairs.

W **frosina.org** Designed for the Albanian diaspora in the US; has articles about Albania, folk tales and recipes.

W **gov.uk/government/world/albania** News from the British embassy in Tirana.

W **instat.gov.al** Albania's National Statistical Institute has a wealth of data on its website, much of it in English as well as Albanian.

W **iucn.org** The International Union for Conservation of Nature & Natural Resources; gives information about endangered species all over the world, including Albania.

W **lcweb2.loc.gov/frd/cs/altoc.html** US Library of Congress Country Study of Albania; from 1992, but useful historical background.

W **osce.org/albania** Information about the mandate and the activities of the OSCE Presence in Albania.

w **reenic.utexas.edu/countries/albania.html** The REENIC (Russia and East European Network Information Centre) site has links to a huge range of other websites.

w **tiranatimes.com** and w **albaniannews.com** The websites of Tirana's English-language newspapers. Most of the content is accessible only to subscribers, but they provide news summaries.

FOLLOW BRADT

For the latest news, special offers and competitions, subscribe to the Bradt newsletter via the website w bradtguides.com and follow Bradt on:

f BradtTravelGuides
🐦 @BradtGuides
📷 @bradtguides
𝒫 bradtguides

ALBANIA ONLINE

For additional online content, articles, photos and more on Albania, why not visit w bradtguides.com/albania?

Index

Page numbers in **bold** indicate major entries; those in *italic* indicate maps.

INDEX OF ADVERTISERS